THE EUROPEAN UNION SERIES

General Editors: Neill Nugent, William E. Paterson

The European Union series provides an authoritative library on the European Union, ranging from general introductory texts to definitive assessments of key institutions and actors, issues, policies and policy processes, and the role of member states.

Books in the series are written by leading scholars in their fields and reflect the most up-to-date research and debate. Particular attention is paid to accessibility and clear presentation for a wide audience of students, practitioners and interested general readers.

The series editors are Neill Nugent, Professor of Politics and Jean Monnet Professor of European Integration, Manchester Metropolitan University, and William E. Paterson, Honourary Professor in German and European Studies, University of Aston. Their co-editor until his death in July 1999, Vincent Wright, was a Fellow of Nuffield College, Oxford University.

Feedback on the series and book proposals are always welcome and should be sent to Steven Kennedy, Palgrave Macmillan, Houndmills, Basingstoke, Hampshire RG21 6XS, UK, or by e-mail to s.kennedy@palgrave.com

General textbooks

Published

Desmond Dinan **Encyclopedia of the European Union**
[Rights: Europe only]

Desmond Dinan **Europe Recast: A History of European Union**
[Rights: Europe only]

Desmond Dinan **Ever Closer Union: An Introduction to European Integration** (4th edn)
[Rights: Europe only]

Mette Eilstrup Sangiovanni (ed.) **Debates on European Integration: A Reader**

Simon Hix **The Political System of the European Union** (2nd edn)

Paul Magnette **What is the European Union? Nature and Prospects**

John McCormick **Understanding the European Union: A Concise Introduction** (4th edn)

Brent F. Nelsen and Alexander Stubb **The European Union: Readings on the Theory and Practice of European Integration** (3rd edn)
[Rights: Europe only]

Neill Nugent (ed.) **European Union Enlargement**

Neill Nugent **The Government and Politics of the European Union** (7th edn)

John Peterson and Elizabeth Bomberg **Decision-Making in the European Union**

Ben Rosamond **Theories of European Integration**

Forthcoming

Laurie Buonanno and Neill Nugent **Policies and Policy Processes of the European Union**

Dirk Leuffen, Berthold Rittberger and Frank Schimmelfennig **Differentiated Integration**

Sabine Saurugger **Theoretical Approaches to European Integration**

Esther Versluis, Mendeltje van Keulen and Paul Stephenson **Analyzing the European Union Policy Process**

Also Planned

The Political Economy of European Integration

Series Standing Order (outside North America only)
ISBN 0–333–71695–7 hardback
ISBN 0–333–69352–3 paperback
Full details from www.palgrave.com

Visit Palgrave Macmillan's
EU Resource area at
www.palgrave.com/politics/eu/

The Government and Politics of the European Union

7th Edition

NEILL NUGENT

palgrave
macmillan

First edition 1989
Second edition 1991
Third edition 1994
Fourth edition 1999
Fifth edition 2003
Sixth edition 2006
Seventh edition 2010

Published by
PALGRAVE MACMILLAN

Palgrave Macmillan in the UK is an imprint of Macmillan Publishers Limited, registered in England, company number 785998, of Houndmills, Basingstoke, Hampshire RG21 6XS.

Palgrave Macmillan in the US is a division of St Martin's Press LLC, 175 Fifth Avenue, New York, NY 10010.

Palgrave Macmillan is the global academic imprint of the above companies and has companies and representatives throughout the world.

Palgrave® and Macmillan® are registered trademarks in the United States, the United Kingdom, Europe and other countries

ISBN 978–0–230–24117–6 hardback
ISBN 978–0–230–24118–3 paperback

This book is printed on paper suitable for recycling and made from fully managed and sustained forest sources. Logging, pulping and manufacturing processes are expected to conform to the environmental regulations of the country of origin.

A catalogue record for this book is available from the British Library.

A catalog record for this book is available from the Library of Congress.

10   9   8   7   6   5   4   3   2   1
19   18   17   16   15   14   13   12   11   10

Printed in China

Summary of Contents

Contents

List of Illustrative Material

Maps

Photos

Documents

Boxes

Figures

Tables

List of Abbreviations

ABB	activity based budgeting	COGECA	General Confederation of Agricultural Cooperatives in the European Union
ACEA	Association of European Automobile Constructors		
ACP	African, Caribbean and Pacific countries	COM	common organisation of the market
AFSJ	area of freedom, security and justice	COPA	Committee of Agricultural Organisations in the European Union
ALDE	Group of the Alliance of Liberals and Democrats for Europe	COP	Corporate Operational Plan
AMCHAM-EU	EU Committee of the American Chamber of Commerce	COPS	Political and Security Committee
		CoR	Committee of the Regions
APPE	Association of Petrochemical Producers in Europe	COREPER	Committee of Permanent Representatives
ASEAN	Association of South-East Asian Nations	CPE	European Farmers Coordination
		CSCE	Conference on Security and Cooperation in Europe
BEPGs	Broad Economic Policy Guidelines	CSDP	Common Security and Defence Policy
BEUC	European Bureau of Consumers' Associations	CT	Constitutional Treaty
BRITE	Basic Research in Industrial Technologies for Europe	DG	Directorate General
		EAFRD	European Agricultural Fund for Rural Development
CAP	Common Agricultural Policy		
CCP	Common Commercial Policy	EAGF	European Agricultural Guarantee Fund
CCT	Common Customs Tariff		
CDU/CSU	German Christian Democratic Union/Christian Social Union	EAGGF	European Agricultural Guidance and Guarantee Fund
CEA	European Insurance Committee	EC	European Community
CEEC	Central and Eastern European country	ECA	European Chemicals Agency
		ECB	European Central Bank
CEEP	European Centre of Enterprises with Public Participation	ECJ	European Court of Justice
		Ecofin	Council of Economic and Finance Ministers
CEFIC	European Chemical Industry Council	ECR	European Conservatives and Reformists' Group
CEN	European Committee for Standardisation	ECSC	European Coal and Steel Community
CENELEC	European Committee for Electrotechnical Standardisation	ecu	European currency unit
CET	Common External Tariff	ED	European Democratic Group
CFI	Court of First Instance	EDA	European Defence Agency
CFP	Common Fisheries Policy	EDC	European Defence Community
CFSP	Common Foreign and Security Policy	EDF	European Development Fund
		EEA	European Economic Area

EEAS	European External Action Service	EU	European Union
EEB	European Environmental Bureau	EUL	European United Left
EEC	European Economic Community	EUMC	European Union Military Committee
EES	European Employment Strategy		
EESC	European Economic and Social Committee	EUMS	European Union Military Staff
		Euratom	European Atomic Energy Community
EFD	Europe of Freedom and Democracy Group		
		EUREKA	European Research Coordinating Agency
EFPIA	European Federation of Pharmaceutical Industry Associations		
		EUROBIT	European Association of Manufacturers of Business Machines and Information Technology
EFSA	European Food Safety Authority		
EFTA	European Free Trade Association		
EIB	European Investment Bank	EUROFER	European Confederation of Iron and Steel Industries
EIF	European Investment Fund		
ELDR	Federation of European Liberal, Democratic and Reform Parties	EUR-OP	Office for Official Publications of the European Union
EMEA	European Medicines Agency	Europol	European Police Office
EMS	European Monetary System	FCO	Foreign and Commonwealth Office
EMU	European Monetary Union	FIEC	Construction Industry Federation
ENP	European Neighbourhood Policy	FRG	Federal Republic of Germany
EP	European Parliament	FRY	Former Republic of Yugoslavia
EPA	Economic Partnership Agreement	FTA	Free Trade Area
EPC	European Political Cooperation	G8	Group of Eight
EPF	European Passengers' Federation	GAERC	General Affairs and External Relations Council
EPP	European People's Party		
EPP-ED	European People's Party/European Democrats	GATT	General Agreement on Tariffs and Trade
ERA	European Research Area	GDP	gross domestic product
ERDF	European Regional Development Fund	GDR	German Democratic Republic
		GM	genetically modified
ERM	Exchange Rate Mechanism	GNI	gross national income
ERRF	European Rapid Reaction Force	GNP	gross national product
ESBG	European Savings Bank Group	GSP	Generalised System of Preferences
ESC	Economic and Social Committee	IGC	Intergovernmental Conference
ESCB	European System of Central Banks	IGO	intergovernmental organisation
ESDI	European Security and Defence Identity	IMF	International Monetary Fund
		JHA	Justice and Home Affairs
ESDP	European Security and Defence Policy	JRC	Joint Research Centre
		LDC	least developed country
ESF	European Social Fund	MEP	Member of the European Parliament
ESFS	European System of Financial Supervisors		
		MFF	multiannual financial framework
ESPRIT	European Strategic Programme for Research and Development in Information Technology	NATO	North Atlantic Treaty Organisation
		NCB	national central bank
		NGO	non-governmental organisation
ESRB	European Systemic Risk Board	NPAA	national programme for the adoption of the *acquis*
ETUC	European Trade Union Confederation		
		NTB	non-tariff barrier (to trade)

OECD	Organisation for Economic Co-operation and Development	SGP	Stability and Growth Pact
OEEC	Organisation for European Economic Cooperation	SME	small and medium-sized enterprise
		TAC	total allowable catch (fish stocks)
OHIM	Office for Harmonisation in the Internal Market	TACIS	Programme for Technical Assistance to the Independent States of the Former Soviet Union and Mongolia
OJ	Official Journal of the European Union	TEC	Treaty Establishing the European Community
OLAF	European Anti-Fraud Office		
OMC	open method of coordination	TEU	Treaty on European Union
OSCE	Organisation for Security and Cooperation in Europe	TFEU	Treaty on the Functioning of the European Union
PDB	Preliminary Draft Budget	UEN	Union for Europe of the Nations Group
PES	Party of European Socialists		
PHARE	Programme of Community Aid for Central and Eastern European Countries	UEN-EA	Union for Europe of the Nations-European Alliance Group
		UK	United Kingdom
PLO	Palestine Liberation Organisation	UKREP	United Kingdom Permanent Representation to the European Union
PSC	Political and Security Committee		
QMV	qualified majority voting		
RACE	Research and Development in Advanced Communications Technologies for Europe	UN	United Nations
		UNCTAD	United Nations Conference on Trade and Development
R&TD	Research and Technological Development	UNICE	Union of Industrial and Employers' Confederations of Europe
S&D	Group of the Progressive Alliance of Socialists and Democrats	USA	United States of America
		VAT	value added tax
SCA	Special Committee on Agriculture	WEU	Western European Union
SEA	Single European Act	WTO	World Trade Organisation
SEM	Single European Market		

Preface to the Seventh Edition

This book aims to provide a clear, systematic and comprehensive introduction to the government and politics of the European Union (EU). It makes no assumptions about readers having any prior knowledge of the subject and it does not require readers to have a grounding in European Studies, Political Science or any other academic discipline.

There have been many major developments in the EU since the previous edition of *The Government and Politics of the European Union* was completed in February 2006. Foremost amongst these developments have been: the negotiation of the Lisbon Treaty and, after some delay, the entry into force of the Treaty on 1 December 2009; the accession of two new member states – Bulgaria and Romania – to the EU on 1 January 2007; the expansion of the eurozone; and considerable policy 'advancements' in several areas – notably market integration, justice and home affairs, and foreign and defence policies. These developments are all extensively explored in this new edition, as are other features of the seemingly constantly evolving process of European integration. The book has been thoroughly revised and updated throughout.

Those familiar with previous editions will notice a major change in format and presentation, with a larger page size, double columns, the inclusion of many new boxes, tables and figures and, for the first time, a selection of photographs. These changes have been made with the intention of making the great amount of information that is contained in the book more digestible and accessible. The new edition is also now supported by a companion website. This contains a range of additional learning material and can be accessed at www.palgrave.com/politics/nugent.

The chapters of the book are organised into five Parts. In Part I, the historical evolution of European integration since the Second World War is examined. Particular themes of Part I include: the impact of the Second World War on the political map of Europe and on the attitudes and practices of political decision makers; the differing and evolving attitudes of decision makers to European inter-state cooperation and

integration; and the progressive, though unevenly paced, development of the European integration process in terms of both deepening and widening.

Part II examines the EU's major treaties. The original treaty bases were laid down in the 1950s, with three founding treaties. Since the mid-1980s, the founding treaties have been amended and supplemented every few years as part of a process that has both reflected and advanced the integration process. The latest treaty, the Treaty of Lisbon, which came into effect in December 2009, is analysed in some detail in Chapter 6.

The EU's institutions and political actors are examined in Part III. The major institutions – the Commission, the Council of Ministers, the European Council, the European Parliament, and the EU Courts – are each given their own chapter, whilst other institutions are taken together in another chapter. There are also separate chapters on interests and member states, which are key EU political actors.

Part IV looks at the EU's policies and policy processes. Given that the EU has some involvement in just about every sphere of public policy and given also that it has numerous policy processes, it is obviously not possible to give a full and detailed account of all policies and all policy processes. Attention is, therefore, focused on 'the big picture'. Regarding policies, this involves identifying key overall features of the EU's policy portfolio and giving particularly important policy areas – such as the operation of the internal market, the Common Agricultural Policy, Economic and Monetary Union, trade policy, and foreign policy – special attention. Regarding policy processes, it involves describing patterns of policy processes, charting changes in the usage of types of policy processes, and examining very closely the most important form of policy processes – legislative processes.

The final Part of the book – Part V – involves, as its title says, a stepping back and a looking forward. The stepping back takes the form of an examination of concepts and theories in EU studies. There is now a vast conceptual and theoretical literature on the EU, much of which can be intimidating and confusing for newcomers to EU studies if it is examined without much prior knowledge of the empirical world to which it is being applied. For this reason, as in previous editions, the description and analysis of conceptualisation and theorisation is placed near the end of the book rather than at the beginning. Those who prefer to have an overview of theoretical considerations at the outset can, of course, read Chapter 23 first. The looking forward component of Part V is contained in the Conclusion, where consideration is given to the major challenges that are likely to be on the EU's agenda in the coming years and how the EU may go about meeting them.

I would like to thank a number of people for assistance they have given me whilst I was preparing this edition of the book. My *European Union Series* co-editor, and good friend, William Paterson, was always encouraging and provided insightful comments on draft chapters. David Allen, Judge George Arestis, and David Phinnemore read particular chapters and provided valuable feedback on them.

Photos 1.1, 2.1, 2.2, 2.3, 2.4, 2.5, 8.1, 8.2, 8.3 and 19.1, 21.2 are © European Union; Photos 9.1, 10.1, 10.2 and 21.1 are © Council of the European Union; Photos 11.1, 11.2, 15.1 and 18.1 are © European Parliament – Audio Visual Unit; Photo 12.1 is © Court of Justice of the European Union. We are grateful for the help of various institutions' audio-visual services in making these available.

Keith Povey was extremely helpful with the production of the book and handled the process with enormous professionalism. As ever, Steven Kennedy of Palgrave Macmillan was a very supportive publisher and always accompanied his chivvying and pressing with great good humour and understanding.

And last, but not least, thanks to Maureen, Helen and Rachael for their support.

February 2010   NEILL NUGENT

Part I
The Historical Evolution

No political system or organisation can properly be understood unless it is set in its historical and operational contexts. The structure and functioning of government institutions, the nature and dynamics of political forces, and the concerns and conduct of those who exercise power do not happen as a matter of chance. They are shaped, and are constantly being remoulded, by evolving forces and events.

Though a relatively new organisation, the European Union (EU) is no less subject to these dictates than are long established nation states, and like them its nature cannot be appreciated without reference to its historical sources or to the world in which it functions. Thus, the EU is often criticised for being weak in structure and quarrelsome in nature, with far too much bickering over matters such as the price of butter and not enough visionary thinking and united action to tackle unemployment, regional imbalances and other major problems. Unquestionably there is much in these criticisms, but that the EU should find harmonious collective policy making difficult is not surprising to anyone with a historical perspective. For before they joined the European Community (EC)/European Union member states made decisions for themselves on most matters. It is not easy, especially for large states or for states that believe themselves to have special interests, to have to cede sovereignty by transferring decision-making responsibilities to a multinational organisation in which other voices may prevail. Any explanation and understanding of what the EU is, and what it has and has not achieved, must recognise this. The EU must, in other words, be seen in the context of the forces that have made it and are still making it. Some of these forces have served to push the states together. Others have resulted in progress towards cooperation and integration sometimes being slow, difficult and contested.

The sovereignty issue may be used to illustrate the importance of both historical background and contemporary operational context in explaining and evaluating the European Union. Many of the EU's opponents and critics subscribe to the view that the nation state, not an international organisation, is the 'natural' supreme political unit. They argue that insofar as transferences of power to Brussels, Luxembourg and Strasbourg – the three main seats of the EU's institutions – undermine national sovereignty, they should be resisted. But what proponents of this view all too often fail to recognise is that national sovereignties were being steadily eroded long before the EC/EU was established, and since it was established sovereignties have been further eroded by forces that are not a consequence of EU membership. Whether it has been because of movements in financial markets, transfers of capital within multinational corporations, changing trade patterns, or United States military dominance, EU states have become increasingly affected by, and at the mercy of, international developments they cannot control. This loss of power may not have involved legal transfers of sovereignty as has been the case within the EU, but it has had a very similar effect. The fact is that in an ever expanding range of policy sectors, states have not been able to act in isolation but have had to adjust and adapt so as to fit in with an array of external influences. The EU should not, therefore, be viewed as constituting a unique threat to the sovereignties of its member states. On the contrary, it is in some ways an attempt to meet this threat by providing a means by which member states, if not able to regain their sovereignty, can at least re-assert control over aspects of decision making by cooperating together at levels and in ways that match post-war internationalism.

The purpose of Part I is thus to provide a base for understanding the EU by tracing its evolution and placing it in its historical and operational settings.

There is always a problem in knowing quite where to start with the history of a subject in a chronological sense. How far back is it necessary to go to be able to properly describe and explain a subject – the subject in this case being the process of European integration. Chapter 1 begins with an outline of some of the major divisions that characterised Europe before the Second World War, so as to emphasise how momentous the post-war transformations that have occurred in Europe as part of the European integration process have been. The European integration process was, however, essentially confined until the 1990s to Western Europe, with the consequence that although the EU now includes amongst its membership states from across the continent, it was constructed by Western European states. Chapter 1 therefore focuses on the nature of, and the factors that explain, what developed into a transformation in the relations between the states of Western Europe after the Second World War.

Chapter 2 analyses the creation in the 1950s, with only six states as founding members, of the three European Communities: the European Coal and Steel Community (ECSC), which was founded by the Treaty of Paris in 1951, and the European Atomic Energy Community (Euratom) and the European Economic Community (EEC) which were both established in March 1957 with the signing of two Treaties of Rome.

Chapter 3 takes an overview of the deepening of the integration process since 1957. This deepening has taken a number of forms, most particularly a growth in the complexity and powers of EC/EU institutional structures and decision-making processes and a great expansion in the number of policy activities in which the EC/EU is involved.

Chapter 4 looks at the widening of integration through the accessions of new member states. In a series of enlargement rounds starting in the 1970s the EC/EU broadened out to such an extent that by the mid-1990s virtually all Western European states were members. This virtual completion, in terms of membership at least, of Western European integration was then followed in the 2000s by the extension of the integration process to former communist states in Central and Eastern Europe.

Chapter 1

The Post-War Transformation of Western Europe

The European integration process was initiated and developed in Western Europe. It was extended to Central and Eastern Europe only after the key features of the European Union (EU) as they are today had been created and become established. Until the collapse of communism in Central and Eastern Europe in 1989–90, countries such as Bulgaria, Estonia, Latvia, Hungary, and Poland were either part of the Soviet Union or were located within the Soviet bloc. As such, they were quite outside the processes that, until the early 1990s, were focused exclusively on drawing Western European states increasingly close to one another in an array of cooperative and integrative relationships.

An understanding and analysis of the European integration process must therefore begin by focusing on Western Europe.

Historical Divisions

The inheritance

Throughout its history Europe has been characterised much more by divisions, tensions and conflicts than it has by any common purpose or harmony of spirit. This applies to Western Europe as much as it does to the European continent as whole.

Language has been perhaps the most obvious divisive force. Linguists may identify structural similarities between European languages, but the fact is that most peoples of Europe, including of Western Europe, have not been able to, until recently at least, directly converse with one another. (Fifty-six per cent of Europeans now say they can hold a conversation in at least one foreign language.) Religion has been another source of division, with the northern countries of Western Europe (except Ireland) being mainly Protestant in their Christian inheritance and the southern countries (including France but excluding Orthodox Greece) being predominantly Catholic. Contrasting cultural traditions and historical experiences have further served to develop distinct identifications – and feelings of 'us' and 'them' – across the map of Europe.

Along with the legacies of power struggles and wars, such differences help to explain why Western Europe has been divided into so many states, each with its own identity and loyalties. Some of these states – France, Spain and the

United Kingdom for example – have existed in much their present geographical form for centuries. Others – including Germany, Italy and Ireland – were constituted only comparatively recently, mostly in the nineteenth and early twentieth centuries as nationalism flourished and as force was used to bring nation and state into closer alignment.

Until at least the Second World War, and in some cases well beyond, linguistic, religious and cultural divisions between the Western European states were exacerbated by political and economic divisions.

Political divisions took the form of varying systems of government and competing ideological orientations. In the nineteenth and early twentieth centuries autocracies existed alongside emerging, and more liberal, parliamentary democracies. Between the two world wars parliamentary democracy found itself under attack and in some cases was overthrown: in Italy in 1922 by Fascism, in Germany in 1933 by Nazism, and in Spain after the 1936–9 civil war by conservative authoritarianism. By the late 1930s, very different political regimes were in place in the major Western European states (see Box 1.1). It was not until the mid-1970s – following the collapse of the dictatorships of the Iberian peninsula and the overthrow of the military regime in Greece – that parliamentary democracy finally became general throughout Western Europe.

Economic divisions were no less marked. From the beginning of the Industrial Revolution until the middle of the nineteenth century Britain was industrially and commercially dominant. Gradually it was challenged – particularly by Germany, but also by Belgium, France and others – so that by the early years of the twentieth century competition between these countries for overseas markets was fierce. At the same time, the economies of the northern countries were increasingly differentiated from those of the south, with the former mostly having substantial industrial bases while the latter remained predominantly agricultural and underdeveloped.

Western Europe was thus long divided and many of its divisions were sources of tension, hostility and war. Finding their expression in economic and ideological competition, drives for national power and prestige, and territorial disputes, and compounded by dangerous mixtures of assertive/weak/incompetent leaderships, the divisions ensured that until after the Second World War rivalry and distrust governed the relationships between most of the states most of the time.

In the twentieth century alone two devastatingly destructive world wars, both of which began as European wars, were fought. The First (1914–18) saw the countries of the triple entente – Britain, France and Russia – plus Italy from 1915, fighting against Germany and Austria–Hungary. The Second (1939–45) saw Germany, assisted from 1940 by Italy, attempting to impose itself by force on virtually the whole of Europe outside the Iberian peninsula.

The background to the Second World War

The background to the Second World War is worth outlining briefly because it puts in perspective how dramatically different, and how suddenly found, were the more cooperative relationships between the Western European states in the post-1945 era.

The period between the First and Second World Wars was characterised by particularly sharp and fluid inter-state relations in Europe. There was no stable alliance system and no clear balance of power. For the most part, European states, including Western European states, regarded one another with, at best, suspicion. Though multilateral and bilateral treaties, agreements, and pacts abounded, there was little overall pattern to them and few had any lasting effect. States came together in varying combinations on

---

Box 1.1

The political systems of Western Europe's major states in the late 1930s

France	Weak parliamentary system (the Third Republic)
Germany	Nazi dictatorship (under Adolph Hitler, from 1933)
Italy	Fascist dictatorship (under Benito Mussolini, from 1922)
Spain	Conservative military dictatorship (under General Franco, from 1937)
United Kingdom	Strong parliamentary system

different issues in a manner that, far from indicating mutual confidence, was increasingly suggestive of fear.

From time to time in the inter-war period proposals for greater cooperation between European states were advanced but little came of them. The international climate – characterised by national rivalries and clashing interests – was not favourable, and most of the leading advocates of closer linkages were seen as having, as indeed they did have, specific national purposes in mind. Aristide Briand, for example, who was French Foreign Minister from 1925 to 1932, supported European cooperation but clearly had as his prime aim a stable European political system that would preserve the peace settlement that had been imposed on Germany by the 1919 Versailles Treaty. Gustav Stresemann, by contrast, who was the German Foreign Minister from 1923 to 1929, saw European cooperation as a way in which Germany could loosen the grip of Versailles and regain its position as a major power.

The lack of any real interest in European cooperation before the Second World War is revealed in the functioning of the League of Nations. Established in 1919 to provide for international collective security, in practice it was dominated by the Europeans and had some potential as a forum for developing understandings and improving relationships between the European states. However, it failed. It did so for three main reasons. First, its aims were vague and were interpreted in different ways. Second, it was intergovernmental in its structure and therefore dependent on the agreement of all member states before any action could be taken. Third, and crucially, the states wanted different things from it: some – notably France, most of the medium-sized Central European countries that had been constituted in 1918–19 out of the collapsed Austria–Hungarian Empire, and to some extent Britain – saw it as a means of preserving the Versailles *status quo*; others – particularly Germany and Italy – wanted to use it to change the 1919 settlement and were prepared to leave or ignore it if it did not serve that purpose.

Inter-war Europe thus experienced rising tensions as national rivalries remained unharnessed and, above all, as German territorial and power ambitions could not be satisfied. When war finally did break out, the Axis Powers (Germany and Italy) gained control for a while over virtually the whole of the continent from the Atlantic to deep inside the Soviet Union. In Western Europe only Britain and those countries that remained neutral (Ireland, Portugal, Spain, Sweden and Switzerland) were not occupied. By May 1945, when German government representatives agreed to unconditional surrender, Nazism and Fascism had been defeated, but economies and political systems throughout Europe had been severely shaken, cities and towns had been destroyed and millions had been killed.

The Post-War Transformation

After the Second World War the relations between the states of Western Europe were transformed. There were, and indeed still continue to be, three principal aspects of this.

Unbroken peace

Western European states have lived peacefully with one another since 1945 and armed confrontation between any two has long since ceased to be even remotely possible. As Altiero Spinelli, one of the great advocates and architects of European integration, observed in 1985 shortly before his death:

> [a] major transformation … has occurred in the political consciousness of Europeans, something which is completely new in their history. For centuries, neighbouring countries were seen as potential enemies against whom it was necessary to be on one's guard and ready to fight. Now, after the end of the most terrible of wars in Europe, these neighbours are perceived as friendly nations sharing a common destiny (Spinelli, 1986: xiii).

Spinelli's view of a common destiny is questionable, but the reality and importance of the transformation from hostile to friendly relations is not. Certainly the states have continued to compete against one another in many areas, and this has sometimes led to strains and tensions, but these disagreements have been mostly on issues where military conflict has not been remotely relevant to the resolution of differences.

Indeed, not only has military conflict been irrelevant to the resolution of differences, but such friction as has occurred has been within a context in which Western European states have usually shared similar views on who can be seen as friends and who are real or potential enemies. Until the revolutions and upheavals in Eastern Europe and the Soviet Union in the late 1980s/early 1990s, communism was the most obvious common threat and this led most significant Western European states to become members of the same military alliance: the North Atlantic Treaty Organisation (NATO). With the communist danger now removed, Western security arrangements have been revamped to adjust to a situation in which Central and Eastern European countries (CEECs) are now partners in both NATO and the EU and in which the main potential security concerns are seen as being of a quite different nature: the bubbling national and ethnic tensions in parts of the former Soviet Empire, the turbulence of the Middle East, and the threat of international terrorism.

A transformed agenda

Throughout the international system the subject matter of discussions and negotiations between states has become much more varied. Whilst, as numerous international political tensions and armed conflicts have shown, the case should not be overstated, international agendas have become less focused than formerly they were on traditional 'high policy' issues and have become more taken up with 'low policy' issues. That is, policies concerned with the existence and preservation of the state (such as territorial issues, balance of power manoeuvrings, and defence considerations) have been joined by policies that are more concerned with the wealth and welfare of populations (such as policies on trade, monetary stability, environmental protection, and airline safety).

This change in the content of international agendas was particularly quickly 'off the mark' in Western Europe after the Second World War where, within a few years, a transformation can be said to have occurred. Classic 'power politics' did not disappear, but they were rapidly not as dominant or as prominent as they had been. By the mid-1950s representatives of Western European governments, and especially representatives from the six states that would become the founding members of the European Communities (Belgium, France, West Germany, Italy, Luxembourg, and the Netherlands), were engaging in detailed negotiations on policy matters – mainly economic policy matters – that would have been almost inconceivable to pre-war leaders. This development subsequently broadened and intensified, to the point that by the 1970s representatives of the European Community governments (numbering nine from 1973 when Denmark, Ireland and the United Kingdom joined) were meeting regularly to consider topics that a generation or two before would not even have been regarded as proper subjects for international negotiations: for example, how might research information be pooled to the general advantage, to what extent and by what means should sheep farmers be subsidised, what should be the maximum weight of lorries permitted on the roads of member states, and could common foreign policy positions be adopted?

New channels and processes

Paralleling, and partly occasioned by, the increasingly diverse international agenda, there has been a gradual transformation over the years in the ways in which states in the international system interrelate with one another. The traditional diplomatic means of interstate communications – via Ministries of Foreign Affairs and embassies – have declined in importance as new channels and processes have become established. In the Western world in particular there are now few significant parts of any state's political and administrative systems that do not have some involvement in the management of external relations. Written communications, telephone conversations, electronically transmitted messages, and bilateral and multilateral meetings between states increase by the year. Contacts range from the *ad hoc* and informal to the regularised and highly structured.

As with changing agendas, changing forms of interstate communication were developed and utilised particularly quickly in Western Europe after the Second World War. Working often within the forums of newly created Western and Western European based organisations (see below), Western European governments were, from the late 1940s, in increasing contact with one another to discuss, and often negotiate about, a range of policy matters. This increasing contact took a major step forward from the early 1950s when the European Communities were established and began functioning, for then representatives of the member states became increasingly enmeshed in collective institutions and policy-making processes on a daily basis.

This enmeshing between European Community member states became ever more intensive from the late 1950s as the European Economic Community (which began operating in 1958) began to broaden its policy portfolio. The enmeshing also became more geographically spread as the EC began enlarging from the early 1970s: enlarging to the point that by 1995 all Western European states of a significant size had joined (the now titled) European Union apart from Iceland, Norway and Switzerland.

Today in the EU, representatives of the governments of all member states meet every working day for such purposes as taking binding decisions (decisions that in many circumstances may be taken by majority vote), exploring possibly advantageous policy coordination, and exchanging views and information. At the lower end of the seniority scale, junior and middle-ranking officials, often working from tightly drawn negotiating briefs and with their actions subject to later approval from national capitals, convene in committees to try to hammer out detailed agreements on proposed legislation. At the top end of the scale, Heads of Government regularly meet, for what are often wide-ranging deliberations, in a wide variety of forums.

Explaining the Transformation, and its Nature

As has been noted above, until recently the European integration process was essentially a *Western* European integration process. The countries of Central and Eastern Europe that have become members of the EU in the 2000s joined an organisation made by countries of Western Europe.

In seeking to explain post-war Western European cooperation and integration different commentators have often highlighted different factors, and sometimes indeed have looked in rather different directions. Four explanatory approaches will be outlined here. These approaches emphasise: the deep roots of European integration; the impact of the Second World

War; the increasing importance of interdependence; and the differing positions of Western European states. For analytical purposes these approaches will be considered separately, but it should be recognised that, in practice, they are by no means mutually exclusive but rather complement, overlap and reinforce one another. It should be recognised, too, that their usefulness as explanations is not constant, but varies over time. So, for example, whilst political ideals and utopian visions of a united Europe had some part to play in the early post-war years, they increasingly counted for less as hard-headed national calculations of economic and political advantages and disadvantages came to loom larger as the principal determinants of the nature and pace of the integration process.

The deep roots of integration?

Some commentators and practitioners have found the roots of post-war developments in the distant past. Supporters and advocates of European integration have been especially prominent in this regard. They have suggested that Europe is, and has long been, a unique and identifiable entity. As evidence of this it is often argued that Europe was the cradle of modern civilisation and from this there developed European values and a European culture, art and literature. Walter Hallstein, a key German figure in the creation of the European Communities in the 1950s and the first President of the Commission of the EEC, typifies this sort of view:

> Europe is no creation. It is a rediscovery. The main difference between the formation of the United States of Europe and that of the United States of America is not that America did not have to merge a number of firmly established nation states, but that for more than a thousand years the idea of a unified Europe was never quite forgotten …

> [The advocates of a European federation] know that Europe shares a sense of values: of what is good and bad; of what a man's rights should be and what are his duties; of how society should be ordered; of what is happiness and what disaster. Europe shares many things: its memories that we call history; achievements it can take pride in and

events that are shameful; its joys and its sufferings; and not least its tomorrows (Hallstein, 1972: 15 and 16).

Clearly there is much idealism in this. People such as Hallstein are suggesting that transcending the differences, divergences and conflicts between peoples and states there has long been a certain commonality and identity of interest in Europe based on interrelationships between geography and historical, political, economic, social and cultural developments. It is a contentious view and certainly not one to which many historians would attach much importance. Divisions and dissension, they would contend, have been more prominent than identity of interest or shared values and experiences. Such limited commonality as has existed has largely been a consequence of geographical proximity.

But if the 'idealistic' interpretation no longer finds much favour, there are still those who stress the importance of the historical dimension of European integration. Inter-state relations in the nineteenth century are sometimes seen as foreshadowing post-1945 developments insofar as peace endured for much of the century and did so, in part at least, as a result of understandings and agreements between the major powers. However, a problem with this view is that it overstates the extent to which the nineteenth century was a century of peace, and it also exaggerates the extent to which the states did cooperate. Arguably, the

so-called Concert of Nations was an embryonic attempt to exercise strategic control through diplomacy and summitry, but that was at a time when conservative autocracies ruled much of Europe and many of today's states did not even exist in their present form. And in any event, the system lasted at best only from 1815 to the Crimean War. It then gave way to the wars of the mid-nineteenth century and later to the balance of power – which was hardly based on European trust and cooperation – as the means of seeking to preserve the peace.

It is perhaps in the field of economic history that the most fertile ground for identifying long-term influences and explanations is to be found. From the late eighteenth century *national* economic integration began to occur, as barriers to economic activity *within* states were dismantled. This helped to promote, and in turn was encouraged by, national political integration, which manifested itself in nationalism and in the elevation of the sovereign state to the status of the supreme collective unit. From the middle of the nineteenth century the achievement and successes of this internal economic and political integration, allied with an increasing interconnectedness in Europe that followed from technological change and economic advance, resulted in increasing inter-state cooperation to promote trade, competition and growth. For some economic historians an embryonic European economy was being established. Pollard, for example, has written of the mid-nineteenth century:

> Europe's industrialisation proceeded relatively smoothly, among other reasons, precisely because it took place within what was in many essentials a single integrated economy, with a fair amount of movement for labour, a greater amount of freedom for the movement of goods, and the greatest freedom of all for the movement of technology, know-how and capital (Pollard, 1981: 38–9).

But unlike the customary pattern within nation states, there was nothing inevitable about European economic integration. Nor was there a clear and developing relationship between it and political integration. On the contrary, from the last quarter of the nineteenth century, states, for a variety of reasons, moved increasingly in the direction of economic protectionism and at the same time developed

Photo 1.1 Walter Hallstein, an early advocate and architect of European integration and President of the European Commission 1958–67

national identities and consciousness such as had not been seen before. In the first part of the twentieth century, and especially between the wars, the European free trading system virtually disappeared, as states sought to protect themselves at the expense of others and national economies were increasingly reshaped along autarkic lines. Alongside these increasingly closed economic systems developed the ever sharper political tensions and rivalries between the states that were noted earlier.

The European historical experience thus emphasises the extremely important, but often overlooked, fact that although industrialisation and economic liberalisation provide potential bases for the furtherance of interconnections, agreements, and harmonious relations between states, they do not ensure or guarantee them. The powers of Europe went to war with their principal trading partners in 1914. Furthermore, between the wars economic linkages did little to bring the nations together or to act as a restraint on governments when divergences developed in their aims and strategies. This must be borne in mind when, later in this chapter, attention is turned to modernisation and interdependence as explanations for post-war political and economic integration. Doubtless they have both been extremely important but, as pre-1939 European history demonstrates, they do not have an inevitable integrationist logic attached to them. Much depends on their relationship to the circumstances of the time and, as will now be shown, these were very different in the post-1945 world from what they had been before the Second World War.

The impact of the Second World War

The Second World War unquestionably marked a turning point in the Western European state system. Just a few years after the end of the war states were cooperating, and in some instances and in some respects were even integrating, in a manner that would have been inconceivable before the war. Fundamental to this transformation were a number of factors resultant upon the war that combined to bring about a radical change in both the climate of opinion and perceptions of requirements. These factors were political and economic in nature.

Political factors

These may be subdivided into four broad areas.

(1) Combating nationalism. The Second World War produced a greater realisation than had existed ever before that unfettered and uninhibited nationalism was a recipe for war, which in the post-1945 world was increasingly seen as meaning mass destruction. At the international level this thinking was reflected in calls for a larger and more powerful body than the pre-war League of Nations, and it played an important part in the establishment of the United Nations in 1944. But the fact that the two world wars had begun as European wars, and that Germany was generally considered to be responsible for those wars, also brought forth demands and moves for specifically European arrangements. Amongst the strongest advocates of the creation of European arrangements were many of those who had been associated with the Resistance movements of Continental Europe which, from 1943 onwards, had come to be linked via liaising networks and from which ideas and proposals had been generated looking forward to a post-war world that would be based more on cooperation and less on confrontation.

There was thus a widely shared optimism at the end of the Second World War that if the European states could work together in joint schemes and organisations, barriers of mistrust could be broken down. On this basis, over 750 prominent Europeans came together in The Hague in May 1948 and from their Congress issued a call to the nations of Europe to create a political and economic union. This stimulated discussions at governmental levels, and in May 1949 the Statute of the Council of Europe was signed by representatives of ten Western European states. Extracts from the Statute are set out in Box 1.2.

As the extracts show, the Council of Europe was established with grandiose, idealistic it may be said, ambitions. However, in practice the Council proved to be a disappointment to those who had hoped it might serve as the basis for a new Western European state system. In part the problem was that its aims were too vague, in part that its decision-making structure was essentially intergovernmental and therefore weak, but the main problem was that some of its members, notably the UK, were not very interested in anything that went beyond limited and voluntary cooperation.

Box 1.2

Extracts from the 1949 Statute of the Council of Europe

Convinced that the pursuit of peace based upon justice and international co-operation is vital for the preservation of human society and civilisation;

Reaffirming their devotion to the spiritual and moral values which are the common heritage of their peoples and the true source of individual freedom, political liberty and the rule of law, principles which form the basis of all genuine democracy;

Believing that, for the maintenance and further realisation of these ideals and in the interests of economic and social progress, there is a need of a closer unity between all like-minded countries of Europe;

Considering that, to respond to this need and to the expressed aspirations of their peoples in this regard, it is necessary forthwith to create an organisation which will bring European States into closer association,

[the signatory states have] in consequence decided to set up a Council of Europe consisting of a committee of representatives of governments and of a consultative assembly, and have for this purpose adopted the following Statute:

Article 1

a. The aim of the Council of Europe is to achieve a greater unity between its members for the purpose of safeguarding and realising the ideals and principles which are their common heritage and facilitating their economic and social progress.

b. This aim shall be pursued through the organs of the Council by discussion of questions of common concern and by agreements and common action in economic, social, cultural, scientific, legal and administrative matters and in the maintenance and further realisation of human rights and fundamental freedoms …

(Ernest Bevin, British Foreign Secretary, commented on proposals for a really effective Council of Europe thus: 'Once you open that Pandora's box, you'll find it full of Trojan horses.') But the weaknesses of the Council should not be overstated. It was to perform, and continues to perform, certain useful functions – notably in the sphere of human rights through its European Convention of Human Rights, and as a forum for the discussion of matters of common interest to its member states. (The value of this latter function long lay in the fact that, unlike other Western European regional groups, virtually all Western European states were members of the Council. In the 1990s, as CEECs became members, an additional value was acting as a forum for establishing links and building understanding between Western and Eastern Europe.)

(2) The new political map of Europe. Although it was not immediately apparent when hostilities ceased in 1945, the Second World War was to result in a fundamental redrawing of the political map of Europe. By the late 1940s it was clear that the legacy of war had left the Continent, and with it Germany, divided in two. In Winston Churchill's phrase, an 'Iron Curtain' now divided East from West. In the East, a swathe of states were either incorporated into the Soviet Union or became part of the Soviet communist zone, which resulted in them being forcibly cut off from developments in Western Europe and being obliged to focus their political and economic ambitions and activities in accordance with Moscow's will.

In the West there was no question of the victorious powers – Britain and the United States – seeking or being able to impose anything like a Soviet-style straitjacket on the liberated countries. Nonetheless, if Western Europe did not quite take on the form of a bloc, liberal democratic systems were soon established everywhere outside the Iberian peninsula and somewhat similar political ideas were prevailing in most of the states. Inevitably this facilitated intergovernmental relations.

Perhaps the most important idea shared by the governments stemmed directly from the East–West division of the continent: there was a determination to preserve Western Europe from communism. Not only had the Soviet Union extended its influence far into the European heartland at the end of the Second World War, but in France and Italy domestic communist parties were commanding considerable support and from 1947 were engaging in what looked to many like revolutionary activities. The United States shared the anti-communist concern of Western European governments and the encouragement and assistance that it gave to the Western European states after the war to cooperate with one another was partly driven by a belief that such cooperation could play a major part in helping to halt the communist advance. In March 1947 President Truman, concerned with events in Greece – where communists were trying to overthrow the government – outlined what became known as the Truman doctrine, which amounted to a political guarantee of support to 'free peoples who are resisting attempted subjugation by armed minorities or by outside pressures'. This political commitment was quickly followed up in 1948 by economic assistance in the form of Marshall Aid (see p. 12), and in 1949 by military protection with the foundation of NATO and a guarantee to the then ten NATO Western European states (Canada and the United States brought the founding membership to twelve) of US military protection against a Soviet attack.

A role for the United States in Western Europe at this time should not be seen as having been unwelcome, for contrary to the impression that is sometimes given by some commentators, US aid was not insidiously imposed on unwilling states but was actively sought. At the same time, the extent of US influence on Western European inter-state relations should not be exaggerated. By its political, economic and military interventions and assistance the United States did exert integrationist pressures and did help to make a number of developments possible, but the US government wanted much more Western European inter-state integration than was actually achieved.

(3) The new international power balance. The post-war division of Europe, the moving of the international power balance from inter-European state relations to

US–Soviet relations, and the onset of the Cold War in 1947–8, combined from the late 1940s to produce the possibility of Europe becoming a battleground between East and West. This in turn promoted a sense that Western Europe was beginning to look like an identifiable political entity in a way that it had not done before. Not all states or politicians shared this perspective, but from many of those who did there emerged a desire that the voice of Western Europe should be heard on the world stage and a belief that this could be achieved only through unity and by speaking with one voice. For some of the smaller European states, which had rarely exercised much international influence and whose very existence had periodically been threatened by larger neighbours, the prospects of such cooperation were particularly attractive.

(4) The German problem. The future of Germany naturally loomed large in the minds of those who had to deal with post-war reconstruction. Three times in seventy years, and twice in the twentieth century, Germany had occupied much of Europe. Rightly or wrongly it had come to be seen as innately aggressive. As a consequence, the initial inclination of most governments after the war was to try to contain Germany in some way. Just how this should be done, however, divided the wartime allies, with the result that matters drifted until what was initially intended as an interim division of Germany into zones gave way, as the Cold War developed, into *a de jure* division: the Federal Republic of Germany (West Germany) and the German Democratic Republic (East Germany) were both formally constituted in 1949.

By this time, the Soviet Union was replacing Germany as the perceived principal threat to democracy and stability in Western Europe. As this occurred, those who were already arguing that a conciliatory approach towards Germany ought to be tried – since a policy of punitive containment had demonstrably failed between the wars – saw their hands strengthened by a growing feeling that attempts must be made to avoid the development of a political vacuum in West Germany that the communists might attempt to exploit. Furthermore, and the US government played an important role in pressing this view from the early 1950s, use of West Germany's power and wealth could help to reduce the contributions that other countries were making to the defence of Europe. The perceived desirability and need to incorporate the Federal Republic into the Western European mainstream, allied with the willingness of Konrad Adenauer – the West German Chancellor from 1949–63 – and his governments to accept incorporation, thus further stimulated the pressure for inter-state cooperation and integration.

Economic factors

Just as pre-war and wartime experiences helped to produce the United Nations, so they also stimulated an interest in the creation of new international economic and financial arrangements. The first fruits of this were realised at the Bretton Woods Conference in 1944, where the representatives of forty-four countries, with the United Kingdom and the United States playing the leading roles, agreed to the establishment of two new bodies. The first was the International Monetary Fund (IMF), which was to alleviate currency instability by creating facilities for countries with temporary balance of payments difficulties to have access to short-term credit facilities. The second was the International Bank for Reconstruction and Development (the World Bank), which was to provide long-term loans for schemes that required major investment. In 1947, at much the same time as the IMF and the World Bank became operative, international economic cooperation was taken a stage further when twenty-three countries negotiated the General Agreement on Tariffs and Trade (GATT), whose purpose was to facilitate trade through the lowering of international trade barriers.

Although Western European governments (or, more usually, national representatives, since governments on the continent were not properly restored until 1945–6) played their part in creating the new international economic arrangements, it was felt in many quarters that there should also be specifically Western European-based economic initiatives and organisations. In 1947–8 this feeling was given a focus, an impetus and an urgency when the rapid post-war economic recovery that most states were able to engineer by the adoption of expansionist policies created massive balance of payments deficits, and dollar shortages in particular. Governments were faced with major currency problems, with not being able to pay for their imports and with the prospect of their economic recovery coming to a sudden and premature end. In these circumstances, and for reasons that were not altogether altruistic – a strong Western Europe was in its political, security and economic interests – the United States stepped in with economic aid in the form of the European Recovery Programme, or Marshall Aid as it came to be known after the US Secretary of State, George Marshall, who championed it. But there was a condition attached to the aid: the recipient states must endeavour to promote greater economic cooperation among themselves. As a result, the first major post-war Western European organisation, the Organisation for European Economic Cooperation (OEEC), was established, with sixteen founding member states, in April 1948. Its short-term task was to manage the US aid, encourage joint economic policies, and discourage barriers to trade; in the longer term, its stated aim was to build 'a sound European economy through the cooperation of its members'. In the event, although the OEEC did some valuable work – the most notable perhaps being to establish payments schemes which in the 1940s and 1950s did much to further trade between the member countries – it never made much progress towards its grander ambitions. Rather like the Council of Europe, its large and somewhat heterogeneous membership, coupled with the strictly intergovernmental nature of its decision-making structure, meant that ambitious proposals were always successfully opposed. Partly as a result of this, and partly in recognition of growing interdependence among all industrialised countries, in 1961 the OEEC gave way to the Organisation for Economic Cooperation and Development (OECD), whose membership was made open to non-European countries and which was to have broader objectives reflecting wider and changing interests.

The OEEC thus stemmed from post-war circumstances that mixed the general with the particular. That is to say, attitudes coming out of the war that favoured economic cooperation between Western European states were given a direction by particular requirements that were related to the war and its immediate aftermath. Only three years later, a similar mixture of general underlying and specific triggering factors combined to produce the first of the European Communities: the European Coal and Steel Community (ECSC). As will be shown in Chapter 2, in a number of ways the ECSC was to mark a major advance in the Western European integration process, not least in that its institutions were empowered not only to act on an intergovernmental basis but also, in some circumstances, supranationally: that is, some binding decisions could be taken without all member states necessarily agreeing with them.

* * *

The most dramatic effect of the Second World War in Europe was, of course, the division of the continent. The war precluded the possibility of Central and Eastern European states participating in the new cooperation and integration schemes that were launched in the West of the continent in the post-war years.

In Western Europe, the effects of some of the political and economic factors associated with the Second World War, such as the presence of Resistance leaders in governments, were essentially short-term. Furthermore, some of the factors, such as the increased need and willingness of the Western European states to cooperate with one another to promote economic growth, were not so much caused by the war as given a push by it. Nonetheless, taken together the factors produced a set of circumstances that enabled Western European cooperation and integration to get off the ground in the 1940s and 1950s.

Western European states naturally differed in the particulars and perceptions of their post-war situations. As a result, there was no general agreement on precisely what the new spirit of cooperation should attempt to achieve. Many different schemes were advanced and many different organisations were established to tackle particular issues, problems and requirements. Thus the war did not produce anything

---

Table 1.1 The creation of major Western and Western European international organisations in the early post-World War II years*

1948	Organisation for European Economic Co-operation
1949	North Atlantic Treaty Organisation
1949	Council of Europe
1951	European Coal and Steel Community
1954	Western European Union
1957	European Economic Community and European Atomic Energy Community
1960	European Free Trade Association

* Indicates year founding treaty was signed.

remotely like a united Western European movement between the states. But it did produce new realities and changed attitudes that enabled, or forced, virtually all the states to recognise at least some commonalities and shared interests. As a consequence, the way was opened for a number of new and inter-state Western European and Western European-dominated organisations to be established (see Table 1.1). Of these organisations, those that were able to offer clear advantages and benefits to members were able to act as a base for further developments. As the ECSC in particular was to quickly demonstrate, cooperation and integration can breed more of the same.

Interdependence

It has become customary to suggest that whilst both political and economic factors were crucial in promoting Western European cooperation and integration in the formative post-war years, the former have now declined in relation to the latter. The impact of modernisation is generally agreed to be a key reason for this. It has broadened the international agenda from its traditional power and security concerns to embrace a range of economic and social issues, and at the same time it has produced an interconnectedness and interrelatedness between states, especially in the economic and monetary spheres, that amounts to an interdependence.

Economic interdependence has arisen particularly from three features of the post-1945 world: the enormously increased volume of world trade; the internationalisation of production, in which multinational corporations have played a prominent part; and – especially since the early 1970s – the fluctuations and uncertainties associated with currency exchange rates and international monetary arrangements. Within Western Europe there have been many regional dimensions to this development of interdependence, two of which have been especially important in promoting the integration process. First, since the Second World War the external trade of all significant Western European countries has become increasingly Western European focused. The EC/EU has played an important role in encouraging this trend, and all EU-15 member states (that is, pre-May 2004 members) now conduct at least 60 per cent of their trade inside the EU. Second, from the 1960s monetary power within Western Europe increasingly came to be held by those who made the monetary decisions for the strongest economy: Germany. Changes in German interest rates or exchange rates had immense and potentially very destabilising implications elsewhere in Western Europe.

As a result of interdependence a wide variety of economic and financial issues have increasingly come to be no longer limited to, and indeed in some respects not even much related to, national boundaries. States have become increasingly vulnerable to outside events and increasingly unable to act in isolation. They must consult, cooperate and, some would argue, integrate with one another in the interests of international and national economic stability and growth. In consequence, when a problem has been seen to require a truly international economic effort most Western European states have been prepared to try to find solutions at this level: in the IMF, in GATT and its successor the World Trade Organisation (WTO), in the Bank for International Settlements, and elsewhere. When a regional response has seemed more appropriate or more practical, Western European-based arrangements have been sought. The most obvious examples of such arrangements have been EC/EU-based. For instance: the decisions that were taken in the 1950s to create a common market and then to launch the Single European Market (SEM) programme in the mid-1980s were rooted in beliefs that the dismantlement of trade barriers between Western European states would further their economic efficiency and prosperity; the development of European research programmes from the early 1980s was in response to an increasing recognition that Western European states must pool their scientific and technological resources and knowledge if they were to be able to compete successfully in world markets against the Americans, the Japanese and other competitors; and the movement towards Economic and Monetary Union (EMU) from the late 1980s was based on the assumption that the coordination and the convergence of national economic and monetary policies and the establishment of a centrally managed single currency was necessary for the completion of the SEM programme and would serve to promote further trade, growth and prosperity in participating states.

Economic interdependence is not the only feature of modern interdependence. Advances in communications and travel have increasingly placed on the international and European agendas issues that either did not exist before the Second World War or were seen as being of purely domestic concern. Now it is commonly accepted that if these issues are to be properly managed they must be dealt with at the inter-state level. Governments thus discuss, and in the EC from the early 1970s began adopting understandings and developing joint policies on, matters as diverse as transfrontier television arrangements, data protection, and action against drug traffickers and football hooliganism.

But despite all the attention that is now given to interdependence as the motor of European integration, and despite the associated assertion that reasonably quickly after the Second World War economic factors came to far outweigh political factors in shaping relations between Western European states, the case should not be overstated. One reason for this is that modern interdependence does not necessarily produce an inescapable and wholly unavoidable set of integrationist processes and developments. There is certainly an integrationist logic attached to interdependence, but for much of integration to actually proceed political choices and decisions have to be made. As the history of negotiations on European integration since the Second World War demonstrate – from the negotiations in the late 1940s to establish the Council of Europe to the negotiations in the early 2000s on a Constitutional Treaty for Europe – politicians, and indeed publics, are capable of adopting an array of often sharply conflicting views of what is necessary and what is desirable when they are faced with particular choices and decisions. A second reason for exercising some caution when evaluating the impact on integration of economic interdependence is that political factors have continued to be important in shaping the nature and pace of integration processes. This was clearly illustrated in the wake of the 1990 reunification of Germany, when a powerful stimulus to a new round of integrationist negotiations was the growing conviction among decision-making elites, most particularly in France, that if Germany was to be prevented from dominating the EU it must be tied more tightly to its neighbours. A third reason for not overemphasising the importance of modern interdependence to the neglect of other factors is that interdependence of a quite different kind – different in that it has arisen not from modernisation but rather from the relatively diminished significance of the European states in the post-1945 period – has continued to play an important part in encouraging cooperation and integration between states. So, for example, with respect to the external political role of the EU, the fact that since the Second World War, Western European states have had relatively limited power and weight when acting individually on the world stage has provided a powerful inducement for them to try to speak as one if they wish to exert a significant influence on world political events. Accordingly, from the early 1970s, they gradually strengthened their mechanisms for inter-state foreign policy cooperation so as to enable them to engage in extensive consultations, and increasingly to adopt joint positions, on foreign policy issues. Similar processes have been under way also in respect of security considerations, with the perception, until the collapse of communism, of the Soviet Union as Western Europe's main political enemy, allied with the inability of any single Western Europe state to offer by itself a wholly credible defence capability, encouraging close military cooperation between the states in the context of both the Western alliance and associated Western Europe defence groupings. The Soviet threat has now disappeared, but potential security dangers of many kinds still abound and these have played an important part in ensuring that not only civil security but also military security is now prominently on the EU's agenda.

National considerations

Differing national positions and preferences

Although most Western European states after 1945 paid at least lip service to the idea of a united Western Europe, there was no consensus amongst them on what this should mean in practice. The rhetoric was often grand, but discussions on specific proposals usually revealed considerable variations in ambitions, motives, intentions and perceptions. Most crucially of all, states differed in their assessments of the consequences for them, in terms of gains and losses, of forging closer relations with their neighbours. These differing assessments resulted in some states being prepared and able to cooperate and integrate more than others, or being prepared to do so at an earlier time. For the fact is that in conducting their relations with their neighbours Western European states were

no more willing to act on the basis of general and idealistic integrationist beliefs than they were than when they were dealing with non-Western European states. Rather, as Alan Milward (2000) has shown, from the very early years of the European integration process there were considerable variations in the judgements of the governments of Western European states on whether, in what circumstances, and in what ways cooperation and integration would serve their national interest.

These variations stemmed largely from real and objective differences in the situations of Western European states. These differing situations are explored later in this chapter and in Chapter 3, but to give just three very brief examples here: Germany and Italy were both interested in establishing themselves back in the European mainstream; as the most obvious Western European 'victor' of the Second World War and with its close links with the USA and the countries of its Empire and then the Commonwealth, UK governments in the early post-war years saw no need to get too close to other Western European states; and as virtual military dictatorships, Spain and Portugal were excluded from most formal cooperationist and integrationist developments.

In consequence, the advancement of cooperation and integration between Western European states in the post-war years was far from coherent or ordered. In the late 1940s and into the 1950s most states were willing to be associated with intergovernmental organisations that made few demands on them – and hence joined the OEEC and the Council of Europe – but there was usually less interest when organisations were proposed that had specific policy purposes or that went beyond intergovernmental cooperation into supranational integration. While all Western European states were touched by at least some of the general cooperation and integration inducing factors that have been examined on the last few pages, the differences between them resulted in their capacity and enthusiasm for cooperation and integration varying in terms of both nature and timing. As a result, the more ambitious post-war schemes – for the ECSC, for a European Defence Community (EDC, which in the event was never established), and for the EEC and Euratom – initially involved only a restricted membership. It was not until circumstances and attitudes in other states changed, and until an obstacle that emerged amongst the founding states themselves – in the form of President de Gaulle's opposition to UK membership – was removed, that the EC gradually expanded in the 1970s, 1980s and 1990s to include eventually virtually all of Western Europe's larger and medium-sized states.

The founding members of the European Community: Belgium, France, West Germany, Italy, Luxembourg and the Netherlands

What were the particular circumstances and needs in Belgium, France, West Germany, Italy, Luxembourg and the Netherlands that resulted in these states being the first to show a willingness to go beyond the cooperative intergovernmental ventures that were established in Western Europe in the late 1940s? Why did these states negotiate and sign the three treaties – the 1951 Treaty of Paris and the two 1957 Treaties of Rome – that founded the European Communities?

It was only cautiously, tentatively, and not without reservations that each came to the view that the benefits of integration, as opposed to just cooperation, would outweigh what appeared to be the major disadvantage – a loss of sovereignty. Some of the perceived advantages that supranational organisations could offer were shared by all of the six, but there were also more nationally based hopes and ambitions.

For the three Benelux countries, their experience of the Second World War had re-emphasised their vulnerability to hostile and more powerful neighbours and the need to be on good terms with West Germany and France. Related to this, their size – Belgium and the Netherlands were only middle-ranking European powers whilst Luxembourg was a very small state – meant that their only real prospect of exercising any sort of influence in Europe, let alone the world, was through a more unified inter-state system. As for economic considerations, they were used to the idea of integration since Benelux economic agreements and arrangements pre-dated the Second World War, and negotiations to re-launch and deepen these had been under way well before the war ended. There was also the fact that not one of the Benelux states was in a strong enough position to ignore Franco-German initiatives for economic integration.

Italy too had a number of reasons for welcoming close relations with other Western European states. First, after more than twenty years of Fascist rule followed by military defeat, European integration offered the prospect of a new start, and from a basis of respectability. Second, in May 1947 (as also occurred in France) the Communist Party left government and for some years thereafter seemed to be intent on fermenting internal revolution. The clear anti-communist tenor of other Western European governments looked comforting, and a possible source of assistance, to Italy's nervous Christian Democratic-led governments. Third, Italy faced economic difficulties on all fronts: with unemployment, inflation, balance of payments imbalances, currency instability and – especially in the south – poverty. Almost any scheme that offered the possibility of finding new markets and generating economic growth was to be welcomed.

Integration was seen as helping France to deal with two of its key post-war policy goals: the containment of Germany and rapid economic growth. In the early 1950s the ECSC was especially important in this regard, offering the opportunity to break down age-old barriers and hostilities on the one hand and giving France access to vital German raw materials and markets on the other. Later in the 1950s, when 'the German problem' was seen as less pressing but German economic competition seemed to be posing an increasing threat, France took steps in the negotiations that produced the EEC to ensure that as part of the price of continued integration certain French interests – including economic protection for its farmers – would be given special treatment.

Konrad Adenauer saw Western European unification as a means by which German self-respect could be regained and by which the Federal Republic could re-establish itself in the international community. Western Europe would also, along with the Atlantic Alliance, provide a much-needed buttress against the perceived threat from the East. More specifically, the ECSC would enable West Germany to rid itself of Allied restrictions and interference, and the more open markets of the EEC would offer immense opportunities for what, in the 1950s, quickly became the fastest growing economy in Western Europe.

Concluding Remarks: The Ragged Nature of the Integration Process in Western Europe

After the Second World War the way in which Western European governments related to and communicated with one another was gradually transformed. A key role in this transformation was played by new international governmental organisations (IGOs). Some of these IGOs were global in their composition, others were regionally based; some had sweeping but vaguely defined responsibilities, others had specific sectoral briefs; most were purely intergovernmental in structure, but those that were within the framework of the European Communities were overlain with supranational powers. At a minimum, all provided frameworks in which national representatives met with one another to discuss matters of mutual interest.

As later chapters of this book will show, the European Communities – which from the 1960s increasingly came to be referred to in the singular as the European Community (EC) – were to develop into the best known, most developed and most important of Western Europe's, and ultimately Europe's, interstate organisations. But the EC was never the only significant Western Europe-wide organisation, and it was not the first such organisation to be established. On the contrary, after the Second World War, numerous proposals were advanced and many arrangements were set in place for organised cooperation and integration among the states. The more ambitious of these sought to bring the whole of Western Europe together in some sort of federal union. The more cautious were limited to the pursuit of restricted aims for just some of the states.

So although the logic of circumstances and of political and economic changes brought the states much more closely together, there can hardly be said to have been a common and coherent integrationist force at work in Western Europe in the post-war years. Far from the states being bound together in the pursuit of a shared visionary mission, relations between them were frequently extremely uncomfortable and uneasy, based as they were on a host of different national needs and perceptions of what might be possible and what was necessary. This remains the case to the present day. In consequence, the processes of cooperation and integration have operated in many different forums, at many different levels, in many different ways, and at many different speeds. Even in the EC/EU, which has been at the integrationist core, the course of the integration process has varied considerably with, for example, the mid-1970s until the early 1980s being years of relatively slow integrationist advance and the mid-1980s until the early 1990s being years of rapid progress.

It is, of course, the conflicting nature of many of the factors that affect the integration process that has resulted in the process being so rocky, uncertain and unpredictable. Moreover, the factors themselves have been subject to considerable and unforeseeable change, no more so than since the early 1990s with the context in which the pressures that affect the furtherance of integration being transformed by the ending of the Cold War and the break-up of the Soviet Union. After four decades of Europe having been politically divided in two, decades in which Western Europe tended to think of itself as *being* Europe, fundamental issues concerning the nature of the continent as a whole came onto the agenda. In these circumstances, new links, contacts and forms of cooperation were rapidly established between the countries of Western and Eastern Europe, advanced not least by many of the latter seeking EU membership within only a few years of having been released from Soviet domination. The manner in which the developments in the former communist bloc transformed what had been a *Western European integration* process into a *European integration* process are explored in Chapter 4.

Chapter 2

The Creation of the European Community

The European Coal and Steel Community

Much of the early impetus behind the first of the European Communities, the ECSC, was provided by two Frenchmen. Jean Monnet, who had pioneered France's successful post-war experiment with indicative economic planning, provided much of the technical and administrative initiative and behind-the-scenes drive. Robert Schuman, the French Foreign Minister from 1948 to early 1953, acted as the political advocate. Both were ardent supporters of European unity, both believed that the OEEC and the Council of Europe – where anyone could be exempted from a decision – could not provide the necessary impetus, and both came to the conclusion that:

> A start would have to be made by doing something both more practical and more ambitious. National sovereignty would have to be tackled more boldly and on a narrower front (Monnet, 1978: 274).

Many of those who were attracted to the ECSC saw it in very restrictive terms: as an organisation that might further certain limited and carefully defined purposes. Certainly it would not have been established had it not offered to potential member states – in particular its two main pillars, France and West Germany – the possibility that it might serve to satisfy specific and pressing national interests and needs. But for some, including Monnet and Schuman, the project was much more ambitious and long-term. When announcing the plan in May 1950, Schuman – in what subsequently became known as the Schuman Declaration – was quite explicit that the proposals were intended to be but the first step in the realisation of a vision of a united Europe that would have Franco-German reconciliation at its heart. But, he famously warned:

> Europe will not be made all at once, or according to a single plan. It will be built through concrete achievements which first create a *de facto* solidarity (the Schuman Declaration is reproduced in Salmon and Nicoll, 1997: 44–6).

In similar vein, Monnet informed governments during the negotiations:

> The Schuman proposals provide a basis for the building of a new Europe through the concrete achievement of a supranational regime within a limited but controlling area of economic effort ... The indispensable first

principle of these proposals is the abnegation of sovereignty in a limited but decisive field (Monnet, 1978: 316).

The German Chancellor, Konrad Adenauer, agreed with this. Addressing the Bundestag in June 1950 he stated:

> Let me make a point of declaring in so many words and in full agreement, not only with the French Government but also with M. Jean Monnet, that the importance of this project is above all political and not economic (quoted in *ibid.*: 319–20).

Schuman made it clear in his Declaration that whilst he hoped other countries would also participate, France and West Germany would proceed with the plan in any event (West Germany having already agreed privately in principle). Italy, Belgium, Luxembourg and the Netherlands took up the invitation, and in April 1951 the six countries signed the Treaty of Paris, which established the ECSC for a period of fifty years from the entry into force of the ECSC Treaty. The ECSC duly came into operation in July 1952 and lasted until the expiry of the Treaty in July 2002, when ECSC responsibilities and activities were transferred to the European Community.

The ECSC Treaty broke new ground in two principal ways. First, its policy aims were extremely ambitious, entailing not just the creation of a free trade area but also laying the foundations for a common market in what at the time were some of the basic materials of any industrialised society: coal, coke, iron ore, steel and scrap. This, it was hoped, would ensure orderly supplies to all member states, produce a rational expansion and modernisation of production, and improve the conditions and lifestyles of those working in the industries in question. Second, it was the first of the European inter-state organisations to possess significant supranational characteristics. These characteristics were to be found in the new central institutions, which had the power, amongst other things, to make and oversee laws in such important areas of activity as the abolition and prohibition of internal tariff barriers, of state subsidies, and of restrictive practices; the harmonisation of external commercial policy; and imposing levies on coal and steel production to finance the ECSC's

activities. Four main institutions were created, as set out in Box 2.1.

In its early years the ECSC was judged to be an economic success. Customs tariffs and quotas were abolished, progress was made on the removal of non-tariff barriers to trade, the restructuring of the industries was assisted, politicians and civil servants from the member states became accustomed to working with one another and, above all, output and inter-state trade rapidly increased (although many economists would now query whether the increases were *because* of the ECSC). As a result, the ECSC helped to pave the way for further integration.

However, the success of the early years was soon checked. In 1958–9, when cheap oil imports and a fall in energy consumption combined to produce an over-capacity in coal production, the ECSC was faced with its first major crisis – and failed the test. The member states rejected the High Authority's proposals for a Community-wide solution and sought their own, uncoordinated, protective measures. The coal crisis thus revealed that the High Authority was not as powerful as many had believed and was not in a position to impose a general policy on the states if they were determined to resist.

This relative weakness of the High Authority/Commission to press policies right through is one of the principal reasons why truly integrated Western European coal and steel industries, in which prices and distributive decisions are a consequence of an open and free market, have not fully emerged. Many barriers to intra-EU trade still remain. Some of these, such as restrictive practices and national subsidies, the High Authority and then the Commission have tried to remove, but with only limited success. Others, particularly in the steel sector, have been formulated and utilised by the Commission itself as its task has switched from encouraging expansion to managing contraction.

But arguably the major problem with the ECSC was that as coal and steel declined in importance in relation to other energy sources, what increasingly was required was not so much policies for coal and steel in isolation, but a coordinated and effective Community energy policy. National differences have prevented such a policy being developed, although there has been progress in recent years.

Early advocates and architects of European integration

Photo 2.1 Jean Monnet, the main deviser of the Schuman Plan and President of the High Authority of the ECSC, 1952–55

Photo 2.2 Robert Schuman, former French Prime Minister, Foreign Minister 1948–52, and presenter of the Schuman Declaration of 9 May 1950 advocating the creation of the ECSC

Photo 2.3 Konrad Adenauer, German Chancellor 1949–63

Photo 2.4 Alcide de Gasperi, Italian Prime Minister 1945–53

Box 2.1

The main institutions created by the ECSC Treaty

The High Authority. There were to be nine members of this appointed institution, including at least one from each member state. Crucially, all must be 'completely independent in the performance of their duties'. In other words, no one would be, or should regard themselves as being, a national delegate or representative. The High Authority was given strong independent powers, including on the prohibition of subsidies and aids, decisions on whether or not agreements between undertakings were permissible, and action against restrictive practices. The membership and powers of the High Authority combined to give it a clear supranational character

The Council of Ministers. Ministers from the national governments constituted the membership of the Council, with each state having one representative. Decision-making procedures in the Council depended on the matter under consideration: sometimes a unanimous vote was required, sometimes a qualified majority, sometimes a simple majority. The main responsibility of the Council was to 'harmonise the actions of the High Authority and that of the Governments, which are responsible for the general economic policies of their countries' (Article 26, ECSC Treaty). More specifically, the Treaty gave the Council formal control over some, but far from all, of the High Authority's actions.

The Common Assembly. Members were not to be elected but to be chosen by national parliaments. The Assembly's powers – notwithstanding an ability to pass a motion of censure on the High Authority – were essentially only advisory.

The Court of Justice. Since many ECSC decisions were to have legal status, a court was needed to settle conflicts between the states, between the organs of the Community, and between the states and the organs. The Court was to be composed of six members – one from each member state. The Court's judgements were to be enforceable within the territory of the member states.

From the ECSC to the EEC

The perceived success of the ECSC in its early years provided an impetus for further integration. Another institutional development of the 1950s also played an important role in paving the way for the creation of the two additional European Communities that were to be created in 1957. This was the projected European Defence Community (EDC).

In the early 1950s, against the background of the Cold War and the outbreak of the Korean War, many Western politicians and military strategists saw the need for greater Western European cooperation in defence matters. This would involve the integration of West Germany – which was not a member of NATO – into the Western Alliance. The problem was that some European countries, especially France, were not yet ready for German rearmament, whilst West Germany

itself, though willing to re-arm, was not willing to do so on the basis of the tightly controlled and restricted conditions that other countries appeared to have in mind for it. In these circumstances the French Prime Minister, René Pleven, launched proposals in October 1950 that offered a possible way forward. In announcing his plan to the National Assembly he stated that the French government 'proposes the creation, for our common defence, of a European Army under the political institutions of a united Europe' (Pleven's statement is reproduced in Harryvan and van der Harst, 1997: 65–9). By the end of 1951 the six governments involved in the establishment of the ECSC had agreed to establish an EDC. Its institutional structure was to be similar to the ECSC: a Joint Defence Commission, a Council of Ministers, an advisory Assembly and a Court of Justice.

In May 1952 a draft EDC Treaty was signed, but in the event the EDC and the European Political

Community that increasingly came to be associated with it were not established. Ratification problems arose in France and Italy, and in August 1954 the French National Assembly rejected the EDC by 319 votes to 264 with 43 abstentions. There were a number of reasons for this: continuing unease about German rearmament; concern that the French government would not have sole control of its military forces; doubts about the efficiency of an integrated force; disquiet that the strongest European military power (the United Kingdom) was not participating; and a feeling that, with the end of the Korean War and the death of Stalin, the EDC was not as necessary as it had seemed when it was first proposed.

Following the collapse of the EDC project, an alternative and altogether less demanding approach was taken to the still outstanding question of West Germany's contribution to the defence of the West. This took the form of a revival and extension of the Brussels Treaty 'for collaboration in economic, social and cultural matters and for collective defence' that had been signed in 1948 by the three Benelux countries, France and the UK. At a conference in London in the autumn of 1954 West Germany and Italy agreed to accede to the Brussels Treaty and all seven countries agreed that the new arrangements should be incorporated into a Western European Union (WEU). The WEU came into effect in May 1955 as a loosely structured, essentially consultative, primarily defence-orientated organisation that, amongst other things, permitted West German rearmament subject to various constraints. It also enabled West Germany to become a member of NATO.

The failure of the EDC, especially when set alongside the 'success' of the WEU, highlighted the difficulties involved in pressing ahead too quickly with integrationist proposals. In particular, it showed that quasi-federalist approaches in politically sensitive areas would meet with resistance. But, at the same time, the fact that such an ambitious scheme as the EDC had come so close to adoption demonstrated that alternative initiatives, especially if they were based on the original Schuman view that political union could be best achieved through economic integration, might well be successful. It was partly with this in mind that the Foreign Ministers of the ECSC six met at Messina in Sicily in June 1955 to discuss proposals by the three Benelux countries for further economic integration. At Messina the Ministers

---

Box 2.2

Extracts from the Messina Resolution*

The governments ... believe the moment has come to go a step further towards the construction of Europe. In their opinion this step should first of all be taken in the economic field.

They consider that the further progress must be towards the setting up of a united Europe by the development of common institutions, the gradual merging of national economies, the creation of a common market, and the gradual harmonization of their social policies.

Such a policy appears to them to be indispensable if Europe's position in the world is to be maintained, her influence restored, and the standard of living of her population progressively raised.

* The full Resolution is reproduced in Salmon and Nicoll, 1997: 59–61).

---

agreed on a resolution, extracts of which are set out in Box 2.2.

To give effect to the Messina Resolution, a committee of governmental representatives and experts was established under the chairmanship of the Belgian Foreign Minister, Paul-Henri Spaak. The UK was invited to participate and did so until November 1955, but then withdrew when it became apparent that its hopes of limiting developments to the establishment of a loose free trade area were not acceptable to the six. In April 1956 the Foreign Ministers accepted the report of the Spaak Committee and used it as the basis for negotiations that in 1957 produced the two Treaties of Rome: the more important of these treaties established the European Economic Community (EEC) and the other the European Atomic Energy Community (Euratom).

Both before and after April 1956 the negotiations between the six governments were extensive and intense. At the end of the negotiations it can be said that, in broad terms, provisions were made in the treaties for those areas upon which the governments were able to reach agreement, but where there were divisions matters were largely left aside for further negotiations and were either omitted from the treaties

Photo 2.5 Signing of the EEC Treaty, Rome, 25 March 1957

altogether or were referred to only in a general way. So the EEC Treaty set out fairly clear rules on trade, but only guiding principles were laid down for social and agricultural policy.

The inclusion in the EEC Treaty of topics such as social and agricultural policy reflected a series of compromises among the six countries, especially between the two strongest ones – France and West Germany. France feared that Germany was likely to become the main beneficiary of the more open markets of the proposed customs union and so looked for compensation elsewhere. This took a number of forms, most notably: insisting on special protection for agriculture – French farmers had historically been well protected from foreign competition and around one-fifth of the French population still earned a living from the land; pressing the case of an atomic energy Community, which would help guarantee France greater independence in energy; and seeking privileged relations with the six for France's overseas dependencies.

Eventually the negotiations were completed, and on 25 March 1957 the two treaties were signed. Only in France and Italy were there any problems with ratification: the French Chamber of Deputies voted 342 for and 239 against, and the Italian Chamber of Deputies voted 311 for and 144 against. In both countries the largest opposition bloc comprised the communists. The treaties came into effect on 1 January 1958.

The EEC and Euratom Treaties

The policy concerns of the EEC Treaty

Of the two Rome Treaties the EEC Treaty was by far the most important. Article 2 of the Treaty laid down broad objectives, as can be seen in Box 2.3.

Many of the subsequent Treaty articles were concerned with following up these broad objectives with fuller, though still often rather general, guidelines for policy development. These policy guidelines can be grouped under two broad headings.

Policy guidelines concerned with the establishment of a common market

The common market was to be based on the following:

1   The removal of all tariffs and quantitative restrictions on internal trade. This would make the Community a free trade area.
2   The erection of a Common External Tariff (CET). This would mean that goods entering the Community would do so on the same basis no matter what their point of entry. No member state would therefore be in a position to gain a competitive advantage by, say, reducing its external tariffs on vital raw materials. The CET would take the Community beyond a mere free trade area and make it a customs union. It would also serve as the basis for the development of a common external

---

Box 2.3

Article 2 of the EEC Treaty

The Community shall have as its task, by establishing a common market and progressively approximating the economic policies of Member States, to promote throughout the Community a harmonious development of economic activities, a continuous and balanced expansion, an increase in stability, an accelerated raising of the standard of living and closer relations between the states belonging to it.

trade policy – known as the Common Commercial Policy (CCP).

3 The prohibition of a range of practices having as their effect the distortion or prevention of competition between the member states.

4 Measures to promote not only the free movement of goods between the member states but also the free movement of persons, services and capital.

Policy guidelines concerned with making the Community more than just a common market

Making it exactly what, however, was left unclear, as it had to be given the uncertainties, disagreements and compromises that formed the background to the signing of the Treaty. There was certainly the implication of a movement towards some sort of general economic integration and references were made to the 'coordination' of economic and monetary policies, but they were vague and implicitly long-term. Such references as there were to specific sectoral policies – as, for example, with the provisions for 'the adoption of a common policy in the sphere of agriculture', and the statement that the objectives of the Treaty 'shall … be pursued by Member States within the framework of a common transport policy' – were couched in somewhat general terms.

* * *

The EEC Treaty was thus very different in character from the constitutions of nation states. Whereas the latter have little, if anything, to say about policy, the EEC Treaty had policy as its main concern. The nature of that concern was such that many have suggested that the policy framework indicated and outlined in the Treaty was guided by a clear philosophy or ideology: that of free-market, liberal, non-interventionist capitalism. Unquestionably there is much in this view: on the one hand the market mechanism and the need to prevent abuses to competition were accorded a high priority; on the other hand there were few references to ways in which joint activities and interventions should be promoted for non-market-based purposes. But the case should not be overstated. First, because competition itself was seen as requiring considerable intervention and management from the centre. Second, because there

were some provisions for non-market policies: in the proposed common policy for agriculture, for example, which was given a special place in the Treaty precisely because of (mainly French) fears of what would happen should agriculture be exposed to a totally free market; in the proposed social policy, which was intended to help soften unacceptable market consequences; and in the proposed common transport policy where specific allowance was to be made for aids 'if they meet the needs of coordination of transport or if they represent reimbursement for the discharge of certain obligations inherent in the concept of a pubic service'. Third, because the Treaty was highly dependent on the future cooperation of the member states for successful policy development, there was never any question – given the Christian Democratic and Social Democratic principles of most EC governments – of an immediate abandonment of national economic controls and a remorseless and inevitable drive towards uninhibited free market capitalism.

The policy concerns of the Euratom Treaty

The policy concerns of the Euratom Treaty were naturally confined to the atomic energy field. Chapters of the Treaty covered such areas of activity as the promotion of research, of the dissemination of information, of health and safety standards, and of a nuclear common market. However, and even more than with the EEC Treaty, differences between the states on key points resulted in the force of many of the provisions of these chapters being watered down by exceptions and loopholes. For example, under Article 52 an agency was established with 'exclusive right to conclude contracts relating to the supply of ores, scarce materials and special fissile materials coming from inside the Community or from outside'. Article 66, however, set out circumstances in which states could buy on the world markets provided Commission approval was obtained. Similarly, Treaty provisions aimed at a pooling and sharing of technical information and knowledge were greatly weakened – largely at French insistence – by provisions allowing for secrecy where national security was involved.

The institutional provisions of the Treaties

The ECSC Treaty served as the institutional model for the EEC and Euratom Treaties, but with modifications which had as their effect a tilting away from supranationalism towards intergovernmentalism. As with the ECSC, both the EEC and Euratom were to have four principal institutions. These are set out in Box 2.4.

The greater intergovernmental character of the institutional arrangements of the 1957 Treaties took the form of less independent powers for the Commission as compared with the equivalent powers of the High Authority in the ECSC Treaty and a requirement that most of the key decisions in the Council would have to be made unanimously. However, there were grounds for believing that the system could, and probably would, serve as a launching pad for a creeping supranationalism. One of these grounds was provision in the EEC Treaty for increased use of majority voting in the Council as the Community became established. Another was the expectation that the Assembly would soon be elected by direct suffrage and that its authority would thereby be increased. And a third was the seemingly reasonable assumption that if the Communities proved to be a success the member states would become less concerned about their national rights and would increasingly cede greater powers to the central institutions.

Box 2.4

The main institutions created by the EEC and Euratom Treaties*

An appointed *Commission* would assume the role exercised by, and in its composition would be similar to the nature of, the ECSC's High Authority. It would be the principal policy initiator, it would have some decision-making powers of its own, and it would carry certain responsibilities for policy implementation. But it would have less power than the High Authority to impose decisions on member states.

A *Council of Ministers*, with greater powers than its equivalent under the ECSC, would be the principal decision-making body. Circumstances in which it must take its decisions unanimously, and circumstances in which majority and qualified majority votes were permissible, were specified.

An *Assembly* would exercise advisory and (limited) supervisory powers. Initially it would be composed of delegates from national parliaments, but after appropriate arrangements were made it was to be elected 'by direct universal suffrage in accordance with a uniform procedure in all Member States'.

A *Court of Justice* was charged with the duty of ensuring that 'in the interpretation and application of this Treaty the law is observed'.

* A similar institutional structure was created for both Communities. A Convention signed on the same day as both of the Community Treaties – 25 March 1957 – specified that the ECSC Assembly and Court of Justice should be common to all three Communities.

Concluding Remarks

The Treaty of Paris and the two Treaties of Rome are thus the Founding Treaties of the three European Communities. At the time of their signings they marked major steps forward in the development of post-war interstate relations. They did so by laying the bases for signatory states to integrate specific and core areas of their economic activities and by embodying a degree of supranationalism in the decision-making arrangements they established for the new Communities.

Insofar as it was the first treaty, the Treaty of Paris holds a special place in the history of European integration. In terms of long-term impact, however, the EEC Treaty has been the most important in that it has been on its wide policy base that much of European integration since 1958 has been constructed.

Though they laid down reasonably clear guidelines on, and requirements for, certain matters, the Founding Treaties were not intended to act as straitjackets with respect to the future shape and development of the Communities. Rather, they provided frameworks within which certain things would be expected to happen and other things could happen if decision makers so chose.

Attention in the next two chapters is therefore turned to the development of European integration since the Rome Treaties came into force in January 1958.

Chapter 3

The Deepening of the Integration Process

Since the European Communities were created in the 1950s, European integration has advanced in many ways. One, much-used and very useful, analytical device for capturing the nature of the ways in which integration has advanced is to distinguish between deepening and widening. Deepening refers to the development of vertical integration: that is, to the ever more intense nature of the integration that exists between member states. Widening refers to the development of horizontal integration: that is, to the growing geographical spread of the EC/EU via the accessions of new member states.

This chapter outlines the most important aspects of the deepening of the integration process. The examination does not take the form of a detailed account of the unfolding of every aspect of EC/EU deepening. For those who want such an account, the best starting point is Dinan, 2004. Nor does the chapter provide a chronological history – a Chronology of Main Events is included at the end of the book. Rather, the chapter provides an overview of the main features of the deepening process.

Three main features are considered: treaty development; the development of policy processes; and the development of policies. Since each of these features is explored further in other chapters of the book, attention in this chapter is restricted to the identification of key points associated with the features and to showing how they have impacted on one another.

Treaty Development

As was shown in Chapter 2, the Treaty of Paris and the two Treaties of Rome constitute the Founding Treaties of the European Communities. Over the years, in response to pressures for the EC/EU treaty framework to be extended, strengthened, and made more democratic, the Founding Treaties have been amended and supplemented by subsequent treaties. Table 3.1 lists the EC/EU's major treaties.

The EU's treaty framework today is thus radically different from the framework that was laid down in the 1950s.

The first major set of revisions to the Founding Treaties were incorporated in the 1986 Single European Act (SEA), which was something of a mixed bag, containing tidying up provisions, provisions designed to give the Community a broader policy remit, and provisions altering aspects of Community decision making. There were two main aspects to these last provisions. On the one

Table 3.1 The EC/EU's major treaties

Name of Treaty	Date signed	Entered into force
Treaty establishing the European Coal and Steel Community	18 April 1951	23 July 1952 (The Treaty was signed for a 50-year duration. When the duration expired in 1952 responsibility for coal and steel was transferred to the European Community).
Treaties establishing the European Economic Community and the European Atomic Energy Community	25 March 1957	1 January 1958
Single European Act	17 and 28 February 1986	1 July 1987
Treaty of Maastricht	7 February 1992	1 November 1993
Treaty of Amsterdam	2 October 1997	1 May 1999
Treaty of Nice	26 February 2001	1 February 2003
Treaty of Lisbon	13 December 2007	1 December 2009

hand, the capacity of the Council of Ministers to take decisions by qualified majority vote (QMV) was strengthened, with the purpose of enabling the Community to pass the laws that would be necessary to give effect to the aim that was agreed at the June 1985 Milan European Council meeting of 'completing' the internal market by December 1992. On the other hand, with a view to be seen to be doing something about the so-called 'democratic deficit', the influence of the European Parliament (EP) (the Assembly started calling itself the European Parliament from 1962) was strengthened via the creation of a two stage legislative procedure – 'the cooperation procedure' – for some legislative proposals. Taken together, the Milan summit and the SEA are often described as heralding the 're-launch' of European integration in that they provided the foundations for a considerable increase in the pace of integration after some years of, if not sclerosis as is sometimes claimed, slow integrationist advance.

The 1992 Maastricht Treaty built on the momentum that the SEA provided for the integration process and advanced it significantly further. It did so in two main ways. First, it created the new organisation of the European Union, which was based on three pillars: the European Communities, a Common Foreign and Security Policy (CFSP), and Cooperation in the Fields of Justice and Home Affairs (JHA). Second, like the

SEA, it furthered policy and institutional deepening: the former, most notably, by laying down a procedure and a timetable for moving to Economic and Monetary Union (EMU) with a single currency; the latter, most notably, by further extending provision for QMV in the Council and by creating a new legislative procedure – co-decision – which, for the first time, gave the EP the power of veto over some legislative proposals.

The 1997 Amsterdam Treaty was neither as far-reaching nor as ambitious as either the SEA or the Maastricht Treaty. Indeed, for Euro-enthusiasts it was something of a disappointment in that it did not complete what had been intended to be its main job, namely adjusting the composition of the EU's institutions in preparation for enlargement. Nonetheless, it was significant for the integration process in that, like the SEA and the Maastricht Treaty, it too carried policy and institutional deepening forward, albeit more modestly. In respect of policy deepening, its main contribution was to strengthen the EU's decision-making capacity in certain justice and home affairs spheres. In respect of institutional deepening, its most important changes were to extend the co-decision procedure to more policy spheres and to virtually abolish the cooperation procedure.

The 2001 Nice Treaty was always intended to be limited in scope in that its remit was largely restricted to dealing with the 'Amsterdam leftovers'. That is to say, its main task was to make changes in the composition of the EU's institutions and in the voting strengths and voting procedures in the Council so as to enable the EU to absorb applicant states, whilst at the same time not undermining the capacity of the EU to function in a tolerably efficient manner. This, as Chapter 5 shows, the Treaty did.

The most recent of the EU's major treaties – the 2007 Lisbon Treaty – continued the pattern of all the treaties since the SEA in that it provided for advances in both policy and institutional integration. As is shown in Chapter 6, the institutional advances were the most significant, including as they did provision for a new position of European Council President and for a more united and identifiable position – entitled High Representative of the Union for Foreign Affairs and Security Policy – than had hitherto existed in respect of representing the EU in external political relations.

But the Lisbon Treaty was also in important respects different from earlier treaties in that it was subject to a much longer and more tortuous period of preparation, negotiation and ratification. The roots of the Treaty lay in the 2000 Nice summit, where the leaders of the member states, aware that the Nice Treaty they had just contracted was much more modest in nature than many would have liked, agreed that another IGC should be convened in 2004. This Nice agreement was quickly overtaken by a momentum that the next IGC should be much more ambitious than its predecessors, with the consequence that at their December 2001 Laeken summit the leaders decided to convene a Convention on the Future of Europe that would prepare the ground for the scheduled 2004 IGC. The Convention submitted its recommendations – which were for a Constitutional Treaty – and these were broadly accepted by the IGC. But the Constitutional Treaty ran into major ratification difficulties, largely because the use of the word 'constitutional' in its title (the treaty was never formally called a 'constitution') elevated its perceived importance and encouraged some member states to hold referendums on it. There had been difficulties in ratifying earlier treaties, but these had not been seen at the time as being insuperable, and in the event they proved not to be so. But the difficulties with ratifying the Constitutional Treaty were of quite a different order, with two founding member states – the Netherlands and France – rejecting the Treaty in referendums held in mid-2005. The consequences of these referendums was initially disputed, with many 'pro-integrationists' arguing for a continuation of the ratification process in the hope that somehow the Treaty could be rescued, and with many others concluding that the Treaty could never come into force. Over time 'realities' increasingly favoured the latter position and the prospects of the whole of the Treaty entering into force were eventually dropped. Another IGC was convened in 2007 and – acting on the basis of tight guidelines issued to it by the European Council – it quickly agreed a new treaty: a treaty that removed the controversial symbolic aspects of the Constitutional Treaty but that left most of its other contents intact. However, the new treaty – the Lisbon Treaty as it became called after being formally signed in the Portuguese capital – also ran into ratification difficulties when the Irish people rejected it in a referendum in June 2008. (Ireland was the only country in which a referendum on the Lisbon Treaty was held.) The entry into force of the Treaty was, in consequence, further delayed: until the Irish people ratified it in a second referendum that was held in October 2009. The Treaty eventually took effect in December 2009.

Development of Policy Processes

The Founding Treaties indicated a pattern of policy making and decision making in which the Commission would propose, the Parliament would advise, the Council would decide – usually by unanimity – and the Court of Justice would interpret when law was made For many years this is how inter-institutional relationships and processes generally worked in practice, and indeed in a few decision-making areas they still do so. But since the re-launch of the integration process in the mid-1980s there have been many additions and amendments to the pattern. Five of these additions and amendments are particularly worth noting.

First, the relationships between the four institutions themselves have altered in a number of ways. As integration has evolved, all of the institutions have extended their interests and simultaneously become increasingly less compartmentalised and less self-contained within the EU system. This has led not only to a certain blurring of responsibilities as the dividing lines between who does what have become less clear, but also to changes in the powers of, and balance between, institutions as there has emerged a more general sharing of powers. So, for example, the Council of Ministers has usurped some of the Commission's proposing responsibilities by becoming progressively more involved in helping to initiate and set the policy agenda; the Court has significantly affected the direction and pace of the integration process by issuing many judgements with considerable policy and institutional implications; and the EP, greatly assisted by treaty changes, has steadily extended its influence, especially its legislative influence. Indeed, such has been the increase in the EP's legislative role that the former Commission–Council axis on which EU legislative processes were based has been replaced by a Council–Commission–EP triangle.

Second, an increasing range of participants not associated with the four main institutions have become involved in policy making and decision making. The most important of these participants are the Heads of Government who, in regular summits – known as European Council meetings – have come to assume key agenda setting and decision-taking responsibilities that have had the effect of reducing the power and manoeuvrability of both the Council of Ministers and the Commission. Prominent amongst other actors who have inserted or attempted to insert themselves into decision-making processes are the many national and transnational sectoral interests and pressures that have come to cluster around the main institutions in order to monitor developments and, when possible, to advise or pressurise decision-makers.

Third, policy processes have become more varied and complex as they have come to function in many different ways at many different levels. In addition to what occurs in the structured settings of Council and Commission meetings, Parliamentary plenaries and committees, and Court sittings, there is a mosaic of less formal channels in which representatives of the institutions, the states, and interests, meet and interact to discuss and produce policies and decisions. Which processes and channels operate in particular cases, and what types of interactions occur therein, varies considerably from sector to sector, and can even do so from decision to decision.

Fourth, policy processes have become, in some respects at least, more efficient and democratic. They have become more efficient insofar as treaty reforms have made it possible for an increasing number of Council decisions to be taken by QMV rather than requiring unanimity. Decision making has thus been less hampered by having to wait for the slowest. Policy processes have become more democratic insofar as the EP – the only EU institution to be directly elected – has become more influential.

Fifth, policy processes have become more supranational in character. Whilst it is the case that many types of decisions can still only be taken if all member states agree, and as such decision making is intergovernmental, many key and binding decisions can be taken without all member states giving their explicit approval. This is the case where non-governmental EU institutions are assigned independent powers: as, for example the Commission is in respect of competition policy and the European Central Bank (ECB) is in respect of eurozone monetary policy. It is the case also where QMV can be used in the Council: and it is now available for most types of policy decisions.

Development of Policies

The EU's policy portfolio has expanded steadily over the years, stimulated and encouraged by treaty provisions, the increasing internationalisation and competitiveness of economic forces, a growing recognition of the benefits of working together, integrationist pressures emanating from central institutions (notably the Commission and the EP), and the stimulus that policy development in one sphere has given to developments in other spheres.

The policies that lie closest to the heart of the EU's policy framework are those related to what used to be called 'the Common Market' and is now known as 'the internal market' or 'the Single European Market' (SEM). In essence, these policies are designed to promote the free movement of goods, services, capital and people between the member states, and to enable the EU to act jointly and present a common front in its economic and trading relations with third countries. Since the mid-1980s – when the creation of the SEM was given priority via the '1992 programme' and the SEA – there has been considerable development of these market-based policies. This has resulted in a great increase in the range and extent of the EU's regulatory presence, which is somewhat ironic given that a key aim of building the SEM has been to liberalise and deregulate the functioning of the market. It has, however, been generally recognised and conceded by EU decision-makers that the market can operate on a reasonably fair and open basis only if key features of it are properly managed and controlled from the centre.

The EU has thus developed many policies with direct implications for the operation of the market. Amongst the regulatory activities in which EU decision-makers have been much concerned are: the establishment of essential conditions for product standards and for their testing and certification (the details are usually worked out by European standards organisations); the liberalisation of national economies, including opening up to competition national monopolies and protected industries in such spheres as energy, transport and telecommunications; the laying down of criteria that companies must satisfy if they wish to trade in the EU market (this has been very important, for example, in the sphere of financial services); and controlling the circumstances in which governments can or cannot subsidise domestic industries.

In addition to these 'pure' market policies, several policy areas in the broader social sphere that have market implications have also become increasingly subject to EU policy interest and, in some cases, regulatory control. This has usually been a consequence of some mix of genuine social concern coupled with a recognition that divergences of national approaches and standards are not helpful for economic growth in the EU. Examples of policy areas that have become subject to such policy attention are employment, the environment, consumer protection, and working conditions.

Another, and crucial, policy aspect of the SEM momentum has been its role in respect of Economic and Monetary Union (EMU). Having long been identified as a Community goal, real progress towards EMU only began in the late 1980s when most of the member states – strongly encouraged by the President of the Commission, Jacques Delors – came to the view that harmonised macroeconomic and financial policies and a single currency were necessary if the SEM was to realise its full potential. Accordingly, a strategy for creating a single currency-based EMU gradually developed. This was put into specific form – with the

laying down of procedures and a timetable – in the Maastricht Treaty. Central to the Maastricht provisions on EMU were conditions – called convergence criteria – that countries would have to meet if they were to become members of the single currency system. The qualifying conditions – low rates of inflation, low interest rates, the avoidance of excessive budgetary and national debt deficits, and currency stability – were designed to ensure that the single currency zone would be based on sound economic and monetary foundations. The conditions were subsequently used as a basis for the development of a Stability and Growth Pact, which is a framework for national economic and monetary policies within the single currency zone designed to ensure that stability is not threatened by national imbalances or 'irresponsible' national policies.

The Maastricht Treaty offered the possibility of the single currency system being launched in 1997, but that proved to be premature. However, the system did come into operation on 1 January 1999, with eleven of the EU's fifteen member states fixing their exchange rates and the common currency – the euro – coming into existence. Of the four non-participating states, Denmark, Sweden and the UK chose not to join, whilst Greece was unable to meet the convergence criteria. Greece's position was, however, quickly deemed to be in order and it too became a member of the system on 1 January 2001. National banknotes and coins were phased-out in the participating countries in early 2002 and were replaced by euro notes and coins.

The states that became EU members in 2004 and 2007 were all required to commit to joining the single currency system, but they were not permitted to join immediately. Rather, they were required to wait for at least two years so as to see whether they could meet the convergence criteria after assuming EU membership. In the event, most of the new member states have found meeting the convergence criteria a struggle and by the time of writing (late 2009) only four 2004/07 accession states – Slovenia (in 2007), Cyprus and Malta (in 2008), and Slovakia (in 2009) – have joined the eurozone. But though the progress of most 2004/07 accession states towards membership of the single currency system has been relatively slow – and the onset of the world economic recession in 2008 has made the situation more difficult – the fact is that it is now the case that sixteen EU states have the same currency. This means they also have the same interest rates and external exchange rates – which are determined by the European Central Bank that was created as part of the EMU system.

A striking feature of the EU's policy portfolio has always been its limited involvement with policy areas that account for the bulk of public expenditure – such as social welfare, education, health and defence. The main exception to this lack of involvement with heavy expenditure policy areas has been agriculture, where the CAP has imposed heavy burdens on the EU's annual budget. Since the early 1980s a series of measures have been adopted that have had the effect of bringing at least some aspects of the CAP'S problems – including heavy overproduction – under control, but agriculture still accounts for over forty per cent of the EU's budgetary expenditure.

Paralleling the attempts to bring the CAP under control has been increased attention to other policy areas that also impose budgetary demands. Regional and social policies have received particular attention, especially via the development and growth since the 1970s of the EU's two main cohesion funds – the European Regional Development Fund (ERDF) and the European Social Fund (ESF). However, even with the growth of regional and social funding, and with more funding being channelled to the likes of research policy and energy policy, the EU budget still only accounts for just over one per cent of total EU gross domestic product (GDP) and less than three per cent of total EU public expenditure.

Beyond economic and economic-related policies, the EU has also moved into other policy areas over the years. The most significant of these areas – significant in that they involve highly sensitive policy matters that are far removed from the original EEC policy focus on the construction of a common market – are foreign and security policy, defence policy, and justice and home affairs policy. These policy areas are still very much in the course of development, but they nonetheless have advanced considerably in both institutional and policy terms. This advancement is seen in the treaties, with the *de facto* growing role of foreign policy from the early 1970s first being given treaty acknowledgement by the SEA, and with both foreign and defence, and justice and home affairs policies being important components of, and being considerably strengthened by, the Maastricht, Amsterdam, Nice and Lisbon treaties.

So extensive and diverse has policy development been since the Community was established that there are now very few policy areas where significant EU policies are not to be found. No other combination of states has arrangements even remotely like those that apply in the EU, where cooperation and integration are consciously practised across such a wide range of policy sectors and where so many policy responsibilities have been transferred from individual states to collective institutions.

The nature of the EU's policy interests and responsibilities are examined at length in Part IV of the book.

Concluding Remarks

The EU is still recognisably based on the three European Communities that were founded in the 1950s. The most obvious ways in which it is so are in its institutional structure and in the continuance of the common market/internal market as the 'core' of policy activity.

However, in many fundamental ways European integration has clearly advanced considerably since it was given its initial organisational expression by the Founding Treaties. This advancement is seen in many ways, not least in the multifaceted nature and extent of integration deepening. This deepening has taken two broad forms. On the one hand, there has been a great development of institutional integration, which is seen in more, and more complex, institutional and policy-making arrangements. On the other hand, there has been a comparable development of policy integration, with the EU's policy responsibilities now extending, to at least some degree, into just about every area of public policy.

Chapter 4

The Widening of the Integration Process

This chapter examines the widening of the integration process. That is to say, it examines EC/EU enlargement.

The chapter begins by emphasising how the enlargement process has proceeded via a series of enlargement rounds. This is followed by an examination of key features of the enlargement rounds and of the new member states. Attention is then turned to the EC/EU's positions on enlargement: why, given that it generally has been regarded as being a highly successful organisation, has the EC/EU been prepared to enlarge when many applicants might be thought to have threatened its success? The different ways in which enlargements have impacted on the nature and operation of the EC/EU are then considered.

Enlargement via Enlargement Rounds

From an original EC membership of six (see Map 4.1), the EU has grown in size to twenty seven member states at the time of writing (early 2010). This great increase has taken place not on a one-by-one basis but rather in a series of enlargement rounds. In these rounds, states with significant shared characteristics have lodged membership applications at about the same times and have subsequently become members at either precisely the same times or at times that have not been too far apart. As Table 4.1 shows, there have been four enlargement rounds: the first resulted in Denmark, Ireland and the UK acceding in 1973; the second, which is commonly called the Mediterranean round, resulted in Greece acceding in 1981 and Portugal and Spain doing so in 1986; the third, which is often referred to as the EFTAn round (because the applicants were all members of the European Free Trade Association) resulted in Austria, Finland and Sweden joining in 1995; and the fourth, which may be called the 10 + 2 round (both because ten of the newcomers were Central and Eastern European countries (CEECs) and two were small Mediterranean islands and also because ten states joined in 2004 and two did so in 2007), resulted in Cyprus, the Czech Republic, Estonia, Hungary, Latvia, Lithuania, Malta, Poland, Slovakia, and Slovenia acceding in 2004 and Bulgaria and Romania acceding in 2007.

In addition to increasing the size of the EC/EU, each of these enlargement rounds has made distinctive contributions to the nature of the integration

Map 4.1 The founding member states

The founding member states

Key
1 Albania
2 Switzerland

Table 4.1 The enlargement rounds

Enlargement round	Date of accession	Member states acceding
The first enlargement round	1 January 2003	Denmark, Ireland, the United Kingdom
The Mediterranean round	1 January 1981	Greece
The Mediterranean round (contd.)	1 January 1986	Portugal and Spain
The EFTAn round	1 January 1995	Austria, Finland, Sweden
The 10 + 2 round	1 May 2004	Cyprus, the Czech Republic, Estonia, Hungary, Latvia, Lithuania, Malta, Poland, Slovakia, and Slovenia
The 10 + 2 round (contd.)	1 January 2007	Bulgaria and Romania

process. The first enlargement round did so by broadening integration out from its founding base, by granting accession to a large state – the UK – with the potential to disrupt the then virtually established Franco-German informal leadership of the Community, and by bringing in two states – Denmark and the UK – that over the years have been firmly in, indeed may be said to have generally led, the 'Euro-cautious' camp on integrationist matters. The second round gave integration a decided tilt to the south and a tilt also to less prosperous states. The third round – which, because the acceding states were all relatively small, prosperous and well functioning, was by far the easiest round to negotiate and manage – meant that virtually all of Western Europe was now part of the EU: when the three EFTANs joined the only significant Western European states to remain outside the EU were Norway, Iceland, and Switzerland. The fourth enlargement round was the most momentous round of all. It was so both in terms of the number of acceding states and in terms of it transforming what had been a process of *Western* European integration into a near *Europe-wide* process of integration. Prior to the collapse of communist regimes in Central and Eastern Europe in 1989–90, followed by the collapse of the Soviet Union in 1991, Central and Eastern European countries (CEECs) had not been eligible for EC membership and in any event had not been sufficiently politically independent to contemplate applying. But, the events of 1989–91 transformed the political and economic landscape of Central and Eastern Europe, and opened the door to a transformation in EU membership in the 2000s.

Each of the enlargement rounds will now be reviewed, with a particular focus on the motivations of the applicants.

The 1973 enlargement: the United Kingdom, Denmark and Ireland

Three factors were especially important in governing the UK's attitude towards European integration in the post-war years. First, the UK saw itself as operating within what Winston Churchill described as three overlapping and interlocking relationships: the Empire and Commonwealth; the Atlantic Alliance and the 'special relationship' with the United States; and Western Europe. Until the early 1960s Western Europe was seen as being the least important of these relationships. Second, successive British governments were not prepared to accept the loss of sovereignty that integration implied. There were several reasons for this, of which the most important were: Britain's long established parliamentary tradition; the record, in which there was considerable pride, of not having been invaded or controlled by foreign powers in modern times; a generally held view that cessation of sovereignty was neither desirable nor necessary, since Britain was still a world power of the first rank; and a certain distaste with the idea of being dependent on the not altogether highly regarded governments and countries of 'the Continent'. Third, Britain's circumstances were such that three of the four main integrationist organisations to be proposed in the 1950s had few attractions in terms of their specific areas of concern: the restrictions on national decision-making powers entailed in the ECSC looked very unappealing to a country whose coal and steel capacity far exceeded that of any of the six; the EDC would have limited governmental manoeuvrability and options at a time when Britain's defences were already stretched by the attempt to maintain a world role; and Euratom looked as though it would involve sharing secrets with less advanced nuclear powers. Only the EEC seemed to have much to offer, but amongst the problems it carried with it was its proposed supranationalism. Attempts were made to persuade the six not to be so ambitious and to direct their attention to the construction of a Western European free trade area, but with no success. As a result, and with a view to increasing its bargaining power with the six, Britain looked to other non-signatories of the Treaty of Rome. This led, in January 1960, to the Stockholm Convention, which established the European Free Trade Association. The founding members of EFTA were Austria, Denmark, Norway, Portugal, Sweden, Switzerland and the UK.

Shortly after the EEC began functioning in 1958 the attitude of the UK government began to change and membership came to be sought. The first enlargement of the Community could, in fact, have occurred much earlier than it did had President de Gaulle not opposed UK applications in 1961 and 1967. He did so for a mixture of reasons: he feared the UK would rival and attempt to thwart his desire to place France at the centre of the European stage; he believed UK membership would unsettle the developing Franco-German alliance – an alliance that was given symbolic force with the signing in 1963 of a Friendship Treaty between the two countries; and he was suspicious of the UK's close links with the United States, thinking they would pave the way for American penetration and domination of Europe if the UK joined the Community. So the UK was barred from Community membership until de Gaulle was replaced as French President by Georges Pompidou in 1969. A different view was then taken in Paris: the UK might serve as a useful counterweight to the increasingly strong and self-confident Germany; UK governments would lend support to France's opposition to pressures from within the Community for increased supranationalism; and France would probably gain economically by virtue of having better access to UK markets and as a result of the UK being a net contributor to the Community budget.

The reasons for the UK's changed position on Europe were a mixture of the political and the economic. Politically, it was increasingly clear that the UK was no longer a world power of the first rank. Paralleling this decline, the nature and status of the 'special relationship' with the USA weakened and became increasingly questionable. Furthermore, the British Empire was giving way to the Commonwealth, a very loose organisation and not one that was capable of providing the UK with much international political support. Economically, trade with the Commonwealth was declining, whilst indicators on growth in trade, investment, gross national product, and income per head all showed that by the early 1960s the member states of the EC were outperforming the UK. Quite simply the figures appeared to show that in economic terms the Community was a success and was so at a time when the UK's pattern of trade, even when not a Community member, was turning away from the Commonwealth and towards Europe. Moreover, the growing economic strength of the EC seemed to be linked with growing political status.

Thus when Pompidou opened the EC door, the UK government entered willingly.

*   *   *

Denmark and Ireland were not interested in joining the Communities that were founded in the 1950s. Both of their economies were heavily dependent on agriculture, so the ECSC had little to offer them. As for the EEC, there were several reasons to doubt that it would be to their benefit, the most important of which was that both countries had strong economic and historical links elsewhere: in Denmark's case with the other Scandinavian countries and with the UK; in Ireland's case with the UK. These links with the UK resulted in both of them tying their willingness to join the EC with the outcome of the UK's attempts to gain membership, so they both applied and then withdrew their applications on two occasions in the 1960s and then became members in 1973.

Like Denmark and Ireland, Norway paralleled the UK in applying for EC membership in the 1960s (twice) and early 1970s. On the third occasion terms of entry were agreed by the Norwegian government, but were then rejected by the Norwegian people in a referendum in 1972 following a campaign in which

Map 4.2 The first enlargement round (1973)

The first enlargement round (1973)

Existing member states

New member states

Key
1 Albania
2 Switzerland

suspicions about the implications for Norwegian agriculture, fishing, and national sovereignty featured prominently.

The Mediterranean enlargement: Greece (1981), Spain and Portugal (1986)

In the 1950s the Greek economy had been unsuitable for ECSC or EEC membership, being predominantly peasant-based. Additionally, Greece's history, culture and geographical position put it outside the Western European mainstream. But just as the countries that joined the Community in 1973 would have liked to have become members earlier, so was the accession of Greece delayed longer than Greek governments would have liked. The initial problem, recognised on both sides when Greece made its first approaches to Brussels soon after the EEC came into being, was the underdeveloped nature of the Greek economy. A transitional period prior to membership was deemed to be necessary and this was negotiated in the form of an Association Agreement that came into force in 1962. Full incorporation into the Community would, it was understood, follow when the Greek economy was capable of sustaining the obligations imposed by membership. However, between April 1967, when there was a military coup in Greece, and June 1974, when civilian government was re-established, the Association Agreement was virtually suspended. It might be thought that this would have further delayed full membership, but in fact it had the opposite effect. After a general election in November 1974 the government immediately made clear its wish for Greece to become a full member of the Community. The Commission issued a formal opinion that Greece was still not economically ready and proposed a pre-accession period of unlimited duration, during which economic reforms could be implemented. In response, the Greek government restated its wish for full membership, and particularly emphasised how membership could help both to underpin Greek democracy and to consolidate Greece's Western European and Western Alliance bonds. The Council of Ministers was sympathetic to these arguments and rejected the Commission's proposal. Membership negotiations were opened in July 1976 and Greece entered the Community in 1981.

As with Greece, for many years both political and economic circumstances counted against Spanish and Portuguese EC membership. Politically, both countries were authoritarian dictatorships until the mid-1970s, to which the democratic governments of the founding six states did not wish to be too closely attached. Not that there was anything in the treaties to specify that members must be liberal democracies: Article 237 of the EEC Treaty simply stated 'Any European State may apply to become a member of the Community'. The assumption was, however, that a democratic political system was a necessary qualification for entry. Economically, both Spain and Portugal were predominantly agricultural and underdeveloped, and both pursued essentially autarkic economic policies until the end of the 1950s: factors that hardly made them suitable candidates for the ECSC and that had the knock-on effect of excluding them from the EEC negotiations, which were opened up only to the UK.

So although both Spain and Portugal requested negotiations on association with the Community as early as 1962, and Spain made it quite clear that its request was with a view to full membership at some future date, both countries were treated with caution by the Community. Eventually they were granted preferential trade agreements, but it was only with the overthrow of the Caetano regime in Portugal in 1974 and the death of the Spanish leader General Franco in 1975 that full membership became a real possibility. Portugal applied in March 1977 and Spain in July 1977. The negotiations were protracted and difficult, covering, amongst many problems, the threat posed to other Mediterranean countries by Spanish agriculture, the size of the Spanish fishing fleet, and the implications of cheap Spanish and Portuguese labour moving north. As with the Greek negotiations, political factors helped to overcome these difficulties: the EC member states wished to encourage political stability in Southern Europe; there was the opportunity to widen and strengthen the political and economic base of the Community; and, by helping to link Southern Europe to the north, there were seen to be strategic advantages for both Western Europe and NATO.

Map 4.3 The Mediterranean enlargement round (1981 and 1986)

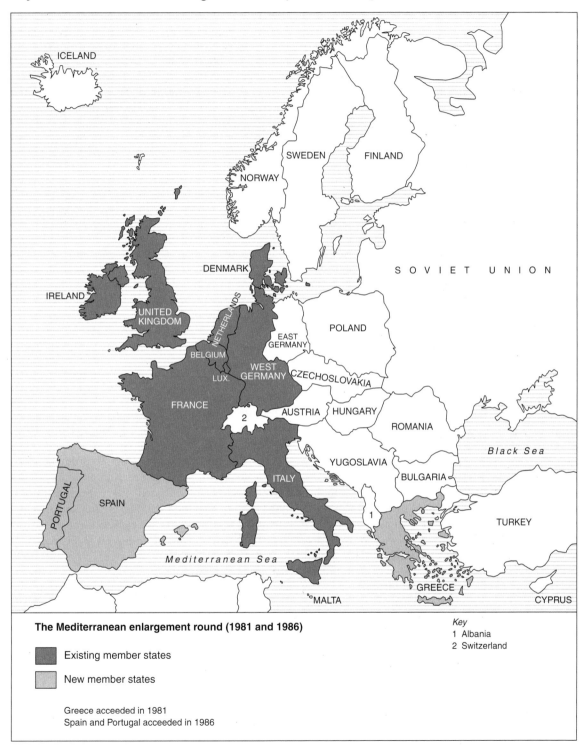

The Mediterranean enlargement round (1981 and 1986)

Key
1 Albania
2 Switzerland

Existing member states

New member states

Greece acceded in 1981
Spain and Portugal acceded in 1986

The EFTAn enlargement: Austria, Finland and Sweden (all 1995)

In 1992 the EC formally opened accession negotiations with Austria, Finland and Sweden, and in 1993 it opened negotiations with Norway. These negotiations were concluded successfully in March 1994, with a view to each of the countries becoming members of the EU after the terms of accession had been ratified at national level.

Two sets of factors stimulated the four states (and Switzerland too – of which more below) to seek membership of the EU. First, what previously had been regarded as virtually insuperable obstacles to EC membership came in the late 1980s and early 1990s to be seen as being less of a problem. For Austria and Sweden (and also Switzerland) the end of the Cold War reduced the importance of their traditional attachment to neutrality. For Finland, the difficulties posed by the country's relative geographical isolation and special position in relation to the Soviet Union disappeared. Second, Austria, Finland, Sweden and Norway, plus Switzerland, Iceland and the micro-state of Liechtenstein, made up the membership of EFTA, with which the EC already had special relations. When EFTA was constituted in 1960 – with Denmark, Portugal and the UK then also as members, but not at that stage Finland, Iceland or Liechtenstein – it had two principal objectives: the establishment of a free trade area in industrial products between the member countries, and the creation of a base for making the whole of Western Europe a free trade area for industrial goods. The first of these objectives was established in 1966 with the removal of virtually all customs duties and quantitative restrictions on trade in industrial products between EFTA countries, and the second was achieved in 1977 with the creation of an industrial free trade area between the EC and EFTA.

Over time, however, despite relations between the EC and EFTA being friendly, and being indeed further developed via cooperation in such areas as environmental protection, scientific and technical research, and transport policy, the EFTA states increasingly came to view key aspects of the EC–EFTA relationship as unsatisfactory. One reason for their dissatisfaction was that the EC was collectively much stronger than EFTA. Another, and related, reason was that the EC was prone to present EFTA with *de facto* situations to

which the EFTA countries had little option but to adjust – as, for example, when the Community laid down product specifications. This latter problem, of having to accept trading rules they had played no part in helping to formulate, became of increasing concern to EFTA countries as the EC's programme to complete the internal market by 1992 – the Single European Market (SEM) programme – gathered pace in the late 1980s and early 1990s. This concern played an important part in encouraging the EFTA countries to reconsider the attractions of EC membership. It also led the EC – concerned that a widening of its membership might threaten its own deepening – to suggest that EC–EFTA relations be strengthened by the creation of a European Economic Area (EEA) which would, in effect, extend the SEM programme to the EFTA states but would stop short of EC membership. The EEA was duly negotiated, but ratification ran into difficulties when in December 2002 the Swiss people narrowly voted – by 50.5 per cent to 49.7 per cent – against Swiss membership. This resulted in Switzerland not being able to join the EEA, in the timetable for bringing the EEA into effect being delayed, and in the Swiss Government being obliged to put aside Switzerland's EU application.

By the time the EEA did come into effect, in January 1994, it had already come to be accepted by most interested parties, including the governments of the EC, that the ambitions of the governments of Austria, Finland, Sweden and Norway would be satisfied only by full EU membership. Accordingly, accession negotiations were opened with all four states in early 1993. They proceeded much more easily and quickly than had negotiations in previous enlargement rounds. This was partly because each of the applicants was already well adjusted to EU membership – being prosperous (and hence not posing potential problems for the EU budget), having already incorporated much of the Community's *acquis* into national law, and having a well-established democratic political system. It was partly also because many of the matters that normally have to be covered in accession negotiations had already been sorted out in the EEA negotiations and agreement.

In the event, Norway, as in 1972, did not ratify the accession treaty and so did not accede with the other three states in January 2005. In the Norwegian ratification referendum campaign issues raised echoed those of 1972, though with the additional argument being

Map 4.4 **The EFTAN enlargement round (1995)**

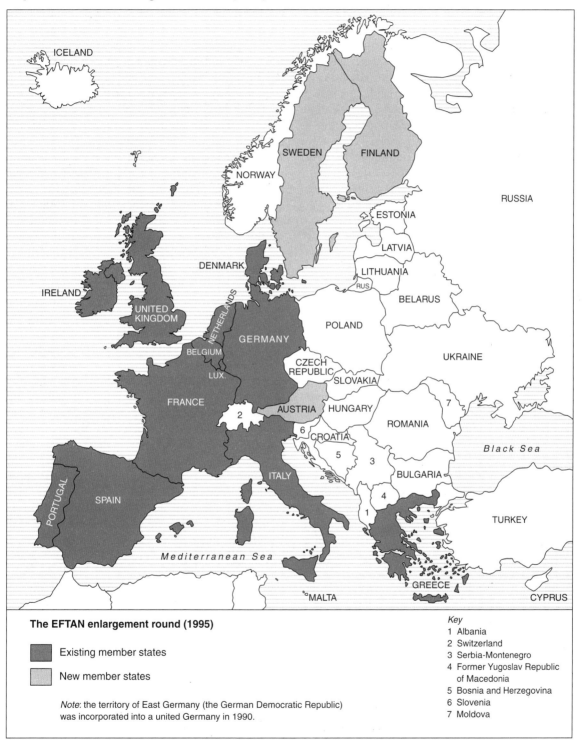

The EFTAN enlargement round (1995)

Existing member states

New member states

Note: the territory of East Germany (the German Democratic Republic) was incorporated into a united Germany in 1990.

Key
1 Albania
2 Switzerland
3 Serbia-Montenegro
4 Former Yugoslav Republic of Macedonia
5 Bosnia and Herzegovina
6 Slovenia
7 Moldova

made by the opponents of membership that Norway had no need to join the EU since it was a prosperous country that, thanks to the EEA, already had the trading ties with the EU that it required.

In consequence, to this day, Norway continues to be a member of EFTA, with Switzerland, Iceland and Liechtenstein being the other members. The EEA also continues to exist, although Switzerland, of course, is not a member. Iceland, Norway and Switzerland all participate in many EU programmes and activities.

A further dimunition in the size of EFTA is possible in the future, with Iceland having applied for EU membership in July 2009 in the wake of its economy having been severely damaged by the global financial crisis.

The 10 + 2 enlargement: Cyprus, the Czech Republic, Estonia, Hungary, Latvia, Lithuania, Malta, Poland, Slovakia, and Slovenia (all 2004); Bulgaria and Romania (both 2007)

As noted above, the 10 + 2 enlargement round involved ten CEECs plus the two Mediterranean islands of Cyprus and Malta.

Central and Eastern European countries

After gaining their independence in 1989–90 following the collapse of communism, most CEECs were soon openly expressing the hope that, as they established liberal democratic and market-based systems and as East–West relations were transformed, the way would be eased for their accession to the EU. Whilst the circumstances of individual CEECs varied, they were all driven by a broadly similar mixture of overlapping and interconnected political, security and economic motivations. Politically, there was a widespread desire to become (re)integrated into the European, and more broadly the Western, world. This resulted in CEEC governments necessarily seeking membership of the EU – the organisation which both symbolised 'the new' Europe and embodied much of its drive. In security terms, EU membership was seen as offering a measure of 'soft' security protection – to bolster the 'hard' protection of NATO, which most CEECs also were seeking to join – especially against any communist revival or nationalist surge. And economically, the EU market was clearly crucial for trade, whilst the EU as an organisation offered a framework and policies to assist with and to underpin economic liberalisation, re-structuring, regeneration and growth.

In the early 1990s the (then) EU-12, prompted and guided by the Commission, were quick to assist CEECs as they set out on their paths of fundamental economic and political reconstruction. The assistance, which took various forms, was given on the assumption that it was but the first step in what was likely to be a long transitional process of building EU–CEEC relations. Certainly, EU membership for CEECs was generally regarded by EU decision-makers not to be a realistic prospect for many years. After all, the CEECs were still in the very early stages of post-communist reconstruction and were nowhere near being ready to meet the demands and disciplines of EU membership. Furthermore, from the very early 1990s the EU was itself preoccupied with other matters, including the EFTAn enlargement round and preparing for EMU.

However, notwithstanding the reservations of most of the member states about moving too quickly, an incremental process of 'rhetorical ratcheting-up' soon began to unfold in which increasingly specific promises about membership were made to CEECs. A key step in the process occurred at the June 1993 Copenhagen European Council where, in the knowledge that applications from CEECs were likely in the near future, EU leaders declared in the Conclusions of the Presidency (in effect, the official communiqué of summit meetings) that 'the associated countries in Central and Eastern Europe that so desire shall become members of the European Union. Accession will take place as soon as an associated country is able to assume the obligations of membership by satisfying the economic and political conditions required' (European Council, 1993: 12).

So as to ensure that the enlargement to CEECs would not threaten the functioning or continuing development of the EU, the Copenhagen summit also laid down – for the first time in the Community's history – conditions that countries aspiring to membership would have to meet. All that had existed hitherto was the very open Article 237 of the EEC Treaty which stated 'Any European State may apply to become a member of the Community.

… The conditions of admission and the adjustment to the Treaty necessitated thereby shall be the subject of an agreement between the Member States and the applicant State'. The Copenhagen conditions – or criteria as they came to be known – were designed so that there would be a convergence between existing and new member states in respect of their political and economic systems and also that new member states would be able to adopt and implement Union laws and policies (these laws and policies being generally referred to as the *acquis*). The Copenhagen criteria are reproduced in Box 4.1.

Between March 1994, when Hungary applied, and January 1996, when the Czech Republic applied, ten CEECs formally applied for EU membership (see the Chronology). The December 1995 Madrid European Council formally reacted to these applications by requesting the Commission to investigate the implications for the EU of enlargement to these countries and to produce opinions on each of the CEEC applicants. This led to the issuing in July 1997 of the Commission's influential communication *Agenda 2000: For a Stronger and Wider Union* (European Commission, 1997a), which claimed that enlargement could be achieved with little extra cost to the Union provided significant reforms were made to the existing main spending areas – agriculture and struc-

---

Box 4.1

The Copenhagen criteria

Membership requires that the candidate country has achieved stability of institutions guaranteeing democracy, the rule of law, human rights and respect for and protection of minorities, the existence of a functioning market economy as well as the capacity to cope with competitive pressure and market forces within the Union. Membership presupposes the candidate's ability to take on the obligations of membership including adherence to the aims of political, economic and monetary union.

The Union's capacity to absorb new members, while maintaining the momentum of European integration, is also an important consideration in the general interest of both the Union and candidate counties (European Council, 1993: 12).

---

tural policies. As for the requested opinions on the applicants, the Commission recommended that negotiations should be opened with five of the ten CEECs – the Czech Republic, Estonia, Hungary, Poland and Slovenia – plus Cyprus, but should be delayed with the other five – Bulgaria, Latvia, Lithuania, Romania, and Slovakia until their economic (and in the case of Slovakia, political) transitions were further advanced. (Malta had suspended its application at this time.) The European Council accepted the Commission's recommendations at its December 1997 Luxembourg meeting and negotiations with what came to be referred to as the '5 + 1 first wave' states duly began in March 1998.

Before long, however, the Luxembourg decision came to be viewed as having been mistaken. One reason for this was that the link that had long been recognised between enlargement and European security was put into sharper focus with continuing turbulence in the Balkans. In particular, the NATO campaign in Kosovo in early 1999 highlighted the continuing dangers in South-East Europe and the broader dangers inherent in letting 'second wave' countries believe they were being left on one side. A second reason was that some of the second wave countries began to narrow the economic gap between them and first wave countries. And a third reason was that the Luxembourg summit had not only differentiated between first and second wave countries, but had also decided that Turkey – which had applied for membership as long back as 1987 – was not yet eligible to be even considered. Strong expressions of dissatisfaction by the Turkish government about how Turkey was being treated, coupled with suggestions that it might be forced to look elsewhere for friends, resulted in the EU having to re-consider its position on Turkey.

Accordingly, the enlargement strategy was revised at the 1999 Helsinki summit where it was decided that: negotiations with the second wave 5 + 1 states would be opened in early 2000 (the 1 being Malta – see below); decisions on the preparedness for membership of all 10 + 2 states to become EU members would be made solely on the basis of their progress in negotiations, not on when the negotiations with them were opened; and Turkey would be given the status of being a 'candidate country'.

Such was the progress in the accession negotiations with the second wave states, which opened in February

Map 4.5 The 10 + 2 enlargement round (2004 and 2007)

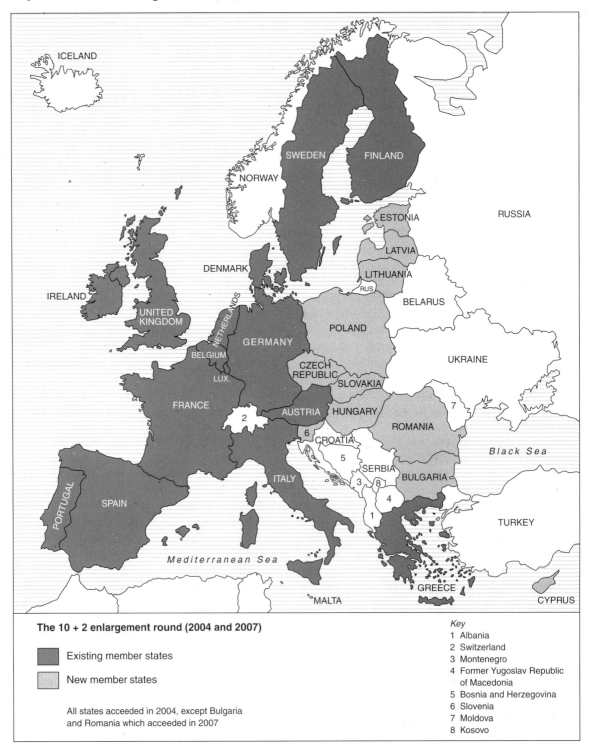

The 10 + 2 enlargement round (2004 and 2007)

Existing member states

New member states

All states acceded in 2004, except Bulgaria
and Romania which acceded in 2007

Key
1 Albania
2 Switzerland
3 Montenegro
4 Former Yugoslav Republic
  of Macedonia
5 Bosnia and Herzegovina
6 Slovenia
7 Moldova
8 Kosovo

This map shows the situation in early 2010.

2000, that it soon became apparent to both partici-pants and observers that far from enlargement proceeding in a series of stages, as had been assumed, there was likely to a 'big bang' enlargement round some time before the June 2004 EP elections – with perhaps all negotiating states other than Bulgaria and Romania joining the EU. In November 2000 the Commission set out a revised enlargement strategy, incorporating a more flexible framework and a 'roadmap' allowing for negotiations with the more prepared states to be completed by December 2002. The Commission's strategy and targets were welcomed by the December 2000 Nice summit and the June 2001 Gothenburg summit confirmed that EU-15 leaders hoped negotiations with applicants that were ready could be concluded by December 2002. This hope was realised at the December 2002 Copenhagen summit when the European Council, on the basis of reports and recommendations from the Commission, decided that an accession treaty could be signed in April 2003 with all negotiating states apart from Bulgaria and Romania, with a view to them becoming members in May 2004 – that is, in time for them to be able to participate fully in the June 2004 EP elections. It was further decided that if Bulgaria and Romania made satisfactory progress in complying with the member-ship criteria, they could anticipate membership in 2007 (European Council, 2002b).

Accession treaties with the ten states – eight CEECs, plus Malta and Cyprus – were duly signed in April 2003. By September 2003, all eight CEECs had held successful ratification referendums and, as scheduled, the eight, along with Cyprus and Malta, became EU members on 1 May 2004.

Bulgaria and Romania did not advance as rapidly in their transitions as had been hoped and throughout much of 2003–4 doubts were being expressed in EU circles as to whether they should be granted the sched-uled 2007 admission. Particular concerns were expressed about the robustness of their administrative and judicial systems and the continuance of excessive corruption in public life. However, concerned about the possible negative implications that delaying Bulgarian and Romanian membership could have, the European Council at its December 2004 meeting decided to authorise the signing of accession treaties in April 2005. These treaties were signed and both states became EU members in January 2007

Cyprus and Malta

Although they are geographically distant from the Western European heartland, the two small Mediterranean states of Cyprus and Malta are usually thought of – and have mostly thought of themselves – as being part of the Western European tradition. In the late 1980s interest in possible EU membership developed in both states. It did so not without considerable internal dissension and doubts, but the attractions of being a member of the economic area with which they conducted most of their external economic relations, having full access to EU programmes and funding opportunities, and becom-ing part of EU decision-making systems were increasingly recognised. For Cyprus there was an additional attraction: EU membership, and possibly even just talks about membership, might open the way to a solution of 'the Cyprus Problem' (see below).

Both countries applied for EC membership in July 1990. Their applications were not received with any enthusiasm in EC circles. This was partly because of a reluctance by the EC to tackle the institutional ques-tions that would be raised by the accession of very small states. In the case of Cyprus it was also because it was the view of most EC decision-makers that prob-lems arising from the division of the island and Turkey's occupation of North Cyprus – over 30 000 Turkish troops had been based there since a Turkish invasion in 1974 occasioned by a right-wing Greek coup on the island – must be resolved before the acces-sion of Cyprus could be contemplated. However, the prospects for both countries improved in June 1993 when the Commission issued its official opinions on the two applications. Whilst recognising that there were many difficulties ahead, the Commission gener-ally supported the applications and, in a significant break with the past, indicated that it did not favour allowing the partition of Cyprus to be a reason for permanently excluding Cypriot accession. The European Council moved the process further forward when it decided at its June 1994 Corfu meeting that 'the next phase of enlargement of the Union will involve Cyprus and Malta' (European Council, 1994). An election in Malta in 1996 then delayed Malta's plans, by bringing to power a government that put the EU application on hold. Nonetheless, the Cyprus application continued to be advanced and accession negotiations opened in March 1998 in parallel with the opening of accession negotiations with the five first wave CEECs. In September 1998 a further change of government in Malta resulted in the country's membership application being revived and the EU opened accession negotiations with it, alongside negotiations with the second wave CEECs, in February 2000.

Cyprus's situation within the enlargement round was always extremely difficult and sensitive. On the one hand, the Greek Cypriot government, acting in accordance with its established position in international law and in the name of the Republic of Cyprus, insisted from the very outset of its attempt to join the EU that it represented the whole island and would be conducting accession negotiations on that basis, even though in practice its writ ran only in the south. On the other hand, the Turkish Cypriot leadership in the north, strongly supported by Turkey, totally rejected the right of the Greek Cypriots to claim to be negotiating on behalf of all of Cyprus. EU leaders hoped that a solution to this situation – which is commonly referred to as 'the Cyprus Problem' – would be found before the end of the accession negotiations, but there were never solid grounds for these hopes. Delaying Cyprus's accession until the Cyprus Problem was resolved remained a possibility throughout the accession negotiations, but not a very realistic one because Greece threatened to veto all of the EU aspirants if Cyprus's accession was postponed. At the same time, however, accepting a divided Cyprus as an EU member risked damaging the EU's relations with Turkey.

At their December 1999 Helsinki European Council meeting, the EU-15 leaders agreed on how they would manage the conflicting pressures associated with the Cyprus application. On the one hand, they declared that whilst a settlement was much desired, it would not in itself be a precondition for Cyprus's accession. On the other hand, they sought to mollify Turkey by stating that 'Turkey is a candidate state destined to join the Union on the basis of the same criteria as applied to the other candidate States' (European Council, 1999d: 3). With no solution reached by the time of the key December 2002 Copenhagen summit – the summit that took final decisions on which of the 10 + 2 applicant states had completed accession negotiations and the target date for their accession – the EU-15 leaders acted on the basis of their Helsinki decision and decided Cyprus could join the EU in May 2004, along with the eight CEECs and Malta. A consequence of this decision was that if no settlement could be reached before Cyprus's accession, then because in legal, though not practical, terms the whole of the island of Cyprus would be joining the EU, a foreign power – Turkey – would be occupying EU 'territory'.

Subsequent to the 2002 Copenhagen summit, a ratification referendum on its accession treaty was held successfully in Malta in April 2003. In Cyprus the government decided that a referendum would not be held unless it could be tied in with a resolution of the Cyprus Problem. With no such resolution seemingly pending, Cyprus's membership was ratified by the Cyprus parliament in July 2003 – thus resulting in Cyprus being the only one of the ten acceding states not to directly seek the approval of the national electorate.

In the autumn of 2003 the UN, which had made various attempts over the years to broker a Cyprus peace settlement, sought to take advantage of Cyprus's scheduled EU membership to launch another round of peace negotiations. The hope was that with the question of Cyprus's EU membership 'resolved', both sides would display increased flexibility. A highly detailed settlement plan – known as the Annan Plan, after the UN's Secretary General – was issued, but despite being revised several times to meet objections it was rejected by the Greek Cypriot government on the grounds that it was too favourable to the Turkish Cypriots. Both sides did, however, agree to put the Plan to binding referendums to be held on the same day in April 2004 in both parts of the island. In the referendums, the Turkish Cypriots voted to accept the Plan by 64.9 per cent to 35.1 per cent on a 87 per cent turnout, but the Greek Cypriots, encouraged by their President, voted to reject it by 75.8 per cent to 24.2 per cent on a 89 per cent turnout. The fact that in the south of the island there was no penalty of exclusion from the EU for voting for rejection was a major factor in determining the outcome. Accordingly, on 1 May 2004 the whole of Cyprus legally joined the EU, but the part of the island that had voted to accept the Plan was, in practice, excluded.

Why has the EU been Willing to Enlarge?

Enlargement has occurred in rounds, or stages, because European states have qualified and applied for EC/EU membership at different times. As the previous few pages of this chapter have shown, they have done so for a number of reasons. One reason has been differences in the nature of national economies and economic needs. A second reason has been differences in national political systems, with a key point here being that membership has always only been open to liberal democratic states. And a third reason has been different perceptions by national politicians of the likely gains and losses that are likely to accrue from EC/EU membership.

But although there have been, and indeed still are, important differences between European states in respect of their attitudes and approaches to European integration, each of the now 27 EU members and each of the states that are currently seeking membership has ultimately taken the view that the advantages of membership outweigh the disadvantages. The nature of the perceived advantages has normally included the likelihood of increased economic growth and of increased political influence. The nature of the perceived disadvantages has normally included concerns about losses of national sovereignty and the national implications of certain EU policies.

So, states have sought EU membership because the perceived benefits of membership have seen to be greater than the perceived costs. But what about the EC/EU's position? Why has it been so willing to open its doors to applicants?

A difficulty in seeking to answer this question is that the EC/EU has never had a clear policy on enlargement. It has reacted to applications rather than proactively setting out its own preferences and goals. As was noted above, the 1957 Treaty stated that 'Any European State may apply to become a member of the Community. ...' but this gave no indication as to whether applications would be welcomed or how the word 'European' would be interpreted. In consequence, there was nothing to stop France twice vetoing applications from the UK in the 1960s, even though the UK was seemingly eminently suitable for membership in that it was a long-established and democratic Western European state with a market economy. The

1993 Copenhagen criteria clarified the situation to a point, but they were conditions for opening accession negotiations with applicants more than they were a positive policy setting out what the EU wanted.

The answer to the question why the EU has generally favoured enlargement is thus best approached, initially at least, by looking at particular membership rounds. Up to and including the EFTAn round there is no great difficulty explaining the EC/EU's willingness to enlarge. It is true that doubts about the wisdom of enlarging were expressed by EU policy makers at the time of each of the first three enlargement rounds. So, the first enlargement round saw concerns in some EC quarters about whether the UK would be a whole-hearted participant. During the Mediterranean round questions were raised about whether the applicants were ready for membership given the relatively underdeveloped nature of their economies and the fledgling nature of their newly established democratic systems. And prior to the EFTAN round some EU practitioners – including the then President of the European Commission, Jacques Delors – made known their fears that enlargement could divert attention from such pressing tasks as developing the Maastricht Treaty provisions on EMU and the CFSP. But notwithstanding these doubts, existing member states were willing to accept new members for a number of reasons: the applicants were Western European states and consequently were generally seen as being part of the post-Second World War Western European 'family'; though some of the applicants were relatively underdeveloped economically at the time of their applications, they all had functioning market-based economies that appeared capable of 'catching up' reasonably quickly; most had well-embedded democratic systems, and those that did not (Greece, Portugal and Spain) found favourable receptions from existing member states to calls to help them to consolidate the re-establishment of democracy; and because the enlargement rounds were limited in scope – with none containing more than three new members (though the first and the third rounds would have contained four had Norway ratified the accession treaties its government negotiated) – the EC/EU could accommodate the new members without itself having to make too many adjustments.

But, with the completion of the EFTAn round the challenges posed to the EU by membership applications changed and became much more testing. For, following the 1995 enlargement, virtually all of the non-member states that could be accommodated into the EU relatively easily were now members. Only Iceland, Norway and Switzerland remained as potential 'easy' applicants. All other possible applicants were to the East or South-East and virtually all of them, with the partial exceptions of the two small Mediterranean islands of Cyprus and Malta (though the former carried its own unique challenges) presented considerable difficulties as regards EU future membership: they all were relatively poor; they all had long been outside the 'Western mainstream'; and they all were still in the process of establishing their democratic credentials.

Given the challenges posed by post-EFTAn applicants, why was the EU – a highly successful organisation in most respects – willing to risk enlargement to CEECs? And why does it remain committed to further enlargement when, with the exception of Iceland, the only realistic acceding states in the foreseeable future are Turkey (with which accession negotiations were opened in 2005) and half a dozen or so small states – most of which were formerly part of Yugoslavia – in the troubled Balkans? Would not a more sensible approach have been, and be, to have established very close relations with applicants and would-be applicants whose membership has seemed to present major challenges for the EU, but to have stopped short of offering them a membership perspective?

Two types of explanation for why the EU has proceeded, and continues to proceed, with enlargement are especially persuasive. These explanations are examined at some length on pp. 440–3, so suffice here to give them just an outline summary:

- *Rationalist explanations* emphasise that whilst it is indeed the case that the potential benefits for the EU of admitting CEECs and South-Eastern European states were, and are, less strong than they have been with most previous acceding states, the cost-benefit balance sheets from the EU's viewpoint have, nonetheless, still been in the black. In economic, political and security terms, the EU has had more to gain than lose by opening accession negotiations with and admitting CEECs, Balkan states and even, ultimately, Turkey.
- *Constructivist explanations* question whether the balance sheets have in fact been positive from the EU's perspective, or at least from the perspective of

all existing EU member states. For constructivists, the values shaping and determining the behaviour of key EU enlargement policy actors have been, and are, more important determining factors in explaining post-1995 enlargement processes than have been measurable balance sheets. A particularly important value is seen as being the inclination of EU politicians and officials to empathise with, and seek to support, geographically proximate states that are attempting to 'Westernise', 'Europeanise', and 'democratise' themselves.

But whichever of these explanations is deemed to be the more plausible – and they probably should not be seen as being in competition with one another but rather as being potentially mutually complementary – it is clear that as the EU has extended the enlargement process to increasingly 'difficult' states, so has it become increasingly watchful of applicants. Accession processes have become more elaborated, accession negotiations have become much more conditional – in the sense that they involve little in the way of real negotiations and are mainly about monitoring the extent to which applicants are absorbing and adjusting to the EU *acquis* – and the EU has become much more actively involved in assisting applicants to make the transitions that are necessary to become EU members.

The Impact of Enlargements on the EU

All enlargements have inevitably affected and changed the Union (and before it the Community) in important ways. Six ways are especially worth noting.

First, enlargements have been an important driving force behind treaty reform, with existing member states wanting to avoid decision-making difficulties post-enlargements by 'easing' decision-making mechanisms. The most obvious instance of this concern feeding into treaty changes is the way in which the inevitably greater difficulty of obtaining unanimity in an expanded Council of Ministers has been a major reason behind the increases in QMV that have been provided for in all rounds of treaty reform since the SEA.

Second, the EU's institutions have naturally grown in size to accommodate representatives of acceding states. This has had a number of consequences, some of which have not been helpful in terms of institutional efficiency. For example, it is generally agreed that the College of Commissioners and the EP are now too big and unwieldy. That this would be so was recognised before the 10 + 2 enlargement occurred, which resulted in both the Constitutional Treaty and the initial version of the Lisbon Treaty providing for the size of the College to be reduced and for the size of the EP to be capped (see Chapter 6). However, the reduction in the size of the College had to be scrapped as part of a package of measures designed to persuade the Irish people to approve the Lisbon Treaty, whilst even with its cap – of 751 – the EP still remains by far the largest parliament in the democratic world.

Another institutional problem related to the increased size of the EU is language. There are now 23 officially recognised EU languages. For routine day-to-day operations this causes inconveniences but not major problems because officials of the institutions work, whatever their nationality, mostly in either French or English. However, considerable problems do arise when institutional business is being conducted by non-officials – such as Members of the European Parliament (MEPs) and representatives in the European Economic and Social Committee – because they may well not have non-native language skills and, even if they do have good French or English, may insist on using their native language. Inevitably, reliance on interpreters reduces spontaneity and can cause delays if interpreters are not available. Delays can also be caused by the requirement that many EU documents (though generally not internal working documents) must be translated into the EU's official languages. Translation delays have been a particular problem for legislative processes. Various devices are used to try and minimise these linguistic problems, including more use of language relays and pressures being placed on officials to produce shorter documents, but some difficulties inevitably remain.

Third, many EU policies outcomes have had to become more flexible so as to satisfy the wider range of national and political interests that enlargement has brought into policy-making processes. The larger and the more heterogeneous the EU has become the more it has naturally become the case that there have been national representatives in policy deliberations that have wanted very different outcomes. One way of dealing with this challenge to decision-making has been

the above-mentioned extensions to QMV provision in the Council. But another response has been to make some policies less binding in nature, with discretion given to national authorities regarding the extent to which and the ways in which the policies are applied. In recent years, considerable use has been made of this more discretionary and less rigid policy approach. The approach has been applied particularly in sensitive policy areas such as social policy and employment policy, often using what is known as the open method of coordination (OMC) – which relies not on 'top down' and binding legislation but rather on semi-voluntary cooperation to achieve agreed goals. (The OMC is explained in Chapter 17.)

The ultimate in policies being flexible is where there is the possibility of a member state or states not participating in a policy, or at least not fully participating. Known as differentiation, this practice has developed in response to the inability or unwillingness of some states to be involved in policies that either create domestic difficulties for them or to which they are opposed. It may have been reasonable to have expected and required all member states to 'swim abreast' when there were only a few of them, but such a requirement has become increasingly unrealistic as the EU's membership has grown and become more diverse and would have been a recipe for major policy difficulties and possible paralysis in some areas if it had continued to be rigidly applied. Accordingly, outside the 'core' internal market policy area, there are now a number of important policy areas where not all member states are equally involved. The most notable of these policy areas are EMU, aspects of JHA, and the ESDP.

Fourth, in so far as member states provide leadership for the EU, it has become more spread out, with different member states or groups of member states providing leadership on different issues, The Franco-German axis, which formerly did much to set the pace of the integration process, is still influential but inevitably it is not as dominant as it was when there were fewer member states. More generally, as the number of smaller states has increased, it has not been as easy for the larger states to push through their preferences.

Fifth, policy debates, concerns and priorities have been affected by new members bringing with them their own requirements, preferences and problems. For example, the growing influence, as a result of the Mediterranean round enlargement, of southern, less

er countries quickly led to calls
 _n of the Common Agricultural
_i northern temperate products
_rranean products, and for strength-
_-focused redistributive policies to directly
_conomic development in the south. The
_AN enlargement quickly played a part in increas-
_ng the attention being given by the EU to such
matters as openness and accountability in decision-
making and to efficiency and sound financial management in decision implementation. And the 10 + 2
enlargement has produced pressures for the EU's
budget to be focused more towards assisting with
economic development in the CEECs and has also
contributed to the EU's relations with Russia being
given a higher priority.

Sixth, enlargement has made the EU a more important and influential international organisation. The
EU's 27 member states account for around one sixth of
the worlds's states (not counting micro-states); the 27
include all the larger, and traditionally more influential, European states to the West of the former Soviet
Union; the population of the EU now approaches 500
million; and the EU is the world's principal commercial power, accounting for around one-fifth of world
imports and exports (not counting commerce
between the member states themselves). These
increases in size and strength combine to give the EU
considerable potential strength on the world's stages.

Concluding Remarks

EU enlargement is best viewed not as series of discrete
events but rather as an ongoing process. For the fact is
that since 1961, when the UK made the first formal
accession application of any state, there has barely
been a time when the EC/EU has not been involved in
some combination of considering the merits of
membership applications, conducting accession negotiations, and 'fitting in' newcomers. This is a situation
moreover, as is shown in Chapter 24, that is likely to
continue for the foreseeable future with, at the time of
writing, negotiations underway with Croatia and
Turkey, applications lodged by the Former Yugoslav
Republic of Macedonia (FYROM), Montenegro,

Albania, Serbia, and Iceland, applications from other
Balkan states pending, and applications from such
former Soviet states as Georgia and the Ukraine possible in time.

Enlargement has been a very difficult policy area
for the EU. There have been three main reasons for
this. First, an EC/EU enlargement policy resting on
clear and consistent principles has never been developed. This absence is largely explained by (changing
and evolving) differences between the member states
on a range of enlargement and enlargement-related
matters. A particular difficulty in trying to develop
such a policy now – with the Turkish application in
mind – would be finding agreement on the 'What is
Europe?' question. Second, the EC/EU has had little
control over the lodging of applications, which has
meant that starting with the Mediterranean round it
has been drawn into accession processes with applicants much earlier than ideally it would have liked.
This resulted in the Mediterranean and 10 + 2 rounds
being extremely protracted: from the lodging of the
membership application to assumption of membership the longest periods to date are the thirteen years
and ten months for Cyprus and Malta, followed by the
ten years and one month for Hungary and Poland;
from the formal opening of accession negotiations to
accession the longest periods are the seven years and
three months for Portugal, the six years and eleven
months for Spain, and the six years and two months
for the 'first wave' CEECs and Cyprus. If Turkey eventually becomes a member, it will far outdistance all
previous records, whatever basis is taking for measur-
ing. Third, following the completion of the EFTAN
round, virtually all of Europe's richer and democratically well-established states were EU members. With
the exception of Iceland, Norway and Switzerland,
only 'difficult' states remained outside.

But notwithstanding the many difficulties that have
been associated with it, enlargement has transformed
the political map of Europe. From the original founding member six, the EU expanded in the 1970s, 1980s,
and 1990s to embrace virtually the whole of Western
Europe. It then → dramatically and momentously –
expanded in the 2000s to incorporate much of Central
and Eastern Europe and to transform what had been a
process of Western European integration into a
process of near Europe-wide integration.

Part II
The Evolving Treaty Framework

From 1957 to the mid-1980s there was only modest treaty development within the EC. However, since the mid-1980s rounds of treaty reform have been carried out every few years. Five major new treaties have been concluded and brought into force – the 1986 Single European Act, the 1992 Maastricht Treaty, the 1997 Amsterdam Treaty, the 2001 Nice Treaty, and the 2007 Lisbon Treaty. In addition, another major treaty – the Treaty Establishing a Constitution for Europe – was agreed by the governments of the member states, but it did not come into effect because of ratification problems.

Part II examines all of these treaties and shows how they have been central to the evolution of the European integration process. The treaties are examined individually in Chapters 5 and 6 and then collectively in Chapter 7.

Chapter 5

From Rome to Nice

As was noted in Chapter 3, the Founding Treaties of the 1950s that created the European Communities have been supplemented and amended in various ways by subsequent treaties. This chapter examines these treaties up to the 2001 Treaty of Nice.

Up to the Single European Act

In addition to accession treaties providing for the enlargements of the Community, a number of other treaties were also concluded in the period between the signing of the Treaties of Rome in 1957 and the Single European Act in 1986. Four of these treaties were of particular significance:

- Treaty Establishing a Single Council and a Single Commission of the European Communities
- Treaty Amending Certain Budgetary Provisions of the Treaties
- Treaty Amending Certain Financial Provisions of the Treaties
- Act Concerning the Election of the Representatives of the Assembly by Direct Universal Suffrage

Treaty Establishing a Single Council and a Single Commission of the European Communities Signed in 1965, coming into force in 1967, and generally known as the Merger Treaty, this treaty established a single Council of Ministers for all three Communities (though different individuals would attend different meetings) and merged the High Authority of the ECSC, the Commission of Euratom, and the EEC Commission into one Commission. The powers exercised by these merged bodies were still to be based on the Founding Treaties: in other words, the Treaties and the Communities themselves were not merged. To clarify and simplify the existing texts relating to the single Community institutions, this treaty was repealed by the 1997 Amsterdam Treaty and its relevant parts were incorporated as appropriate into the Community Treaties.

Treaty Amending Certain Budgetary Provisions of the Treaties and *Treaty Amending Certain Financial Provisions of the Treaties* The first of these treaties was signed in 1970 and the second in 1975. Together, they laid down a budgetary procedure and allocated budgetary powers between the EC institutions. Of particular importance, given its relative weakness in most policy areas, were powers allocated to the European Parliament. The 1975 Treaty also established a Court of Auditors to examine the accounts of all revenue and expenditure of the Community.

Act Concerning the Election of the Representatives of the Assembly by Direct Universal Suffrage Signed in 1976, but not ratified by all the member states until 1978, this Act provided the legal base for direct elections to the EP and laid down certain rules for their conduct. The Act did not directly increase the Parliament's powers.

The Single European Act (SEA)

It was recognised at the June 1985 Milan European Council meeting that the legislative measures that would be required to give effect to the priority Single European Market (SEM) programme would have little chance of being passed unless Community decision-making procedures were changed. Accordingly, and because too it was thought certain other treaty-related matters required addressing, it was decided to establish an Intergovernmental Conference (IGC) to negotiate and prepare treaty reforms. (See Chapter 7 for an account of how IGCs operate.) The IGC duly undertook its work in the second half of 1985 and culminated at the December 1985 Luxembourg summit when the national leaders agreed to what they called the Single European Act (SEA). After legal and translation work had been undertaken on the political deal reached at the summit, the SEA was formally signed in February 1986, but it did not come into force until mid-1987 because of ratification difficulties in Ireland.

Box 5.1

The most important provisions of the Single European Act

- Completion of the internal market by 1992 was identified as a specific goal and was incorporated into the EEC Treaty. (A programme for completing the internal market had already been agreed at the June 1995 Milan summit, but according the goal treaty status enhanced its prospect of success.)
- A number of new policy areas – most of which were already being developed – were formally incorporated into the EEC Treaty, so the capacity for decision making in these areas was increased. The new policy areas included environment, research and technological development, and 'economic and social cohesion'.
- A new legislative procedure – the cooperation procedure – was established with a view to improving the efficiency of decision making in the Council of Ministers and increasing the powers of the EP. Regarding the first of these aims, the Council's ability to take decisions by QMV was extended to most decisions subject to the procedure. Regarding the second aim, the single reading of legislative proposals under the established consultation procedure was extended to two readings and it was made more difficult for the Council to ignore the EP's views. Several legislative areas were covered by the new procedure including, crucially, most of the measures 'which have as their object the establishment and functioning of the internal market'.
- The EP's role and potential influence in the Community was further increased by the establishment of a new 'assent procedure'. Under the procedure, the EP's approval, by an absolute majority of members, became necessary both for the accession of new members to the Community and for association agreements between the Community and third countries.
- European Political Cooperation (EPC) – the official Community term for the foreign policy cooperation that had increasingly been practised since the early 1970s, but outside the treaty framework – was put on a legal basis (but not by treaty incorporation).
- Meetings between the Heads of Government in the framework of the European Council, which had been taking place since 1975, were given legal recognition (but not by treaty incorporation).
- The capacity of the Court of Justice, which had been weakened by workload overstretch, was extended by a provision for the establishment of a new Court of First Instance.

The SEA contained a wide range of measures, the most important of which are set out in Box 5.1.

The SEA provided a major boost to the European integration process. It did so in two main ways. First, it strengthened the treaty base for policy activity, most particularly in respect of the completion of the internal market where a deadline of December 1992 was set for its completion. Second, it strengthened the Community's institutional system, especially in respect of the increased capacity of the Council of Ministers to take decisions by QMV and the increased legislative powers given to the EP.

The Maastricht Treaty

The background to and the making of the Treaty

Many of the Community's decision-making elites – both in Community institutions and in member states – were disappointed with the SEA. It did not, they believed, sufficiently advance the process of integration, so even before the SEA was ratified the view was being expressed in many influential quarters that further integration would soon be necessary. In the second half of the 1980s a number of factors combined to give weight and force to this body of opinion. These factors were both internal and external in nature.

The internal factors were mostly associated with the stimulus to further integration provided by the 're-launching' of the Community in the mid-1980s. This re-launching, which was embodied in the SEM programme and in the SEA, contained its own integrationist logic in that it gave greater urgency to some long-standing but unresolved issues facing the Community and it also served to bring new issues onto the Community's agenda. Four factors were of particular importance in this respect. First, many member states increasingly came to the view that the full benefits of the SEM would only be realised if action was taken to bring about Economic and Monetary Union (EMU). Second, there was growing acceptance of the need for a 'social dimension' that would soften and offset some of the liberal market/deregulatory implications of the SEM. Third,

the dismantling of border controls in the internal market created pressure for new and greatly improved mechanisms at Community level to deal with such problems as cross-border crime, drug trafficking, international terrorism, and the movement of peoples (the latter included growing concern about the 'threat' of mass migration from Eastern Europe and North Africa to Western Europe). Fourth, the long-standing problem of a 'democratic deficit', which had been only partially addressed in the SEA, was increasingly seen as needing attention as the Community exercised increasing power over a broad range of policy areas, but did so in a political context where its decision-makers were not democratically accountable.

The external factors arose largely from the break-up of the communist bloc and the Soviet Union. As with internal factors, there were four main aspects to this. First, the collapse of communism in Central and Eastern Europe from the autumn of 1989 resulted in pressures for the Community to consolidate and strengthen itself so as to be better able to meet the challenges of the rapidly transforming Europe. Second, the unification of Germany, which formally took place in October 1990, increased the potential for German domination of the Community and led many to conclude that it was necessary to advance the integration process in order to ensure the consolidation of a European Germany rather than a German Europe. Third, the break-up of the Soviet Union in 1991 added to the sense of uncertainty about the future nature and stability of the European continent and added to existing pressures for a strengthening of the Community's policy and institutional capacities. Fourth, the ending of the Cold War heralded the disappearance of the framework that had provided much of the rationale, focus and setting for the foreign and defence policies of most Western European countries for over forty years and in so doing raised many questions about the suitability of existing arrangements in the post-Cold War era.

From the mid-1980s several factors thus combined to build up a head of steam for another round of treaty-based integration between the member states. The processes that produced what became the Maastricht Treaty involved the convening of two IGCs – one on Political Union and the other on Economic and Monetary Union. These IGCs met throughout 1991 and culminated at the December 1991 European Council in Maastricht, where, in a summit marked by ill-temper, brinkmanship, and threat of breakdown – all of which were largely accounted for by the UK's unwillingness to commit to the proposed European single currency or to be bound by the European Social Charter – political agreement on the contents of the Treaty was eventually reached. After subsequent careful examination by a working party of legal and linguistic experts, the Maastricht Treaty was formally signed, by Foreign and Finance Ministers, in February 1992. Ratification problems then ensued – notably in Denmark, where the Treaty was rejected in a referendum held in June 1992 but was later endorsed in a second referendum held in May 1993, and in Germany, where a case brought before the German Constitutional Court that the Treaty infringed the country's constitution was not dismissed (though even then only with qualifications) until October 2003. Resolution of the German Constitutional Court case enabled the Treaty to come into effect on 1 November 1993 – ten months later than originally planned.

The contents of the Treaty

Like the SEA, the Maastricht Treaty was something of a mixed bag in legal terms. It included: a new 'umbrella' Treaty on European Union (TEU), the provisions of which were largely beyond the jurisdiction of the ECJ; substantial revisions to the post-SEA Founding Treaties; and numerous protocols and declarations.

At the heart of the Treaty was the creation of a new organisation: the European Union. The EU was to be based on what quickly came to be referred to as its three 'pillars' – though the word 'pillar' was not used in the Treaty. The pillars were: the European Communities; a Common Foreign and Security Policy (CFSP); and Cooperation in the Fields of Justice and Home Affairs (JHA). The Union was assigned a range of objectives, would be based on a set of guiding principles – including subsidiarity and respect for democracy and human rights – and would be governed by an institutional structure presided over by the European Council.

Most of the provisions of the Treaty were concerned with the three pillars, which in the case of pillar one meant amending the Treaties of the three European Communities, and in the cases of pillars two and three meant laying down guiding principles and operating rules for the CFSP and for JHA within the TEU.

There now follows a summary of the main provisions of the Maastricht Treaty (a longer outline is contained in the sixth edition of this book).

Pillar one: the European Communities

This was by far the most important pillar since it incorporated most of the EU's policy responsibilities. Under the Treaty, the *acquis* of the existing three Communities was preserved and in several important respects was extended and strengthened by revisions of the EEC, ECSC and Euratom Treaties.

Article 1 of the revised EEC Treaty stated the following: 'By this Treaty, the High Contracting Parties establish among themselves a European Community'. This meant that the European Economic Community – the EEC – was renamed the European Community. A rather confusing situation was thereby produced, in which the European Community became part of the European Communities, which in turn became part of the European Union.

Two important new principles were introduced into what now became the Treaty Establishing the European Community (TEC). First, the much discussed principle of subsidiarity was formally incorporated, though only in somewhat vague terms. European Council meetings subsequently developed guidelines designed to assist with the application of the principle, with subsidiarity generally being taken to mean that policies should be decided at the national level, and perhaps even at regional or local levels, whenever possible. Second, the TEC established Union citizenship, with every national of a member state becoming a citizen of the Union. Though symbolically significant, the practical effect of this was limited since citizens of the Union would only 'enjoy the rights conferred by this Treaty'. One of these rights was the right to live and work anywhere in the territory of the member states, subject to certain limitations. Union citizens were also given the right to vote and stand as candidates in EP and local elections, again subject to certain limitations. Because the principles of subsidiarity and Union citizenship were incorporated into the TEC, and not just confined to the Common Provisions of the TEU, they were subject to the jurisdiction of the ECJ.

Other revisions made by the Maastricht Treaty to the TEC covered institutional and policy changes.

1 *Institutional changes.* The revisions falling under this heading were mostly designed to improve the efficiency and democratic nature of the Community's institutional structures and decision-making processes. Regarding efficiency, the most significant changes concerned the Council of Ministers, which was empowered to take a greater range of decisions on the basis of QMV. Regarding the Community's democratic nature, the most significant changes concerned the EP, which was given increased powers and influence in several areas – notably in respect of the making of legislation where, under a newly created co-decision procedure, it was given, for the first time, a veto power. The main institutional changes are set out in Box 5.2.

2 *Policy changes.* The EC's policy competences were extended and strengthened. They were so mainly so in the four ways that are set out in Box 5.3. Of these ways, the most important and potentially far-reaching was the laying down of a plan and a schedule for building an Economic and Monetary Union (EMU) that would be based on a single currency, and hence also on single exchange and interest rates. In the view of many practitioners and observers, the decision to build EMU marked a major step in a federalist direction. However, this view was partly undermined by the fact that two states – Denmark and the UK – were granted protocols (in Denmark's case only after the Treaty was initially rejected in a national referendum) stating that they were not obliged to join the single currency system.

Box 5.2

The most important institutional provisions of the Maastricht Treaty

- A new legislative procedure – the co-decision procedure – was established. In effect the co-decision procedure extended the cooperation procedure by allowing – if the Council and the EP could not agree at second reading – for the convening of a conciliation committee and for a third reading of legislation by both the Council and the EP. Unlike the cooperation procedure, however, which enabled a determined Council to ignore the EP's expressed views, the co-decision procedure would allow the EP, for the first time, to veto legislative proposals it did not wish to accept.
- The policy areas subject to the cooperation procedure were revised, with some areas previously covered by the procedure being transferred to the new co-decision procedure, and some new policy areas previously subject to the consultation procedure being transferred to it.
- The scope of the assent procedure was extended.
- From January 1995 the term of office of Commissioners was extended from four to five years so as to bring the lifespan of a Commission closely into line with the lifespan of a Parliament. The national governments were to nominate by common accord, after consulting the EP, the person they intended to appoint as the President of the Commission. Other members of the Commission were to be nominated by the national governments in the established manner, but now in consultation with the nominee for Commission President. The entire prospective Commission was to be subject to a vote of approval by the EP before being formally appointed by common accord of the national governments.
- A Committee of the Regions was established to provide the Council and the Commission with advice on matters of major importance for the regions
- The ECJ was given the power to impose fines on member states that failed to comply with its judgments or failed to implement Community law.
- The EP was to appoint an Ombudsman to receive complaints from citizens 'covering instances of maladministration in the activities of the Community institutions or bodies, with the exception of the Court of Justice and the Court of First Instance acting in their judicial role'.

Box 5.3

Main pillar one policy changes made by the Maastricht Treaty

- The main features of Economic and Monetary Union (EMU) were defined and a timetable for establishing it was specified. Regarding the features, EMU was to include the irrevocable fixing of exchange rates leading to the introduction of a single currency and to the establishment of a European Central Bank (ECB) which would operate within the framework of a European System of Central Banks (ESCB). Regarding the timetable, EMU was to be established in three stages, with stage three beginning no later than 1 January 1999 for those states which could meet the specified convergence criteria. In a protocol attached to the Treaty it was recognised that the United Kingdom 'shall not be obliged or committed to move to the third stage of Economic and Monetary Union without a separate decision to do so by its government and Parliament'. In another protocol the Danish government reserved the right to hold a national referendum before participating in the third stage of EMU.
- Some policy areas in which Community involvement had not had an explicit Treaty base and some in which the Community had not previously been much involved were brought into the TEC for the first time. Development policy was in the first of these categories. Public health, consumer protection, trans-European networks, and the competitiveness of industry were amongst those in the second.
- Community responsibilities in some policy areas that were first given treaty recognition in the SEA were further developed. This applied particularly to research and technological development, the environment, and economic and social cohesion. As part of the strengthening of economic and social cohesion, a new fund – the Cohesion Fund – was established to provide financial assistance for environmental programmes and trans-European transport infrastructures.
- A policy area that created particular difficulties during the negotiations both before and at Maastricht was social policy. Eleven member states wished to build on and give a firm treaty base to the Social Charter, which had been adopted (by eleven votes to one) by the European Council in 1989, whilst the UK government wished to see no extension to the Community's existing responsibilities in this area. After almost bringing the Maastricht summit to the point of collapse, the impasse was resolved by the eleven contracting a separate protocol and agreement on social policy.

Pillar two: a Common Foreign and Security Policy

The SEA stated that the member states 'shall endeavour jointly to formulate and implement a European foreign policy'. The TEU greatly stiffened this aim by specifying that the EU and its member states 'shall define and implement a common foreign and security policy ... covering all areas of foreign and security policy', and by further specifying that the common policy 'shall include all questions related to the security of the Union, including the eventual framing of a common defence policy, which might in time lead to a common defence'.

The objectives of the Common Foreign and Security Policy (CFSP) were defined only in general terms. More specific definition and elaboration of the

principles and general guidelines of the CFSP were to be the responsibility of the European Council.

There were to be three principal ways in which the objectives of the CFSP were to be pursued:

- Systematic cooperation was to be established between the member states on any matter of foreign and security policy that was of general interest. Whenever it deemed it necessary the Council should, on the basis of unanimity, define common positions. Member states should ensure that their national policies conformed to such common positions. On the basis of general guidelines from the European Council, the Council could decide that a matter was to be the subject of joint action.
- In deciding on joint action, or at any stage during the development of a joint action, the Council

could determine that implementation decisions should be taken by QMV.

- The Western European Union (WEU), which 'is an integral part of the development of the Union', was requested 'to elaborate and implement decisions and actions of the Union which had defence implications. The Council shall, in agreement with the institutions of the WEU, adopt the necessary practical arrangements'

This second pillar of the TEU thus put European Political Cooperation (EPC), which had been well-established for some time, within the broader framework of a Common Foreign and Security Policy. The pillar was also extremely significant in that it introduced two important new elements into the West European integration process. First, although foreign policy remained essentially intergovernmental in character, some foreign policy decisions – albeit only 'second-order' decisions – became potentially subject to QMV. Second, defence made its first formal appearance on the policy agenda, albeit somewhat tentatively.

Pillar three: Cooperation in the Spheres of Justice and Home Affairs

The member states were to regard the following areas as matters of common interest: asylum policy; rules governing, and controls on, the crossing by persons of the external borders of the member states; immigration policy and residence rights of third-country nationals; combating drug addiction; combating international fraud; judicial cooperation in civil matters; judicial cooperation in criminal matters; customs cooperation; and police cooperation to combat terrorism, drug trafficking and other serious crime through an EU-wide police intelligence office (Europol). Any measures taken in regard to these matters was to be in compliance with the European Convention of Human Rights.

In the nine areas of common interest the Council could adopt joint positions, promote forms of cooperation, and draw up conventions to be recommended to the member states for adoption in accordance with their respective constitutional requirements.

As with the CFSP pillar of the TEU, the significance of the Justice and Home Affairs (JHA) pillar lay not only in the substantive content of its provisions but also in the broader contribution it would make to the

integration process in Europe. There were, as there were with the CFSP pillar, policy and institutional aspects to this. Regarding the policy aspects, a legal base was given to cooperation in areas of activity that in the past had either been dealt with purely on a national basis or had been the subject of only rather loose and informal cooperation between the member states. Regarding the institutional aspects, whilst intergovernmentalism continued to prevail, a small element of supranationalism appeared with the possibility of qualified majority decisions on certain aspects of policy implementation, and a somewhat larger element appeared with provision in the TEC for a common visa policy and for decisions on visas to be determined by QMV from 1996.

The Treaty of Amsterdam

The background to and the making of the Treaty

Article N of the TEU specified that another IGC should be convened in 1996 to examine the operation of the Treaty. This specification was included mainly at the behest of those member states that were dissatisfied at what they felt to be the insufficient integrationist progress of the Maastricht Treaty. The advance notice given in the TEU of the convening of another IGC in 1996 allowed the Amsterdam Treaty to be considered and prepared over a much longer period than had been either the SEA or the Maastricht Treaty.

As part of the preparation the European Council decided at its June 1994 Corfu meeting to establish a 'Reflection Group', charged with clearing some of the ground for the IGC by examining and elaborating ideas for Treaty revisions. The Reflection Group was composed of 18 members: one representative from each member state (mainly junior ministers from Ministries of Foreign/External Affairs, or very senior diplomats); two representatives from the EP (one Socialist and one Christian Democrat); and one representative from the Commission (the Commissioner with responsibility for the IGC). The main thrust of the Group's report when it was issued in December 1995 was to recommend that the IGC should focus on trying to achieve results in three main areas: making

Europe more relevant to its citizens; enabling the EU to work better and prepare for enlargement; and giving the EU greater capacity for external action. However, beyond agreement on these questions and on a few broad principles and specific issues, it was clear that there were deep divisions in the Group on the traditionally difficult topics. The positions taken by the national representatives were not identified, but the report was studded with such phrases as 'one of us believes that', 'one of us is opposed to', and 'a broad majority of members of the Group favours'. Given the already well-known position of most governments on most EU issues, and especially the UK's continuing opposition to further integration, most of these phrases could be interpreted without too much difficulty.

The experience of the Reflection Group did not thus augur well for the IGC, which was formally launched at a special Heads of Government meeting in Turin in March 1996. Little was achieved in 1996 or early 1997 on the more controversial questions: should there be extensions to QMV in the Council, should the balance of votes in the Council be weighted more towards the larger member states, should the powers of the EP be extended, and should parts of the CFSP and JHA pillars be transferred to the first pillar and/or be placed on a more supranational basis? Few IGC participants were, however, overly concerned about the lack of progress. There were two reasons for this. First, EU negotiations on constitutional/institutional issues – and indeed on most major contested issues – customarily begin slowly and then speed up as deadlines approach. Second, there were strong grounds for believing that the main obstacle to achieving progress – the UK government's opposition to further integration – would be at least partly removed by the likely outcome of the general election that had to be held before the scheduled conclusion of the IGC at the June 1997 Amsterdam summit.

The UK obstacle was indeed duly removed when, in the May 1997 election, the Conservatives were defeated after 18 years in government and replaced by Labour. Tony Blair, the new Prime Minister, declared that his government would pursue a policy of 'constructive engagement' with the EU, and this was immediately reflected in the closing weeks of the IGC when the UK's approach became much more positive than it had been under the Conservatives. There was not a complete policy about-turn, but on most issues

the UK's previous 'awkwardness' and isolationism largely disappeared.

The UK's changed stance helped to make the Amsterdam summit, which marked the last stage of the IGC, much smoother than the Maastricht summit. There were still differences to be resolved at Amsterdam and not a few tensions in the air, but political agreement on the contents of the Treaty was reached relatively easily. After the necessary legal and translation work had been undertaken, the Treaty was formally signed in October 1997.

At the time of the signing of the Treaty it was generally anticipated – largely because the new treaty's contents were much more modest than those of the Maastricht Treaty – that there would be no major ratification difficulties. But though ratification was never seriously endangered, it was considerably delayed. The main problem was that some of the member states had to deal with domestic political and legal difficulties before ratification could be effected. In France, the ratification process could not even begin until the national constitution had been amended to take account of some of the Treaty's justice and home affairs provisions. France was the last member state to ratify, in March 1999, and the Treaty eventually came into force in May 1999.

The contents of the Treaty

It was always likely that the Amsterdam Treaty would not be as innovative or as important as either the SEA or the Maastricht Treaty. The intention from the outset was that it would essentially be a revising rather than a pioneering treaty. Moreover, even in respect of revisions, the great issue of internal EU debate in the mid- to late 1990s – EMU – was not on the IGC's agenda.

The Treaty had no great *projet* to guide and drive it, in the manner that the SEA had the SEM and the TEU had EMU. There was a major new EU *projet* in hand by the time the negotiations on the Treaty started – preparing for the anticipated accession of CEECs – but although this issue featured prominently in the IGC's deliberations it was not placed centre stage in the Treaty itself. This was because, with enlargement still some way off, the national governments were just not subject to enough pressure to find the political will to reach agreement on key institutional issues. The issue

Box 5.4

The most important provisions of the Amsterdam Treaty

Institutional
- The cooperation procedure was virtually abandoned and the remit of the co-decision procedure was extended to 23 new areas.
- The co-decision procedure was streamlined and the EP's position under the procedure was strengthened.
- There was increased provision for the use of QMV in the Council.
- The EP's *de facto* right to approve the European Council's nominee for Commission President was given treaty status; the nominations of the national governments to the College must now be made 'by common accord' with the President-designate; and the Commission would now be required to work 'under the political guidance of its President'.

Internal policies
- A number of JHA and JHA-related policy areas were transferred to the EC, with the purpose of facilitating, within a period of five years after the entry into force of the Treaty, the adoption of measures that would result in the progressive establishment of 'an area of freedom, security and justice' in which there would be free movement of persons behind a common external border. The UK and Ireland were given opt-outs from these free movement of persons provisions and Denmark also was not to be fully associated with them.
- Underpinning the free movement of persons title, the Schengen *acquis* (which consisted of rules and supporting measures dealing with the abolition of checks at internal borders) was integrated into the EU framework through a protocol. Ireland and the UK were allowed to opt-out from the Schengen Protocol.
- Pillar three of the TEU was refocused and re-titled 'Provisions on Police and Judicial Cooperation in Criminal Matters'.
- A new title on employment was inserted into the TEC and the Social Chapter of the TEC (which existed only as a protocol attached to the Treaty because of the opt-out the UK government had negotiated at Maastricht) was fully incorporated into the TEC.

External relations
- QMV was established as the norm, subject to exceptional circumstances, for adopting and implementing joint actions and common positions.
- A new device of 'constructive abstention', was introduced whereby a state abstaining in a vote could issue a declaration that would result in it not being obliged to apply the decision taken, whilst recognising that the decision did commit the EU.
- A new post of CFSP High Representative was created to assist the Council, and especially the Council Presidency, in all CFSP matters.
- Specific security issues were identified for the first time as falling within the remit of the EU, with the incorporation of the so-called Petersberg tasks of 'humanitarian and rescue tasks, peacekeeping tasks and tasks of combat forces in crisis management, including peacekeeping'.

Closer cooperation
The possibility of the development of policy activities without all member states participating (as seen in the Maastricht Treaty provisions for EMU and the Social Charter) was advanced with the incorporation of provisions in the first and third pillars of the TEU to allow a less than full complement of member states – but constituting 'at least a majority' – to establish closer cooperation between themselves, and for this purpose to be able to make use of the EU's institutions, procedures and mechanisms. Flexibility of this kind was to be used only as a last resort and was made subject to various restrictions – including that it should not affect the *acquis communautaire*.

was, therefore, postponed to another day, via the attachment to the TEC of a 'Protocol on the institutions with the prospect of enlargement of the European Union' in which provision was made for another IGC to be convened 'at least one year before the membership exceeds twenty'. Its task would be to carry out 'a comprehensive review of the provisions of the Treaties on the composition and functioning of the institutions'. Significantly, however, the bases on which an agreement could be reached on two of the most difficult institutional issues – the size of the Commission and voting weights in the Council – were identified in the Protocol with a statement that at the time of the next enlargement of the Union 'the Commission shall comprise one national of each of the Member States, provided that, by that date, the weighting of the votes in the Council has been modified ... notably [by]compensating those Member States which give up the possibility of nominating a second member of the Commission'.

The contents of the Amsterdam Treaty were, as compared with the SEA and the TEU, thus relatively modest. It was a modernising and consolidating treaty rather than a transforming one. But, though the Treaty lacked the *élan* and drive of the SEA and Maastricht Treaties, it did nonetheless contain changes of significance for the governance of the EU. The most significant of these changes are outlined in Box 5.4. (More detailed outlines are given in the fourth to sixth editions of this book.)

The Treaty of Nice

The background to and the making of the Treaty

With enlargement negotiations opening in 1998 with six candidate countries and negotiations with another six likely to open in the near future, the Heads of Government of the member states decided at their June 1999 Cologne summit that the IGC provided for in the Amsterdam Treaty Protocol should be convened in early 2000 and concluded by the year's end. Accordingly, the IGC opened in February 2000 and closed at the December 2000 Nice European Council. The remit of the IGC was initially limited to the so-

called 'Amsterdam leftovers' – that is to the composition of the Commission, the weighting of votes among the members of the Council, and the further extension of QMV to new policy areas. From the beginning of the IGC, however, the Commission and some of the member states lobbied for an additional item to be placed on the agenda, namely the strengthening and simplification of the closer cooperation procedure that had been created under the Amsterdam Treaty. Eventually, this item did become part of the agenda, as did a number of other issues as the IGC progressed.

Distinctive features of the IGC are outlined in Chapter 7 and have been described in detail by David Galloway (2001) and by Church and Phinnemore (2002). The most important of these features was the narrow focus of the IGC as compared with its predecessors, and indeed also its successors. Whereas all other IGCs have ranged widely across EC/EU affairs, the 2000 IGC was focused very much on institutional issues. This did not, however, make its operation any smoother, for institutional matters bring national status and power positions very much to the fore. With the French Council Presidency, which oversaw the second half of the IGC, being increasingly suspected by smaller member states of looking too much to the interests of the larger member states, it was perhaps no surprise that the Nice European Council, which marked the culmination and close of the IGC, broke the length record for all European summits – being spread over four days.

The narrow focus of the Nice Treaty helped to make its ratification relatively straightforward, except in Ireland where domestic political circumstances resulted in the Irish people rejecting the Treaty in a referendum held in June 2001. The Treaty therefore had to be put on hold until, in a second referendum held in October 2002, the Irish people gave it their approval. The Treaty came into force in February 2003.

The contents of the Treaty

The composition and functioning of the institutions

The Commission. The IGC did not, as many thought it should, take a decision on the maximum size of the

College of Commissioners. Rather, it agreed that from 2005 the College would consist of one national per member state, thus resulting in the five largest states losing their right to have two Commissioners. It was further agreed that once the EU numbered 27 members a decision would be taken on the exact size of the College and on arrangements for a fair rotation system between the member states.

Arrangements for the appointment of the College were changed, most notably with the replacement of unanimity by QMV in the European Council and Council of Ministers for key decisions on the nomination of Commission President and the nomination and subsequent appointment of the whole College.

The powers of the Commission President were also strengthened, including by enabling him to decide on the Commission's 'internal organisation', to allocate the responsibilities of Commissioners and to require a Commissioner to resign after obtaining the approval of the College.

The Council of Ministers. A central feature of the IGC was – with enlargement looming and the prospect of many small states joining the EU – a determination by the large member states to protect their position when votes are taken in the Council. Various options were explored on this, with it eventually being agreed that the mixed solution that is set out in Box 5.5 would apply from 1 January 2005.

As in all IGCs since the SEA, much attention was given to further extensions of the use of QMV However, of the 70 or so treaty provisions still subject to unanimity, only 45 were discussed. The remainder – including such areas as common defence, revision of the treaties, and comitology – were left aside because they were deemed to be constitutional or too sensitive in nature. Many of the extensions that were agreed covered relatively uncontentious and not very politically significant matters. Amongst politically important matters to move to QMV were measures to facilitate freedom of movement of the citizen, measures assisting judicial cooperation in civil matters, the conclusion of international agreements in the area of trade in services and the commercial aspects of property, and actions in the field of industrial policy. A partial and deferred switch to QMV was agreed for matters relating to visas, asylum, immigration and other policies related to free movement of persons.

Box 5.5

QMV voting provisions in the Council of Ministers as established by the Nice Treaty*

1 The voting weights of the member states under QMV were changed. Overall, small states continued to be over-represented, but there was some tilting of the balance towards large member states. Germany remained particularly under-represented in terms of voting weight in relation to population size – which was largely because France was especially resistant to Germany having more votes than the other large states.

    A related decision assisting large states was that the threshold for a qualified majority was raised. The EU-15 requirement – 62 votes out of 87, or 71.26 per cent – would be replaced by a system in which the QMV threshold would be 255 out of 345, or 73.91 per cent, when the EU reached 27 members. (For an account and full analysis of the QMV debate and decisions of Nice, see Galloway, 2001: 76–93.)

2 Provision was made for any member state to request verification that a qualified majority represented at least 62 per cent of the total population of the Union. If it did not, no decision could be taken. This stipulation clearly advantaged the more populous states.

Slightly offsetting these two provisions that were to the advantage of large states, it was, also agreed at Nice – on the insistence of smaller states – that decisions taken by QMV must be approved by a majority of states.

* Under the Lisbon Treaty, these voting arrangements will stay in place until 2014, and in some circumstances can be used until 2017.

(For a full list of the QMV extensions, see: European Commission, 2001; Bond and Feus, 2001; Galloway, 2001.)

The European Parliament. One of the few institutional provisions agreed in the Amsterdam IGC to help prepare the EU for enlargement was the setting of a ceiling of 700 on the size of the EP. Under pressure not to reduce the size of national representations by too much, this ceiling was raised by the Nice IGC to 732, but on a phasing-in basis.

The ECJ and the CFI. A number of changes were made to the Treaty articles covering the EU's two courts with a view to preparing them for enlargement, improving their functioning, and amending and clarifying their responsibilities. Four of these changes were especially important.

First, the size of the Court of Justice (ECJ) remained unchanged at 'one judge per Member State', but that of the Court of First Instance (CFI) – which hitherto had not been specified in the Treaty – was now specified as being 'at least one judge per Member State'.

Second, ECJ cases previously dealt with in full plenary session would now normally be dealt with in a Grand Chamber – comprised, though this was not specified in the Treaty itself, eleven judges.

Third, to lighten the workload of the ECJ, the types of cases coming before the CFI was widened to include most direct actions and, for the first time, preliminary rulings in specific areas.

Fourth, so as to allow the CFI to take on its new responsibilities, the Council, acting unanimously, was given the power to establish judicial panels to hear and determine certain classes of cases that hitherto have been handled by the CFI. Decisions taken by judicial panels would be subject to a right of appeal to the CFI 'where there is a serious risk of the unity or consistency of Community law being affected'.

Decision-making procedures

The Nice Treaty was much more restrained than had been the SEA and the Maastricht and Amsterdam treaties in making changes to the form and application of the EU's decision-making procedures.

The most striking changes to *form* were to the Amsterdam-created flexible cooperation procedure –

now re-named enhanced cooperation under the Nice Treaty – which had provided a base for states to engage in a policy activity without all states participating. The Amsterdam arrangements had been widely criticised for being too restrictive and almost unworkable. Two changes were made to those arrangements to make enhanced cooperation more flexible and potentially more usable. First, the minimum number of member states required for enhanced cooperation was set at eight, as compared with the Amsterdam stipulation that a majority of states was required. Second, in the first and third pillars, the possibility of any single state vetoing enhanced cooperation was removed and replaced by the possibility of an appeal to the European Council, which would be able to act by QMV.

As for changes to the *application* of decision-making procedures, there were a number of extensions to the use of procedures. First, the Treaty provided for the possibility of enhanced cooperation being used in the second (CFSP) pillar for the implementation of joint actions and common positions that did not have military or defence implications, although any state that objected to its use could ask that the matter be referred to the European Council for a unanimous decision. Second, the remit of the co-decision procedure (which gives the EP a veto over proposals) was extended, including to certain anti-discrimination measures, judicial cooperation in civil matters (except family law), and specific industrial policy support measures. The EP's hopes and request that the procedure should apply to all decisions where QMV applies was resisted, with the consequence that in some important policy areas – including agriculture and competition – the consultation procedure, which only gives the EP consultative and advisory powers, would still apply. Third, the assent procedure (under which decisions require the assent of the EP) was also extended, including to enhanced cooperation when the matter concerned covered an area falling under the co-decision procedure and to decisions relating to whether 'there is a clear risk of a serious breach by a Member State' of the principles on which the EU is founded. (The Amsterdam Treaty had established the use of the assent procedure for breaches of EU principles, but had restricted its application to determining whether 'a serious and persistent breach' already existed'). If a breach was held to be at risk or to exist, the Council could determine appropriate action, including

– a new Nice provision – making recommendations where a risk existed, or – an Amsterdam-established provision – suspending EU voting rights.

New competences

The IGC's focus on institutional issues meant that not as much attention was given as had been in previous IGCs to extending the EU's policy competences. Only two significant extensions were made.

First, following on from the 1999 Tampere summit which focused on justice and home affairs matters, new forms of cooperation in the fight against organised crime were identified. Following on also from Tampere, the means of operationalising such cooperation were strengthened by giving treaty recognition and support to the European Judicial Cooperation Unit (Eurojust) which the Tampere Council had decided to establish for the purposes of facilitating coordination and action between national prosecuting authorities in respect of serious cross-border crime.

Second, the objectives of social policy were widened with the addition to the list of social policy objectives of two new objectives: combating social exclusion and the modernisation (but specifically not the harmonisation) of social protection systems.

The 'case of the Charter of Fundamental Rights of the European Union'

At its Cologne meeting in June 1999, the European Council declared that 'the fundamental rights applicable at Union level should be consolidated in a Charter and thereby made more evident' (European Council, 1999b: 18). The European Council further declared that a draft document should be prepared in advance of the December 2000 European Council meeting, when it would then be considered 'whether and, if so, how the Charter should be integrated into the treaties' (*ibid.*: Annex iv).

The composition of the body – called a Convention – charged with drawing up the Charter was broadly outlined at Cologne and then specified at the October 1999 Tampere summit. It had 62 members, drawn from four sources: fifteen representatives of the heads of state and government; a representative of the President of the Commission; sixteen members of the EP; and thirty members of national parliaments. This membership was quite unique in that for the first time EU representatives were meeting with national representatives to draft a Union text. A much broader, and arguably more democratic, base was thus being used than in IGCs, which are composed of governmental representatives.

The Charter of Fundamental Rights of the European Union was agreed by the Convention in October 2000. Its high tone and ambitions may be seen by quoting from its Preamble:

> Conscious of its spiritual and moral heritage, the Union is founded on the indivisible, universal values of human dignity, freedom, equality and solidarity; it is based on the principles of democracy and the rule of law. It places the individual at the heart of its activities, by establishing the citizenship of the Union and by creating an area of freedom, security and justice.
>
> The Union contributes to the preservation and to the development of these common values while respecting the diversity of the cultures and traditions of the peoples of Europe as well as the national identities of the Member States and the organisation of their public authorities at national, regional and local levels; it seeks to promote balanced and sustainable development and ensures free movement of persons, goods, services and capital, and the freedom of establishment (*Official Journal*, C364: 43, 18 December 2000).

Following the Preamble, the substantive contents of the Charter were set out in six chapters, the contents of which are summarised in Box 5.6.

Some governments wanted to take advantage of the 2000 IGC to give treaty status to the Charter. However, resistance from the UK government, with some support from four other states, resulted in it not being mentioned at all in the Nice Treaty. However, it was 'solemnly proclaimed' at Nice by the Council, EP and Commission. Quite where this left the Charter in legal terms was uncertain, though it was clear it would have at least some legal impact for it did, in effect, come close to giving formal recognition to a series of rights that hitherto had become recognised in the Union's legal system but in a somewhat tangential manner. The status of the Charter was to become one of the more controversial issues considered in the processes that led to the Constitutional and Lisbon Treaties. As will

---

Box 5.6

The Charter of Fundamental Rights of the European Union: summary of the key contents of the Charter's six titles

I (Articles 1–5): dignity. Rights covered under this chapter include: the right to life, including the prohibition of the death penalty; the integrity of the person including prohibition of the reproductive cloning of human beings; and the prohibition of torture or inhumane treatment.

II (Articles 6–19): freedoms. Included here are the right to liberty and security; respect for private and family life; protection of personal data; freedom of thought, conscience and religion; freedom of expression; freedom to conduct business; and the right to property.

III (Articles 20–26): equality. Amongst the rights recognised in this chapter are equality before the law, non-discrimination, equality between men and women, and the rights of the child.

IV (Articles 27–38): solidarity. This chapter includes workers' rights to information and consultation within undertakings, the right of collective bargaining and action, fair and just working conditions, health care rights, and consumer protection.

V (Articles 39–46): citizens' rights. Rights listed here include the right of a citizen to vote and stand as a candidate at EP and municipal elections in the member states in which he or she resides, the right to good administration, the right of movement and residence within the Union, and the right of diplomatic or consular protection by the authorities of any member state in a third country in which the member state of which he or she is a national is not represented.

VI (Articles 47–50): justice. This chapter includes the right to an effective remedy and to a fair trial, the presumption of innocence and right of defence, and adherence to the principles of legality and proportionality of criminal offences and penalties.

---

be seen in the next chapter, it was given treaty status under the Constitutional Treaty but not fully under the Lisbon Treaty.

Concluding Remarks

The EC/EU's treaty framework evolved considerably in the period from the Treaties of Rome to the Treaty of Nice, with all of the treaties advancing the integrationist process in some way. The SEA and the Maastricht Treaty were the most ambitious of the treaties. They were so because of the wide range of policy and institutional measures they contained and also because they each did something for the integrationist spirit over and above the specific treaty additions and amendments they contained. So, the SEA, along with the already agreed SEM programme to which the SEA gave a treaty-base, heralded the re-

launch of the integration process after years of relative stagnation and provided a major stimulus to the integrationist momentum. The Maastricht Treaty laid the foundations for EMU and also created a symbolically important new organisational form – the European Union – based on three pillars.

The Amsterdam Treaty was disappointing to those who looked for major reforms in advance of the enlargement of the EU that was beginning to loom. Nonetheless, it did help to pick up integrationist progress after the caution that had followed upon the 1992 Danish ratification referendum on the Maastricht Treaty and it also signalled the wish of the UK government to enter the EU mainstream.

As for the Nice Treaty, it was narrower than its predecessors in that it was concerned almost exclusively with institutional matters. The IGC that produced it was, as Galloway (2001: 21) has observed, driven largely by concerns about the relative power and influence of member states in the Union.

However, criticism of the IGC for not having addressed wider issues of EU's governance – concerning, for example, the power balance between the Union and the member states or the 'constitutionalisation' and simplification of the treaties – misunderstand what the IGC was established to do. It achieved its main purpose, which was to take decisions about EU institutions that created the necessary bases for the planned expansion of the EU to incorporate Central, Eastern and Southern European countries. Beyond providing for this widening of the EU, the Treaty also provided for some deepening by further edging forward the integration process through, for example, the increased powers given to the EP and the wider legal base of QMV in the Council.

The broader issues that critics of the Treaty would have liked to have seen explored in the 2000 IGC were scheduled for another IGC that a declaration attached to the Nice Treaty programmed to be convened in 2004.

Chapter 6

The Constitutional and Lisbon Treaties

The Making of the Constitutional Treaty

As was noted at the end of Chapter 5, it was recognised at the time agreement was reached on the Nice Treaty that it contained little more than the minimum that was necessary to enable the EU to enlarge. The Treaty made provision for fitting the new member states into the Commission, the Council, the EP and the other EU institutions, but it did little to tackle wider matters relating to how the much larger and more heterogeneous EU could function with efficiency and effectiveness.

Thus recognising the limitations of the treaty they had contracted, the national leaders agreed at Nice to open up a debate on the future of the EU and to convene another IGC in 2004. To facilitate the debate and help prepare the IGC, the December 2001 European Council meeting issued the *Laeken Declaration on the Future of the European Union* which provided for the establishment of a Convention on the Future of Europe (European Council, 2001).

The Constitutional Convention

The Laeken Declaration declared that the soon-to-be enlarged European Union needed to become 'more democratic, more transparent and more efficient' (European Council, 2001: 21). The Union also needed to resolve three basic challenges: 'how to bring citizens, and primarily the young, closer to the European design and the European institutions'; 'how to organise politics and the European political area in an enlarged Union'; and 'how to develop the Union into a stabilising factor and a model in the new, multipolar world' (European Council, *ibid.*).

These general aims and challenges resulted in the Convention being asked to examine a number of key issues. These included establishing a better division and definition of EU competences, simplifying the Union's instruments, increasing democracy, transparency and efficiency, and simplifying and reorganising the treaties – with this to include the option of leading 'in the long run to the adoption of a constitutional text in the Union' (European Council, 2001: 24).

The Convention was composed of 105 members (see Box 6.1). As had been the case with the Convention that had drawn up the Charter of Fundamental Rights (see page 65), the dominant presence amongst the membership was parliamentarians rather than governmental representatives. The Convention was thus not intended to replicate an IGC.

The Convention opened its proceedings on 28 February 2002. Its work was undertaken in four forums, as set out in Box 6.2.

Box 6.1

Membership of the Constitutional Convention

- a chairman, the former French President, Valery Giscard D'Estaing, and two vice chairmen: Guiliano Amato, a former Italian Prime Minister, and Jean-Luc Dehaene, a former Belgian Prime Minister;
- representatives of the Heads of State or Government of the member states (15);
- representatives of the Heads of State or Government of the candidate states (13);
- representatives of the national parliaments of the member states (30);
- representatives of the national parliaments of the candidate states (26);
- representatives of the European Commission (2);
- representatives of the European Parliament (16).

In addition to these 105 members (all of whom were backed-up by alternative members):

1 Representatives of the (then) soon-to-be acceding states were able to play a full part in the proceedings of the Convention, but were not empowered to prevent any consensus emerging between the 15 member states.
2 Observer status was given to: the European Economic and Social Committee (3 representatives); the Committee of the Regions (6); the social partners (3); and the European Ombudsman.

The Laeken Declaration had stated that the Convention's 'final document will provide a starting point for discussions in the Intergovernmental Conference, which will take the ultimate decisions' (European Council, 2001: 25). As, however, the work of the Convention proceeded, it became increasingly clear from statements by governmental leaders that the final document would be likely not just to provide a 'starting point' for IGC discussions but in many respects would determine them. It also quickly became clear that the Convention was not going to restrict itself to a minimalist interpretation of its remit but

was going to draw up a full draft constitution for the Union. These developments resulted in the work of the Convention attracting growing attention, not least from national governments – some of which replaced sitting Convention representatives with more senior figures.

The Convention's draft had been scheduled to be presented to the June 2003 Thessaloniki European Council, but in the event only Parts I and II of what was a four-part text were ready. Parts III and IV were considered and approved at a final Convention plenary in July. On the insistence of Giscard D'Estaing, chairman of the Convention, who feared open divisions would weaken the weight of the Convention's position, texts were adopted by consensus rather than by voting. The final text was formally presented to the Italian Council Presidency on 18 July 2003.

This final text took the form of a *Draft Treaty Establishing a Constitution for Europe* (European Convention, 2003). The nature of its contents will be considered later in this chapter, since most of them were incorporated by the ensuing IGC. Suffice it to note here that the recommendations were, for the most part, relatively modest and essentially incrementalist in manner. This is precisely the reason most of them were acceptable to the IGC: they were set within the general thinking frameworks of national governments. (For detailed accounts of the operation of the Constitutional Convention, see: Castiglione *et al.*, 2007; Norman, 2003.)

The Intergovernmental Conference

The IGC opened on 4 October 2003. In terms of its composition it was similar to previous IGCs, with Heads of State or Government formally at the apex, Foreign Ministers meeting regularly to review and prod progress, and most of the detailed work being undertaken by senior national officials. The states that were scheduled to join the EU in May 2004 were accorded full IGC membership.

However, in terms of its functioning the IGC was very different from earlier IGCs in that its agenda was largely set by the Draft Treaty Establishing a Constitution for Europe that had been agreed by the Constitutional Convention. It was also supposed to be different from its immediate predecessors by being completed more speedily: the European Council asked that it be concluded 'as soon as possible and in time for it to become known to European citizens before the June 2004 elections for the European Parliament' (European Council, 2003a: 2).

As always, governments approached the IGC with a mixture of views. On particular issues individual governments were decidedly in favour of some measures being adopted, decidedly opposed to others, and open on some. So, for example, nine states – the Czech Republic, Ireland, Italy, Lithuania, Malta, Poland, Portugal, Slovakia, and Spain – wanted the inclusion of a reference to Europe's Christian inheritance and values. Seven (smaller) states – Austria, Denmark, Estonia, Ireland, the Netherlands, Portugal and Slovenia – wanted to retain the system of a rotating Council presidency. And eight (including all former 'non-aligned') states – Austria, Denmark, Estonia, Finland, Ireland, Poland, Sweden and the UK – were opposed to the inclusion of a collective defence clause.

To try and ensure such differences between states were not given too much of an airing, which would have slowed progress, the approach of the Italian Presidency was to stick as closely as possible to the Convention's Draft Treaty. Attempts by governments to re-open particular matters that had been agreed in the Convention were generally discouraged. However, two issues proved to be highly troublesome, and could not be resolved when the European Council met in Brussels on 12–13 December. The first concerned the size of the College of Commissioners. The Convention had recommended that from 2009 the size be reduced to fifteen, but with non-voting Commissioners also to be appointed. Most member states had concerns about this, but small states particularly did so because the Commission traditionally has been seen as helping to protect the interests of smaller states against larger ones. The second concerned voting arrangements in the Council of Ministers. The Convention had recommended that QMV voting weights be abandoned in favour of a double majority system in which majorities would be deemed to exist for proposals that were supported by a majority of states representing at least 60 per cent of the EU's total population. Germany was especially anxious to accept this recommendation, believing that the Nice arrangements had assigned a disproportionately large voting weight to Poland and Spain – 27 votes to each despite both countries having popula-

---

Box 6.2

The Working Forums of the Constitutional Convention

- *The Office of the President.* Giscard D'Estaing did much to set the focus and pace and to shape the outcomes of the Convention. He had clear ideas on a number of issues, including strengthening the European Council, moving the Commission to a more collegial model, and simplifying procedures in the interests of efficiency and democracy. In the closing period, when disagreements between Convention members were creating difficulties, he was highly proactive in ensuring progress was made.
- *The Praesidium.* This was composed of 13 Convention members, including the Chairman and two Vice-Chairmen. Its job was to provide direction and impetus, most particularly by ensuring the work of the Convention was being properly organised and tasks were being completed.
- *Working Groups.* Eleven of these were established to examine particular issues in depth.
- *Plenary Sessions.* Normally held over a two-day period at least once each month, plenaries held general debates, deliberated on working group reports, and gradually moved towards the adoption of a final text.

The work of the four forums was supported by a well organised and flexible secretariat.

---

tions of just under 40 million, whilst Germany with its population of just over 80 million was assigned – with 29 – only two more votes.

At the December summit, agreement could not be reached on these two issues. If the Council voting system issues had been resolved then an agreement probably could have been found also on the size of the College issue, but Poland and Spain refused to abandon the system that had given them such over-generous treatment. Accordingly, and amidst whispered accusations from some participants that the Italian Presidency had not handled proceedings well, the summit failed to finalise the text of the Constitutional Treaty.

It was thus left to the succeeding Council Presidency – Ireland – to pick up the pieces and try to find a consensus. In so doing it was greatly assisted by a general election in Spain in March, which saw the incumbent conservative government replaced with a socialist government that was – partly because it was keen to establish close relations with France and Germany – more flexible on the Council voting issue. This left Poland isolated: a position that, as both a new member state and a member state that knew it faced political battles ahead on the likes of CAP and the cohesion funds, it did not wish to be in.

Accordingly, the Irish presidency was authorised by the European Council in late March to reconvene the IGC. An agreement was subsequently brokered on the Commission and Council issues: on the former, the size of the College was capped, but on the basis of a formula that was different to that proposed by the Convention, and from 2014 rather than 2009; on the latter, Council voting weights were dropped, but the thresholds for majorities was raised from what the Convention had advocated both in respect of the number of member states and the proportion of the EU population they represented (see below for the details on both issues). The IGC was concluded at the European Council meeting in Brussels on 17–18 June 2004. After the customary work by lawyers and translators, the Constitutional Treaty was formally signed in Rome on 29 October 2004.

The Contents of the Constitutional Treaty

The Constitutional Treaty (CT) would have replaced the EU's existing treaties – that is, the TEU, the TEC, and the Euratom Treaty in their post-Nice forms – with a single treaty. Far from being the relatively short document that many – especially Euro-enthusiasts – had hoped it would be, the CT was extremely long. It consisted of a preamble, four parts that ran to a total of 448 articles, 36 protocols, 2 annexes, and 50 declarations (Treaty Establishing a Constitution for Europe, 2004). The way in which the four parts of the CT were organised is set out in Box 6.3.

Box 6.3

The Four Parts of the Constitutional Treaty

Part I (articles 1–60) laid down the general rules and principles underlying the Union. The EU's objectives, powers, institutions, and decision-making procedures were all identified.

Part II (articles 61–114) incorporated the Charter of Fundamental Rights, which had been 'solemnly proclaimed' at Nice, into the Treaty.

Part III (articles 115–436) covered the Union's policies and functioning. Most of this part incorporated provisions of existing treaties – notably the Treaty Establishing the European Community.

Part IV (articles 437–448) consisted of general and final provisions, including procedures for adopting and revising the Treaty.

The specific contents of the CT will not be described here as most of them are covered in the description later in the chapter of the contents of the Lisbon Treaty – which succeeded the CT when the latter failed to be ratified. (For detailed accounts of the contents of the CT, see: Church and Phinnemore, 2005; Phinnemore, 2004; and the sixth edition of this book.) However, the main overall features of the CT will be outlined. Six were especially important.

First, despite the use of the symbolically important word 'constitution', the hope of Euro-enthusiasts that a reasonably simple document would be produced that would be widely recognised as being a 'proper' constitution was not realised. It partly would have been so had the CT been confined to Part I and the Charter of Fundamental Rights, for they covered much of the sort of ground that is found in national constitutions. However, such is the nature of the EU that the governments of member states generally wish to codify many detailed matters concerning the Union's functioning, and hence wished the long and detailed Part III – in essence an amended version of the TEC, covering many technical matters of little interest to the ordinary citizen – to be part of the CT. But, in any event, Parts I and II were weak on some traditionally core constitutional matters: there was no enunciation of a clear philosophy of government; there was no robust underpinning of EU citizenship (which remained weak); there was no provision for an EU budget capable of financing significant spending policies; and the instruments given to the EU to protect and promote the interests of its citizens via foreign and defence policies remained relatively weak.

Second, most of the CT's contents were taken from the treaties it was designed to replace – namely, the TEU and the TEC as they had been amended over the years – plus the Charter of Fundamental Rights. In consequence, most of the Treaty confirmed the existing treaty *acquis*.

Third, the new content was largely of the type that had featured in all of the treaties since the SEA. That is, it consisted, for the most part, of relatively modest changes designed to make the EU more efficient and more democratic. To give just one example: much publicity was given to the new post of Union Minister for Foreign Affairs, but this was really just a merging of two existing positions – the Council's High Representative for the CFSP and the Commission's External Relations Commissioner.

Fourth, an important theme running through some of the changes was to give the EU greater coherence and identity. This was seen in the 'transfer' of the JHA pillar to the TEU (though the CFSP pillar continued to be located in the TEU), the assignment of legal personality to the EU, the creation of a semi-permanent President of the European Council, and the above mentioned merging of the existing separate Council and Commission foreign policy posts into a single Union Minister for Foreign Affairs.

Fifth, changes in institutional provisions and decision-making arrangements did not have much overall effect on the intergovernmental/supranational balance within the Union. A small tilting in a supranational direction was seen in the increased capacity of the Council to take decisions by QMV. But this increased capacity applied mostly to relatively low-key and technical areas. In highly sensitive areas – including treaty reform, enlargement, financial matters, social policy, and most areas of CFSP and all of ESDP – unanimity continued to prevail. Moreover, intergovernmentalism may be said to have been given a boost by the strengthening of the capacity of the EU's most intergovernmental institution – the European Council – through the creation of the new post of European Council President.

Sixth, and crucially, the significance of the CT lay not only in its specific provisions for EU structures, institutions, decision-making processes, and policies. It also had potentially great symbolic significance with its use of the word 'constitution' and with treaty status being given to the already much-used EU 'anthem' (Beethoven's 'Ode to Joy') and flag (the distinctive twelve yellow stars on a blue background). This symbolic entrenchment suggested to many Europeans – of both Europhile and Eurosceptic persuasions – a highly significant advance in the process of 'building Europe'. Largely because of this symbolic importance, the Treaty attracted much more political attention during the treaty-making process than had earlier amending treaties and led to major – and ultimately insuperable – problems when ratification processes began

Ratifying the Constitutional Treaty

As with all of the EU's treaties, the CT could not enter into force until it had been ratified by all of the member states. Aware that ratification by all 25 member states was by no means a formality, it was specified in Part IV of the Treaty that if by two years after the signing of the Treaty four-fifths of the member states had completed ratification but one or more states 'have encountered difficulties in proceeding with ratification', the matter would be referred to the European Council – for unspecified action. With the Treaty being formally signed in October 2004, all member states were thus obliged to try and ratify by October 2006 at the latest.

In the past, member states have almost invariably ratified post-accession treaties by a parliamentary vote. The exceptions have been those occasional instances when referendums have been used: in Ireland for all four treaties from the SEA; in Denmark for the SEA, Maastricht and Amsterdam treaties; and in France for the Maastricht Treaty. With the Constitutional Treaty more widespread use of referendums was always likely: partly because of the perceived highly symbolic importance of the treaty – it was widely seen as being much more than 'just another' amending treaty – and partly because of the much larger number of member states in the enlarged EU. Quite how widespread promises of referendums were to become, however – amounting ultimately to almost half of the member states – was not anticipated. The major factor bringing about the increase was domestic political pressures. In the UK, for example, Prime Minister Blair, anticipating the next general election, responded to a Conservative Party promise that it would call a referendum on the Constitutional Treaty by promising one himself. This in turn heightened pressures in France on President Chirac to hold a referendum.

A referendum is, of course, much more difficult for a government to control than a parliamentary vote. Citizens can 'cause problems' in two ways: by taking a contrary view to the government on the issue at stake, or by expressing a view on an issue or issues other than the one that features in the referendum question. Both of these 'problems' influenced voting when ratification referendums were held in France on 29 May 2005 and three days later in the Netherlands on 1 June.

By the time the French and Dutch referendums were held, ten member states had, in fact, already ratified the Treaty, though only in one – Spain – by referendum. The majority in favour in Spain was comfortable enough, with 76.7 of those who voted favouring ratification, but the turnout was, at 42.3 per cent, very low. In France and the Netherlands the possibility of *No* votes increased over the course of the referendum campaigns. One reason for this was growing opposition to the form of the Treaty, which was seen by many as embracing elite rather than popular wishes. Another reason was concerns about the supposed 'Anglo-American' social and economic values contained in the Treaty: although, in reality, the CT contained no significant changes in values from previous treaties, opponents of the Treaty presented it as doing so – to the background of concerns about whether existing welfare systems could be sustained. And a third reason was that various 'non-Treaty' matters featured in the campaigns – including political opposition to the governments in power, insecurities arising from the May 2004 enlargement and projected Turkish accession, and resentment in the Netherlands over the country being the largest per capita contributor to the EU budget. The outcomes of the two referendums were clear rejections of the CT. In

France, 54.9 per cent voted against ratification on a 69.7 per cent turnout, whilst in the Netherlands 61.7 per cent voted against on a 63 per cent turnout.

The question then became 'what now?' EU leaders quickly divided on this. Should the ratification process continue, on the basis that all citizens were entitled to express their view and with the CT's own 'four-fifths' provision (see above) suggesting the Treaty was not necessarily lost because a couple of states had failed to ratify. Prominent amongst those advocating continuation were the Luxembourg President of the Council, Jean-Claude Junker, President Chirac, and Chancellor Schröder. Foremost amongst those taking a contrary view was Prime Minister Blair, who hinted the ratification process should at least be put on hold because the Treaty could not enter into force unless it was ratified by all member states and that no longer looked to be possible

As it happened, a European Council meeting was already scheduled for the week after the referendums. With realities beginning to be absorbed, and with governments that had promised referendums increasingly realising that roll-on effects from France and the Netherlands would likely now make the referendums in their own countries much more difficult to win, the summit decided on caution. In a Declaration it was stated that the matter would be set aside until the first half of 2006 so as to allow for a 'period of reflection [which] will be used to enable a broad debate to take place in each of our countries …' (European Council, 2005b). Those states that had not yet conducted their ratification processes were given discretion as to what to do. In the event, this resulted in all of those states that were committed to holding referendums postponing them, except Luxembourg where the arch Euro-integrationist, Prime Minister Junker, proceeded with the referendum that was already scheduled for early July. In this most integrationist of member states, 56.52 per cent voted *Yes* and 43.48 voted *No*, on a 90.5 per cent turnout.

From the Constitutional Treaty to the Lisbon Treaty

The 'period of reflection' was more protracted than had been anticipated. Indeed, for the first few months there was not much public reflection at all beyond exchanges between EU practitioners as to whether the CT was now dead or could be revived. Understandably, the governments of those member states that had ratified the CT – ultimately numbering eighteen – were inclined, initially at least, to support pressing ahead with the CT whilst the governments of states where ratification problems had occurred, or promised to occur, were more cautious. However, during 2006 a tentative position began to emerge under which the governments of all member states gradually came to informally coalesce around the view that, on the one hand, the 'constitutional' aspects of the CT would have to be dropped but, on the other hand, the more 'routine' reformist aspects of the Treaty should largely remain. Crucial to the emergence of this position was a resolve on the part of virtually all member states that the new treaty should be capable of being presented as being much more 'low key' than the CT, and therefore capable of being ratified in the customary way of ratifying EU treaties – by parliamentary votes – and not requiring national referendums (except in Ireland, where it is politically, and many argue constitutionally, required).

The task of determining the contents of the CT's successor began early in the German Council Presidency of the first half of 2007. The initial steps were handled by a team of 'sherpas' – made up of senior officials from the member states – whose task was to draft a 'Berlin Declaration' that would be issued in March 2007 to celebrate the fiftieth anniversary of the EEC Treaty. When it appeared, the Berlin Declaration was somewhat bland, but it and the processes associated with its making were important in advancing the treaty-making process. One way in which they were was that the negotiation of the Declaration provided Chancellor Merkel and her support team with opportunities to sound out member state governments on options for a replacement to the CT. A second way in which the Declaration assisted the treaty-making was in some of the language the Declaration contained. Especially helpful was the assertion '… we are united in our aim of placing the European Union on a renewed common basis before the European Parliament elections in 2009', which signalled an agreed political determination to resolve the matter (German Presidency of the European Union, 2007: 2). Shortly after the issuing of the Declaration, member states were invited by the

Presidency to complete a questionnaire outlining their stances on key treaty issues.

As the German Presidency stepped up the pace, a few governments began to make clear, not least for domestic political reasons, particular matters they would wish to see addressed in the new treaty. Very much to the fore in this regard was the UK Government, which made much of what it called its 'red lines' These consisted essentially of sovereignty-related matters, including greater opt-outs for the UK from JHA provisions and a guarantee that the Charter of Fundamental Rights would provide no new legal rights in the UK.

Anxious that the treaty-making process should be conducted as fast as possible and should not result in a re-opening of traditionally divisive issues, the Presidency increasingly made it clear that the convening of a traditional IGC in which governments bring their lists of preferences and demands to the table was not being envisaged. Rather, the IGC would be largely confined to considering what elements of the CT would have to be amended or dropped to ensure national ratifications.

The sherpas duly produced a draft IGC mandate that was adopted by the June 2007 European Council meeting and was included in the summit's Presidency Conclusions (European Council, 2007a: Annex 1). Highly significantly, the mandate was very specific and tight, with much that was to go into the new treaty – which was entitled The Reform Treaty – not being merely outlined but actually being written. Included in the mandate was acceptance of the UK's 'red lines'.

The specificity of the mandate succeeded in doing what it was supposed to do: de-politicise much of the ensuing IGC. Some political discussions did occur in the IGC. Poland, for example, successfully pressed that an extension to the possible use of Nice voting rules until 2017 be included in the Treaty itself and in an accompanying protocol rather than being confined to a declaration. And the UK successfully pressed to further widen the JHA opt-outs it had already been granted in the IGC mandate and to tighten language guaranteeing that CFSP matters would be beyond the reach of the ECJ. But, for the most part the IGC was largely a technical exercise conducted by lawyers and subject experts. Indeed, the relative lack of political input is no more clearly seen than in the fact that following the formal launch of the IGC on 23 July, Foreign Ministers (who, as with

---

Box 6.4

The Making of the Lisbon Treaty

2000	December	The Treaty of Nice is politically agreed
2001	February	The Treaty of Nice is formally signed. Attached to the Treaty is a *Declaration on the Future of the European Union* that: calls for a 'deeper and wider debate about the future of the European Union'; commits to a decision being taken at the December 2001 European Council meeting on how the debate should be continued; and states that an IGC will be convened in 2004 to consider the broad questions raised in the debate.
	December	European Council at Laeken agrees on the *Laeken Declaration on the Future of the European Union*. The Declaration includes a decision to 'convene a Convention composed of the main parties involved in the debate on the future of the Union' (European Council, 2001: Annex 1, p. 24). The Convention will be chaired by Valery Giscard d'Estaing and will 'pave the way' for the next IGC (*ibid.*).
2002	February	Constitutional Convention opens.
2003	June	The Convention's *Draft Treaty Establishing a Constitution for Europe* is presented to the European Council, which considers it to provide 'a good basis for starting in the Intergovernmental Conference' (European Council, 2003a: 2).
	October	IGC opens
	December	European Council fails to end the IGC, as scheduled. The main reason for the breakdown in negotiations is Polish and Spanish opposition to the voting weights assigned to them in the Council of Ministers, though an insufficiently focused Italian Council Presidency is a contributory factor.
2004	June	Agreement on remaining unresolved issues in the Constitutional Treaty (CT) is reached at the European Council, under the Irish Council Presidency.
	October	The CT is formally signed by national leaders in Rome.
2005	May and June	Ratification referendums in France and the Netherlands result in 'No' votes.
	June	In the light of the two negative referendum results, the European Council calls for a 'period of reflection' on how next to proceed with the treaty reform process and says it will return to the matter in the first half of 2006 (European Council, 2005b: Declaration ... on the Ratification of the Treaty Establishing a Constitution for Europe). →

past IGCs, were politically responsible for the conduct of the IGC) met only once more – at an informal meeting on 7–8 September – until they convened on 15 October to finalise matters.

The Reform Treaty was then politically agreed by the Heads of State and Government at an informal meeting on 18 October. It was subsequently formally signed – in Lisbon, on the insistence of the Portuguese Presidency which was determined to have the Treaty named after its national capital – on 13 December 2007.

The efforts to ensure that the Treaty was, or could

be presented as being, sufficiently different from the CT to minimise the number of ratification referendums that would be held were successful. Although referendums were considered by a handful of member state governments, the only state in which a referendum was eventually held was the one in which, for domestic constitutional reasons, it was always going to be unavoidable: Ireland. Elsewhere, ratification was by parliamentary votes, supplemented in a handful of cases by other measures. These other measures contributed to ratification delays in a few states, notably Germany – where the national Constitutional

---

Box 6.4 *continued*

2006	June	The European Council asks the forthcoming German Presidency (Jan–June 2007) to prepare a report that 'should contain an assessment of the state of discussion with regard to the Constitutional Treaty and explore possible future developments' (European Council, 2006: 17).
2007	March	The Berlin Declaration indicates an intention to resolve the Treaty problem before the 2009 EP elections.
	June	The European Council decides that 'after two years of uncertainty over the Union's treaty reform process, the time has come to resolve the issue and for the Union to move on.' (European Council, 2007: 2). It is agreed to open an IGC almost immediately, charged with the task of drawing up a 'Reform Treaty'. A tight mandate is agreed that 'will provide the exclusive basis and framework for the work of the IGC' (*ibid.*: Annex 1).
	July	The IGC opens.
	October	An informal summit agrees on the contents of the new treaty.
	December	The Lisbon Treaty (as the Reform Treaty now becomes known) is signed in Lisbon by national leaders.
2008	June	The Lisbon Treaty is rejected by Irish voters in a ratification referendum. (Ireland is the only member state to hold a referendum on the Treaty.)
2009	June	The European Council provides Ireland with a number of concessions, clarifications and assurances on the Treaty in the hope this will result in it being ratified in a second referendum.
	June	The German Constitutional Court withholds approval of the Lisbon Treaty until a law is passed strengthening the German Parliament's participation in EU law making procedures
	September	The German Parliament passes the law required by the Constitutional Court.
	October	The Irish people approve the Lisbon Treaty in a (second) referendum.
	October	The Polish President, Lech Kaczynski, signs the law that ratifies the Lisbon Treaty in Poland.
	November	The Czech President, Vaclav Klaus, signs the law that ratifies the Lisbon Treaty in the Czech Republic.
	December	The Lisbon Treaty enters into force

Court deliberated on whether the Treaty breached Germany's constitution and then ruled, in July 2009, that it did not as long as the German parliament was given stronger supervisory powers over EU decision making – and Poland and the Czech Republic where eurosceptic Presidents delayed giving their required approval to the Treaty

As had happened with the ratification of the Nice Treaty, the Irish referendum, which was held in June 2008, resulted in a rejection of the Lisbon Treaty: by 53.6 per cent to 46.4 per cent on a 53.1 per cent turnout. As also had happened with the ratification of the Nice Treaty, deliberations in Ireland and the EU about what to do next gradually – and almost inevitably – led to it being decided that Ireland should, after being given assurances on issues that had seemingly played an important part in producing the rejection of the Treaty, vote again. The assurances took two forms. The first, which was agreed at the December 2008 summit, addressed concerns that under the Lisbon Treaty Ireland would not always have a Commissioner. The assurance took the form of a statement that provided the Lisbon Treaty entered into force, the Treaty stipulation that the size of the College of Commissioners would be reduced to two thirds of the number of EU members would be replaced by the existing Nice system of one Commissioner per member state. The second form of assurance, which was agreed at the June 2009 summit, involved committing to a legally binding Protocol to be attached to the EU's treaties that would allay Irish concerns that its policies in regard to taxation, military neutrality, ethical issues (especially abortion), and aspects of social matters would not be affected by the Treaty. With these two assurances given, the Irish Government held a second referendum in October 2009 and, as it had done with its second referendum on the Nice Treaty, won a comfortable majority: the Lisbon Treaty was endorsed by 67.1 per cent to 32.9 per cent on a 58 per cent turnout. In addition to the assurances just noted, other factors that contributed to the endorsement included a better organised pro-Treaty campaign and concerns about Ireland's vulnerability if it was to become economically isolated in the EU: concerns that were sharpened by the global international financial crisis and the recent near economic collapse of another small state – Iceland – that did not have EU protection.

The Irish 'Yes' resulted in the Polish President, Lech Kaczynski, quickly approving the Treaty, which left the signature of the Czech President, Vaclav Klaus, as the only remaining obstacle in the way of final ratification. On 3 November, after 'winning' from the European Council an extension of Protocol 30 of the Lisbon Treaty to the Czech Republic – and thereby limiting the possible impact on the Czech Republic of the Charter of Fundamental Rights – and after a ruling by the Czech Constitutional Court that the Treaty was not in conflict with national constitutional law, Klaus signed the law ratifying the Treaty in the Czech Republic.

In consequence, the Lisbon Treaty entered into force on 1 December 2009: almost eight years after the start of the treaty-making round at the December 2001 Laeken summit!

The Contents of the Lisbon Treaty

The Lisbon Treaty is made up overwhelmingly of the contents of the Constitutional Treaty. There are two main reasons for this.

First, the process of trying to find an acceptable new treaty dated back to 2001 (if the Laeken Declaration is taken as the first step) and governments did not want to see the process further extended any longer than was necessary. There just was little taste for starting again from square one and putting all national preferences back on the table. To have done this would have been to re-open issues that, in the context of the Constitutional Treaty-making process, had already been long negotiated and on which agreements had been reached only with great difficulty. The position of the German Presidency when it started the new treaty-making process rolling – 'let's confine ourselves to making such changes to the Constitutional Treaty as are necessary to ensure ratification' – was generally welcomed by the governments of the member states. Accordingly, a twin-track approach was taken, both by the German Presidency as it prepared an IGC mandate for the June 2007 European Council meeting and then in the subsequent IGC itself. On the one hand, there was the removal of those symbolic high-profile aspects of the Treaty – the constitutional aspects – that had led many member state governments to holding, or promising to hold, referendums. On the other hand, special measures of various kinds – in the form of opt-outs and clarificatory statements – were created for member states that had either been unable to ratify the Constitutional Treaty and/or that promised to have considerable ratification difficulties with the Lisbon Treaty.

Second, the factors that had led to the contents of the CT remained. There was still felt to be a need for new treaty measures that would, for example:

- give the European Council greater institutional capacity (hence the retention in the Lisbon Treaty of the CT's provision for the creation of a new semi-permanent post of European Council President);
- enhance the EU's external profile (hence the retention of the CT provision that, in effect, merged the Council post of High Representative for the CFSP with the Commission post of Commissioner for External Political Relations.
- improve the operational performance and cohesion of the College of Commissioners (hence the retention of the CT reduction of the size of the College, albeit not until 2014, to two thirds of the number of member states [so as to encourage the Irish in their second referendum on the Lisbon Treaty, this change was subsequently dropped and replaced by

Box 6.5

The Principal Ways in Which the Lisbon Treaty is Different To the Constitutional Treaty

The form and symbolic content of the treaties
- The LT does not repeal the existing treaties and consolidate them into one treaty. Rather it amends and adds to the existing treaties.
- The Treaty Establishing the European Community (TEC) is re-named the Treaty on the Functioning of the European Union (TFEU).
- All references to the word 'constitutional' are removed.
- The CT article on the symbols of the Union – flag, anthem and currency – is removed.
- The Charter of Fundamental Rights is not incorporated into the Treaties, but rather it was 'solemnly proclaimed' by the Presidents of the Commission, Council and EP in December 2007. However, notwithstanding its non incorporation, Article 6 of the amended TEU states the Charter 'shall have the same legal value as the treaties'.
- Throughout the existing treaties 'Community' is replaced by 'Union'.
- The CT provisions creating new legislative acts – in particular *laws* (equivalent to current regulations) and *framework laws* (equivalent to current directives) – are dropped.
- The CT-created title of 'Union Minister for Foreign Affairs' is replaced with 'High Representative of the Union for Foreign Affairs and Security Policy'.

Changes of substance
- The CT changes to voting arrangements in the Council – with the replacement of the triple majority system and use of voting weights by a double majority system – is retained, but its introduction is postponed until 2014. Between 2014–17 a transition process will operate during which the possibility of voting weights being used is retained. A new delaying formula to assist states in a minority will apply from 2017 (see Box 6.6)
- The CT provision to reduce, from 2014, the size of the College of Commissioners to two-thirds of the number of member states is dropped. (It was retained in the Lisbon Treaty as originally adopted, but the existing arrangement of one Commissioner per member state was later restored as part of the attempt to persuade the Irish to ratify the Treaty.)
- New legal bases are created for combating climate change and for member states acting in a spirit of solidarity in respect of energy policy.

Opt-ins, opt-outs, and clarifications
- In a Protocol, the UK and Ireland are given the power to chose whether to participate in third pillar issues that are transferred to the first pillar.
- In a Protocol it is stated that the Charter of Fundamental Rights contains no new legal rights in UK or Polish law. In October 2009 the European Council extended the Protocol to the Czech Republic.
- In a Protocol it is stated that the CFSP does not undermine the independence of member states in respect of the conduct of national foreign policies.
- In a Protocol (the principle of which was agreed at the June 2009 summit) Ireland is assured that the Treaty does not affect its policies on taxation, military neutrality, ethical issues (especially abortion), and aspects of social policy.

the existing system in which each member state has one Commissioner]);

- enhance the Council's decision-making capacity (hence the retention of CT provisions increasing the ability of the Council to take decisions by QMV);
- replace the weighted voting system in the Council by a simpler system (hence the retention, though in an amended form, of the CT replacement of the existing triple majority system with a double majority system based on a combination of the number of states voting for a proposal and the populations they represent);
- further tackle the 'democratic deficit ' problem (hence the retention of CT extensions to the applicability of the co-decision procedure [which strengthens the EP] and of the CT-created citizens' initiative procedure – which empowers citizens to call on the Commission to initiate a legislative proposal).

In consequence, the contents of the Lisbon Treaty were based overwhelmingly on the contents of the Constitutional Treaty. The form of the CT was changed, but most of its substantive contents remained. In the words of a senior Commission adviser 'Broadly speaking, it can be said that some 95 per cent of the 2004 Constitutional Treaty has been retained, in terms of both institutional structure and the substance of the policies' (Ponzano, 2007: 16).

Box 6.5 outlines the main ways in which the Lisbon Treaty is different from the Constitutional Treaty. The changes contained in the Lisbon Treaty were made primarily for three main reasons.

- *To make the Treaty more acceptable to citizens.* Changes made for this reason included dropping the CT constitutional language and symbols. Related to this elimination of the constitutional language and symbols, the CT consolidation of the existing treaties into a single treaty was reversed and the treaties remained separate. These changes enabled governments to (correctly) portray the new treaty as being essentially an amending treaty in the tradition of the SEA and the Maastricht, Amsterdam and Nice Treaties. As such it also gave governments good grounds to claim that the traditional bases for national ratifications of EU treaties – by parliamentary votes

rather than by referendums except where the latter are a constitutional (Ireland) or a political (sometimes Denmark) requirement – applied also to the new treaty.

- *To accommodate a (limited) number of pressing national and institutional interests.* Although the intention was not to permit matters relating to particular national and other interests to be reopened either in the mandate given to the IGC or in the IGC itself, accommodations were made in few cases. The UK was the major beneficiary of this, partly because of its sheer persistence and partly because it was recognised that its Government needed a strong case to be able to argue with credibility that the Treaty was so different from the Constitutional Treaty that the referendum that had been promised on the CT (and which almost certainly would have been lost) no longer applied.
- *To recognise new issues impacting on the political agenda.* In recognition of increasing concerns about climate change and energy supply, new legal bases were created for tackling climate change and for prioritising member state solidarity on energy policy.

As for the overall importance of the Lisbon Treaty, views on this greatly vary, with some regarding it as marking a potentially great advance in the integration process and others seeing it as including only modest reforms. The reasons for these different judgements are to be found partly in the prior views of commentators, with those inclined to a Eurosceptic view tending to see the Treaty as containing significant supranational advances and those of a more Europhile disposition tending to see it as embodying too many missed opportunities and as containing little more than marginal adjustments. Another reason for the large number of different judgements on the importance of the Treaty is the uncertainty that exists regarding how some of the Treaty's more high profile provisions – such as the creation of the new post of European Council President, the special status accorded to the Charter of Fundamental Rights, and the new powers given to national parliaments – will work out in practice.

However, no matter what the Treaty's importance will ultimately prove to be, there is no doubt, as Box 6.6 shows, that it has a very considerable amount of

Box 6.6

The Main Provisions of the Lisbon Treaty

Treaty Structure

- Most of the Treaty is concerned with amending and adding to the Treaty on European Union (TEU) and the Treaty Establishing the European Community TEC). The TEC is re-named the Treaty on the Functioning of the European Union (TFEU).
- The third 'pillar' of the TEU – Provisions on Police and Judicial Cooperation in Criminal Matters – is moved into the TFEU. This enables most of the EU's justice and home affairs (JHA) policies to be brought together in a new Title V of the TFEU covering the 'Area of Freedom, Security and Justice'.
- The second 'pillar' of the TEU – the Common Foreign and Security Policy – is largely unchanged. It continues to be located in the TEU rather than being 'transferred' to the TFEU and it continues to be based primarily on intergovernmental operating principles.
- Throughout the EU's treaties, the word 'Community' is replaced by 'Union'.

The Nature and Competences of the Union.

- A new Article 2 TEU sets out the values on which the Union is founded. They are 'the values of respect for human dignity, freedom, democracy, equality, the rule of law and respect for human rights, including the rights of persons belonging to minorities'.
- A new Article 3 TEU (which is a revised ex-Article 2) amends the objectives of the Union. They include the promotion of peace, offering Union citizens an area of freedom, security and justice without internal frontiers, the establishment of an internal market aiming at full employment and social progress, and the combating of social exclusion and discrimination.
- The Union is given a legal personality in international law.
- The competences of the Union are set out. They fall into three broad categories: exclusive, shared, and supporting or supplementary. The main exclusive competences are the common commercial policy, the customs union, competition rules necessary for the functioning of the internal market, and monetary policy for euro members.
- Policy competences are strengthened in a few areas, including energy, tourism, and climate change.

Legal Acts and Procedures

- The remit of the co-decision procedure is extended, including to agriculture, fisheries, the structural funds, transport, and third pillar issues that are transferred to the first pillar. The procedure is re-named the 'ordinary legislative procedure'.
- The remit of the assent procedure is extended and the procedure is re-named the 'consent procedure'.
- The annual budgetary procedure is simplified and the EP and Council become co-equal decision makers. The distinction between compulsory and non-compulsory expenditure is abolished.
- The multi-annual financial frameworks (within which annual budgets must operate) become legally binding and must be approved by the EP.
- A new hierarchy of norms is established distinguishing between legislative acts, delegated acts, and implementing acts. The Council and the EP are to jointly decide on how to control delegated and implementing acts (that is, on what sort of comitolgy is to apply).
- Citizens become empowered to invite the Commission to submit a legislative proposal by collecting one million signatures in a 'significant number' of member states.

→

Box 6.6 *continued*

The Institutions

The Commission
- In a new requirement, the President of the Commission must now be nominated by the European Council 'taking into account the elections to the European Parliament'. The nominee is then 'elected by the European Parliament by a majority of its component members' rather than, as previously, 'approved by the European Parliament'

The European Council
- It is established as a separate institution distinct from the Council of Ministers.
- It is to elect its own President, by QMV, for a 2½ year term which may be renewable once.
- The responsibilities of the President are to be confined to European Council business.

The Council of Ministers
- As from November 2014, QMV voting arrangements in the Council are changed from the Nice triple majority formula to a double majority formula in which, when the Council is acting on a proposal from the Commission or the High Representative, a majority must contain at least 55 per cent of the member states comprising at least 65 per cent of the EU population. The majority must also include at least 15 member states and a blocking minority must include at least four. When the proposal does not emanate from the Commission or the High Representative, the qualified majority must consist of at least 72 per cent of the member states comprising at least 65 per cent of the EU population.
    Until 2017 a member state may insist that in a particular vote the Nice voting rules should apply.
    In a formula that is based on the Ionnina Compromise, a new mechanism allows a number of member states representing 55 per cent of the population or 55 per cent of the number of member states needed to constitute a blocking minority to ask for a delay and reconsideration of a draft law before it is adopted.
- There are some 40–45 (depending on exactly what is counted) extensions to QMV, most particularly in the areas of freedom, internal security and justice. Areas where unanimity – and hence the national veto – remain include the CFSP (except implementing measures), the CSDP, enhanced cooperation, treaty reform, taxation, and aspects of social policy.
- The Presidency of the Council is to be held by groups of three members for a period of eighteen months, with each member of the group chairing for six months.
- The Foreign Affairs Council is to be chaired by the occupant of the new post High Representative of the Union for Foreign Affairs and Security Policy.
- The proceedings of the Council are to be open when it is exercising its legislative functions.

European Parliament
- Its size is set at 750 plus its President. Seats are to be distributed between the member states on the basis of degressive proportionality, with no state to have either more than 96 members or less than 6.
- Its powers are strengthened by extensions to the remit of the co-decision (now ordinary) and assent (now consent) procedures and by increased powers over trade policy and the budget.

The CFSP and the CSDP
- A new post of High Representative of the Union for Foreign Affairs and Security Policy, charged to contribute to the development of the CFSP and to conduct the CFSP as mandated by the Council, replaces the two posts of High Representative for the CFSP and Commissioner for External

→

Box 6.6 *continued*

(Political) Relations. The High Representative is to be appointed by the European Council acting by QMV, with the agreement of the President of the Commission. The High Representative is to have a base in both the Council and the Commission: by chairing the Foreign Affairs Council whilst also being a Vice President of the Commission.

- A new European External Action Service is to be created to assist the High Representative.
- In both the Treaty itself and in attached protocols the legal independence of member states in the foreign and defence policy areas is stressed.
- Defence policy is given a higher treaty profile, under the title of Common Security and Defence Policy (CSDP). Within the CSDP, a new mechanism of 'permanent structured cooperation' is created for states that wish to make more binding commitments than others and that meet certain criteria in terms of military capabilities.

Other
- The roles of national parliaments are increased in two ways. First, the Commission becomes required to reconsider a proposal if one-third of national parliaments claim it may breach the subsidiarity principle. If the Commission then presses on with the proposal and a majority of parliaments continue to object, the Commission must refer the proposal to the Council and EP where a 55 per cent majority in the Council or a simple majority in the EP can block the proposal. Second, all national parliaments are empowered to veto a European Council decision to change Council decision-making in a given area or case from unanimity to QMV (itself a new power for the European Council).
- Simplified procedures are introduced for future modest amendments to the treaties. These procedures take various forms depending on the nature of the amendments, but they normally require unanimous approval by the national governments and approval too by the EP and/or national parliaments.
- Member states are given the right to secede from the Union and general arrangements for so doing are set out.

Opt-outs, exceptions, and clarifications
The Treaty contains a number of opt-outs, exceptions, and clarifications designed to deal with particular concerns of governments'. Some of these measures are explicitly directed to a particular member state or states whilst others are generally applicable but are included at the pressing of a particular member state or states. The measures are contained amongst the 38 Protocols and 65 Declarations that accompany the Treaty. Prominent amongst 'the national measures' are:

- Protocols 19 and 20 allow the UK and Ireland to choose whether or not they wish to participate in measures designed to strengthen the Schengen system (the two states are not full members of the Schengen system).
- Protocol 21 allows the UK and Ireland not to take part in measures concerned with the creation of the area of freedom, security and justice, but allows them to opt-in.
- Protocol 30 states that no court – European or national – may rule that UK or Polish law are inconsistent with the contents of the Charter of Fundamental Rights. During the Treaty's ratification process, the Protocol was also extended to the Czech Republic.
- Declarations 13 and 14 (which were inserted at UK insistence) state that the responsibilities and powers of the member states for formulating and conducting their foreign policies are not affected by the CFSP.
- A protocol (that was agreed in principle at the June 2009 European Council meeting as an inducement to Ireland to ratify the Treaty) states that the Treaty does not affect Ireland's policies on taxation, military neutrality, ethical issues (especially abortion), and aspects of social policy.

content. To be sure, the constitutional language and symbolism of the Constitutional Treaty have gone and the Lisbon Treaty is largely confined – like its SEA, Maastricht, Amsterdam and Nice predecessors – to amending and adding to existing treaties – with what is in policy terms the most important of these treaties, the TEC, re-named the Treaty on the Functioning of the Union (TFEU). But, the number of amendments and additions is large, and many of them seem bound to have a very noticeable impact. To give just a few instances of potentially very significant changes:

- The new and strengthened competences given to the EU – in such policy areas as internal security and energy – should better enable appropriate and cohesive policies to be developed.
- The new posts of European Council President and of High Representative of the Union for Foreign Affairs and Security Policy should provide the potential for much stronger and more focused EU leadership. Their creation also, however, raises the possibility of considerable inter-institutional tensions, with the European Council President, the European Commission President and, where foreign policy is involved, the High Representative, becoming involved in extensive turf-wars and jockeying for position.
- The new voting rules in the Council from 2014 involve a significant tilt in the balance of power within the Council towards larger member states.
- The increases in QMV provisions in the Council should facilitate decision making in some policy areas, including very important JHA areas.
- The extensions to the reach of the co-decision procedure and the revisions to the budgetary procedures (both multi-annual and annual) significantly extend the powers of the EP.

In summary, whilst the Lisbon Treaty disappointed those who had been strong supporters of the Constitutional Treaty and who wished for major integrationist advance, the Treaty is more than a mere tidying-up exercise. It is true that it does not contain anything comparable to the SEA's internal market mission or the Maastricht Treaty's arrangements for creating EMU. But it does contain significant changes and additions to the structure and contents of the existing treaties. These changes and additions are mostly with a view to simplifying and clarifying the

nature, enhancing the operation, and strengthening the democratic character of the enlarged EU. (For further commentaries on the significance of the Lisbon Treaty, see Kurpas, 2007; Ponzano, 2007.)

Documents 7.1 and 7.2 set out the contents of the EU's two main treaties – the TEU and the TFEU – as they are post-Lisbon.

Concluding Remarks

The Lisbon Treaty was made in a quite different manner to the EU's preceding treaties. It was so in two main ways. First, the processes leading to its finalisation were extremely protracted. They started with the 2001 Laeken Declaration and were not completed until late 2009 when the Irish people voted *Yes* in their country's second ratification referendum and the Czech and Polish Presidents, who had withheld their confirmation of their country's ratification until after the Irish vote, gave their assent. Second, the processes were much more complex, involving as they did a Constitutional Convention – which was relatively open in its operation and in which political actors independent of national governments had a significant role to play – and two IGCs that were conducted along traditional – that is, closed and somewhat secretive – lines.

But though the treaty-making process was different, the outcome was, ultimately, strikingly similar to predecessors. For the Lisbon Treaty is a consolidating rather than a radical document. It contains measures that go some way to meeting the stated goals of the Laeken Declaration – of making the EU 'more democratic, more transparent, and more efficient' (European Council, 2001: 21) – but there is no suggestion of an attempt to transform the nature of the EU. There is, for example, no fundamental upheaval in the EU's institutional structures, nor any great extension in its policy competences. As such, the Lisbon Treaty is the latest in a line of treaties that have since the mid-1980s amended and extended the EU's founding treaties. In the tradition of earlier amending treaties, it has adjusted, and in some respects advanced, the integrationist process in an incrementalist manner. Arguably, the adjustments and the advances provided for in the Lisbon Treaty are of a lesser order than those contained in the SEA and the Maastricht Treaty, where bases were laid for significant policy extensions and for new decision-making procedures.

Of course, if the Constitutional Treaty had been approved its symbolic aspects would have distinguished the Treaty from predecessors. The use of the word 'constitutional', the official adoption of a flag and an anthem, and the appointment of someone with the title of 'Foreign Minster' would have given the EU certain state-like characteristics. But they would have been characteristics only in appearance, for the substantive contents of the CT were little different from what ultimately appeared in the Lisbon Treaty.

And, in any event, not all of the symbols have disappeared with the Constitutional Treaty. Certainly there has been no noticeable decline in use of either the anthem or the flag since the CT was dropped. Indeed, both featured prominently at the Lisbon Treaty signing ceremony!

Chapter 7

Treaties and the Integration Process

Since the SEA it has been customary for rounds of treaty reform to occur on a regular basis. One reason for this has been that the logic and momentum of the integration process has required periodic revision of the treaties so as both to 'catch up' with evolving realities and to enable desired developments to occur. Another reason has been that because all treaties are a consequence of intergovernmental bargaining, some governments are inevitably disappointed with the outcomes of treaties and so start pressing for another round of treaty reform almost before a negotiated treaty has been ratified and applied. And a third reason has been that the Maastricht, Amsterdam and Nice Treaties explicitly provided for further rounds of treaty reform: in the Maastricht case in response to pressures from dissatisfied governments at the Treaty's outcome, and in the Amsterdam and Nice cases in consequence of a general recognition that the Treaties were leaving unfinished business.

This chapter builds on the earlier chapters that have examined specific treaties in detail by stepping back and examining how rounds of treaty reform have fitted into and have contributed to the integration process.

The Making of Treaties

Intergovernmental Conferences

Treaty-making is very much an intergovernmental process, as the name of the forum for deciding on the contents of treaties – Intergovernmental Conferences (IGCs) – makes clear. The key actors in IGCs are representatives of the governments of the member states, and unanimity amongst them is necessary for treaties to be agreed.

Each IGC has had its own distinctive features, but all have displayed most of the features of a broad pattern, which will now be outlined.

The treaty-making process may be said to formally start with a decision by the European Council to establish an IGC. These decisions have been made for a variety of specific reasons, which were outlined in Chapters 5 and 6. However, the specific reasons have been framed within a shared recognition on the part of the governments of most member states that the EC/EU has needed treaty reform for reasons of operational efficiency and effectiveness.

IGCs work within a remit given to them by the European Council. Prior to the Lisbon Treaty IGC, these remits were mostly couched in fairly general terms, which left ample room for political debate and contestation within IGCs. However, as was shown in Chapter 6, the Lisbon Treaty IGC was obliged

---

Box 7.1

The operation of Intergovernmental Conferences

- Working parties of national experts have been established to examine particular issues as and when they have been deemed to be necessary. They have identified relevant points and have tried to establish a consensus wherever possible, but they have not normally engaged in negotiations in the sense of trading points on matters that are contentious or have a clear political dimension.

- A group known as the 'personal representatives of the minister' or the 'preparatory group' has undertaken most of the detailed negotiations. The members of the group have been mainly very senior national officials – mostly the Permanent Representatives of the member states to the EU. The group in the 2000 IGC consisted of ten Permanent Representatives, three senior officials from foreign ministries, and two junior ministers. The frequency of group meetings has depended on progress and on the overall IGC timetable, but fortnightly meetings have tended to be the norm.

- Foreign Ministers have, nominally at least, overseen the process and provided political guidance and impetus. However, as Galloway (2001: 34) has shown in his work on the 2000 IGC, it was difficult during that IGC (and by implication is also in other IGCs) for Foreign Ministers to exercise this role in a manner that enabled them to assert authority over the Conference: many of the issues on the agenda were highly specialised and outside the normal departmental remits of participants, so there often was a lack of enthusiasm and willingness to resolve matters being discussed; some Foreign Ministers had poor attendance records and their representatives often did not have, or did not feel they had, authority to agree deals on contested matters; the multiple subject inter-linkages made deals on particular points often difficult to reach; and there were relatively few IGC ministerial meetings – IGC business, indeed, was normally dealt with as an additional item on the Foreign Minister's regular monthly meeting. (The Maastricht Treaty was an exception to this arrangement of Foreign Minister's stewardship of IGCs, for two IGCs prepared the Treaty: a Political IGC that operated as described here, and a parallel but separate IGC that prepared the EMU provisions of the Treaty and which was overseen by Finance Ministers.)

  This potential lack of influence of Foreign Ministers was seen even more clearly in the Lisbon Treaty IGC where the highly specific nature of the mandate given to the IGC meant there was little for Foreign Ministers to do other than keep a general watching brief. Most of 'the politics' of the treaty-making had been dealt with under the German Presidency when the mandate was being negotiated, and the IGC was left to deal largely with technical and legal matters.

- IGCs culminate at a European Council meeting, where all outstanding issues are negotiated and traded. Almost invariably, the main players – the Heads of Government – are subject to information overload as a battery of information on issues that needs to be resolved is directed at them. Much of the business is conducted in an almost feverish atmosphere, with deadlines postponed, much of the business conducted in informal bilaterals and huddled groups, and often with at least one delegation threatening to return home if it is not given further satisfaction or if a deal is not made.

The only summit that has actually failed after attempting to finalise the contents of a treaty was the December 2003 European Council meeting, under the Italian Presidency, which was supposed to bring the CT IGC to a conclusion. The IGC had only opened in the October, which would have made it the quickest full IGC on record if the summit had been successful. But the summit broke up in disagreement, and the IGC had to be suspended for four months until a possible way forward was identified the following spring. Poor management by the Presidency was widely blamed by many for the summit's failure, though real disagreements on institutional matters plus a lack of enthusiasm on the part of several other EU leaders of seeing the Italian Prime Minister, Silvio Berlusconi, bathed in success, were important contributory factors.

to operate within a very tight remit. This remit took the form of a mandate agreed at the June 2007 meeting of the European Council that, on most of the more potentially divisive issues, virtually wrote what should be in the Treaty.

The length of IGCs has varied considerably, partly reflecting timetables given to them by the European Council and partly reflecting the ease/difficulty with which agreements have been reached. From the formal opening of an IGC to political agreement on the contents of a new treaty at a European Council meeting, the shortest IGCs have been those that produced the SEA and the Lisbon Treaty, both of which were of just four months duration: the former lasted from September to December 1986 whilst the latter lasted from July to October 2007. However, the necessary legal and linguistic work that follows political agreement on the contents of a treaty before it is formally signed is technically part of the IGC process, which means that, strictly speaking, the SEA and Lisbon IGCs lasted six months, not four months. duration. (To be even more 'strictly speaking' there have actually been shorter IGCs, albeit of a very special kind: at the end of the Maastricht IGC, dedicated IGCs were convened to amend the ECSC and Euratom Treaties: they opened on 3 February 1992 and closed four days later!) The longest IGC was that which produced the Amsterdam Treaty, which opened in March 1996, was not concluded politically until the June 1997 summit, and did not see the Treaty signed until October 1997.

Deliberations in IGCs have taken different forms, but they have normally occurred at four levels, in the ascending order set out in Box 7.1

With their extensive structure, IGCs have inevitably taken up many working hours. Leaving aside expert group work, the 2000 IGC took up 370 hours, involving thirty meetings of the personal representatives, ten of the Foreign Affairs Ministers, and three of the European Council (Wessels, 2001).

The main responsibility for pulling everything together and setting the pace in IGCs has fallen to the Council Presidency. As Galloway (2001: 33) says, the Presidency acts as 'the engine driving the Conference'. It exercises this role by convening and chairing all meetings at all levels, tabling discussion and proposal papers that act as the basis for negotiations (other states, the Commission and the EP also produce papers but they are more for information purposes), and generally trying to identify and mediate compro-

mises. A problem in the 2000 IGC was that the French Presidency, which was responsible for the second half of the IGC, was in some respects badly organised and was seen by several member states – especially some of the smaller states – as being too robust in pressing its own views on certain issues and insufficiently focused on trying to broker agreements that would be generally acceptable (Ross, 2001). And, as was noted above, the Italian Presidency during – what proved to be – the first half of the CT IGC was similarly seen by many participants and observers to be deficient. In its case the principal charge was that it was too casual and under-prepared for the December 2003 summit.

Because IGCs are intergovernmental in character, the EU's two main non-governmental institutions – the Commission and the EP – struggle to exert much influence. The Commission is a participant in IGCs at all levels and does its utmost – not least via the submission of position papers – to influence outcomes. However, because it does not enjoy the same negotiating status as the member states, and is certainly in no position to attempt to veto agreements, its negotiating hand is weak and its influence on eventual outcomes is usually marginal.

The EP is even more disadvantaged than the Commission in that it does not fully participate in all IGC meetings. This is precisely why it so favoured the Constitutional Convention that laid the foundations for the CT IGC. Indeed the EP used to not participate in IGCs at all, but it has gradually been accorded consultative and limited observational status. Like the Commission, the EP makes submissions to IGCs and, again like the Commission, it has usually been disappointed by IGC outcomes. Its position has not been helped by not having assent power over treaties – although the Lisbon Treaty has partly rectified this by giving it consent powers ('consent' is the post Lisbon Treaty word for 'assent') over certain modest treaty amendments that in the future may not require the convening of IGCs. But, to date, such influence as the EP has exercised over treaty content has been mostly in relation to expansions of its own powers, where it has kept up constant pressure.

Ratifying treaties

Every one of the post-foundation treaties except for the Amsterdam Treaty has run into serious ratification problems. These problems have taken a number of forms, the most dramatic and high-profile of which have been negative referendum results. Most member states have ratified the treaties by parliamentary votes, but each round of treaty reform has been accompanied by at least one referendum. This pattern started with the SEA, when the Irish Government was forced by the country's Supreme Court to hold a ratification referendum. Since then, in every round of treaty reform apart from the Nice and Lisbon rounds at least one other member state has joined Ireland in holding a referendum – either because it has been politically unavoidable or because of governmental choice.

The ratification difficulties have resulted in the schedule for the implementation of all of the post-foundation treaties apart from the Amsterdam Treaty being seriously affected. In the case of the Constitutional Treaty, it resulted, of course, in the Treaty not being implemented at all, although most of its contents subsequently reappeared in the Lisbon Treaty.

Somewhat ironically given that it works to the advantage of 'the awkward squad' rather than 'good club members', ratification difficulties can bring national gains. The most obvious way in which this has occurred has been in the form of 'concessions' – contained in Protocols and Declarations attached to the Treaties – to bring dissenters onside. So, for example, when the Danish people rejected the Maastricht Treaty they were persuaded to reverse their vote by being permitted by the other member states to opt-out of EMU and by given special arrangements on certain other policy matters.

But it is not just the fact of ratification difficulties that can bring national benefits, but also the promise of them. In this context there is no doubt that the negotiating hand of UK Governments in IGCs has been strengthened by a recognition by other member states that unless the UK Government can make a convincing case at home that it 'did well' in the IGC, UK ratification could be very difficult. This was no more clearly demonstrated than in the Lisbon Treaty IGC, when from the early preparatory stages there was an inclination to accommodate most of the UK Government's high-profile 'red lines'.

Treaties and the Nature of European Integration

In terms of understanding the foundations, development and essential nature of the EU, the 'stories' of the Treaties are extremely revealing. They are so because they highlight and confirm the following long-established characteristics and features of the integration process.

Economics before politics

Some of the major advances in integration have tended to take the form of agreeing to integrate aspects of economic activity and then, at times seemingly almost as an afterthought, realising that this requires political integration too if there is to be political direction and control. In practice there has naturally been considerable overlap and blurring between the economic and the political, but from 1950–1, when the ECSC was created, the economic has at times and in important ways preceded the political.

In terms of the treaties, the strengthening of the EU institutions that has been provided for in all of the treaties since the SEA has been largely a consequence of this being seen to be necessary if (mainly economic) policy development is to be achieved. The extent to which much treaty reform has involved 'catching-up' with economic integration and needs is no more clearly seen than in the way that every post-foundation treaty has involved extensions to QMV. Indeed, the main rationale for the convening of the IGC that produced the first major post-foundation treaty – the SEA – was that QMV extensions were a prerequisite for the passage of the SEM programme. Subsequent treaties have continued with this extension programme, to such an extent that virtually all economic policy matters where legislation is made are now subject to QMV apart from in such 'hard core' areas as taxation and social security.

Flexibility

When the member states, or a sufficient number of them, have wished to act together in a policy area and the established mechanisms have been judged to be not suitable for the purpose, then alternative ways of proceeding have usually been found. This was, for example, the case with the establishment and development of EPC from the early 1970s, the EMS from the late 1970s, and the Schengen System (designed to assist free movement of persons) from the mid-1980s.

All of the EU's treaties since the Maastricht Treaty have built on and extended this tradition of being adaptable and innovative in respect of policy development. The Maastricht Treaty did so via the construction of two non-Community pillars (some states regarded it as either premature or undesirable to bring the policy areas covered by the pillars into the EC) and also via, for the first time, the non-inclusion of member states in a core policy area specifically identified in the Treaties (the UK and Danish opt-outs from EMU). The Amsterdam Treaty incorporated new policy opt-outs (for Denmark, Ireland, and the UK), and further 'constitutionalised' flexibility by the enhanced cooperation provisions (allowing some policies to be developed without all member states participating) that were added to the TEC and the third pillar and the constructive abstention provision that was added to the second pillar. The Nice Treaty streamlined the Amsterdam-enhanced cooperation arrangements, primarily by making them easier to apply. The Lisbon Treaty continued with the tradition of broadening the treaty base for greater flexibility, including by allowing an unspecified number of member states to engage in 'permanent structured cooperation' in the defence policy sphere and by giving some states, notably the UK, opt-in/opt-out options in respect of a number of JHA matters.

Incrementalism

The integration process has been characterised by an almost constant edging forward, with 'advances' followed by pressures for more advances. Phases and forms of integration have frequently followed almost inevitably and logically from earlier – and often less significant – phases and forms. In a pattern well understood by those who are persuaded by historical institutionalist interpretations of the evolution of the integration process (see, for example, Pierson, 1998),

and especially by the importance of 'path dependence' in shaping the nature of the evolution, the treaty architects have, as Wessels (2001: 212–14) has shown, developed an almost ideal three-step type of integration cascade. In the first phase, governments realise the advantages of cooperating with other EU countries in a particular policy area and attempt to do so on a very loose intergovernmental basis, often on the margins of, or even outside, the EU framework. When this form of cooperation proves to be insufficient, the governments move to the second phase, which sees the policy area given clear treaty recognition and moved firmly into the organisational framework of the Union, but still on an essentially intergovernmental basis in that the role of the Commission is limited, the EP is at best given only consultative rights, Council decisions are by unanimity, and the Court has few – if any – powers. In the third phase, governments realise they must permit stronger decision-making processes if aims are to be achieved, so a more supranational route is taken with greater powers and roles assigned to the Commission, EP and Court, and QMV permitted in the Council.

Table 7.1 demonstrates how the treaties have advanced the integrationist cause in this incrementalist manner by, on the one hand, expanding the EU's policy remit and potential and, on the other hand, strengthening the EU's institutional and decision-making arrangements. These two aspects of increasing integration are, of course, linked, as the steadily increasing powers of the EP demonstrate. The EP has been by far the greatest institutional beneficiary of treaty reform, with every treaty since the SEA having significantly strengthened its powers: by creating new legislative procedures that are to its advantage; by widening the remit of those procedures; and by enhancing its powers in respect of many decisions that are not taken through normal legislative procedures – such as the appointment of the Commission President and the size and composition of the multi-annual financial frameworks and the annual budgets. These steadily increasing powers have resulted in large part from policy transfers to the EC/EU having produced growing demands – not least from MEPs themselves – for EU decision-making processes to have more accountable and democratic bases.

The precise way in which the integrationist logic works does, of course, vary according to an array of

Table 7.1 Summary of the contents of the main EU treaties

Name of Treaty/ Date signed/ Date came into effect	Institutional provisions	Policy provisions
Treaty of Paris April 1951 July 1952	Creates: – High Authority – Council of Ministers (with some QMV) – Common Assembly – Court of Justice	– Lays foundations for a common market in coal, steel, coke, iron ore, and scrap.
Treaty of Rome Establishing the European Economic Community March 1957 January 1958	Creates: – Commission – Council of Ministers – (QMV more restricted than under the Treaty of Paris) – Assembly } – Court of } to serve all three Justice } communities	– Lays foundations and timetable for a customs union with removal of internal barriers to trade and the establishment of a common external tariff; foundations also laid for deeper economic integration through the creation of a common market and some common policies – including agriculture and transport.
Treaty of Rome Establishing the European Atomic Energy Community March 1957 January 1958	Creates: – Commission – Council of Ministers – Assembly } – Court of } to serve all three Justice } communities	– Provides for the possibility of a common market in nuclear materials, but with safeguards built in. Other activities in the nuclear field to be promoted.
Single European Act February 1986 July 1987	– European Council is given legal recognition. – The legal capacity of the Council to take decisions by QMV is extended – notably to internal market measures. – A new legislative procedure – the cooperation procedure – is created, which gives the EP more powers. – An assent procedure is also created, which results in the assent of the EP being required.	– The aim of completing the internal market by 1992 is given treaty status. – New policy areas are added to the EEC Treaty, notably environment, economic and social cohesion, and research and development. – European Political Cooperation (foreign policy) is given legal recognition.
Treaty of Maastricht February 1992 November 1993	– Creates the European Union as a three pillar structure. – Extends legal base of QMV. – Creates co-decision legislative procedure, which increases the power of the EP.	– A framework and timetable for creating Economic and Monetary Union is incorporated in the EC Treaty. – Pillars two and three create the treaty foundations for a Common Foreign and Security Policy (CFSP) and Cooperation in the Fields of Justice and Home Affairs (JHA).

→

Table 7.1 *continued*

Name of Treaty/ Date signed/ Date came into effect	Institutional provisions	Policy provisions
		– Several new policy areas are added to the EC Treaty, including development, public health, and consumer protection.
Treaty of Amsterdam October 1997 May 1999	– Extends legal base of QMV. – Extends the co-decision procedure to more policy spheres, and amends aspects of the procedure to the EP's advantage. – Creates enhanced cooperation procedure. – Creates new post of High Representative for the CFSP.	– CFSP provisions are strengthened. – Much of JHA pillar is transferred to EC pillar. – New policy areas are added to EC pillar, including anti-discrimination, promoting employment, and consumer protection.
Treaty of Nice February 2001 February 2003	– Changes national representations in EU institutions in preparation for enlargement. – Changes QMV weightings – Extends legal base of QMV. – Small extensions to application of co-decision procedure. – Makes enhanced cooperation procedure easier to apply.	– Only marginal extensions of existing policy areas, mainly in the JHA and social policy fields.
Treaty of Lisbon December 2007 December 2009	– European 'Community' disappears. – The third 'pillar' is moved into the TFEU, but the second 'pillar' remains in the TEU. – Creates two new important posts: European Council President; High Representative of the Union for Foreign Affairs and Security Policy (which merges the existing leading foreign policy posts in the Council and the Commission). – Extends legal base of QMV. – New voting system is created in the Council, though not to come into effect until 2014 – and even then there are transitional arrangements. – Significant extensions to application of co-decision procedure, which is re-named 'the ordinary legislative procedure'.	– JHA policy area is greatly strengthened. – Defence policy is given fuller recognition.

circumstances. The justice and home affairs policy area, however, may be taken as an example of how it can work. From modest beginnings in the mid-1970s when, quite outside the framework of the treaties, governments began to cooperate with one another on such matters as cross-border crime and illegal movements of persons, the policy area has steadily developed: cooperation was stepped up in the 1980s through what became known as the Trevi process; justice and home affairs (JHA) was given treaty status in pillar three of the Maastricht Treaty, though very much on an intergovernmental basis; much of pillar three was transferred into pillar one by the Amsterdam Treaty, some provision was made for QMV, and new justice and home affairs issues – including provisions for tighter and stronger police cooperation – were added to pillar three; the Nice Treaty further extended QMV in the policy area; and the Lisbon Treaty abolished pillar three, grouped most JHA policy matters together in the TFEU – in a broader and strengthened new title on the 'Area of Freedom, Security and Justice' – and established the 'ordinary legislative procedure' (the former co-decision procedure) with QMV as the norm for the policy area.

The incrementalist logic of the treaties in an integrationist direction is perhaps most starkly witnessed by the difficulty in identifying a single clear example of a treaty provision that has reversed an aspect of European integration to any significant degree. Perhaps the greater emphasis given in the EEC Treaty than in the ECSC Treaty to unanimity in the Council may be thought of as such an example, but that was as the European Community was being established, and the EEC Treaty as a whole did, of course, mark a major step forward in integration. The attention given to subsidiarity in the Maastricht Treaty may perhaps be thought of as another example, but its inclusion was partly for symbolic reasons and the way in which it was described in the Treaty did not give it great bite. And a third example may be thought to be the attempted strengthening of the institutional capacity of the essentially intergovernmental European Council in the Lisbon Treaty through the creation of a semi-permanent president. But, these possible exceptions notwithstanding, the fact is that there have been no 'hard' treaty 'reversals', such as a change from QMV to unanimity in Council voting procedures, the removal of a competence from the EP, or a policy sphere being removed from an EU treaty because of it

coming to be deemed to be an exclusively national responsibility.

Increased length and complexity

The treaties are the outcomes of negotiations between national governments. In the negotiations, the governments attempt to make the EU more effective and efficient, but they also seek to promote and defend national interests. These objectives are not always easily compatible, with the consequence that the EU's treaties have become lengthier and more complex so as to enable agreements on their contents to be reached.

On length, post-Lisbon, the TEU contains 55 articles and the TFEU no less than 358. (The original EEC Treaty contained 240). In addition, the Lisbon Treaty contains 37 Protocols and 65 Declarations, most of which are attached to the TEU and/or TFEU.

On complexity, this is no more clearly demonstrated than with the TEU. In some respects it is a framework treaty, laying down general principles and a structure for the EU. But in other respects it is a substantive treaty, specifying in Title V quite detailed provisions in the CFSP and CSDP policy areas: areas that the member states prefer not to have 'communitarised' – primarily because they want them to continue to be essentially intergovernmental in character. (See Document 7.1 for the TEU's contents.)

As for the TFEU, as it (in its various forms) has had new policy competences and decision-making arrangements added in rounds of treaty reform, so has it become ever more impenetrable for all but subject specialists. The Treaty was tidied up a little as part of the Amsterdam revisions, but not in such a way as to make it accessible to 'the ordinary citizen', and the Nice and Lisbon Treaties have done nothing to 'improve' this situation. (See Document 7.2 for the TFEU's contents.) Many of its articles cover the sort of subject matter that would normally be expected to be found in policy legislation rather than a document which – in effect – serves as a key part of the EU's 'constitution'.

The sphere in which treaty negotiations have produced the most complex outcomes is in respect of decision-making processes, which have become more numerous over the years. Following the Nice Treaty, there were no less than 38 combinations of

---

Document 7.1

The (post-Lisbon) Treaty on European Union: contents

---

possible voting modalities in the Council and participation opportunities for the EP. Of the 38 combinations, 22 were legislative in nature (Wessels, 2001: 201). When the positions of other EU institutions were added, the number of decision-making processes increased even further. Significantly, the CT and Lisbon Treaty IGCs made little progress in simplifying this mosaic.

Not only have the treaties produced a steady increase in the number of decision-making processes, but they have also produced some extremely complicated processes. The prize for complexity should, perhaps, be awarded to Article 7 TEU which, in its post-Lisbon Treaty form, includes the following:

1 On a reasoned proposal by one-third of the Member States, by the European Parliament or by the Commission, the Council, acting by a majority of four-fifths of its members after obtaining the consent of the European Parliament, may determine that there is a clear threat of a serious breach by a Member State of the values referred to in Article 2 [which states the Union is founded on 'the values of respect for human dignity, freedom, democracy, equality, the rule of law, and respect for human rights, including the rights of persons belonging to minorities'] ...

2 The European Council, acting by unanimity on a proposal by one-third of the Member States or by the Commission and after obtaining the consent of the European Parliament may determine the existence of a serious and persistent breach by a Member State of the values referred to in Article 2, after inviting the government of the Member State in question to submit its observations ...

5 The voting arrangements applying to the European Parliament, the European Council and the Council for the purposes of this Article are laid out in Article 354 of the Treaty on the Functioning of the European Union [Article 354 contains further voting rules].

The many protocols and declarations that customarily have been attached to the treaties provide another dimension of the highly complicated nature of the EU's treaties. Protocols have the same binding legal effect as treaty articles, but declarations are essentially political statements. Designed for a variety of purposes – such as providing clarification on treaty articles, laying down bases for extra-treaty policy activity, and 'exempting' particular member states from specified treaty commitments – protocols and declarations can make the understanding of treaties even more difficult for all but the trained expert.

Document 7.2

The Treaty on the Functioning of the European Union: contents

Document 7.2 *continued*

Variable pace

The pace of the integration process has varied considerably since the Community was founded in the 1950s with, in general terms, the periods up to the mid-1960s, from the mid-1980s to the early 1990s, and from the late 1990s to the mid-2000s being times of rapid integration, and the late 1960s to the early 1980s and the mid-1990s being more sluggish. Treaties reflect this variable pace. The Maastricht Treaty, for example, was negotiated at a time when the governments of most member states were generally optimistic and ebullient in their attitudes to European integration, with the consequence that they wanted to see, and made sure that they did see, major integrationist advances incorporated into the Treaty. By contrast, when the Amsterdam Treaty was being negotiated the mood was less upbeat – not least because the 1992 Danish referendum had obliged supporters of further integration to become more cautious – and so less was sought from, and less was put into, the Treaty. With the Constitutional Treaty, the atmosphere had again changed, with the successful launch of the euro, the considerable progress being made on JHA issues, and the impending 'big bang' EU enlargement all indicating rapid integration advance. The CT was intended to both symbolically signal and further assist with this advance.

Interplay between supranational and national actors

Some analysts of European integration have made much of the role played in the integration process by supranational actors, most particularly the Commission, the EP, and the Court of Justice. Other analysts have played down the role of these actors and have argued that whilst they may have exercised some influence on the course of events, the EU's key actors have been representatives of the governments of the member states meeting in the European Council and the Council of Ministers. (There is a review of these different interpretations of the integration process in Chapter 23.)

At first sight, the decision-making processes associated with the making of the EU's treaties would appear to provide support only for the second of these analytical interpretations: the membership of IGCs consists of national governmental representatives, with the Commission present but having no vote; decision-making in the IGCs is based on bargaining between the national governmental representatives, with agreements on some particularly difficult issues being reached only after hard direct negotiations between Heads of Government; and the supranational EU institutions – especially the Commission and the EP – have been generally disappointed with the outcomes of the IGCs, with both having pressed in recent IGCs for greater extensions to QMV and to their own powers than have been incorporated in the treaties.

However, although the making of the EU's treaties may appear to provide strong support for an intergovernmental interpretation of the integration process, the case should not be overstated. First, treaty-making processes are not typical EU decision-making processes since they lead to what Peterson (1995) has called 'history-making' decisions, and are therefore the very processes in which the role of national governments is likely to be most prominent. Second, although it does not have voting powers, the Commission is an active participant in IGCs and the EP was allowed to make a direct input into the Amsterdam, Nice and CT IGCs. Finally, there is evidence – provided, for example by Beach (2005) – to indicate that the Commission and the EP have been able to exercise influence in IGCs. The influence is, however, 'contingent upon the negotiating context and whether they [supranational EU institutions] use appropriate leadership strategies' (Beach, 2005: 245).

Benefits for everybody

The integrationist advances achieved in the treaties have been made possible by the member states judging it to be in their interests to promote integration. Certainly in all of the treaty-making negotiations there have been disagreements between the states as to just how much, and what kind of, integration they have wanted. But it has nonetheless been recognised that there are benefits for all to be gained from the integration process – with the furtherance of economic growth and the promotion of harmonious relations between the states of Europe being the most obvious benefits.

However, because of their own distinctive needs and preferences, states have sometimes argued that in addition to taking a share of general benefits they should also be awarded special benefits and/or be given special considerations. The award of special benefits in treaties has usually taken the form of providing a base for some sort of policy development that will be especially helpful to a particular state or group of states. So, for example, the SEA provided such a policy base when, largely at the behest of the poorer member states, it included provisions for the development of redistributive policies. The Maastricht Treaty did much the same thing, with the creation of a Cohesion Fund that would be directed at the four poorest member states (Greece, Ireland, Portugal and Spain). The granting of special dispensations has most commonly taken the form of the opt-ins/opt-outs that, as has been described both in this chapter and earlier chapters, some states have been given as the price for persuading them to sign and/or ratify treaties.

An elite-driven process

Insofar as political and administrative elites tend to set the policy agenda, and insofar as they usually take decisions without directly consulting their electorates, political activity in all nation states – in Europe and beyond – may be said to be elite-driven. But this is particularly the case in the EU because of the weak lines of accountability between decision-makers and the citizenry. There is no opportunity to elect a European government or parliament with full decision-making powers. Arguably this would not matter too much if there were grounds for believing that most citizens were strongly supportive of the integration process, or were happy to leave decisions about integration to the appropriate elites. However, public opinion polls have suggested that in some member states considerable reservations and doubts have existed at various times.

The extent to which the integration process is elite-driven, and the extent to which elites do not always reflect popular concerns, has been demonstrated by difficulties in ratifying the treaties. Problems began with the ratification of the Maastricht Treaty, when not only did the Danes vote *No* in their first referendum and the French almost vote *No*, but opinion polls

indicated that German and UK voters too might have rejected the Treaty if they had been given the opportunity to do so. The increased caution shown by national representatives in the 1996–7 IGC can perhaps be seen as partly reflecting greater sensitivity to the popular concerns that the Maastricht ratification process had highlighted. However, the extent of this sensitivity should not be overstated, as is demonstrated by the fact that despite all the post-Maastricht talk about promoting openness and democracy in the EU, there was no movement towards opening up the treaty-making process to popular participation. On the contrary, only the Danish and Irish governments included referendums as part of their national ratifications of the Treaty. And only the Irish government consulted the people on the ratification of the Nice Treaty – who duly rejected it at the first time of asking, though more for domestic political reasons than because they opposed the treaty.

The most dramatic, and in its consequences most important, demonstration of the elite-driven nature of the integration process occurred when, for reasons that were set out in Chapter 6, several member states moved to hold referendums on the Constitutional Treaty. In two of the EU's founding states – France and the Netherlands – the Treaty was rejected by the people. This was not so much because voters objected to specific Treaty provisions, but rather for a range of 'non-Treaty' reasons including concerns about such aspects of the integration process as the 2004 enlargement, possible Turkish accession, the perceived increasing influence of liberal market principles, and – in the Netherlands – the financing of the EU budget. The French and Dutch referendums showed, as other planned national referendums may have shown if they had proceeded, that aspects of the integration process are not so strongly supported by citizens as they are by elites.

Significantly, the general reaction of EU leaders to the difficulties encountered with ratifying the Constitutional Treaty was not to conclude that the referendums had shown that many European citizens did not want the Treaty and therefore they – the leaders – should dispense with it. Quite to the contrary, the reaction was, on the one hand, to press ahead with as much of the Treaty as was possible and, on the other hand, to do whatever was necessary to minimise the need for further ratificatory referendums. There was a broad agreement that as much as possible of the Treaty should be saved, but wherever it could be avoided the people should not be asked for their views in referendums for they might say *No* again. Of course, this is precisely what the Irish did in their first referendum on the Lisbon Treaty – so they were asked to vote again!

Concluding Remarks: an Ongoing, but Perhaps in the Future a Very Different, Process

However the EU's political nature is to be described – and this matter is examined in Chapter 23 – all of the ratified treaties have contributed significantly to development of the European integration process. None of the treaties has, however, in any sense marked the end of the process or even identified where that end may be. The discussions and negotiations that have taken place before and at all the major IGCs have been characterised by considerable differences between the participants on the nature and pace of integration. What has emerged from the processes that have produced the treaties have been compromises: compromises that have included aspects of different visions of the future of Europe, and compromises that, while failing to advance integration as much as some governments had hoped, have advanced it further than others would have liked. There has therefore, as was noted at the beginning of this chapter, been no shortage of important political actors wanting to return to treaty-making, and there has been no shortage of good reasons for periodically re-examining the treaties.

Such has been the regularity of rounds of treaty reform since the SEA that an expectation has become established that the treaties will be changed at regular intervals. Indeed, the agreements on the Maastricht, Amsterdam and Nice Treaties were accompanied by formal European Council commitments that further IGCs would soon be held. But the problems associated with the Constitutional Treaty followed by the Lisbon Treaty were so drawn-out – over virtually the whole of the 2000s – that there is now little appetite for the subject of treaty reform. Indeed, it was with an almost

audible sigh of relief that the European Council announced in December 2007, immediately after the signing of the Lisbon Treaty, that 'The Lisbon Treaty provides the Union with a stable and lasting institutional framework. We expect no change in the foreseeable future ... .' (European Council, 2007b: 2)

But, of course, the intention of putting treaty reform aside for the foreseeable future does not mean that pressures for reform – most likely so as to further 'improve' the operation of the EU or to strengthen its competences – will not continue. If they become pressing, how might they be handled? Article 48 of the post-Lisbon TEU provides for future treaty reform to take place in one of three ways:

- The 'ordinary revision procedure' is largely the CT-making procedure, though with the possibility of a Convention not needing to be called if the European Council, after obtaining the consent of the EP, decides by a simple majority that the scale of the proposed amendments does not warrant the convening of a Convention.

- Variant one of the 'simplified revision procedure' applies only to Part III of the TFEU (see Document 7.2) and may not include any increase in the competences conferred on the Union. Under this procedure, the European Council may take an amending decision by unanimity, which then has to be approved by all the member states. So, this variant differs from past practice in that an IGC does not have to be convened.

- Variant two of the 'simplified revision procedure' exists for two types of amendments: extending the use of QMV provisions in the TFEU and in Title V of the TEU (though this latter CFSP coverage does not include defence policy matters); and, under the TFEU, changing a special legislative procedure (which normally would mean the consultation procedure) to the ordinary legislative procedure. This procedure enables Treaty revisions to be made if they are agreed by the European Council acting by unanimity, if an absolute majority of MEPs give their consent, and if no national parliament objects.

Given the experience of the 2000s, clearly none of these options provides an 'easy' way of amending the treaties. The likelihood of governments feeling obliged, or choosing, to hold national referendums is reduced under the simplified revision procedure – though it is probable there would be a court challenge in Ireland if the Irish Government tried to avoid holding one. But the fact is that all of the procedures involve unanimous agreement by the national governments and, in effect, also by national parliaments. With Euroscepticm being very much politically alive in some member states, not least the UK and some of the new member states, finding unanimous agreement would be extremely difficult – not least since further treaty reform would almost certainly take the EU deeper into territory that touches on 'hard core' sovereignty matters.

So, further treaty reform does not seem likely for some time. Whether this matters is a debatable point. For those who want to see the EU based on an integrated federalist structure it certainly does matter, but then this federalist vision is no longer realistically on the table. For those who take a more pragmatic view of what the EU should be doing and where it should be going it does not matter since, for them, the treaties are, for the most part, now strong and flexible enough.

Part III

The Institutions and Political Actors of the European Union

There are five main EU institutions: the Commission, the Council of Ministers, the European Council, the European Parliament, and the Court of Justice of the European Union. Chapters 8–12 consider each of these institutions. Chapter 12 has also been taken as the most appropriate place to examine the nature and status of EU law.

Chapter 13 looks at those institutions which, though not given a chapter in their own right, nonetheless also exercise a significant influence in the EU: the European Economic and Social Committee, the Committee of the Regions, European agencies, the European Investment Bank, the European Central Bank, and the Court of Auditors.

Chapter 14 moves away from institutions to examine the roles and influence of interests in the EU system. The word 'interests' is used rather than 'lobbyists' or the term 'pressure groups' because it seems to better capture the range of involvement and activity that is displayed.

The final chapter in this Part looks at what are in many ways the most important EU actors of all: the member states.

Chapter 8

The Commission

Frequently portrayed as the civil service of the EU, in reality the Commission is rather more and rather less than that: rather more in the sense that the treaties and political practice have assigned to it much greater policy-initiating and decision-making powers than those enjoyed, in theory at least, by national civil services; rather less in that its role in policy implementation is greatly limited by the fact that agencies in the member states are charged with most of the EU's day-to-day administrative responsibilities.

The Commission is centrally involved in EU decision-making at all levels and on all fronts. With an array of power resources and policy instruments at its disposal, and strengthened by the frequent unwillingness or inability of other EU institutions to provide clear leadership, the Commission is at the very heart of the EU system.

Appointment and Composition

The College of Commissioners

Seated at the summit of the Commission are the individual Commissioners, who are each in charge of particular policy areas and who meet collectively as the College of Commissioners. Originally they numbered nine, but with enlargements their size has grown: to thirteen, to fourteen, to seventeen, to twenty, to twenty five, and to twenty seven following the 2007 enlargement. The reason for the lack of symmetry between the number of Commissioners and the number of member states prior to 2004 is that each of the larger states (France, Germany, Italy, Spain and the UK) used to have two Commissioners. However, so as to avoid the size of the College becoming too big after enlargement it was agreed at the 2000 Nice summit that from January 2005 all member states would have just one Commissioner and that when the EU numbered 27 member states the number of members of the Commission would be less than the number of member states. The IGC that produced the Lisbon Treaty, following in the steps of the IGC that produced the Constitutional Treaty, duly decided that from 2014 the size of the College would be reduced to the equivalent of two-thirds of the number of member states. However, this reduction was removed from the Lisbon Treaty by the European Council as part of its attempt to persuade the Irish to vote *Yes* in their second referendum on the Treaty in 2009 (see pp. 77–8). In consequence, the 'one Commissioner for each member state' Treaty provision remains.

Appointment procedure

Prior to the College that took office in January 1993, Colleges were appointed every four years by common accord of the governments of the member states. The Maastricht Treaty changed this procedure, primarily in order to strengthen the links between the Commission and the EP. This strengthening was achieved in two ways. The first was by formalising and somewhat stiffening practices that developed in the 1980s regarding the appointment of the Commission and its President: the member state governments now became obliged to consult the EP on who should be President, and the College-designate became obliged to present itself before the EP for a vote of confidence. The second was by bringing the terms of office of the EP and the Commission into close alignment: Colleges would now serve a five-year term and would take up office six months after EP elections, which are held on a fixed basis in the June of years ending in four and nine. (So as to bring about the alignment, a transitional two-year College served from January 1993 to January 1995.)

On the occasion of the first application of the new appointments procedure – in respect of the College that assumed office in January 1995 – the EP pressed its new powers to the full. When Jacques Santer, the Luxembourg Prime Minister, was nominated as President-designate in mid-1994 (at short notice and as a compromise candidate following the UK government's refusal to support the Belgian Prime Minister, Jean-Luc Dehaene), the EP was in fact barely consulted. However the EP made it quite clear to the European Council (the forum in which the nominee of the national governments is agreed) that whoever was nominated would be required to appear before the Parliament and a vote on confirmation would be held. The assumption would be that if the nominee was not confirmed his candidature would be withdrawn. Chancellor Kohl, acting in his capacity as Council President, confirmed that the EP would indeed have a *de facto* veto over the nomination. In the event Santer was confirmed, but only by a narrow majority: there were 260 votes in favour, 238 against, and 23 abstentions. As for the vote of approval on the whole College, the EP held 'hearings', with each of the Commissioners-designate being required to appear before the appropriate EP committee before the plenary vote was held. There was strong criticism of

five of the Commissioners-designate, but given that there was no provision for singling them out in a vote, the EP, after being given certain reassurances by Santer, gave a vote of confidence to the new College by 417 votes to 104.

The Amsterdam Treaty confirmed the *de facto* confirmatory power the EP had assigned to itself on the appointment of the Commission President. The Treaty also gave the President-designate a potential veto over the national nominees for appointment to the College. (Under the Maastricht Treaty he was supposed to be consulted on the national nominees to the College, but in practice this amounted to little in 1994.) The Nice Treaty further altered the procedure by specifying that the decisions in the European Council on the nomination of the President and on the other Commissioners plus the decision on the appointment of the whole College, could henceforth be made by qualified majority vote rather than by consensus. The Lisbon Treaty then introduced the requirement that in making its nomination for College President the European Council should take into account the recently held EP elections and also stated, in what was intended to have symbolic resonance, that the proposed candidate should be *elected* by – not, as previously, merely be *approved* by – the EP. The Lisbon Treaty, like the Constitutional Treaty before it, also stipulated that one of the Commissioners should be the person holding the new post of High Representative of the Union for Foreign Affairs and Security Policy (see Chapter 6).

Accordingly, the relevant post-Lisbon Treaty provisions on the appointment of the President and the College are as set out in Document 8.1.

Treaty rules do, of course, often tell only part of the story of what happens in practice, since the circumstances in which the rules are to be applied and interpreted can vary considerably. This is clearly illustrated with the last three rounds of appointing the Commission President and College.

The appointment of the Prodi College. At the time the Amsterdam Treaty was negotiated it was assumed that its provisions on the appointment of the College would be given their first use for the College that was due to assume office in January 2000. However, in March 1999 the College led by Jacques Santer was pressurised – most particularly by the EP, which was threatening to dismiss it by passing a motion of

---

Document 8.1

The post-Lisbon Treaty provisions on the appointment of the President of the College and of the other Commissioners

Taking into account the elections to the European Parliament and after having held the appropriate consultations, the European Council, acting by a qualified majority, shall propose to the European Parliament a candidate for President of the Commission. This candidate shall be elected by the European Parliament by a majority of its component members. If he does not obtain the required majority, the European Council, acting by a qualified majority, shall within one month propose a new candidate who shall be elected by the European Parliament following the same procedure.

The Council, by common accord with the President-elect, shall adopt the list of the other persons whom it proposes for appointment as members of the Commission. They shall be selected, on the basis of the suggestions made by Member States, in accordance with the criteria set out in paragraph 3, second subparagraph [which states that Commissioners shall be chosen 'on the ground of their general competence and European commitment from persons whose independence is beyond doubt'] ... .

The President, the High Representative of the Union for Foreign Affairs and Security Policy and the other members of the Commission shall be subject as a body to a vote of consent by the European Parliament. On the basis of this consent the Commission shall be appointed by the European Council, acting by a qualified majority ... (Article 17, TEU).

... The European Council, acting by a qualified majority, with agreement of the President of the Commission, shall appoint the High Representative of the Union for Foreign Affairs and Security Policy ... (Article 18, TEU).

---

censure – into resigning, nine months before the scheduled end of its term of office.

The circumstances that produced deep dissatisfaction with the Santer College and led to its resignation are described on p. 187. Essentially, they centred on indications in a report drawn up by a committee of independent experts that there was some substance to long-held suspicions that at least one Commissioner (Edith Cresson) had shown favouritism in issuing contracts, that Santer had been insufficiently vigilant in the exercise of some of his responsibilities, that there were problems of financial mismanagement in certain parts of the Commission, and that the College as a whole had displayed a general lack of responsibility for the Commission's actions (Committee of Independent Experts, 1999a).

Almost immediately after resigning the Santer College announced that it would stay in office in a caretaker capacity until a replacement College was appointed. This gave the governments of the member states breathing space, both to decide on a collective basis how they should proceed and to consider on an individual basis whom they wished to nominate to the new College. There were two collective decisions to be made. First, who should replace Jacques Santer as Commission President? Second, should the replacement College be appointed on an interim basis to see out the remaining months of the Santer College's term or should the process of appointing a new full-term College be brought forward?

A special summit to consider these questions did not have to be called, since one was already timetabled for ten days after the College's resignation. At the summit, the national leaders decided to nominate the former Italian Prime Minister, Romano Prodi, to be the new Commission President. They further decided that they wanted a full-term rather than an interim College.

Prodi's nomination was endorsed by the EP in May by 392 votes to 72, with 41 abstentions. It soon became apparent, however, that it would take some time for the other Commissioners to be nominated and then approved by the EP, so it was decided to ask the Santer College (minus Santer himself, who resigned to run in the EP elections) to stay in office until a new College could be appointed in the autumn. The nominations for the other Commissioners were then duly made, though with only limited influence exercised by Prodi. EP committees held 'hearings' on each Commissioner-designate in late August/early September and then, after a plenary debate on the new College, the Parliament voted to endorse the Prodi Commission by 414 votes to 142, with 35 abstentions. It was agreed that the EP's endorsement covered a full five-year term as well as the three and a half months that would have remained of the Santer Commission's term.

The appointment of the first Barroso College. The events leading to the appointment of the College that in 2004 succeeded Prodi's College illustrate just how politicised the appointments process is, both in terms of the keen interest taken by EU actors in the political composition of the incoming College and in terms of inter-institutional relations.

In the months leading up to the June 2004 European Council meeting which was due to agree on who should be nominated to be the new Commission President, the names of many prominent EU figures were mentioned as 'strong possibilities'. Eventually, however, especially after the June 2004 EP elections produced a centre-right majority, two very experienced and moderate right of centre figures emerged as strong favourites: the Belgian Prime Minister, Guy Verhofstadt, and the British External Relations Commissioner, Chris Patten. In all probability either would have received the qualified majority support in the European Council that would have sufficed under the Nice Treaty to be appointed. However, no vote was ever put at the June summit. This was because the British Prime Minister, Tony Blair, was resolutely opposed to Verhofstadt (who had 'led' the opposition in the EU to the invasion of Iraq, and who also was seen as being too integrationist) and the French President, Jacques Chirac, was opposed to Patten (because he was British). Since a President-designate who was known not to have the support of a large member state even before he assumed office clearly would be greatly handicapped politically, the summit broke up with no name put

forward. Intense informal exchanges then ensued between EU politicians, which resulted in agreement being reached on the Portuguese Prime Minister, José Manuel Barroso. A special summit was convened to formally endorse him and shortly afterwards he was approved by the EP – by 413 votes to 251 – after formally addressing the Parliament in plenary session.

Agreement had barely been reached on Barroso before some governments were announcing the name of their Commissioner-designate, which was hardly indicative of Barroso having had much input into the selection process. In the case of the new member states quick announcements were reasonable enough since most of them chose to re-nominate the people who had only been Commissioners since May 2004. In the case of the EU-15, however, the spirit of nominating 'in common accord' with the President-designate was applied in little more than a formal sense. Insofar as Barroso did have views which had an effect, it was towards the end of the process when he expressed open concern that his College might contain a smaller proportion of women than its predecessor. In the event it did not.

As, in the autumn of 2004, the EP moved towards, and then held, its now customary committee 'hearings', criticisms were made of five of the Commissioners-designate. In two cases this was because of a suspicion of a possible conflict of interest with the portfolio they had been assigned: the Dutch Commissioner-designate Neelie Kroes who had been assigned competition policy and the Danish Commissioner-designate Mariann Fischer-Boel who had been assigned agriculture policy. In one case it was because the Commissioner-designate was seen as not being up to the job: the Hungarian, László Kovács, who had been assigned energy policy. In another, and more serious, case it was because the Latvian Commissioner-designate, Ingrida Udre, was believed to be associated with funding irregularities in her national political party. And in the most serious case of all, the Italian Commissioner-designate, Rocco Buttiglione, was, following very conservative comments he made in his hearing about homosexuality and the role of women, deemed by MEPs to be wholly inappropriate for the justice and home affairs portfolio he had been assigned by Barroso.

As the plenary confirmation vote approached, Barroso refused to make changes, save for transferring certain anti-discrimination and civil liberties dimensions of the JHA portfolio from Buttiglione to himself. This proved not enough to satisfy MEPs so, with the prospect of a defeat looming, Barroso withdrew his College-designate on the very morning of the day the vote was scheduled to be held. Over subsequent days, Buttiglione and Udre stood down and Kovács was transferred to the taxation portfolio. This was acceptable to the EP, which then duly approved the revamped College by 449 votes to 149, with 82 abstentions. The Barroso College was thus eventually able to assume office – three weeks later than had been intended – on 22 November 2004.

The EP's ability to force changes to the composition of, and allocation of portfolios in, the Barroso College provides a particularly graphic illustration of how it has become increasingly important for the Commission to be highly sensitive to the views of MEPs. Formally, the EP in 2004 only had the power to approve or disapprove the College as a whole; it could not identify individual Commissioners who it would refuse to endorse. But Buttiglione was, in effect, singled out and rejected. In forcing Barroso to react to their views on this matter, MEPs asserted their influence over the Commission and also damaged the standing of the new Commission President even before he assumed office.

The appointment of the second Barroso College. The processes leading to the appointment of the second Barroso College in 2009 were complicated by the uncertainties about whether the Irish would ratify the Lisbon Treaty. The Nice Treaty had provided for the size of the College to be reduced when the EU reached 27 member states, and this provision was duly incorporated in the Lisbon Treaty with a stipulation that the size of the College would correspond to two-thirds of the number of member states, though only from 2014. However, as was explained in Chapter 6, as part of the attempt to persuade the Irish to reverse their initial rejection of the Lisbon Treaty and to endorse it in a second referendum, the European Council took advantage of a power given to it by the Treaty to declare that if the Irish did ratify the Treaty there would be a reinstatement of the arrangement whereby every member state has one Commissioner. The consequence of this European Council decision was that until the Irish referendum was held in October 2009 the size of the new College was unknown. Were

all member states to have a Commissioner, which would be the case if the Irish ratified the Lisbon Treaty, or would some states not have a Commissioner, which would be the case if the Irish rejected the Treaty and the Nice Treaty applied? Furthermore, if the Irish did not ratify, which would be the member states not to have a Commissioner on the first occasion of using a rota system?

Unsurprisingly, the member states collectively decided not make any 'national' nominations until after the Irish result was known. There was no reason, however, for the European Council to delay in agreeing who they wished to propose as President of the College and this they did at their June summit when, without any great difficulties, Barroso, who had made clear his eagerness for another term and whose centre-right political position certainly reflected the

Photo 8.1 José Manuel Barroso, President of the European Commission, answering questions in the European Parliament, November 2009

(even larger) centre-right majority in the newly elected Parliament, was chosen. So as to avoid politicking on the matter over the summer, the European Council hoped that Barroso would be confirmed by the new EP at its first meeting in July. However, resistance by political group leaders in the Parliament, who saw no need to rush the process given that the Irish referendum was not to take place until early October, led to the Swedish Council Presidency accepting that it could be counterproductive to press for an early vote and accepted that Parliament's vote on the nomination should be delayed until after the summer break. When the vote was held, in mid-September, Barroso, after making his case in meetings with the larger political groups and in plenary, was comfortably endorsed, by 382 votes in favour, 219 against, and 117 abstentions.

Following the endorsement of Barroso, events had to be put on hold until the Irish had voted *Yes* and other problems that arose with the ratification of the Lisbon Treaty had been resolved (see pp. 76–8). Once the Treaty was finally ratified, in early November, the names of the national nominees quickly began emerging. A difference from previous Colleges was that one Commissioner (in addition to the already designated President), had, under the Lisbon Treaty, to be appointed by the European Council. This was the High Representative of the Union for Foreign Affairs and Security Policy who, as was explained in Chapter 6, as well as having a foot firmly placed in the Council camp was also to a Vice President of the Commission. At a special summit meeting held in late November, called primarily to fill the posts of European Council President and High Representative, the serving UK Commissioner, Catherine Ashton, was appointed to be the High Representative.

By early December, the names of all the nominees were known and Barroso had allocated their portfolios. Time was, however, judged to be too short to allow the Commissioners-designate to prepare for EP hearings in December, so they were not held until mid-January. At the hearings – which involved every Commissioner-designate answering questions for three hours from the EP committee(s) covering their portfolio – several Commissioners-designate were judged by MEPs to have performed rather poorly. However, one Commissioner-designate – the Bulgarian, Rumiana Jeleva, who was her country's serving Foreign Minister – was so criticised by MEPs for her performance in answering questions both about her personal financial interests and her knowledge of her future job as Commissioner for Humanitarian Aid, that she felt obliged to withdraw her nomination shortly after her hearing. This meant that Bulgaria had to nominate another Commissioner-designate and the EP plenary vote on the new College had to be delayed until after a hearing for the new Bulgarian nominee – Kristalina Georgieva, a senior World Bank official – was held. This hearing, which was judged by MEPs to be satisfactory, took place at the beginning of February, which enabled the EP to vote on the new College on 9 February. In the vote, the College was approved by 488 votes to 137 with 72 abstentions.

Photograph 11.1 on page 186 shows a Commissioner-designate's hearing in session.

The Barosso II College thus did not assume office until 9 February 2010: four months later than had originally been intended. If it had not been for the uncertainty as to which treaty would apply to the new College, in all probability the EP vote on the President-designate would have been held at the July plenary, the names of the other Commissioners-designate (including the High Representative) would have emerged over the summer, the EP would have held its 'hearings' and have voted on the whole College in September,

---

Box 8.1

The Commissioners

- One Commissioner per member state, including the President and the High Representative.
- Five year term, which may be renewed.
- Each Commissioner is nominated by his/her member state, but must be acceptable to the President-designate.
- The College as a whole must be approved by the EP after individual 'hearings'.
- Commissioners must be independent and not act as national 'representatives'.
- Each Commissioner has a portfolio.

Photo 8.2 The Barosso II College of Commissioners, front row, from left to right: Maroš Šefčovič, Neelie Kroes, Catherine Ashton, José Manuel Barroso, Viviane Reding, Joaquín Almunia, Siim Kallas, second row, from left to right: Karel De Gucht, Androulla Vassiliou, Kristalina Georgieva, Janusz Lewandowski, Janez Potočnik, Olli Rehn, Günther Oettinger, Maria Damanaki, Michel Barnier, Algirdas Šemeta, third row, from left to right: Štefan Füle, Cecilia Malmström, Johannes Hahn, Máire Geoghegan-Quinn, John Dalli, Dacian Cioloş, László Andor, Connie Hedegaard, Andris Piebalgs. Antonio Tajani is not shown in this photograph. Full details of the Commissioners and their portfolios are given in Table 8.1, pp.114–15.

and the new College would have assumed office on time, on 1 October. But, 'events' resulted in the schedule having to be adjusted.

Photograph 8.2 shows the College that took office in February 2010.

Impartiality and independence

Although individual Commissioners frequently are referred to as 'the Finnish Commissioner', 'the Hungarian Commissioner', and so on, Commissioners are in fact not supposed to be national representatives. Rather, the Commission 'shall promote the general interest of the Union' and Commissioners 'shall be chosen on the ground of their general competence and European commitment from persons whose inde-

pendence is beyond doubt' (Article 17, TEU). Much the same sentiments pertain to the requirement that Commissioners should 'neither seek nor take instructions from any Government or other institution, body, office or entity' (*ibid.*).

In practice, full impartiality is neither achieved nor attempted. Although Commissioners are formally appointed by the Council with the agreement of the President-designate and the EP, in reality all but the President and the High Representative are national nominees. It would therefore be quite unrealistic to expect Commissioners, upon assuming office, suddenly to detach themselves from previous loyalties and concern themselves solely with 'the wider European interest' – not least since a factor in their nomination by national governments is likely to have been an expectation that they would keep an eye on the national interest. The Treaty's insistence on the complete independence of Commissioners is therefore interpreted flexibly. Indeed, total neutrality is not even desirable since the work of the Commission is facilitated by Commissioners maintaining their links with sources of influence throughout the EU, and they can most easily do this in their own member states. But the requirements of the system and the necessities of the EU's institutional make-up are such that real problems arise if Commissioners try to push their own states' interests too hard. It is both legitimate and helpful to bring favoured national interests onto the agenda, to help clear national obstacles from the path, to explain to other Commissioners what is likely to be acceptable in 'my' national capital. But to go further and act consistently and blatantly as a national spokesman, or even to be seen as being over-chauvinistic, as a few Commissioners occasionally have, is to risk losing credibility with other Commissioners. It also makes it difficult for the Commission to function properly since it clearly cannot fulfil its set tasks if its divisions match those of the Council of Ministers.

Characteristics of Commissioners

There are no rules or understandings as to what sort of people, with what sort of experience and background, member state governments should nominate to be Commissioners. It used to be the case that most Commissioners tended to be former national politicians just short of the top rank. However, as the EU, and the Commission with it, has become increasingly important, so has the political weight of the College's membership increased, and now most Commissioners are former ministers, and some of them very senior ministers.

Given the diverse political compositions of the EU's national governments, there is naturally a range of political opinion represented in the Commission, with its political balance reflecting the political composition of the governments of the member states at the time the College is appointed. Crucially, all governments have made it their custom to nominate people who are broadly pro-European and have not been associated with any extremist party or any extreme wing of a mainstream party. So whilst Colleges certainly contain party political differences, these are

usually within a range that permits at least reasonable working relationships.

Amongst important characteristics of the Barroso II College at the time of it assuming office in February 2010 were: nine of the 27 members were women; 14 were returning Commissioners, whilst another had previously been a Commissioner in the Prodi College; and in terms of their political background, 13 Commissioners were centre-right, eight were liberals, and six were centre-left.

The President

The most prestigious and potentially influential College post is the Presidency. Although most important Commission decisions must be taken collectively by the College, the President:

- is the most prominent, and usually the best known, of the Commissioners;
- is the principal representative of the Commission in its dealings with other EU institutions and with outside bodies;
- is generally expected to give a sense of direction to his fellow Commissioners and, more broadly, to the Commission as a whole. Article 17 (6) TEU states the President 'lays down guidelines within which the Commission is to work';
- allocates Commissioners' portfolios (see next section);
- may require fellow Commissioners to resign;
- is directly responsible for overseeing some of the Commission's most important administrative services – notably the Secretariat General which, amongst other functions, is responsible for the coordination of Commission activities and for relations with the Council and the EP;
- may take on specific policy responsibilities of his own, usually in harness with other Commissioners.

Inevitably, given the importance of the office, the European Council is very careful about who is nominated to be Commission President. It has come to be generally accepted that only the most prominent of national politicians will be considered, as is witnessed by the last four Presidents: Jacques Delors was a former French Finance Minister, Jacques Santer and Romano Prodi were former Prime Ministers – Santer of Luxembourg and Prodi of Italy – whilst José

Manuel Barroso was the serving Prime Minister of Portugal.

Portfolios

All Commissioners have portfolios: that is, particular areas of responsibility. Some portfolios, such as Budget, Competition, and Environment are more or less fixed but others, especially those of a broader and less specific nature, can be varied, or even created, depending on how a new President sees the role and tasks of the Commission and depending too sometimes on the pressures to which he is subject from Commissioners-designate and national governments. Table 8.1 sets out the porfolios at the beginning of the Barroso II College in early 2010.

Prior to the implementation of the Amsterdam Treaty, the distribution of portfolios among the Commissioners was largely a matter of negotiation and political balance. The President's will was the most important factor, but he could not allocate posts simply in accordance with his own preferences. He was intensively lobbied – by the incoming Commissioners themselves, and sometimes by governments trying to get 'their' Commissioners into positions that were especially important from the national point of view. Bearing in mind all these difficulties, it is not surprising that unless a resignation, death or enlargement enforced it, reshuffles did not usually occur during the lifetime of a Commission.

Clearly this situation meant that Commissioners were not necessarily assigned to the most appropriate posts, and also that not much could be done if a Commissioner was not performing satisfactorily. The situation was, however, partly addressed in a declaration attached to the Amsterdam Treaty and has since been strengthened, with the situation now being that, apart from in respect of the special portfolio of High Representative, 'the responsibilities incumbent on the Commission shall be structured and allocated among its members by its President … . The President may reshuffle the allocation of those responsibilities during the Commission's term of office' (Article 248, TFEU).

There is no question but that Prodi and Barroso (the latter twice), though certainly lobbied by Commissioners-designate and national governments on portfolio allocations – especially concerning such key portfolios as Internal Market, Trade and Competition – have both acted much more autonomously than their predecessors when making the portfolio assignments. Up to the time of writing, no significant re-shuffling of portfolios has occurred once a College has assumed office.

Cabinets

To assist them in the performance of their duties, Commissioners have personal *cabinets*. These consist of small teams of officials numbering, under rules introduced by Prodi designed to ensure *cabinets* are not too large or too powerful, six officials plus support staff, except for the President's *cabinet* which has twelve officials. Members of *cabinets* used to be mostly fellow nationals of their Commissioners, which enabled *cabinets* to act as important links with Commissioners' home bases, but Prodi made it clear shortly after being nominated as Commission President that he wished to see *cabinets* acquire a more markedly multinational character. To give effect to this, new rules were introduced requiring that each *cabinet* should include at least three nationalities and indicating that the *chef de cabinet* or the *deputy chef de cabinet* should preferably be of a different nationality to the Commissioner.

Typically, a *cabinet* member is a dynamic, extremely hard-working, 35–50-year-old, who has been seconded or recruited from some part of the EU administration, from the civil service of a member state, or from a political party or sectional interest with which the Commissioner has links.

Cabinets undertake a number of tasks: they gather information and seek to keep their Commissioner informed of developments within and outside his or her allocated policy area; they liaise with other parts of the Commission, including other *cabinets*, for purposes such as clearing up routine matters, building support for their Commissioner's policy priorities, and generally trying to shape policy proposals as they come up the Commission system; and they act as a sort of unofficial advocate/protector in the Commission of the interests of their Commissioner's country. Over and above these tasks, the President's *cabinet* is centrally involved in brokering the many different views and interests that exist amongst Commissioners and in the Commission as a whole to ensure that, as an institution, the Commission is clear, coherent, cohesive and efficient (see pp. 119–21 for further discussion of the roles of Commissioners' *cabinets*).

Table 8.1 Barroso II College: portfolios and associated services

Portfolios	Names and nationality	Supporting services and services for which responsible
President	José Manuel Barroso (Portugal)	Secretariat-General; Legal Service; Bureau of European Policy Advisers; Spokespeople's Service.
High Representative of the Union for Foreign Affairs and Security Policy and Vice-President of the Commission.	Baroness Catherine Ashton (UK)	DG External Relations.
Agriculture and Rural Development.	Dacian Ciolos (**Romania**)	DG Agriculture and Rural Development.
Budget and Financial Programming.	Janusz Lewandowski (**Poland**)	DG Budget.
Climate Action.	Connie Hedegaard (**Denmark**)	DG Climate Action.
Competition. Also Vice-President of the Commission.	Joaquín Almunia (**Spain**)	DG Competition.
Development	Andris Piebalgs (**Latvia**)	DG Development; the development part of the EuropeAid-Cooperation Office.
Digital Agenda. Also Vice-President of the Commission.	Neelie Kroes (**Netherlands**)	DG Information Society; European Network and Information Security Agency.
Economic and Monetary Affairs	Olli Rehn (**Finland**)	DG Economic and Monetary Affairs; Eurostat.
Education, Culture, Multilingualism and Youth	Androulla Vassiliou (**Cyprus**)	DG Education and Culture; DG Translation; DG Interpretation; Translation Centre for the Bodies of the EU; European Centre for the Development of Vocational Training; European Training Foundation; European Institute of Technology.
Employment, Social Affairs and Inclusion	László Andor (**Hungary**)	DG Employment, Social Affairs and Inclusion; European Foundation for the Improvement of Living and Working Conditions; European Agency for Health and Safety at Work.
Energy	Günter Oettinger (**Germany**)	DG Energy; Euratom Supply Agency.
Enlargement and Neighbourhood Policy	Štefan Füle (**Czech Republic**)	DG Enlargement; the neighbourhood parts of DG External Relations and of the EuropeAid-Cooperation Office.
Environment	Janez Potočnik (**Slovenia**)	DG Environment; European Environmental Agency.
Health and Consumer Policy.	John Dalli (**Malta**)	DG Health and Consumers; Community Plant Variety Office; European Centre for Disease Prevention and Control; European Food Safety Authority; European Medicines Agency; Executive Agency for Health and Consumers.

→

Table 8.1 *continued*

Portfolios	Names and nationality	Supporting services and services for which responsible
Home Affairs.	Cecilia Malmström **(Sweden)**	Parts of DG Justice, Liberty and Security; European Agency for the Management of Operational Cooperation at the External Borders; European Police Office; European Police College; European Monitoring Centre for Drug and Drug Addiction.
Industry and Entrepreneurship. Also Vice-President of the Commission	Antonio Tajani **(Italy)**	DG Enterprise and Industry; European Chemicals Agency.
Inter-institutional Relations and Administration. Also Vice President of the Commission.	Maroš Šefčovič **(Slovakia)**	For inter-institutional relations, will draw on the support of the Secretariat-General. For administration: DG Human Resources and Security; DG Informatics; Office for Administration and Payment of Individual Entitlements; Office for Infrastructure and Logistics in Brussels; Office for Infrastructure and Logistics in Luxembourg; European Personnel Selection Office; European Administration School.
Internal Market and Services.	Michel Barnier **(France)**	DG Internal Market and Services; Office of Harmonisation in the Internal Market.
International Cooperation, Humanitarian Aid and Crisis Response.	Kristalina Georgieva **(Bulgaria)**	DG Humanitarian Aid.
Justice, Fundamental Rights and Citizenship. Also Vice-President of the Commission.	Viviane Reding **(Luxembourg)**	Parts of DG Justice, Liberty and Security; Part of DG Employment; European Fundamental Rights Agency; European Institute for Gender Equality; European Judicial Cooperation Unit; DG Communication; Publications Office.
Maritime Affairs and Fisheries	Maria Damanaki **(Greece)**	DG Maritime Affairs and Fisheries; Community Fisheries Control Agency.
Regional policy.	Johannes Hahn **(Austria)**	DG Regional Policy.
Research, Innovation and Science.	Maire Geoghegan-Quinn **(Ireland)**	DG Research; Joint Research Centre (JRC); European Research Council; Research Executive Agency; European Research Council Executive Agency.
Taxation and Customs Union, Audit and Anti-Fraud.	Algirdas Šemeta **(Lithuania)**	DG Taxation and Customs Union; Internal Audit Service; European Anti-Fraud Office.
Trade.	Karel de Gucht **(Belgium)**	DG Trade.
Transport.	Siim Kallas (Estonia)	DG Transport; European Railway Agency; European Aviation Safety Agency; European Maritime Safety Agency; Trans-European Transport Network Executive Agency.

The Commission bureaucracy

Below the Commissioners lies the Commission bureaucracy. This is by far the biggest element of the whole EU administrative framework, though it is tiny compared with the size of administrations in the member states. In 2008 the Commission's staffing establishment numbered just under 26,000 – fewer than in many national ministries and, indeed, many large city councils (EU member states average around 300 civil servants per 10,000 inhabitants, as against 0.8 per 10,000 for all EU institutions). Of these 26,000, some 20,000 were employed in administration – including just over 6,000 at senior policy-making levels; 3,800 were engaged in research and technological development; and 1,940 were in offices attached to the Commission. The 20,000 includes over 2,500 engaged in the translation and interpretation work necessitated by the EU's officially recognised 23 working languages: the 23 languages produce 506 possible language combinations, although most of the Commission's internal business is conducted in French or English. (Figures on authorised staffing in the EU's institutions are set out each year in the EU's budget, which is published in the *Official Journal*, and also in the annual *General Report on the Activities of the European Union*, which is compiled by the Commission. The figures given here are from the 2008 *General Report*.[European Commission, 2009a: Chapter VI]) The Commission also makes use of temporary staff of various kinds, including national officials on secondment and experts contracted for specific purposes.

Permanent staff are recruited on the basis of open competitive procedures, which for the senior levels are highly competitive. An internal career structure exists and most of the top jobs are filled via internal promotion. However, pure meritocratic principles are disturbed by a policy that tries to provide for a reasonable national balance amongst staff. All governments have watched this closely and have sought to ensure that their own nationals are well represented throughout the EU administrative framework, especially in the upper

---

Box 8. 2

Advantages and disadvantages of the Commission's multinational staffing policy

Advantages

1 The staff have a wide range of experience and knowledge drawn from across all the member states.
2 The confidence of national governments and administrations in EU decision-making is helped by the knowledge that compatriots are involved in policy preparation and administration.
3 Those who have to deal with the Commission can often more easily do so by using their fellow nationals as access points. A two-way flow of information between the Commission and the member states is thus facilitated.

Disadvantages

1 Insofar as some senior personnel decisions are not made on the basis of pure meritocratic principles but result in part from a wish for there to be a reasonable distribution of nationals from all member states in the upper reaches of the Commission, two damaging consequences can follow. First, the best available people do not necessarily fill all posts. Second, the morale and commitment of some staff can be damaged.
2 Senior officials can occasionally be less than wholly and completely EU-minded. For however impartial and even-handed they are supposed to be, they cannot, and usually do not wish to, completely divest themselves of their national identifications and loyalties.
3 There are differing policy styles in the Commission, reflecting different national styles. These differences are gradually being flattened out as the Commission matures as a bureaucracy and develops its own norms and procedures, but the differences can still create difficulties, especially when there is an influx of staff into middle-ranking and senior grades following EU enlargements.

reaches. For the most senior posts something akin to an informal national quota system has operated, though this is now not as prevalent as it was following a broad programme that has been under way since the Prodi College assumed office to modernise Commission personnel, management and administrative policies. This multinational staffing policy of the Commission, and indeed of the other EU institutions, has both advantages and disadvantages, as is shown in Box 8.2

Organisation

The Directorates General and other services

The Commission is divided into organisational units in much the same way as national governments are divided into ministries and departments. Collectively the organisational units are referred to as the services. Most of the organisational units carry the title Directorates General (DG) whilst those that do not are known as specialised services. A list of the DGs and specialised services is given in Box 8.3.

The size and internal organisation of DGs and specialised services varies. Most commonly, they have a staff of between 200 and 500, divided into four to six directorates, which in turn are each divided into three or four units. However, policy importance, workloads and specialisations within DGs produce many departures from this norm. Thus in terms of size, DG Agriculture employs almost 1,000 staff whilst DG Education and Culture employs around 150. As for organisational structure, DG Agriculture has eleven directorates and 48 units, whilst DG Taxation and Customs Union has five directorates and 19 units.

There is no hard and fast reason as to why some

Box 8.3

Directorates General and main specialised services of the Commission

Policies	*External relations*
Agriculture and Rural Development	Development
Climate Action	Enlargement
Competition	EuropeAid – Cooperation Office
Economic and Financial Affairs	External Relations
Education and Culture	Humanitarian Aid
Employment, Social Affairs and Inclusion	Trade
Energy	*General services*
Enterprise and Industry	European Anti-Fraud Office*
Environment	Eurostat*
Maritime Affairs and Fisheries	Press and Communication
Health and Consumers	Publications Office*
Information Society	Secretariat General*
Internal Market and Services	*Internal services*
Joint Research Centre	Budget
Justice, Liberty and Security	Bureau of European Policy Advisers*
Regional	Human Resources and Security
Research	Informatics
Taxation and Customs Union	Internal Audit Service
Transport	Interpretation
	Legal Service*
	Translation

* Not a Directorate General.

services have DG status and others do not. It is true that non-DG services tend to be more concerned with providing support for policies than directly handling policies, but in practice these two activities intertwine and overlap. Certainly non-DG services should not be thought of as being junior to DGs, not least since some of them – most notably the Secretariat General, which has a general responsibility for ensuring the Commission as a whole functions effectively and efficiently, and the Legal Service – are amongst the most prestigious locations within the services.

The hierarchical structure

The hierarchical structure of the Commission is as set out in Box 8.4. It is a reasonably clear structure, although in practice complications can occur. At the topmost echelons in particular the lines of authority and accountability are sometimes blurred. One reason for this is that an imperfect match sometimes exists between Commissioners' portfolios and the responsibilities of services. EC/EU enlargements and the consequent increases in the size of the Commission over the years, plus a streamlining of portfolios initiated by

---

Box 8.4

The hierarchical structure of the Commission

- All important matters are channelled through the weekly meetings of the College of Commissioners. At these meetings decisions are almost invariably taken by consensus, but majority voting is possible.
- In particular policy areas the Commissioner holding the portfolio in question carries the main leadership responsibility.
- DGs are formally headed by Directors General, who are responsible to the appropriate Commissioner.
- Directorates are headed by Directors, who report to the Director General or, in the case of large DGs, to a Deputy Director General.
- Units are headed by Heads of Unit, who report to the Director responsible.

Prodi, have allowed for greater specialisation on the part of individual Commissioners and a better alignment with the responsibilities of services. However, even now, with more services than there are Commissioners, some Commissioners have to carry responsibilities that touch on the work of several services, as Table 8.1 shows.

Another structural problem concerning Commissioners is the curious halfway position in which they are placed. To use the British parallel, they are more than permanent secretaries but less than ministers. For whilst they are the principal Commission spokesmen in their assigned policy areas, they are not members of the Council of Ministers – the body that, often in association with the EP, takes most final decisions on important policy matters. (The High Representative chairs the Foreign Ministers Council, but is not a voting member of it.)

These structural arrangements mean that any notion of individual responsibility, such as exists in most member states in relation to ministers – albeit usually only weakly and subject to prevailing political currents – is difficult to apply to Commissioners. It might even be questioned whether it is reasonable that the Commission should be subject to collective responsibility – as it is by virtue of Article 234 of the TFEU which obliges it to resign if a motion of censure on its activities is passed in the EP by a two-thirds majority of the votes cast, representing a majority of all members. Collective responsibility may be thought to be reasonable insofar as all Commission proposals and decisions are made collectively and not in the name of individual Commissioners, but at the same time it may be thought to be unreasonable insofar as the ability of the Commission to undertake its various tasks successfully is highly dependent on other EU actors. In practice no censure motion has been passed although, as was shown above and as is discussed in Chapter 11, one came close to being so in January 1999 and it was the near certainty of one being passed that prompted the Santer College's resignation in March 1999.

Decision-making mechanisms

The hierarchical structure that has just been described produces a 'model' route via which proposals for decisions make their way through the Commission machinery. This route is set out in Box 8.5. From the 'model' route all sorts of variations are possible, and in practice are commonplace. For example, if draft proposals are relatively uncontroversial or there is some urgency involved, procedures and devices can be employed to prevent logjams at the top and expedite the business in hand. One such procedure enables the College of Commissioners to authorise the most appropriate amongst their number to take decisions on their behalf. Another procedure is the so-called

---

Box 8.5

'Model route' for the development of a proposal within the Commission

- An initial draft is drawn up at middle-ranking policy grade level in the 'lead' DG. Liaison with other DGs that have an 'interest' is conducted by various means, including the convening of inter-service groups Outside assistance – from consultants, academics, national officials and experts, and sectional interests – is sought, and if necessary contracted, as appropriate. The parameters of the draft are likely to be determined by a combination of existing EU policy commitments, the Commission's annual work programme, and guidelines that have been laid down at senior Commission and/or Council levels.
- Progress is 'monitored' by the Secretariat General, which needs to be assured that appropriate 'tests' (including of subsidiarity and proportionality) are met and that correct procedures are used.
- The draft is passed upwards – principally through superiors within the DG, through the *cabinet* of the Commissioner responsible, and through the weekly meeting of the *chefs de cabinet* – until the College of Commissioners is reached. During its passage the draft may be extensively revised.
- The College of Commissioners can do virtually what it likes with the proposal. It may accept it, reject it, refer it back to the DG for redrafting, or defer taking a decision.

'written procedure', by which proposals that seem to be straightforward are circulated amongst all Commissioners and are officially adopted if no objection is lodged within a specified time, usually a week. Urgent proposals can be adopted even more quickly by 'accelerated written procedure'.

Another set of circumstances producing departures from the 'model' route is when policy issues cut across the Commission's administrative divisions – a very common occurrence given the sectoral specialisations of the DGs. For example, a draft directive aimed at providing a framework in which alternative sources of energy might be researched and developed probably would originate in DG Energy, but would have direct implications for DG Research, DG Budget, and perhaps DG Enterprise and Industry. Sometimes policy and legislative proposals do not just touch on the work of other DGs but give rise to sharp conflicts, the sources of which may be traced back to the conflicting 'missions' of DGs: for example, there are sometimes disputes between DG Competition and DG Regional Policy, with the latter tending to be much less concerned than the former about rigidly applying EU competition rules if European industry is thereby assisted and advantaged. Provision for liaison and coordination is thus essential if the Commission is to be effective and efficient. There are various procedures and mechanisms aimed at providing this necessary coordination. Four of these are particularly worth noting.

First, at the level of the DGs, various management practices and devices have been developed to try to rectify the increasingly recognised problem of horizontal coordination. In many policy areas this results in important coordinating functions being performed by a host of standing and *ad hoc* arrangements: inter-service groups and meetings are the most important of these arrangements, but there are also task forces, project groups, and numerous informal and one-off exchanges from Director General level downwards.

Second, the main institutional agency for promoting coordination is the Secretariat General of the Commission, which is specifically charged with ensuring that proper coordination and communication takes place across the Commission. In exercising this duty the Secretariat satisfies itself that all Commission interests have been consulted before a proposal is submitted to the College of Commissioners.

Third, the President of the Commission has an ill-defined, but generally expected, coordinating responsibility. A forceful personality may be able to achieve a great deal in forging a measure of collective identity out of the varied collection of people from quite different national and political backgrounds who sit around the Commission table. But it can only be done tactfully and with adroit use of social skills. Jacques Delors, who presided over three Commissions between 1985 and 1995, unquestionably had a forceful personality, but he also displayed traits and acted in ways that had the effect of undermining team spirit amongst his colleagues. For example, he indicated clear policy preferences and interests of his own; he occasionally made important policy pronouncements before fully consulting the other Commissioners; he criticised Commissioners during Commission meetings and sometimes, usually by implication rather than directly, did so in public too; and he frequently appeared to give more weight to the counsel of personal advisers and to people who reported directly to him – drawn principally from his *cabinet* and from the Commission's Forward Studies Unit (since reconstituted and now known as the Bureau of European Policy Advisers) – than to the views of his fellow Commissioners.

Fourth, the College of Commissioners, in theory at least, is in a strong position to coordinate activity and take a broad view of Commission affairs. Everything of importance is referred to the Commissioners' weekly meeting and at that meeting the whole sweep of Commission interests is represented by the portfolios of those gathered around the table.

Photo 8.3 Jacques Delors: President of the European Commission, 1985–95

Commissioners' meetings are always preceded by other meetings designed to ease the way to decision-making:

- Informal and *ad hoc* consultations may occur between Commissioners who are particularly affected by a proposal.
- Groups of Commissioners in related and overlapping policy areas exist for the purpose of facilitating liaison and cooperation and enabling discussions at College meetings to be well prepared and efficient. Amongst Groups of Commissioners to have been established by Barroso are ones on the Lisbon Strategy, External Relations, and Competitiveness.
- The Commissioners' agenda is always considered at a weekly meeting of the heads of the Commissioners' *cabinets*. These *chefs de cabinet* meetings are chaired by the Commission's Secretary General and are usually held two days before the meetings of the Commission itself. Their main purpose is to reduce the agenda for Commission meetings by reaching agreements on as many items as possible and referring only controversial/difficult/major/politically sensitive matters to the Commissioners.
- Feeding into *chefs de cabinet* meetings are the outcomes of meetings between the *cabinet* members responsible for particular policy areas.
- Officials from the different *cabinets,* who are generally well known to one another, often exchange views on an informal basis if a proposal looks as though it may create difficulties. (Officially *cabinets* do not become involved until a proposal has been formally launched by a DG, but earlier consultation is common. If this consultation is seen by DGs to amount to interference, tensions and hostilities can arise – not least because *cabinet* officials are usually junior in career terms to officials in the upper reaches of DGs.)

However, despite these various coordinating arrangements, a feeling persists in many quarters that the Commission continues to function in too compartmentalised a manner, with insufficient attention being paid to overall EU policy coherence. Amongst the problems are the following.

1 The Commission has a rather rigid organisational framework. Despite the development of horizontal

links of the kind that have just been noted, structural relationships, both between and within DGs, remain essentially vertical. Although encouragement has been given, principally via the President's office and the Secretariat General, to the creation of agencies and teams that can plan on a broad front, these are not fully developed, and in any event they have found it difficult to assert their authority in relation to the DGs, especially the larger and traditionally more independent DGs. As for the President himself, he has only limited powers to direct the actions of DGs.

2 Departmental and policy loyalties sometimes tend to discourage new and integrated approaches to problems and the pooling of ideas. Demarcation lines between spheres of responsibility are fairly tightly drawn and policy competences can be too jealously guarded.

3 Sheer workload makes it difficult for Commissioners and senior officials to look much beyond their own immediate tasks. One of the duties of a Commissioner's *cabinet* is to keep the Commissioner abreast of general policy developments, but it remains the case that the Commissioner holding the portfolio on, say, research, can hardly be blamed if she or he has little to contribute to a Commission discussion on the milk market regime.

Power Resources

Like all political actors, the Commission needs power resources to be able to exercise influence. As Box 8.6 shows, the Commission is well endowed with such resources.

The power resources available to the Commission illustrate the special nature of the Commission as an institution, and especially the ways in which it combines features of being both a political institution and an administrative institution. As regards it having resources that are normally associated with political institutions, it does not have the resources that are most associated with, and are most important for, national politicians – the legitimacy that stems from having been directly elected by citizens and the power to not only propose policy measures but also to actually take final decisions on them. But, the Commission

> **Box 8.6**
>
> ## Power resources of the Commission
>
> - Its powers of initiative: exclusive and non exclusive.
> - Its neutrality (which results in it being seen as less partisan and more trustworthy than most other EU actors).
> - It is present in virtually all decision-making forums and at all decision-making stages (and so is very well-informed about the positions of other actors and is often looked to by them for advice).
> - Its access to information about EU policies and needs (an access that is assisted by it being surrounded by hundreds of expert and advisory committees).
> - Smaller states often look to the Commission for leadership and protection – and most EU states *are* small.

does have a key resource of politicians: the power to initiate policies. Where legislation is concerned, this power is mostly exclusive to it. Where other measures are concerned, the power is shared with other EU actors – most particularly the Council. Even, however, where the Commission's initiating powers are not exclusive, its position can be greatly strengthened by other actors often finding it logistically difficult to develop initiatives without receiving considerable assistance from the Commission.

As regards the Commission having resources that are normally associated with public administrations, the most important of these are its access to, and its understanding of, information about the operation of EU policies: what is working well?; what needs reforming?; what would be the consequences, for the EU as a whole and for parts of it, of introducing a particular policy or policy amendment? Often only the Commission, drawing on its many sources of information, is in a position to make accurate judgements on such questions.

Moreover, such judgements by the Commission are more likely to be generally trusted than are judgements by, say, a national government or a political group in the EP. This brings in another type of power resource of the Commission: those that stem from the unique nature of the EU and the Commission's special position in it. The Commission's duty to be neutral and non-partisan mean that policy proposals stemming from it generally are given a more favourable reception than are proposals coming from a more sectional or perceived special interest source. This is not, of course, to say that there are not circumstances in which Commission proposals do not run into stiff resistance, but even then the Commission's special position in the EU system gives it considerable advantages. Amongst these advantages are that, unlike national administrations, the Commission is physically present in virtually all policy-making forums and at all policy-making stages (including all Council meetings and EP committees) and so is well-placed to be able to anticipate the reactions of other institutions to proposals it makes and to be able to explain and defend its stances.

The Commission's power resources will be further explored and illustrated in the next section on the Commission's responsibilities.

Responsibilities

Some of the Commission's responsibilities and powers are prescribed in the treaties and in EU legislation. Others are not formally laid down but have developed from practical necessity and the requirements of the EU system.

Whilst recognising that there is some overlap between the categories, the responsibilities of the Commission may be grouped under six major headings: proposer and developer of policies and legislation, executive functions, guardian of the legal framework, external representative and negotiator, mediator and conciliator, and promoter of the general interest.

Proposer and developer of policies and legislation

Article 17 TEU states that 'The Commission shall promote the general interest of the Union and take appropriate initiatives to that end.' This means, amongst other things, that the Commission is charged

with the responsibility of proposing measures that are likely to advance the development of the EU. Where legislation is envisaged, this power to propose is exclusive to the Commission 'except where the Treaties provide otherwise' (Article 17, TEU). The most important areas where the Treaties do so provide otherwise are in respect of certain JHA matters. Where proposals do not involve legislation, as in the CFSP area, the Commission's proposing and initiating powers are shared with the member states.

In addition to its formal treaty powers, political realities arising from the institutional structure of the EU also dictate that the Commission is centrally involved in formulating and developing policy. The most important of these realities is that there is nothing like an EU Head of Government or Council of Ministers capable of providing the EU with clear and consistent policy direction, let alone a coherent legislative programme. Senior Commission officials who have transferred from national civil services are often greatly surprised by the lack of political direction from above and the amount of room for policy and legislative initiation that is available to them. Their duties are often only broadly defined and there can be considerable potential, especially for more senior officials, to stimulate development in specific and, if they wish, new and innovative policy areas.

An indication of the scale of the Commission's proposing activities is seen in the fact that in 2008 it made 420 proposals for directives, regulations and decisions, plus ten recommendations. It also presented 318 communications and reports, nine Green Papers, and one White Paper (European Commission, 2009a: Chapter VI).

Although in practice they greatly overlap, it will be useful here, for analytical purposes, to look separately at policy initiation and development on the one hand, and legislative initiation and development on the other.

* * *

Policy initiation and development takes place at several levels in that it ranges from sweeping 'macro' policies to detailed policies for particular sectors. Whatever the level, however, the Commission – important though it is – does not have a totally free hand in what it does. As is shown at various points elsewhere in this book, all sorts of other actors – including the European Council, the Council of Ministers, the EP, national governments, sectional groups, regional and local authorities, and private firms – also attempt to play a part in the policy process. They do so by engaging in such activities as producing policy papers, issuing exhortations and recommendations, and lobbying. Such activities are frequently designed to exert direct policy pressure on the Commission. From its earliest deliberations on a possible policy initiation the Commission has to take note of many of these outside voices if its proposals are to find broad support and be effective in the sectors to which they are directed. The Commission must concern itself not only with what it believes to be desirable but also with what is possible. The policy preferences of others must be recognised and, where necessary and appropriate, be accommodated.

Of the many pressures and influences to which the Commission is subject in the exercise of its policy initiation functions, the most important are those that emanate from the European Council and the Council of Ministers. When these institutions indicate that they wish to see certain sorts of proposal laid before them, the Commission is obliged to respond. However, important though the European Council and Council of Ministers are as policy-initiating bodies, the extent to which they undermine the initiating responsibilities and powers of the Commission ought not to be exaggerated. For the institutional structures and compositions of the European Council and Council of Ministers can make it difficult for them to be bold and imaginative. They tend often to be better at responding than at originating and proposing, which results in the Commission not only taking instructions from them but also using them to legitimise its own policy preferences. EU enlargement illustrates this mutual interdependence of the Commission on the one hand and the European Council and Council of Ministers on the other in terms of policy initiation and development, with the Commission almost invariably having taken the lead with proposals when decisions have had to be taken. Furthermore, there have been few European Council meetings since the early 1990s that have either not received a report of some kind from the Commission on an aspect of enlargement or have not asked that such a report be prepared.

The Commission's policy-initiating activities cover both major and cross-sectoral policies and policy programmes and also specific policy areas. Examples of the former include: the 2004 *Communication From the Commission to the Council and the European Parliament: Building Our Common Future. Policy Challenges and Budgetary Means of the Enlarged European Union 2007–2013*, which set out a framework for EU expenditure and policy priorities over the next budgetary cycle and the 2008 *Communication From the Commission to the European Council: A European Recovery Plan* , which identified a range of measures it urged should be taken in response to the global financial and economic crisis. Examples of the latter include: attempting to generate a more integrated approach to a policy area – as with the 2005 Green Paper on energy efficiency *Doing More With Less,* and the 2007 Communication *A European Strategy Energy Technology Plan (SET) – Towards a Low Carbon Future*; attempting to strengthen existing policy frameworks – as with the 2009 White Paper *Adjusting EU ICT Standardisation Policy To the Realities of the 21st Century*; and attempting to promote ideas, discussion and interest as a possible preliminary to getting a new policy area or initiative off the ground – as with the 2005 discussion document A *European Institute of Technology?* that was issued as part of the mid-term review of the Lisbon Process.

But whatever their particular focus, most – though not all – policy initiatives need to be followed up with legislation if they are to have bite and be effective.

* * *

If the Commission is well-placed with regard to policy initiation and development, it is even better placed with regard to *legislative initiation and development,* for it alone normally has the power to initiate and draft legislative proposals. The other two main institutions involved in the legislative process, the Council and the EP, can request the Commission to produce proposals, but they cannot do the initiating or drafting themselves. Moreover, after a legislative proposal has been formally tabled the Commission still retains a considerable measure of control, for it is difficult for the Council or the EP to amend it without the Commission's agreement: the Council can only do so by acting unanimously and the EP can only do so in specified circumstances and then only with the support of an absolute majority of its component members.

As with the preparation of policy proposals, the Commission makes considerable use of outside sources, and is often subject to considerable outside pressures, when preparing legislative proposals. The preparation of legislative proposals is thus often accompanied by an extensive sounding and listening process, especially at the pre-proposal stage – that is, before the Commission has formally presented a proposal to the Council and the EP. In this process an important role is played by a vast network of advisory committees that have been established over the years.

The Commission's advisory committee network

The committees are of two main types.

Expert committees. These consist of national officials, experts and specialists of various sorts. Although nominated by national governments the committee members are not normally viewed as official governmental spokesmen in the way that members of Council working parties are (see Chapter 9), so it is usually possible for them to conduct their affairs on a reasonably informal basis. Many of these committees are well-established, meet on a fairly regular basis, and have a more or less fixed membership; others are *ad hoc* – set up, very frequently, to discuss an early draft of a Commission legislative proposal – and can hardly be even described as committees in that they may only ever meet once or twice. In terms of their interests and concerns, some of the committees are wide-ranging, such as the Advisory Committee on Restrictive Practices and Dominant Positions and the Advisory Committee on Community Actions for the Elderly, while others are more specialised and technical, such as the Advisory Committee on Unfair Pricing Practices in Maritime Transport and the Committee of Experts on International Road Tariffs.

Consultative committees. These are composed of representatives of sectional interests and are organised and funded by the Commission without reference to the national governments. Members are normally appointed by the Commission from nominations made by representative EU-level organisations: either umbrella groups such as BusinessEurope (*sic* – the former Union of Industrial and Employers' Confederations of Europe), the European Trade Union Confederation (ETUC), and the Committee of Agricultural Organisations in the European Union

(COPA), or more specialised sectoral organisations and liaison groups such as the European Tour Operators' Association (ETOA) or the Partnership for Energy and the Environment (EPEE, which represents the heating, cooling and refrigeration industry in Europe). The effect of this appointments policy is that the consultative committees are overwhelmingly composed of full-time employees of associations and groups. As would be expected, agriculture is a policy sector where there are many consultative committees, with over twenty committees for products covered by a market regime plus half a dozen or so more general committees. Most of the agricultural advisory committees have a membership of around fifty, but there are a few exceptions: the largest are those dealing with cereals, milk and dairy products, and sugar, whilst the smallest are the veterinary committee and the committee on hops.

In addition to these two types of committees there are many hybrids with mixed forms of membership.

Most of the advisory committees are chaired and serviced by the Commission. A few are serviced by the Council and technically are Council committees, but the Commission has observer status on these so the distinction between the two types of committee is of little significance in terms of their ability to advise the Commission.

The extent to which policy sectors are covered by advisory committees varies. One factor making for variation is the degree of importance of the policy within the EU's policy framework – it is hardly surprising, for example, that there should be many more agricultural advisory committees than there are educational advisory committees. Another factor is the dependence of the Commission in particular policy areas on outside expertise and technical knowledge. A third factor is the preferences of DGs – some incline towards the establishment of committees to provide them with advice, while others prefer to do their listening in less structured ways.

The influence exercised by advisory committees varies enormously. In general, the committees of national experts are better placed than the consultative committees. There are a number of reasons for this. First, Commission consultation with the expert committees is usually compulsory in the procedure for drafting legislation, whereas it is usually optional with the consultative committees. Second, the expert committees can often go beyond offering the Commission technical advice and alert it to probable governmental reactions to a proposal, and therefore to possible problems that may arise at a future decision-making stage if certain views are not incorporated. Third, expert committees also have the advantage over consultative committees of tending to meet more regularly – often convening as necessary when something important is in the offing whereas consultative committees tend to gather on average no more than two or three times a year. Usually, consultative committees are at their most influential when they have high-ranking figures amongst their membership, when they are given the opportunity to discuss policy at an early stage of development, when the timetable for the enactment of a proposal is flexible, and when the matter under consideration is not too constrained by existing legislation.

Executive functions

The Commission exercises wide executive responsibilities. That is, it is closely involved in the management, supervision and implementation of EU policies. Just how involved varies considerably across the policy spectrum, but as a general rule the Commission's executive functions tend to be more concerned with monitoring and coordinating developments, laying down the ground rules, carrying out investigations and giving rulings on significant matters (such as proposed company mergers, state aid, and applications for derogations from EU law) than they are with detailed 'ground level' policy implementation.

Three aspects of the Commission's executive functions are worth special emphasis.

Rule-making powers

It is not possible for the treaties or for primary legislation to cover every possible area and eventuality in which a rule may be required. In circumstances and under conditions that are defined by the treaties and/or EU legislation, the Commission is therefore delegated rule-making powers. This puts the Commission in a similar position to national executives where, because of the frequent need for quick decisions in that grey area where policy overlaps with administration, and because too of the need to relieve

the normal legislative process of over-involvement with highly detailed and specialised matters, it is desirable to have truncated and special rule-making arrangements for administrative and technical law. The Lisbon Treaty formalised this distinction between 'political' and 'non-political' legislation, calling the former 'legislative acts' and dividing the latter into 'delegated acts' and 'implementing acts'.

The Commission used to issue at least 4000 legislative acts per year in the form of directives, regulations, and decisions (see Chapter 12 for an examination of the different types of EU legislative instrument). In recent years, however, with most of the SEM programme in place and with the Commission conscious of the expectation arising from the subsidiarity principle that it should issue laws only when they are absolutely necessary, the number has been lower. But that said, the figure for 2009 was still over 2,000 – just over half of which were regulations and most of the rest of which were decisions.

Most Commission legislation is confined to the filling-in of details or to the updating of specifications of various kinds that follow automatically from primary legislation that is made by the European Parliament and Council, or sometimes (but not much, post-Lisbon) just the Council. Much of it concerns Common Agricultural Policy matters. Box 8.7, which lists just a few of the many Commission laws that were issued on one day in late 2009, illustrates the sorts of matters covered in Commission legislation.

But not quite all of the Commission's rule-making powers are confined to the routine and the straightforward. In some policy areas opportunities exist to make not just 'administrative' law but what verges on 'policy' law. For example, in managing EU trade policy the Commission has considerable discretion in deciding whether to apply preventive measures in order to protect the EU market from dumping by third countries. And in implementing the EU's competition policy, the Commission has taken advantage of a rather generally phrased Article 81 TEC (now 101 TFEU) to clarify and develop the position on restrictive practices through the issuing of regulations and decisions.

As will be shown below, the Commission works closely with committees of governmental representatives when exercising its rule-making powers.

Box 8.7

Examples of typical Commission legislation

Regulations

Commission Regulation (EC) No 1158/2009 of 30 November 2009 establishing the standard import values for determining the entry price of certain fruit and vegetables.

Commission Regulation (EC) No 1159/2009 of 30 November 2009 fixing the import duties in the cereals sector applicable from 1 December 2009.

Commission Regulation (EC) No 1173/2009 of 30 November 2009 designating intervention centres for durum wheat and rice.

Directives

Commission Directive 2009/152/EC of 30 November 2009 amending Annex I to Council Directive 91/414/EEC as regards the common name and the purity of the active substance hydrolysed proteins.

Decisions

Commission Decision of 30 November 2009 amending Decision 2007/777/EC as regards imports into the Community of biltong from certain parts of South Africa and from Uruguay.

Commission Decision of 30 November 2009 allowing Member States to extend provisional authorisations granted for the new active substances metaflumizone and gamma-cyhalothrin.

Source: Official Journal of the European Union L314, 1 December 2009.

Management of EU finances

On the revenue side of the budget, EU income is subject to tight constraints (see Chapter 22 for an explanation of budgetary revenue). In overseeing the collection of this income the Commission has two main duties: to see that the correct rates are applied within certain categories of revenue, and to ensure that the proper payments are made to the EU by those national authorities that act as the EU's collecting agents.

On the expenditure side, the administrative arrangements vary according to the type of expenditure concerned. The Commission must, however, always operate within the approved annual budget (the EU is not legally permitted to run a budget deficit) and on the basis of the guidelines for expenditure headings that are laid down in multi-annual planning instruments, known as multi-annual financial frameworks (MFFs), on which all EU annual budgets are based. Of the various ways in which the EU spends its money two are especially important in that together they account for over 75 per cent of total budgetary expenditure.

First, there is CAP spending, which accounts for over 40 per cent of the annual budget and is used for agricultural support and rural development purposes. Up to 2006 this had been based on the European Agricultural Guidance and Guarantee Fund (EAGGF), but in June 2005 the Agriculture Ministers agreed to change CAP funding arrangements from 2007 to coincide with the application of a new MFF for the years 2007–13. The agreed change was to replace the EAGGF with two new funds that would be better tailored to the 'new CAP': the European Agricultural Guarantee Fund (EAGF) and the European Agricultural Fund for Rural Development (EAFRD).

General management decisions on the use of CAP funds – such as whether, and on what conditions, to dispose of product surpluses – are taken by the Commission, usually via an appropriate committee made up of representatives of national governments. The day-to-day application of agricultural policy and management decisions occurs at national levels through appropriate agencies.

Second, there is cohesion policy spending, which accounts for over 35 per cent of total EU expenditure. The EU's cohesion policy is aimed at reducing economic and social disparities in the Union, at both national and regional levels. As with CAP spending, cohesion policy funding arrangements have been changed under the 2007–13 MFF, with financial instruments reduced from a previous six to three: the European Regional Development Fund (ERDF), the European Social Fund (ESF), and the Cohesion Fund (see Chapter 19 for details).

Programming, partnership, co-financing and evaluation are key principles of cohesion policy. The practical effect of this in management terms is that cohesion policy is based on a tiered system in which the roles and responsibilities of actors, including the Commission, vary at different levels. The post-2007 system differs in details from, but is similar in spirit to, its predecessor. The key features of the system are: overall strategic decisions are taken by the Council, on the basis of Commission proposals; broad programming decisions for member states and regions are developed jointly between the Commission and member states (with it being left to member states as to who participates on their side, but with regional and local authority involvement expected); implementation decisions are monitored by the Commission but are undertaken through appropriate member state institutional arrangements involving national, regional and local authorities, and also social partners and representatives of civil society.

* * *

Moving beyond the specific aspects of the Commission's financial management functions to look at the overall picture, it is clear that the Commission's ability to manage EU finances effectively is greatly weakened by the fact that the Council and the EP (especially the former) control the upper limits of the revenue base and take framework spending decisions. In the past this sometimes caused considerable difficulties because it meant that if it became obvious during the course of a financial year that expenditure was exceeding income the Commission could not step in at an early stage and take appropriate action by, for example, increasing the value added tax (VAT) ceiling on revenue or reducing agricultural price guarantees. All the Commission could do, and regularly did, was to make out a case as to what should be done. This dependence on the Council and EP remains, but the general situation is not as fraught as it was, because the use of MFFs since 1988 has meant there have been clearer controls on the growth of both income and expenditure.

Another, quite different, factor in weakening the Commission's financial management capability is that it does not itself directly undertake much of the front-line implementation of EU spending programmes and schemes. Rather, it mostly works through external – mainly national and subnational – agencies which, acting on its behalf, execute some 80 per cent of the EU budget. This point about the reliance of the Commission on external agencies is explored in the next section, but it is worth emphasising here too, not least since a major thrust of criticisms often made of the Commission is that it is too lax in its monitoring and control mechanisms in respect of many of these agencies. Under a programme of financial management reforms that was drawn up in the early months of the Prodi Commission and which was set out in a 2000 White Paper (European Commission, 2000) many changes to procedures and practices have been introduced. They include: the adoption of activity-based management and budgeting, to provide for improved financial planning and the better alignment of political priorities and the allocation of resources; the enhancement of accountability procedures within the Commission; a sharper separation between the approval and the auditing of expenditure functions; and less contracting out of implementing functions to private sector agencies (such contracting out had become increasingly common in the 1990s, largely as part of an attempt to deal with Commission under-staffing).

* * *

Before leaving the Commission's responsibilities for financial management, it should also be noted that the Commission has some responsibilities for coordinating and managing finances that are not drawn exclusively from EU sources. These responsibilities mostly cover environmental programmes, scientific and technological research programmes, and educational programmes in which the member states are joined by non-member states. A particularly important programme area in which the Commission has assumed coordination and management responsibilities has been the provision of Western assistance to states of the former Soviet bloc and Soviet Union.

Supervision of 'front-line' policy implementation

The Commission's role with regard to the implementation of EU policies is primarily that of supervisor and overseer. It does undertake some direct policy implementation, most notably in connection with competition policy – which is considered below in the section on the guardian of the legal framework. However, the bulk of the practical/routine/day-by-day/front-line implementation of EU policies is not undertaken by the Commission itself but is delegated to appropriate agencies within the member states. Examples of such national agencies are: Customs and Excise Authorities, which deal with most matters pertaining to movements of goods and services across the EU's external and internal borders; veterinary inspection teams, which check quality standards on foodstuffs; and Ministries of Agriculture and Agricultural Intervention Boards, which are responsible for controlling the volume of agricultural produce on domestic markets and which deal directly with farmers and traders about payments and charges. To ensure that policies are applied in a reasonably uniform manner throughout the member states the Commission attempts to supervise, or at least hold a watching brief on, the national agencies and the way they perform their EU duties. It is a task that carries with it many difficulties, four of which are especially important.

First, in most policy areas the Commission is not sufficiently resourced for the job. There just are not enough officials in the DGs, and not enough money to contract the required help from outside agencies, to see that the likes of the agriculture, fishing and regional policies are properly implemented. The Commission is therefore heavily dependent on the good faith and willing cooperation of the member states. However, even in those policy spheres where it is in almost constant communication with national officials, the Commission cannot be aware of everything that is going on, and with respect to those areas where contacts and flows of communication between Brussels and national agencies are irregular and not well ordered it is almost impossible for Commission officials to have an accurate idea as to what is happening 'at the front'. Even if the Commission comes to suspect that something is amiss with an aspect of policy implementation, lack of resources can mean that it is not possible for the matter to be fully investigated. In respect of fraud, for example, there are less than 500 officials in the European Anti-Fraud Office (OLAF) which is attached to the Commission.

The second difficulty is that even when they are willing to cooperate fully, national agencies are not always as capable of implementing policies as the Commission would wish. One reason for this is that some EU policies are, by their very nature, very difficult to administer. The Common Fisheries Policy is one such policy, with its numerous rules on fishing zones, days at sea, total allowable catches, and conservation requiring surveillance measures such as obligatory and properly kept logbooks, port inspections and aerial patrols. Another reason why national agencies are not always capable of effective policy implementation is that national officials are often poorly trained and/or are overburdened by the complexities of EU rules. The jumble of rules that officials have to apply is illustrated by the import levy on biscuits, which varies according to cereal, milk, fat and sugar content, while the export refund varies also according to egg content. Another example of rule complexity is seen in respect of the export of beef, which is subject to numerous separate regulations, which themselves are subject to an array of permanent and temporary amendments.

The third difficulty is that agencies in the member states do not always wish to see EU law applied. Competition policy, for example, is rich in such examples, but sometimes there is little action the Commission can take against a deliberately recalcitrant state given the range of policy instruments available to governments that wish to assist domestic industries and the secretiveness with which these can often be arranged.

The fourth and final difficulty is that EU law can be genuinely open to different interpretations. Sometimes indeed it is deliberately flexible so as to allow for adjustments to national circumstances.

Comitology

As is implicit in the above discussion, a number of different procedures apply with regard to how the Commission exercises its executive functions. Many of the procedures involve the use of implementing committees composed of governmental representatives. The implementing committee system has come to be known as 'comitology'.

From the mid-1980s, comitology became an increasing problem for the EU. This was for two main reasons. First, there was the sheer size and complexity of the comitology structure. By 2008 there were some 270 comitology committees, with 35 in each of the environment and the transport and energy policy sectors, 33 in enterprise and industry, and 31 in agriculture and rural development (European Commission, 2009c: 4). Up to 2006 there were four main comitology procedures: under the advisory procedure, committees could only *advise* the

Commission on implementing decisions; under the management procedure, committees could *block* Commission decisions by a qualified majority vote (QMV); under the regulatory procedure, committees had to give their *approval* for Commission decisions by QMV; and under (the rarely used) safeguard measures, committees could use a variety of consultative, confirming, amending, and revoking powers. In 2006 a further comitology procedure was introduced – the regulatory procedure with scrutiny (RPS) – which applied to broadly based measures and which built on the existing regulatory procedure to significantly extend the EP's powers, including giving it veto rights where a comitology committee had given a positive opinion. In 2008 the comitology committees adopted a total of 2,185 opinions and the Commission adopted 2,022 implementing measures via comitolgy – including 71 using the new RPS procedure (European Commission, 2009c: 6–7). Most comitology committees (37 per cent) operated under several procedures, though 31 per cent worked exclusively under the regulatory procedure and 22 per cent – including most of the agriculture committees – worked exclusively under the management procedure.

Second, there were frequent disputes, especially before the 2006 reform, between the Council on the one hand and the Commission and EP on the other, over the nature and application of the procedures. The main bones of contention between the institutions focused around: 1) complaints by the Commission and the EP that the Council made too much use of the procedures that gave it most control and insufficient use of the advisory committee procedure; 2) complaints by the EP that it was provided with insufficient information about deliberations in comitology committees and that its scrutiny powers were insufficiently strong – especially since much of the implementing legislation being channelled through the comitology committees, numbering over 2,000 legal instruments per year, was based on EP and Council legislation.

Partly so as to try and deal with these problems, the Lisbon Treaty made a distinction between two types of administrative legislation that could be issued by the Commission (see Chapter 12). In brief, *delegated acts* would be of 'general application to supplement or amend certain non-essential elements of the legislative act' (legislative acts are the parent acts) while *implementing acts* would be used where 'uniform conditions

for implementing legally binding acts are needed'. The Treaty also set out general arrangements for how the exercise of the conferred powers would be controlled by the Council and EP:

- Under Article 290 TFEU, *delegated acts* may be issued by the Commission, with the parent act explicitly laying down the conditions to which the delegation is subject. The conditions may be as follows: a) 'the European Parliament or the Council may decide to revoke the delegation; b) the delegated act may enter into force only if no objection has been expressed by the European Parliament or the Council within a period set by the legislative act'.
- Under Article 291 TFEU, *implementing acts* may be issued by the Commission, or in some circumstances by the Council, whilst the EP and Council 'shall lay down in advance the rules and general principles concerning mechanisms for control by Member States of the Commission's implementing powers'.

At the time of writing, the new comitology arrangements required for handling the new system of administrative law has to be developed However, since delegated acts will usually be the more broadly based of the two types of act, it is probable that they will be subject to a version of the RPS procedure. Implementing acts are likely to be subject to versions of the advisory, management and regulatory procedures.

A point to be emphasised about the role and policy impact of comitology committees is that although their most important function is, as has just been described, to deal with administrative legislation, they do also undertake other activities. In addition to considering proposed Commission decisions, agenda items for committee meetings can include analysing the significance of data of various kinds, looking at how existing legislation is working, considering how existing legislation may be modified to take account of technical developments, and assessing market situations (a prime task for the agricultural committees).

Naturally, the frequency of committee meetings varies enormously according to the nature of the policy sectors they cover. In the case of agricultural products such as cereals, sugar and wine that require frequent market adjustments committee meetings can be almost weekly, whilst in other cases meetings may be held only very occasionally.

* * *

Concluding this section on comitology on a broad point, comitology committees can be seen as a means by which the governments of the member states, and to a lesser extent the EP, seek to ensure the Commission does not become too independent of them. In conceptual terms, the committees are one of a number of mechanisms and devices found throughout the EU system used by the EU's principals – mainly the national governments, but increasingly also the EP – to maintain control over their agents, especially the Commission, where control is desired. This is achieved in a number of ways. For example, although some of the committees do exercise important powers, for the most part they tend to work within fairly narrowly defined limits. Anything very controversial can be referred to a Council meeting, and increasingly also the EP. There is also the fact that the Council, and again increasingly the EP, are jealous of their powers and would move quickly against the Commission if it was thought comitology committees were being used to undermine those powers. And then there is the key point that the Council and EP know that that it is just not in the Commission's long-term interests to abuse its powers by forcing unwelcome or unpopular measures through a committee. The Commission wants and needs the cooperation of the Council and EP.

The guardian of the legal framework

In association with the EU's courts, the Commission is charged with ensuring that the treaties and EU legislation are respected. This role links closely with the Commission's supervisory and implementing responsibilities. Indeed the lack of a full EU-wide policy-implementing framework means that its legal watchdog role serves, to some extent, as a substitute for the detailed day-to-day application of policies that at national level involves such routine activities as inspecting premises, checking employee lists, and auditing returns. It is a role that is extremely difficult to exercise: transgressors of EU law do not normally wish to advertise their illegal actions, and they are often protected by, or may even be, national authorities.

The Commission may become aware of possible illegalities in one of a number of ways. In the case of non-transposition or incorrect transposition of a directive into national law this is obvious enough, since directives normally specify a time by which the Commission must be supplied with full details of national transposition measures. A second way is through self-notification. For example, states are obliged to notify the Commission about all national draft regulations and standards concerning technical specifications so that the Commission may satisfy itself that they will not cause barriers to trade. Similarly, state aid must be referred to the Commission for its inspection. Self-notifications also come forward in respect of restrictive business practices because although parties are not obliged to notify the Commission of such practices, they frequently do so, either because they wish for clarification on whether or not a practice is in legal violation or because they wish to seek an exemption (if a notification is not made within a specified time limit exemption is not permissible). A third way in which illegalities may come to the Commission's attention is from the many representations that are made by individuals, organisations, firms and member states who believe that their interests are being damaged by the alleged illegal actions of another party. For example, Germany has frequently complained about the amount of subsidies that many national governments give to their steel industries. And a fourth way is through the Commission's own efforts. Such efforts may take one of several forms: investigations by one of its small monitoring/investigatory/fraud teams; careful analysis of the information that is supplied by outside agencies; or simply a Commission official reading a newspaper report that suggests a government or a firm is doing, or is not doing, something that looks suspicious under EU law.

Infringement proceedings are initiated against member states for not notifying the Commission of measures taken to transpose directives into national law, for non-transposition or incorrect transposition of directives, and for non-application or incorrect application of EU law – most commonly in connection with the internal market, industrial affairs, indirect taxation, agriculture, and environmental and consumer protection. Before any formal action is taken against a state it is informed by the Commission that it is in possible breach of its legal obligations. If, after the Commission has carried out an investigation, the breach is confirmed and continues, a procedure comes into force under Article 258 TFEU whereby the Commission

> shall deliver a reasoned opinion on the matter after giving the State concerned the opportunity to submit its observations.
>
> If the State concerned does not comply with the opinion within the period laid down by the Commission, the latter may bring the matter before the Court of Justice of the European Union.

Since most infringements have implications for the functioning of the market, the Commission usually seeks to ensure that these procedures operate according to a tight timetable: normally a state is given about two months to present its observations and a similar period to comply with the reasoned opinion.

Most cases, it must be emphasised, are settled at an early stage. So in an average year the Commission issues around 1,000 letters of formal notice, 500 reasoned opinions, and makes 150 references to the Court of Justice. One reason for so many early settlements is that most infringements occur not as a result of wilful avoidance of EU law but rather from genuine differences over interpretation, or from national administrative and legislative procedures that have occasioned delay.

Although there are differences between member states in their enthusiasm for aspects of EU law, most wish to avoid open confrontation with EU institutions. If states do not wish to submit to an EU law it is therefore more customary for them to drag their feet rather than be openly obstructive. Delay can, however, be a form of obstruction, in that states know it could be years before the Commission, and even more the Court of Justice, brings them to heel. Environmental legislation illustrates this, with most states not having fully incorporated and/or implemented only parts of long-standing EU legislation – on matters such as air pollution, bathing water and drinking water.

With regard to what action the Commission can take if it discovers breaches or prospective breaches of EU law, that depends very much on the circumstances. Four different sorts of circumstances are set out in Box 8.8.

* * *

As with most of its other activities, the Commission's ability to exercise its legal guardianship function is blunted by a number of constraints and restrictions. Three are especially important:

- The problem of limited resources means that choices have to be made about which cases are worth pursuing, and with how much vigour. For example only around 100 officials undertake the detailed and highly complex work that is necessary to give effect to the Merger Regulation.

- Relevant and sufficiently detailed information can be difficult to obtain – either because it is deliberately hidden from prying Commission officials or because, as is the case with many aspects of market conditions, reliable figures are just not available. An example of an EU law that is difficult to apply because of lack of information is the 1979 Council Directive on the Conservation of Wild Birds (79/409/EEC). Amongst other things, the Directive provides protection for most species of migrant birds and forbids killing for trade and by indiscriminate methods. Because the shooting of birds is popular in some countries, several governments were slow to transpose the Directive into national law and have been reluctant to do much about applying the law since it has been transposed. On the first of these implementing problems – transposition – the Commission can acquire the information it needs since states are obliged to inform it of the measures they have taken. On the second of the implementation problems, however – application of the law by national authorities against transgressors – the Commission has been much less able to make judgements about whether states are fulfilling their responsibilities: it is very difficult to know what efforts are really being made by national authorities to catch shooters and hunters.

- Political considerations can inhibit the Commission from acting as vigorously as it might in certain problem areas and in particular cases. An important reason for this is that the Commission does not normally wish to upset or politically embarrass the governments of member states if it is at all avoidable. The Commission does, after all, have to work closely and continuously with the national governments both on an individual and – in the Council of Ministers – on a collective basis, so it is in its interests to operate in a flexible and

Box 8.8

What can the Commission do about breaches of EU legislation?

- *Non-compliance by a member state.* Until the entry into force of the Maastricht Treaty in 1993, the Commission was not empowered to impose sanctions against member states that were in breach of their legal obligations. Respect for Commission decisions was dependent on the goodwill and political judgement of the states themselves, backed up by the ability of the Commission to make a referral to the Court of Justice – though the Court too could not impose sanctions. However, the Maastricht Treaty gave the Commission power, when a member state refuses to comply with a judgment of the Court, to bring the state back before the Court and in so doing to specify a financial penalty that should be imposed. The size of the penalty must reflect the seriousness of the legal infringement, the duration of the infringement, and the state's ability to pay (using GDP as an indicator). The Court takes the final decision. The first state to be fined by the Court was Greece, which in 2000 was held to have failed to fulfil its obligations on waste directives and was ordered to pay €20,000 per day until it complied with the Court's judgment. On a much bigger scale, in May 2002 the Commission asked the Court to fine France €242,650 per day for being in breach of EU insurance laws.

- *Firms breaching EU law on restrictive practices and abuse of dominant market positions.* Treaty provisions, legislation and Court judgments have established a considerable volume of EU law in the sphere of restrictive practices and abuse of dominant market positions. If at all possible, the Commission avoids resorting to law and taking formal action against firms. This is partly because of the ill-feeling that can be generated by open confrontation and partly because the use of law and formal action involves cumbersome and protracted procedures to establish a case. Offending parties are therefore encouraged to fall into line or to reach an agreement with the Commission during the extensive informal processes – which can last several years – that always precede formal proceedings. If, however, informal processes fail, fines and required actions can result. Such was the case with Microsoft in 2004, when the Commission ruled that it had abused its dominant position in the group server operating systems and media player markets. A €497 million fine was imposed and it also was required to introduce a modified version of its Windows operating system and to reveal details of its Windows software codes so as to enable competitors to produce compatible products. The 2004 fine was subsequently upheld by the EU's Court of First Instance in 2007 when Microsoft appealed, and in 2008 the Commission imposed a €899 million penalty payment on Microsoft for non compliance with the 2004 decision.

  In May 2009 the Commission imposed an even larger, and record, fine – of €1.03 billion – on the US computer chipmaker Intel for 'illegal anti-competitive practices'. Intel had, the Commission concluded after a long investigation, given rebates to major computer manufacturers provided they bought the computers' central processing units (the computers' 'brains') from Intel. This arrangement, in the view of

  →

politically sensitive manner. An example of political pressures inhibiting the Commission in this way is provided by the above-cited Conservation of Wild Birds Directive: in addition to the practical problem of acquiring information on the killing of birds, the Commission's sensitive political antennae serve to hold it in check in that it is well aware of the unpopularity and political difficulties that would be created for some governments, such as the Spanish and Maltese, if action were taken against the thousands who break this law. Another example of the inhibiting role of political pressures is the cautious line that the Commission has often adopted towards multinational corporations that appear to be in breach of EU competition law: to take action against multinationals is to risk generating political opposition from the member states in which the companies are based, and also risks being self-defeating in that it may cause companies to transfer their activities outside the EU.

Box 8.8 *continued*

the Commission, left the computer manufacturers with no choice but to buy from Intel and, in consequence, reduced consumers' choice and also discouraged innovation. In the words of the Competition Commissioner, Neelie Kroes 'Intel has harmed millions of European consumers by deliberately acting to keep competitors out of the market for computer chips for many years. Such a serious and sustained violation of the EU's antitrust rules cannot be tolerated (*EUobserver*, 13 May 2009). In July 2009 Intel launched an appeal against the decision at the EU's Court of First Instance, claiming that the fine violated its human rights and also arguing that such fines should only be issued as a result of criminal investigations and not from administrative proceedings.

- *Firms breaching EU rules on state aid.* The TFEU provides the Commission with the power to take action against what is deemed to be unacceptable state subsidisation of business and industry. This power can take the form of requiring that the state aid in question be repaid, as was the case in January 2002 when the French bank Credit Mutuel was instructed to repay €164 million to the French government. The Commission decided that the aid, which had been granted to help pay for special reduced tax bank accounts, gave Credit Mutuel an unfair advantage over its competitors. Generally, however, indeed in about 95 per cent of the cases it investigates, state aid applications and allegations result in the aid being authorised.

- *Potential breaches of EU rules on company mergers.* Under the EU Merger Regulation (originally Council Regulation 4064/89, now amended by Council Regulation 139/2004), the Commission is assigned considerable powers to oversee and vet proposed concentrations between companies that are deemed to have an EU-wide dimension. Information regarding proposed mergers and takeovers above certain limits has to be notified to the Commission. On receipt of the information the Commission must decide within one month whether it proposes either to let the deal go ahead because competition would not be harmed, or to open proceedings. If it decides on the latter it has four months to carry out an investigation, in the course of which it is entitled to enter the premises of firms and seize documents. Any firm that supplies false information during the course of a Commission inquiry, or conducts a merger or takeover without gaining clearance from the Commission, is liable to be fined up to 10 per cent of its annual sales. In practice the Commission normally authorises the proposed mergers that are referred to it, though conditions are often laid down requiring, for example, some of the assets of the merging firms to be sold off. The best known prohibition is the Commission's decision in 2001 not to authorise the proposed €42 billion merger between the US companies General Electric and Honeywell, even though the US authorities had cleared the merger subject only to minor divestment. Explaining the decision, the Competition Commissioner said the companies made too few concessions, too late, and that 'The merger … would have severely reduced competition in the aerospace industry and resulted ultimately in higher prices for customers, particularly airlines' (*The Guardian*, 4 July 2001).

External representative and negotiator

The Commission's roles in respect of the EU's external relations are considered in some detail in Chapter 21, so attention here will be limited simply to identifying the roles. There are, essentially, six.

First, the Commission is centrally involved in determining and conducting the EU's external trade relations. On the basis of Article 207 TFEU (ex Article 133 TEC), and with its actions always subject to Council approval, the Commission represents and acts on behalf of the EU both in formal negotiations, such as those that are conducted under the auspices of the World Trade Organisation (WTO), and in the more informal and exploratory exchanges that are common between, for example, the EU and the USA over world agricultural trade, and between the EU and Japan over access to each other's markets.

Second, the Commission has important negotiating and managing responsibilities in respect of the various special external agreements that the EU has with many countries and groups of countries. These agreements take many forms but the more advanced include not only privileged trading conditions but also financial aid and political dialogue.

Third, under Article 220 TFEU, the High Representative of the Union for Foreign Affairs and Security Policy and the Commission (which is rather confusing as the High Representative is a member of the Commission) represent the EU at, and participate in the work of, a number of important international organisations. Four of these are specifically mentioned in Article 220: the United Nations and its specialised agencies, the Council of Europe, the Organisation for Security and Cooperation in Europe, and the Organisation for Economic Cooperation and Development.

Fourth, the Commission has responsibilities for acting as a key point of contact between the EU and non-member states. Over 160 countries have diplomatic missions accredited to the EU and the Commission is expected to keep them informed about EU affairs, either through the circulation of documents or by making its officials available for information briefings and lobbying. The EU, for its part, maintains an extensive network of diplomatic missions abroad, numbering over 130 delegations and offices, which hitherto have been staffed by Commission employees. As the Lisbon Treaty comes into operation, this overseas representation role is being taken over by the new European External Action Service (EEAS) which is provided for in the Treaty. The EAAS is staffed from the Commission and the Council Secretariat, plus seconded officials from national diplomatic services.

Fifth, as was shown in Chapter 4, the Commission is entrusted with important responsibilities with regard to applications for EU membership. Upon receipt of an application the Council normally asks the Commission to carry out a detailed investigation of the implications and to submit an opinion. If and when negotiations begin, the Commission, operating within Council-approved guidelines, acts as the EU's main negotiator, except on showpiece ministerial occasions or when particularly sensitive or difficult matters call for an inter-ministerial resolution of differences. When negotiations are completed the Commission makes a recommendation to the Council – in practice to the European Council – as to whether an applicant should be accepted for membership. The whole process – from the lodging of an application to accession – can take years.

Finally, whilst the essentially intergovernmental nature of the CFSP and CSDP mean that the Commission's role in respect of foreign and defence policies is essentially supportive and secondary to that of the Council and is not in any way comparable to the role it undertakes with regard to external trade, it still has a significant part to play. It does so in two particular respects. First, under the post-Lisbon TEU, the new post of High Representative is based in the Commission as well as in the Council. Second, the effectiveness of many CFSP policies are highly dependent on the use of policy instruments – concerned often with trade and development aid – that are managed by the Commission.

Mediator and conciliator

Much of EU decision-making, not least in the Council of Ministers, is based on searches for agreements between competing interests. The Commission is very much involved in trying to bring about these agreements, and a great deal of its time is taken up looking for common ground that amounts to more than the lowest common denominator. This mediating and conciliating role obliges the Commission to be sometimes guarded and cautious with its proposals. Radical initiatives, perhaps involving what it really believes needs to be done, are almost certain to meet with fierce opposition. More moderate proposals on the other hand, perhaps taking the form of adjustments and extensions to existing policy, and preferably presented in a technocratic rather than an ideological manner, are more likely to be acceptable. Hence the Commission must often subject itself to a somewhat grudging incrementalism.

The Commission is not the only EU body that consciously seeks to oil the wheels of decision-making. As is shown in Chapter 9, the Council itself has mediating mechanisms, notably via its Presidency. But the Commission is particularly well placed to act as mediator and conciliator. One reason for this is that it is normally seen as being non-partisan: its proposals may therefore be viewed less suspiciously than any that come from, say, the chairperson of a Council working party. Another reason is that in many instances the Commission is simply in the best position to judge which proposals are likely to command support, both inside and outside the Council. This is because of the continuous and extensive discussions that the Commission has with interested parties from the earliest considerations of a policy proposal through to its enactment. Unlike the other institutions, the Commission is represented at virtually every stage and in virtually every forum of the EU's decision-making system.

Although there are naturally limitations on what can be achieved, the effectiveness with which the Commission exercises this mediating role can be considerably influenced by the competence of its officials. While, for example, one Commission official may play a crucial role in driving a proposal through a Council working party, another may so misjudge a situation as not only to prejudice the Commission's own position but also to threaten the progress of the whole proposal. Many questions must be handled with care and political sensitivity. When should a proposal be brought forward, and in what form? At what point will an adjustment in the Commission's position open the way to progress in the Council? Is there anything to be gained from informal discussions with 'awkward delegations'? These, and questions such as these, call for highly developed political skills.

Promoter of the general interest

In performing each of the above tasks the Commission is supposed to stand apart from sectional and national interests. While others might look to the particular, it should look to the general; while others might look to the benefits to be gained from the next deal, it should keep at least one eye on the horizon. As many have described it, the Commission should be the 'conscience' of the Union.

In looking to the general interest, the expectation is that the Commission should avoid partisanship and look to the good functioning and cohesion of the Union as a whole. This is seen to require acting in ways that strike a balance, and if necessary reconciles differences, between different actors and interests: for example, between the large and small member states, between the northern and southern states, between

the old and new states, and between the net contributors to and the net beneficiaries of the EU budget.

Worthy, however, though it may be in theory, this neutral role is difficult to operationalise. One reason why it is so is that it is highly questionable whether such a thing as the 'general interest' exists: there are few initiatives that do not threaten the interests of at least one member state – were this not to be the case there would not be so many disagreements in the Council.

In practice, therefore, the Commission tends not to be so detached, so far-seeing or so enthusiastic in pressing the *Union esprit* as some would like. This is not to say that it does not attempt to map out the future or attempt to press for developments that it believes will be generally beneficial. On the contrary, it is precisely because the Commission does seek to act and mobilise in the general interest that the smaller EU states tend to see it as something of a protector and hence are normally supportive of the Commission being given greater powers. Nor is it to deny that the Commission is sometimes ambitious in its approach and long-term in its perspective. But the fact is that the Commission operates in the real EU world, and often that necessitates looking to the short rather than to the long term, and to what is possible rather than what is ideally desirable.

The Varying (and Declining?) Influence of the Commission in the EU System

Previous sections of this chapter have shown that the Commission has access to a wide range of power resources and draws on these to exercise a very considerable influence in the EU system. But it is an influence that varies according to a number of circumstances, such as its Treaty-based powers, the extent to which the member states look to it to provide a lead, and the formal control mechanisms to which it is subject. Box 8.9 outlines key factors determining this varying influence that the Commission exercises, with particular reference to its ability to provide leadership for the EU.

But whether the influence is quite as strong today as it was in the mid-to-late 1980s and early 1990s – when Jacques Delors was President and new policy

> ## Box 8.9
>
> ## Circumstances favourable to the exercise of Commission leadership
>
> - when it has strong and clear powers (for example, its competition policy powers are very strong but its defence policy powers are weak)
> - when QMV applies in the Council (because the Commission is then less subject to member state control)
> - when control mechanisms are weak
> - when there is uncertainty of information amongst the member states (because they are more likely to be susceptible to Commission leadership)
> - when there is an absence of strong conflicts in the Council and the EP (because there is less likelihood of a body of opinion being resistant to Commission proposals)
> - when there is the possibility of exploiting differences between member states

programmes were rapidly coming on-stream – is a matter of some academic debate. Certainly there are many academics who would argue that there has been a marked decline in the influence of the Commission since the days when it was leading the march to complete the internal market and was championing such initiatives as EMU and the social dimension. Commentators have suggested that there has been a particular diminution in the Commission's initiating role and a corresponding weakening of its ability to offer real vision and leadership. It has become, it is claimed, too reactive in exercising its responsibilities: reactive to the pressures of the many interests to which it is subject; reactive to the immediacy of events; and above all reactive to the increasing number of 'instructions' it receives from the Council of Ministers and the European Council.

Unquestionably, there is something in this view. The explanation for why it has happened lies in a number of factors, which are set out in Box 8.10. Some of these factors have been inescapable, such as the growing powers of the European Council and EP and the fact that there is less room for major new policy initiatives as the EU's policy portfolio has become ever more crowded. But some factors have been at least

partly avoidable, most notably the damage done to the Commission's status and prestige by the 1999 forced resignation of the College and the ineptness of Barroso's allocation of portfolios in 2004.

But, the extent to which there has been a decline in the position of the Commission should not be exaggerated. Certainly it has had to trim more than it would like, and it has suffered its share of political defeats – not least in its wish for stronger treaty-based powers. But it still commands extensive power resources, it still has key duties to undertake, and in

> ## Box 8.10
>
> ## Factors explaining a relative decline in the influence of the Commission
>
> - The policy 'pioneering' days are largely over.
> - The increasing influence of the European Council.
> - The increasing influence of the European Parliament.
> - Loss of status: the 1999 crisis, internal College divisions, the 2004 EP 'hearings'.
> - It has suffered some 'defeats' and failures in recent years. For example; little influence in recent IGCs; it was unsuccessful in 2005 in preventing a loosening of the Stability and Growth Pact; the economic liberalisation programme has not advanced as far or as rapidly as the Commission has wanted.
> - The growing importance of the use of 'new modes of governance' – based on flexible and non-legislative policy instruments, notably via the open method of coordination – has weakened the Commission's influence. This is because the Commission does not have exclusive initiating rights nor strong implementing powers in the increasing number of policy areas where such an approach is being practised.
> - Like national administrations, the Commission has been affected and infected by prevailing notions of rolling back the responsibilities of public sector organisations and of concentrating on making them more efficient in what they do, not more powerful in what they could do.

some respects its powers have actually increased as it has adapted itself to the ever-changing nature of, and demands upon, the EU. As has been shown, the Commission exercises, either by itself or in association with other bodies, a number of crucially important functions. Moreover, it has been at the heart of pressing the case for, and putting forward specific proposals in relation to, many of the major issues that have been at the heart of the EU agenda in recent years: consolidating and further extending the internal market; ensuring the success of EMU; driving forward the enlargement process; promoting the Lisbon Strategy for increased economic growth and employment; and shifting the CAP from a price support system to an income support system.

Concluding Remarks

The Commission is in many ways the most distinctive of the EU's institutions, combing as it does both political and administrative features and responsibilities. Partly because of its distinctiveness, it has been the focus of extensive debate amongst both academics and political practitioners. To the fore in academic debate have been different views on the extent to which the powers exercised by the Commission are exercised at the behest and on the direction of other EU actors – notably the governments of the member states – or are exercised in an at least quasi-independent manner. Box 8.11 summarises the 'polar' views taken by contributors to this debate.

Amongst practitioners, debate has tended to be focused mainly on the extent to which an institution that is unelected should be exercising significant powers. For those who take a broadly intergovernmentalist position on what the nature of the EU should be, the powers of the Commission need to be restricted and the exercise of what powers it has need to be firmly controlled. But, for those who are more integrationist in spirit, a strong and not over-shackled Commission is vital if the EU is to have policies that are sufficiently creative and ambitious to tackle the many policy problems the EU faces.

Box 8.11

The academic debate on the influence of the Commission

There is an extensive academic debate regarding the extent to which the Commission exercises leadership and undertakes its various roles in an independent manner. Broadly speaking, there are two 'polar' views, with variations stretched out in between.

- The 'intergovernmentalist' view sees the Commission as essentially being an 'agent', operating on the basis of guidelines and instructions given to it by its 'principals' – with the governments of the member states operating collectively in the European Council and Council of Ministers being the most important principals. (Prominent advocates of this view include Andrew Moravcsik and Paul Magnette.)
- The 'supranationalist' view sees the Commission as not being so controlled by its 'principals'. Rather, the 'agent' is able to escape control in important respects, as a focus on decision-*making* processes rather than just on decision *taking* demonstrates. (Prominent advocates of this view include Derek Beach, Susanne Schmidt, Wayne Sandholtz and Alec Stone Sweet, and Mark Pollack.)

But whatever position is taken in these and related debates, it is indisputable that the Commission is a core institutional presence in the EU. When the EU is 'in operation', the Commission is almost invariably involved in some significant way. The frequent appearance on the EU agenda of politically sensitive matters, coupled with the desire of politicians not to cede too much power to others if they can avoid it, may have resulted in at least some member states being reluctant in recent years to grant too much further autonomy to the Commission, but the Commission nonetheless remains central and vital to the whole EU system.

Chapter 9
The Council of Ministers

The Council of Ministers is the principal meeting place of the national governments.

When the Community was founded in the 1950s many expected that in time, as joint policies were seen to work and as the states came to trust one another more, the role of the Council would gradually decline, especially in relation to the Commission. This has not happened. On the contrary, by guarding and building on the responsibilities that are accorded to it in the treaties, and by adapting its internal mechanisms to enable it to cope more easily with the increasing volume of business that has come its way, the Council not only has defended, but in some respects has extended, its power and influence. This has naturally produced some frustration in the Commission, and also in the EP. It has also ensured, especially when set alongside the increasingly important position of the European Council in the EU's institutional system, that national governments have remained centrally placed to shape and influence most aspects of EU business.

Responsibilities and Functions

The functions undertaken by the Council can be classified in various ways. Hayes-Renshaw and Wallace (2006: 322–7) identify four main functions: legislative – developing and making legislation; executive – taking direct responsibility in some policy areas for exercising executive power; steering – 'devising the big bargains that orient the future work of the Union' (p. 325); and forum – 'providing an arena through which the member governments attempt to develop convergent national approaches to one or other policy challenges in fields where the Union does not have clear collective policy powers' (*ibid.*).

A three-fold classification is used here. As compared with the Hayes-Renshaw and Wallace classification, their legislative function is broadened, their executive function is retained, a different category – mediator – is added, and their steering and forum functions are subsumed within the first and third categories. The steering function is, however, revisited in Chapter 10, for much of what the Council does in this regard takes the form of preparing European Council decisions and declarations.

Policy and law maker

The principal responsibility of the Council is to take policy and legislative decisions. As is shown in other chapters, the exercise of these responsibilities is shared in various ways with other EU institutions – especially the Commission and the EP.

The extent to which the Council must work with, and is dependent upon the cooperation of, the Commission and the EP in respect of policy and decision-making varies between policy areas and according to what type of decisions are being made. In broad terms, the Council has most room for independent manoeuvre when it is not acting within 'the Community method' (see Chapter 17), for then the roles and powers of the Commission and the EP are normally restricted. Amongst policy areas where the Community method does not apply are foreign and defence policy, both of which have increased enormously in importance in recent years as the EU has come to issue numerous declarations on foreign policy matters and has come to engage in an array of foreign policy actions.

The Community method – which is used for the making of EU legislation – places limitations on the Council in two main ways. First, it is normally restricted to acting on the basis of proposals that are made to it by the Commission. Second, the EP has very important legislative powers. Prior to the Maastricht Treaty, the Council was formally the EC's sole legislature, but under the co-decision procedure that was created by the Treaty the EP became co-legislator with the Council in those policy areas where the procedure applied. As a result of subsequent treaty reforms, the procedure – which, tellingly, was re-named the 'ordinary legislative procedure' by the Lisbon Treaty – now applies to most significant legislation.

An indication of the Council's legislative role is seen in the volume of legislation it approves, either by itself or jointly with the EP. Prior to the entry into force of the Lisbon Treaty, in an average year the Council would adopt around 15 directives, 150 regulations and 50 decisions in its own name, and under co-decision with the EP around 30 directives, 50 regulations and 5 decisions. Under the TFEU, the proportion of acts that are adopted jointly with the EP will increase.

It should not be thought that because the TFEU states that the Council can normally only develop legislation on the basis of Commission proposals, the Council is thereby deprived of all powers of initiation. In practice, ways have been found if not to circumvent the Commission entirely at least to allow the Council a significant policy-initiating role.

Article 241 TFEU (formerly 208 TEC) is especially useful: 'The Council acting by a simple majority may request the Commission to undertake any studies the Council considers desirable for the attainment of the common objectives, and to submit to it any appropriate proposals.' In the view of many observers the use that has been made of this article, and the very specific instructions that have sometimes been issued to the Commission under its aegis, are against its intended spirit. Be that as it may, the political weight of the Council is such that the Commission is bound to pay close attention to the ministers' wishes.

In addition to Article 241/208, three other factors have been also useful in facilitating the Council's policy-initiating role in non-foreign policy issue areas:

1 The adoption by the Council of opinions, resolutions, agreements and recommendations. These are not legal texts but they carry political weight and it is difficult for the Commission to ignore them. Sometimes they are explicitly designed to pressurise the Commission to come up with proposals for legislation.

2 The increasingly developed Council machinery, which has grown in size over the years and become more specialised. There are now many places in the Council's network where ideas can be generated. The most obvious of these is the Council Presidency, which has become potentially more influential as preceding, existing and succeeding Presidencies work increasingly closer with one another (see below). The Presidency can be much to the fore in prompting the Council to consider new policy directions and priorities.

3 The increasing willingness of the member states to found aspects of their cooperation not on EU law but on non-binding agreements and understandings. Such non-legal arrangements, which do not have to be initiated by the Commission, are increasingly found not only in the foreign and defence policy areas but also in a number of domestic policy spheres where national differences can make it very difficult for legislation to be agreed. Such, for example, is the case with the non monetary dimensions of EMU and also with the Lisbon Strategy – which focuses mainly on the promotion of economic growth and employment and much of which is built not on legislation but

on the much looser open method of coordination (OMC) (see Chapter 17).

Executive

The Commission is the principal EU institution responsible for the implementation of EU policies and laws. As was shown in Chapter 8, it is the Commission that liaises with and oversees the work of the various agencies that undertake most of the 'front-line' EU policy implementation in the member states and it is the Commission that undertakes the limited amount of direct EU-level policy implementation in non foreign policy areas.

However, as was also shown in Chapter 8, in undertaking many of its implementation functions the Commission is obliged to work with and through comitology committees composed of national governmental officials. These committees are not formally part of the Council machinery or system, but they do give the Council indirect executive powers by virtue of the fact that the Commission has to work through them. In some circumstances committee challenges to Commission executive decisions result in references to the ministers for final resolution.

The foreign and defence policy areas provide for the most obvious and direct Council executive activity. Many of the declarations issued by the Council on foreign policy matters are, in effect, executive decisions in that they involve the operationalisation of principled positions developed and pronounced earlier by the European Council and by the Council of Ministers itself. Often these operationalisations involve close liaison with the Commission, especially where trade and development policy instruments are involved. Where operational activity involves putting civilian, police, and military personnel into 'troubled areas' – as many EU operations now do in the form of EU 'special representatives', 'monitors', 'observers', and 'peace missions'– policy execution is very much in the hands of the Council, working usually in very close liaison with appropriate agencies from member states.

Mediator

The Council exercises important responsibilities in the key activities of mediation and consensus-building. Of course, as the forum in which the national representatives meet, the Council has always served the function of developing mutual understanding between the member states both on prospective and established and on general and specific EU matters. Moreover, a necessary prerequisite for successful policy development has always been that Council participants display an ability to compromise in negotiations. But as the EU has grown in size, as more difficult policy areas have come onto the agenda, and as political and economic change has broken down some of the pioneering spirit of the early days, so has positive and active mediation come to be ever more necessary: mediation primarily between the different national and ideological interests represented in the Council, but also between the Council and the Commission, the Council and the EP, and the Council and non-institutional interests. The Commission has taken on much of this task, but so too have agencies of the Council itself – most notably the Presidency and the Secretariat.

* * *

The Council has both gained and lost responsibilities over the years. The most obvious gain has been the extended scope of its policy interests. As is noted at several points in this book, the EU's policy remit is now such that there are very few spheres of public policy in which the EU is not involved to at least some extent. This in turn means that there are few policy spheres in which the Council is not seeking to launch or shape initiatives and to take decisions of some sort.

There are, however, two respects in which the Council may be said to have lost responsibilities over the years, or at least to have become obliged to share them. First, as is shown in Chapter 10, the European Council – the body that brings together the Heads of Government – has assumed increasingly greater responsibility for taking the final political decisions on such 'history-making' issues as new accessions, institutional reform, the launching of broad policy initiatives, and the strategic direction of external relations. Second, as was noted above and is shown at greater length in Chapter 11, the powers of the EP have greatly increased, especially in respect of the making of legislation where the vast majority of Commission proposals now need not only Council but also EP approval if they are to become law.

Composition

The ministers

Ministerial meetings are at the apex of the Council machinery. Legally there is only one Council of Ministers, but in practice there are more in the sense that the Council meets in different formations or configurations to deal with different policy areas.

The Council used to meet in over twenty formations but a concern that this was too many led to the European Council deciding at its December 1999 Helsinki meeting to reduce the number in an attempt to improve the consistency and coherence of the Council's work. The number of formations was capped at sixteen. However, it was decided at the June 2002 Seville summit that sixteen was still too high and the number was further reduced to nine .

Post-Seville, the General Affairs and External Relations Council (GAERC) had the widest brief. It had always handled foreign policy and external trade and also had a loosely understood responsibility for dealing with horizontal issues relating to policy initiation and coordination and for tackling particularly politically sensitive matters. At Seville, these external and horizontal responsibilities were both extended and the GAERC was also specifically charged with responsibilities in relation to the operation of the European Council. In the words of the Seville summit's official conclusions, the GAERC would now deal with:

(a)   preparation for and follow-up to the European Council (including the coordinating activities necessary to that end), institutional and administrative questions, horizontal dossiers which affect several of the Union's policies and any dossier entrusted to it by the European Council, having regard to EMU operating rules;
(b)   the whole of the Union's external action, namely common foreign and security policy, European security and defence policy, foreign trade, development cooperation and humanitarian aid (European Council, 2002b: Annex II: Measures Concerning the Structure and Functioning of the Council).

To enable the GAERC to deal with the external and horizontal aspects of its work, it was further agreed at Seville that the two aspects would henceforth be dealt with in separate meetings. As a result: separate meetings were indeed held, with one subtitled General Affairs and the other External Relations; the meetings were almost invariably scheduled to follow on from one another – though often on succeeding days rather than on the same day; the agendas of the two meetings were significantly different from one another; and an array of ministers attended on behalf of the member states, with Foreign Ministers often being replaced by European or other ministers for General Affairs Councils and with different external ministers – notably those of Trade, Defence and Development – often accompanying or replacing Foreign Ministers for External Relations Councils.

Recognising that – in no small part due to it having too heavy and too broad a workload – the GAERC was in effect operating as two separate formations of the Council, the Lisbon Treaty formalised the split. A new Foreign Affairs Council formation would now deal with the EU's external relations while a new General Affairs formation 'shall ensure consistency in the work of the different Council configurations' (Article 16.6 TEU). The General Affairs Council would also, in liaison with the occupant of the new post of European Council President and with the Commission, be involved with the preparation of and follow-up to European Council meetings.

The Economic and Finance Council (Ecofin) also has a broad remit in that, especially since the development of EMU, few economic and financial issues are excluded from its portfolio. Its meetings often are preceded by meetings of the Eurogroup, which brings together the Economic or Finance Ministers of the states that are members of the eurozone. Non-Eurogroup ministers have sometimes complained of the Eurogroup trying to set the agenda and frame the decisions of Ecofin on monetary questions – as the Eurogroup certainly did, for example, in 2005 in respect of the changes that were made to the rules of the Stability and Growth Pact.

Beyond the General Affairs, Foreign Affairs, and Ecofin Councils, other matters are dealt with, as can be seen from Box 9.1, by sectoral or technical Councils, which are composed of Ministers of Agriculture, Transport, Environment and so on. The relatively small number of Council formations and the broad policy responsibilities of each formation means that member states often send more than one minister to

---

Box 9.1

Formations of the Council

General Affairs
Foreign Affairs
Economic and Financial Affairs
Justice and Home Affairs
Employment, Social Policy, Health and Consumer
  Affairs
Competitiveness
Transport, Telecommunications and Energy
Agriculture and Fisheries
Environment
Education, Youth and Culture

---

the same Council meeting, though when this happens ministers normally only attend for the agenda items that directly concern them.

The national representatives who attend ministerial meetings can differ in terms of their status and/or policy responsibilities. This can inhibit efficient decision-making. The problem arises because the states themselves decide by whom they wish to be represented, and their decisions may vary in one of two ways:

1 *Level of seniority.* Normally, by prior arrangement, Council meetings are attended by ministers of a similar standing, but circumstances do arise when the various delegations are headed by people at different levels of seniority. This may be because a relevant minister has pressing domestic business or because it is judged that an agenda does not warrant his or her attendance. Occasionally he or she may be 'unavoidably delayed' if a meeting is unwanted and/or has a politically awkward issue on the agenda. Whatever the reason, a reduction in the status and political weight of a delegation may make it difficult for binding decisions to be agreed.

2 *Sectoral responsibility.* Usually it is obvious which government departments should be represented at Council meetings, but not always. Doubts may arise because agenda items straddle policy divisions, or because member states organise their central government departments in different ways. As a result, it is possible for ministers from rather different national ministries, with different

responsibilities and interests, to be present. The difficulties this creates are sometimes compounded, especially in broad policy areas, by the minister attending not feeling able to speak on behalf of other ministers with a direct interest and therefore insisting on the matter being referred back to national capitals.

States are not, therefore, always comparably represented at ministerial meetings. But whether a country's representative is a senior minister, a junior minister or, as sometimes is the case, the Permanent Representative, the Deputy Permanent Representative or even a senior diplomat, care is always taken to ensure that national interests are defended. The main way this is done is by the attendance at all meetings of not only the national representative but also small national delegations. These delegations comprise national officials and experts plus, at important meetings or meetings where there is a wide-ranging agenda, junior ministers to assist the senior minister. So, for example, Trade Ministers usually accompany Foreign Ministers to meetings of the Foreign Affairs Council when trade issues are to be considered. Similarly, Budget Ministers – who had their own separate Council pre-Seville – usually accompany Economic and Finance Ministers to the Ecofin Council when the EU's budget is on the agenda. Normally four or five officials and experts support the 'inner table team' (that is, the most senior national representatives who actually sit at the negotiating table), but this number can vary according to the policy area concerned, the importance of the items on the agenda, the size of the meeting room, and the size of a member state – with small states usually struggling to match the 'turnout' of large member states. The task of the supporting teams is to ensure that the head of the delegation is properly briefed, fully understands the implications of what is being discussed, and does not make negotiating mistakes. Sometimes, when very confidential matters are being discussed or when a meeting is deadlocked, the size of delegations may, on a proposal from the President, be reduced to 'Ministers plus two', 'Ministers plus one' or, exceptionally, 'Ministers and Commission'.

*   *   *

Altogether there are usually around 100 formal Council meetings in an average year: 117 in 2008

(European Commission. 2009b: Chapter VI). Many of these meetings are held towards the end of a country's six-month Presidency as attempts are made to complete business and as some Councils have to assist in preparing the June and December European Council meetings. Council meetings are normally held in Brussels, but the April, June, and October meetings are held in Luxembourg.

The regularity with which meetings of individual formations of the Council are held reflects their importance in the Council system and the extent to which there is EU policy interest and activity in their area. So, the Foreign Affairs and the General Affairs Councils meet the most frequently, with usually at least one meeting per month. The Ecofin, Agriculture and JHA Councils meet most months, whilst the other Councils do not normally meet more than twice during each Council Presidency.

Unless there are particularly difficult matters to be resolved, meetings do not normally last more than a day. A typical meeting begins about 10.00 a.m. and finishes around 6.00 p.m. or 7.00 p.m. Foreign Ministers and Ecofin Ministers are the most likely to meet over two days, and when they do it is common to start with lunch on day one and finish around lunchtime on day two.

Outside the formal Council framework, ministers, particularly Foreign Ministers and Ecofin Ministers, have periodic weekend gatherings, usually in the country of the Presidency, to discuss matters on an informal basis without the pressure of having to take decisions. In 2008 there was total of 50 informal ministerial meetings (European Commission. 2009b: Chapter VI). Such informal gatherings are especially common in the opening weeks of Council Presidencies, when Presidencies are keen to discuss their priorities with colleagues and to gain feedback on what will and will not 'run'.

The Committee of Permanent Representatives

Each of the member states has a national delegation – or Permanent Representation as they are formally known – in Brussels, which acts as a kind of embassy to the EU. The Permanent Representations are headed by a Permanent Representative, who is normally a diplomat of very senior rank, and are staffed, in the case of the larger states, by about sixty officials plus back-up support. About half of the officials are drawn from the diplomatic services of the member states and about half are seconded from appropriate national ministries, such as Agriculture, Trade and Finance.

Of the many forums in which governments meet 'in Council' below ministerial level, the most important is the Committee of Permanent Representatives (COREPER). Although no provision was made for such a body under the Treaty of Paris, ministers established a coordinating committee of senior officials as early as 1953, and under the Treaties of Rome the Council was permitted to create a similar committee under its Rules of Procedure. Under Article 4 of the 1965 Merger Treaty these committees were merged and were formally incorporated into the Community system: 'A committee consisting of the Permanent Representatives of the Member States shall be responsible for preparing the work of the Council and for carrying out the tasks assigned to it by the Council.'

There are in fact two COREPERs: COREPER II and COREPER I. Both normally meet once a week, on Wednesdays. COREPER II is the more senior. At its meetings the member state delegations are headed by the Permanent Representatives and its agendas are the more 'political' of the two COREPERs. It works mainly for the Foreign Affairs, the Ecofin and the JHA Councils, plus, as noted above, the General Affairs Council and and through it for the European Council. It also often deals with issues for other Council meetings that are particularly sensitive or controversial. COREPER II is assisted in its tasks by the Antici Group, which is made up of senior officials from the Permanent Representations and which, in addition to assisting COREPER II, acts as a key information-gathering and mediating forum between the member states.

At COREPER I meetings, national delegations are headed by the Deputy Permanent Representatives. COREPER I works mainly for the Councils not covered by COREPER II. Because of the nature of the business covered by these Councils, COREPER I tends to deal with more technical policy and legislative matters than does COREPER II. COREPER I is assisted by its equivalent of the Antici Group: the Mertens Group.

In addition to preparing Council meetings, COREPER also exercises a number of more general functions on behalf of the ministers in the Council and EU systems. As Bostock (2002: 215) has put it: COREPER 'should be thought of as a co-ordinator of Council business, partly as a fixer and trouble-shooter'. It is able to exercise such roles because, again to quote Bostock (p. 226), it 'is a body composed of officials with the seniority and proximity to ministers to take a politically informed view, but with the diplomat's and bureaucrat's obligation to master the technicalities of the dossier before him'. Such qualities make COREPER members ideal when – as COREPER I members usually do – they represent the Council in conciliation meetings with the EP under the ordinary legislative procedure (on the procedure, see Chapters 11 and 18).

But whilst not querying COREPER's central role in the Council system, it has to be recognised that there has been a marginal decline in its position and effectiveness in recent years. One reason for this is that, as will be shown below, in the increasingly important and busy foreign and security and economic and finance policy areas, very senior Council committees have come to act almost on a comparable level to COREPER and to have acquired a considerable measure of discretion in how they operate. Another reason is that COREPER has inevitably become less 'clubbable' as the EU has grown in size, which has reduced COREPER's ability to 'get things done' through informal means.

Committees and working parties

A complicated network of committees and working parties assists and prepares the work of the Council of Ministers and COREPER.

Council committees

Council committees are composed of national officials, are serviced by Council administrators, and have as their task providing advice to the Council and the Commission as appropriate, and in some instances as directed. An outline of the most important Council committees is given in Box 9.2.

In addition to the committees listed in Box 9.2, many other committees also assist the work of the Council. Among them are the Committee on Scientific and Technical Research, the Employment Committee, and the Economic Policy Committee. There also are various groupings that are not always referred to as committees, but sometimes as working parties or simply as meetings, that are found especially in emerging policy areas. In addition, there has been an increasing tendency in recent years for *ad hoc* committees of senior national officials – sometimes referred to as 'High-Level Groups' – to be established for the purpose of developing initiatives and policies (though not of course for the purpose of drafting legislation) in new and sensitive areas.

Working parties

The role of Council working parties (also known as working groups) is more specific than that of most of the committees in that their main job is to carry out detailed analyses of formally tabled Commission proposals for legislation. The number of working parties in existence at any one time varies according to the overall nature of the EU's workload and the preferences of the Presidency in office, but in recent years there have usually been over 150. (It is impossible to give a precise figure because many working parties are *ad hoc* in nature.) Members of working parties, of whom there are usually between two and four per member state, are almost invariably national officials and experts based either in the Permanent Representations or in appropriate national ministries. Occasionally governments appoint non-civil servants to a working party delegation when highly technical or complex issues are under consideration.

The name 'working party' suggests that meetings would be attended by a relatively small number of people, who would soon likely develop a 'clubbable' atmosphere. But, in fact, with perhaps four or even five being in each national 'team' and with representatives from the Commission and General Secretariat also attending working party meetings, there can be well over 100 people present – not counting translators!

Working parties meet as and when required, which for permanent working parties with a heavy workload means regularly, whilst for those where nothing much comes up within their terms of reference means only occasionally. Usually there is an interval of at least two weeks between meetings so as to allow the Council's Secretariat time to circulate minutes and agendas – in all of the languages of the member states. But, if a working party is dealing with a contested piece of legislation which the Presidency is

Box 9.2

Key Council committees

- *The Special Committee on Agriculture* (SCA). Because of the volume and complexity of EU activity in the agricultural sector, most of the 'routine' and 'non political' pre-ministerial-level work on agriculture is undertaken not in COREPER but in the SCA. The SCA, which is staffed by senior officials from the Permanent Representations and national Ministries of Agriculture, usually meets at least weekly.
- Since the creation of the customs union in the 1960s the Council has had a special committee to watch over and liaise with the Commission when it conducts external negotiations in the framework of the common commercial policy (that is, common external trade policy). The committee has always been known by the number of the treaty article under which it is constituted: so, originally it was the *Article 113 Committee;* after the TEC was re-numbered by the Amsterdam Treaty it became the *Article 133 Committee*; and with the further re-numbering (as well as re-naming and reorganisation) with the TFEU it has become the *Article 207 Committee*. Any significant action undertaken by the EU in international trade negotiations is preceded by internal coordination via this committee. It normally meets once a week: the full members – who are very senior officials in national Ministries of Trade or the equivalent – meet monthly and deal mostly with overall trade policy issues; the deputies – who are middle-ranking officials from the Ministries, or sometimes from the Permanent Representations – meet three times a month and deal mostly with more specific trade matters. At meetings of both formations of the committee the national representatives are accompanied by small teams of national experts. Working parties, which meet as and when it is necessary, assist the committee. The committee performs two main functions: it drafts the briefs that the Commission negotiates on behalf of the EU with third countries (the committee's draft is referred, via COREPER, to the Ministers for their approval); and it acts as a consultative committee to the Council and the Commission – by, for example, indicating to the Commission what it should do when problems arise during the course of a set of trade negotiations.
- *The Economic and Financial Committee*, which was established at the start of the third stage of EMU in January 1999, focuses on economic and financial policy, capital movements, and international monetary relations. The members of the Committee – of which there are two from each member state (one from the administration and one from the national Central Bank), plus two from the Commission, and two from the European Central Bank – are senior and influential economic and financial experts: they are, in other words, people who can normally communicate directly with whomsoever they wish, and who are customarily listened to.
- *The Political and Security Committee* (PSC, though more commonly known after its French acronym – COPS) is the Council's main CFSP committee. It is composed of senior officials from the Permanent Representations, though sometimes it also meets at the level of Political Directors of the member states.
- Up to the entry into force of the Lisbon Treaty, two committees of senior national officials dealt with strategic JHA matters: the *Article 36 Committee* (CATS – *Comité Article Trente Six*) covered pillar three business whilst the *Strategic Committee on Immigration, Frontiers, and Asylum* (SCIFA) handled pillar one JHA issues. The Lisbon Treaty's abolition of the pillar structure resulted not in the abolition of these committees but in their work being made subject to review. The Lisbon Treaty also created a new *Committee on Internal Security* (COSI) to facilitate and promote the coordination of internal security operational actions.
- *The Standing Committee on Employment* is unusual in two respects. First, it is composed not only of governmental representatives but also of sectional interest representatives – the latter being drawn from both sides of industry. Second, the governmental representations are headed by the ministers themselves, or, if they are unable to attend, their personal representatives. The Committee meets twice a year to discuss matters of interest and, where possible, to make recommendations to the Employment, Social Policy, and Health and Consumer Affairs Council. The nature of the membership of the Committee, with ministerial representation, means that when general agreement can be reached, the matter is likely to be taken up by the Council.

keen to advance, meetings are likely to be held weekly. Up to fifteen or so different working parties are in session in Brussels on most working days. On completion of their analyses and deliberations of the work in hand – usually Commission proposals – working parties report to COREPER or to one of the Council's senior committees.

The General Secretariat

The main administrative support for the work of the Council is provided by the General Secretariat, which is headed by the Council's Secretary-General who is appointed by the European Council.

The Secretariat has a staff of almost 3,500 most of whom are located in Directorates General dealing with different policy areas. Of the 3,500, around 500 are at diplomatic level. The Secretariat's base, which also houses Council meetings, is located close to the main Commission and EP buildings in Brussels.

The Secretariat's main responsibility is to service the Council machinery – from ministerial to working party levels. This involves activities such as preparing draft agendas, drafting or assisting with the drafting of documentation, keeping records, providing legal advice, processing and circulating decisions and documentation, translating, and generally monitoring policy developments so as to provide an element of continuity and coordination in Council proceedings. This last task includes seeking to ensure a smooth transition between Presidencies by performing a liaising role with officials from the preceding, the incumbent and the incoming Presidential states.

In exercising many of its responsibilities, the Secretariat works particularly closely with the Council Presidency (see below). This is essential because key decisions about such matters as priorities, meetings and agendas are primarily in the hands of the Presidency. Before all Council meetings at all levels Secretariat officials give the Presidency a full briefing about subject content, the current state of play on the agenda items, and possible tactics – 'the Poles are isolated', 'there is strong resistance to this in Spain and Portugal, so caution is advised', 'a possible vote has been signalled in the agenda papers and, if taken, will find the necessary majority', and so on.

The extent to which Presidencies rely on the Secretariat varies considerably. Because of their more limited administrative resources, smaller member states tend to be more reliant but larger states also have much to gain by making use of the Secretariat's resources and its knowledge of what approaches are most likely to be effective in particular situations.

The main reason why Presidencies are sometimes a little reluctant to make too much use of the Secretariat is that there is a natural tendency for Presidencies to rely heavily on their own national officials as they seek to achieve a successful period of office by getting measures through. Something approaching a dual servicing of the Presidency is apparent in the way at Council meetings, at all levels, the President sits with officials from the General Secretariat on one side and national advisers on the other.

The Operation of the Council

The Council Presidency

The rotation system

Up to the entry into force of the Lisbon Treaty in December 2009, the Council Presidency rotated between the member states on a six-monthly basis: January until June, July until December. The rotation used to be in alphabetical order, but following the 2004 enlargement it was decided to arrange it in groupings of three states. Box 9.3 lists the Presidency rotation set for the years 2007–20.

The grouping of Presidencies into three states grew out of a long-standing practice of preceding, current and succeeding Presidencies working closely with one another. This practice – known as the troika, or the trio – developed partly to assist small member states when they occupied the Presidency, but mainly to try and improve continuity and enhance consistency between Presidencies.

The troika system was formalised and strengthened in a Declaration annexed to the Treaty of Lisbon, which stated that the Presidency would now 'be held by pre-established groups of three Member States for a period of 18 months' (see Document 9.1). The existing system of one state chairing all meetings for a six months period would, however, be retained, apart from for the Foreign Affairs Council which would be chaired by the High Representative of the Union for

---

Box 9.3

Rotation of Council Presidencies 2007–20

Germany	Jan–June	2007
Portugal	July–Dec	2007
Slovenia	Jan–June	2008
France	July–Dec	2008
Czech Republic	Jan–June	2009
Sweden	July–Dec	2009
Spain	Jan–June	2010
Belgium	July–Dec	2010
Hungary	Jan–June	2011
Poland	July–Dec	2011
Denmark	Jan–June	2012
Cyprus	July–Dec	2012
Ireland	Jan–June	2013
Lithuania	July–Dec	2013
Greece	Jan–June	2014
Italy	July–Dec	2014
Latvia	Jan–June	2015
Luxembourg	July–Dec	2015
Netherlands	Jan–June	2016
Slovakia	July–Dec	2016
Malta	Jan–June	2017
UK	July–Dec	2017
Estonia	Jan–June	2018
Bulgaria	July–Dec	2018
Austria	Jan–June	2019
Romania	July–Dec	2019
Finland	Jan–June	2020

Source: Official Journal of the European Union, L, 4 December 2007: 1–2.

Foreign Affairs and Security Policy (on the High Representative, see Chapters 6 and 21). In a discretion that was inserted particularly to assist very small member states with limited administrative resources, the three states in the Presidency group would be able to alter this arrangement if they so chose.

The Council Presidency system post-Lisbon thus is that the Presidency is held for eighteen months by groups of three member states, with each of the states assuming 'the lead' for six months. The groups are assembled and states assume the 'lead' position in the order as set out in Box 9.3. So, the first post-Lisbon Treaty group Presidency, which assumed office in January 2010, was composed of Spain, Belgium and Hungary, with Spain taking the lead from January–June 2010.

The tasks of the Presidency

The main tasks of the Presidency are as follows.

1 *To arrange (in close association with the General Secretariat) and to chair most Council meetings from ministerial level downwards.* As noted above, this task is undertaken by the lead Presidency state.

   Prior to the Seville summit (see above) the Presidency chaired virtually all Council meetings apart from a few committees and working parties that have a permanent chairman. However, as part of the Seville summit's streamlining of the Council structures it was decided that where it was clear that dossiers would be dealt with mainly during the next Presidency or where issues would be dealt with at ministerial level during the next Presidency, then some of the Council's sub-ministerial meetings – though not COREPER – should be chaired by the country holding the next Presidency. In the same spirit of trying to ensure that a single member state assumes responsibility for taking issues through the Council machinery, it was decided in the specific case of the examination of the EU's annual budget that all meetings would be chaired by the country holding the Presidency during the second six-month period of the year.

   The Lisbon Treaty introduced a further change to Council chairing arrangements by stipulating that meetings in the Foreign Affairs policy sphere, including ministerial-level meetings, would be chaired by the High Representative or his/her representative.

   As the chair of meetings, the Presidency has considerable – though not complete – control over how often Council bodies meet, over agendas, and over what happens during the course of meetings.

2 *To build a consensus for initiatives.* A successful Presidency is normally regarded as one that gets things done. This can usually only be achieved by extensive negotiating, persuading, manoeuvring, cajoling, mediating and bargaining with and between the member states, and with the Commission and the EP.

Document 9.1

The grouping of Council Presidencies as set out in Declaration 9 of the Treaty of Lisbon

Article 1

1 The Presidency of the Council, with the exception of the Foreign Affairs configuration, shall be held by pre-established groups of three Member States for a period of 18 months. The groups shall be made up on a basis of equal rotation among the Member States, taking into account their diversity and geographical balance within the Union.

2 Each member of the group shall in turn chair for a six-month period all configurations of the Council, with the exception of the Foreign Affairs configuration. The other members of the group shall assist the chair in all its responsibilities on the basis of a common programme. Members of the team shall decide alternative arrangements between themselves.

Source: Declaration 9 attached to the Treaty of Lisbon '... *concerning the European Council decision on the exercise of the Presidency of the Council'.*

As Tallberg has observed (2006, 2008), within the Council itself a number of factors have combined to increase the importance of 'the Presidency compromise'. Foremost amongst these factors are the increased range and complexity of EU business, the increased number of member states and therefore also of national preferences, and the increased availability of QMV – which has resulted in it becoming common practice for the Presidency to attempt to find a qualified majority and then work to bring the dissatisfied on board.

3 *To offer leadership.* Very much overlapping with the building of consensus task, Presidencies have a responsibility to offer leadership. As has just been shown, this can involve leading the way in efforts to forge acceptable deals between member states. But, it can also involve attempting to prioritise new issues and ensure existing issues are taken forward.

Work programmes are important frameworks via which Presidencies provide and organise leadership in issue areas. Each group Presidency issues an eighteen-month work programme before it enters office. So, France, the Czech Republic and Sweden issued an 89-page working document in June 2008 which outlined both general goals and also specific goals in respect of, for example, the bringing forward of policy programmes, the launching of legislative proposals, revisions to be made to exist-

ing legislation, and the lines to be pursued in upcoming international negotiations . This work programme was then followed up by work programmes from each of the three states as their turn came to take the chair. So, Sweden issued a 46-page work programme in June 2009 that identified tackling the economic crisis and the climate threat as the main overall challenges and that also identified a range of specific goals and intentions – regarding for example, the advancement of legislation – in some detail.

In unforeseen circumstances – such as responding to an external crisis like 9/11, or to an unforeseen economic problem like the world recession that took hold in 2008 – Presidency leadership may require initiating policy responses and cajoling the EU institutions and the member states to be proactive in responding to the problem in hand. During its Presidency in the second half of 2008, France was seen – and was generally praised – for offering strong leadership of this second kind as the depth of the economic recession became increasingly clear.

4 *To ensure continuity and consistency of policy development.* An important mechanism used for this purpose has been the troika, now formalised with the group Presidencies which, as Document 9.1 shows, are required to operate on the basis of a

common programme. This notion of a common programme builds on an increased attention to medium-term planning that has been in the making for some time: the Seville summit decided that more weight should be given to an annual operating programme of Council activities that would be proposed by the two next presidencies and finalised by the General Affairs Council every December; this programme would be set within the framework of three-year multi-annual strategic programmes adopted by the European Council and would include the political priorities for the year and a list of indicative agendas for the various formation of the Council.

5 *To represent the Council in dealings with outside bodies.* This task is exercised most frequently with regard to other EU institutions and with non-member countries in connection with external EU policies. Regarding the first of these, this particularly takes the form of ministers appearing before EP committees and, to a lesser extent, EP plenary sessions. Regarding the second, the Lisbon Treaty transfers some of this responsibility to the High Representative, though the Council Presidency retains an important external representative function in non CFSP/CSDP sectoral areas with important external dimensions – such as energy and environment.

Advantages and disadvantages of holding the Presidency

Holding the Presidency – especially in the post-Lisbon arrangements, the lead Presidency – has advantages and disadvantages. One obvious advantage is that there is considerable prestige and status associated with the position, with media focus and interest on the Presidency invariably being high. A second advantage is that because the occupation of the Presidency puts states at the very heart of EU affairs, Presidencies have the potential to do more than they can as ordinary member states to help shape and set the pace of EU policy priorities. The extent of this potential should not, however, be exaggerated for though Presidencies set out their priorities when they enter office, they do not start with a clean sheet but rather have to deal with much uncompleted business from previous Presidencies and with rolling work programmes. Furthermore, their time in office is relatively short,

and certainly for states in the chair six months is just not long enough for the full working-through of policy initiatives – especially if legislation is involved. And a third advantage is that there is some leeway for bringing Council positions closer to the positions of the Presidency. As Tallberg (2004: 1019) has put it, Presidencies can use their privileged access to information about states' preferences and their access to instruments of procedural control to 'steer negotiations away from their worst alternative and towards their preferred outcome'. Schalk *et al.* (2007) and Thomson (2008) confirm Talberg's finding about the ability of Presidency's to tilt decisional outcomes in their favour, though both stress that this is time dependent and only takes place in the closing stages of decisional proceedings. As Thomson describes it: 'Member states that hold the presidency when a legislative proposal is adopted as law pull decision outcomes towards their favoured policy positions' (Thomson, 2008: 611).

As for the disadvantages of holding the Presidency, one is the heavy administrative burdens that are attached to the job. To take just the chairing of meetings, during its Presidency in the first half of 2009 the Czech Presidency chaired 38 formal ministerial meetings and no less than 2,400 meetings of COREPER and working parties (*EUobserver*, 30 June 2009). The administrative burdens have, moreover, increased over the years as the EU has moved into an increasing number of policy areas and has acquired many more members. Indeed, it was the growing extent of the administrative burdens along with the greatly increased number of smaller member states that lay mainly behind the movement towards group Presidencies. A second disadvantage is that although, as has just been noted, there is some room for Presidencies to attempt to bring issues closer to their own preferred positions, it is generally expected that Presidencies will adopt a broadly consensual approach on disputed issues – which on some issues can limit the ability of governments to defend their own national interests. Such was the case in the first half of 1999 under the German Presidency and in the second half of 2005 under the UK Presidency, when both governments felt inhibited about over-pressing their dissatisfaction with the deals that emerged on the financial perspectives for the 2000–6 and 2007–13 periods respectively. And a third disadvantage is the blow to esteem and standing that is incurred when a state is judged to have run a poor Presidency. Member states generally viewed as having operated poor Presidencies in recent times are France (in the second half of 2000), Italy (in the second half of 2003), and the Czech Republic (in the first half of 2009).

The hierarchical structure

A hierarchy exists in the Council. As indicated above and as outlined in Box 9.4 it consists of: ministers – with the Foreign Affairs Council and to an extent also the Ecofin Council informally recognised as being the most senior Councils; COREPER and a few specialised high-level committees such as the SCA and the PSC; and committees and working parties. The European Council is also sometimes thought of as being part of this hierarchy, but in fact it is not properly part of the Council system, even though it does have the political capability of issuing what amount to instructions to the ministers and in certain circumstances is charged with making binding decisions.

The Council's hierarchical structure is neither tight nor rigidly applied. The General Affairs, the Foreign Affairs, and the Ecofin Councils are, for example, not empowered to issue instructions to other Council formations, whilst important committees and working parties can sometimes communicate directly with ministers. Nonetheless, the hierarchy does, for the most part, work. This is best illustrated by looking at the Council's procedures for dealing with a Commission proposal for a significant piece of legislation.

The *first stage* is initial examination of the

Box 9.4

The hierarchical structure of the Council

- The Ministers, who meet in ten formations
- COREPER I (Deputy Permanent Representatives), COREPER II (Permanent Representatives), and certain high-level committees – including the PSC and the SCA.
- Committees and working parties, of which there are about 150 of the latter in existence at any one time.

Box 9.5

Principal factors determining the progress of a proposal through the Council

- The urgency of the proposal.
- The controversiality of the proposal and support/opposition amongst the states.
- The extent to which the Commission has tailored its text to accommodate national objections/reservations voiced at the pre-proposal stage.
- The complexity of the proposal's provisions.
- The ability of the Commission to allay doubts by the way it gives clarifications and answers questions.
- The judgements made by the Commission on whether, or when, it should accept modifications to its proposals.
- The competence of the Presidency.
- The agility and flexibility of the participants to devise (usually through the Presidency and the Commission) and accept compromise formulae.
- The availability of, and willingness of the states to use, majority voting.

Commission's text. This is undertaken by a working party or, if it is of very broad application, several working parties. If no appropriate permanent working party exists, an *ad hoc* one is established.

As can be seen from Box 9.5, several factors can affect the progress of the proposal in the Council, from working party level upwards. They include the urgency, complexity and controversiality of the proposal, the competence and flexibility of the Commission as it explains and defends 'its' proposal, and the extent to which member states are able and willing to compromise on the contents of the proposal.

An influencing factor that has greatly increased in importance over the years is whether the proposal could be subject to qualified majority voting (QMV) when it appears before the ministers. Formal votes are not called below ministerial level, but the possibility of them being taken can affect the progress of a proposal at all levels. If a vote is not possible and unanimity is required, then working-party deliberations may take as long as is necessary to reach an agreement – which can mean months or even years. If, however, QMV is possible, delegations that find themselves isolated in the working party must anticipate the possibility of their state being out-voted when the ministers consider the proposal, and may therefore feel it necessary to engage in damage limitation. This usually involves adopting some combination of three strategies. First, if the proposal is judged to be important to national interests, then this is stressed during the working party's deliberations – in the hope that other delegations will take a sympathetic view and will either make concessions or not seek to press ahead too fast. Second, if the proposal is judged to be not too damaging or unacceptable, then attempts will be made to amend it, but it is unlikely that too much of a fuss will be made. Third, an attempt may be made to 'do a deal' or 'come to an understanding' with other delegations so that a blocking minority of states is created.

The General Secretariat of the Council is always pressing for progress and tries to ensure that a working party does not need to meet more than about four times to discuss any one proposal. But, if any significant contestation between states is involved on a proposal, it is highly probable that there will be at least seven or eight working-party meetings before the proposal is passed up the Council system. The first, and possibly also the second, meeting normally consists of a general discussion of key points. Subsequent meetings are then taken up with line-by-line examination of the Commission's text. If all goes well, a document is eventually produced indicating points of agreement and disagreement, and quite likely having attached to it reservations – in the form of footnotes – that states have entered to indicate that they are not yet in a position formally to commit themselves to the text or a part of it. (States may enter reservations at any stage of the Council process. These can vary from an indication that a particular clause of a draft text is not yet in an acceptable form, to a general withholding of approval until the text has been cleared by the appropriate national authorities.)

The *second stage* is the reference of the working party's document to COREPER – which in the case of Commission proposals for legislation is normally COREPER I – perhaps via one of the Council's high-level committees. Placed between the working parties and the ministers, COREPER acts as a sort of filtering agency for ministerial meetings. It attempts to clear as much of the ground as possible to ensure that only the most difficult and sensitive of matters detain the ministers in discussion. So when the conditions for the adoption of a measure have been met in a working party, COREPER is likely to confirm the working party's position and advance it to the ministers for formal enactment. If, however, agreement has not been reached by a working party, COREPER can do one of three things: try itself to resolve the issue (which its greater political status might permit); refer it back to the working party, perhaps with accompanying indications of where an agreement might be found; or pass it upwards to the ministers.

Most matters requiring a Council decision are resolved at working party or COREPER level. Hayes-Renshaw and Wallace (2006: 53) estimate that on average about 70 per cent of Council business is agreed at working party level and a further 15–20 per cent at COREPER level. Kuasmanen (1998), an official in the General Secretariat of the Council, gives similar figures, estimating that between 75–85 per cent of matters are resolved at committee and working party level, most of the remaining matters at COREPER level, leaving only about 5 per cent of issues requiring substantial discussion and decision at ministerial level. Häge (2008: 554) suggests rather different figures for decisions (taken in 2003) that he studied with '35 per cent of the legislative decisions … taken by the ministers themselves, about 22 per cent on the level of Coreper and the SCA, and approximately 43 per cent by working parties'. However, as even Häge himself partly concedes, the ministerial figures are almost certainly much too high and do not sufficiently differentiate between decision that are considered by ministers and those that are really taken by ministers.

Whatever progress proposals have made at working party and COREPER levels, formal adoption is only possible at ministerial level. Ministerial meetings thus constitute *the third and final stage* of the Council's procedure. Items on ministerial meeting agendas are grouped under two headings: 'A points' and 'B points'. Matters that have been agreed at COREPER level, and on which it is thought Council approval will be given without discussion, are listed as 'A points'. These can cover a range of matters – from routine 'administrative' decisions to controversial new legislation that was agreed in principle at a previous ministerial meeting but upon which a formal decision was delayed pending final clarification or tidying up. 'A points' do not necessarily fall within the policy competence of the particular Council that is meeting, but may have been placed on the agenda because the appropriate formation of the Council is not due to meet for some time. Ministers retain the right to raise objections to 'A points', and if any do so the proposal may have to be withdrawn and referred back to COREPER. Normally, however, 'A points' are quickly approved without debate. Such is the thoroughness of the Council system that ministers can assume 'A points' have been thoroughly checked in both Brussels and national capitals to ensure they are politically acceptable, legally sound, and not subject to scrutiny reservations. Ministers then proceed to consider 'B points', which may include items left over from previous meetings, matters that have not been possible to resolve at COREPER or working-party levels, or proposals that COREPER judges to be politically sensitive and hence requiring political decisions. All 'B points' will have been extensively discussed by national officials at lower Council levels, and on most of them a formula for an agreement will have been prepared for the ministers to consider.

*   *   *

Ministerial meetings can have very wide and mixed agendas, as Document 19.5 on pp. 348–9 illustrates. Four observations are particularly worth making about the sorts of agenda items that arise.

- There are variations regarding what ministers are expected to do. The range of possibilities includes the taking of final decisions, the adoption of common positions, the approval of negotiating mandates for the Commission, the resolution of problems that have caused difficulties at lower levels of the Council hierarchy, and – simply – the noting of progress reports.
- Some items concern very general policy matters, whilst others are highly specialised and technical in nature.
- Most items fall within the sectoral competence of the ministers who have been convened, but a few do not. 'Extra sectoral' items are usually placed on agendas when everything has been agreed, a decision needs to be taken, and the relevant sectoral

Council is not scheduled to meet in the immediate future.
- As well as policy issues, agenda items can also include administrative matters, such as appointments to advisory committees.

The position of the General Affairs Council, and of the GAERC before the Lisbon Treaty entered into force, suggests that there would, in certain circumstances – such as when a policy matter cuts across sectoral divisions, or when sectoral Councils cannot resolve key issues – be a fourth decision-making stage directed at 'pulling everything together'. In practice, recourse to such a stage has not been common, although on very sensitive and important matters it has sometimes occurred – as for example in 2005 when there were several rounds of negotiations on the 2007–13 financial perspective in the GAERC. It is possible that the remit given to the General Affairs Council by the Lisbon Treaty to ensure 'consistency in the work of the different Council configurations' (see above) will result in more systematic attempts to ensure there is effective policy coordination at ministerial level, but it certainly will not result in the formalisation of a new 'final' decision-making stage where decisions taken by all Council formations are 'weighed' against each other and given final clearance.

One problem for the General Affairs Council in seeking to undertake its Article 16.6 TEU responsibility of coordinating the work of the Council is that it has no legal seniority over other Council formations. A second problem is that members of the General Affairs Council, who as the Lisbon Treaty changes take effect are likely to increasingly consist of European Affairs Ministers, have no greater seniority in rank to their national colleagues in other Councils, and may even be junior to many. And a third problem is that sectoral Councils usually are resistant to their policy responsibilities being considered elsewhere, for that risks losing control of outcomes. As Van Schendelen has noted with regard to the Agriculture Council, sectoral ministers want to find their own solutions rather than refer dossiers to a 'cross-sectoral' Council formation 'where agricultural interests might be traded off against quite different ones' (Van Schendelen, 1996: 54).

This absence of clear Council leadership and of an authoritative coordinating mechanism has played a part in encouraging the European Council to assume responsibilities in relation to the Council of Ministers, even though it is not formally part of the Council hierarchy. Increasingly the Heads of Government at their meetings have gone beyond issuing general guidelines to the Council of Ministers, which was intended to be the normal limit of European Council–Council of Ministers relationships when the former was established in 1974. Summits have sometimes been obliged to try to resolve thorny issues that have been referred to them by the Council of Ministers, and have also had to seek to ensure that there is some overall policy direction and coherence in the work of the Council. The European Council can only go so far, however, in performing such problem-solving, leadership, and coordinating roles: partly because of the infrequency of its meetings; partly because some Heads of Government prefer to avoid getting too involved in detailed policy discussions; but, above all, because the national leaders are subject to the same national and political divisions as the ministers.

Decision-making procedures

Taking decisions

As is shown in Box 9.6, the treaties provide for three basic ways in which the Council can take decisions: by unanimity, by qualified majority vote, or by simple majority vote.

- *Unanimity* used to be the normal requirement when a new policy was being initiated or an existing policy framework was being modified or further developed. However, treaty reforms since the SEA have greatly reduced the circumstances in which a unanimity requirement applies and it is now confined to just a few policy areas and types of decisions. Included amongst these are policy directional decisions within the framework of the CFSP/CSDP, enlargement decisions, 'constitutional' decisions, and many decisions with financial implications – including all those touching on taxation. Unanimity is also required when the Council wishes to amend a Commission legislative proposal against the Commission's wishes.

  Abstentions do not constitute an impediment to the adoption of Council decisions that require unanimity. Furthermore, the Amsterdam Treaty

---

Box 9.6

Decision-making in the Council

Ministers may take decisions in one of three ways:

- By *unanimity*. Although rounds of treaty reform have greatly reduced the number of decisions that require unanimity, it still applies to many types of decision – including all major decisions in such key policy areas as foreign, defence, enlargement, and taxation.
- By *qualified majority*. Since the Nice Treaty and until 2014 QMV contains the requirement of a double majority and the possibility of a triple majority: a) a minimum of 255 of the 345 weighted votes; b) the qualified majority must include a majority of the member states if the vote is on a Commission proposal and in other cases two thirds of the member states; c) a member state may request verification that the member states in the qualified majority represent at least 62 per cent of the EU population.
- By *simple majority*. This applies only to relatively minor and procedural matters.

In practice, there is always a preference for consensus whatever procedure applies.

---

provided for 'constructive abstentionism' under the CFSP pillar, whereby an abstaining state 'shall not be obliged to apply the decision, but shall accept that the decision commits the Union. ... If the members of the Council abstaining in this way represent at least one third of the Member States comprising at least one third of the population of the Union, the decision shall not be adopted' (Article 31 in the post-Lisbon Treaty TEU).

- *Qualified majority voting* now applies to most types of decision where legislation is being made and to some – mainly executive – CFSP/CSDP decisions.

  Since 1 November 2004, the rules for QMV that were incorporated into the Treaty of Nice (see Box 5.5) as part of the EU's preparations for enlargement have applied. The making of these rules were described in Chapter 5 and the rules themselves are set out in Box 9.6 and Box 9.7.

Qualified majority voting: voting rules and national voting weights*

Where the measure being voted on must, under the Treaties, be based on a Commission proposal, a qualified majority consists of at least 255 votes in favour representing a majority of the member states. In other cases, the 255 votes must represent at least two-thirds of the member states.

A member of the European Council or the Council of Ministers may request that a check is made to ensure that the member states comprising the qualified majority represent at least 62 per cent of the total population of the Union. If it does not, the measure may not be accepted.

The voting weights of member states are as follows:

Germany, France, Italy, United Kingdom	29
Spain, Poland	27
Romania	14
Netherlands	13
Belgium, Czech Republic, Greece, Hungary, Portugal	12
Austria, Bulgaria, Sweden	10
Denmark, Ireland, Lithuania, Slovakia, Finland	7
Cyprus, Estonia, Latvia, Luxembourg, Slovenia	4
Malta	3
TOTAL	**345**

* In the EU-27.

Key features of the QMV arrangement post-Nice as compared with pre-Nice include:

- An increase in the differentials of the voting weights of member states, with the position of larger states enhanced a little.
- A small increase in the threshold for a qualified majority – from the pre-Nice 71.3 per cent to 73.9 per cent in the EU-27.
- The creation of two additional criteria when qualified majorities exist, which have the effect of creating the need for virtually a triple majority. The first of these additional criteria requires that QMV decisions on Commission proposals must be supported by at least a majority of states, and on Council proposals must be supported by at least two-thirds of states. This criterion is helpful to small member states. The second additional criterion requires that a qualified majority must comprise at least 62 per cent of the Union's total population when verification to this effect is requested by a member state. This criterion assists the position of large member states.

As was described in Chapter 6, and more particularly in Box 6.6, the Lisbon Treaty abolishes the weighted votes and triple-majority system and replaces it with a simpler double-majority system in which a qualified majority exists if at least 55 per cent of the member states representing at least 65 per cent of the EU population are in favour of a proposal. However, this system does not enter into force until November 2014, and until 2017 a member state may insist that in a particular vote the Nice voting rules should still apply. Furthermore, states in a QMV minority that meet certain conditions can call for the taking of a decision to be delayed and for draft laws to be reconsidered before they are adopted.

- *Simple majority voting*, in which all states have one vote each, is used mainly for procedural purposes and, since February 1994, for anti-dumping and anti-subsidy tariffs within the context of the Common Commercial Policy (CCP).

Until the mid-1980s, proposals were not usually pushed to a vote in the Council when disagreements between the states existed, even when majority voting was permissible under the treaties. A major reason for this was the so-called Luxembourg Compromise of 1966, which was a political deal between the member states that was interpreted as meaning that, whatever the treaties might say about voting arrangements, any state had the right to exercise a veto on questions that affected its vital national interests – and states themselves determined when such interests were at stake. (For a fuller account of the Luxembourg Compromise and its consequences, see the fifth edition of this book, and Teasdale 1995). However, though majority voting has now come to be used and the Luxembourg Compromise is all but dead, the member states still prefer to take decisions by unanimity. They do so because it is recognised that the functioning and development of the EU is likely to be enhanced if policy-making processes are consensual rather than conflictual. Thus, national authorities are unlikely to undertake the necessary task of transposing EU directives into national law with much enthusiasm if the directives are perceived as domestically damaging, or if they are imposed on a dissatisfied state following a majority vote in the Council. Nor is it likely that national bureaucracies will be helpful about implementing unwanted legislation. More generally, the over-use of majority voting on important and sensitive matters could well create grievances that could have disruptive implications right across the EU's policy spectrum.

For good reasons, as well as perhaps some bad, decision-making in the Council thus usually proceeds on the understanding that difficult and controversial decisions are not imposed on dissenting states without full consideration being given to the reasons for their opposition. When it is clear that a state or states have serious difficulties with a proposal, they are normally allowed time. They may well be put on the defensive, asked fully to explain their position, pressed to give way or at least to compromise, but the possibility of resolving an impasse by a vote is not the first port of call. Usually the item is held over for a further meeting, with the hope that in the meantime informal meetings or perhaps COREPER will find the basis for a solution. All states, and not just the foremost advocates of retention of the veto – initially France and since the early 1980s the UK – accept that this is the only way Council business can be done without risking major divisions.

But though there are good reasons for preferring consensus, it came to be accepted from the early 1980s that the unanimity principle could not be applied too universally or too rigidly. It was recognised that QMV would need to be increasingly used, and in practice it has been so. Several interrelated factors explain this increased use of majority voting.

- Attitudes have changed. There has been an increasing recognition, even amongst the most rigid defenders of national rights and interests, that decision-making by unanimity is a recipe not only for procrastination and delay, but often for unsatisfactory, or even no, decision-making. The situation whereby consensus remains the rule even on issues where states would not object too strongly to being voted down, has come to be seen as unsustainable in the face of the manifest need for the EU to become efficient and dynamic in order, for example, to assist its industries to compete successfully on world markets.

- The 'legitimacy' and 'mystique' of the Luxembourg Compromise were dealt a severe blow in May 1982 when, for the first time, an attempt to invoke the Compromise was over-ridden. The occasion was an attempt by the UK government to veto the annual agricultural prices settlement by proclaiming a vital national interest. The other states did not believe that such an interest was at stake and took the view that Britain was attempting to use agricultural prices to force a more favourable outcome on concurrent negotiations over UK budgetary contributions.

- By increasing the number and variety of interests and views represented in the Council, EU enlargements have made unanimity all the more difficult to achieve and hence have increased the necessity for majority voting.

- All treaties since the SEA have extended the number of policy areas in which majority voting is constitutionally permissible (see Part II for details). Moreover, the discussions that have accompanied treaty reforms have been based on the assumption that the new voting provisions would be used.

- In July 1987, the General Affairs Council, in accordance with an agreement it had reached in December 1986, formally amended the Council's Rules of Procedure. Among the changes was a relaxation of the circumstances by which votes could be initiated: whereas previously only the President could call for a vote, since the amended Rules came into effect it has been the case that any national representative and the Commission also, have the right, and a vote must be taken if a simple majority agrees.

Figures on the use of QMV are, in fact, lower than might be supposed, with analyses indicating that votes take place on only between 10 and 15 per cent of all Council decisions where QMV is possible. Wolfgang Wessels, for example, puts the figure at 10 per cent (Wessels, 2001: 206–9); Jean-Paul Jacqué, a director in the Council's Legal Service, says that between 1999 and 2003, 85 per cent of the decisions that could have been taken by QMV were taken by unanimity (Jacqué,

2004: 316); and Mikko Mattila calculates that in the May 2004–December 2006 period – that is, post the 2004 enlargement – 90 per cent of all Council decisions were taken unanimously, with the figure for legislative acts being 85.8 per cent (Mattila, 2008: 27–30). Most votes are on agriculture and fisheries and internal market issues.

Such low figures for the use of votes, which are confirmed by other observers – see, for example, Naurin and Wallace (2008: especially chapters 3 and 4), Hagemann and Clerck-Sachsse (2007), and Hayes-Renshaw and Wallace (2006) – do not, however, provide a full picture of the impact of QMV on voting behaviour in the Council. This is because what really amounts to majority voting can occur without a formal vote being taken. Often referred to as implicit majority voting, this can take the form of a state that is opposed to a proposal that otherwise commands general support preferring to try to extract concessions through negotiation – perhaps at working party or COREPER stage – rather than run the risk of pressing for a vote and then finding itself out-voted. Or it can take the form of the Presidency announcing that 'we appear to have the necessary majority here', and this being left unchallenged by a dissenting state and therefore not formally voted on: unless an important point of principle or a damaging political consequence is at stake, a state in a minority may prefer not to create too much of a fuss. Or, in a practice that has increased since the 2004 enlargement, implicit majority voting can take the form of a government that is opposed to a proposal registering its opposition not in a dissenting vote but in a dissenting statement that is attached to the minutes of the Council meeting. Hagemann and Clerck-Sachsse (2007: 14) estimate that if dissenting statements are added to dissenting votes, then in 2006 as much as 45 per cent of legislation adopted by the Council was opposed by at least one government.

So, the importance of QMV lies not only in the number of votes that are held. Its existence affects Council processes in many ways, most obviously in that when it is available – and its 'reach' has spread greatly over the years – it not only permits votes to be taken but it also forces states that are dissatisfied with a proposal to look for deals with other states and/or for ways to protect themselves. Where, by contrast, unanimity applies, states can be encouraged to grandstand and to look for 'compensations' in areas that have little to do with the proposal in hand.

That all said, the impact of QMV should not be overstated. As Box 9.5 shows, many factors combine to determine the progress of proposals through the Council. Crucially, a strong preference for consensual decision-making remains a key feature of Council decision-making processes, and can be expected to remain so. Quite apart from the fact that unanimity is still required by the treaties in some important areas, there continues to be a strong preference for trying to reach general agreements where 'important', 'sensitive', and 'political' matters, as opposed to 'technical' matters, are being considered. This may involve delay, but the duty of the national representatives at all Council levels is not only to reach decisions but also to defend national interests.

The conduct of meetings

The formal processes by which Council meetings are conducted and business is transacted are broadly similar at ministerial, COREPER, and working party levels.

With working parties normally attended by at least 100 people and COREPER and ministerial meetings by about 150, meetings have to be held in large rooms, as photograph 9.1 shows. At one end or one side of the meeting table sits the state that is in the Presidency chair – whose delegation is led by the most senior figure present from the state; at the other end or side sit the Commission representatives; and ranged between the Presidency and the Commission are the representatives of the member states, with national delegations sitting together. The delegation from the country holding the Presidency chair sits to the right of, but separate from, the Presidency team.

As indicated earlier, the Presidency plays a key role in fixing the agenda of Council meetings, both in terms of content and the order in which items are considered. The room for manoeuvre available to the Presidency should not, however, be exaggerated, for quite apart from time constraints there are several other factors that serve to limit options and actions. For example, it is difficult to exclude from the agenda of Council meetings items that are clearly of central interest or need resolution; the development of rolling programmes means that much of the agenda of many meetings is largely fixed; and anyone in a COREPER or a ministerial meeting can insist that a matter is discussed provided the required notice is given. Therefore, a Presidency cannot afford to be too ambitious or the

Photo 9.1 Agriculture and Fisheries Council, 20 November 2009

six-month term of the state in the chair will probably come to be seen as a failure. With this in mind, the normal pattern for an incoming chair of a reasonably important sectoral Council is to take the view that of, say, eight proposed directives in his or her policy area, he or she will try to get four particular ones through. This is then reflected in the organisation of Council business, so that by the end of the six-month term two may have been adopted by the Council while another two may be at an advanced stage.

At ministerial level, Council meetings can often appear to be chaotic affairs: as indicated above, not counting interpreters there can be up to 150 people in the room – with each national delegation represented by a team of perhaps four or five at any one time, the Commission by a similar number, and the Presidency being made up of both General Secretariat and national officials; participants frequently change – with ministers often arriving late or leaving early, and officials coming and going in relation to items on the agenda; ministers are constantly being briefed by officials as new points are raised; there are huddles of delegations during breaks; requests for adjournments and postponements are made to enable further infor-

mation to be sought and more consideration to be given; and communications may be made with national capitals for clarifications or even, occasionally, for authorisation to adopt revised negotiating positions. Not surprisingly, delegations that are headed by ministers with domestic political weight, that are well-versed in EU ways, that have mastered the intricacies of the issues under consideration, and that can think quickly on their feet, are particularly well-placed to exercise influence.

A device that used to be employed at Council meetings, especially when negotiations were making little progress, was the *tour de table* procedure, whereby the chair invited each delegation to give a summary of its thinking on the matter under consideration. This ensured that the discussion was not totally dominated by a few, and more importantly it allowed the position of each member state to be established. It could thus help to reveal possible grounds for agreement and provide useful guidance to the President as to whether a compromise was possible or whether an attempt should be made to proceed to a decision. Enlargement has made the use of this procedure largely impractical because it is so time consuming. Presidencies now tend to be very cautious about using the procedure unless there seems to be no other way forward, and even then only representatives from states opposed to a proposal are encouraged to speak.

Enlargement has also had another effect on the conduct of meetings: by greatly increasing the number of people who attend it has made meetings more formal. It is not practically possible to engage in 'real' negotiations in a room of 150 or so, with microphones being used, with a considerable physical distance often between people who are addressing each other, and with a heavy reliance on translators. The fact is that since the 2004 enlargement an increasing amount of time at Council meetings – especially at ministerial level meetings – is taken up with delegations virtually reading out what amount to pre-prepared statements.

The nature of meetings thus places a considerable burden on the Presidency to find a way forward on disputed matters. Much of this task is most fruitfully undertaken between and before formal meetings and can take the form of, for example, leaning on the Commission to amend its proposal, persuading a disgruntled state to take a softer line, and seeking to isolate the most 'hard-line' state in the hope that it will back down. But, the Presidency can use formal meetings too. So, for example, an astute and sensitive chairperson is often able to judge when a delegation that is causing difficulties is not terribly serious: when, perhaps, it is being awkward for domestic political reasons and will not ultimately stand in the way of a decision being made. A poor chairperson, on the other hand, may allow a proposal to drag on, or may rush it to such an extent that a state which, given time, would have agreed to a compromise may feel obliged to dig in its heels.

Informal processes and relationships

A final feature of Council decision-making procedures, that has already been suggested but merits being made explicit, is the extremely important role of informal processes and relationships. Three examples will be taken to demonstrate this.

First, many understandings and agreements are reached at the lunches and dinners that are very much a part of ministerial meetings. These meals are attended only by ministers and a minimal number of translators (most ministers can converse directly with one another, usually in French or English).

Second, when difficulties arise in ministerial negotiations a good chairperson will make advantageous use of scheduled or requested breaks in proceedings to explore possibilities for a settlement. This may involve holding off-the-record discussions with a delegation that is holding up an agreement, or it may take the form of a *tour* of key delegations – perhaps in the company of the relevant Commissioner and a couple of officials – to ascertain 'real' views and fall-back positions.

Third, what happens between meetings, at all levels, is frequently crucial in shaping and determining decisional outcomes. When problems arise, EU policy practitioners – in the institutions, in the national Permanent Representations, and in national capitals too – are in frequent contact with one another via telephone, email, and informal conversations, Indeed, many of the policy practitioners who are based in Brussels come to know each other extremely well as a result of dealing with the same *dossiers* and attending the same meetings. They may use these contacts – which can become social as well as professional – to assist with the resolution of policy difficulties. So, for example, national officials based in the Permanent Representations may know their counterparts in other Permanent Representations well enough to be able to judge when a state is posturing and when it is serious, and when and how a deal may be possible. A sort of code language may even be used between officials to signal their position on proposals. So if, for example, a national representative declares that 'this is very important for my minister', or 'my minister is very strongly pressurised on this', the other participants recognise that a signal is being given that further deliberations are necessary at their level if more serious difficulties are to be avoided when the ministers gather.

Concluding Remarks

In recent years a number of important reforms have been made to the structure and functioning of the Council. These have sought to deal with the perceived problems of power being too dispersed, insufficient cohesion between and sometimes within sectoral Councils, and decision-making processes still often being rather cumbersome and slow. The most important of the changes have been the increased use of majority voting, the reduction in the number of Council formations, and the strengthening of the troika and its formalisation into group Presidencies.

Arguably the reforms have still not gone far enough. Many have argued that what is most needed to deal with at least some of the weaknesses is the creation of a 'super' Council of European Ministers, armed with the authority to impose an overall policy pattern on subsidiary sectoral Councils. However, though such a Council could indeed be useful for identifying priorities and knocking a few heads together, it would be unwise to hold out too many hopes for it, even if the practical obstacles to its establishment could be overcome. For, other than at the most general of policy levels, any dream of the national politicians who are at the apex of the Council system being able to rationally formulate and implement clear and overarching policy frameworks in some sort of detached way that would serve the 'EU interest' just does not accord with political realities.

Chapter 10

The European Council

Origins and Development

Although no provision was made in the Founding Treaties for summit meetings of Heads of Government, a few such gatherings did occur in the 1960s and early 1970s. At the Paris summit in 1974 it was decided to institutionalise these meetings with the establishment of what soon became known as the European Council.

The main reason for the creation of the European Council was a growing feeling that the Community was failing to respond adequately or quickly enough to new and increasingly difficult challenges. Neither the Commission, whose position had been weakened by the intergovernmental emphasis on decision-making that was signalled by the Luxembourg Compromise, nor the Council of Ministers, which was handicapped both by sectoralism and by its practice of proceeding only on the basis of unanimity, were providing the necessary leadership. A new focus of authority was seen as being necessary in order to make the Community more effective, both domestically and internationally. What was needed, argued France's President Giscard d'Estaing, who with West Germany's Chancellor Schmidt was instrumental in establishing the European Council, was a body that would bring the Heads of Government together on a relatively informal basis to exchange ideas, to further mutual understanding at the highest political level, to give direction to policy development, and perhaps sometimes to break deadlocks and clear logjams. It was not anticipated that the leaders would concern themselves with the details of policy.

The formal creation of the European Council was very simple: a few paragraphs were issued as part of the Paris communiqué. The key paragraphs of the communiqué are set out in Document 10.1.

Two points about the communiqué are particularly worth emphasising. First, it was vague and left important questions unanswered, especially regarding the precise role and functioning of the European Council. Second, it had no treaty standing. It announced a political agreement between the national leaders but it did not formally or legally integrate the European Council into the Community framework.

The European Council was thus part of the 'unofficial' approach to integration – that was also seen in the 1960s and 1970s with the Luxembourg Compromise and the development of foreign policy cooperation via European Political Cooperation (EPC) – rather than the 'official' treaty-based approach. Over the years, however, there has been something of a 'constitutionalisation' of the position and role of the European Council, albeit on a cautious basis. This has occurred in six steps. First, declarations by the European Council itself

Document 10.1

Extracts from the communiqué of the 1974 Paris summit

Recognising the need for an overall approach to the internal problems involved in achieving European unity and the external problems facing Europe, the Heads of Government consider it essential to ensure progress and overall consistency in the activities of the Communities and in the work on political cooperation.

The Heads of Government have therefore decided to meet, accompanied by the Ministers of Foreign Affairs, three times a year and, whenever necessary, in the Council of the Communities and in the context of political cooperation.

The administrative secretariat will be provided for in an appropriate manner with due regard for existing practices and procedures.

(The full communiqué is reproduced in Harryvan and van der Harst, 1997: 181–3.)

in the late 1970s and early 1980s – notably London (1977) and Stuttgart (1983) – did something, though not a great deal, to clarify its role. Second, in 1986 the European Council was given legal recognition for the first time via the SEA, though only in two short paragraphs that were confined to clarifying membership and reducing the minimum number of meetings per year from three to two. The paragraphs were not incorporated into the Community Treaties. Third, the Maastricht Treaty, expanding on the SEA, contained three 'sets of references' to the European Council: in the TEU it was assigned responsibility for identifying the general direction of the EU's development and was provided with important powers in the CFSP pillar; in the TEC it was given certain duties and decision-making powers in respect of EMU. Fourth, the Amsterdam Treaty confirmed the Maastricht provisions in respect of its general directional role and with regard to EMU, and greatly strengthened the European Council's position in respect of the CFSP. Fifth, the Nice Treaty gave *de jure* status to the *de facto* situation wherein the European Council nominated the person who was to be put forward for the position of President of the Commission. Sixth, the Lisbon Treaty established the European Council as a fully fledged EU institution. (hitherto it had been omitted from the list of EU institutions under Article 5 TEU – now, in revised form, Article 13 TEU) and it created the potentially very important new position of semi-permanent European Council President.

It might have been thought that the limited treaty base of the European Council – not recognised until the SEA, largely outside the Community framework, and a lack of legal clarity about its roles – would have hindered the ability of the European Council to exercise influence and establish itself as an important decision-making institution. In practice it has not been a hindrance at all because the status of those who attend meetings – particularly the national leaders – is such that there is little to stop them from deciding amongst themselves what the European Council will and will not do. As a result, the evolution, operation and influence of the European Council have owed much more to the preferences of the participants and to political and practical necessities than they have to treaty stipulations. Indeed, in order to give itself maximum flexibility and manoeuvrability, the European Council has been careful to avoid being based on or subject to tight treaty rules and requirements. It has been careful also to place itself mainly (though not exclusively) in the TEU – which, until the Lisbon Treaty, was largely beyond the jurisdiction of the Court of Justice of the European Union – rather than in the TEC (now TFEU).

The opportunity to decide for itself what it does has resulted in the European Council exercising a number of roles and performing a number of functions. The precise nature of these roles and functions are explained in some detail later in the chapter, so suffice it to note here that they add up to an extremely important and impressive portfolio. Indeed, they put the European Council at the very heart of EU decision making – not on a day-to-day basis in the manner of the other four main EU institutions, but rather from a more distanced position where it is centrally involved in setting the overall parameters of the EU system. Final and legally binding EU decisions may be made by other EU institutions, but major political decisions concerning the institutional and policy development of the EU are now almost invariably taken by, or at least are channelled through and given clearance by, the European Council.

Membership

Prior to the Lisbon Treaty there were two 'tiers' of membership of the European Council: the Heads of State or Government of the member states and the President of the Commission; and the Foreign Ministers of the member states and one other member of the Commission who attended to provide assistance.

From the late 1990s, it became increasingly common for certain sectoral ministers, especially Ecofin Ministers, to also make an appearance at summits when agenda items warranted it. In response to this practice and to make for greater flexibility in the operation of summits, the 2002 Seville summit made provision for Foreign Ministers to be replaced in the meeting room by other ministers for specific agenda items. It did so simply by specifying that 'Each delegation shall have two seats in the meeting room' (European Council, 2002a: Annex III – Rules for Organising the Proceedings of the European Council).

This change at Seville highlights a practice that has been always been part of European Council meetings: in an attempt to encourage a more open and relaxed atmosphere than applies in Council of Ministers meetings, there has been a tight restriction on the number of people who are allowed to be present in formal summit sessions. Prior to changes made by the Lisbon Treaty, the only people permitted access to the meeting room were: the two formal members per delegation (with sectoral ministers sometimes replacing Foreign Ministers); the Council Secretary General (who pre-Lisbon was also the High Representative for the CFSP); the Council Deputy Secretary General; the Secretary General of the Commission; a very small number of Council Presidency, Council Secretariat, and Commission senior officials (sitting back from the main table); national civil servants, but only on the basis of one adviser per country being allowed entrance at any one time; and interpreters.

The Lisbon Treaty changed this situation by making two important changes to the membership of the European Council. First, as can be seen in Document 10.2, it more clearly restricts membership

---

Document 10.2

The Treaty Provisions on the Membership of the European Council

1 The European Council shall provide the Union with the necessary impetus for its development and shall define the general political directions and priorities thereof. It shall not exercise legislative functions.
2 The European Council shall consist of the Heads of State or Government of the Member States, together with its President and the President of the Commission. The High Representative of the Union for Foreign Affairs and Security Policy shall take part in its work.
3 The European Council shall meet twice every six months, convened by its President. When the agenda so requires, the members of the European Council may decide each to be assisted by a minister and, in the case of the President of the Commission, by a member of the Commission. When the situation so requires, the President shall convene a special meeting of the European Council.
4 Except where the Treaties provide otherwise, decisions of the European Council shall be taken by consensus.

Source: Article 15, *Treaty on European Union* (post-Lisbon Treaty).

than hitherto had been the case to just one tier, consisting of the Heads of State or Government plus the European Council President and the President of the Commission. The phrase 'Heads of State *or* Government' is used (as it always has been) because in a few member states – including Cyprus, Finland, France, Lithuania and, on an internally contested basis, the Czech Republic and Poland – Heads of State are also Heads of Government or have certain functions normally associated with Heads of Government. Other ministers – though not now with Foreign Ministers given any precedence – can still attend summit sessions, but more specifically only to assist and when the agenda so requires. Second, the occupant of the Lisbon Treaty-created post of European Council President (see below) becomes a European Council member, though like the European Commission President, he cannot (under Article 235 TFEU) cast a vote on the (relatively rare) occasions when the European Council takes a decision by a vote. The Lisbon Treaty also specifies that the occupant of

the new position it created of High Representative of the Union for Foreign Affairs and Security Policy will take part in the work of the European Council, but he/she is not made a member of it.

As a result of the Lisbon Treaty changes, the people present in formal summit sessions has been altered in the following ways: there will be more occasions when sectoral ministers rather than Foreign Ministers accompany the Heads of State or Government; there probably will be more sessions when Heads meet without ministerial accompaniment; the European Council President will be present and his/her small team of officials (drawn from the General Secretariat of the Council) will replace the officials of the (previously rotating) Council Presidency; and the High Representative will attend for external affairs agenda items.

But though physical presence in the summit meeting room is kept as tight as possible, several hundred officials attend European Council meetings. Each member state has a suite in the vicinity of the summit

Photo 10.1 Meeting room for the European Council, October 2009

© COUNCIL OF THE EUROPEAN UNION

meeting room, which is available to its official delegation and from which officials may be summoned as required. At Seville it was decided that official delegations would be restricted in size to twenty people. However, these are supplemented by numerous other officials who make up what are customarily described as the non-official or technical delegations.

The European Council membership is thus based on the Council of Ministers model in the sense that it is made up of national delegations, plus the Commission. Unlike in the Council of Ministers, however, the participants in formal European Council sessions are not accompanied by teams of national officials. The original thinking behind this restriction on access to the summit meeting room was that it would encourage relaxed informality, and in any event was not strictly necessary as the European Council was not a law maker. However, in practice it has proved difficult to achieve the desired mood, not least because of the increased number of participants following EC/EU enlargements and the increased importance of decisions taken at European Council meetings. As photograph 10.1 shows, the physical setting of summits does not encourage informality!

The European Council President

The creation of the post

Prior to the Lisbon Treaty, the Presidency of the European Council was held concurrently with the Presidency of the Council of Ministers. So, it rotated between the member states every six months. As with the Council of Ministers Presidency, this arrangement had advantages and disadvantages. The advantages included that every six months there was the possibility for a new Head of State or Government to inject an innovative dynamism into EU processes at the very top level and also that every few years (though with enlargements the gaps between the years greatly increased) every member state was given its chance to be 'in the spotlight'. The disadvantages included the disruptions that never-ending turnovers created, the enormous burden placed on the shoulders of the national leader of the state occupying the Presidency,

and the high dependence of the European Council on the competence of a person who was in the position of European Council chair not because of his/her credentials for doing the job but rather as a side-effect of national politics.

The participants in the 2002–03 Constitutional Convention took the view that the disadvantages of the existing situation outweighed the advantages and opted to discard the rotating European Council Presidency and replace it with a new post of semi-permanent and appointed European Council President. The Convention's recommendation on this matter was not seriously challenged in either of the subsequent IGCs that led to the Lisbon Treaty. Certainly there were voices expressing reservations, based principally on concerns that the new post would result in (further) confusion over the location of leadership in the EU, would weaken the position of the Commission and especially that of its President, and would signal a shift towards greater control by the member states of EU affairs. But, these two latter concerns worked 'both ways' and were important reasons why some national governments supported the creation of the new post. France and the UK were especially to the fore in wanting to strengthen the institution position of the European Council and to see greater European Council control over the political direction of the Union.

The Lisbon Treaty accordingly provided for the creation of a new post of European Council President.

The treaty provisions on the post

The key Treaty provisions on the European Council President post are reproduced in Document 10.3.

Five features of these Treaty provisions especially merit comment.

First, the range of responsibilities and tasks of the President are not at all clear. What, for example, does the phrase 'drive forward its work' mean? Clearly, the role to be played by the President will depend greatly on the personality and ambitions of the incumbent and on the manoeuvrability and flexibility he/she is given by the member states.

Second, other than being able to convene special meetings of the European Council, the President is given no specific powers. He/she does, however, potentially have considerable authority, based on the status

---

Document 10.3

The Treaty provisions on the President of the European Council

5 The European Council shall elect its President, by a qualified majority, for a term of two and a half years, renewable once. In the event of an impediment or serious misconduct, the European Council can end the President's term of office in accordance with the same procedure.

6 The President of the European Council:
  a) shall chair it and drive forward its work;
  b) shall ensure the preparation and continuity of the work of the European Council in cooperation with the President of the Commission, and on the basis of the work of the General Affairs Council;
  c) shall endeavour to facilitate cohesion and consensus within the European Council;
  d) shall present a report to the European Parliament after each of the meetings of the European Council.

The President of the European Council shall, at his level and in that capacity, ensure the external representation of the Union on issues concerning its common foreign and security policy, without prejudice to the powers of the High Representative of the Union for Foreign Affairs and Security Policy.

The President of the European Council shall not hold a national office.

Source: Article 15, *Treaty on European Union* (Post-Lisbon Treaty).

---

of those who have both made the selection and who the incumbent is challenged to both lead and serve.

Third, the stipulation that the European Council President 'shall not hold a national office' does not, of course, mean that he/she cannot have held such an office. If a very senior such national office has been held and has been so with distinction, this is likely to bolster the authority of the incumbent and also to make him/her well tuned to what is possible, and by what means.

Fourth, the President is elected to office by the members of the European Council by qualified majority vote. In practice, it is probable that the use of QMV will be avoided if at all possible since the authority of the President clearly would be undermined if it is known that he/she is, even before assuming office, not supported by the governments of all member states.

Fifth, there is the potential for tensions, and even turf disputes, between the President, the European Commission President, and the High Representative. Regarding relations with the European Commission President, whilst the European Council President is restricted to operating within the framework of the European Council activities the fact is, as will be shown below, that these activities cover virtually all spheres of EU operations. Regarding relations with the High Representative, the requirement that the European Council President 'shall, at his level and in that capacity, ensure the external representation of the Union' is a recipe for obvious 'who does what' problems and uncertainties.

The appointment of the first occupant of the post

The Lisbon Treaty was signed in December 2007 but, for reasons that were explained in Chapter 6, was not ratified until November 2009. Since no one could be formally nominated to the position of European Council President until after the ratification was completed – not least because that would be seen to be presumptuous and might even endanger ratification – there was consequently a period of almost two years during which the inter-related questions of what should be the nature of the post and who should be appointed to it were much discussed.

In broad terms, there were two views taken by member state governments on these questions, with various shadings in-between and with views sometimes

Photo 10.2 Herman van Rompuy, President of the European Council, December 2009–

As soon as the Lisbon Treaty had been ratified in early November 2009, the Swedish Prime Minister, Fredrick Reinfeldt, in his capacity as head of government of the state holding the Council Presidency, began informal soundings with the other heads of government and convened an informal summit. At the summit, on November 19, the meeker – consolidationist, apologists would say – view prevailed and Van Rompuy was appointed, by consensus. The member states most strongly supporting his appointment were many of the EU's smaller states – which feared a strong President could work too much in the interests of the larger member states – plus, crucially, France and Germany – whose leaders seemed to have become increasingly concerned that they could be overshadowed on the European stage by too powerful a European Council President.

The unanimity of Van Rompuy's appointment was facilitated by being part of a package deal in which he – a centre-right and male politician from a small member state – was 'balanced' by the appointment at the same summit of Catherine Aston – a centre-left and female politician from a large member state (the UK) – to the new post of High Representative of the Union for Foreign Affairs and Security Policy.

being hedged according to the possible incumbent. In one what might be called the 'bolder' view, the post was seen as needing to provide the EU with more vigorous leadership, and in particular as enabling the EU to project itself more effectively and dynamically on the world stage. Those taking this view inclined to appointing a 'big hitter', which was normally taken as requiring a serving or a former head of government with a forceful personality from a large member state. The names most commonly mentioned in this context were the former Spanish Prime Minister, Felipe González, and the former UK Prime Minister, Tony Blair. In what might be called the 'meeker' view, what was thought to be needed was a competent politician who had displayed good mediating and chairing skills in national, and perhaps also EU, politics. Amongst names mentioned in this context were the Dutch Prime Minister, Jan Peter Balkenende, the Luxembourg Prime Minister, Jean-Claude Juncker, and, late in the process, the Belgian Prime Minister, Herman Van Rompuy.

Organisation

Frequency, location and length of summits

Frequency

From the Maastricht Treaty until the entry into force of the Lisbon Treaty, the European Council was required to meet at least twice a year. These two required meetings were held at the end of each six month Council Presidency, in June and December.

However, from the late 1990s it became increasingly common for there to be three or four meetings per year. Beginning with a special summit held in March 2000 in Lisbon to examine how the EU could best utilise new technologies to promote economic growth and employment, there was a regular annual spring summit. The main purpose of this meeting, in theory at least – it was sometimes side-tracked by other pressing issues – was to examine what became known after the March 2000 summit as the Lisbon Strategy on growth and employment. An autumn summit also became a regular event in the 2000s. The only year in which one was not held was 2005, which was because the UK Presidency decided that an autumn summit was not strictly necessary, and indeed might be troublesome given ongoing differences between member states – especially France and the UK – over the content of the 2007–13 financial framework. Tony Blair did however host, in October at Hampton Court Palace, what was officially labelled an 'Informal Meeting of Heads of State of Government'. The meeting, which lasted for just five hours, including lunch, had as its main purpose a discussion on how the EU could best respond to the challenges of globalisation.

The 2002 Seville summit regularised the *de facto* situation of four summits per year by specifying that the European Council would henceforth meet in principle four times a year: twice during each Council Presidency. Strictly speaking the Hampton Court informal meeting was thus in breach of the Seville decision. The Seville summit also decided that extraordinary meetings could be convened in extraordinary circumstances. Such a meeting – in the form of a one day informal meeting of the Heads of State or Government to discuss the EU's response to the worsening global financial crisis – was convened by President Sarkozy in November 2008, during the French Presidency. A similar meeting, to discuss the EU's position in advance of global talks on financial reform, was held under the Swedish Presidency in September 2009.

As can be seen in Document 10.2, the Lisbon Treaty makes it a treaty requirement that there should be at least four summits a year: twice in each six months. The Treaty also empowers the European Council President to convene special summits when required: a power that Herman Van Rompuy used for the first time to call, in February 2010, a summit that was supposed to be focused on considering Commission plans for a successor to the Lisbon Strategy but which in practice focused mainly on Greek budgetary problems.

Location

Up to 2001 summits were held in the country of the Presidency. However, with security becoming an increasing problem and with the prospect of enlargement

meaning that without a change a large number of summits would be held in small states, the 2000 IGC annexed a declaration to the Nice Treaty stipulating that 'as from 2002, one European Council meeting per presidency will be held in Brussels. When the Union comprises 18 members [which, of course, it has since May 2004], all European Council meetings will be held in Brussels'. The declaration related, however, only to the end-of-Presidency summits. The Brussels move was 'completed' in late 2009 when new European Council Rules of Procedure stated that, apart from in exceptional circumstances, 'The European Council shall meet in Brussels' (European Council, 2009b: 52).

Length

The 'standard model' for full summits has been that they have been held over a two-day period, beginning in the morning or early afternoon of day one and ending in the late afternoon of day two. From this model, there have been various departures in practice, most of them arising from the length and nature of agendas and the politics of meetings. The longest summit to date was at Nice in December 2000, where disagreements over the contents over what became the Nice Treaty resulted in the meeting extending into a fifth day.

As part of an attempt to streamline the operations of the European Council, the 2002 Seville summit changed the arrangements concerning the length of summits. Heads would still gather for two days, but on day one they would not be joined by ministers. The full European Council would normally last for just one full day, with the meeting closing at the end of the afternoon. In practice, these revised arrangements proved difficult to apply, with the consequence that, up to the time of writing, most post-Seville summits have been conducted much like their predecessors. It remains to be seen how they will proceed post the Lisbon Treaty changes, but the Rules of Procedure adopted in late 2009 state:

> Each ordinary meeting of the European Council shall run for a maximum of two days, unless the European Council or the General Affairs Council, on the initiative of the President of the European Council, decides otherwise (European Council, 2009b: 53).

The timing and length of special summits depends largely on the reasons for which they have been called, but they rarely extend into a second day and often last for just a few hours.

Preparing summits

Prior to the Lisbon Treaty, much of the responsibility for preparing European Council meetings rested with the Presidency and the GAERC. The 'standard' procedure for end-of-Presidency summits was for senior officials from the Presidency, working in liaison with the Secretariat of the Council of Ministers, the Antici Group (see Chapter 9), and the Commission, to identify topics that could be, ought to be, or needed to be discussed. These were then channelled through COREPER, and in the case of CFSP matters through the Political and Security Committee (see Chapters 9 and 21). Final coordinating preparatory work, including agreement on agendas, was undertaken by the GAERC which, at a meeting held at least four weeks before the European Council, would, acting on a Presidency proposal, agree on a draft agenda and then, on the eve of the European Council meeting, would hold a final preparatory session and adopt the definitive agenda. (A fuller description of the pre-Lisbon Treaty arrangements is given in the sixth edition of this book.)

The creation of the new position of European Council President in the Lisbon Treaty naturally necessitated changes to these arrangements. But what the nature of the changes should be were not altogether self-evident, with it being widely felt by many national governments and other EU actors that all preparatory arrangements should not be put wholly in the hands of the new President. Accordingly, the new post-Lisbon Rules of Procedure of the European Council made provision – as Document 10.4 shows – for the Head of Government of the Council Presidency State, the Commission President, and the General Affairs Council also to have an involvement in preparations.

Setting the agenda

The agendas for the June and December summits have usually been crowded. The sorts of matters that appear on their agendas are considered in a separate section later in the chapter, but the circumstances that can bring them onto agendas will be outlined here.

- Some issues are almost invariably on the agenda because of their intrinsic importance. So, time is usually allowed for a discussion of the general economic situation in the EU, and some time is normally also set aside for a consideration of developments relating to the internal market, EMU, the promotion of employment, and enlargement.
- The contextual environment within which the EU operates can 'force' issues onto the agenda. So, for example, the global financial and economic crisis that erupted in 2008 resulted in subsequent summits giving a top priority to examining, and taking decisions on, a range of remedial measures.
- The Commission may be pressing a policy initiative towards which at least some of the member states are sympathetic. This was, for example, an important part of the background to the June 2001 Goteborg summit agreeing on a strategy for sustainable development and adding an environmental dimension to the Lisbon Strategy.
- There may be a need, or a wish in some quarters, to use a summit to make or to formalise institutional change. Several summits, for example, have made decisions about the convening of IGCs, have reviewed the progress being made in IGCs, and of course have marked the culmination of IGCs.
- Decisions may be needed on matters that have come to be accepted as requiring European Council resolution, or at least approval. So, for example, the June and December 2005 summits were much taken up with the increasing need to reach an agreement on the 2007–13 financial perspective.
- Business may be left over from, or have been referred from, a previous summit. For example, the June 1998 Cardiff summit invited the Commission 'to report to future European Councils' on progress made in integrating environmental protection into EU policies so as to achieve sustainable development (European Council, 1998: 12). Another example concerns the Turkish membership application: at its December 2002 Copenhagen meeting the European Council promised Turkey that at its December 2004 meeting it would authorise the opening of accession negotiations if Turkey had made sufficient progress with its internal reform programme; the item thus duly appeared on the

Document 10.4

Preparing European Council meetings

Article 2

Preparation for and follow-up to the proceedings of the European Council

1 The President of the European Council shall ensure the preparation and continuity of the work of the European Council in cooperation with the President of the Commission, and on the basis of the work of the General Affairs Council.
2 The General Affairs Council shall prepare and ensure the follow-up to meetings of the European Council, in liaison with the President of the European Council and the Commission.
3 The President shall establish close cooperation and coordination with the Presidency of the Council and the President of the Commission, particularly by means of regular meetings ...

Article 3

Agenda and preparation

1 In order to ensure the preparation provided for in Article 2(2), at least four weeks before each ordinary meeting of the European Council ... the President of the European Council, in close cooperation with the member of the European Council representing the Member State holding the six-monthly Presidency of the Council and with the President of the Commission, shall submit an annotated draft agenda to the General Affairs Council.

   Contributions to the proceedings of the European Council by other Council configurations shall be forwarded to the General Affairs Council at the latest two weeks before the meeting of the European Council.

   The President of the European Council, in close cooperation as referred to in the first subparagraph, shall prepare draft guidelines for the European Council conclusion and, as appropriate, draft conclusions and draft decisions of the European Council, which shall be discussed in the General Affairs Council.

   A final meeting of the General Affairs Council shall be held within the five days preceding the meeting of the European Council. In the light of that final discussion, the President of the European Council shall draw up the provisional agenda.
2 Except for imperative and unforeseeable reasons linked, for example, to current international events, no other configuration of the Council or preparatory body may, between the session of the General Affairs Council at the end of which the provisional agenda for the European Council is drawn up and the European Council meeting, discuss any subject submitted to the European Council.
3 The European Council shall adopt its agenda at the beginning of its meeting.

   As a rule, issues entered on the agenda should have been examined beforehand, in accordance with the provisions of this Article.

Source: Rules of Procedure of the European Council (European Council, 2009b).

December 2004 meeting's agenda and the authorisation was given subject to certain conditions.

● Reports may have to be considered, or at least noted. For instance, amongst reports submitted to the June 2002 Seville summit were: from the

Council on illegal immigration and smuggling; from the Council on taxation; from the Commission on the management of the EU's external borders; from the Commission on using the internet to develop twinning between European secondary schools; from the Presidency on enlargement; and from the Presidency on the Lisbon Strategy.

- External relations usually require discussions, declarations and decisions. For example, amongst matters considered at the June 2009 summit were the security situation in Pakistan and Afghanistan, the holding of nuclear tests by North Korea, and the recent elections in Iran.

The spring and autumn summits have normally been convened around a specific theme or issue, so their agendas have been narrower. Since 2000, the spring summits have had as their main focus consideration of the economic, social and environmental situation in the Union. More specifically, as was noted above, their remit during the first decade of the century was to follow up on the key economic goals laid down at the 2000 Lisbon summit. These goals aimed to achieve for the EU by 2010: the creation of twenty million new jobs; the promotion of economic and social reform; and the creation of the world's leading knowledge-based economy. Usually, however, circumstances and events have resulted in the spring summits also devoting at least some of their time to non-economic matters. This happened, for example, with the March 2004 summit, which was held shortly after bombs in Madrid had killed over 200 people. Dealing with terrorism was added to the agenda and several measures were adopted, including a declaration on combating terrorism.

The autumn summits have taken a number of forms. Some, for example, have been convened to deal with a particular policy area, as with the October 1999 Tampère summit which considered measures that would need to be taken to create 'an area of freedom, security and justice in the European Union' (European Council, 1999c). Some have been convened to discuss potentially troublesome matters, such as the October 2000 Biarritz summit which had as its main purpose reviewing progress in the 2000 IGC. And some have been convened to consider particularly urgent matters, such as the September 2001 Brussels summit that was hurriedly called to consider the EU's response to the September 11 terrorist attacks in the USA.

It is likely that under the post-Lisbon Treaty arrangements more summits focused around specific themes and issues will be held.

The conduct of business

Summits have naturally varied in terms of how precisely they are arranged and conducted. The most obvious variation has arisen from the contents of agendas, with some summits being assigned fewer working sessions than others. Some summits have, indeed, been cut short because the Presidency has thought no agreement could be reached on a controversial issue (as with the Italian Presidency and the Constitutional Treaty negotiations at the December 2003 summit) or have been extended because the President has resolved to reach a settlement (as with the French Presidency and the Nice Treaty negotiations at the December 2000 summit).

Thus bearing in mind that variations do occur, though perhaps they will do so much less in the future with the semi-permanent President, the 'standard model' for the conduct of business at European Council meetings that last more than one day is as set out in Box 10.1.

A very important point to emphasise about the conduct of business in the European Council is that decisions are almost invariably taken by unanimity. Until the Lisbon Treaty this was a consequence of a mixture of political choice and necessity, with it being recognised that immense internal political problems and disharmony would arise in the EU were the European Council to use majority voting for the high-profile decisions it commonly takes. This *de facto* situation was given treaty status by the Lisbon Treaty, which included in its new TEU article on the European Council: 'Except where the Treaties provide otherwise, decisions of the European Council shall be taken by consensus' (Article 15: 4, TEU). And the Treaties do not much 'provide otherwise': with appointments to certain senior positions being the main area where they do (see below).

Activities

As was noted above, the European Council is relatively free to decide what it may and may not do. The few treaty and other legal provisions that relate to its responsibilities are, for the most part, vague, whilst the political status of its members is such as to put it generally beyond much challenge.

As a result, the activities undertaken by the

Box 10.1

The 'standard model' for European Council meetings

- Much depends on whether a one day or two day summit is planned. If it is a one day summit, participants gather on the eve of the summit for a working dinner. The following describes two day summits.
- On the basis of the agenda that has been agreed in advance, a plenary session is held in the morning of day 1. Since 1987 this session has included an address from the President of the European Parliament.
- Lunch is a drawn-out affair, which allows time for informal discussions and bilateral meetings. During lunch, and indeed during most breaks, there are meetings between the summit participants and their national delegations.
- Another plenary is held in the afternoon. Ministers in attendance may have separate meetings.
- In the evening, dinner provides another opportunity for further informal discussions. The Heads of Government and the President of the Commission on the one hand, and other ministers in attendance on the other, usually dine separately.
- What happens after dinner depends on what progress has been made during the day. Occasionally there are reconvened plenaries in an attempt to make progress with uncompleted business, and often bilateral late-night meetings are held. During the night, officials work on a draft of conclusions on the first day's business ('pre-drafts' are written even before summits open) and/or on a form of words that can serve as a basis for further negotiations the next day.
- Another plenary session is held in the morning and sometimes the afternoon of day two. This usually picks up from the previous day's discussions, but with the draft that has been worked on during the night now tabled. With the participants trying to move towards conclusions, breaks in the proceedings are sometimes called so as to permit delegations to study the implications of proposals or to allow informal discussions to take place.
- The summit normally ends in the afternoon or early evening with the publication of a statement – in the form pre-Lisbon of 'Presidency Conclusions' and post-Lisbon of 'European Council Conclusions'. Everything in the statement is customarily agreed to by all summit participants.
- Press conferences, including one by the Head of State or Government from each member state, are held for the up to 4000 journalists who attend European Councils and who do so much to turn the summits into major media events. Different versions of what has happened are often given on these occasions.

European Council have tended to vary, according both to the preferences of the participants and changing circumstances and requirements. So, in the second half of the 1970s, when President Giscard d'Estaing and Chancellor Schmidt determined much of the direction and pace of European integration, considerable time was given to general discussions of major economic and monetary problems. For much of the 1980s, by contrast, when some participants – notably Margaret Thatcher and the representatives of the Commission – began to press particular distributional questions, and when policy issues were increasingly referred 'upwards' from the Council of Ministers for resolution, the summits came to be much concerned with quite detailed decision making. Towards the end of the 1980s another shift began to occur as summits devoted increasing time and attention to the general direction and development of the Community. This shift has continued and has resulted in the European Council increasingly assuming the role of a sort of board of directors: setting the overall framework and taking decisions about the major initiatives to be pursued, but tending to leave the operationalisation of its pronouncements and decisions to management (which in this case is essentially the Commission and the Council of Ministers).

The main topics and areas with which the European Council concerns itself can be grouped under six headings.

The evolution of the European Union

Although this item appears only occasionally on European Council agendas as a topic in its own right, reviewing and guiding the general evolution of the EU is what several specific items are, in effect, concerned with. The most important of these items – constitutional and institutional reform, EMU, and enlargement – are dealt with separately below, but others that are worth noting include: the monitoring of progress in the creation of the internal market; 'troubleshooting' when progress in building the European Union is threatened – as with measures agreed at the June 2009 summit to try and persuade the Irish people to approve the Lisbon Treaty; setting out framework principles when this is deemed necessary – as with periodic statements since the early 1990s emphasising the importance of subsidiarity; and framing the parameters of EU income and expenditure by determining the size and shape of the EU's multi-annual financial frameworks – as with the agreement at the special March 1999 Berlin summit on the 2000–6 financial perspective and the agreement at the December 2005 Brussels summit on the 2007–13 financial perspective (see Chapter 22 on these two agreements).

'Constitutional' and institutional matters

These come up in the European Council in three main forms.

First, the European Council takes important decisions relating to treaty development and reform. As is shown in Box 10.2, it has been a key player in respect of the establishment and remits of IGCs, finalising the contents of treaties, and deciding what is to be done when treaties run into ratification difficulties.

Second, a range of specific institutional matters are considered, and are decided, at summits. For example,

---

Box 10.2

The European Council and the 'Constitutionalisation of European Integration

- The June 1985 Milan summit established the IGC that paved the way for the SEA, which was agreed at the December 1985 Luxembourg summit.
- The IGCs that worked on what became the Maastricht Treaty were established over a series of four summits in 1989 and 1990 (two regular and two special). The final negotiations on the Treaty were conducted at the December 1991 Maastricht summit.
- Preparations and arrangements for the 1996–7 IGC were decided at summits between 1994 and 1996 – notably Corfu in June 1994, Cannes in June 1995, and Madrid in December 1995. The contents of the Amsterdam Treaty was finalised at the June 1997 Amsterdam summit.
- The Amsterdam summit made provision for the convening of another IGC to prepare for enlargement, whilst decisions on the convening and agenda of the 2000 IGC were taken at the June 1999 Cologne summit. The contents of the Treaty were finalised at the December 2000 Nice summit.
- The Nice summit provided for another IGC, which led to later summits determining the preparations for the Constitutional Treaty IGC – including creating the Constitutional Convention. The final contents of the CT were agreed at summits in December 2003 and June 2004 (the first of these summits reached agreement on virtually everything except national voting weights in the Council).
- After the failure to ratify the CT: the June 2005 summit decides on a 'period of reflection'; the June 2006 summit asked the forthcoming German Presidency to prepare a report to enable progress to be made; the June 2007 summit decided to convene an IGC, on the basis of a very tight mandate; the October 2007 summit agreed on the contents of the Lisbon Treaty; the June 2009 summit agreed on a list of measures designed to persuade the Irish people to ratify the Treaty.

at the December 2003 summit a decision was taken on the location of several EU offices and agencies – including the European Food Safety Authority (which both Italy and Finland wanted), the European Chemicals Agency, and Eurojust.

Third, the European Council takes important personnel decisions. Most notably it: appoints its own President; appoints the High Representative of the Union for Foreign Affairs and Security Policy; appoints the President, the Vice President and the Executive Board members of the European Central Bank (ECB); and proposes to the EP the person it wishes to see appointed as Commission President. Although it has not as yet been formally used, all of these matters can be decided by QMV if necessary. Personnel decisions can become extremely politicised and difficult. So, taking the nomination for Commission President, the UK government vetoed the nomination of the Belgian Prime Minister, Jean-Luc Dehaene, as Commission President at the June 1994 Corfu summit, with the consequence that a special summit had to be held in Brussels a fortnight later when Jacques Santer was nominated. Similarly, in 2004, no agreement could be reached at the June summit on who should be nominated to succeed Romano Prodi, with the consequence that a special summit subsequently had to be convened after informal agreement had been reached that the nominee should be José Manuel Barroso. Taking the President of the ECB, France objected at the special Brussels summit in May 1998 to the appointment of Wim Duisenberg of the Netherlands Central Bank as the ECB's first President rather than Claude Trichet of the French Central Bank, and it was only after a deal was negotiated that involved Duisenberg agreeing to step down before his term of office had expired that the matter was resolved.

The economic and monetary policies of the European Union

Summits have long reviewed the overall economic and social situation within the EU and looked in a general way at questions relating to economic growth, trade patterns, inflation, exchange rates, and unemployment. Until the early 1990s, however, differences between the member states about what should be done, coupled with a widely shared determination to ensure that national hands remained firmly placed on key economic controls, meant that these discussions usually produced little beyond general exhortations on topics such as controlling inflation, tackling unemployment and encouraging investment.

However, in recent years these economic deliberations, whilst still falling far short of producing a common economic policy for all member states, have acquired more bite. One reason why they have done so is that the European Council is one of the political forums – the Ecofin Council and the Eurogroup are the other main forums (see Chapters 9 and 13) – where the operation and membership of the EMU system are considered. Another reason is that since EMU requires convergence between key national economic policies and the Lisbon Strategy for economic growth and employment also requires some economic policy coordination, consideration of economic policy in the EU and of proposals for concerted EU economic action are now considered as being wholly appropriate European Council agenda items. Indeed, under Article 121 TFEU (formerly Article 99 TEC) a general review of macroeconomic policy at European Council level is required: 'The European Council shall, acting on the basis of [a draft report] from the Council [of Ministers] discuss a conclusion on the broad guidelines of the economic policies of the Member States and of the Union'. And a third, and more recent, reason why European Council macroeconomic and monetary policy discussions have become more significant is that the global financial and economic crisis that broke out in 2008 has inevitably obliged the EU's national leaders, along with EU policy-makers at all levels, to examine what EU level responses are appropriate and would be beneficial. In this context, the December 2008 European Council meeting discussed the situation at length and approved a European Economic Recovery Plan that was forwarded to it by the Commission in the form of a communication (European Commission, 2008b). Central elements of the Plan that the national leaders at the December summit identified as particularly supporting included: an increase in European Investment Bank lending; the simplification of procedures and faster implementation of programmes financed from the EU budget; additional action by the European Social Fund to support employment; and the possibility of individual member states reducing value added tax rates in certain sectors (European

Council, 2008: 5). Subsequent summits have further discussed and monitored the effects of the Recovery Plan, with requests usually being made to other policy actors for actions of various sorts. For example, the Presidency Conclusions of the June 2009 summit included the following:

> The European Council calls for further progress to be made in the regulation of financial markets, notably on the regulation of alternative investment funds, the role and responsibilities of depositories and on transparency and stability of derivatives markets. The European Council also calls on the Commission and the Member States to accelerate their work and make rapid progress on countering the pro-cyclical effects of regulatory standards, e.g. as regards capital requirements and impaired assets. It also invites the Member States to take action rapidly on executives' pay and on remunerations in the financial sector, taking into account the recommendations made by the Commission (European Council, 2009a: 7).

Enlargements

Most important decisions relating to EU accession applications are taken at European Council meetings, usually – although not always – on the basis of recommendations from the Commission. Moreover, since the early 1990s there have been few summits when enlargement has not featured some way prominently on the agenda, whether it has been in the form of considering applications, authorising the opening of accession negotiations, hearing reports from the Commission on the progress of negotiations, deciding whether negotiations have been successfully concluded, setting accession dates, or – as has very much been the case in recent years with the Turkish application – dealing with problems that have arisen during the accession process.

By way of illustrating the range of enlargement matters with which the European Council becomes involved, amongst the many key decisions taken in the process that led to the 2004 enlargement were: the agreement at the June 1993 Copenhagen summit that CEECs could become members of the EU; the setting-out at the December 1994 Essen summit of a pre-accession strategy; the confirmation at the

Luxembourg 1997 summit of the Commission's recommendation that negotiations should open with five CEECs and Cyprus in 1998; the similar confirmation at the Helsinki 1999 summit that negotiations should be extended in 2000 to the five remaining CEEC applicants and Malta; and the agreement at the December 2002 summit that ten states had completed the accession negotiations successfully and could join the EU on 1 May 2004.

External relations

In addition to the 'special case' of enlargement, the European Council is involved in the EU's external relations in three principal ways.

First, many economic issues are not purely internal EU matters. They have vitally important global dimensions and summits often look at these either with a view to considering the EU's relations with other economic powers (especially the United States, Russia and Japan), or with a view to coordinating the EU's position in international negotiations (such as at G8 and G20 summits or in the World Trade Organisation).

Second, since the Maastricht Treaty the European Council has been assigned by the TEU a guidance role on the overall principles and direction of the EU's foreign and security policy. The post-Lisbon Treaty formulation of this role is set out in Document 10.5.

Third, the European Council has long issued declarations on important aspects of international political affairs. Sometimes the declarations have had policy instruments attached to them, but usually only 'soft' instruments in the form, for example, of mild economic sanctions or modest economic aid.

Specific internal policy issues

Despite the original intention that the European Council should operate at a fairly general level, in practice it often concerns itself with quite specific internal policy issues. There are three main reasons for this: 1) some issues are so sensitive and/or so intractable that it requires the authority of national leaders to deal with them; 2) the European Council is, because of its non-sectoral nature, often the best-placed institution to put together broad-ranging policies or broker deals that

---

Document 10.5

The Treaty provisions on the Foreign and Security Policy Roles of the European Council

1 The European Council shall identify the Union's strategic interests, determine the objectives of and define general guidelines for the common foreign and security policy, including for matters with defence implications. It shall adopt the necessary decisions.

   If international developments so require, the President of the European Council shall convene an extraordinary meeting of the European Council in order to define the strategic lines of the Union's policy in the face of such developments.

2 The Council shall frame the common foreign and security policy and take the decisions necessary for defining and implementing it on the basis of the general guidelines and strategic lines defined by the European Council.

   The Council and the High Representative of the Union for Foreign Affairs and Security Policy shall ensure the unity, consistency and effectiveness of action by the Union.

Source: Article 26, *Treaty on European Union* (post-Lisbon Treaty).

---

cut across policy sectors; and 3) the status of the European Council in the EU system is now such that the general expectation and assumption is that most policy matters of significance ought at least to be given clearance, if not be determined, at European Council level.

These differing reasons have resulted in three broad types of internal policy involvement by the European Council. First, it sometimes plays a significant role in policy initiation. For example, since the late 1980s it has prompted initiatives in such areas as immigration, drugs and terrorism. Second, policy involvement can take the form of tackling issues that the Council of Ministers has been unable to resolve or which it is deemed necessary that the European Council should resolve. Such an instance occurred in connection with the institutional crisis that developed in the EU in 1996 following the export ban placed on British beef because of the high incidence of Bovine Spongiform Encephalopathy (BSE) in British cattle: the Commission drew up a plan for resolving the crisis, and it was referred to the June Florence summit for approval. Third, and this has been of increasing importance in recent years as the number of policy issues that are 'referred up' from the Council of Ministers for final resolution has declined (largely as a consequence of QMV resulting in fewer blockages at Council of Ministers level), the European Council has

become less concerned with arbitrating and acting as a final court of appeal on internal policy issues and more concerned with encouraging and guiding. This is illustrated by the frequent messages it sends to other EU institutions via summit Conclusions: almost invariably these Conclusions are studded with phrases such as the European Council 'invites a report on', 'calls for action to be taken in regard to', 'confirms its full support for', 'welcomes the progress made by', 'endorses the steps taken in connection with' and so on.

The European Council and the EU System

As the previous section showed, the European Council concerns itself with various activities, the relative importance of which can vary from summit to summit. Five broad functions, which can be analytically separated but which in practice greatly overlap, are associated with these activities. The functions are set out in Box 10.3.

One function, it should be emphasised, that the European Council does not exercise is that of legislator. As Document 10.2 shows, the TEU prevents it from taking legislative decisions. Its decisions are

Functions of the European Council

- It is a forum, at the highest political level, for building mutual understanding and confidence between the governments of the EU member states.
- It identifies medium- and long-term EU goals.
- It is a policy initiator and dispenser of policy guidelines.
- It makes an important contribution to the coordination of EU policy goals and activities.
- It is a decision-maker – both on matters that have come to be accepted are its ultimate responsibility (most notably constitutional and major institutional, policy and budgetary issues), and on matters that, because of their importance or their political complexity and sensitivity, are not resolved by the Council of Ministers.

high' politics – by attempting to providing strategic direction for the EU and taking major – 'history-making' (Peterson and Bomberg, 1999: chapter 1) – decisions. It tries to avoid becoming too involved in policy details. But this position of dealing with 'the big picture' and leaving detailed and operational matters to others is not applied with complete consistency. What happens at individual summits is not part of any wholly regularised or consistent pattern. Thus, some summits are relatively low-key affairs and do little more than pronounce on some aspects of current international developments, indicate one or two policy initiatives in fringe policy areas, and cobble together a concluding statement exuding general goodwill. Other summits, by contrast, are surrounded by an atmosphere of crisis and prophecies of catastrophe should they fail to produce firm decisions on key and pressing issues. Occasionally they do fail, but the forecasted catastrophes never quite happen, and the next summit, or next but one, is usually able to find an agreement via the customary EU method of compromise.

* * *

The creation and development of the European Council has inevitably had implications for the role and functioning of the other principal EU institutions.

- The Commission has experienced some undermining of its special position regarding policy initiation: an undermining that may be further compounded by the creation of the position of European Council President. However, to date the Commission has to some extent been compensated for the undermining by being permitted to enter into political discussions with national leaders at the summits, and also by being able – and sometimes required – to submit reports and documents to the summits.
- The Council of Ministers has lost power to the European Council by virtue of the increasing tendency of most major issues to go through summits in some form. As Hayes-Renshaw and Wallace (2006: 1) note, one role of the European Council is to act 'as a higher level of the Council of Ministers, by attempting to settle those issues on which the ministers have been unable to reach agreement'. However, the extent of the Council of Ministers loss of power should not be exaggerated.

political decisions. When it is intended that its decisions should be given legal effect, the customary EU legislative procedures have to be applied. And in those procedures there is no guarantee that a European Council agreement will automatically produce ease of passage. One reason for this is that the policy guidelines laid down by the European Council are sometimes insufficiently precise to clear all political obstacles. Another reason is that governments occasionally decide after a summit that their delegations have given too much away and that ground must be recovered by taking a tough line in the Council of Ministers.

Institutionalised summitry in the form of the European Council has inevitably strengthened the position of national governments in the EU system. It has also added an extra intergovernmental element to the nature of the EU by virtue of the fact that the leaders virtually always act on the basis of unanimous agreement – either because they are required to do so or, in those instances where voting is possible, because they prefer to do so.

However, although the European Council is unquestionably a very important EU institution, its role, or more accurately its roles, in the EU system are not wholly fixed. For the most part it focuses on 'very

One reason why it should not be so is that there is no rigid hierarchical relationship between the two bodies in the sense that the Council of Ministers always feels obliged to refer all significant matters 'upwards' for final decisions. It is true that most broad-based or very significant initiatives are referred to the European Council, but often that is for little more than political approval or for information. Certainly it would be quite erroneous to suppose that the European Council takes all 'first-order' decisions and the Council of Ministers is confined to 'second-order' decisions. A second reason why the extent of the loss should not be overstated is that there is no consistent line of division between the two regarding who does what, other than the Council of Ministers being responsible for making legislation. A third reason is that most issues considered by the European Council have already been prepared, channelled and filtered by the appropriate formations of the Council of Ministers. And a fourth reason is that since the European Council meets for only six to eight days a year, it cannot normally hope to do anything more than sketch outlines in a restricted number of areas.

- The EP has been largely by-passed by the European Council and so could be regarded as having experienced some net loss of power. It is true that the European Council President gives a verbal report on each summit meeting to the next EP plenary session, and it is also the case that the EP President addresses the opening sessions of summits in order to inform the national leaders of the EP's thinking on key issues. However, there is no evidence that either of these procedures produce much in the way of influence. Far more important is the almost complete lack of input by the EP into European Council agendas or deliberations, and the tendency of the Council of Ministers to take the view that proposals that stem from European Council decisions do not permit it much manoeuvrability when dealing with the EP.
- Since the European Council operates largely outside the framework of the TFEU and since its decisions are political rather than legal in character, its existence has had few implications for the Court

of Justice. Or rather it has had few direct implications. Necessarily, however, in so far as important decisions are taken that are beyond the Court's 'reach', this constitutes a weakness in the influence of the Court.

Concluding Remarks

The record of the European Council is mixed. On the one hand there have been failures, or at least the non-fulfilment of hopes. This was particularly so in the period from about 1980 to 1988: summits became rather routinised and immersed in specifics; too much time was devoted to policy detail rather than to mapping out the future; and disputes about distributional issues were seemingly always on the agenda. On the other hand there have been positive achievements: understandings between national leaders have been furthered; important goals have been identified/given an impetus/brought to a conclusion – such as on enlargements, the internal market, institutional reform, and EMU; and agreements have been worked out on matters that were either unsuitable for, or could not be resolved by, the Council of Ministers.

That there should be both pluses and minuses in the record is not altogether surprising. The summits are, after all, conducted on a relatively loosely structured basis and it is thus perhaps inevitable, given the participants, that they should be drawn into attempting to do a host of different things. It is also inevitable that summits should experience many of the problems of intergovernmental conflict that are so characteristic of the Council of Ministers.

Aware of the European Council's weaknesses, the government of the member states – led by the governments of the large member states – used the treaty reform process that led to the Lisbon Treaty to strengthen the European Council's institutional capacity. They did this by replacing the six-month rotating Presidency of the European Council by a more permanent President. Whether, in practice, this change will further strengthen the already key position of the European Council in the EU system remains to be seen.

Chapter 11

The European Parliament

Powers and Influence

For long after it was first constituted as the Assembly of the European Coal and Steel Community, the European Parliament – the title it adopted for itself in 1962 – was generally regarded as a somewhat ineffectual institution. This reputation is no longer justified, for whilst it is true that the EP's formal powers are not as strong as those of national legislatures, developments over the years have come to give it a considerable influence in the EU system. As with national parliaments this influence is exercised in three main ways: through the legislative process, through the budgetary process, and through control and supervision of the executive.

Parliament and EU legislation

The EP is an extremely active legislator. During the 2004–9 Parliament it approved in plenary session a total of 2,924 texts, nearly half of which – 1,355 – were legislative documents (European Parliament, 2009c).

There are a number of ways in which the Parliament can influence the nature and content of the EU's legislative output.

First, it sometimes participates in policy discussions with the Commission at the pre-proposal legislative stage. The Commission may, for example, float a policy idea before an EP committee, or committee members themselves may suggest policy initiatives to the Commission.

Second, the EP can formally adopt its own ideas for suggested legislation. There are two main ways in which it can do this. One way is to adopt own initiative reports – that is, reports that the Parliament itself initiates. Since 1982, the Commission has agreed in principle to follow-up on any reports to which it does not have major objections, though it has not always done so in ways that the EP intended. As can be seen in Table 11.1 (p. 182), 151 own initiative reports, most of which were not calling for legislative proposals, were adopted in 2008. The other way of adopting ideas for legislation is under Article 225 TFEU (formerly Article 192 TEC) which, states that 'The European Parliament may, acting by a majority of its component members, request the Commission to submit any appropriate proposal on matters on which it considers that a Union act is required for the purpose of implementing the Treaties.' An example of such a request being made was in November 2008 when, by 590 votes to 23 and with 46 abstentions, the EP voted to request the Commission to draft a legislative proposal to strengthen the current law on equal pay. Political realities make it difficult for the Commission not to act on

---

Box 11.1

The EU's legislative procedures and the EP

● *The consultation procedure.* Under this procedure the EP is asked for an opinion on Commission proposals for legislation. Once that opinion is given the Council may take whatever decision it wishes, even if the EP's opinion is negative.

   If the Council acts prematurely and does not wait for Parliament to make its views known, the 'law' will be ruled invalid by the ECJ. Any uncertainty on this point was removed by the isoglucose case ruling in 1980, when the Court annulled a Council regulation on the ground that it had been issued before Parliament's opinion was known. The isoglucose case ruling does not give the EP an indefinite veto over legislation under the consultation procedure, for it is obliged by treaty to issue opinions and in some of its judgements the Court has referred to the duty of loyal cooperation among EU institutions. However, the ruling does give the EP a very useful delaying power, of up to about three months.

   What use the EP is able to make of the consultation procedure depends, in part at least, on its own subject competence and its tactical skills. The standard way of proceeding is to take advantage of Article 293 TFEU (ex 250 TEC), which states: 'As long as the Council has not acted, the Commission may alter its proposals during the procedures leading to the adoption of a Union act.' If the Commission can be persuaded to alter a proposal so as to incorporate the EP's views, the prospect of those views becoming part of the text that is finally approved by the Council is greatly enhanced. With this in mind, the EP attempts to convince or to pressurise the Commission. Normally, pressurising takes the form of voting on amendments to proposals but delaying voting on the resolution that formally constitutes the opinion until after the Commission has stated – as it is obliged to do – whether or not it accepts the amendments. If the Commission does accept the amendments the EP votes for the legislative resolution and the amendments are incorporated into the Commission's proposal. If the Commission does not accept the amendments, or at least not all of them, the EP may judge the Commission's position to be unsatisfactory and as a result may seek to delay the progress of the proposal by referring it back to the appropriate Parliamentary committee for further consideration.

→

Article 225 requests, but, as Judge and Earnshaw (2008: 195–6) show, it has not always rushed to do so. Moreover, only a handful of Article 225/(192) requests have been passed to date, largely because absolute majorities can be difficult to obtain. An example of a legislative proposal stemming from such an EP request is a 2000 directive on settling the insurance claims of victims of traffic accidents occurring outside the victim's country of origin, which had its roots in an October 1995 EP resolution.

   Third, the annual budgetary cycle provides opportunities to exercise legislative influence. In large measure this dates back to the *Joint Declaration of 30 June 1982 by the European Parliament, the Council and the Commission on various measures to improve the budgetary procedure.* Amongst the 'various measures', it was agreed that if the EP put appropriations into the budget for items for which there was no legal base – in other words if the EP opened new budget lines – the Commission and the Council would seek to provide the necessary base. It was further agreed that expenditure limits in respect of legislation should not be set in the legislative process, but in the budgetary process – where the EP has, until recently, had more power. For the most part this understanding between the institutions has worked well and has enabled the EP to promote favoured policies: for example in 1998 it promoted a policy on employment generation in the area of small and medium-sized enterprises and in the 2000s it has advanced programmes and pilot actions in respect of aspects of regional policy. It is an understanding, however, that requires the three institutions to work closely together, as was demonstrated in 1998 when the ECJ ruled in favour of four member states

Box 11.1 *continued*

- *The ordinary legislative procedure.* Up to the entry into force of the Lisbon Treaty this procedure was known as the co-decision procedure. The word 'co-decision' highlights a key difference between this procedure and the consultation procedure: whereas under the consultation procedure the EP is formally restricted to advising, under the ordinary procedure it is a co-decision maker with the Council. The EP thus has the power to veto legislative proposals, which naturally greatly increases its bargaining power when, as is almost invariably the case, it is seeking not to reject but rather to amend legislative proposals. The significance of the Parliament's powers under the procedure is symbolised by the fact that legislation that is subject to the procedure is made in the name of the EP and the Council, whereas legislation that is made under the consultation procedure is made in the name of the Council only.

  Another important difference between the two procedures is that whereas the consultation procedure is a single reading procedure the ordinary procedure is potentially a three reading procedure. If the Council and the EP reach agreement on the proposal at first reading, the proposal can be adopted at that stage, but if there is no agreement the Council adopts a 'common position' that must then be referred back to the EP. When doing so, the Council is obliged to provide the EP with an explanation of its common position – including reasons for any EP amendments that have been rejected. If the Council and the EP are still at odds after the second reading, the proposal falls if the Parliament has rejected it by an absolute majority of its members and it is referred to a conciliation committee if the EP has amended it by an absolute majority. The conciliation committee is composed of an equal number of representatives from the Council and the Parliament. If agreement is reached in the conciliation committee, the text must be approved by the EP by a majority of the votes cast and by the Council acting by qualified majority. If no agreement is reached the proposal falls.

- *The consent procedure.* Under this procedure, which was known as the assent procedure pre-Lisbon Treaty, the EP must consider proposals at a single reading. As with the ordinary procedure, the EP has veto powers under this procedure but it cannot make amendments. In some circumstances the consent requires an absolute majority of Parliament's members.

  The procedure is not – and never has been – used for 'normal' legislation but is reserved for special measures, including certain citizenship-related issues and the accession of new member states.

---

that claimed that a number of EU programmes stemming from EP initiatives and approved under the budgetary procedure were illegal because they did not have an authorised legal base.

Fourth, the EP can influence, albeit perhaps rather indirectly, the Commission's annual legislative programme – which is essentially a planning tool of an indicative nature. The procedure is as follows. 1) The Commission adopts its annual work programme, which includes all proposals of a legislative nature, usually in November. Several factors determine the contents of the programme, most notably: commitments that are pending; initiatives that are deemed to be necessary to give effect to existing policy developments; preferences that have been indicated by the Council and the EP, perhaps in inter-institutional meetings; and priorities identified in Council planning programmes (see Chapter 10). 2) The programme is considered by appropriate EP committees, with a dialogue often taking place between MEPs and Commission representatives. 3) A resolution on the programme is voted on in an EP plenary session, usually in December.

Fifth, and most importantly of all, the EP's views must be sought in connection with important/significant/sensitive legislation, with its powers varying according to the legislative procedure applying. Since the Lisbon Treaty came into effect there have been three procedures to which legislation may be subject. The nature of these procedures and the policy areas to which they apply are described in some detail in Chapter 18. Box 11.1 provides a summary of the procedures as they affect the EP.

Which procedure applies to a particular legislative

Table 11.1 Parliamentary proceedings from January to December, 2008 – resolutions and decisions adopted

Part-session	Legislation				Assent	Budget and discharge	Other procedures				Total
	Consultation[1]	Co-decision					Own initiative	Resolutions	Human rights	Miscellaneous	
		First reading[2]	Second reading[3]	Third reading							
January I	4	5	1				8	2	3		23
January II	1	3	1				3	3		1	12
February	2	12	1		2		10	5	3	2	37
March	10	4	1	1		2	9	2	4	2	35
April I	5	2				1	5	6		1	20
April II	3	1	1		1	31	11	7	3	1	59
May I	3						6	2		2	13
May II	4	9	1			2	14	8	3		41
June I	4	4				2	7	4		1	22
June II	8	24	3				7	7	3		52
July	11	11	8			1	10	6	3	4	54
September I	10	10				1	12	8	3	1	45
September II	7	15	6			1	13	6		1	49
October I	2				1		6	4		2	15
October II	9	12	2		1	3	8	10	3	2	50
November	13	7	1		1	1	7	8	3	3	44
December I	5	2					3	2			12
December II	9	19	3		4	3	12	3	3	3	59
Total	110	140	29	1	10	48	151	93	34	26	642

[1] Including 65 cases in which Parliament proposed amendments to the Commission proposal.
[2] Including 93 cases in which Parliament proposed amendments to the Commission proposal.
[3] Including 19 cases in which Parliament amended the Council's common position.

Source: European Commission (2009a), section on European Parliament.

proposal depends on which treaty article(s) the proposal is based. It is in the EP's interest that as much as possible is based on the ordinary procedure, where its powers are strongest, and as little as possible is based on the consultation procedure, where its powers are weakest. Since the co-decision procedure was created by the Maastricht Treaty, all subsequent revising treaties – those of Amsterdam, Nice and Lisbon – have benefited the EP by 'upgrading' policy areas from the consultation and cooperation procedures to the co-decision/ordinary procedure. Since the Lisbon Treaty entered into force, the great majority of legislative proposals fall under the ordinary procedure, Table 18.1 on pp. 308–9 lists the policy areas to which the ordinary procedure does not apply.

Table 11.1 shows the number of times the three procedures were used in 2008 for legislative proposals that were considered by the EP.

It is very difficult to estimate the precise effect of EP deliberations on the final form of legislative acts. One reason for this is that a great deal of EP persuading and lobbying is impossible to monitor because it is carried out via informal contacts with Commission and Council representatives. That is to say, EP influence is exercised not just by the formal acts of approving, rejecting, and amending legislative proposals. Second, statistical analyses of the extent to which EP amendments are incorporated into final legislation struggle with the following problems:

- Distinguishing between amendments that have a political edge and those that are essentially technical or procedural in nature.
- The fact that, as Corbett (2001: 363) has noted, the significance of EP amendments varies according to circumstances. For instance, some amendments under the ordinary procedure are adopted primarily for tactical reasons ahead of negotiations with the Council.
- How to count when some, but not all, of an amendment is accepted by the Council. This is a particular problem under the ordinary procedure, with many amendments leading to compromises negotiated between the EP and Council.

Notwithstanding, however, these difficulties – which many would say make it impossible to be precise about the extent of the EP's legislative influence – some indication of the influence being exercised by the EP can be gauged from the fact that under the ordinary procedure only about 10 per cent of legislative proposals go to the final conciliation stage: about 60 per cent are agreed at first reading and about 30 per cent at second reading. In other words, around 90 per cent of legislative proposals are in an acceptable form for the EP by the end of second reading. Of the 10 per cent that go to conciliation, figures for the first half of the 2004–9 Parliament are instructive: 86 proposals went to conciliation, containing a total of 1,344 EP amendments adopted at second reading; of the 1,344, 23 per cent were adopted in conciliation without change, 60 per cent were agreed after compromise between the EP and the Council, and 17 per cent were withdrawn (Judge and Earnshaw, 2008: 232).

But even if the precision of such statistical estimates of the EP's legislative influence can be questioned, two matters are incontrovertible. First, the EP is centrally involved with the Commission and the Council in the making of EU legislation. It is so both in formal settings – such as when it examines Commission proposals in committees and when it meets with the Council in conciliation committees – and through a variety of informal mechanisms – such as through trialogue meetings that bring together the key EP, Commission and Council actors on a proposal to explore the possibilities for a deal. Second, EP activity does have a significant impact on the outcome of legislative processes. Whilst only a handful of legislative proposals are actually blocked by the EP, many proposals are significantly altered, including on matters of political substance.

*   *   *

Having established that the EP does have a genuine legislative influence – an influence that many national parliaments cannot match – three weaknesses to which it is subject now will be outlined.

The first and most obvious weakness is that the EP does not have full legislative powers. Unlike national parliaments, it does not have the final say over what is and what is not to become law. On the one hand, it does not have the capacity to exercise a fully 'positive' legislative role by initiating, developing and passing into law its own proposals. On the other hand, its 'negative' legislative role is also circumscribed, for whilst the ordinary and consent procedures do give it a veto over most legislative proposals, under the consultation procedure the Council has the power to overturn EP amendments that have or have not been accepted by the Commission, and to ignore the EP's rejection of legislative proposals. Moreover, the Council can also choose not to act at all on legislative proposals it does not like – and there are always many proposals upon which the Parliament has given an opinion that still await a Council decision. (Proposals subject to the ordinary procedures are not exempt from such Council inaction, since the restricted timetable that is attached to the procedure only comes into play once the Council has adopted its common position.)

The second weakness is that although the EP usually attempts to deliver opinions as soon as possible to ensure they are available to the Council at an early stage of its deliberations, it is not unusual – although more so than it used to be – for the Council, before the opinion of the EP has been delivered, to take preliminary decisions or to adopt common positions 'in principle' or 'pending the opinion of the European Parliament'. This is especially common when the initial referral to the EP is delayed, when there is some urgency about the matter, or when a Council Presidency is anxious to push the proposal through. Whatever the reason, in such circumstances the EP's opinion, especially under the consultation procedure, is reduced.

The third weakness is that the EP does not have full powers over Commission legislation, even though numerically Commission legislation makes up most of EU legislation. There are different views on the significance of this. Pointing to the political and expenditure implications of some Commission legislation, MEPs have long argued that this is another example of executive power and legislative and democratic weakness. The Council and Commission, however, have emphasised that Commission legislation is usually highly technical and of a kind that needs quick decisions; as such, it is similar to the decrees, ordinances and other minor legislative acts that national administrations issue and which are commonly accepted as an inevitable aspect of decision-making in the modern world. Reforms introduced in 2006 and also in the Lisbon Treaty have gone some way to rectifying this area of traditional EP weakness (see the section on comitology in Chapter 8).

Parliament and the EU budget

As is shown in Chapter 22, there are two very different dimensions of EU budgetary-making: the making of multiannual financial frameworks (MFFs) (formerly known as financial perspectives) and the making of annual budgets. The first of these is the more important in that the contents of annual budgets have to be set within guidelines laid down in MFFs.

Multiannual financial frameworks

Following a series of intense disputes in the early-to-mid 1980s between the Council and EP over the contents of the EC's annual budget, in 1988 the EP, the Commission and the Council of Ministers put their names to *The Interinstitutional Agreement on Budgetary Discipline and Improvement of the Budgetary Procedure*. This committed all three institutions to a financial perspective for the years 1988 to 1992. The financial perspective was, essentially a medium-term financial framework for the annual budgets. It provided for a significant increase in non-compulsory expenditure (essentially spending on policy areas other than the CAP) and a significant decrease in compulsory expenditure (CAP expenditure), both of which were strongly supported by the EP. The main institutional benefits of the Agreement for the EP were twofold. First, its influence over compulsory expenditure, which in the past had been very limited, was potentially increased because its approval was now required for any upward movement of the compulsory expenditure ceiling. Second, the very act of the Council agreeing to sign a financial perspective with the EP gave to the latter an extra element of leverage in budgetary discussions.

However, when the 1988–92 financial perspective was revised in 1992–3 the EP's influence was not as great as MEPs had hoped or anticipated. Whilst it was accepted by the Commission and the Council that a precedent had been set in 1988 and that the next financial perspective would require the EP's endorsement, the key institutions in determining the size and shape of what became a seven-year financial perspective covering the years 1993–9 were the Commission, the Council of Ministers and the European Council. As it turned out there was much in the new financial perspective of which the EP approved – most notably further cuts in agricultural expenditure and further increases in non-agricultural expenditure – but this was more the outcome of battles fought in the Council of Ministers and at the December 1992 Edinburgh European Council meeting than EP influence.

As with the 1988–92 and 1993–9 financial perspectives, the key actors in shaping the 2000–6 and 2007–13 perspectives were again the Commission – which set the broad agenda via initial and then revised proposals – and the governments which, in both the Council of Ministers and the European Council, contested key issues and acted virtually as if they were the sole decision-makers. The EP exerted as much influence as it could – by producing reports and recommendations, questioning the Council and Commission, and holding debates and votes – but it was kept largely to the margins. On both occasions, the EP managed to persuade the Council to make some modest adjustments to the perspective that had been agreed at European Council level, but the endorsements the Parliament gave to the perspectives were essentially endorsements of Commission-sponsored and member state-negotiated deals.

It is likely that the Lisbon Treaty will increase the EP's influence over the contents of MFFs, but probably not by very much. For whilst the Treaty gives treaty status to MFFs and the power of consent over them to the EP, these 'elevations of status' are really just a formalisation of the *status quo*. Moreover, when the consent procedure applies, the norm is for the member state governments to negotiate agreements without too much reference to the EP, and then to make a few concessions to bring the EP aboard.

Annual budgets

Thanks mainly to the 1970 *Treaty Amending Certain Budgetary Provisions of the Treaties* and the 1975 *Treaty Amending Certain Financial Provisions of the Treaties*, the EP enjoyed from the 1970s considerable treaty powers in relation to the EU budget. These powers included: 1) the right to propose 'modifications' to compulsory expenditure (though with the final decision being taken by the Council); 2) the right to propose 'amendments' to non-compulsory expenditure (with the EP having the final decision); 3) the right of approval or rejection, with the Council, over the whole budget.

Following the introduction of direct elections for MEPs in 1979, extensive use was made of the powers just listed. Virtually all aspects of the rules, including the power of rejection, were tested to see how far they could be taken. Major confrontations with the Council, far from being avoided, seemed at times almost to be sought as the EP attempted to assert itself. The 1988 introduction of financial perspectives served, however, as had been intended, to take much of the heat out of the annual budgetary decision-making process, and since 1988 the annual budget has been agreed by the two co-decision makers – the Council and EP – on time and without too much controversy.

But notwithstanding the relative smoothness of the annul budgetary process after 1988, a running sore for the EP that frequently surfaced was the distinction between compulsory and non-compulsory expenditure and the EP's weak powers in regard to the former. This sore was removed by the Lisbon Treaty, which abolished the distinction and made for full parity between the EP and Council as the budgetary authorities.

Control and supervision of the executive

Virtually all parliaments have difficulty exercising controlling and supervisory powers over executives. They are hampered by the executives, which do not welcome the prospect of being investigated and therefore seek to protect themselves behind whatever constitutional, institutional or party political defences are available. They are hampered also by the parliamentarians themselves, who tend not to have the requisite information, the specialist knowledge, or the necessary resources that are required to properly monitor, and if necessary challenge, executive activity.

The EP shares these problems but also has two additional ones of its own. First, a key aspect of control and supervision of executives concerns policy implementation: is policy being implemented efficiently and for the purposes intended by the relevant law? The Commission is the most obvious body to be called to account on this question. But in many policy spheres the Commission's executive role is very limited and consists essentially of attempting to coordinate the work of outside agencies operating at different administrative levels. Such agencies, of which national governments are the most important, are often reluctant to open the books to or cooperate with EP investigators. Certainly there is little question of government ministers allowing themselves to be grilled by the EP on the competency and honesty of their national bureaucracies.

The second problem specific to the EP is that on broad controlling and supervisory issues – such as whether the EU executive is acting responsibly in the execution of its duties, and whether it is fulfilling its treaty obligations – problems arise from the blurring of roles between the Commission, the Council of Ministers and the European Council. Insofar as the Council of Ministers and the European Council undertake what are in effect executive powers, the EP's supervisory powers are weakened. This is because Parliament's access and treaty powers are not so strong in relation to the Council of Ministers and the European Council as they are to the Commission.

The Commission

In relation to the Commission, the EP has eight main supervisory powers and channels at its disposal.

First, prior to the Lisbon Treaty, the nominee for Commission President had to be approved by the EP. The narrow vote of approval given to Jacques Santer in 1994 showed that confirmation of the European Council's nominee could not be assumed. The Lisbon Treaty strengthened this power of the EP by specifying that the European Council's proposal of a candidate for Commission President must be made '(t)aking into account the elections to the European Parliament' (Article 17:7 TEU). The candidate is then 'elected' by the EP by a majority of its component members, and if the necessary majority is not obtained the European Council is required to submit the name of another candidate who is then subject to the same procedure.

Second, the Commissioners-designate 'shall be subject as a body to a vote of consent by the European Parliament' (Article 17:7 TEU). Since this power of approval, in a slightly different form, was first given to the EP, by the Maastricht Treaty, each Commissioner-designate has been subject to a three hour or so grilling – known as a 'hearing' – by the appropriate EP

Photo 11.1 Viviane Reding, the (Luxembourg) Commissioner-designate for Justice, Fundamental Rights and Citizenship, appearing in her January 2010 hearing before members of the EP's Civil Liberties, Justice and Home Affairs Committee, Legal Affairs Committee, and Women's Rights and Gender Equality Committee. The photograph is taken from an interpreter's booth.

committee(s) before the confirmation vote. The confirmation vote itself cannot be on individual Commissioners but must be on the College as a whole. However, as was shown in Chapter 8, in 2004 and 2010 changes were made to both of President Barroso's Colleges-designate following what were deemed by MEPs to be unacceptable hearing performances by individual Commissioners.

Third, the EP can dismiss the College – but not individual Commissioners – by carrying a motion of censure by a two-thirds majority of the votes cast, including a majority of all MEPs. This power of dismissal is obviously too blunt a controlling instrument for most purposes and it has never been carried through. However, it came close to being so in January 1999 when a number of factors came together to produce a groundswell of dissatisfaction amongst MEPs with the Santer College. Amongst the factors were: a Court of Auditors report that revealed (yet again!) evidence of 'missing' EU funds and was strongly critical of aspects of Commission management practices; the suggestion that some Commissioners were favouring relatives and friends for appointments and the awarding of contracts; and a rather dismissive response by Jacques Santer to the criticisms that were being made about himself and some of his colleagues. It was only after Santer agreed to the creation of a special committee of independent experts to investigate the allegations of fraud, nepotism and mismanagement that the threat of dismissal receded, though even then the motion of censure was supported by 232 MEPs, with 293 voting against.

The special committee's report was issued two months later, in March, and was highly critical of aspects of the College's work and behaviour (Committee of Independent Experts, 1999a). Particular criticisms were made of: Santer in his capacity as the official responsible for the Commission's Security Office, for taking 'no meaningful interest in its functioning' and allowing it to develop as 'a state within a state' (point 6.5.7); Edith Cresson, the Commissioner responsible for Research, for showing favouritism to someone known to her when issuing contracts (points 8.1.1–8.1.38); and Commissioners as a whole for being reluctant to assume responsibility for their actions – 'The studies carried out by the Committee have too often revealed a growing reluctance among the members of the hierarchy to acknowledge their responsibility. It is becoming diffi-

cult to find anyone who has even the slightest sense of responsibility' (point 9.4.25). Meeting almost immediately after the report was published, faced with a refusal by Santer and Cresson to resign, and aware that MEPs were likely to carry a motion of censure on it by the necessary two-thirds majority, the Santer College collectively resigned. The resignation was widely interpreted as a triumph for the EP and as a highly significant step forward in its long campaign to exercise greater control over Commission activities.

A further step forward was taken in 2004 when the Commission President-designate, José Manuel Barroso, gave way to pressures from MEPs that he should respond positively to any request from them to dismiss an individual member of his College. He promised that if what amounted to a motion of no confidence in a Commissioner was passed, he would require the individual to resign or at least would appear before Parliament to explain why he was not insisting on the Commissioner's resignation.

Fourth, under Article 233 TFEU, the EP 'shall discuss in open session the annual general report submitted to it by the Commission'. This debate used to be one of the highlights of the Parliamentary year, but it has never produced significant results and is now of little consequence.

Fifth, under Article 318 TFEU 'The Commission shall submit annually to the European Parliament and to the Council the accounts of the preceding financial year relating to the implementation of the budget. The Commission shall also forward to them a financial statement of the assets and liabilities of the Union.' On the basis of an examination of the accounts and the financial statement, and having examined also the annual report of the Court of Auditors, Parliament 'acting on a recommendation from the Council, shall give a discharge to the Commission in respect of the implementation of the budget' (Article 319 TFEU). Under its discharge powers the EP can require the Commission and other institutions to take appropriate steps to ensure action on the comments appearing in the decision on discharge. Sometimes the EP's discharge powers lead to confrontation with the Commission, as most notably in 1998 when Parliament's refusal to give discharge was an important factor in bringing about the January 1999 censure motion (see above). (The 1998 discharge dispute is considered further in the section on the Court of Auditors in Chapter 13.)

Sixth, the remits of EP standing committees are broad enough to allow them to attempt to exercise supervisory functions if they so choose. However, the Commission is not anxious to encourage investigations of itself, and the committees are not sufficiently well resourced to be able to probe very deeply. The Committee on Budgetary Control, which is specifically charged with monitoring policy implementation, is in a typically weak position: with only a handful of senior officers employed to assist it, it cannot hope to do anything other than cover a small fraction of the Commission's work.

Seventh, the EP is empowered to establish temporary committees of inquiry 'to investigate ... alleged contraventions or maladministration in the implementation of Union law, except where the alleged facts are being examined before a court and while the case is still subject to legal proceedings' (Article 226 TFEU). The work of committees of inquiry are not just concerned with Commission activities, but they certainly can focus on them, as demonstrated in 1996 when many of the recommendations that were made by the committee established to investigate the BSE crisis were directed at the Commission. According to one well-placed Commission insider, 'Parliament's debates with the Commission on 16 July 1996 and 18 February 1997 [on the BSE crisis, and framed by the work of the committee] can be seen as classic examples of a legislature holding the executive to account' (Westlake, 1997: 23). Following publication of the

committee's report there was a move to censure the Commission, but – aware that blame for the crisis was widely shared – the EP opted to employ what it called a 'conditional censure', which involved imposing a deadline on the Commission to carry out the EP's recommendations.

Finally, questions can be asked of the Commission. These take different forms: written questions, oral questions in question time, and oral questions with debate (see Table 11.2).

The Council

The EP is less able to control and supervise the Council of Ministers than it is the Commission. There are three main reasons for this.

The first reason arises from the role of the Council as the main meeting place of the governments of the member states. To make it, or any of its members, directly responsible to the EP would be to introduce a measure of supranationalism into the EU that is unacceptable to member state governments. Council members are to be responsible to their national parliaments. This means that the Council as a collective body is not responsible to anyone, whilst individual members are not responsible to an EU institution.

Second, the very nature of the Council – with its ever-changing composition, its specialist Councils, and its rotating Presidency – means that continuity of relations between it and the EP is difficult to establish.

Third, politicians from the Council are often very cautious about being too open with the EP in respect of such sensitive policy areas as the CFSP, the CSDP, and aspects of EMU. This reluctance, which can occur at national levels too, is partly because decisions in these spheres sometimes need to be made quickly and in secret and partly because some member states favour intergovernmentalism as the prevailing decision-making mode in these sensitive areas. The EP is thus left to make the best it can of its powers to be consulted, to be kept informed, to ask questions, and to make recommendations.

The amount of access the EP gets to the Council depends in large part on the attitude of the Council Presidency. There are, however, certain set points of contact which, if they do not enable the EP to exercise control over the Council, at least provide it with opportunities to challenge the Council on its general conduct of affairs. First, the Presidency of the Council

Table 11.2 Questions addressed by the European Parliament during 2008

To the Commission	7322
of which:	
written	6570
oral with debate	659
during question time	93
To the Council	1037
of which:	
written	547
oral with debate	413
during question time	50

Source: adapted from European Commission (2009a: European Parliament section).

– formerly usually represented by the Foreign Minister, but Heads of Government have done this in recent years – appears before EP plenaries at the beginning and end of each six-month term of office. This practice was made into a requirement by new Rules of Procedure adopted by the European Council as the Lisbon Treaty came into effect:

> The member of the European Council representing the Member State holding the Presidency of the Council shall present to the European Parliament the priorities of the Presidency and the results achieved during the six-month period (European Council, 2009b: 53).

Second, ministers from the Presidency usually attend the EP committees that deal with their spheres of responsibility at least twice during their country's Presidency. MEPs can use these occasions for informal discussions with the Council, or to have wide-ranging question and answer sessions on the Council's priorities and performance. Third, ministers from the Presidency also regularly attend EP plenary sessions and participate in important debates. Fourth, the EP can, through the Presidency, ask questions of the Council (see Table 11.2).

In one important respect the EP's supervisory position over the Council is boosted by the Lisbon Treaty, with it being accorded, as is shown in Chapter 21, considerable contact with the High Representative for Foreign Affairs and Security Policy.

The European Council

If the EP is not able to call the Commission fully to account and is greatly restricted in its ability to exercise control over the Council of Ministers, it is even weaker in being able to exercise any supervisory power over the European Council. This is largely because of the nature of the European Council: it is an intergovernmental institution that is largely outside the framework of the TFEU; it meets normally for only between six and eight days a year; and the Heads of Government, who make up most of its membership, not only have no great wish to be accountable to MEPs but can also ensure that they do not become so since it is at European Council meetings that final decisions on the contents of the treaties – which set out the main operating principles of the EU – are taken.

The TEU and the TFEU make provision in a few instances – such as in regard to EMU – for the European Council, or the Heads of Government meeting in the composition of the Council of Ministers, to inform or consult the EP, but these are anticipated as being for only occasional use. In only two sets of circumstances does the European Council come into regular contact with the EP. The first is at the opening session of European Council meetings, when the EP President is permitted to address the summit to inform it of the views of MEPs on current issues. The second has treaty status in that the Lisbon Treaty formalised and modified the former practice of the Head of Government of the Council Presidency appearing before the EP after the 'end of term' European Council meeting. Under the post-Lisbon Article 15:6(d) TEU, the President of the European Council 'shall present a report to the European Parliament after each of the meetings of the European Council.'

What this all adds up to is that the EP can exert very little direct influence on the European Council, let alone control over what it does. The fact is that there are only limited linkages between the two institutions, and there is no reason to suppose that the participants at summits make a habit of looking over their shoulders in anticipation of how the EP will view the outcome of their deliberations and negotiations.

Other bodies

The EP has a number of supervisory powers in relation to other EU bodies. Some of these bodies are of a quasi-executive nature.

The most prominent of the quasi-executive bodies is the European Central Bank where, under Article 283 TFEU, the EP must be consulted on the nominees for the Bank's President, Vice-President and Executive Board members. As with the powers given to it on the appointment of the College of Commissioners, the Parliament has sought to use these treaty provisions to maximum advantage by use of confirmation hearings. Significantly, the first President-designate of the Bank, Wim Duisenberg, stated at the time of his confirmation hearing in 1998 that he would withdraw his candidature if the EP did not give him its approval. He also undertook to keep the EP fully informed about the work of the Bank and to appear personally before the EP's Economic Committee at least once a quarter.

This undertaking was given, in an amended form, treaty status by the Nice Treaty, and now constitutes part of Article 284:3 of the TFEU: 'The President of the European Central Bank and the other members of the Executive Board may, at the request of the European Parliament or on their own initiative, be heard by the competent committees of the European Parliament.'

Other quasi-executive bodies in which the EP has a role in the nomination process include the executive boards of some of the EU agencies which have been established in recent years. Amongst these agencies are the European Environment Agency and the European Medicines Agency.

Beyond quasi-executive bodies, the EP also has a role in the appointment and overseeing of certain other EU bodies. Two of these bodies are especially important. First, the EP is consulted on the appointment of members of the Court of Auditors. It is a consultation that, as with other appointment powers, has been examined via committee 'hearings' followed by a vote. However, as is shown on pp. 240–1, there have been occasions when negative EP opinions of nominations have been ignored by the Council. Second, the European Ombudsman, who investigates cases of alleged maladministration, is appointed by the EP, with the Council having no input at all. Indeed, the Ombudsman is virtually a quasi-parliamentary post in that not only is the incumbent appointed by the EP but the duties of the post are regulated by Parliament and are annexed to the Parliament's Rules of Procedure.

Elections

Until 1979 MEPs were nominated by the national parliaments from amongst their members. Various consequences followed from this: parties not represented in their national legislature could not be represented in the EP; virtually all MEPs were pro-integrationist, since sceptics in national parliaments were generally unwilling to allow their names to be considered for nomination; and MEPs had limited time to devote to their European responsibilities.

However, Article 138 of the EEC Treaty included the following provision: 'The Assembly shall draw up proposals for elections by direct universal suffrage in accordance with a uniform procedure in all Member States.' The Assembly approved such proposals as early as 1960, but found itself frustrated by another Article 138 requirement which stated: 'The Council shall, acting unanimously, lay down the appropriate provisions, which it shall recommend to Member States for adoption in accordance with their respective constitutional requirements.' That the first set of direct elections were not held until 1979 is witness to the feeling of some member state governments – initially mainly the French, later the Danes and the British – that direct elections were rather unwelcome, both because they had supranational overtones and because they might be followed by pressure for institutional reform in the EP's favour. Even after the principle of direct elections was eventually won and it was agreed they would be held on a fixed five-year basis, no uniform electoral system could be agreed, nor has been agreed since. Consequently, the seven sets of direct elections held to date – in 1979, 1984, 1989, 1994, 1999, 2004, and 2009 – have all been contested on the basis of different national electoral arrangements. The 1999 elections, however, did bring a significant movement in the direction of standardisation in that the UK did not use its traditional single member constituency first-past-the-post system but rather proportional representation on a regional basis, which meant that for the first time proportional representation – albeit in different forms – was used in all member states. This situation was repeated in 2004 and 2009. (See Table 11.3 for the electoral systems used in 2009.)

In addition to the differences arising from the usage of varying versions of proportional representation, two other differences between the states' EP electoral arrangements merit note. The first is that voting does not take place on the same day. In 2009, for example, voting was between Thursday 4 June and Sunday 7 June, with the Netherlands and the UK voting on the 4th, Ireland on the 5th, the Czech Republic on the 5th and 6th, Cyprus, Latvia, Malta and Sovakia on the 6th, Italy on the 6th and 7th and all other states on the 7th. The second difference, and one that is important in terms of the democratic base of the EP, is that there is a considerable variation in the numbers of citizens MEPs represent. This is because national allocations of EP seats are distributed using the principle of degressive proportionality, whereby the number of citizens per MEP increases as the size of member states increases. The reason for using this principle is much

Table 11.3 Member States and the 2009 European Parliament Elections

	Number of MEPs*	Number of citizens per MEP (in thousands)**	Eligibility for election (years)	Electoral system	Constituency structure	Electoral turnout (%)
Austria	17/19	438	18	PR with preferential vote 4% threshold	Single constituency	45.3
Belgium	22/22	445	21	PR with preferential vote	5 (3 electoral colleges)	90.3
Bulgaria	17/18	425	21	PR	Single constituency	38.9
Cyprus	6/6	131	25	PR	Single constituency	59.4
Czech Republic	22/22	432	21	PR with preferential vote 5% threshold	Single constituency	28.2
Denmark	13/13	391	18	PR with preferential vote	Single constituency	59.5
Estonia	6/6	223	21	PR with preferential vote	Single constituency	43.2
Finland	13/13	379	18	PR with preferential vote	Single constituency (electoral districts)	40.3
France	72/74	817	23	PR 5% threshold	8	40.1
Germany	99/99	830	18	PR 5% threshold	16 *Länder*	43.3
Greece	22/22	467	21	PR	Single constituency	52.6
Hungary	22/22	419	18	PR 5% threshold	Single constituency	36.2
Ireland	12/12	338	21	PR with STV	4	57.6
Italy	72/73	764	25	PR with PV	5	66.5
Latvia	8/9	252	21	PR with PV	Single constituency	53.1
Lithuania	12/12	259	21	PR with PV 5% threshold	Single constituency	20.9
Luxembourg	6/6	80	21	PR with vote splitting	Single constituency	91.0
Malta	5/6	82	18	PR with STV	Single constituency	78.8
Netherlands	25/26	608	18	PR with PV	Single constituency	36.9
Poland	50/51	705	21	PR with PV 5% threshold	Single constituency (13 electoral districts)	24.5
Portugal	22/22	442	18	PR	Single constituency	37.0
Romania	33/33	615	23	PR 5% threshold	Single constituency	27.4
Slovakia	13/13	386	21	PR with PV 5% threshold	Single constituency	19.6
Slovenia	7/8	289	18	PR	Single constituency	28.3
Spain	50/54	839	18	PR	Single constituency	46.0
Sweden	18/20	483	18	PR with PV 4% threshold	Single constituency	45.5
United Kingdom	72/73	785	21	PR (Northern Ireland PR with STV)	11+1 (Northern Ireland)	34.3
TOTAL	736/754					43.2

PR = Proportional representation without preferential voting.
PR with PV = Proportional representation with preferential voting.
STV = Single transferable vote.

* The first figures are the numbers of MEPs who were elected in June 2009 under the Nice Treaty provisions. The second figures are the numbers provided for in the 2009–14 term (under decisions taken by the European Council in December 2007 and December 2008) on the coming into effect of the Lisbon Treaty.
** These figures are calculated on the basis of the post-Lisbon Treaty allocations.

Sources: various, but especially European Parliament (2009a).

the same as applies to the membership and/or voting arrangements of most other EU institutions: to ensure smaller member states can have confidence that their voices have the potential to be heard and that their representations are not totally swamped in EP decision-making processes. As can be seen in Table 11.3, in 2009 the number of citizens per MEP ranged from one per 830,000 in Germany to one per 80,000 in Luxembourg. The overall average was 659,000 citizens per MEP.

* * *

A subject that has been much discussed in the context of EP elections is voter turnout. Many have argued that a high turnout would serve to enhance the EP's legitimacy and democratic base, and as a consequence would also place the EP in a strong position to press for increased powers.

In the event, turnout has been relatively low and has declined in every election since the first direct elections in 1979. In 1979 only 62 per cent of those eligible to vote did so; in 1984 the figure was 61 per cent; in 1989 it was 58 per cent; in 1994 it was 56.5 per cent; in 1999 it was 49.8 per cent; in 2004 it was 45.5 per cent, and in 2009 it was 43.2 per cent. As Table 11.3 shows, in 2009 turnout was highest in Belgium and Luxembourg – where voting is obligatory – and was lowest in Slovakia and Lithuania.

Three main factors combine to explain the low turnouts. First, because EP elections do not offer any prospect of a change of government, switches in policy, or the making or unmaking of political reputations, they stimulate little popular interest or political excitement. Second, the election campaigns have little overall coherence or coordination. They are essentially national contests, but of a secondary sort. 'European' issues have never made much of an impact. In 2009, for example, there was little sense of the centre-right majority in the 2004–9 Parliament defending its record, or of the left seeking to gain control. Third, those actors who do much to focus attention on and generate interest in national electoral campaigns approach the EP elections in, at best, a half-hearted manner: few 'big names' have been candidates in recent elections; national political parties have been generally reluctant to commit resources to their Euro campaigns; party activists have tended to be uninterested; a conscious attempt has been made by some governments to play down the importance of the elec-

tions because they are frequently interpreted as being, in part at least, 'mid-term' national elections, or unofficial referendums on the government's performance in office; and media interest has been limited.

These three factors have thus combined to make EP elections appear much less important – in the sense of something significant and identifiable being at stake – than national elections. They have also resulted in EP elections having a relatively low visibility in most member states.

Political Parties and the European Parliament

Party political activity takes place at three main levels in relation to the EP: the transnational, the political groups in the EP, and the national.

The transnational federations

Very loosely organised transnational federations, grouped around general principles, exist for coordinating, propaganda, and electioneering purposes. They are based on affiliation by national parties, from both within and outside the EU.

The three main federations were created in similar circumstances in the mid-1970s out of existing, but extremely weakly based, liaising and information-exchanging bodies, and as a specific response to the continuing development of the EC and the anticipated future use of direct elections to the EP. These three federations are: the European People's Party (EPP), whose membership consists of 74 centre-right parties from 39 European countries; the European Liberal, Democrat and Reform Party (ELDR), whose membership consists of 56 liberal parties from across Europe; and the Party of European Socialists (PES), which has 36 full member parties and ten associate and observer parties drawn from most European countries.

Supporters of European integration have hoped that the federations might develop into organisations providing leadership, vision and coordination at the European level, and perhaps might even serve as agents of unification to their heterogeneous memberships. They have failed to do so. Their principal weakness is that, unlike national parties or the EP political groups, they are not involved in day-to-day political activity in an institutional setting. Hence they have no clear focus and cannot develop attachments and loyalties. From this, other weaknesses flow: low status; limited resources – they are heavily dependent on the EP political groups for administrative and financial support; and loose organisational structures based on periodic congresses and bureaux meetings.

The federations, therefore, have not been able to do very much, even though there certainly are tasks that EU-wide transnational parties could usefully perform, such as long-term policy planning, the harmonisation of national party differences, and educating the electorate about Europe. Such influence as they have exercised has been largely confined to very loose policy coordination – effected partly through periodic meetings of national leaders, usually before European Council meetings – and to EP elections when manifestos have been produced and a few joint activities have been arranged. Even the manifestos, however, have reinforced the general picture of weakness for they invariably have been somewhat vague in content (necessarily so given the need to reconcile differences), and have been utilised by only a few of the constituent member parties (because EP elections are contested, for the most part, along national lines).

Beyond the three main federations, other groupings of an even looser nature have surfaced from time to time, usually in order to coordinate election activities. They have included Green, Regional, Communist, and Extreme Right alliances. All have been internally divided and have been hard-pressed to put together even minimal common statements.

The political groups in the European Parliament

Partisan political activity in the EP is mainly channelled via political groups. The rules for the composition of political groups have changed over the years in response to the increasing size of the Parliament. In the 2009–14 Parliament, at least 25 MEPs drawn from at least one quarter of the member states are necessary to form a group.

Groups have been formed and developed for a number of reasons. The principal basis and unifying element of most of the groups is ideological identification. Despite the many differences that exist between them, MEPs from similar political backgrounds and traditions are naturally drawn to one another. All the more so when cooperation serves to maximise their influence, as it does in the EP in all sorts of ways – from electing the President to voting on amendments to Commission proposals.

Organisational benefits provide another inducement to political group formation. For example, funds for administrative and research purposes are distributed to groups on the basis of a fixed amount per group (the non-attached being regarded as a group for these purposes), plus an additional sum per member. No one, therefore, is unsupported, but the larger the group the more easily it can afford good back-up services.

There are also advantages in the conduct of Parliamentary business that stem from group status, since the EP arranges much of what it does around the groups. Although non-attached members are not formally excluded from anything by this – indeed they are guaranteed many rights under the Rules of Procedure – in practice they can be disadvantaged: in the distribution of committee chairmanships for example, where the largest political groups get first choices on the most important and prestigious committees; in the preparation of the agendas for plenary sessions; and in speaking time during debates.

In recent years there have usually been between seven and nine political groups in the EP: seven at the beginning of the 2009–14 Parliament. The main reason for there being so many is that, with proportional representation being used for EP elections, MEPs reflect the wide range of political opinion that exists across the EU with regard to ideological and national orientation. Since direct elections were introduced in 1979 there have never been fewer than 60 national political parties represented in the EP; since the 1994 elections there have never been fewer than 100; and following each of the 2004 and 2009 elections there have been around 160.

The main characteristics of the political groups in the EP, as of early 2010, are set out in Box 11.2. The sizes of the groups are shown in Table 11.4 and Figure 11.1.

As suggested in the outlines of the groups in Box 11.2, group formation and composition is highly fluid. The extent of this is demonstrated by the fact that although the number of groups has remained relatively stable over the years, since direct elections were first introduced only the two largest groups – the EPP

Box 11.2

Political groups in the EP

- *Group of the European People's Party (EPP).* The EPP, which has been the largest group in the EP since 1999, used to be based on European Christian Democracy, and in particular the large Christian Democratic parties of Germany and Italy. Over the years, however, other centre-right parties, mostly from a conservative tradition, have been absorbed into the group. Indeed it was at the behest of these parties, especially the UK Conservative Party, that the group changed its name in 1999 from EPP to EPP-ED. However, after the 2009 EP elections, when the UK Conservatives left the group to help form the ECR group, the EEP-ED reverted to its former EPP name. The group, which is by far the largest in the Parliament and which contains at least one member from 26 of the 27 member states (the UK being the exception), has had some difficulty maintaining internal ideological cohesion, but is broadly a pro-integrationist group of the moderate political right.
- *Group of the Progressive Alliance of Socialists and Democrats (S&D).* Calling itself the Socialist Group until the 2009 EP elections, this group adopted the new S&D name after the 2009 elections to accommodate the wishes of the new Italian Democrat Party which is made up of former communists and left-wing Christian Democrats. Although including at least one MEP from every member state and maintaining its position as the second largest group in the Parliament, the 2009 elections were a disaster for the group, with its 25 per cent share of the seats in the new Parliament constituting its lowest representation since direct elections were first used in 1979. Although broadly a grouping of social democrats, the members of the group have sometimes found cooperation difficult. In part this has been because of diversity within the group about the nature of the commitment to socialism and social democracy, with opinions ranging from 'traditional state interventionists' to 'moderate' and 'modernising' social democrats. In part it has stemmed from differences over the bases and direction of European integration. And in part it has been caused by national party groups being reluctant to concede national interests to wider European interests.
- *Group of the Alliance of Liberals and Democrats for Europe (ALDE).* This group, which has long been the third largest group in the Parliament, is a strongly pro-European integrationist and centrist group. It is comprised primarily of national parties from the political centre and the right, but there are also certain

→

and the PES – have survived in recognisable form. Moreover, both of these have been subject to considerable changes in their memberships as a result of enlargements, election results, and – especially in the EPP's case – defections from and to smaller groups.

As is also suggested in Box 11.2, all the political groups have significant internal divisions, usually of both an ideological and a national character. Internal division within a group does, of course, undermine coherence, which has a weakening effect. But, though this is recognised, whatever their ideological principles might suggest to them it is all but impossible for French MEPs, for example, to vote in favour of cuts in agricultural support measures or for Polish MEPs not to support increases in the Structural Funds.

In addition to ideological heterogeneity and national attachments, three other factors also make for looseness and a limited ability on the part of the groups to control and direct their members. The first of these factors arises from the political powers of the EP and the institutional setting in which it is placed. With no government to sustain or attack and no government-sponsored legislation to pass or reject, MEPs do not have the semi-automatic 'for' or 'against' reaction that is so typical of much national parliamentary behaviour. The second factor is structural. Unlike parties in national legislatures, the political groups are not part of a wider organisational framework from which emanate expectations of cooperative and united behaviour, and generally recognised notions of responsibility and accountability. Rather, most of them are weak, quasi-federal bodies functioning in a

Box 11.2 *continued*

leftist elements. In the Parliament it often occupies a key position in determining whether majorities can be obtained in votes. Whilst certainly not being in any sort of alliance with the EPP, it has tended to work more closely with it than it has with the Socialists. In the 2004–09 Parliament the group had members from twenty member states, a position it almost maintained in the 2009 elections when it returned members from nineteen states.

- *Group of the Greens/European Free Alliance (Greens/EFA).* This group was formed in 1999 largely as a marriage of convenience. It brings together greens and regionalists of various sorts. Beyond supporting green issues and greater regional autonomy, the group is not very homogeneous, with some of its MEPs coming from a clear left background and others seeing themselves as being neither left nor right.
- *European Conservatives and Reformists' Group (ECR).* This group was formed after the 2009 EP elections, with three main component elements – the UK Conservative Party, the Polish Law and Justice Party, and the Czech Civic Democratic Party – plus an assortment of populists and conservatives, some of who had been in the (now disbanded) Union for Europe of the Nations Group (UEN) in the 2004–09 Parliament. The group stops short of the virulent euroscepticism that characterises the EFD, but it is a firmly anti-federalist group – of the political right
- *Confederal Group of the European United Left/Nordic Green Left (GUE/NGL).* This group is made up mainly of left Socialist and former Communist parties, plus a small number of Nordic leftist Greens. It supports European integration, but wants much greater emphasis to be given to social and environmental issues. Disparate views within the group coupled with a very loose group structure make for little internal group cohesion.
- *Europe of Freedom and Democracy Group* (EFD). Created after the 2004 EP elections as the Independence and Democracy Group (Ind/Dem), this group is comprised of eurosceptics of various persuasions, including the UK Independence Party which campaigns for complete British withdrawal from the EU. Its message is that there should be a 'Europe of Sovereign Nation States' and that further European integration should be firmly opposed. On principle, the group does not attempt to persuade its constituent national delegations to vote as bloc.
- Non-attached (NA) MEPs are drawn from many different persuasions, with the strongest element being right-wing populists and hard-right extremists.

multicultural environment. This is evidenced in a number of ways: the constituent member parties of the larger groups hold their own separate meetings and have their own leaderships; in seeking to encourage group unity, group leaders can invoke no effective sanctions against, and can withhold few rewards from, MEPs who do not fall into line; and in looking to their political futures, it is not only their political group or its leadership that MEPs must cultivate but also their national parties at home. The third factor is that MEPs may have claims on their loyalties and votes that compete with the claims of the political groups. One source of such claims are the numerous interest groups with which many MEPs are closely associated. Other sources are the EP intergroups, which bring together, usually on a relatively informal basis, MEPs

from different political groups who have similar views on particular issues. Over 100 intergroups exist, of which 25 or so meet on a regular basis. The intergroups come in many different forms and vary considerably in the nature and range of their policy focus. Amongst their number are the Federalist Intergroup for European Union, the Friends of Israel Intergroup, the Central American Intergroup, the Media Intergroup, the Rural Areas Intergroup, the Animal Welfare Intergroup, and the Elderly People Intergroup.

However, despite the many weaknesses of the groups, it is important to emphasise that they are of considerable importance in determining how the EP works. Some of their functions and tasks and the privileges they enjoy are specifically allocated to them under the Rules of Procedure or by parliamentary

Table 11.4 Political groups in the European Parliament

	EPP	S&D	ALDE	Greens/EFA	ECR	GUE/NGL	EFD	NA	Total
Austria	6	4		2				5	17
Belgium	5	5	5	4	1			2	22
Bulgaria	6	4	5					2	17
Cyprus	2	2				2			6
Czech Rep.	2	7			9	4			22
Denmark	1	4	3	2		1	2		13
Estonia	1	1	3	1					6
Finland	4	2	4	2			1		13
France	29	14	6	14		5	1	3	72
Germany	42	23	12	14		8			99
Greece	8	8		1		3	2		22
Hungary	14	4			1			3	22
Ireland	4	3	4			1			12
Italy	35	21	7				9		72
Latvia	3	1	1	1	1	1			8
Lithuania	4	3	2		1		2		12
Luxembourg	3	1	1	1					6
Malta	2	3							5
Netherlands	5	3	6	3	1	2	1	4	25
Poland	28	7			15				50
Portugal	10	7				5			22
Romania	14	11	5					3	33
Slovakia	6	5	1					1	13
Slovenia	3	2	2						7
Spain	23	21	2	2		1		1	50
Sweden	5	5	4	3		1			18
United Kingdom		13	11	5	25	1	13	4	72
TOTAL	265	184	84	55	54	35	32	27	736

Notes: Situation in January 2010. The full names of the political groups are given in the text.

Source: European Parliament web pages on the Europa website.

decisions. These include guaranteed representation on key EP bodies and committees, and speaking rights in plenary sessions. Other functions have not been formally laid down but have developed out of political necessity, advantage, or convenience. This is most obviously illustrated by the way the groups are the prime determiners of tactics and voting patterns in the EP, the decisions on which are normally taken in the week prior to plenary sessions which is set aside for political group meetings. At these meetings efforts are made to agree a common group position on matters of current importance. For example: should a deal be attempted with another political group on the election of the EP's President?; what is the group's attitude towards a Commission proposal for a directive?; what tactics can the group employ to prevent an unwelcome

Figure 11.1 Left–right composition of the EP after the 2009 elections

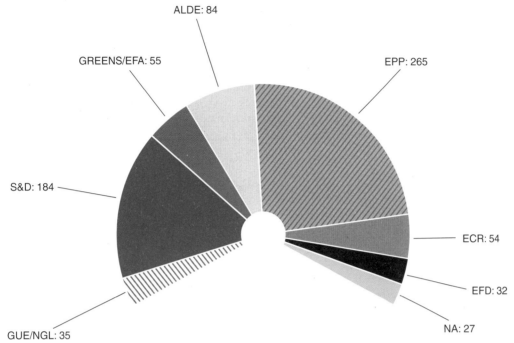

ALDE: 84

GREENS/EFA: 55

EPP: 265

S&D: 184

ECR: 54

EFD: 32

GUE/NGL: 35

NA: 27

own initiative report being approved by a committee? In dealing with such questions internal group differences may have to be tackled, and sometimes they may not be resolved. But of the many influences bearing down on MEPs, political group membership is normally the single most important factor correlating with how they vote, and is considerably higher than voting along national lines. There are some differences between researchers on how high the correlation with political group membership actually is (differences arising largely from whether roll-call votes, which account for about one third of total votes in plenary sessions, are representative of all votes or are slanted), but overall it seems that in the three largest groups – the EPP, the S&D, and the ALDE – MEPs vote with their group over 85 per cent of the time, whilst for all groups the average is just over 70 per cent. (Useful sources on voting behaviour and group membership include: Hix *et al.*, 2007; Hix, 2008; Judge and Earnshaw, 2008).

Regarding the implications of the political group composition of the EP for the overall balance of power in the Parliament, in very broad terms it can be said

that from 1979–89 a nominal centre-right majority existed, from 1989–94 there was a nominal left-green majority, from 1994–9 there was no nominal majority either to the right or to the left, and since the 1999 elections there has been a centre-right majority. The nature of the political balance existing at any one time unquestionably affects the interests and priorities of the EP, with groups from the left tending, for example, to be more sympathetic to social and environmental issues than groups from the right. However, the significance of the nature of the overall balance is not as great as it normally is in national parliaments. There are four main reasons for this. First, important issues, sometimes of an organisational or domestic political nature rather than an ideological nature, can divide groups that otherwise appear to be obvious voting partners. The various liaising channels and mechanisms that exist in the EP via which groups attempt to reach agreements and strike deals cannot always bridge these divisions. On many issues it is by no means unusual for the views of political groups on the centre-left and centre-right, or at least of many MEPs within these groups, to be closer to each other than to the views of other left and right groups. The second reason is that many matters that come before the EP cut across traditional left–right divisions. Such is the case with much of the essentially technical legislation with which Parliament deals. Such too is the case with issues like action to combat racism in Europe, the provision of assistance to the countries of the developing world, and the further development of economic and political European integration. The third reason is that the EP frequently and consciously attempts to avoid being divided along left–right lines when it votes because it is in its institutional interests to do so. For example, under the ordinary legislative procedure an absolute majority of MEPs must support EP amendments and rejections for votes to be effective. In consequence, it is necessary for groups from both left and right – and especially from the EPP, the S&D, and the ALDE – to work together if the EP is to make full use of its powers. And the fourth reason is that most EU decision-making processes are characterised by bargaining and compromising. So, for example, the EP is almost constantly involved in inter-institutional dealings with the Commission and the Council. As a result, MEPs are accustomed to exchanging points and cutting deals in all sorts of ways: ways that often result in alliances being made that are not based on ideological identities.

Given these circumstances it is not surprising that the most dominant voting pattern in the EP is not along 'hard' left–right lines. Simon Hix has noted in his writings (see, for example, Hix, 2005; Hix *et al.*; 2007; Hix 2008) that 'ideological' voting along left–right lines has increased in the EP over the years and the EP has come to operate more on ideological grounds and less on national grounds. But, the fact is that much voting remains grouped around an alliance of centre-left and centre-right. The EPP, the PES, and the ELDR (the pre-2004 name of the ALDE) used to vote together on average about 75–80 per cent of the time (Hix and Lord, 1997: 137). This figure has subsequently slipped, but the 'big three' groups still come together in a 'grand coalition' on about two-thirds of the votes (Hix *et al.*, 2007). Left–right divisions account only for about one-third of votes, though the greater strength of the right in the 2009–14 Parliament (if they voted together, the EPP, the ALDE and the ECR would have an absolute majority) could result in this figure increasing.

On a final point concerning the political groups, it is to be noted that the key position they occupy in organising and controlling much of the activity of the EP raises further questions – in addition to those arising from EP elections – concerning the relationship between the EP and EU democracy. For, as Judge and Earnshaw (2008) note, whilst voters in European elections are mobilised primarily around national party programmes and affiliations, the candidates who are elected by this process operate within the EP in transnational groups of which voters are almost completely unaware. Indeed, groups sometimes are not even in existence at the time of EP elections: as with, for example, the ECR group in the 2009–13 Parliament.

National parties

National political parties are involved in EP-related activities in three main ways. First, most candidates in EP elections, and virtually all of those who are elected, are chosen by their national parties. This means that MEPs inevitably reflect national party concerns and are normally obliged, if they wish to be re-selected, to continue to display an awareness of these concerns.

Second, EP election campaigns are essentially national election campaigns conducted by national parties. Use may be made of transnational manifestos, but voters are directed by the parties primarily to national issues and the results are mainly assessed in terms of their domestic implications. That the European dimension is limited is no more evident than in the fact that the most dominant pattern in EP elections is a movement away from governing parties and large opposition parties towards smaller opposition parties (see Hix and Marsh, 2007; Hix 2009). So, in the 2009 elections, in 22 of the 27 member states the party of the head of government suffered significant losses as compared with the previous national parliamentary election. Ten of these 22 parties came from the centre-right political family, seven came from the social democrats and five came from the liberals (Niedermayer, 2009: 3). Therefore, whilst it is true that social democrats generally performed poorly in the 2009 elections, the elections did not display, as previous EP elections had also not displayed, any consistent left–right movement in voting patterns across the member states.

Finally, in the EP itself national party groups exist

within the political groups. This is an obvious potential source of political group disharmony and sometimes creates strains. Problems do not arise so much from the national groups having to act on specific domestic instructions. This does sometimes occur, but in general the organisational links between the national groups and national party leaderships are weak and the former have a reasonably free hand within general party guidelines. The problem is simply that each national party group inevitably tends to have its own priorities and loyalties. Moreover, when there is a clash between the positions of a national group and its political group, the former usually takes precedence for the national MEPs (see Hix *et al.*, 2007).

Composition

In addition to party political attachments, four other aspects of the composition of the EP are particularly worthy of comment.

The dual mandate

After the 1979 election some 30 per cent of MEPs were also members of their national legislature. This figure was inflated, however, because many MEPs had contested the election primarily for domestic political reasons and had no firm commitment to completing their terms of office. By the end of the Parliamentary term the number of dual mandates had been more than halved. What therefore seemed to be a big drop after the 1984 elections, to around 12 per cent of MEPs holding a dual mandate, in fact reflected a trend that was already well under way: a trend that was assisted from 1984 with the holding of a dual mandate being discouraged in most member states and being forbidden by national law in some. Only six per cent of MEPs who were elected in 1999 were simultaneously members of their national parliaments.

Dual mandates have the advantage of strengthening links between the EP and national parliaments, but the disadvantage of reducing the amount of time and energy that is available for each post. Reacting to an increasingly accepted view that being an MEP should be a full-time job, a 2002 Council Decision abolished the dual mandate as from the 2004 EP elections, save

for limited and temporary derogations given to Ireland and the UK. Accordingly, only eight people were elected to the EP in June 2004 who were also members of their national parliaments: six Irish and two British (with the latter both being members of the House of Lords) (Corbett *et al.*, 2005: 22). There were no dual mandates in the EP that was elected in June 2009.

Continuity

Change and turnover in personnel affects the way most organisations work. The EP is no exception to this: the more effective MEPs tend to be those who have developed policy interests and expertise in European affairs over time and have come to know their way around the EU system.

Lack of continuity in membership was a problem after the first EP elections in 1979, with nearly one-quarter of MEPs being replaced before the 1984 elections. However, as noted above, that was always likely as many of the prominent politicians who stood in 1979 had no intention of making a political career in the EP. Things have since settled down and now only a relatively small proportion of MEPs resign before the end of their term of office. However, the turnover of MEPs between parliaments is certainly higher than in most national parliaments: just over 50 per cent of those who were elected in 1989 were returnees, in 1994 the figure was just over 40 per cent, in 1999 it was 46 per cent, in 2004 it was 54 per cent for MEPs from EU-15 states (Corbett *et al.*, 2005: 48), and in 2009 it was 50 per cent.

Gender

As in national parliaments, women are proportionately under-represented in the EP. In the Parliaments elected in 1994, 1999 and 2004, the figure hovered around 30 per cent, while in the 2009–14 Parliament it is 35 per cent.

The member states with the highest proportion of women MEPs elected in 2009 were Finland (62 per cent), Sweden (56 per cent), Estonia (50 per cent) and the Netherlands (48 per cent). The states with the lowest proportion were Malta (0 per cent – though it has only five seats), Italy (17 per cent), and the Czech

Republic (18 per cent). In most member states a higher proportion of women were elected to the EP in 2009 than had been elected to the national parliaments in the previous national elections.

Competence and experience

It is sometimes suggested that MEPs are not of the same calibre and do not carry the same political weight as their counterparts in national legislatures. Because the EP is not high-profile, the argument runs, it mostly attracts second-rate parliamentarians, or those who regard it merely as a stepping stone to a national career or advancement.

There is some truth in this view. Major national figures have tended either not to contest EP elections or not to complete their terms of office. (The provision in the 1976 'Direct Elections Act' making national governmental office incompatible with EP membership has not helped in this regard.) Additionally, a few MEPs have transferred from the EP to national legislatures.

But the situation should not be exaggerated. The competition to become an MEP is normally fierce and requires all the customary political skills. Most MEPs have considerable public experience, either in national or regional politics, or in an executive capacity with a major sectional interest. In the 2009 elections, amongst those elected were eight former prime ministers and one former president.

Perhaps the key point to be emphasised is that it should not be assumed that those who choose to stand for and work in the EP are necessarily settling for second best. Many are firmly committed to their responsibilities and have developed competences and experience that may be different from, but are not necessarily inferior to, those of national parliamentarians.

Organisation and Operation

The multi-site problem

The work of the EP is carried out on three sites in three different countries. Full plenary sessions are held in Strasbourg whilst mini-plenary sessions are held in Brussels. Committees usually meet in Brussels.

Around half of the just over 6,000 staff who work in the EP Secretariat (with another 150 in temporary posts) are based in Luxembourg, with the rest mainly in Brussels. (These figures do not include the 600 who work in the secretariats of the political groups.)

This situation is clearly unsatisfactory and is a source of grievance and annoyance for most MEPs. Reasonably conscientious MEPs may well have to change their working location half a dozen times in an average month. An average work diary is likely to look something like this: four days attending the monthly plenary in Strasbourg; from two to five days in committee(s), probably in Brussels but sometimes elsewhere; two to four days in political group meetings and group working parties, probably in Brussels; whatever time remains is spent in the constituency (if the MEP has one), visiting somewhere as part of an EP delegation, in Brussels or Luxembourg consulting with officials on a report, or at home.

If the EP had just one base, and especially if that was Brussels, it is likely that the EP's efficiency, influence and visibility would all be increased. However, the Council has the power of decision on the matter, and hard lobbying from the Luxembourg and French governments has ensured that arguments for 'sense to prevail' and a single site in Brussels to be agreed have not been acted upon.

Arranging parliamentary business

Relative independence

Compared with most national parliaments the EP enjoys considerable independence in the arrangement of its affairs. This is not to say it can do whatever it likes. The treaties oblige it to do some things – most notably deliver its views on Commission proposals for legislation – and prevent it from doing others – such as censuring the Council. But on many agenda, timetable and other organisational matters the EP is, to a considerable degree, its own master.

A major reason for this independence is the special institutional setting in which the EP operates. The EU executive does not have to be as concerned to control what the EP does as do national governments with their legislatures. This is because although many EP pronouncements and activities can be unwelcome to the Council and the Commission, outside legislative procedures they do not normally have such politically damaging or unmanageable consequences as can be the case when national parliaments act in ways of which national governments disapprove.

A second, and closely related, reason is the lack of any clear and consistent identification, of either a positive or a negative kind, between the EP and the EU executive. In national parliaments business is shaped to a considerable degree by political attachments. But the Commission is made up of officials who are nominally non-partisan, whilst the Council is multi-party, multi-ideological, and multi-national in its membership. As for the 'persuasive devices' that national executives have at their disposal to encourage loyalty, neither the Commission nor the Council has patronage to dispense.

A third reason is that the EP is entitled to adopt its own Rules of Procedure. This it has done, amending and streamlining the Rules in order to make itself more efficient and more influential.

Important organisational positions and bodies

Most decisions about the operation and functioning of the EP are not taken in plenary session but are delegated to EP offices and bodies.

The *President of the EP* is elected to office for a two-and-a-half-year term. For the 1999–2004 Parliament, the EPP-ED and ELDR arranged a deal to enable each of them to assume the Presidency for a term. The EEP-ED and the PES made a similar deal at the beginning of the 2004/09 Parliament, which resulted in the Socialist Josep Borrell – a vastly experienced Spanish politician, but a newly elected MEP – being elected President for the first two and a half years of the Parliament and Hans-Gert Pöttering, a Christian Democrat, being elected for the second two and a half years. No open deal was contracted at the beginning of the 2009–14 Parliament when Jerzy Buzek, a former Polish Prime Minister and a member of the EPP group, was elected President and became the first person from a Central or East European state to become 'head' of an EU institution.

According to Rule 20 of the Rules of Procedure, the President 'shall direct all the activities of Parliament and of its bodies under the conditions laid down in these Rules' (European Parliament, 2009b). In practice this means that the President has many functions, such

as presiding over debates in the chamber, referring matters to committees as appropriate, and representing the EP in dealings with other EU institutions and outside bodies. An effective President must be an administrator and a politician, skilled in organising and also in liaising and bargaining.

The *Bureau* consists of the President and the EP's fourteen Vice-Presidents. Like the President, the Vice-Presidents are elected for a two-and-a-half-year term of office, though by tradition the posts are distributed amongst the political groups and member states. Various financial and administrative organisational matters are dealt with by the Bureau, such as drawing up the EP's draft estimates and deciding on the composition and structure of the Secretariat. To assist it in the performance of its duties, and in particular to take responsibility for financial and administrative matters concerning members, five *Quaestors*, who are also elected, sit in the Bureau in an advisory capacity.

Organisational matters, other than matters of routine which are dealt with by the Bureau, are the responsibility of the *Conference of Presidents*. This is composed of the EP President and the chairs of the political groups. MEPs who are not attached to any political group can delegate two of their number to attend meetings. Matters that fall within the remit of the Conference of Presidents include the following: deciding on the seating arrangements in the Chamber – a potentially sensitive and highly symbolic issue when groups do not wish to be seated too far to the left or too far to the right of the hemicycle; arranging the EP's work programme, including assigning the drafting of reports to committees and drawing up the draft agendas for plenary sessions; and authorising the drawing up of own initiative reports. By and large the Conference responds to matters coming before it from EP committees and groups rather than imposing itself on Parliament. Decisions are made by consensus whenever possible, but if none exists matters are put to a vote, with group chairs (though not the non-attached delegates who do not have voting rights) having as many votes as there are members of the group.

Two other Conferences also have an organisational role: the Conference of Committee Chairs and the Conference of Delegation Chairs. The *Conference of Committee Chairs* brings together the chairs of EP committees on a monthly basis to undertake such tasks as arranging for necessary liaison between committees, settling intercommittee disputes, and generally monitoring the progress of business through the committee system. The *Conference of Delegation Chairs*, which meets monthly to discuss common organisational and planning matters, brings together the chairs of the EP's 35 delegations. These delegations, each of which number about 15 MEPs, are of three types: interparliamentary delegations to maintain contacts with non EU countries that are not seeking EU membership; joint parliamentary committees to maintain contacts with the parliaments of countries that are seeking membership and/or have association agreements with the EU; and EP delegations to five multilateral assemblies including the ACP–EU Joint Parliamentary Assembly (see Chapter 21); and the Euro-Mediterranean Parliamentary Assembly.

The committees of the EP

Much of the EP's work is carried out by committees. These are of two main types. The first and by far the most important are standing or permanent committees, of which there are twenty in the 2009–14 Parliament (see Table 11.5). The second are *ad hoc* committees, which are established to investigate specific problems and topics.

MEPs are assigned to the standing committees at the beginning and half way through each five-year term. Assignment to the *ad hoc* committees is as required. According to the Rules of Procedure, all committee members are elected to their positions on the basis of proposals made by the Conference of Presidents to Parliament which are 'designed to ensure fair representation of Member States and of political views'. What this means in practice is that the political groups negotiate the share-out of committee memberships on a basis proportionate to their size. Most MEPs become a member of one standing committee – though a few are on as many as three – and a substitute member of another.

The standing committees, which in most cases have 40–60 members, perform various duties, such as exploring ideas with the Commission, fostering own initiative reports, and discussing developments with the President-in-Office of the Council. The most important task of most of them, however, is to examine Commission proposals for legislation. The customary way of proceeding (other than when a

Table 11.5 Standing committees of the European Parliament

Foreign Affairs
  – Human Rights sub-committee
  – Security and Defence sub-committee
Development
International Trade
Budgets
Budgetary Control
Economic and Monetary Affairs
Employment and Social Affairs
Environment, Public Health and Food Safety
Industry, Research and Energy
Internal Market and Consumer Protection
Transport and Tourism
Regional Development
Agriculture and Rural Development
Fisheries
Culture and Education
Legal Affairs
Civil Liberties, Justice and Home Affairs
Constitutional Affairs
Women's Rights and Gender Equality
Petitions

proposal is completely straightforward and uncontroversial, which may result in it being dealt with by special procedures allowing for rapid approval) is as follows:

1 Each proposal is referred to an appropriate committee. Should a proposal overlap the competency and interest of several committees, up to three may be asked for their views, but one is named as the committee responsible and only it reports to the plenary session.

2 The responsibility for drawing up the committee's report is entrusted to *a rapporteur*. Though formally chosen by their fellow committee members, in practice *rapporteurs* are, as are committee chairs, appointed as a result of negotiations between the political groups: negotiations that in this case are carried out by group 'coordinators' from the different committees. When drawing up the report the *rapporteur* can call on various sources of assistance: from the EP Secretariat, from

her or his own research services (the EP provides funds to enable each MEP to have at least one research assistant), from the Secretariat of his or her political group, from research institutes, and even from the Commission. Some *rapporteurs* hardly use these facilities and do most of the work themselves; others do little more than present what has been done on their behalf.

3 A first draft is produced for consideration by the committee according to an agreed timetable. Drafts are normally presented in four main parts: Amendments to the Commission Proposal (if there are any); a Draft Legislative Resolution; an Explanatory Statement; and Annexes (if there are any), which include the opinions of other committees. How much discussion the draft provokes, and how many committee meetings are required before a text is adopted that can be recommended to the plenary, depends on the complexity and controversiality of the subject matter. Factors that are likely to shape the reactions of committee members include national and ideological perspectives, lobbying by outside interests, and views expressed by the Commission.

4 The *rapporteur* acts as the committee's principal spokesperson when the report is considered in the plenary. In this capacity he or she may have to explain the committee's view on amendments put forward by non-committee members, or be called upon to use his or her judgement in making recommendations to Parliament on what it should do when the Commission goes some, but not all, of the way towards accepting committee-approved amendments. Occasionally – as when, for example, the Commission offers a mixed package – committee meetings may be hurriedly convened during plenary sessions.

5 Where the ordinary legislative applies, the role and activity of committees at the second reading stage are similar to those at the first reading. That is, they examine the proposal (which is now in the form of the Council's common position) and make recommendations to the plenary. The responsibility for drawing up reports is conferred automatically on the committee involved in the first reading and the *rapporteur* remains the same. The reports normally have two main sections: Recommendations for the Second Reading (which may include approval of, rejection of, or amendments to, the common posi-

tion – amendments are often aimed at re-establishing the EP's position as defined at the first reading, or producing a compromise with the Council); and Justifications or Explanatory Statements.

6 The committee that has dealt with a proposal at the first and second readings is not directly concerned with the proceedings if a conciliation committee is convened under the co-decision procedure. However, the EP delegation to a conciliation committee always includes some members of the committee concerned, including the chairperson and the *rapporteur*.

* * *

As for the influence exercised by the standing committees, this varies between committees according to the factors set out in Box 11.3.

Plenary meetings

There are twelve full plenary meetings, or part-sessions as they are officially known, each year: one each month apart from August, plus an extra one in the autumn when MEPs consider the annual budget. The sessions are held in Strasbourg and last from Monday to Thursday. The EP ceased holding Friday plenary meetings in 2001, largely because of poor attendance on that day.

In addition to full plenaries, six mini-plenaries are held each year. They normally take up two half-days (from lunchtime on day one to lunchtime on day two) and are held in Brussels.

The agenda for plenaries is drafted by the President and the Conference of Presidents in consultation with the Conference of Committee Chairs and the EP Secretariat. Their recommendations have to be approved by the plenary itself. With time so tight, items that many MEPs consider important inevitably do not get onto the agenda, and those that do make it normally have to be covered at pace. Strict rules govern who can speak, when, and for how long: the effect of the rules is often to restrict speakers to committee and political group spokesmen.

Full plenaries have three standard elements. First, the bread-and-butter business is the consideration of reports from committees. As indicated earlier, these reports usually lead either to resolutions embodying opinions or to resolutions embodying own initiatives.

Box 11.3

Factors determining the influence of EP committees

- *The significance of the policy area within the EU system.* The Internal Market Committee, for example, deals with matters that loom larger in the EU scale of things than the Culture and Education Committee.
- *The extent of EU policy development.* There can be more opportunities to exercise influence when EU policy is in the process of formation than when it is well-established. So, the Committee on Environment, Public Health and Food Safety is advantaged in this regard whereas the Committee on Agriculture is disadvantaged.
- *The power of the EP within the policy area.* The influence of the Committee on Budgets is enormously enhanced by the real budgetary decision-making powers that the treaties give to the EP. The Committee on Foreign Affairs, by contrast, though dealing with extremely important subject material, is limited in what it can do because of the essentially intergovernmental character of the policies with which it deals.
- *Committee expertise.* Many committee members do not have the requisite specialised skills to be able to explore relevant issues in depth or to question the Commission on the basis of a fully informed understanding of policy. For example, few members of the Committee on Industry, Research and Energy have a technical background (though they may develop an expertise as a result of their committee membership). The Committee on Legal Affairs, on the other hand, is composed mainly of lawyers or legal experts.
- *Committee chairmanship.* Committee chairs can be vital in guiding the work of committees. They can help to push business through; they can assist *rapporteurs* in rallying support for reports that are to be debated in plenaries; they can help to create committee harmony and a constructive working atmosphere; and they can do much to ensure that a committee broadens its horizons beyond simply reacting to initiatives presented to it by others.
- *Committee cohesiveness.* One of the reasons why, for example, the Committee on Development is more influential than a number of other committees is that it tends to display a high degree of cohesiveness. With members of the committee being united on the desirability of improving conditions in the developing countries, discussions tend to revolve around questions of feasibility rather than ideological desirability. The Agriculture Committee, on the other hand, attracts MEPs who are both supportive and critical of the CAP and hence it often tends to be sharply divided.

Second, time is set aside for debates on topical and urgent matters. As with the reports, these debates frequently result in the adoption of resolutions. Finally, statements are made by the Council and the Commission and there are also question times with both institutions. Who answers questions on behalf of the Commission and the Council depends on the policy content of the questions (which are known in advance), preferences expressed by the EP, and who is available. As part of the question time arrangements, on being re-appointed Commission President in 2009 José Manual Barroso agreed to be appear before each monthly plenary for a one hour question and answer slot. (Tables 11.1 and 11.2 provide a statistical breakdown of the 'outputs' of EP activity.)

In addition to the three standard activities, there

are a number of other possible agenda items, such as addresses by distinguished foreign guests, reports by the European Council President on European Council meetings, and reports by the Head of Government of the Council Presidency.

The EP in plenary does not, it should be said, give the impression of being the most dynamic of places: attendance in the chamber is poor; political group leaders and committee spokespersons dominate speaking time; the order of speakers and the amount of time they have to speak are largely pre-arranged; translation problem limits spontaneity (all 23 official EU languages are used, with MEPs who speak 'mainstream' languages often preferring to use their national language); and much immediacy is lost by the practice of taking most votes in clusters at allocated voting

Photo 11.2 European Parliament chamber, Strasbourg

times rather than at the end of debates (these voting times are often not even on the same day as the debate.) Nonetheless, working procedures have been gradually improved over the years, most notably by the removal of much minor business from the floor of the chamber.

Concluding Remarks: Is the EP a 'Proper' Parliament?

The EP has clearly assumed an increased role in the EU over the years. Several factors account for this, not least the Parliament's own efforts to increase its powers.

In attempting to enhance its role and influence, the EP has pursued a dual strategy. On the one hand there has been an *incrementalist* approach, in which the EP has used its existing powers to the full and done what-

ever it can to determine how far these powers can be pressed. As part of this approach the EP has, for example, interpreted its Maastricht-granted confirmation power on incoming Colleges of Commissioners as giving it the power to 'interview' Commissioners-designate, and it has contracted a number of interinstitutional agreements with the Commission and the Council (on such matters as the budgetary procedure and conciliation meetings) that have enhanced its institutional position.

On the one hand there has been *a maximalist* approach, which has been directed at achieving fundamental reform of interinstitutional relations, and especially increasing the powers of the Parliament *vis-à-vis* the Council of Ministers. In 1984 this approach led to the EP approving the *Draft Treaty Establishing the European Union,* which played a part – though perhaps not as important a part as its supporters have claimed – in helping to bring about the SEA, which included amongst its contents considerably increased legislative powers for the EP. In the periods leading up to subsequent rounds of treaty reform the EP, taking advantage of the debate about the 'democratic defeat', has, as in 1984, called for, amongst other things, co-decision-making legislative powers with the Council across the policy spectrum (significant progress was achieved in the Maastricht, Amsterdam and Lisbon Treaties), the right to elect the President of the Commission on a proposal from the European Council and for the nominee to reflect the outcome of EP elections (granted in the Lisbon Treaty), and the co-decision-making procedure (now ordinary procedure) to apply whenever QMV applies in the Council (conceded by the governments of the member states in the Lisbon Treaty).

But notwithstanding the increased powers and influence it has secured, the EP is still widely viewed as not being quite a proper parliament. The main reasons for this are: it cannot overthrow a government; its formal legislative powers remain weaker than those of national parliaments; and in some important spheres of EU policy activity – notably EMU and foreign and defence policies – it is largely confined to information-receiving and consultative roles. However, the extent to which there is a 'formal powers gap' between the EP and national parliaments has greatly narrowed over the years, and in many important respects the Lisbon Treaty has narrowed it further. Indeed, the EP may be said to have been the principal institutional beneficiary of the Treaty, with gains for it including: significant extensions to its legislative powers; stronger budgetary powers; and EP approval becoming necessary for a number of important decisions that hitherto only required Council approval, such as the use of enhanced cooperation and a wide range of international agreements.

However, when assessing the importance of the EP attention should not be restricted to its formal capabilities. For when the comparison with national parliaments is extended to encompass what actually happens in practice, the powers exercised by the EP are, in several key respects, comparable to the powers exercised by many national parliaments. Indeed, it is not difficult to make out a case that in exercising some of its functions – most particularly scrutinising legislative proposals – the EP exerts a greater influence over affairs than do the more executive-dominated parliaments of many member states.

Chapter 12

European Union Law and the EU's Courts

The Need for EU Law

An enforceable legal framework is the essential basis of decision-making and decision application in all democratic states. Although not itself a state, this also applies to the EU because the EU is more than merely another international organisation in which countries cooperate with one another on a voluntary basis for reasons of mutual benefit. Rather it is an organisation in which states have voluntarily surrendered their right, across a broad range of important sectors, to be independent in the determination and application of public policy.

Regarding the determination of public policy, if there was no body of law setting out the powers and responsibilities of the institutions and the member states of the EU, and if there was no authority to give independent rulings on what that law is and how it should be interpreted, effective EU decision-making on policies would not be possible. Of course law is not the only factor shaping the EU's decision-making processes. As in any organisation, practice evolves in the light of experience of what is possible and what works best. The tendency not to press for a vote in the Council even when it is legally permissible is an obvious example of this. But the law does provide the basic setting in which decisions are made. It lays down that some things must be done, some cannot, and some may be. So, to give just four very different examples, it is by virtue of EU law that the Commission takes decisions on the permissability of proposed mergers between large companies, that the Council and EP determine the size and shape of the EU's annual budget, that fishermen are restricted in what and how much they can catch in the seas surrounding the EU, and that products not meeting specified standards cannot be sold in the EU's market.

Regarding the application of public policy, the existence of EU law is also crucial because if the decisions taken by the EU's policy makers only took the form of intergovernmental agreements, and if those agreements could be interpreted by member states in whatever way was most beneficial and convenient for them, common policies would not in practice exist and the whole rationale of the EU would be undermined. The likes of the EU's competition and agriculture policies, and the approximation of EU standards on matters as diverse as maximum axle weights for lorries and minimum safety standards at work, can be fully effective only if they are based on *common laws* that are capable of *uniform* interpretation in *all* member states.

The Sources of EU Law

An EU legal order is thus an essential condition of the EU's existence. The sources of that order are to be found in a number of places: the treaties, EU legislation, judicial interpretation, international law, and the general principles of law.

The treaties

Are the treaties the EU's constitution?

The EU's treaty structure is, as was shown in Part II of this book, made up of two main component parts: the Treaty on European Union (TEU) and the Treaty on the Functioning of the European Union (TFEU). Do these two treaties constitute the EU's constitution?

National constitutions in liberal democracies normally do two main things: they establish an institutional structure for decision-making, and they set out – often in a bill of rights or a declaration of liberties – the freedoms of the individual and restrictions on the power of decision-makers over the citizenry. The relevant component parts of the EU's treaties cover the first of these tasks, and to a considerable extent the second too. The establishment of the institutional structure can be seen, most obviously, in the identification of the Commission, the European Council, the Council of Ministers, the European Parliament, and the Court of Justice of the European Union as the key decision-making institutions, and by the specification (in general terms) of their roles and powers and of what must be the nature of the relations both between them and also between them and the member states. As for the establishment of individual rights, the treaties have long had much to say about economic freedoms but in recent rounds of treaty reform they have increasingly also emphasised civil freedoms. The key article in this respect is Article 6 TEU, which states that: a) the Charter of Fundamental Rights of the European Union (see Chapters 5 and 6) has the same legal value as the treaties (though Protocol 30 of the Lisbon Treaty limits the potential impact of the Charter in the Czech Republic, Poland and the UK); b) the Union shall accede to the [1950] European Convention for the Protection of Human Rights and Fundamental Freedoms; c) fundamental rights shall constitute general principles of the Union's law.

In addition to including not dissimilar content to national constitutions, the EU's treaties may also be said to be constitutional in nature in respect of the status of their contents and how they are determined. Treaty law is not 'ordinary' EU law that is made by 'ordinary' law-making procedures, but rather is primary law. That is to say, it is a higher status law in the sense that all 'ordinary' EU law must have a treaty base and in that also treaty law is made by a special procedure. As is shown in Part II of the book, the special procedure to date has taken the form of Intergovernmental Conferences (IGCs), which have been extensively pre-prepared, which usually have been spread out over several months, which have culminated at European Council meetings, and whose outcomes have been subject to national ratification processes that in some member states have been very high-profile and difficult. Simplified procedures were included in the Lisbon Treaty for future modest amendments to the treaties, but these still will normally require unanimous approval by the national governments and by the EP and/or national parliaments.

As well as covering 'traditional' constitutional matters, the treaties are also much concerned with something that is not normally considered to be appropriate subject matter for constitutions: policy. This takes the form of the setting-out of general principles on the one hand and the identification of policy sectors and activities that are to be developed on the other. The main general principles are those that are designed to promote competition and the free movement of goods, persons, services and capital, all behind a common external tariff (CET) and a common commercial policy (CCP). The policy sectors and activities that are identified, with varying degrees of precision on how they are to be developed, include: agriculture, social affairs, transport, regional affairs, the environment, and economic and monetary union (all in the TFEU), and foreign, security and defence policy (in the TEU). The inclusion of policy content is the main reason why the EU's treaties are so much longer than national constitutions: the TEU has 55 articles and the TFEU has 357!

The treaties thus do not formally constitute the EU's constitution in that they do not set out in a single and readily understandable document that is called a constitution the fundamental bases of the EU's principles and powers. Moreover, as Christiansen and Reh (2009: especially Chapters 1 and 3) have pointed out, in so far as the EU may be said to have a constitution there are other sources in addition to the treaties. These other sources, which include Court judgments and inter-institutional agreements, are part of an implicit, incremental and ongoing constitution- alising process.

But although the treaties may not be the EU's constitution in a formal sense, they nonetheless have many clear constitutional features. Amidst the politi- cal heat and debate surrounding the demise of the Constitutional Treaty (see Chapter 6), sight was perhaps sometimes lost of the fact that in important respects the EU may be said to have already had a constitution, albeit of a rather non-traditional kind.

EU legislation

Laws adopted by the EU institutions under Article 288 TFEU constitute secondary legislation. They are concerned with translating the general principles of the treaties into specific rules and are adopted by the European Parliament and the Council, by the Council, or by the Commission according to the procedures described in other chapters of this book (see especially Chapters 8 and 18). While there is no hard and fast distinction between EP and Council, Council, and Commission legislation, the first two tend to be broader in scope, to be concerned with more impor- tant matters, and to be aimed at laying down a legal framework in a policy sphere. Commission legislation – of which in terms of volume there is much more than EP and Council and Council-only legislation – is largely of an implementing, administrative, and tech- nical nature and is usually subject to tight guidelines laid down in enabling EP and Council or Council legislation.

The Constitutional Treaty tried to clarify the somewhat confusing nature of EU legislative instru- ments by distinguishing between legislative acts, which it named laws and framework laws, and implementing acts, which it named regulations and decisions. The Lisbon Treaty maintained this hierar- chical distinction between legislative acts and imple- menting acts, but abandoned the terminology of

laws and framework laws for legislative acts and reinserted the long-used terminology – based mainly on regulations, directives and decisions – for both legislative and implementing acts. An opportunity for terminological clarification was thus not taken, even though there was provision for 'implementing' or 'delegated' to be henceforth added to the titles of executive acts.

The TFEU post-Lisbon thus distinguishes between, as preceding treaties have, the following types of legis- lation: regulations, directives, decisions, and recom- mendations and opinions. The nature of and the differences between these types of legislation are set out in Box 12.1.

* * *

In order to accommodate the mosaic of different national circumstances and interests that exist on many policy issues, the EU's legislative framework needs to be creative, flexible, and capable of permitting differentiation.

There are four main ways in which it is so:

- As Box 12.1 shows, the EU makes use of a variety of formal and quasi-formal legislative instruments.
- There are considerable variations between direc- tives regarding the time periods permitted for incorporation into national law. For example, amending directives may have to be incorporated almost immediately, whereas innovative or contro- versial directives, or directives that require substan- tial capital expenditure in order to be properly applied – as is common with environmental direc- tives – may not be required to be incorporated for some years.
- Devices that allow for adaptation to local condi- tions and needs are often either attached to legal texts or are authorised by the Commission after an act has come into force. Examples of such devices include exemptions, derogations, and safety clauses.
- Provided the Commission is satisfied that the rele- vant provisions are not 'a means of arbitrary discrimination or a disguised restriction on trade between Member States' and do not 'constitute an obstacle to the functioning of the internal market' (Article 114: 6 TFEU), member states are permitted to apply national legislation that is 'tougher' than EU legislation in respect of certain matters where

---

Box 12.1

The different types of EU legislation

Regulations

A regulation under Article 288 TFEU is:

1 Of 'general application'; that is, it contains general and abstract provisions that may be applied to particular persons and circumstances.
2 'Binding in its entirety'; that is, it bestows rights and obligations upon those to whom it is addressed, and member states must observe it in full and as written.
3 'Directly applicable in all Member States'; that is, there is no need for national implementing measures to be taken in order for a regulation to have binding force within the member states. Regulations specify the date on which they are to take legal effect. Normally this is the same day as, or very shortly after, they are published in the *Official Journal of the European Union*. This in turn is usually only a day or two after they have been adopted.

Most regulations are adopted by the Commission and concern highly specific and technical adjustments to existing EU law. The majority relate to the CAP.

Directives

A directive 'shall be binding, as to the result to be achieved, upon each Member State to which it is addressed, but shall leave to the national authorities the choice of form and methods' (Article 288 TFEU).

In theory, a directive is thus very different from a regulation: it is not binding in its entirety but only in 'the result to be achieved'; it is addressed to member states and does not claim general applicability; it is not necessarily addressed to all member states; and appropriate national measures need to be taken to give the directive legal effect. As a consequence directives tend to be rather more general in nature than regulations. They are less concerned with the detailed and uniform application of policy and more with the laying down of policy principles that member states must seek to achieve but can pursue by the appropriate means under their respective national constitutional and legal systems.

$\rightarrow$

---

there is not complete harmonisation. Policy areas where this occurs include protection of the environment and of the working environment.

There used to be several thousand legislative instruments issued each year, comprising around 4,000 regulations, 2,000 decisions, and 120 directives. However, the number of the first two of these has dropped considerably in recent years, mainly because of a drive by all decision-making institutions to simplify the EU legislative framework. In an average year, there now are around 1,200–1,400 regulations (the great number of which are Commission regulations), 800–900 decisions, and still about 120 directives. The vast majority of these legal instruments consist of administrative measures of a routine, 'non-

political', recurring kind. Many are replacements for instruments that have either been repealed (usually because, as with most CAP-related legislation, they have become outdated as a result of changing market conditions) or have expired.

Judicial interpretation

The Court of Justice of the European Union consists of two main courts: the Court of Justice and the General Court – the latter of which was called the Court of First Instance (CFI) until its name was changed by the Lisbon Treaty. The former is the more senior of the two courts in that it deals with most cases raising major issues – including those of a 'constitutional' and/or

Box 12.1 *continued*

The distinction between regulations and directives should not, however, be exaggerated because in practice a number of factors often result in a blurring. First, directives are almost invariably addressed to all states. An important reason for this is that directives are frequently concerned with the harmonisation or approximation of laws and practices in fields of EU activity. Second, some directives are drafted so tightly that there is very little room for national authorities to incorporate adjustments when transposing directives into national law. Third, directives contain a date by which the national procedures to give the directive effect must have been completed. The Commission has to be notified of national implementing measures, and states that fail to comply by the due date are liable to have proceedings initiated against them, which can ultimately result in a case before the Court. Fourth, the Court has ruled – so as to prevent member states taking advantage of their own failures to comply – that directives may be directly applicable when national implementing legislation has been unduly delayed or when it has departed from the intent of the original directive.

Decisions

A decision 'shall be binding in its entirety upon those to whom it is addressed' (Article 288 TFEU). It may be addressed to any or all member states, to undertakings, or to individuals. Many decisions are highly specific and, in effect, are administrative rather than legislative acts. Others are of a more general character and can be akin to regulations or even, occasionally, directives.

Decisions are adopted in a whole range of circumstances. For example: to enforce competition policy; to institute a pilot action programme; to authorise grants from one of the EU's funds; to allow an exemption from an existing measure; or to counter dumping from a third country.

Recommendations and opinions

Recommendations and opinions are explicitly stated by Article 288 TFEU as having no binding force but this does not mean lack of legal effect. Indeed, on occasions the Court has referred to them. The same applies to some of the other non-binding devices used by the EU institutions for such purposes as floating ideas, starting a legislative process, promoting coordination, and encouraging harmonisation. These include memoranda, communications, conventions, programmes, guidelines, agreements, declarations, and resolutions.

'political' nature – and in that also General Court judgments are, subject to specified conditions, subject to appeal to the Court of Justice. When, therefore, reference is made to EU law arising from judicial interpretation, the reference is normally to Court of Justice case law.

Although case law has not traditionally been a major source of law in most of the EU member states, the rulings of the EU's courts have played an important part in shaping and making EU law. This stems partly from the courts' duty to ensure that EU law is interpreted and applied correctly. It stems also from the fact that much of EU statute law is far from clear or complete.

The lack of precision in much of the EU's statute law is due to a number of factors: the relative newness of the EU and its constituent parts; the often sharply differing views of policy actors within EU decision-making processes can lead to weak compromises and the avoidance of necessary secondary legislation; and the speed of change in some spheres of EU activity makes it very difficult for the written law to keep abreast of developments. In many fields of apparent EU competence the EU's courts thus have to issue judgments from a less than detailed statutory base. In the different types of case that come before them – cases of first and only instance, cases of appeal, and cases involving rulings on points of EU law that have been referred by national courts – the EU's courts therefore inevitably often go well beyond merely giving a technical and grammatical interpretation of the written rules. They fill in the gaps in the law and, in so doing, they not only clarify the law but also extend it.

International law

International law is notoriously vague and weak, but the EU's courts have had occasional recourse to it when developing principles embodied in EU law. Judgements have also established that insofar as the EU has been increasingly developing an international personality of its own and taken over powers from the states, the same rules of international law apply to it as apply to them, for example with regard to treaty law and the privileges and immunities of international organisations. This process is likely to be further advanced in the future, with the Lisbon Treaty having accorded (in Article 47 TEU) legal personality to the EU.

The many international agreements to which the EU is a party – including association, cooperation and trade agreements – are sometimes viewed as another dimension of international law. However, since they are implemented by legislative acts they are better viewed as constituting part of EU legislation, even though the Court of Justice has ruled that they are superior in the hierarchy of EU law than secondary law (Case 24/72).

The general principles of law

Article 19 TEU states that 'The Court of Justice of the European Union … shall ensure that in the interpretation and application of the Treaties the law is observed.' The implication of this and of certain other Treaty articles (notably 263 and 340 TFEU) is that the EU's courts need not regard written EU law as the only source of law to which they may refer.

In practice this has meant that the courts, when making their judgments, have had regard to general principles of law when these have been deemed relevant and applicable. Exactly what these general principles of law are, however, is a matter of controversy. Suffice to note here that the principles that have been cited by the courts include non-discrimination (whether between nations, product sectors, firms or individuals), adherence to legality, and respect for procedural rights.

The Content of EU Law

The content of EU law is described at some length in Part IV of the book, in the context of the examination that is presented there of EU policies. Attention here will, therefore, be confined to three points of general significance.

The first point is that EU law is not as wide-ranging as national law. It is not, for instance, much concerned with criminal law, property law, or family law. Nor does it have much to do with policy areas such as education or health. What EU law is primarily, although by no means exclusively, concerned with – and in this it reflects the aims and provisions of the treaties – is economic activity. More particularly, EU law is strongly focused in the direction of such areas of activity as the customs union, the internal market, competition policy, agriculture policy, and fisheries policy. It also makes up a significant element of the law applying in the member states in such policy areas as energy, transport, regional development and the environment.

The second, and related, point is that in virtually all policy areas EU law sits side-by-side with national law. As Box 16.4 (p. 287) shows, the TFEU identifies five areas where the Union has exclusive competence. However, it is only in respect of the customs union and the common commercial policy that a comprehensive code of EU law exists in a major policy area that applies in all EU states. Even in areas where there is a high degree of EU regulation, such as with the functioning of agricultural markets, national laws covering various matters still exist. As Tables 16.1 and 16.2 show (pp. 283–4) , EU law thus constitutes an important part of the overall legal framework of member states in some policy spheres, whilst being of only marginal significance in others.

The third point is that the range of EU law has broadened considerably over the years. As already noted, EU law is primarily economic in character, but less dominantly so than it was. The great expansion in recent years of law related to the creation of the area of freedom, security and justice is testament to this. So too is the considerable volume of EU environmental law that now exists: there are over 200 EU environmental laws in force, dealing with matters as diverse as air and water pollution, the disposal of toxic waste, and the protection of endangered bird species. This expansion of EU law into an increasing number of policy areas has occurred, and is still occurring, for several reasons, prominent among which are: recognition of the benefits that joint action can bring to many fields of activity; pressures from sectional interests; and acceptance that the internal market can function smoothly, efficiently and equitably only if there are common rules not just on directly related market activities but also on matters such as health and safety at work, entitlements to social welfare benefits, and mutual recognition of educational and professional qualifications.

The Status of EU Law

In Case 6/64, *Costa* v. *ENEL,* the Court of Justice stated:

> By creating a Community of unlimited duration, having its own institutions, its own personality, its own legal capacity of representation on the international plane and, more particularly, real powers stemming from limitation of sovereignty or a transfer of powers from the states to the Community, the Member States have limited their sovereign rights, albeit within limited fields, and have thus created a body of law which binds both their individuals and themselves.

EU law thus constitutes an autonomous legal system, imposing obligations and rights on both individuals and member states, and limiting the sovereignty of member states. There are two main pillars to this legal system: direct effect and primacy.

Direct effect

This term – which is sometimes also called direct applicability – refers to the principle whereby certain provisions of EU law may confer rights or impose obligations on individuals that national courts are bound to recognise and enforce. Having initially established the principle in 1963 in the case of *Van Gend en Loos* (Case 26/62), the Court, in a series of judgments, has gradually strengthened and extended the scope of direct effect so that it now applies to most

secondary legislation except when discretion is explicitly granted to the addressee. Many of the provisions of the treaties have also been established as having direct effect, although the Court has ruled that it does not apply to all spheres.

Primacy

Somewhat surprisingly, until the Treaty of Lisbon there was no explicit reference in the treaties to the primacy or supremacy of EU law over national law. Clearly the principle was vital if the EU was to function properly, since if member states had the power to annul EU law by adopting or giving precedence to national law, then there could be no uniform or consistent EU legal order: states could apply national law when EU law was distasteful or inconvenient to them. From an early stage, therefore, the Court took an active part in establishing the primacy of EU law. National courts, it consistently asserted, must apply EU law in the event of any conflict, even if the domestic law was part of the national constitution. An example of a Court statement on primacy may be taken from *Simmenthal* v. *Commission* (Case 92/78) where the Court concluded that:

> Every national court must, in a case within its jurisdiction, apply Community law in its entirety and protect rights which the latter confers on individuals and must accordingly set aside any provision of national law which may conflict with it, whether prior or subsequent to the Community rule.

In general, national courts have accepted this view and have given precedence to EU law. A few problems have remained – notably in relation to fundamental rights guaranteed by national constitutions – but for the most part the authority and binding nature of EU law has been fully established.

The Treaty of Lisbon consolidated the principle by giving it explicit treaty recognition for the first time. However, the recognition did not take the form of inclusion in the Treaty but rather recognition in a declaration on primacy that was attached to the Treaty (see Box 12.2).

Box 12.2

Declaration 17 of the Treaty of Lisbon

Declaration concerning primacy
The Conference recalls that, in accordance with well settled case law of the Court of Justice of the European Union, the Treaties and the law adopted by the Union on the basis of the Treaties have primacy over the law of Member States, under the conditions laid down by the said case law.

The Conference has also decided to attach as an Annex to this Final Act the Opinion of the Council Legal Service on the primacy of EC law as set out in 11197/07 (JUR 260):

Opinion of the Council Legal Service
of 22 June 2007

It results from the case-law of the Court of Justice that primacy of EC law is a cornerstone principle of Community law. According to the Court, this principle is inherent to the specific nature of the European Community. At the time of the first judgment of this established case law (Costa/ENEL, 15 July 1964, Case 6/641* there was no mention of primacy in the treaty. It is still the case today. The fact that the principle of primacy will not be included in the future treaty shall not in any way change the existence of the principle and the existing case-law of the Court of Justice.

* "It follows ... that the law stemming from the treaty, an independent source of law, could not, because of its special and original nature, be overridden by domestic legal provisions, however framed, without being deprived of its character as Community law and without the legal basis of the Community itself being called into question."

The Court of Justice of the European Union

The Court of Justice of the European Union consists of three courts: the Court of Justice, the General Court (formerly called the Court of First Instance), and the European Union Civil Service Tribunal. Attention in this chapter is focused only on the first two of these courts, as the Tribunal just deals with internal EU staffing disputes.

All of the courts are located in Luxembourg. None of them should be, though the Court of Justice in particular sometimes is, confused with the Strasbourg-based European Court of Human Rights which is part of the Council of Europe institutional system.

Membership

The Court of Justice and the General Court both consists of 27 judges – one from each member state. The Court of Justice is assisted by eight advocates-general. All the judges and advocates-general are appointed for a six-year term of office that may be, and frequently is, renewed. To ensure continuity, turnover is staggered in three-yearly cycles.

Under Article 253 TFEU, the judges and advocates-general are appointed 'by common accord of the governments of the Member States' from amongst persons 'whose independence is beyond doubt and who possess the qualifications required for appointment to the highest judicial offices in their respective countries or who are juriconsults of recognised competence'. The Lisbon Treaty supplemented Article 253 with a preliminary stage under which, in a new Article 255, before being appointed by the member states the suitability of nominated candidates must be considered by a seven-member panel consisting of former EU and national supreme court judges and legal experts, one of whom must be proposed by the EP.

In practice there is something of a gap, in spirit at least, between the treaty provisions and reality. First, because notwithstanding the formal stipulation that appointment is 'by common accord of the governments of the Member States', each state is actually permitted one nomination to both the Court of Justice and the General Court and these nominations are automatically accepted. (Although the new 'vetting panel, which must issue an opinion on each nominee, could result in occasional problems in this regard in the future.) Second, because when making their choices governments have tended not to be overly worried about the judicial qualifications or experience of their nominations and have instead looked for a good background in appropriate professional activities and public service. There is no evidence of 'political' appointments being made, in the way that they are to the United States Supreme Court, but the fact is that soundness and safeness seem to be as important as judicial ability. At the time of initial appointment the typical judge is a legally qualified 'man of affairs' (in early 2010, for example, there were only seven female members of the Court of Justice!) who has been involved with judicial, governmental, or academic work in his native country in some way, but who has often not served in a judicial capacity for long (if at all) or at a high level. Third, because each of the larger states have usually been able to ensure that one of the eight advocates-general is from their member state.

In addition to the judges, each of whom are assisted by three legal secretaries, and the advocates-general, each of whom is assisted by four legal secretaries, the Court, together with the General Court and the Civil Service Tribunal (many supporting services are shared), employs a staff of around 1,500 in permanent posts and 450 in temporary posts. Most of these are engaged in either administrative duties – such as registering and transmitting case documents – or in providing language services.

Organisation and numbers of cases

In most respects, the two courts are organised in similar ways.

The Court of Justice

The judges elect one of their number to be President of the Court for a term of three years. The President's principal function is to see to the overall direction of the work of the Court by, for example, assigning cases to the Court's chambers and appointing *judge-rapporteurs*. The President is also empowered, upon application from a party, to order the suspension of Union measures and to order such interim measures as he deems appropriate.

Assisting the judges in the exercise of their tasks are the advocates-general. The duty of advocates-general is 'acting with complete impartiality and independence, to make, in open court, reasoned submissions on cases which … require his involvement' (Article 252 TFEU). This means that an advocate-general, on being assigned to a case, must make a thorough examination of all the issues involved in the case, take account of all relevant law, and then present his conclusions to the Court. The conclusions are likely to include observations on the key points in the case, an assessment of EU law touching on the case, and a proposed legal solution.

The increasing number of cases coming before the Court – in the 1960s there were around 50 in an average year, today there are approaching 600 new cases each year (see Table 12.1) – has made it impossible for everything to be dealt with in full plenary session. As Table 12.2 shows, the great majority of cases are therefore dealt with by one of the Court's eight chambers. In general, a matter is referred to a chamber of three judges if it is based upon relatively straightforward

Table 12.1 Cases before the Court of Justice 2004–8: numbers and stages of proceedings*

	2004	2005	2006	2007	2008
New cases	531	474	537	580	592
Completed cases	665	574	546	570	567
Cases pending	840	740	731	741	767

* The figures represent the total number of cases without account being taken of the small number of cases where cases are joined because of their similarity.

Source: Court of Justice (2009): 82.

Table 12.2 Completed cases before the European Court of Justice, 2008: bench hearing actions*

	Judgments/ Opinions	Orders	Total
Full Court	–	–	–
Grand Chamber	66		66
Chambers (5 judges)	259	13	272
Chambers (3 judges)	65	59	124
President	–	7	7
TOTAL	390	79	469

* The figures given represent the total number of cases, without account being taken of the joining of cases on the ground of similarity.

Source: Court of Justice (2009): 90.

Table 12.3 Cases before the Court of First Instance 2004–8: number and stages of proceedings

	2004	2005	2006	2007	2008
New cases	536	469	432	522	629
Completed cases	361	610	436	397	605
Cases pending	1174	1033	1029	1154	1178

Source: Court of First Instance (2009): 171.

Table 12.4 Completed cases before the Court of First Instance 2008: bench hearing actions

	Judgments and Orders
Grand Chamber	–
Appeal Chamber	26
President of the Court	52
Chambers (five judges)	17
Chambers (three judges)	510
Single judge	–
Total	605

Source: Court of First Instance (2009): 178.

facts, raises no substantial points of principle, or where the circumstances are covered by existing case law. Cases that involve more complex findings of fact, or novel or important points of law, and do not require to be heard by the full Court, are assigned to a chamber of five judges.

Following amendments made by the Maastricht Treaty, the only circumstance in which the Court was required to sit in full plenary session was 'when a Member State or a Community institution that is a party to the proceedings so requests' (Article 221 TEC). In the Nice Treaty this was changed to enable such a request to be met by proceedings to be dealt with by a grand chamber, numbering thirteen judges since the 2004 EU enlargement. The Court is now obliged to sit in full plenary session for only a very restricted number of cases (set out in Article 16 of the Court's Statutes), though it may also decide to sit as the full Court when cases are deemed to be 'of especially importance'. In practice, plenary sessions have become rare.

The General Court

The main organisational difference between the Court of Justice and the General Court is that no advocates-general are appointed to the latter. When the exercise of the function of advocate-general is seen as being necessary – which it is not in all cases – the task is

undertaken by one of the judges; the judge so designated cannot take part in the judgement of the case.

As Table 12.3 shows, the number of cases coming before and dealt with by the General Court is similar to the numbers of the Court of Justice. Accordingly, just as the Court of Justice deals with its heavy workload problem by assigning most cases to chambers, so too does the General Court. But whereas in the Court of Justice over half of all cases are dealt with by chambers of five judges, in the General Court the overwhelming majority of cases are, as Table 12.4 shows, dealt with by chambers of three judges

The procedure of the Courts

Most of the work of the two Courts is conducted largely away from the public eye via the communication of documents between those directly involved in cases, interested parties, and Court officials. Not much happens in open court, and in some cases the parties do not require a public hearing at all.

Without going into all the details and possible variations, an outline of how direct action cases (which tend to be the most important cases in terms of setting important case law) are typically channelled through the Court of Justice will now be given to give a flavour of Court procedures:

- Relevant documentation and evidence is assembled. In complicated cases, involving for example the alleged existence of cartels, hundreds or even thousands of separate items of evidence may be collected. The Court (though more so in the General Court than in the Court of Justice), under the direction of a duly appointed *judge-rapporteur*, may have to take a very proactive role in gathering the information that it needs and in soliciting the views of interested parties. This may involve holding a preparatory inquiry at which oral and documentary evidence is presented. (In preliminary ruling cases the procedure is very different: the national court making the reference should have provided with its submission a summary of the case and of all relevant facts, a statement of the legal problem, and the – abstract – question it wishes the Court to answer.)

- A public hearing is likely to be (but is not always) held at which the essentials of the case are outlined, the various parties are permitted to present their views orally, and the judges and advocates-general may question the parties' lawyers.

- Following the public hearing, the advocate-general appointed to the case examines it in detail. He and his staff look at all relevant EU law and then come to a decision that they consider to be correct in legal terms. A few weeks after the public hearing the advocate-general presents his submission to an open session of the Court.

- Acting on the advocate-general's submission, and on the basis of a draft drawn up by the *judge-rapporteur*, the Court prepares its decision.

Photo 12.1 The First Chamber of the Court of Justice delivering a judgment

Table 12.5 Duration (in months) of proceedings in the Court of Justice 2004–8

	2004	2005	2006	2007	2008
References for a preliminary ruling	23.5	20.4	19.8	19.3	16.8
Urgent preliminary ruling procedures					2.1
Accelerated preliminary ruling procedures					4.5
Direct actions	20.2	21.3	20	18.2	16.9
Direct actions – accelerated procedures	5.6				
Appeals	21.3	20.9	17.8	17.8	18.4

Source: Court of Justice (2009): 82.

Deliberations are in secret and if there is disagreement – as sometimes there is – the decision is made by majority vote. Judgments must be signed by all the judges who have taken part in the proceedings and no dissenting opinions may be published. (In their oath of office members swear to preserve the secrecy of the deliberation of the Court.)

Three problems associated with the proceedings of both of the Courts ought to be mentioned. First, there is a lengthy gap between cases being lodged and final decision being issued, as Tables 12.5 and 12.6 show. In the Court of Justice, for example, direct action cases take, on average, almost seventeen months, whilst in the General Court most non-staff actions take twenty-six months. A major factor explaining this length of time is that all documents have to be translated – into all 23 official languages of the Union in preliminary ruling cases. In special cases, however, interim judgments are issued and accelerated procedures are used. Second, lawyers' fees usually mean that going before the Courts in direct action cases can be an expensive

Table 12.6 Duration (in months) of proceedings in the Court of First Instance 2004–8

	2004	2005	2006	2007	2008
Other actions	22.6	25.6	27.8	29.5	26.0
Intellectual property	17.3	21.1	21.8	24.5	20.4
Staff cases	19.2	19.2	24.8	32.7	38.6
Appeals				7.1	16.1

Source: Court of First Instance (2009): 179

business, even though there is no charge for the actual proceedings in the Court itself. This does not, of course, place much of a restriction on the ability of national governments or EU institutions to use the Courts, but it can be a problem for individuals and small firms. There is a small legal aid fund, but it cannot remotely finance all potential applicants. Third, the use of majority voting, coupled with the lack of opportunity for dissenting opinions, has encouraged a tendency, which is perhaps inevitable given the different legal backgrounds of the judges, for judgments sometimes to be less than concise, and occasionally even to be fudged.

Types of Cases Before the Courts

The EU's courts cannot initiate actions. They must wait for cases to be referred to them. Cases coming before the courts take a number of forms, the most important of which are outlined below. They are outlined by taking the courts together rather than separately. There are three reasons for this. First, although the jurisdiction of the General Court (then the CFI) was initially greatly restricted when it was established in 1988 to relieve the workload of the Court of Justice, treaty reforms have so extended its potential jurisdiction that now there are only a few types of cases with which it cannot deal. Second, in describing the responsibilities of the courts, the TFEU mostly refers to 'the Court of Justice of the European Union' – that is, it does not distinguish between the Court of Justice and the General Court.

Third, most of the decisions of the General Court are subject to appeal to the Court of Justice on points of law.

As a preliminary, let it just be said that, in very broad terms, the Court of Justice's main – and unstated – role is to deal with matters that are of considerable importance to the EU's legal order, whilst the General Court is charged with dealing with matters that are generally more routine in nature. This division results in the Court of Justice being the competent court to deal with failures of member states to fulfil obligations, most preliminary references, and appeals against General Court decisions in direct actions. The General Court has responsibility for annulments, failures to act, disputes relating to compensation for non-contractual liability, and appeals from the European Union Civil Service Tribunal. Tables 12.7 and 12.8 indicate the numbers of the types of cases dealt with by the two courts.

Table 12.7 New cases brought before the Court of Justice 2004–8 according to types of proceedings*

	2004	**2005**	**2006**	**2007**	**2008**
References for a preliminary ruling	249	221	251	265	288
Direct actions	219	179	201	221	210**
Appeals	52	66	80	79	77
Appeals concerning interim measures and intervention	6	1	3	8	8
Opinions/rulings	1	1			
Special forms of procedure	4	7	2	7	8
Total	531	474	537	580	592

* The figures given represent the total number of cases, without account being taken of the joining of cases on the ground of similarity.
** Of which 207 were actions for failure to fulfil an obligation and 3 of which were actions for annulment.

Source: Court of Justice (2009): 82

Table 12.8 New cases before the Court of First Instance 2004–8 according to types of action

	2004	**2005**	**2006**	**2007**	**2008**
Actions for annulment	199	160	223	249	269
Actions for failure to act	15	9	4	13	9
Actions for damages	18	16	8	27	15
Arbitration clauses	8	8	9	8	12
Intellectual property	110	98	143	168	198
Staff cases	146	151	1	2	2
Appeals			10	27	37
Special forms of procedure	40	27	34	29	87
Total	536	469	432	522	629

Source: Court of First Instance (2009): 173

Failure to fulfil an obligation

Under Articles 258 and 259 TFEU, the Court of Justice rules on whether member states have failed to fulfil obligations under the Treaty. As can be seen from Table 12.7, failure to fulfil an obligation cases constitute virtually all of the direct action cases that come before the Court: 207 out of 210 in 2008.

Actions may be brought either by the Commission or by member states. In either eventuality, the Commission must first give the state(s) against which the charge is made an opportunity to submit observations and then deliver a reasoned opinion. Only if this fails to produce proper compliance with EU law can the matter be referred to the Court.

In practice, failures to fulfil obligations are usually settled well before they are brought before the Court. When an action is brought the Commission is almost invariably the initiator. It is so partly because if a member state is behind the action it is obliged to refer the matter to the Commission in the first instance, and partly because member states are extremely reluctant to engage in direct public confrontation with one another (although they do sometimes try to encourage the Commission to, in effect, act on their behalf). Such cases have led to rulings against, for example, Italy (that its duties on imported gin and sparkling wine were discriminatory), against the UK (that it had introduced insufficient national measures to give full effect to the 1976 directive on sexual discrimination), and Belgium (for failing to implement directives to harmonise certain stock exchange rules).

The Maastricht Treaty gave to the Court, for the first time, the power to impose penalties on member states for not complying with Court judgments in respect of failures to fulfil obligations. The possibility of fines only arises after extensive exchanges between the Commission and the state in question, after the state has been given every opportunity to submit its observations, and after a time limit for compliance has been specified and has not been met. If these conditions apply, the Commission may bring the matter back before the Court. In so doing the Commission must specify the amount of the lump sum or penalty payment to be paid 'which it considers appropriate in the circumstances' (Article 260 TFEU). If the Court finds that the member state has not complied with its judgment, it may impose a lump sum and/or recurring penalty payment. An example of such an imposition is that imposed on France in July 2005 for allowing fishermen to catch and sell fish that were smaller than permitted under EU legislation. The Court fined France €20 million and also required it to pay €57.8 million every six months until it complied with the rules. Another example is the financial penalties imposed on Greece in July 2009 for failing to fully abide by a previous Court ruling to recover illegal subsidies paid to the state-owned Olympic Airlines. The Court imposed a €2 million fine and a €16,000 daily penalty to be paid until the funds were recovered.

Application for annulment

Under Article 263 TFEU, the Court 'shall review the legality of legislative acts, of acts of the Council, of the Commission and of the European Central Bank, other than recommendations and opinions, and of acts of the European Parliament and of the European Council intended to produce legal effects *vis-à-vis* third parties. It shall also review the legality of acts of bodies, offices or agencies of the Union intended to produce legal effects *vis-à-vis* third parties.' Judicial review of acts of the European Council and of the agencies was only introduced by the Lisbon Treaty and is potentially very important, with the extension of the Court's powers to the European Council in particular marking a very significant advance in its remit and, more broadly, a very significant advance also in the constitutionalisation of the EU.

The Court cannot conduct reviews on its own initiative, but only in response to actions brought by a member state, the EP, the Council or the Commission. Reviews may be based on the following grounds: 'lack of competence, infringement of an essential procedural requirement, infringement of the Treaties or of any rule of law relating to their application, or misuse of powers' (Article 263 TFEU). If an action is well founded, the Court is empowered under Article 264 TFEU to declare the act concerned to be void.

The most high profile annulment case in recent years was in 2004, when the Commission brought an action against the Council in connection with EMU's Stability and Growth Pact (SGP). In the autumn of 2003 the Commission had recommended that the Council require France and Germany to take the necessary measures to reduce their budgetary deficits under Article 104(9) TEC. However, no majority existed for this in the Council, so as an alternative the Council decided, in effect, that the excessive deficit procedures should be suspended whilst France and Germany took other correcting action. Deciding that this Council decision undermined both its own authority and the credibility of EMU, the Commission brought an action for annulment against the Council. When it delivered its opinion, in July 2004 (in Case C-17/04, *Commission* v. *Council*), the Court basically ruled in favour of the Commission, but refrained from insisting that the Council follow the Commission's recommendations. The judgment played an important part in the subsequent Council deliberations which led to the reform of the SGP in the spring of 2005.

An important aspect of Court activity in annulment cases arises in connection with the Treaty base(s) upon which EU legislation is proposed and adopted. There are several procedures by which EU law can be made (see Chapter 18 for details), each of which is different in terms of such key matters as whether qualified majority voting rules apply in the Council and what are the powers of the EP. Which procedure applies in a particular case depends on the article(s) of the Treaty upon which legislative proposals are based. It thus naturally follows that if a legislative proposal is brought forward by the Commission on a legal base that a member state or the EP believe to be both damaging to their interests and legally questionable, and if political processes cannot bring about a satisfactory resolution to the matter, they may be tempted to appeal to the Court.

Similarly, institutions sometimes appeal to the Court when they believe their prerogatives have been infringed during a legislative procedure. The EP has been very active in this regard, taking a number of cases to the Court, usually on the grounds that either it should have been consulted but was not, or that the Council changed the content of legislation after it left the EP and the EP was not reconsulted. In general, the Court has tended to support the EP in such cases.

Article 263 also allows any 'natural or legal person' (that is private individuals or companies) to institute proceedings for annulment. Cases brought on this basis have included appeals by companies against Commission decisions to refuse to authorise subsidies and challenges to Commission decisions on abuse of dominant trading positions, restrictive practices, and company mergers. An instance of the CFI making an important decision in an application for annulment

case occurred in June 2002 when it overruled the Commission's 1999 veto of the merger between the UK holiday firms Airtours and First Choice on the grounds that the Commission had failed to provide enough evidence that the merger would harm competition. This was the first defeat for the Commission in one of the EU's courts in a merger case, but there have subsequently been others. Generally, however, rulings have tended to strengthen the hand of EU institutions and to serve as useful underpinnings to some EU policies, notably competition policy and commercial policy.

In certain policy spheres, of which competition is the most important, the Commission is empowered to impose financial penalties to ensure compliance with EU regulations. Under Article 262 TFEU, the regulations governing such policy spheres may allow unlimited jurisdiction to the Court with regard to the penalties. This means that aggrieved parties may appeal to the Court against Commission decisions and the penalties it has imposed. As such, this is another form of action for annulment. The Court may annul or confirm the decision and increase or decrease the penalties. In the great majority of judgments the Commission's decisions are upheld. (See Chapter 8 for examples of fines imposed on firms for breaches of competition law.)

As Tables 12.7 and 12.8 show, actions for annulment constitute a considerable volume of the cases in the Court of Justice of the European Union. All but the most high-profile and important are dealt with by the General Court.

Failure to act

Under the treaties there are provisions for institutions to be taken to court for failure to act. These provisions vary in nature between the treaties. Under the TFEU, should the EP, the European Council, the Council, the Commission, or the European Central Bank fail to act on a matter provided for by the Treaty, the member states and the other institutions and, in restricted circumstances, 'natural or legal persons', may initiate an action under Article 265 to have the infringement established. Such actions are not common, but one that attracted much attention was initiated by the EP, with the support of the Commission, against the Council in 1983. The case concerned the alleged failure of the

Council to take action to establish a Common Transport Policy, despite the provision for such a policy in the EEC Treaty. The judgment, which was delivered in May 1985, was not what the EP or the Commission had hoped for. The ECJ ruled that whilst there was a duty for legislation to be produced, it had no power of enforcement because the Treaty did not set out a detailed timetable or an inventory for completion; it was incumbent upon the national governments to decide how best to proceed.

Action to establish liability

'In the case of non-contractual liability, the Union shall, in accordance with the general principles common to the laws of the Member States, make good any damage caused by its institutions or by its servants in the performance of their duties' (Article 340 TFEU). Under Article 268 the Court has exclusive jurisdiction to decide whether the Union is liable and, if so, whether it is bound to provide compensation.

This means that the Union may have actions brought against it on the ground of it having committed an illegal act. The complex mechanisms of the CAP have produced by far the greatest number of such cases, threatening indeed to overwhelm the Court in the early 1970s. As a consequence the Court became increasingly unwilling to accept non-contractual liability cases, at least on the basis of first instance, and made it clear that they should be brought before national courts.

In the 1970s the Court also ruled that the circumstances in which the Community could incur non-contractual liability and be liable for damages were strictly limited. Of particular importance in this context were judgements in 1978 on two joined cases concerning skimmed milk (Cases 83 and 94/76, and 4, 15 and 40/77). Community legislation obliged the food industry to add skimmed milk to animal feed as part of an effort to reduce the surplus of powdered milk. A number of users challenged the legality of this on the ground that the Community's solution to the problem was discriminatory. In its first judgment the Court ruled that the powdered milk regulations were, indeed, invalid because they did not spread the burden fairly across the agricultural sector. In its second judgment, however, it ruled that only in exceptional and special circumstances, notably when a relevant body

had manifestly and seriously exceeded its powers, should the Community be liable to pay damages when a legislative measure of a political and economic character was found to be invalid.

Reference for a preliminary ruling

The types of case referred to in the sections above are known as direct actions. That is, the Union's Courts are called upon to give a judgment in a dispute between two or more parties who bring their case directly to court. References for preliminary rulings are quite different, in that they do not involve the EU's Courts giving judgments in cases, but rather require them to give interpretations on points of EU law to enable national courts to make a ruling.

References are made under Article 267 TFEU, which states that national courts may, and in some circumstances must, ask the Court to give a preliminary ruling where questions arise on the interpretation of the Treaty or the validity and interpretation of acts of the institutions of the Union. The Court cannot make a pronouncement on a case that happens to have come to its attention unless a reference has been made to it by the appropriate national court. It is the exclusive prerogative of the national court to apply for a preliminary ruling, with parties to a dispute in a national court having no power to insist on a reference or to object to one being made. Once a reference has been made, the Court is obliged to respond, but it can only do so on questions that have been put to it and it may not pronounce on, or even directly attempt to influence the outcome of, the principal action. Interpretations made by the Court during the course of preliminary rulings must be accepted and applied by the national court that has made the referral.

Virtually all preliminary ruling cases are dealt with by the Court of Justice and, as can be seen in Table 12.7, such cases constitute approaching fifty per cent of the cases that come before it each year. Preliminary rulings serve three principal functions. First, they help to ensure that national courts make legally 'correct' judgments. Second, because they are generally accepted by all national courts as setting a precedent, they promote the uniform interpretation and application of EU law in the member states. Third, they provide a valuable source of access to the Court for private individuals and undertakings who cannot directly appeal to it, either because there is no legal provision or because of insufficient funds.

Staff cases

As the figures for 2004 and 2005 in Table 12.8 show, by the first half of the 2000s over one quarter of the cases coming before the CFI involved disputes between the EU and its staff. This type of case increasingly came to be seen as not being appropriate for the already over-loaded CFI, so the Nice Treaty provided for the estab-lishment of a special tribunal to deal with staff cases. Accordingly, on the basis of a Commission proposal of October 2003, the above-noted European Union Civil Service Tribunal was created in November 2004 and came into operation in 1 October 2005. The Tribunal, which is attached to the General Court, consists of seven judges who are appointed for six years by the Council. Decisions of the Tribunal are subject to appeal to the General Court, subject to conditions.

Appeals

Under Article 256 TFEU, certain decisions of the General Court are subject to appeal to the Court of Justice.

Appeals cannot be made on the substance of a case, but only on points of law. There are three broad grounds for appeal: the General Court lacked jurisdic-tion, it breached procedural rules, or it infringed Union law. Most, but not all, of the appeals fail. They do so because the Court of Justice will only accept appeal on points of law, not points of substance, and also because the General Court follows previous case law of the Court of Justice.

There are usually around seventy appeals each year, constituting about fifteen per cent of the Court of Justice's workload.

The seeking of an opinion

Under Article 218 TFEU, a member state, the EP, the Council or the Commission may obtain the opinion of the Court of Justice on whether a prospective interna-tional agreement is compatible with the provisions of the Treaties. Where the opinion of the Court is adverse, the agreement cannot enter into force without being suitably amended or without the Treaties being amended.

An example of an extremely important opinion is that issued in 1994 in respect of external powers. The Commission took the case before the Court, arguing that Article 113 of the EEC Treaty, which gave the Commission sole negotiating powers in respect of certain international commercial agreements, should extend to trade in services and trade-related aspects of intellectual property rights. The Court ruled (Opinion 1/94) that the Community and the member states shared competence to conclude such agreements and therefore the Commission did not have sole negotiat-ing powers.

The Impact and Influence of the Courts

The EU's courts have two main functions. First, they are responsible for directly applying the law in certain types of case. Second, they have a general responsibility for interpreting the provisions of EU law and ensuring that the application of the law, which on a day-to-day basis is primarily the responsibility of national courts and agencies, is consistent and uniform.

Inevitably, for the reasons explained earlier, these duties result in the courts – and especially the Court of Justice – making what, in effect, is judicial law. This is most clearly seen in four respects.

First, as noted above, the Court of Justice has clari-fied and strengthened the status of EU law. Landmark decisions of the 1960s and 1970s, such as *Van Gend en Loos* and *Costa* v. *ENEL*, were crucial in paving the way to the establishment of a strong legal system, but later decisions have also been important. For example, in its 1992 judgment in *Francovich and Bonifaci* v. *Italy* (Joined Cases 6/90 and 9/90) the Court ruled that indi-viduals are entitled to financial compensation if they are adversely affected by the failure of a member state to transpose a directive within the prescribed period. And in its 2005 judgment in *Commission (supported by the European Parliament)* v. *Council (supported by eleven member states)* (Case C-176/03) the Court strengthened the EU's implementation capacity by ruling that in some circumstances criminal law sanc-tions could be used for offences against EU law.

Second, EU policy competence has been strengthened and extended by Court judgments. Social security entitlements illustrate this. Most governments have not wished to do much more about entitlements than coordinate certain aspects of their social security systems. The Court, however, through a number of judgments, often based on the TEC (now TFEU) rather than on legislation, has played an important part in pushing the states towards the harmonisation of some of their practices, for example with regard to the rights of migrant workers. It has also extended the provisions of certain laws in ways the states did not envisage when they gave them their approval in the Council.

Another example of the Court strengthening and extending policy competence is a judgment it gave in May 1990 in a preliminary ruling case. The case – *Barber* v. *Guardian Royal Exchange Assurance Group* (Case 262/88) – had been referred by the UK Court of Appeal. The Court ruled that occupational pensions are part of an employee's pay and must therefore comply with Article 119 of the EEC Treaty dealing with equal pay for men and women. Regarding the particular issue that gave rise to the case, the Court stated that it was contrary to Article 119 to impose different age requirements for men and women as conditions for obtaining pensions on compulsory redundancy under a private pension scheme.

The area where the EU's courts have exercised the greatest influence in strengthening and extending EU policy competence is in regard to the internal market. In some instances this has been a result of practices being ruled illegal and in others it has been a consequence of judgments pressurising, enabling or forcing the Commission and the Council to act – as, for example, in de-regulating air transport following the 1986 *Nouvelles Frontières* case in which the ECJ held that the treaty rules governing competition applied to air transport.

Third, judgments have saved the EU the need to make law in existing areas of competence. A particularly influential judgment in this context was issued in February 1979 in the (now famous) *Cassis de Dijon* case (Case 120/78), which concerned the free circulation of the French blackcurrant liqueur of that name. The Court ruled that national food standards legislation cannot be invoked to prevent trade between member states unless it is related to 'public health, fiscal supervision and the defence of the consumer'.

The principle of 'mutual recognition' – whereby a product lawfully produced and marketed in one member state must be accepted in another member state – was thus established, with the result that the need for legislation to harmonise standards in order to facilitate trade was much reduced. Of course the *Cassis de Dijon* judgment did not, and does not, rule out challenges to the principle of 'mutual recognition', or to its application. For example, in the much publicised case *Commission* v. *Germany* (Case 178/84), the German government attempted to protect its brewers by arguing that whereas their product was pure, most so-called foreign beers contained additives and should be excluded from the German market on health grounds. In March 1987 the Court upheld the 'mutual recognition' principle and ruled that a blanket ban on additives to beer was quite disproportionate to the health risk involved; the German insistence on its own definition of beer amounted to a barrier to trade. In a similar ruling in July 1988 (Case 407/85) the Court ruled against an Italian prohibition on the sale in Italy of pasta products that are not made from durum (hard) wheat; the Court stated that German pasta – which is made from a mixture of hard and soft wheat – presented no threat to Italian consumers' health, nor did the product mislead consumers.

Fourth, the powers and functioning of the institutions have been clarified, and in important respects have been significantly affected, by the Court. Four important judgments will be cited to illustrate this. First, in 1980, in the isoglucose case (Case 138/79), the Court ruled that the Council could not adopt legislation until it had received the EP's opinion (see Chapter 11 for further consideration of this case). Second, in 1988, in the 'Wood Pulp' cases (Joined Cases 89, 104, 114–117, 125–129/85), the Court upheld and strengthened the power of Community institutions to take legal action against non-EC companies. (In this case the Commission had imposed fines on a number of American, Canadian and Finnish producers of wood pulp in respect of concerted practices that had affected selling prices in the Community. The Court ruled that the key factor in determining the Community's jurisdiction was not where companies were based, nor where any illegal agreements or practices were devised, but where illegalities were implemented.) Third, in 1992, in *Spain, Belgium and Italy* v. *Commission* (Joined Cases 271, 281 and 289/90) – which involved the liberalisation of the monopolistic telecommunications services market – the Court ruled that the Commission's powers in relation to competition policy were not limited to the surveillance of rules already in existence but extended to taking a proactive role to break monopolies. The fact that the Council could have taken appropriate measures did not affect the Commission's competence to act. Fourth, in 2000, in *Germany* v. *European Parliament and Council* (Case 376/98) Germany successfully sought annulment of the Tobacco Advertising Ban Directive which would have gradually phased-out virtually all tobacco publicity and sponsorship by 2006. The Court ruled that the Commission had been incorrect to use Article 100a TEC (now 114 TFEU) – which provides for internal market harmonisation and elimination of competition measures – as the legal base of the Directive. This was because other treaty articles excluded harmonisation measures designed to protect and improve human health and Article 100a could not be a general power to regulate the internal market.

The EU's courts have thus had a very considerable impact on the content of EU law. They have done so for a number of reasons, not least because, as Alter (1996: 479) has pointed out, those EU politicians who have been dissatisfied with judicial activism (representing a minority on most issues) have found it difficult to constrain, let alone reduce, the powers of the courts.

The independent influence of the courts should not, however, be overstated. As Wincott (1999) has argued of the Court of Justice, it is not normally in a position to create a fully fledged policy by itself. There are two main reasons for this. First, the Court must usually have a treaty or legislative base upon which to act. This means that its judgments are normally constrained to at least some extent by an existing, albeit sometimes very sketchy, policy framework. Second, judgments can only be issued on cases that are referred to the Court. It cannot initiate cases itself. Consequently, as Wincott says, 'where the Court has made a striking contribution to the character of a particular policy, usually its contribution has been to unsettle an established policy regime or to break up a gridlock … rather than to create a policy itself'. Court judgments have certainly impacted on EU policy, but the most important impact has often been not so much direct as rather 'the provocation of further legislation' (Wincott, 1999: 94–5).

Concluding Remarks

The legal framework described in the previous pages constitutes the single most important feature distinguishing the EU from other international organisations. The member states do not just cooperate with one another on an intergovernmental basis but have developed common laws designed to promote uniformity. The supremacy that applies in the interpretation, application and adjudication of these laws constitutes a central element of the supranational character of the EU.

This has necessarily involved the member states in surrendering some of their sovereignty, since they are obliged to submit to a legal system over which they have only partial control. In consequence of this, the governments of member states are sometimes obliged to apply laws they do not want and are occasionally prevented from introducing laws they desire.

The EU's courts have played an extremely important part in establishing the EU's legal order. This is because between them they exercise three key legal roles (Lenaerts, 1991). First, there is the role of constitutional court – adjudicating, for example, inter-institutional disputes and disputes about the division of powers between EU institutions and member states. Second, there is the role of supreme court, as most obviously with preliminary rulings that have as their purpose the uniform interpretation and application of EU law. And third, there is the role of administrative court, as when both the Court of Justice and the General Court are called upon by private parties to offer protection against illegal executive acts by EU institutions.

In exercising their responsibilities, the courts, and particularly the Court of Justice, sometimes not only interpret law but also make it. Of course judges everywhere help to shape the law, but this is especially so in the EU where there are lots of gaps to be filled in the EU's legal framework and where the courts in consequence have much more manoeuvrability available to them than is customary within states. They have used this to considerable effect: to help clarify relations between the institutions and between the institutions and the member states; to help clarify and extend EU policy in many different spheres; and arguably also to help develop and foster the EU's *esprit*.

Chapter 13
Other Institutions

In addition to the EU's main institutions, which have been examined in the last five chapters, there exist a large number of other institutions. These institutions have a variety of roles and purposes. The more important of these additional institutions are examined in this chapter.

The European Economic and Social Committee

Origins

In the negotiations that led to the Rome Treaties it was decided to establish a consultative body composed of representatives of socio-economic interests.

There were four principal reasons for this decision. First, five of the six founding states – West Germany was the exception – had such bodies in their own national systems. The main role of these bodies was to provide a forum in which sectional interests could express their views and in so doing could supplement the popular will as expressed via parliaments. Second, the essentially economic nature of the Community meant that sectional interests would be directly affected by policy developments and would be key participants in, and determiners of, the development of integration. Third, it was not thought that the Assembly (as the EP was then called) would be an effective forum for the expression of sectional views. Fourth, the institutional framework of the Rome Treaties was based on the Treaty of Paris model, and that had provided for a socio-economic advisory body in the ECSC Consultative Committee.

Accordingly, the EEC and Euratom Treaties provided for a common Economic and Social Committee (ESC). It was to have an advisory role and it was to be made up of representatives of various types of economic and social activity.

Since 2003, the ESC has called itself the European Economic and Social Committee (EESC).

Membership

The EESC has 344 members. France, Italy, Germany and the UK have the largest national representations, with 24 members each, whilst Malta has the smallest representation, with five members (see Table 13.1). Under Protocol 36 of the TFEU, the total size of the EESC is capped at 350, which means that – with EU enlargements in the pipeline – the national allocations of

Table 13. 1 Memberships of the European Economic and Social Committee and the Committee of the Regions

France, Germany, Italy, UK	24
Poland, Spain	21
Romania	15
Austria, Belgium, Bulgaria, Czech Republic, Greece, Hungary, Netherlands, Portugal, Sweden	12
Denmark, Finland, Ireland, Lithuania, Slovakia	9
Estonia, Latvia, Slovenia	7
Cyprus, Luxembourg	6
Malta	5
Total	334

membership will have to be adjusted at some point in the future.

The members of the EESC are proposed by national governments and are formally appointed by the Council of Ministers, by QMV since the ratification of the Nice Treaty. The term of office is five years, which may be renewed.

To ensure that a broad spectrum of interests and views is represented, the membership is divided into three groups that are just about equal in size. Each national complement of members is supposed to reflect this tripartite division. The three groups are as set out in Box 13.1.

Box 13.1

The three groups of the EESC

- *Group I: Employers.* Just less than half of this group are drawn from industry. The rest are mostly from public enterprises, commercial organisations, banks, insurance companies etc.
- *Group II: Employees.* The great majority in this group are members of national trade unions.
- *Group III: Various interests.* About half of this group are associated with either agriculture, small and medium-sized businesses, or the professions. The rest are mostly involved with public agencies and local authorities, consumer groups, environmental protection organisations and so on.

All members are appointed in a personal capacity and not as delegates of organisations. However, since most members are closely associated with or are employees of national interest organisations (organisations that in many cases are affiliated to Euro-organisations) it is inevitable that they do tend to act as representatives of, and be spokesmen for, a cause.

*   *   *

The administrative support for the EESC is organised by its Secretariat General. In 2009 there were 135 staff working exclusively for the EESC, while another 520 were located in departments that the EESC shares with the Committee of the Regions.

Organisation

Every two years the EESC elects a President, two Vice Presidents, and a Bureau from amongst its members. The Presidency rotates amongst the three groups, with the two groups that do not occupy the Presidency each assuming a Vice Presidency. There are 37 members of the Bureau: the President, the two Vice Presidents, and 34 members drawn from the three groups in equal proportion.

The main role of the President is to see to the orderly conduct of the EESC's business and to represent the EESC in its relations with other EU institutions, member states, and outside bodies. The Vice Presidents assist the President in these tasks. The main tasks of the Bureau are to provide guidelines for the EESC's work, to coordinate that work, and to assist with external representation.

The groups operate in a somewhat similar fashion to the political groups in the EP. That is to say, they meet on a regular basis – there are about 90 group meetings per year – to review matters of common concern, to discuss ongoing EESC work, and (particularly in the more cohesive groups I and II) to attempt to agree voting positions on proposals and issues that are due to be considered in plenary sessions. Group representatives in sections and study groups (see below) also sometimes meet together to coordinate their activities.

Most of the work of the EESC consists of giving opinions on EU-related matters. In a manner similar to the way in which the detailed work on opinions in the EP is undertaken by committees, so in the EESC it is undertaken by sections, each of which draws its membership from the groups. There are six sections: Agriculture, Rural Development and the Environment; Economic and Monetary Union and Economic and Social Cohesion; Employment, Social Affairs and Citizenship; External Relations; The Single Market, Production and Consumption; and Transport, Energy, Infrastructure and the Information Society. The sections appoint *rapporteurs* to prepare draft opinions on their behalf. How *rapporteurs* go about this depends on circumstances and preferences. Usually use is made of a study group or sub-committee; assistance may be called for from the EESC Secretariat; and – a common occurrence – help may be sought from, or be offered by, outside interests. In the sections, attempts are usually made to develop common positions on opinions, though on controversial issues this is not always possible to achieve. In an average year there are usually around 70–80 section meetings and some 300 meetings of study groups and subcommittees. (In addition, there are 300–400 miscellaneous meetings and meetings sponsored by the three groups. Many of these are concerned in some way with the preparation of opinions.)

Plenary meetings are held in Brussels, over a two-day period, usually nine or ten times a year. Agendas are dominated by consideration of reports from the sections. The standard procedure for dealing with reports is for each to be introduced by its *rapporteur*, for a debate to be held, and for a vote to be taken. On uncontroversial items the vote may be taken without discussion or debate.

Functions

The EESC engages in a number of activities:

1. It issues information reports on matters of contemporary interest and concern.
2. It liaises, via delegations, with a host of other international bodies and groupings.
3. It seeks to promote understanding between sectional interests by, for example, organising conferences, convening meetings, and being represented at congresses and symposia.
4. It seeks to take advantage of various contacts it has with other EU institutions to press its views. The most regularised of these contacts is with the

Commission: Commission officials, and sometimes Commissioners themselves, attend plenaries and meetings of sections. Occasionally ministers address plenaries.

5. Above all, as noted above, it issues opinions on a range of EU matters. Opinions are issued in one of three sets of circumstances:
   - *Mandatory referral.* Under Article 304 TFEU 'The Committee shall be consulted by the European Parliament, by the Council or by the Commission where the Treaties so provide.' Extensions made in the rounds of treaty reform since the SEA have resulted in most important policy areas now being subject to EESC mandatory referral. So, amongst the policy spheres on which the EESC must be consulted are agriculture, freedom of movement of workers, internal market issues, economic and social cohesion, social policy and the European Social Fund (ESF), regional policy and the European Regional Development Fund (ERDF), the environment, and research and technological development. In addition, under the Euratom Treaty the EESC has to be consulted on such matters as research and training programmes, health and safety, and investment.
   - *Optional consultation.* Also under Article 304 TFEU, the EESC may be consulted by the EP, the Council or the Commission 'in all cases in which they consider it appropriate'. Until the entry into force of the SEA some 80 per cent of EESC opinions were based on optional consultation. With the widening of the scope of mandatory referral this figure has fallen to around 50 per cent.
   - *Own initiatives.* The EESC has the right to issue opinions on its own initiative. Thus, in theory it can pronounce on almost any matter it wishes.

The EESC normally issues over 200 consultative documents per year, of which the vast majority are opinions on Commission proposals and communications, about 30–40 are own initiative opinions, and 3–4 are information reports. To illustrate the sort of topics on which opinions are issued, the plenary session of 15–16 July 2009 may be taken. Amongst the matters covered in Commission proposals and communications on which the EESC issued opinions were: minimum standards for the reception of asylum seekers;

consumer rights; the prevention of falsified medicinal products; and administrative cooperation between member states in the field of taxation. Amongst matters covered by EESC own opinions in the session were: urban areas and youth violence; the future of non-urban areas in the knowledge society; and emissions from road transport.

The EESC tends to operate in a reasonably consensual manner, with most of its opinions issued unanimously or with a very large majority. A point of contrast, however, worth noting between EESC and EP opinions is that the EESC is not as concerned as the EP to reach a single position that excludes all minority views. It is quite possible for minority positions to be attached as annexes to EESC opinions that have received majority support in the plenary.

Influence

The influence exercised by the EESC on EU policy and decision-making is limited. Evidence of this is provided, for example, by the Commission's follow-up reports to EESC opinions, which rarely constitute unambiguous acceptance of EESC recommendations but often include evasive comments along the lines of 'The Commission has taken note of the EESC opinion' or 'The opinion will be useful to the Commission staff in their exchanges of views with the Council'. Such EESC recommendations as are taken up usually cover relatively minor points, and are often as much a consequence of pressure exerted by other institutions and interests as by EESC pronouncements (this point is discussed further in Chapter 18).

There are a number of reasons why the EESC has only limited power. First, there has always been, as Jeffery (2002) has observed, a lack of clarity as to its role in the EU system: is it mainly a body to represent interests that otherwise would be neglected or is it a sort of panel of experts charged with improving the quality of decision-making? Added to this lack of clarity is the fact that both of these roles have become increasingly difficult for the EESC to use with effect: the first because the nature of its membership has increasingly come to have a rather old-fashioned look and also because corporatist structures themselves are now not so in vogue as they were; the second because the EESC is but one of many sources of specialised advice available to the EU's decision-making institutions.

Second, following on from the last point, the EESC is not the only, and in many circumstances is not even the most important, channel available to sectional interests wishing to exert pressure on EU decision-makers. EU policy processes are highly sectoralised and multi-levelled and offer numerous contact points for interests. Direct access to Council representatives and Commission officials, and representation in Commission advisory committees, are generally seen by interests as being more useful channels for exercising policy influence than activity in the EESC – not least because these other channels often offer greater opportunities than does the EESC for influencing policy at the pre-proposal stage.

Third, the EESC's formal powers are relatively weak. The Council and the Commission are not obliged to act upon its views and even when its opinion is required under mandatory referral the delivery of the opinion can be made subject to a timetable that is so tight as not to allow sufficient time for a considered response: the Council and the Commission can, if they consider it necessary, set a time limit as short as one month for the submission of an EESC opinion.

Fourth, it is by no means uncommon for proposals to be referred to the EESC at a stage of policy advancement when agreements between the key decision-makers in the Commission, Council and EP have already been made in principle and are difficult to unscramble.

Finally, the members of the EESC serve only on a part-time basis, which places time limits on what they can do. Furthermore, the fact that they serve – in theory at least – in a personal rather than a representational capacity means that there are rarely strong reasons for the Commission or the Council to listen to them if they do not wish to do so.

* * *

The EESC basically does two things. First, it provides a forum in which representatives of sectional interests can come together on a largely cooperative basis to exchange views and ideas. Second, it is a consultative organ that provides some limited – though in most cases only very limited – opportunities for interests to influence EU policy and decision-making.

Whether, taken together, these two functions of the EESC make it the bridge between European civil society and the EU's institutions that it likes to claim for itself must be doubted.

The Committee of the Regions

Origins

Regionalism, regional issues and regional politics have come to assume a significant role and importance in the EU. The main factors accounting for this are as follows:

- There are great variations in wealth and income between member states and between regions in the member states. The disparities have long produced calls for compensatory and rectifying measures to be taken at EU level, and these calls have increased as the internal market programme has intensified and as enlargements have resulted in relatively poor states acceding.
- Since the ERDF was established in 1975, regional and local groupings have had a clear focus for their attention at EU level: the attraction of funds. The Commission has encouraged subnational levels of government to play a full part in ERDF management, especially since the launching of its partnership programme under the 1988 reform of the Structural Funds.
- Partly as a consequence of the financial opportunities offered by the ERDF and other funds, but partly too because they do not wish to be wholly controlled by their national governments, many subnational levels of government have established direct lines of communication with decision-makers in Brussels. Well over 100 regional governments have established their own offices in Brussels.
- Over the years several transnational organisations that bring together the subnational governments of different member states have been established to promote common interests and, where appropriate, to make representations and exert pressure at the EU level. These organisations include the Association of European Border Regions, the Assembly of European Regions, the Association of Regions of Traditional Industry and the Association of Frontier Regions.

In response to this developing regional dimension of Community affairs, in 1988 the Commission established the Consultative Council of Regional and Local Authorities. For some governments, notably the German and Belgian, the Consultative Council did not go far enough and they took advantage of the 1990–1 IGC on Political Union to press the case for a stronger body to be established. Differing views were expressed in the IGC – with France, Spain and the UK putting up some resistance to the creation of a new body – but it was eventually agreed to establish, with full Treaty recognition, a Committee of the Regions (CoR).

Membership, organisation, functions and powers

The size and national composition of the *membership* of the CoR is the same as that of the EESC (see Table 13.1). The members are appointed for a renewable five-year term of office by the Council of Ministers on the basis of proposals from the member states.

As to the qualities and characteristics of the CoR's members, at the time of the creation of the institution the TEC simply stated the Committee should consist of 'representatives of regional and local bodies' (Article 263). The lack of insistence in the Treaty that members should be elected representatives of regional and local bodies led to considerable debate in some member states as to who should be proposed for membership, but in the event virtually all of those nominated to the CoR were and have continued to be elected representatives of subnational levels of government of some kind. Those countries with clear regional structures – including Belgium, France, Germany, Italy, the Netherlands and Spain – have allocated at least half of their places to regional representatives, while countries without regional structures have mostly sent representatives from local councils and authorities. The ambiguity about whether or not members should hold elected office was removed by the Nice Treaty and confirmed by the Lisbon Treaty: members must be elected members of regional or local authorities or be politically accountable to an elected assembly (Article, 300, TFEU).

* * *

The *organisational structure* of the CoR is similar to that of the EESC. The planning and overseeing of the work of the Committee is undertaken by its 60 member Bureau, which is made up of the CoR's

President, first Vice President, 27 other Vice Presidents (one from each member state), 27 other members (one from each member state), and the chairs of the four political groups (see below). The members of the Bureau are elected for a two-year term.

Most of the work of the CoR is channelled through six specialised committees, called commissions. These are the commissions for: Territorial Cohesion; Economic and Social Policy; Sustainable Development; Culture, Education and Research; Constitutional Affairs, European Governance, and the Area of Freedom, Security and Justice; and External Relations and Decentralised Cooperation. The commissions report to CoR plenary sessions, of which there are normally five each year.

Unlike in the EESC, political groups paralleling the main groups in the EP exist in the CoR. There are four such groups: the European People's Party (EPP), the Party of European Socialists (PES), the Group of the Alliance of Liberals and Democrats for Europe (ALDE), and – not quite the same as in the EP – the Union for Europe of the Nations-European Alliance Group (UEN-EA). The groups, which have official status in the CoR, meet before plenaries to discuss and try to agree positions on tactics on upcoming business.

As was described above, most of the CoR's administrative support is shared with the EESC.

*   *   *

The *functions and powers* of the CoR are, like those of the EESC, of an advisory nature. The key Treaty references to what the CoR can do are set out in Document 13.1

The range of policies provided for in the TFEU on which the CoR must be consulted is narrower than for the EESC, but still includes many important areas. Amongst these areas are economic and social cohesion, energy infrastructure networks, public health, transport, enlargement, combating social exclusion, the environment, and cross-border cooperation.

As they can with the EESC, the EP, the Council or the Commission can set a time limit on the CoR for the delivery of its opinion, which can be as little as one month. Upon expiry of the time limit, the absence of an opinion cannot prevent the EP, the Council or the Commission from proceeding.

An indication of the volume of work undertaken by the CoR is seen in its adoption in 2008 of 61 opinions and three resolutions. Of the opinions, seven were own initiatives. Topics covered in its opinions included the energy and climate change policy package, the Lisbon Strategy objectives, cultural diversity, and the promotion of cohesion policy. Not surprisingly, a theme running through most of the opinions was, as is usually the case, that subnational levels of government should play an important role in the identification, management, and evaluation of EU policies that affect them.

Within the spheres of its competence, and especially where mandatory consultation applies, the influence of the CoR appears to be at least comparable to that of the EESC. Like the EESC it is weakened

Document 13.1

Treaty powers of the Committee of the Regions

The Committee of the Regions shall be consulted by the European Parliament, by the Council or by the Commission where the Treaties so provide and in all other cases, in particular those which concern cross-border cooperation, in which one of these institutions considers it appropriate ...

Where the Economic and Social Committee is consulted ... the Committee of the Regions shall be informed by the European Parliament, the Council or the Commission of the request for an opinion. Where it considers that specific regional interests are involved, the Committee of the Regions may issue an opinion on the matter.

The Committee of the Regions may be consulted by the European Parliament.

It may issue an opinion on its own initiative in cases in which it considers such action appropriate.

Source: Article 307, *Treaty on the Functioning of the European Union* (post-Lisbon Treaty, 2008).

by the fact that those it is charged to represent – primarily subnational authorities in its case – also have other policy process options to utilise, including the Council of Ministers itself in those cases where the national governments of countries with strong regional governmental structures allow regional representatives to participate in their Council 'delegations' on some issues. As Jeffery (2002: 345) has stated, the CoR is only one of a number of channels available for regional interests to make a mark on Europe.

European Agencies

'Agency' is a word used in public sectors to describe a myriad of organisations that undertake policy functions whilst not being part of 'mainstream' political and administrative systems. They are in some way(s) detached from the formal policy and decision-making structures.

In 1975 the EC established two agencies charged with a variety of information-gathering, information-dissemination, networking and advisory tasks. These agencies, which had no regulatory roles or powers and were essentially a mix of research-cum-promotional bodies, were the European Centre for the Development of Vocational Training (CEDEFOP) and the European Foundation for the Improvement of Living and Working Conditions (EUROFOUND).

Since the early 1990s many more agencies have been created. Their creation, which reflects a development that has also been taking place at national levels, indicates, as Majone (2006a: 191) puts it, 'the existence of functional needs that are not met by centralized policy-making institutions'. EU functional needs that can be at least partly satisfied by using agencies include: policy requirements can be examined and policy deliberations can be undertaken independent of those who are politically responsible for policy; using less traditional, less hierarchical, and less centrally controlled modes of operation can provide greater organisational flexibility; the ability to use technical experts in policy areas that are heavily reliant on specialised expertise can be increased; some of the workload of the Commission can be relieved, enabling it to concentrate on its core responsibilities; in areas of shared policy competence, agencies can promote and facilitate EU-member state cooperation which might well be resisted if attempted by EU institutions; and – a functional need that Majone thinks is especially important – the credibility of long-term policy commitments can be enhanced if aspects of the policy are removed from the political process and given an independent base.

There are now over forty EU agencies in existence, with at least one agency to be found in just about every area of EU policy activity. They take a number of different forms. Such indeed is the variety of their organisational natures, their relations to the main institutions, their competences, and their powers that it is possible to classify them in several different ways.

An initial distinction needs to be made between executive and regulatory agencies. The former, of which there were six at the beginning of 2010, are established on the basis of a common Council regulation. This is because they have a common purpose and narrow tasks to undertake: all executive agencies are created for a limited period to manage EU programmes. The fact that the EU's executive agencies are all located close to the Commission in Brussels reflects both that they are very much part of the EU's administrative machinery and that they are controlled by the Commission – via 'parent' Directorates General. An example of an executive agency is the Education, Audiovisual and Culture Agency, which implements aspects of nearly twenty EU programmes in such areas as education and training, active citizenship, youth, audiovisual and culture. Other executive agencies include the Executive Agency for Competitiveness and Innovation and the Executive Agency for Health and Consumers.

Regulatory agencies – which are sometimes also known as traditional agencies (because they began to be created before executive agencies) or decentralised agencies (because they are physically distributed around the member states) – are more important politically than executive agencies. This is because they usually have a capacity to feed into policy processes and in some instances they have direct, albeit tightly controlled, regulatory powers. They are independent, with their own Management Boards (on which the Commission is usually represented but is always in a minority) and are established on their own legal bases.

Box 13.2

The differing types of regulatory agencies

- *Agencies adopting individual decisions that are legally binding on third parties.* Notwithstanding the wide use of the term 'regulatory agency' to encompass all of the EU's non executive agencies, most of the regulatory agencies do not in fact have direct regulatory power. But, a few do, although their scope for regulating is invariably tightly drawn and limited usually to not much more than issuing individual 'technical' clarifications and updates within the framework of existing EU legislation. None are empowered to issue general regulatory measures and none have significant discretionary regulatory powers. Examples of agencies that have such regulatory powers include the Office for Harmonization in the Internal Market (Trade Marks and Designs) (OHIM), the Community Plant Variety Office (CPVO), the European Aviation Safety Agency (EASA), and the European Chemicals Agency (ECA).

- *Agencies providing technical or scientific advice to the Commission and, where necessary, to the member states.* Agencies in this category feed information directly into EU policy forums, principally the Commission, and make recommendations. They undertake regulatory work, but they are not regulators themselves. For example, the European Food Safety Authority (EFSA) can assess risks arising from food safety issues but it cannot itself manage the risks. So, where manufacturers are pressing for genetically modified (GM) crops to be given access to the EU market, the EFSA makes assessments, but final decisions on whether or not to give product authorizations are taken by the Council of Ministers acting by QMV. (Normally such matters would not reach the ministers, but would be taken by the Commission operating within the comitology framework. GM-related issues are however, very controversial and high-profile; hence the ministerial involvement.) Of course, since much of the information that the agencies feed into EU forums is highly technical and specialised in nature, it can be difficult for policy-makers to challenge and ignore. Certainly, for instance, it is not conceivable that a GM product would be authorised against EFSA advice. And in respect of the authorisation of pharmaceuticals, which is handled by the European Medicines Agency (EMEA), Gehring and Kraphol (2007) have shown that although formally the EMEA only advises the Commission, in practice it is almost invariably the real decision-maker and operates much like an independent agency. Indeed, they argue that 'the multi-tiered oversight mechanism restricts the non-scientific actors involved in the authorization of pharmaceuticals more than

→

A useful way of classifying regulatory agencies is provided by the Commission in a 2008 communication on agencies (European Commission, 2008b: 7). The classification is based on the key functions of agencies and, given that agencies often perform a number of functions, 'an analysis of the centre of gravity of agencies' activities'. The Commission's classification is used in Box 13.2 to help explain the differing types of regulatory agencies that exist.

As Box 13.2 shows, regulatory agencies undertake a wide range of differing tasks in many policy areas. Their growing significance and profile in the EU context is seen in the seemingly constantly increasing number of them – there were thirty-six at the beginning of 2010 – and in the corresponding increasing number of personnel working in them: in early 2010 around 4,000 people were based in the agencies, with the largest single number being in the OHIM – where over 600 were located.

But, though a few agencies, such as the EFSA and the EMEA, do have a real regulatory impact, for the most part the agencies are relatively weak in their powers and are very restricted in what they can do. They have been entrusted with only very limited decision-making powers. Certainly they are not comparable to some of the strong agencies that have been created in member states. The main reason for this relative weakness is that the member states and the Commission do not wish to lose decision-making capacity.

Box 13.2 *continued*

the agency – as long as the agency adheres to its mandate of producing scientifically convincing decisions' (p.208). In addition to the EFSA and EMEA, other examples of agencies of this type include the European Railway Agency (ERA) and the European Maritime Safety Agency (EMSA).

- *Agencies in charge of operational activities.* Some operational tasks are seen as being best handled not by the Commission but by agencies that have, or at least can be seen as having, a measure of distance, independence and in some instances subject specialism. Examples of agencies of this type include the Community Fisheries Control Agency (CFCA) and the European Agency for the Management of Operational Cooperation at the External Borders (Frontex).

  An additional and very important reason for the existence of agencies of this sort is that some operational matters have fallen under the EU's second and third pillars and, therefore, have not been within the Commission's competence. The Lisbon Treaty weakens this rationale in so far as the three JHA agencies – the European Police Office (Europol), the European Police College (CEPOL), and the European Union's Judicial Cooperation Unit (Eurojust) – are, as with all former third pillar JHA policies, placed in the TFEU. But, with many of the activities of these agencies involving highly sensitive matters and the use of specialist practitioners, strong reasons remain for their continuance as separate agencies. As for the three agencies created under the CFSP/ESDP umbrella – the European Defence Agency (EDA), the European Institute for Security Studies (EUISS), and the European Union Satellite Centre (EUSC) – the CFSP/ESDP policy areas remain, post-Lisbon, outside the TFEU and largely based on intergovernmental procedures.

- *Agencies responsible for gathering, analysing, and making available relevant information and/or networking.* In policy terms, these are the weakest of the regulatory agencies in that they are not usually such direct policy practitioners. Many of them are akin to think-tanks, with their work being focused largely on assembling and providing background information and, sometimes, on bringing policy practitioners together for exchanges on issues of shared interest. Examples of agencies of this type include the European Centre for the Development of Vocational Training (CEDEFOP) the European Environmental Agency (EEA), and the European Centre for Disease Prevention and Control (ECDC).

- *Agencies providing services to other agencies and institutions.* There is only one agency that falls full-square in this category: the Translation Centre for the Bodies of the European Union (CDT).

The European Investment Bank

The European Investment Bank (EIB) was created in 1958 under the EEC Treaty. Its members are the member states of the EU. The Bank is located in Luxembourg.

Responsibilities and functions

The responsibilities and functions of the EIB are referred to in several articles of the TFEU. Article 309 is especially important: it sets out the task of the EIB as being to contribute, on a non-profit-making basis, via the granting of loans and the giving of guarantees, to the 'balanced and steady development of the internal market in the interests of the Union'. What this means in practice is that the Bank's main job is to act as a source of investment finance for projects that further EU goals. In so doing, it is by far the largest provider of EU loan finance. In 2008 the EIB granted loans totalling €59.3 billion, of which €53.2 billion was in the EU-27 member states and €6.1 billion was in 'partner countries' – which are mainly underdeveloped countries where the funds are used for development aid and cooperation (European Investment Bank, 2009).

Within the broad remit that is given in the TFEU,

EIB policy is framed within Corporate Operational Plans (COPs) that prioritise objectives. Central to the COP for the 2009–11 period is an increase in the scale of EIB operations as part of the European Economic Recovery Plan that seeks to enable the EU to mitigate the effects of, and recover from, the global credit and economic crisis that set-in during 2008.

With regard to the loans that are made within the EU, two main conditions have to be satisfied for the EIB to consider providing finance.

First, projects must comply with the policy objectives laid down in Article 309 and in the current COP, and also with credit directives from the Bank's Board of Governors. These objectives are interpreted fairly broadly, but at least one of the following criteria normally has to be met:

1 Projects must further economic and social cohesion by contributing to the economic development of the EU's less prosperous regions. Almost two-thirds of EIB loans within the EU are assigned for regional development purposes and for helping the poorest areas. This finance is used primarily to assist with communications and other infrastructure, the productive sector, and capital spending on energy installations.
2 Projects must support innovation, contribute to the competitiveness of EU industry, and help implement the 'Lisbon Strategy'. Under this heading, particular support is given to the introduction and development of advanced technology and to the integration of industry at the European level.
3 Projects must be of common interest to several member states or to the EU as a whole. In this connection, major transport and telecommunications developments and the EU's energy objectives are given a high priority. The EU's environmental policies also receive considerable support, with around half of the 'environmental loans' being made to the water sector (catchment, treatment and supply) and the rest going to projects dealing with such problems as atmospheric pollution, waste management, land conservation, and urban improvement.

Second, projects must be financially and technically viable, and loans must be guaranteed by adequate security. This is because although the EIB is not a profit-making body it is not a loss-making one either:

apart from in certain specified and strictly limited circumstances, the Bank's loans are not subsidised from the EU budget but must be financed from its own capital. This capital comes from two sources: paid-in or due-to-be-paid-in capital by the member states, and borrowing – in the EIB's own name and on its own credit – on capital markets inside and outside the EU. Of these two sources, borrowing is by far the largest element, and since the sums raised must be repaid from the Bank's own financial operations it must take appropriate steps to protect itself.

A major attraction for potential EIB borrowers is that loans are offered at very competitive rates. They are so partly because the Bank enjoys a first-class international credit rating and is thus itself able to borrow at favourable rates and partly also because the Bank is not profit-making and is thus able to pass on its favourable rates. Other advantages of EIB loans are that they are generally made available at fixed interest rates, repayments can often be deferred for the first two or three years, and the repayment periods are usually medium-to-long term (between five and twelve years for industrial projects and up to twenty years or more for infrastructure projects).

Two other features of EIB loans are also worth noting. First, the Bank does not usually lend more than 50 per cent – the average is about 30 per cent – of the investment cost of a project unless it is part of a special programme. Borrowers need to find additional sources of loan finance, with the consequence that the Bank very frequently operates on a co-financing basis with other banks. Second, the Bank generally only deals directly with large loans – of more than about €25 million. This does not however mean that only large-scale investment is supported because, mainly via its global loan facility, the Bank opens lines of credit to intermediary institutions – such as regional development agencies and, more commonly, national financial institutions – which lend-on the money in smaller amounts. Global loans account for around 30 per cent of total EIB lending and are directed principally towards small and medium-sized enterprises (SMEs). They have been prioritised as part of the EIB's contribution to the European Economic Recovery Plan. An administrative problem with global loans is that the intermediary agencies that act on the EIB's behalf and are delegated responsibility for appraising applications and negotiating with potential borrowers on the basis of the EIB's lending criteria tend sometimes to make their decisions according to traditional banking criteria and with little eye to EU objectives.

* * *

In addition to the activities just described – which may be thought of as the Bank's 'standard' activities – certain other activities are undertaken, including the following:

- Some projects are eligible for both EIB loan finance and EU grant aid. When this is the case – and it applies mainly in connection with the ERDF and the Cohesion Fund – the Bank works closely with other interested parties, especially the Commission, to work out appropriate financial arrangements.
- The December 1992 Edinburgh European Council laid the foundations for a European Investment Fund (EIF), which was established in 1994 and which is designed primarily to assist high-technology SMEs and those with a high growth potential. This is done via a venture capital facility, loan guarantees, and direct investment operations. Guarantees are particularly important, with guarantees of over €2 billion covering 20 operations made in 2008. The EIF is being expanded as part of the European Economic Recovery Programme.

The EIF's subscribed capital is drawn from three sources: 40 per cent is provided by the EIB, 30 per cent by other EU sources (channelled through the Commission), and 30 per cent by public and private banks. The EIF has its own administrative and decision-making structure within the EIB.

Organisation

The EIB's main decision-making bodies are as follows:

The *Board of Governors* decides on the Bank's subscribed capital and lays down general directives on the Bank's activities. It is also responsible for formally appointing the members of the Board of Directors and the Management Committee. The Board of Governors is composed of one minister per member state – usually the Minister of Finance – and normally meets once a year. Certain major Board decisions have to be made unanimously, whilst others can be made by a majority of members representing at least 45 per cent of subscribed capital.

The *Board of Directors* has general responsibility for ensuring that the Bank is managed according to the provisions of the TFEU, the Bank's Statute, and directives issued by the Governors. More specifically, the Board has sole responsibility for deciding on loans and guarantees, raising funds, and fixing interest rates. There are 28 Directors: one Director is nominated by each member state and is invariably a senior figure in a national financial institution or an appropriate national ministry, and one Director is nominated by the Commission. The Board of Directors normally meets every four to six weeks.

The *Management Committee* controls current operations, makes recommendations to the Board of Directors and is responsible for implementing decisions made by the Directors. The Committee consists of the Bank's President and eight Vice-Presidents. It meets at least weekly.

* * *

Supporting, and operating under, these decision-making bodies is the EIB's administration. This is divided into thirteen departments, included amongst which are: the General Secretariat and Legal Affairs; the Directorate for Lending Operations in Europe; the Directorate for Lending Operations Outside Europe; the Finance Directorate; and the Projects Directorate. In all, the EIB employs around 900 staff.

The importance of the EIB

The EIB is a bank, not a grant-dispensing body. This means that it must observe certain basic banking principles. At the same time, however, it is an EU institution charged with furthering a number of policy objectives. These two roles – banker and EU institution – do not always sit easily together.

The scale of EIB borrowing and lending is small when compared with the total operations of commercial banks across the member states. The importance of the Bank should not, however, be underestimated. Indeed, it is the largest international financial institution on capital markets and within the EU it is a useful source of medium- and long-term finance for EU-oriented projects. It complements other public and private funding resources for the promotion of capital investment projects that, in general terms, promote economic development and further integration within the EU.

The European Central Bank

The creation of the Bank

As the EU moved forward during the 1990s with the construction of Economic and Monetary Union (EMU), the nature of the institutional structure within which it would operate was extensively debated. In the debate, one of the key issues was where the balance should lie between politicians and bankers in the determination of the common monetary policies that the single currency system would require. There were different views on the question, but agreement was reached by the national governments at an early stage of the deliberations, and it was specified in the Maastricht Treaty, that bankers should be responsible for the day-to-day management of common monetary policies. However, it was also agreed – more enthusiastically by some governments than by others – that in exercising their management role the bankers should not have a completely free hand: they should be subject, albeit at a general level, to some political direction and accountability.

As a result of the debates and agreements of the 1990s, and with some refinements since, a rather complex institutional structure was created for EMU. This structure is set out in Box 17.1 on p. 290. At the heart of the structure is the European Central Bank (ECB), which is located in Frankfurt. The Bank operates within the European System of Central Banks (ESCB), which embraces the national central banks of all EU member states, whether they are eurozone members or not.

Objectives and tasks

Article 127 TFEU states:

> The primary objective of the European System of Central Banks ... shall be to maintain price stability. Without prejudice to the objective of price stability, the ESCB shall support the general economic policies in the Union with a view to

contributing to the achievement of the objectives of the Union as laid down in Article 3 of the Treaty on European Union.

These two sentences of Article 127 contain the seeds of possible disputes over ESCB policies, since Article 3 TEU identifies Union tasks as including 'aiming at full employment and social progress' and promoting 'economic, social and territorial cohesion, and solidarity among Member States'. These are tasks that in some circumstances might be seen as not sitting easily alongside policies aimed at ensuring low inflation. In public statements, several EU politicians have already sought to exert pressure on ESCB decision-makers for not paying enough attention to policies beyond the control of inflation. For example, in June 2004 the then French Finance Minister, Nicolas Sarkozy, accused the Bank of concentrating too much on keeping inflation below its target of two per cent and not enough on promoting economic growth and employment. Later in 2004 the Italian Prime Minister, Silvio Berlusconi, plus several leading German politicians, called on the Bank to sell euros and buy dollars so as to stop the rise in value of the euro which was damaging export potential. However, ESCB decision-makers are given a certain amount of protection from such political pressures in that the Treaty emphasises that the ESCB must be independent. When performing ESCB-related tasks 'neither the European Central Bank, nor a national central bank, nor any member of their decision-making bodies shall seek or take instructions from Union institutions, bodies, offices or agencies, from any government of a Member State or from any other body' (Article 130 TFEU).

Article 127 also states that the basic tasks to be carried out through the ESCB are 'to define and implement the monetary policy of the Union', 'to conduct foreign exchange operations', 'to hold and manage the official foreign reserves of the Member States' and 'to promote the smooth operation of payment systems'. In addition, the ESCB is charged with providing advice to the Union and national authorities on matters that fall within its competence, especially where legislation is envisaged, and contributing to the smooth conduct of policies pursued by the competent authorities relating to the prudent supervision of financial institutions.

The organisational structure of the ECB

'The ESCB shall be governed by the decision-making bodies of the ECB which shall be the Governing Council and the Executive Board' (Article 129 TFEU).

The Governing Council

The main responsibilities of the ECB Governing Council are:

- To adopt guidelines and make the necessary decisions to ensure the performance of the tasks entrusted to the ESCB.
- To formulate the Union's monetary policy, including, as appropriate, decisions relating to intermediate monetary objectives, key interest rates and the supply of ESCB reserves.

The Governing Council, which meets twice a month, is made up of the members of the Executive Board and the governors of euro member NCBs. The President of the Ecofin Council and a member of the Commission may attend Governing Council meetings, but do not have the right to vote.

The Executive Board

The main responsibilities of the ECB Executive Board are:

- To implement monetary policy in accordance with the guidelines and decisions laid down by the Governing Council, and in so doing to give the necessary instructions to the national central banks.
- To execute policies delegated to it by the Governing Council (European Central Bank, 1999).

Though these responsibilities suggest that the Executive Board is the servant of the Governing Council, in practice it is very much involved in the formulation of policy, not least in helping to set the agenda and shape the decisions of the Council (McNamara, 2002: 171–3).

The Executive Board consists of the ECB President, Vice-President, and four other members. They are appointed 'from among persons of recognised standing and professional experience in monetary or banking matters' by the European Council acting by qualified majority 'on a recommendation from the Council, after it has consulted the European Parliament and the Governing Council of the European Central Bank' (Article 283 TFEU). The term of office is a non-renewable eight years.

As was shown on pp. 174, in 1998 the appointment of the first Executive Board, and more especially of the first President, became highly politicised when France pressed for the appointment of its candidate, Jean-Claude Trichet, as President, rather than the Dutchman, Wim Duisenberg, who was favoured by other states. The impasse was only resolved by what most participants regarded as an unsatisfactory informal understanding – the terms of which later came to be disputed – in which Duisenberg agreed to step down well before his eight-year term expired, at which point he would be replaced by Trichet. In the event, Trichet replaced Duisenberg in 2003.

* * *

In addition to its Governing Council and Executive Board, the ECB also has a General Council. Its membership comprises the ECB President and Vice-President and the governors of all the NCBs (that is, from both euro and non-euro zone states). The four other members of the ECB Executive Board may participate in General Council meetings, but do not have the right to vote.

The General Council has a number of tasks to perform, including supervision of the functioning of the post-single currency Exchange Rate Mechanism, considering the monetary and exchange rate policies of the member states that are not in the euro zone, and undertaking various advisory, administrative, and technical duties.

The governing bodies of the ECB are supported by an ECB staff complement of around 1,400 employees.

Functioning

The experiences to date of the ESCB, and more especially of its core institution the ECB, have highlighted a number of difficulties that may be expected to continue, perhaps even increase in intensity, in the foreseeable future.

One of these difficulties is tensions arising from the fact that whilst the ECB is broadly responsible for the monetary policies of the eurozone the member states retain the main responsibility for economic policies. When the Bank's policies have been thought not to chime wholly with the economic goals of national governments it has found itself the object of public criticism from the state(s) concerned.

A related difficulty has been some uncertainty and also disagreement as to whether the ECB should pursue exchange rate objectives. Should, as Duisenberg argued in 1998, the external value of the euro be mainly a consequence of the ECB's monetary policy, or should there be 'general orientations' and, if so, should these be set by the bankers or the politicians? A sharp decline in the value of the euro against the dollar in its initial period of operation stoked disagreements amongst practitioners and commentators on these questions. They are disagreements that have continued, with some national leaders, including President Sarkozy, having argued the case for active exchange rate management and others, including Chancellor Merkel, having been opposed to such intervention.

A third area of difficulty has concerned, as McNamara (2002: 180) has put it, 'how the ECB can maintain independence and profit from the benefits of political autonomy and at the same time be viewed as legitimate and accountable to the European public'. The fact is that the ECB enjoys a very considerable independence in respect of the eurozone's monetary policy and some important EU actors, including some national leaders, have expressed concerns about this – especially when eurozone interest rates have been seen to be too high or too low for particular national interests. Matters about which there has been unease include whether bankers should have so much power and, given that the bankers have been given considerable power, whether they should not be made more accountable.

And a fourth difficulty has been that the ECB has become the main focus for complaints about the economic performance of the eurozone. That the performance has been disappointing is undeniable, with growth consistently below two per cent since the single currency was launched and with unemployment around ten per cent in several eurozone states – including the key states of France and Germany. Whether, however, the ECB should be held partly to account for this is highly questionable. Most economists point to underlying economic structural problems as the main 'culprit'. And Kaltenthaler (2006), in one of the few full-length studies of the ECB to have been published to date, insists that accusations that the ECB has over-concentrated on achieving low inflation and has neglected the overall health of the economy are unjust. But the fact is that, as the main physical embodiment of the eurozone, the Bank has been a useful and much-used scapegoat.

The Court of Auditors

The 1975 *Treaty Amending Certain Financial Provisions of the Treaties …*, which entered into force in 1977, replaced the two existing Community audit bodies – the Audit Board of the EEC and Euratom and the ECSC Auditor – with a single Court of Auditors. The Maastricht Treaty enhanced the Court of Auditors' standing by raising it to the rank of a fully fledged Community institution. The Court is based in Luxembourg.

Membership and organisation

There are as many members of the Court of Auditors as there are EU states. Each member is appointed by the Council of Ministers, by QMV post-Nice, on the basis of one nomination per member state and after consultations with the EP. As with Commissioners-designate, the EP uses its right of consultation to hold hearings with nominees: before the Budgetary Control Committee.

At its November 1989 part-session, the EP voted, for the first time, to reject nominations – one made by France and one by Greece. The EP vote was not binding on the Council, but France nonetheless submitted a new name. Greece claimed difficulty in finding a suitable alternative candidate, so at the following December part-session the EP decided to accept both appointments so that the two posts could be filled by the new year. The EP hoped that this episode established its right to veto any nominee whom it considered to be unsuitable, but this proved not to be the case for in 1993 the Council confirmed the appointment of two candidates about whom the EP had expressed reservations. In 2004 the Council again overrode the EP's views when in appointing members from the new member states it confirmed the Slovak nominee even though he had been rejected by the EP. (The EP did, however, have a partial 'success' in 2004 when the Cypriot nominee withdrew his name following a negative vote by the Budgetary Control Committee.)

At the time of their appointment, members of the Court of Auditors must belong to, or have belonged to, an external audit body in their own country, or be appropriately qualified in some other capacity. The appointment is for a renewable six-year period. As with other 'non-political' EU bodies, a condition of appointment is that the members will act in the general interest and will be completely independent in the performance of their duties.

The members elect one of their number to be the President of the Court. The term of office is three years and is renewable. The President sees to the efficient running of the Court and also represents it in its external relations.

The members are assigned a general area of activity for which they hold a particular responsibility regarding the preparation and implementation of the decisions of the Court. Each area falls under one of five audit groups, which act primarily as coordinating agencies and filters for plenary sessions of the whole Court. All important decisions are taken in plenaries, by majority vote if need be.

* * *

As with several other EU institutions, the administration supporting the Court of Auditors is rather small in size given the potential importance of the work to be done. In 2009 just under 900 people were employed by the Court, of whom almost 100 were in temporary posts. Of the 900, around 400 were directly engaged in audit duties, 150 were in the language service, and 100 were in administrative departments. Inevitably such modest staffing resources greatly restricts the number of things the Court can attempt to do.

Activities of the Court

The main tasks of the Court of Auditors are to examine all EU revenue and expenditure accounts, the same for bodies set up by the EU unless the relevant legal instruments preclude such examination, and to provide the Council and the EP with a Statement of Assurance on the reliability of the accounts and the legality and regularity of the associated transactions. This activity involves what is known as external auditing, with the 'spending agencies' themselves undertaking what is known as the internal auditing (see Figure 13.1.)

Figure 13.1 Overview of Internal Control and External Audit of the EU Budget

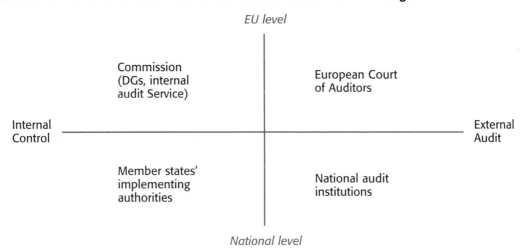

Source: European Court of Auditors, _Annual Activity Report for 2008_, Europa website, p. 9.

In exercising its responsibilities the Court engages in two main types of activity.

The first is to carry out audits to see whether revenue has been received and expenditure has been incurred in a lawful and regular manner, and also to examine whether the financial management of EU authorities has been sound. The auditing powers of the Court cover the general budget of the EU, plus certain financial operations that are not included in the budget such as aid to developing countries that is financed by national contributions.

The auditing of the general budget and the related process of granting a discharge to the Commission on its implementation of the budget, proceed as follows:

- The Commission is required to draw up, for each financial year, accounts relating to the implementation of the budget, a financial statement of the assets and liabilities of the EU, and an analysis of the financial year. The main responsibility for collecting and presenting this information (the internal audit) lies with financial controllers in the Commission. The documentation must be forwarded to the Council, the EP, and the Court of Auditors by no later than 1 June of the following financial year.

- The Court undertakes its audit (the external audit) partly on the basis of an examination of Commission documentation and partly on the basis of its own independent investigations. The latter is an ongoing process and involves the examination of records supplied by and requested from EU institutions and member states (which in the case of member states means liaising closely with national audit bodies and appropriate national agencies), and when necessary carrying out on-the-spot investigations. The purpose of this Court audit is not to replicate what has already been covered by the internal audit, but rather to add an extra dimension to the EU's overall auditory control by examining the adequacy of internal procedures – particularly with regard to their ability to identify significant irregular and unlawful transactions – and to evaluate the extent to which correct financial management (in terms of economy, efficiency and effectiveness) is being practised. The Court transmits to all relevant institutions any comments that it proposes to include in its annual report to which it believes there should be a reply or to which an institution may wish to reply. After receipt of the replies, the Court completes the final version of its annual report. This has to be communicated to the other EU institutions by 30 November.

The format of the annual report changed with the report on the 1997 financial year so as to allow the Court's work to be more manageable and measured. Whereas the report used to contain the detailed results of enquiries, it now consists largely of general observations grouped into chapters – on, for example, the CAP, structural measures, and external aid – and a summary of the audit conclusions of special reports which are drawn up during the year (see below) and special annual reports on particular activities and EU agencies. Whilst the annual reports have increasingly testified in recent years to improvements in the EU's, and more especially the Commission's, financial control and operating systems, they have also emphasised that the Court is able only to examine a small proportion of EU expenditure and is just not in a position to give a statement of assurance on the reliability and regularity of all financial transactions.

- The EP, acting on a recommendation of the Council, is supposed to give discharge to the Commission in respect of the implementation of the budget by 30 April of the following year. To this end, the EP's Budgetary Control Committee examines all relevant documentation, particularly that produced by the Court of Auditors, and makes a recommendation to the EP. Normally discharge is given by the due date, but not always and there have been occasions when discharge has been deferred until after the Commission has taken remedying measures to deal with the problem. Most dramatically in this context, in March 1998 the EP deferred discharge on the 1996 budget after a series of cases involving alleged Commission mismanagement and fraud came to light, particularly in respect of a number of aid programmes. When the discharge vote was eventually held, in December 1998, the EP – angered by what it saw as an insufficiently robust Commission response to its concerns and aware that in November the Court had again strongly criticised the Commission in its report on the 1997 financial year – voted against giving discharge, even though the Budgetary Control Committee had voted narrowly (by 14 votes to 13) to recommend that discharge be given. The President of the

Commission, Jacques Santer, responded by calling on the EP either to back or to sack the College of Commissioners. As was shown in Chapters 8 and 11, the sacking option came close to being taken when other causes of dissatisfaction with the Commission became caught up in a vote of censure on the College in January 1999. Though the vote was not passed, the circumstances that led to it being held paved the way for the events that resulted in the resignation of the College two months later.

The second main activity of the Court of Auditors is to deliver special reports and opinions on a range of subjects. Regarding special reports, about a dozen or so of these are issued each year. Amongst topics covered in special reports in 2009 were the management of the Galileo programme (which is responsible for Europe's Global Satellite Navigation System), the Commission's management of non state actors involved in development cooperation policies, and aspects of agricultural policy. Regarding opinions, about half-a-dozen of these are issued each year. They normally are drawn up in one of two sets of circumstances: an EU institution may ask the Court to submit an opinion on a matter, usually concerning financial aspects of draft legislation; the Court's opinion is required prior to the adoption of new or updating legislation with a potentially significant financial impact.

The effectiveness of financial controls

As the Court continually makes clear, controls over EU revenue and expenditure could be improved. For example, given that over 80 per cent of budgetary expenditure is 'paid out' by national agencies, procedures could be tightened so as to prevent member states from imposing the limitations they sometimes apply to the audit enquiries considered necessary by the Court. The Court's own attempts to extend its influence beyond questions of financial rectitude into considerations of policy efficiency could be encouraged, and even formalised. And the particular problem of fraud – much of which occurs in connection with agriculture payments and foreign aid contracts – could be tackled more effectively if resources at both EU and member state levels were increased and if more of the proposals that have long been advocated by the Court for streamlining administrative practices were adopted.

However, considerable progress has been made in recent years in improving financial control and overseeing, especially since the College of Commissioners was forced to resign in 1999 because – in large part – it was seen to have been lax in respect of financial management. The Court's estimate is that the level of error in financial payments is currently only between two and five per cent except for cohesion policies where it is at least eleven per cent. Though obviously still too high, the two to five per cent overall figure is much lower than the ten per cent and more that was the general estimate of the level of financial irregularities a decade or so ago. Much of the credit for this progress, which is a consequence of both tighter financial control mechanisms and the development/strengthening of a culture of financial responsibility throughout the EU, can be claimed by the Court of Auditors. Its reports have been sharp, critical, and increasingly difficult for those who are responsible for managing EU expenditure to ignore. One reason for this is, as Laffan (2002: 251) has observed, that its reports have provided the raw material for the EP to exercise its discharge procedure in a manner that has strengthened its control over the Commission.

One final point about EU expenditure that should be recognised amidst the hype that sometimes greets allegations of financial mismanagement: the total sums involved are relatively modest (see Chapter 22 for details). EU decision makers, far from being able to be financially profligate with surplus funds are, for the most part, obliged to work to tight budgets and within limited resources.

Chapter 14

Interests

Different Types

Brussels has come to compete with Washington as the world's 'most lobbied city'. The exact number of lobbyists in Brussels is impossible to gauge with precision, partly because many who lobby do not do so on a full-time basis but also act as lawyers, accountants, businessmen, and so on, and partly also because many of those who are really full-time lobbyists prefer to call themselves 'consultants', 'advisers', 'policy specialists', and the like. Nonetheless, the normal estimates of between 15,000 and 20,000 people making a living from 'lobbying Brussels' give an indication of the scale of lobbying activity.

Lobbyists represent and seek to act on behalf of a range of non-governmental interests. These interests are of four main types.

Subnational levels of government

As noted in the section on the Committee of the Regions in Chapter 13, many subnational governmental bodies from the member states seek to influence, or even play a direct role in, EU policy processes. The degree of their involvement and activity varies enormously, depending largely on the degree of autonomy and manoeuvrability they have in their member states and on the impact of particular EU policies on regional and local matters.

In member states where there are large and strong subnational levels of government – such as Belgium, Germany, and Spain – regional, and to a lesser extent local, authorities maintain nationally based EU offices of various kinds and also an office in Brussels. In respect of regional policy and also aspects of such policy areas as environmental, social and industrial, these offices, especially the Brussels-based offices, have direct lines of communication with EU institutions, notably the Commission. Where subnational levels of government are not so well-established at member state level, and in policy areas where there is not an ongoing subnational dimension, regional and local authorities work with the EU more through their national governments and, where appropriate, through EU-wide liaison organisations.

Private and public companies

Many large business firms, especially multinational corporations, are very active in lobbying EU institutions. Around 250 firms have established offices in Brussels. Adopting, usually, multiple strategies, business lobbying is channelled through both national and Euro interest groups (see below), and is also conducted on a direct basis. Direct lobbying has the advantage of not requiring a collective view to be sought with other firms and also enables sensitive issues to be pursued when there is no desire to 'go public' – as, for instance, when competition and trading matters are involved. The car industry is an example of a sector where direct lobbying by firms, and not just European firms, is common – as is indicated by the fact that most large car firms in Europe have lobbying/information offices in Brussels.

National interest groups

Many circumstances result in national interest groups attempting to involve themselves in EU processes. For example, several national environmental interest groups have pressed for more effective implementation of existing EU legislation on the disposal of sewage into the sea. In some policy areas, especially those concerned with business and trade matters, many national interest groups are from non-EU countries: one of the most influential of all is the EU Committee of the American Chamber of Commerce (AMCHAM-EU).

In seeking to play a part in EU processes, most national interest groups are confined to working from their national offices or via a European interest group, but a few of the larger industrial and agricultural groups have, in addition to a domestic and a European group base, their own representatives and agents permanently based in Brussels.

Eurogroups

Eurogroups are groups that draw their membership from several countries and operate at – and in so doing seek to represent the interests of their sector or cause at – the EU level. As with lobbyists, the number of Eurogroups is difficult to estimate, with there being no complete central register of such groups and with the differences between groups that might be considered to be Eurogroups being so great that considerable difficulties arise in deciding which ones should be counted. As an indication, however, of the scale of activity, Greenwood (2007: 12) estimates there are 1,450 formally constituted EU level groups that exist to address EU activities.

Given their particular EU orientation it is worth looking at Eurogroups in detail.

Policy interests

The policy interests of Eurogroups naturally reflect the policy priorities and concerns of the EU. Whist precise categorisation is all but impossible because of the often vague self-descriptions of Eurogroups and because too of the often blurred boundaries between categories, Greenwood (2007: 10–11) estimates that over half of Eurogroups represent business, about one third (a rising proportion in recent years) represent citizens interests (the environment, consumers, youth, etc.), and about ten per cent represent the professions. Within these broad categories a multiplicity of specific interests and groups are to be found. For example, within the business category, agricultural interests are a major and diverse component, ranging in nature from the broadly based Committee of Agricultural Organisations in the European Union (COPA) and the General Confederation of Agricultural Co-operatives in the European Union (COGECA), which work very closely with one another, which share a secretariat, and which seek to represent most types of farmer on most issues, to highly specialised groups representing the likes of yeast producers and pasta manufacturers.

The reason why such an array of Eurogroups has been constituted and is active at the EU level is quite simple: pressure groups go where power goes. As policy responsibilities – in agriculture, in the regulation of the market, in the protection of the environment and so on – have been transferred from national capitals to the EU, so has a Euro-lobby developed to supplement – not to replace – the domestic lobbies.

Membership

The membership of Eurogroups also varies considerably. It does so in four main respects. First, there are variations in the breadth of the membership base. Some groups – the so-called umbrella groups – have a broad membership base and are usually trans-sector or sectoral-wide in character. Examples of prominent umbrella groups are BusinessEurope (*sic*) which was formerly the Union of Industrial and Employers Confederation of Europe (UNICE), the European Trade Union Confederation (ETUC), the European Environmental Bureau (EEB), the European Bureau of

Consumers' Associations (BEUC), and COPA/COGECA. Because of the breadth of their membership some of these umbrella groups have considerable difficulty in maintaining internal cohesion and presenting a common front: ETUC, for example, has traditionally had to try to reconcile differences between socialist, communist, and Christian trade unions, whilst COPA/COGECA has had problems with managing the varying agricultural sectoral implications of reforms to the CAP. Most groups, however, are more narrowly focused than the umbrella groups and seek to speak on behalf of a specific industry, process, service, or product. Examples of such groups are the Construction Industry Federation (FIEC), the Savings Banks Group (ESBG), and the European Cocoa Association (ECA).

Second, there are variations in terms of whether membership is direct or via affiliation. In most cases membership is based on affiliation by national sectoral or, in the case of a few of the larger Eurogroups, national peak (cross-sectoral) organisations. Since the mid-1980s, however, there has been a growth in direct membership groupings and organisations. The most important development in this regard has been the coming together of major industrial, often multinational, companies, frequently as a supplement to their involvement in affiliation-based sectoral groups. Examples of Eurogroups that are dominated by large companies are the European Automobile Manufacturers' Association (ACEA), which represents most of the EU's major non-Japanese car, truck and bus manufacturers, and the Association of Petrochemical Producers and Exporters (APPE). A few lobbying-related linkages between major companies are relatively informally based and in some respects are perhaps more like thinktanks and forums for the generation of ideas than Eurogroups. The best known example of such a 'think tank' is the European Round Table of Industrialists which brings together, on an invitation-only basis, fifty or so heads of major European industries. The Round Table produces reports that are intended to identify how the right conditions can be created for business to flourish.

Third, there are variations in the representativeness of groups. Since most Eurogroups are based on national affiliates, the number of people they can claim to represent naturally reflects the factors determining group membership at the national level. Hence, sectional interests are usually better placed than promotional interests. Similarly, amongst sectional interests, Eurogroups representing interests that are well mobilised at the national level, such as dairy farmers and textile manufacturers, naturally tend to be much more genuinely representative than groups acting on behalf of poorly mobilised sections of the population such as consumers or agricultural labourers.

Fourth, there are variations in the width of the EU base of groups. At one end of the spectrum, a few groups draw members from virtually all EU states and often also several European states beyond. ETUC, for example, comprises 82 member organisations from 36 countries plus 12 European industry federations, whilst BuinessEurope comprises 40 national member federations from 34 countries. Membership of this latter sort, stretching into non-EU states, has advantages and disadvantages: on the one hand it can help to promote international cooperation and increase group resources; on the other hand, and this is a charge that has frequently been laid against ETUC, it can serve to dilute group concentration on, and therefore influence within, the EU. More typical, however, of Eurogroups than ETUC or UNICE is the European Passengers' Federation (EPF), which seeks to promote rail use and to look after the interests of rail passengers by promoting rail infrastructure and rail facilities. The EPF has 29 member organisations drawn from sixteen EU member states plus Switzerland. Clearly this narrower membership weakens the representational claims that the EPF can make.

Resources

The best resourced groups are mostly either large business groups – such as the European Chemical Industry Council (CEFIC), COPA/COGECA, BusinessEurope, the European Insurance Committee (CEA), and the European Federation of Pharmaceutical Industry Associations (EFPIA) – or global public interest groups such as Friends of the Earth and the World Wide Fund for Nature. The most poorly resourced groups, which are not of a particular type but exist amongst business, public interest, and other groups, usually do not have strong corporate backing and/or have a narrow membership base.

There are thus wide variations in group resources. On the one hand, there are very well resourced groups – such as CEFIC, BusinessEurope and COPA/COGECA – that have forty and more staff and ample and well-appointed accommodation. On the other hand, there are numerous groups – of which the EPF is but one – that do not even stretch to one employee and that work through affiliates, consultants, and part-time and temporary representatives whose services are called upon as and when they are needed. (It is not difficult to find people prepared to act as contract agents: there are around 140 professional public consultancies and 160 law firms based in Brussels that are willing to take on 'EU business'.)

Organisational structure

The organisational structure of most Eurogroups is extremely loose. The central group organs usually enjoy only a very limited independence from the national affiliates, whilst the affiliates themselves are autonomous in most respects and are not subject to central discipline. In addition, key decisions made at the centre are frequently taken only on the basis of unanimous votes, though some groups do have provisions for weighted majorities on some issues. These loose structures can weaken the effectiveness of Eurogroups by making them slow to react and making it difficult for them to put forward collective views that are anything more than rather vague lowest common denominators. At the same time, however, moves to create stronger structures risk groups not affiliating, or national affiliates concentrating almost exclusively on their national activities.

The more specialised and poorly resourced groups usually operate on a fairly rudimentary basis, often merely via an annual meeting and an executive committee that meets as required. The large umbrella

Figure 14.1 Organisation structure of COPA

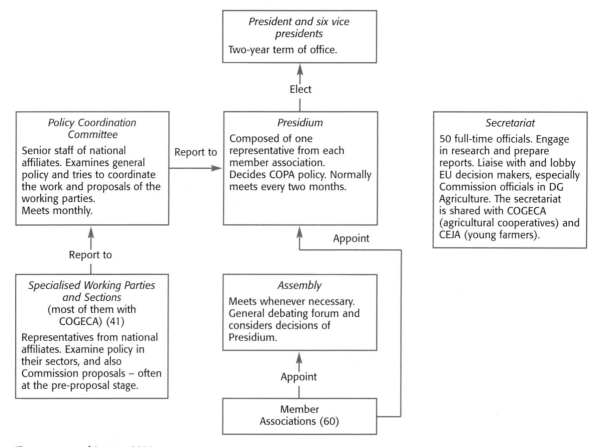

Figures are as of January 2010.

groups, in contrast, usually have a quite elaborate organisational framework that typically includes a general meeting at least once a year, an executive committee that meets once every four to six weeks, specialist policy committees whose frequency of meeting depends on the business in hand, a President, and a full-time Secretariat headed by a Secretary General. COPA is an example of a group with a highly developed structure (see Figure 14.1).

Functions

Eurogroups normally attempt to do two main things. First, they seek to gather and exchange information, both in a two-way process with EU organs and with and between national affiliates. Second, they seek to have their interests and views incorporated into EU policy, by persuading and pressurising those who make and implement policy. Not all Eurogroups, of course, attempt or are able to exercise these functions in equal measure: for example, in those sectors where EU policy is little developed, Eurogroups often choose to give a higher priority to the first function than they do to the second.

Access to Decision-Makers

The long, complex and multi-layered nature of EU processes provides many points of access for interests, and hence many opportunities for them to keep themselves informed about developments and press their cases with those who influence, make, and implement decisions. The main points of access are national governments, the Commission, and the European Parliament.

National governments

A major problem for interests is that they cannot normally directly approach either the European Council or the Council of Ministers. This is partly because there are practical problems with lobbying what are in effect international negotiations, it is partly because the meetings are held (mainly) behind closed doors, but it is mainly because neither body wishes to make itself available, as a collective entity, for

regularised or intensive interest targeting. Only a few direct linkages therefore exist, and these are largely restricted to the most powerful interests. So, the President-in-Office of a sectoral Council may occasionally meet the president of a powerful Eurogroup, or a written submission from an influential interest may be officially received and circulated prior to a European Council or Council of Ministers meeting. More usually, however, the only way an interest can hope to establish contact with, and perhaps exert pressure on, the European Council or the Council of Ministers is indirectly: through a government or governments looking favourably on its cause or feeling obliged to act on its behalf.

Much time and effort is therefore spent by interests, especially national interests, attempting to influence the positions adopted by governments in EU negotiations. In the case of the European Council, this task usually has to be undertaken at least at one stage removed because national leaders do not normally allow themselves to be lobbied directly. With the Council of Ministers, however, one of a number of factors may result in doors being opened. Amongst such factors are: some interests, such as most of the major national agricultural groups, enjoy – for a mixture of political, economic, technical and other reasons – insider status with the relevant government departments, which means they are consulted as a matter of course on proposals and developments within their sphere of interest; when a technically complicated matter is under consideration, governments usually seek the advice of relevant interests at an early stage of the Council process – with perhaps Council working party members communicating directly with interest representatives; and when the cooperation of an interest is important for the effective implementation of an EU proposal, its views may well be actively sought, or received and listened to if an approach is made.

This last point touches on another reason (in addition to trying to influence Council decision making), why interests may approach national governments: they may wish to influence the way EU decisions are implemented. One way in which they can attempt to do this is by making their views known to governments when measures are being devised to incorporate EU directives into national law. And if relevant ministries can be persuaded to delay, or not to monitor too closely, the implementation of directives on, say, the disposal of pollutants or safety standards in the workplace, some interests may well have much to gain financially.

The Commission

The Commission is the main target for most interests. It is so, primarily, because of its central importance in so many respects: in policy initiation and formulation; in following proposals through their legislative cycle; in managing the EU's spending programmes; and in policy implementation. An important contributory reason why the Commission attracts so much attention is simply that it is known to be approachable.

The Commission makes itself available to interests because several advantages can accrue to it from so doing. First, interests often have access to specialised information and to knowledge of how things are 'at the front' which the Commission needs if it is to be able to exercise its own responsibilities efficiently. This is especially so when the Commission is seeking to 'move into' or expand a policy area. Second, the Commission's negotiating hand with the Council of Ministers is strengthened if it can demonstrate that its proposals are supported by influential interests – as, for example, many of its attempts to approximate European standards are supported by multinational corporations, and indeed in some cases may have originated from them. Third, and this is in some ways the other side of the coin of the previous point, if the Commission does not consult with and try to satisfy interests, and advances proposals to which influential interests are strongly opposed, the proposals are likely to meet with strong resistance in the Council. Fourth, with specific regard to Eurogroups, when groups come forward with broadly united and coherent positions they can greatly assist the Commission by allowing it to deal with already aggregated views and enabling it to avoid entanglement in national and ideological differences between sectional interests. For this reason, DGs generally keep 'recognised' Eurogroups informed about matters that are of interest to them and are usually prepared to consult them too. (There are, however, no explicit Commission rules on recognition, in the sense that there is no proper system of accreditation or registration, but informal consultation lists do exist. The main reasons for non-recognition are

---

Box 14.1

Ways in which interests can communicate their views to the Commission

- The extensive advisory committee system that is clustered around the Commission primarily exists for the precise purpose of allowing interests to make their views known (see pp. 124–5).
- Commissioners and DG officials receive numerous delegations from interests of all sorts.
- Representatives of the Commission travel to member states to meet interests and to attend conferences and seminars where interests are represented.
- A few of the larger Eurogroups invite Commission representatives to attend some of their working parties and committee meetings.
- Informal meetings and telephone conversations between Commission and interest representatives occur constantly.
- Interests present the Commission with a mass of written communications in the form of information, briefing, and policy documents.
- The Social Dialogue provides for an exchange of views between the Commission and the two sides of industry. Since 1985 it has regularly brought together representatives from the Commission, trade union representatives from ETUC and representatives from the two main employers' and industrial organisations – BusinessEurope and the European Centre of Enterprises with Public Participation (CEEP). The Maastricht Treaty's Social Charter greatly extended the scope of the Commission's consultations with management and labour and it is even possible for legislative proposals to be developed within its framework.

either that the Commission does not regard the group as a proper Eurogroup – perhaps because it consists of just two or three large companies – or that it is not seen as being very effective in 'delivering' aggregated and coordinated views.)

Until about the mid-1970s the Commission displayed a strong preference for talking to Eurogroups rather than national groups, and to national governments rather than subnational levels of government. This attitude, however, has since been relaxed and most interests of significance, and most interests that can provide useful information that is presented in a clear manner, are able to have their views at least considered by the Commission. The ways in which the contacts and communications occur are many and are of both a formal and an informal nature. The most frequent ways are set out in Box 14.1.

Naturally, the extent and nature of the communications between interests and the Commission vary considerably according to a number of factors. A small national interest in a specialised area may only require and seek occasional contact at middle-ranking official level with one particular DG. In contrast, an active umbrella group may wish to be permanently plugged into the Commission at many different points. As an indication of how extensive the links can be, some of the access channels available to COPA are worth noting: about every three months the Presidium of COPA meets the Commissioner for Agriculture; the Secretary General of COPA and the Director General of DG Agriculture meet regularly and often speak to each other on the telephone; at all levels, the staff of COPA are in almost constant touch with staff in DG Agriculture and, less frequently, are also in close contact with staff in other DGs – notably DG Budget and DG Environment; and COPA is strongly represented, both in its own right and via affiliates, on all the agricultural advisory committees and also on certain other leading advisory committees such as the Standing Committee on Employment and the Harmonisation of Legislation Committee.

The European Parliament

It has been very noticeable, not least in the swelling ranks of lobbyists who attend EP plenaries, that as the role and influence of the EP in the EU system has grown it has increasingly attracted the attention of interests. The EP now has access to a wide range of powers that interests would like to see exercised in ways that are to their advantage.

The most prominent and important of these powers are those relating to the making of legislation. As is shown in Chapters 11 and 18, the EP exercises a wide range of legislative powers and a very considerable influence over the content of EU legislation. This is most obviously so when the ordinary legislative procedure is being used, for it is there that the EP's powers are at their greatest. Whilst the Parliament does not normally wish to exercise its veto powers under the procedure, it usually makes lots of amendments to proposed legislation and it has a high rate of success in seeing them incorporated in adopted acts. But beyond its important position in legislative procedures the EP also has other potentially useful tools at its disposal that can feed into EU law making and create the possibility of interests using MEPs to influence the legislative environment. These tools include: the production of own initiative reports, that can pave the way for the Commission to come forward with proposals; the power to formally request the Commission to submit legislative acts; and the access to a range of forums – such as political group meetings and EP committees – where ideas about legislation are discussed and exchanged both in formal sessions and on the margins of meetings.

The main lobbying possibilities available to interests in respect of the EP are set out in Box 14.2.

Which is the most appropriate lobbying channel?

Many possible 'targets' are thus available to interests to enable them to try and advance their causes. Which are the most suitable, the most available, and the most effective channels varies according to circumstances.

For example, a local authority that wishes to attract ERDF funds would, if it is well-advised, give a high priority to establishing contact with DG Regional Policy. It should also court good relations with regional and national civil servants since the ERDF functions on an EU-national-regional partnership basis. A chemical company concerned about the possibility of tighter EU air quality standards is likely to want to be able to transmit its views to: relevant parts

---

Box 14.2

Ways in which interests can communicate their views to the EP

- It can be very fruitful for interests to lobby MEPs, especially *rapporteurs* and members of committees dealing with relevant legislation. The relative lack of political group discipline in the EP enhances the possibility of individual MEPs being 'persuadable'.
- MEPs and officials engaged in preparing reports for EP committees often approach appropriate interests for their views, or allow themselves to be approached. This can be for a number of reasons but is usually because they wish to make use of the knowledge and expertise of interests and/or because the future progress of reports is likely to be eased if they do not come up against stiff oppositional lobbying from interests.
- Interests have some opportunities for direct contact with EP committees and political groups. Committees, for example, sometimes hold 'hearings' and occasionally travel to member states for the precise purpose of meeting interest representatives, whilst political groups sometimes allow themselves to be addressed when they judge it to be appropriate.
- Attempts can be made to encourage MEPs to draw up own initiative reports. If this results in progress, the Commission and/or the Council might conceivably then be prompted into action of a desired sort.
- Intergroups, which are loosely organised and voluntary groupings of MEPs with shared concerns about particular issues or areas of activity, are natural targets for interests. For example, interests acting on behalf of disabled people will clearly wish to be in contact with the Handicapped Intergroup, while those acting on behalf of citrus fruit producers will wish to be in touch with, amongst others, the Israel and the Mediterranean Intergroups.
- A general circulation of literature amongst MEPs may have the effect of improving the image of an interest or changing the climate of opinion in the interest's area of concern.
- Attempts can be made to persuade individual MEPs to take matters up with governments and the Commission.

---

of the Commission – both directly and perhaps also via sympathetic Eurogroup representatives on Commission advisory committees; the host national governments(s) – which are likely to be sympathetic to the chemical company's position if tighter standards risk leading to unemployment; and to MEPs representing the area(s) in which the company is located. And an environmental group in a member state where the government is not noted for its sympathy to green issues is likely to be most effective working as part of a Eurogroup in order to, for example: launch public information and relations campaigns that help persuade the EP to adopt a sympathetic position, and perhaps pass a resolution; pressurise the Commission to produce legislative proposals and increase its efforts to ensure that existing legislation is properly implemented; and find a route to the Council of Ministers via some of the national affiliates that are leaning on their governments.

Influence

The factors that determine the influence exercised by interests in the EU are similar to those which apply at the national level. The more powerful and more effective interests tend to have at least some of the following characteristics:

Control of key information and expertise

Effective policy-making and implementation requires a knowledge and understanding that often can only be provided to EU authorities by interests. This obviously puts interests on which EU policy-makers are to some extent dependent in a potentially advantageous position – as evidenced by the fact that the influence that interests exercise via official forums is often much greater in specialised advisory committees than it is in more general settings such as the EESC or the CoR.

Adequate resources

The better resourced an interest is, the more likely it is to be able to make use of a variety of tactics and devices at a number of different access points. So, with regard to proposed legislation, a well-resourced interest is likely to be in a position to feed its views through to the Commission, the EP, and perhaps the Council from the initiating stage to the taking of the final decision. Similarly, a regional or local authority hoping for EU funds is more likely to be successful if it employs people who know what is available, how to apply, and with whom it is worth having an informal word.

Economic weight

Important economic interests – be they major companies or cross-sectoral representational organisations – usually have to be listened to by EU policy-makers, not least because their cooperation is often necessary in connection with policies designed, for instance, to encourage EU-wide investment, expand employment in less prosperous regions, stimulate cross-border rationalisations, or improve industrial efficiency. Examples of economic weight being an important factor in political influence include: the way in which the chemical industry – via its Eurogroup CEFIC – has managed to persuade the Commission to investigate numerous cases of alleged dumping; the way in which EUROFER (the steel manufacturers' association) has worked closely with the Commission and governments to limit the damage caused to its members by steel rationalisation programmes; and the way in which the pharmaceutical industry – acting through EFPIA – has persuaded the Commission to allow it to regulate itself rather than be regulated.

Political weight

Many interests have political assets that can be used to advantage, usually via governments. For example, a national pressure group that is closely linked to a party in government may be able to get that government to act virtually on its behalf in the Council of Ministers. At a broader level, electoral factors can be important, with ministers in the Council not usually anxious to support anything that might upset key voters, especially if an important national or local election is looming. Farmers' organisations in France, Italy,

Germany and elsewhere are the best examples of interests that have benefited from the possession of electoral significance.

Genuine representational claims

National pressure groups and Eurogroups that genuinely represent a sizeable proportion of the interests in a given sector are naturally in a stronger position than those that do not. The representativeness of CEFIC, for example, is one important reason why the chemical industry has been permitted to exercise a certain degree of self-regulation.

Cohesion

Some interests find it difficult to put forward clear and consistent views and are thereby weakened. As was noted earlier, this often applies to Eurogroups, especially umbrella Eurogroups, because of their varied membership and loose confederal structures. Increasing difficulty in maintaining internal coherence and consensus has contributed to a decline in COPA's lobbying influence over the years.

Access to decision-makers

Most of the characteristics just described play some part in determining which interests enjoy good access to decision-makers and which do not. Clearly, those that do have good access – especially if it is at both national and EU levels – are more likely than those that do not to be fully aware of thinking and developments in decision-making circles, and to be able to present their case to those who matter. At the EU level, COPA is, notwithstanding its declining influence, an obvious example of such an 'insider' interest, whilst at the national level COPA affiliates usually also enjoy an advantageous position.

Interests and EU Policy Processes

There are both positive and negative aspects to the involvement of interests in EU processes. Of the positive aspects, two are especially worth emphasising. First, interest activity broadens the participatory base of the EU and ensures that policy-making is not completely controlled by politicians and officials. Second, interests can provide EU authorities with information and viewpoints that improve the quality and effectiveness of their policies and decisions. Of the negative aspects, the most important is that some interests are much more powerful and influential than others. This lack of balance raises questions about whether interests unduly, perhaps even undemocratically, tilt EU policy-making in certain directions – towards, for example, a legislative framework that tends to favour producers more than such 'natural' opponents as consumers and environmentalists.

But irrespective of whether interest activity is judged to be, on the whole, beneficial or not, its importance is clear. Interests are central to many key information flows to and from EU authorities, and they bring considerable influence to bear on policy-making processes from initiation through to implementation. There are no EU policy sectors where interests of at least some significance are not to be found.

Chapter 15

The Member States

The EU exists first and foremost to further the interests of its member states. It is, therefore, hardly surprising that, as previous chapters of this book have shown, the member states are core EU actors. This chapter examines the ways in which member states behave and act in the EU.

A useful starting point for the examination is to recognise that states pay a price for EU membership. The nature of the price varies between states but usually has two main aspects. The first and most obvious is that there is a substantial loss of national decision-making powers. In a few policy spheres – such as agriculture and external trade – most key decisions are now taken at the EU level, whilst in many other spheres – such as environmental policy and competition policy – decision-making responsibilities are shared between the EU and the member states. There is, in short, a loss – or at least a pooling – of national sovereignty. The second aspect, which is a consequence of the first, is that states are obliged to participate in and apply some policies that their representatives believe are not, at least in certain respects, in the national interests. For example, some governments with coastal waters believe they are not fairly treated under the Common Fisheries Policy. Several governments believe the Common Agricultural Policy has outlived its time, distorts EU budgetary expenditure to their disadvantage, and should be fundamentally reformed. And virtually all governments at some time have been unhappy about competition decisions – most commonly concerning state aid or proposed company mergers – that have been issued by the Commission.

Given this seeming heavy price of membership, why are states members of the EU? Why are they willing to participate in collective decision-making in important policy areas? Essentially they are so because their national decision-makers, supported by, or at least with the acquiescence of, large sections of their populations have believed it to be in their national interests to do so. National decision-makers have judged that there is more to be gained from being inside the EU than from being outside. Perceptions of the particular balance of advantages and disadvantages arising from EU membership have varied from state to state, but all have judged that the net balance sheet is in the black.

A consequence of being a member state is that national political, economic and legal systems are increasingly being 'Europeanised'. As part of this, national political structures, political actors, policy processes, and policies are progressively orientating, or are being orientated, in a European direction. The extent of the orientating, and of the associated national adaptations, varies both between and within states. But no states are exempt from the need to accommodate many aspects of national systems to EU rules and requirements.

Because it is mainly concerned with the impact of the EU on the member states, Europeanisation – or 'EU-ization' as Bulmer and Lequesne (2005a:11) suggest it may be better termed – is normally thought of as being a top-down process. (There is now an extensive academic literature on Europeanisation. See, for example: Ladrech, 2010; Featherstone and Radaelli, 2003; Goetz and Hix, 2001; Green Cowles *et al.*, 2001; Olsen, 2002.) However, Europeanisation has an important bottom-up element too in that a key reason national political actors, agencies and sectors have adjusted to the EU is so as to enhance their ability to communicate with and influence decision-making at the EU level. It is with this latter aspect of Europeanisation that this chapter is mostly concerned. That is to say, whilst top-down Europeanisation is not ignored, the main focus is on national inputs into EU policy and decision-making processes and how they have been designed and adjusted in attempts to enable them to feed into the processes in an effective manner.

The precise nature of these inputs varies between states, reflecting such factors as different national political systems, traditions, and cultures. In broad terms, however, they can be seen as being directed through seven principal channels: governments, parliaments, courts, subnational levels of government, citizens' views, political parties, and interests. This chapter is mainly taken up with examining each of these channels. However, it is useful to begin by placing the inputs that have been and are being made through the particular channels into a wider context of general national orientations and approaches towards European integration and EU membership. It is also useful to have towards the end of the chapter a section that considers the relative influence exercised by states in the EU.

National Orientations and Approaches

The circumstances in which the EU's 27 member states founded or became members of the EC/EU were outlined in Chapters 1 and 4. Their general stances towards and behaviour within the EU will now be outlined. It will be shown that whilst there are some similarities in the stances and behaviour of member states, there are also many very significant differences. These differences reflect more than anything else the

fact that the member states *just are* different from one another in numerous respects. Table 15.1 shows some of the more obvious size and economic differences that exist, but a fully comprehensive table of significant differences between member states would require many pages.

As in Chapters 1 and 4, the states are grouped according to when they assumed membership.

The founding member states: Belgium, France, Germany, Italy, Luxembourg, and the Netherlands

Since helping to create the EC in the 1950s, four of the founding states – Belgium, Luxembourg, the Netherlands and Italy – have remained firm and consistent supporters of the integration process. They have almost invariably backed, and sometimes have been prominent in the initiation of, the many proposals put forward over the years for further integrationist advance. The only significant exception to this is the rejection by the Dutch people in a referendum in June 2005 of the proposed Constitutional Treaty. The reasons for, and the significance of, this vote were considered in Chapter 6.

Germany – or, to be strictly accurate, West Germany up to 1990 and united Germany since – has also been a reasonably dependable member of the integrationist camp. (German unification took the form of the German Democratic Republic – East Germany – integrating into the Federal Republic of Germany, so there was no question of a new state joining the Community and therefore no question of normal enlargement procedures applying.) However, in recent years the enthusiasm for integration has wobbled a little, with a reluctance to continue acting as the EU's main 'paymaster' being displayed and with reservations about continuing enlargements of the EU, especially to Turkey, being expressed.

In the early years of the EC, France assumed a very wary attitude towards the integration process. This was a consequence of President de Gaulle's hostility to any international organisation that assumed supranational characteristics and, thereby, undermined French national sovereignty. The economic benefits of Community membership for France were recognised and welcomed, but they were not to be paid for with

Table 15.1 Key information on EU member states

	Population[1] (millions)	Surface area (1,000 sq.km)	Size of GDP[2] (billion euro)	GDP per capita in PPS[3]
Germany	82.2	357.0	2,238,507	116.1
France	63.8	544.0	1,678,544	107.4
UK	61.2	243.8	1,705,659	117.7
Italy	59.6	295.1	1,404,270	100.6
Spain	45.2	506.0	1,132,591	103.4
Poland	38.1	312.7	535,737	57.6
Romania	21.5	230.0	219,909	45.8
Netherlands	16.4	33.8	515,016	135.0
Greece	11.2	130.7	261,400	93.9
Belgium	10.7	30.3	302,651	114
Portugal	10.6	91.9	192,775	75.5
Czech Republic	10.4	77.3	198,933	80.1
Hungary	10.0	93.0	145,698	62.8
Sweden	9.2	410.3	262,149	121.0
Austria	8.3	82.5	248,889	123.1
Bulgaria	7.6	111.0	70,426	40.5
Denmark	5.5	43.1	152,151	118.7
Slovakia	5.4	49.0	89,139	71.8
Finland	5.3	304.5	141,811	115.1
Ireland	4.4	68.4	143,746	136.6
Lithuania	3.4	62.7	41,802	61.2
Latvia	2.3	62.3	25,368	55.8
Slovenia	2.0	20.1	42,596	90.7
Estonia	1.4	43.4	19,109	68.2
Cyprus	0.8	9.3	18,029	96.2
Luxembourg	0.5	2.6	31,309	271.5
Malta	0.4	0.3	7,813	75.5
Total EU-27	497.4	4,215.1	11,826,027	

Sources:
[1] *Council of Ministers* (2008).
[2] *Eurostat*, December 2009.
[3] PPS = purchasing power standards, *Eurostat*, December 2009.

Further information on the member states is available on the book's website at **www.palgrave.com/politics/nugent**.

transfers of national sovereignty to the likes of the Commission, the European Parliament or a Council of Ministers taking its decisions by majority vote. Since de Gaulle's resignation in 1969, France's concerns about loss of sovereignty have been less to the fore, though they have never quite disappeared and even today France still tends to take a more intergovernmentalist stance than the other five founding states with respect to the powers of the EU institutions. Notwithstanding this tendency, however, French Presidents have sought to be prominent in moving integration ahead and have linked up with others, especially German Chancellors, for this purpose. It thus came as a considerable setback to President Chirac when the French people

Photo 15.1 Charles de Gaulle, President of France, 1958–69.

rejected the Constitutional Treaty in a referendum held in May 2005 – a matter which, like the Dutch referendum on the Constitutional Treaty, was considered in Chapter 6.

The first enlargement round acceding states: Denmark, Ireland, and the UK

Since joining the Community, the UK has been something of an awkward partner and has played an important role in slowing aspects of the integration process. This was especially so during the Conservative Party's term of office between 1979 and 1997, for it took a largely minimalist view of what the EC/EU should be doing and what organisational shape it should take. The strong preference was for the EC/EU to be concerned primarily with market-related matters, and more particularly for it to direct most of its efforts towards creating an integrated and largely deregulated European market. The proper and efficient operation of this market was not seen to require common economic, financial, and social policies, let alone a single currency. As for the political dimensions of Community/Union membership, the governments led by Margaret Thatcher and John Major were willing to support the development of intergovernmental cooperation when that seemed useful – as, for example, in the field of foreign policy and aspects of internal security policy – but they almost invariably sought to resist supranational developments and any loss of national sovereignty.

With the election of a Labour government in 1997, the British stance in the EU became more cooperative, as was exemplified by the willingness of the governments led by Tony Blair and then Gordon Brown to incorporate extensions to supranational decision-making in the Amsterdam, Nice and Lisbon Treaties, to provide a lead in the development of EU defence policy, and to strike a generally positive stance in EU forums. However, overall under Labour, Britain remained in the slow integration stream, as was demonstrated by the unwillingness not to join the single currency system and by the insistence in the negotiations that led to the Nice and Lisbon Treaties that Britain be given opt-outs from certain measures designed to strengthen the EU's justice and home affairs policies.

Denmark's record since joining the Community has been not wholly dissimilar from that of the UK in that, aware of domestic scepticism about the supposed benefits of EC/EU membership, Danish governments have tended to be cautious in their approach to integration. The most dramatic manifestation of Danish concern with the integration process occurred in 1992 when, in a national referendum, the Danish people rejected Denmark's ratification of the Maastricht Treaty. This rejection, which was reversed in a second referendum in 1993, upset the schedule for applying the Treaty, took much wind out of the sails of those who wished to press ahead quickly with further integration, and resulted in Denmark distancing itself from certain future integrationist projects. As part of this distancing, Denmark, like the UK, did not become a member of the common currency system when it was launched in 1999, and then, in a referendum held in September 2000, the Danish people rejected a recommendation made by their government to join.

For the most part, Ireland has been a strongly prointegrationist member state. One reason for this has been that it has been afforded generous treatment under the Common Agricultural Policy (CAP) and the Structural Funds. Another, related, reason is that EU membership is commonly viewed as having been a key contributing factor behind the so-called 'Irish economic miracle' that saw rapid economic growth in the 1990s and early 2000s and the transformation of Ireland from being one of the EU's poorest member states to one of the richest.

But, notwithstanding its generally strong pro-integrationist stance, Ireland has created two major problems for the EU, both of them involving decisions not to ratify EU treaties. In both instances the difficulties arose because the Irish Government is obliged to seek popular approval of major EU treaties by referendum. The first rejection involved the decision of the Irish people in a referendum held in June 2001 to reject ratification of the Nice Treaty. The vote put the implementation of the Nice Treaty on hold until it was approved in another referendum held in October 2002. The second rejection was of the Lisbon Treaty, in a referendum held in June 2008. Again, the implementation of the Treaty had to be put on hold until the vote was reversed in another 'second try' referendum in October 2009. Unlike the two 'No' referendum votes in Denmark, the Irish rejections were explained primarily not in terms of Eurosceptic sentiments but rather a variety of domestic political circumstances.

The Mediterranean round acceding states: Greece, Spain, and Portugal

Since becoming a member state, Greece has generally supported the advancement of the integration process. That said, particular Greek policies, concerns, and special needs have sometimes created difficulties: Greece's relative poverty (it is the poorest EU-15 state) has contributed to pressures on the EU's redistributive policies and funds; the somewhat unstable and debt-ridden nature of the Greek economy has meant that it has sometimes had to seek special economic assistance from its partners; although it wished to join the single currency from its launch, it was the only EU member state that was unable to meet the qualifying convergence criteria for entry into the first wave; Greece's long-standing hostility towards Turkey – now fading,

but not gone – and its complicated web of friendships and hostilities with parts of the former Yugoslavia have presented difficulties in the way of EU attempts to develop united and effective policies in South-East Europe; and Greece's special links with Cyprus led to it making threatening noises in the early 2000s about EU enlargement to CEECs should Cyprus's application be blocked.

Since their accession both Spain and Portugal have broadly gone along with integrationist developments, with the former perhaps being a little more integrationist than the latter. The fear expressed in some quarters before their accession that they would come to constitute a disruptive Iberian bloc has not been realised. As would be expected, they do frequently adopt similar positions on issues of common concern but, as with other member states, their preferences on specific policy matters often diverge. The single greatest difficulty they, and more especially Spain, have created for the EU is the tough position they have (understandably) adopted in seeking to protect themselves when – most notably in the context of enlargement to CEECs – it has been suggested that the support they receive from the Structural Funds should be reduced.

The EFTAN round acceding states: Austria, Finland, and Sweden

Since their accession, none of the 1995 entrants has created any major problems for the EU, although there was disappointment in 'integrationist quarters' when the Swedish people decided in a referendum held in September 2003 not to join the single currency system. In terms of distinctive contributions in particular policy areas, Sweden, working closely with Finland and the EU's third Scandinavian member state – Denmark – has been to the fore in advancing EU environmental policy and in pressing the case for greater openness and transparency in the EU. The three Scandinavian states have also led the way, working in cooperation with the Baltic states that acceded in 2004 (Estonia, Latvia, and Lithuania), in developing the EU's 'Northern Dimension' and Arctic policies, which are policies designed to promote and protect EU and national policy interests in the Baltic and Arctic seas regions.

The 10+2 round acceding states: Bulgaria, Cyprus, the Czech Republic, Estonia, Hungary, Latvia, Lithuania, Malta, Poland, Romania, Slovakia, and Slovenia

Prior to the accession of the 10+2 states, concerns were expressed in some EU quarters that the CEECs would act together on EU policy matters and would virtually constitute a voting bloc in the Council of Ministers. Such concerns have not been realised. They have not been so because, apart from generally supporting increased cohesion funding (that is, funding that is primarily designed to help economically less prosperous parts of the EU) and also generally pressing for the EU to adopt a robust stance in its relations with Russia, the CEECs have no more constituted a cohesive group than have the EU-15. Post the 2004–7 enlargement, the nature of divisions along national lines within the Council and other EU institutions remain, as they have always been, more crosscutting than cumulative. That is to say, on issues where there are divisions between member states, more often than not states ally with one another in different combinations rather than consistently ally in the same combinations.

But, though the CEECs as a whole have not constituted a bloc within the enlarged EU, groups of CEECs do seek to coordinate their activities in some policy areas. So, the Baltic States – Estonia, Latvia, and Lithuania – frequently liaise with one another before Council meetings, including by holding ministerial-level breakfast meetings. Prior to meetings of the General Affairs, and more especially of the Foreign Affairs, Councils these breakfast meetings often also include the Foreign Ministers of the three Scandinavian states – Denmark Finland and Sweden. A more structured form of liaison is attempted by the Visegrad Group, which is made up of the Czech Republic, Hungary, Poland and Slovakia and which is named after the Hungarian town where the group was launched in 1991. The Group 'is best described as a framework for both internally and externally oriented subregional cooperation between its four Central and European member states … (it) can be considered a permanent feature of the European political landscape' (Dangerfield, 2009: 3; see also, Dangerfield,

2008). The Visegrad Group member states exchange experiences and information across a number of policy fields and seek to act cooperatively in some. Their greatest cooperative activity since accession has been in respect of strongly supporting, though not leading, the development of an Eastern Partnership within the European Neighbourhood Policy which was launched in 2003 to provide an overall framework for channelling the EU's relation with its neighbours in the Mediterranean and to the East. (The Eastern Partnership was formally launched in May 2009, in part as a counterpart to the Mediterranean Union that was launched in 2008.)

Regarding individual CEECs having a particular impact on the EU, the two clearest instances concern institutional matters. The first involved Poland which, even before it assumed membership, joined forces with (the similarly sized) Spain at the December 2003 European Council meeting to block agreement on the Constitutional Treaty until both states had been given more votes under the Council's revised QMV rules. The second instance involved the Czech Republic and Poland, both of which – because they had strongly Eurosceptic Presidents whose approvals were required – were very laggardly in ratifying the Lisbon Treaty. Indeed, the signature of the Czech President, Vaclav Klaus, was the very last act in the Lisbon Treaty ratification process.

Bulgaria and Romania have created problems of a different kind for the EU, with the corruption in public life that raised questions about their preparedness for membership in 2007 continuing to remain rife. The EU-25 were well aware of these problems when they decided to let the 2007 enlargement go ahead, but hopes that membership would lead to them being more robustly and effectively tackled have been over-optimistic.

As for the two non-CEECs that were part of the 2004–7 enlargement round – Cyprus and Malta – the latter has created no particular problems for the EU since it became a member in 2004 but, predictably in the absence of a resolution to the Cyprus Problem, the former has. Like the representatives of all member states, Cypriot representatives in EU forums are particularly active in respect of matters that touch directly on national interests. In Cyprus's case, these matters include corporate law and taxation (many international companies have bases in Cyprus), the regulation of maritime transport (the Cypriot flag is a major flag of convenience for international shipping), and the regulation of and assistance for service industries (tourism accounts for approximately one third of Cypriot GDP). But, looming over Cyprus's 'routine' involvement in such 'normal' policy areas has always been the Cyprus Problem, with Cypriot representatives constantly having to address it one way or another – most particularly by ensuring that EU policies do not involve the EU officially dealing directly with authorities in northern Cyprus and by ensuring that pressure is maintained on Turkey to assist with a resolution of the Problem. On the particular issue of the Turkish EU membership application, Cyprus has been to the fore in pressing for the pace of the accession negotiations to be slow until Turkey has given full recognition to Cyprus and the Cyprus Problem has been resolved. This pressing has been successful, though it has been greatly assisted by the fact that some other member states – especially Austria, France and Germany – have, for their own reasons, also wanted to see the negotiations with Turkey be dragged out.

Governments

Governments are naturally in the strongest position of all national actors to control or influence EU processes. This is most obviously seen in their relationships with the Commission and the Council of Ministers.

Influencing the Commission

As was shown in Chapter 8, the system of appointment to the Commission ensures that all member states are represented within it. This, however, does not mean that Commissioners or Commission officials act as governmental representatives. Rather, for the most part they look to the EU-wide interest and are not open to instructions from national capitals. But they may, quite naturally, be inclined to take a particular interest in the impact of proposals on their own country. And governments looking for sympathetic ears in the Commission may well make fellow nationals their first port of call (though not necessarily: competent government officials, especially from

the Permanent Representations, cultivate a broad range of contacts in the Commission).

As well as the use of national contacts, there are many other ways in which governments try to persuade, influence or bring pressure to bear on the Commission. Use is made of the many formal channels on which governments are represented, such as the groups of experts who advise the Commission on all sorts of matters, the comitology committees through which the Commission exercises many of its executive functions, and the numerous decision-making meetings that take place within the Council system from working party level upwards – meetings that the Commission virtually always attends. Informal methods range from a minister ringing up a Commissioner, to a working party representative meeting a Commission official for lunch.

It should be emphasised that government influence on Commission thinking is not necessarily a bad thing. On the contrary, it can be positively helpful by, for example, improving the prospect of legislative proposals being adopted. However, it can become unhealthy if governments try to lean too heavily on their fellow nationals in the Commission, or if clusters of nationals have a disproportionate influence on policy development in a key sector (as, for example, has frequently been alleged of the French in respect of agriculture).

Influencing the Council

The potential for any government to influence what happens in the Council depends on a number of factors.

The size of the state it represents

On most policy issues the EU's larger member states carry more weight than do smaller member states. This is not just because the larger states have greater voting weight in the Council but also because the smaller states tend to defer to the size and resources of the larger states. The case should not, however, be overstated for, as Thorhallsson (2000) and Archer and Nugent (2002) have shown, the smaller states do – ironically because of their more limited administrative capacities – often display characteristics that make it possible for them to participate successfully in EU decision-making processes. Amongst these characteristics are: more informal domestic lines of policy communication; more flexible internal decision-making; the issuing of guidelines rather than instructions to Council negotiators; and a focus on a narrower range of policy issues.

The importance of the state to particular negotiations

When an issue is important to a state, its government will be actively involved in Council processes and it is likely to ensure that it is represented by senior figures in Council meetings. When, by contrast, a state is not much affected by an issue it may send junior people to represent it and its representatives may not engage actively in Council deliberations. For example, in Common Fisheries Policy (CFP) deliberations the Spanish and Irish governments are likely to be much more central actors than the Austrian or Slovak governments.

The desire of the government to play an active role

Where governments have strong policy preferences they are likely to be to the fore in the preparation of position papers and to be highly active in relevant policy debates and deliberations. This may result in them playing a crucial role in helping to set policy agendas and establish 'framework ideas'. Examples of governments exercising such a role include Germany in respect of the 'sound money' principles of EMU and the UK in respect of the liberal principles of the internal market.

The capacity of the government to play an active role

A government may have clear views on an EU initiative and may wish to play an active role in supporting or opposing it, but be restrained by domestic political considerations such as a finely balanced coalition government, opposition from key interest groups, or possible electoral damage.

Relations with other governments

Cohesive and fixed alliances within the EU between particular governments do not exist. The governments of small states, for example, do not come together as a group, except on some treaty reform issues. Rather, governments come together in different combinations on different issues. Taking Irish governments as an example, their positions have traditionally been close to the positions of the governments of: Spain, Greece and Portugal on cohesion policy; Sweden and Finland on defence; France on agriculture; the Benelux states on institutional questions; and the UK on taxation and some justice and home affairs matters.

However, some governments do make more of a conscious effort than others to seek general understandings and cooperation with one or more of their EU partners. So, for example, in 2001 the prime ministers of the three Nordic member states – Denmark, Sweden and Finland – decided they would meet before each European Council meeting to discuss issues of common concern. The Benelux leaders also often meet before summits. As was noted above, Baltic and Visegrad leaders also often get together on a regular basis, with the latter even having institutionalised their meetings with a rotating presidency.

The best known and most influential of member states having a close relationship is that between France and Germany, which has been consciously fostered and maintained by most French and German governments since the early 1960s. The so-called Franco-German axis is no longer as commanding as it was when there were only six member states, or when Chancellor Schmidt and President Giscard d'Estaing and later Chancellor Kohl and President Mitterrand worked closely together, but it still plays an important part in helping to shape and set the pace of EU developments.

An increasingly important aspect of governmental strategies in the EU is multilateral bilateralism, which sees governments linking up with just one or two other governments on specific issues, often for the purpose of launching initiatives.

The procedures applying

Of particular importance here is whether qualified majority voting is permissible under the relevant treaty article(s) and is politically acceptable in the circumstances applying. If it is, concessions and compromises might be preferable to being outvoted. If it is not, any government can cause indefinite delay, though by so doing it may weaken goodwill towards it and thus damage its long-term interests. An example of governments forgoing the use of a veto they would have liked to have exercised is Austria and Cyprus, which in 2004 and 2005 resisted vetoing the opening of accession negotiations with Turkey.

The competence of governmental negotiators

Given the extensive tactical manoeuvrings involved in EU processes, and given that many negotiations are not about the broad sweep of policy but are about highly technical matters, the competence of individual negotiators can be crucial. Are they well-briefed and able to master details? Can they judge how far their negotiating partners can be pushed? Can they avoid being isolated? Can they build coalitions? Can they time their interventions so as to clinch points? The evidence suggests that variations in such competencies are not so much between states as between individual negotiators.

The arrangements for linking representatives in the Council with national capitals

This point is worth developing in a little detail because there are significant variations in the ways in which governments attempt to manage and control their input into the Council via their representatives. Two aspects of this are particularly worth mentioning.

First, some countries – including Belgium, Italy, and the Netherlands – generally allow their representatives to work within a relatively flexible framework. This is demonstrated by the way in which representatives are often able to negotiate on important policy matters not just at the ministerial level but also at lower levels. As well as assisting the functioning of the Council as a whole – by reducing the need for awkward issues to be referred upwards – manoeuvrability of this kind can be used to the national advantage by competent negotiators. At the same time, however, too much independence on the part of representatives can lead to the need for awkward backtracking at a later negotiating stage if a misjudgement is made. In contrast, the representatives of some other states – including France and the UK – are generally reluctant and/or are not able to negotiate on policy issues below ministerial level. Whether, as is sometimes claimed, this greater rigidity improves the consistency and effectiveness of a

country's negotiating position is doubtful. Undoubtedly, the more that countries lean in this direction, and all do at times, the more that negotiations at the lower Council levels are limited to technical matters and the more the overall Council process is protracted.

At the most senior Council level – ministerial meetings – there is, of course, not such a problem of control from national capitals. It is important to ensure that the minister is fully briefed on the national implications of proposals and is accompanied by national officials who fully understand all aspects of agenda items, but the political weight of the participants usually means that, if the will is there, commitments can be entered into without having to refer back for clearance. This is not to say that those in attendance at ministerial meetings can do as they like. At a minimum they are obliged to operate within the general guidelines of their government's policies. They may also be subject to special national constraints: perhaps occasioned by an inability of the minister to attend personally; perhaps linked to domestic political difficulties caused by the existence of a coalition government; perhaps caused by a national parliamentary committee having indicated concerns; or perhaps a consequence of a particular national interest having resulted in the establishment of a rigid governmental position in advance.

Second, in all member states arrangements have been established to enable governments to coordinate their policy towards and their participation in the EU. According to Peters and Wright (2001: 162) four general observations can be made about these arrangements: major political and constitutional EU issues are handled by the Heads of Government, assisted by their Foreign and Finance Ministers; the formal link between the domestic capital and Brussels is generally coordinated through the Foreign Ministry, the Finance/Economics Ministry, or both; most ministries in all member states have adjusted their internal structures to meet EU requirements; and despite some convergence, the nature of the coordination arrangements varies considerably between the member states.

Some flesh can be put on these general observations by comparing the arrangements made by three member states: Malta, which is a small member state with a very centralised coordinating system: the UK, which is a large state with a quite centralised coordinating system;

and Germany, which is a large member state with a more fragmented system.

* * *

In *Malta* a centralised governmental system and a majority party political system have provided a favourable base for tight coordinating mechanisms.

At the heart of the system is the Permanent Representation in Brussels and the EU Secretariat – which is based in the Office of the Prime Minister (OPM) – in Malta. Most matters that require attention are channelled from the Permanent Representation to the EU Secretariat, which then hands on the matter to the appropriate ministry to coordinate and prepare a response. The response is returned to the EU Secretariat, which then normally refers it for clearance to the Inter-Ministerial Committee on EU Affairs (IMCEU). Despite its name, the IMCEU is composed not of ministers but of civil servants. It is chaired by the Permanent Representative and composed of Permanent Secretaries (the most senior civil servants) from all major ministries – though usually the latter are represented by their Directors for EU Affairs. (All ministries have such Directors, with support teams – the size of which naturally varies). If the matter is politically sensitive or especially important, it is referred to the Cabinet Committee on EU Affairs for finalisation.

The extent of the centralized arrangements in Malta is seen in the very powerful position of the Permanent Representative. He is head of the Permanent Representation, which channels all official EU-Malta links. He chairs the IMCEU, which clears most national positions on routine issues. And he sits in the Cabinet, which ultimately approves all national positions – either by rubber-stamping non-contentious issues agreed in the IMCEU or by discussing and taking decisions on matters that necessitate a political input. Reflecting the high degree of clientelism in Maltese politics – which has been exacerbated by the centre-right Christian Democrats having been in power for all but two years since 1987 – the Permanent Representative is not a career civil servant.

* * *

Like Malta, *the UK* also has a centralised governmental system and a majority party political system. As in Malta these have contributed to the creation of centralised coordinating mechanisms.

The mechanisms themselves are formalised, structured, and seemingly well integrated. At the general policy level, the Foreign and Commonwealth Office (FCO), the Cabinet Office, and the UK Permanent Representation to the European Union (UKREP) are the key bodies: the FCO frequently changes its organisational arrangements for dealing with the EU, with, at the time of writing, a range of units located within an umbrella European and Globalisation Directorate; the Cabinet Office contains a European Secretariat which, amongst other things, convenes each year around 200 interdepartmental meetings of civil servants attended by representatives from appropriate ministries, including one regular weekly meeting which is attended by the Permanent Representative; and UKREP – which is formally an FCO overseas post – acts as the eyes and ears of the UK in Brussels. Working together, these three bodies attempt to monitor, coordinate and control overall EU developments: by giving general consideration to important matters due to come up at forthcoming meetings; by looking at whether a broadly consistent line is being pursued across different policy areas; by trying to ensure that ministries have issued sufficiently clear guidelines for representatives in Council meetings; and, in the cases of the FCO and UKREP, giving briefings to representatives when appropriate. 'Above' these three bodies, but not involved in such a continual manner, there is a Cabinet Committee on European Issues chaired by the Foreign Secretary, the Cabinet itself, and the Prime Minister. 'Below' them, each ministry has its own arrangements for examining proposals that fall within its competence and for ensuring that specialist negotiators are well briefed and fully aware of departmental thinking. When EU matters loom large in a ministry's work, special divisions or units exist for coordination purposes.

* * *

In *Germany* a number of factors combine to make coordination on EU matters more difficult than it is in the UK:

- The existence of a coalition government and the need to satisfy (though not on a consistent basis across policy areas) the different elements of the coalition.
- The relative autonomy of ministers and ministries within the federal government.

- The lack of an authoritative coordinating centre: the Chancellor's Office and the Foreign Ministry both have a responsibility for major EU issues, whilst the Economics Ministry also has a responsibility for many coordination matters.
- The considerable powers of the federal states (the Länder) in certain policy areas.
- The strong sectoral specialisation allied with loyalties to different federal ministries amongst the staff of the German Permanent Representation in Brussels.

The sort of difficulties that can arise from these factors was seen during the 2005–9 Government, when much of the coordination of Germany's input into EU policy process was undertaken by the Social Democrat (SPD)-led Foreign Ministry whilst much also was undertaken by the Christian Democrat (CDU/CSU)-led Economics Ministry. After the autumn 2009 election, this situation continued, though with the end of the grand CDU/CSU-SPD coalition, the Foreign Office was now led by the Free Democrats (FDP).

The German system is still able to arrange the sort of coordinating activities that take place in some form in all member states – with, for example, regular meetings being held of representatives from relevant ministries at (normally junior) ministerial and senior official levels. But, in consequence of the particular challenges it faces, Germany's European policies are sometimes less than consistent and Germany's position in EU negotiations often emerges much later than do the positions of governments in more centralized systems such as the UK.

Fortunately for Germany, having strong and effective domestic arrangements for coordinating inputs into EU processes is not the only factor in determining policy influence in the EU. Its position as the strongest single EU state seemingly enables it to avoid being too seriously damaged by this internal weakness.

* * *

But whatever the particulars of their arrangements for controlling and influencing their EU policy activities, all governments have found the task increasingly difficult in recent years. The reasons for this are set out in Box 15.1.

Box 15.1

Reasons why national governments are finding it difficult to control their 'inputs' to the EU

- The EU's policy portfolio continues to grow, with decisions being taken in almost all areas of public policy. This applies both to major and long-term decisions, on the likes of EMU and enlargement, and to more specific and technical decisions on such matters as the internal market and environmental standards.
- Not only are more decisions being made, but many are being made much more quickly. The greater use of QMV means that governments can no longer always delay progress on a proposal until they are ready and satisfied.
- The increased scope of EU policy interests means that there are no longer just a few domestic ministries – such as Agriculture, Trade, and Finance – which are directly involved with the EU. The 'Europeanisation' of domestic politics and administration has resulted in most ministries in most states being affected by, and becoming actively involved in, EU affairs. So, for example, Wessels (2001) has estimated that approximately one-third of all senior (A-level) German Federal Ministry officials are involved directly in different phases of the Brussels policy cycle, whilst nearly two-thirds are in contact with the EU system in some way as part of their normal administrative work.

Parliaments

Parliaments have much less influence than governments over EU developments. Of course, governments normally reflect the political composition of their national legislatures and must retain their confidence, so – in an indirect sense – government activity in relation to the EU could be said to reflect the parliamentary will. But that is a quite different matter from direct parliamentary control.

One of the main reasons for the comparative lack of direct parliamentary control has been that until the

Lisbon Treaty entered into force national parliaments had no formal EU treaty powers, so governments were in a strong position to choose what to consult their parliaments about. All governments consulted their parliaments on fundamental matters when the treaties referred to ratification in accordance with 'respective constitutional requirements' (enlargements, treaty amendments, and the EU's budgetary base carry this provision), but otherwise there were great variations between the states. The Lisbon Treaty should serve to narrow these variations and generally increase the role of national parliaments in the EU system by its inclusion – most particularly in a new Article 12 TEU and in new protocols – of a number of provisions specifically designed to increase the role of national parliaments. The most important of these provisions are new rights to examine policy documents and draft legislative acts and a new power to require that draft legislation be reconsidered. The Commission has long forwarded appropriate documentation to national parliaments, and indeed since 2006 has forwarded draft legislative proposals to them at the same time as doing so to the EP and Council, but the parliaments had no formal powers to directly input into EU processes. Under Article 12 TEU, it is now the case that if one-third of national parliaments object to a new legislative proposal on the grounds that it breaches the EU's subsidiarity principle the Commission must reconsider the proposal. If the Commission then decides to continue with the proposal the matter must be referred to the Council and the EP for a final decision if a majority of national parliaments continue to object.

In addition to the pre-Lisbon lack of treaty-based powers, a number of logistical difficulties arising in relation to advising on EU legislation have also contributed to the weakness of national parliaments. The difficulties include: much EU legislation is so technical that it is almost incomprehensible to the average legislator; there is little opportunity to consider even the most important legislation at the formative and crucial pre-proposal stage; proposed legislation has often been well-advanced in the Council system before being examined by parliaments (the new Lisbon provisions should reduce this practice); legislative proposals can change in nature as they make their way through EU decision-making procedures, but it is usually just not practical for national parliaments to track every change at every

step; and QMV in the Council means that a parliament whose government has been outvoted has no way at all of calling the real decision-makers to account.

But notwithstanding these problems and difficulties, all national parliaments have established some sort of specialised arrangements for attempting to deal with EU affairs. In different ways and with different degrees of effectiveness, these arrangements focus on examining proposed EU legislation, scrutinising ministerial positions and performances, producing reports on EU-related matters, and generally monitoring EU developments. Amongst the many differences that exist between the national arrangements three are particularly worth noting. They are set out in Box 15.2

Despite the changes and adjustments made by parliaments in recognition of the importance of the

---

Box 15.2

Variations in national parliamentary arrangements for monitoring and controlling EU matters

- All parliaments have established an EU committee or committees of some sort. However, whereas in some cases these serve as the main forum for dealing with EU matters, in others they serve more as coordinating committees with the detailed work being undertaken by appropriate 'subject' committees.
- The regularity with which and the circumstances in which ministers with EU policy responsibilities appear before appropriate parliamentary bodies to explain and be questioned about these policies varies considerably.
- Some parliaments have established close working relationships with their national MEPs, whilst others have not. In a few parliaments – including the Belgian, German, and Greek – the specialised EU committees include MEPs, whilst in a growing number of parliaments MEPs are used as experts when appropriate.

EU, it is still, however, inevitably the case that parliaments are, as compared with governments, confined to a junior role, though one that is generally increasing.

The position of the Irish Parliament is fairly typical. It has changed its arrangements on a number of occasions over the years, with the situation now being that its work on EU affairs is channelled mainly via two committees made up of representatives of both houses of the Irish Parliament, the Dáil and the Senate. The Joint Committee on European Affairs meets regularly when Parliament is sitting to consider broad issues concerning Ireland and the EU. One a month there is a meeting with the Minister of Foreign Affairs or the Minister of State for European Affairs prior to Council meetings. The work of the other committee, the Joint Committee on European Scrutiny, is guided by two main principles: to scrutinise all legislative proposals that could have significant implications for Ireland and to undertake the scrutiny in time so as to influence the Government's negotiating position in the Council of Ministers.

The three Scandinavian EU member states – Denmark, Finland, and Sweden – have similar arrangements to each other and are the major exceptions to the general pattern of legislative weakness. Of the three, the Danish Parliament – the Folketing – is probably the strongest. There are two main sources of its strength. First, there has been a powerful anti-integration sentiment among the people of Denmark since accession in 1973. No Danish government has been able to ignore the articulation of this in the Folketing, especially since Danish governments are invariably coalitions or minorities. Second, the Folketing has a committee system – formerly based on a very influential European Committee, since 2004 broadened out to include 'mainstream' policy committees – that includes amongst its activities close working relationships between Danish parliamentarians and ministers in advance of the latter attending Council meetings. The principal advantage of the system is that it helps to ensure that agreements reached by Danish ministers in the Council are not subsequently queried or endangered at home. The principal disadvantage is that it can make it difficult for Danish representatives to be flexible in the Council and can result in them being isolated if new solutions to problems are advanced during the course of negotiations.

Courts

National courts might be thought to have a significant role to play as the guarantors and defenders of national rights against EU encroachment, but in practice they do not.

The reason for this, as was explained in Chapter 12, is that the principle of primacy of EU law is accepted by national courts. There were some initial teething problems in this regard, but it is now extremely rare for national courts to question the legality of EU proceedings and decisions. The treaties, EU legislation and the case law of the EU courts are seen as taking precedence when they clash with national law. The frequent practice of national courts to seek preliminary rulings from the Court of Justice in cases where there is uncertainty over an aspect of EU law is testimony to the general desire of national courts not to be out of step with EU law.

That said, national courts have occasionally sought to assert national rights and interests against the EU. For example, in a few instances national courts have refused to acknowledge the legality of directives that have not been incorporated into national law by the due date, even though the Court of Justice has ruled that in such circumstances they may be deemed as having direct effect. Constitutional law, especially as applied to individual rights, has been another area where some assertion of national independence has been attempted by national courts, though less often since the principle of EU law having precedence over national constitutional law was confirmed by Court of Justice rulings in the early 1970s.

In recent years the most important instances of national court involvements have been in connection with Irish ratification of the SEA, German ratification of the Maastricht Treaty, and German and Czech ratifications of the Lisbon Treaty. The Irish involvement occurred in December 1986 when the Irish Supreme Court, by a margin of three to two, found in favour of a Raymond Crotty, who had challenged the constitutional validity of the SEA. The judges ruled that Title III of the Act, which put foreign policy cooperation on a legal basis, could restrict Ireland's sovereignty and might inhibit it from pursuing its traditionally neutral foreign policy. The SEA must therefore, they indicated, be endorsed by a referendum. As a result, the SEA was unable to come into effect in any of the twelve

Community states in January 1987, as had been intended, and was delayed until after the Irish had given their approval in the duly held referendum. Since the 1986 SEA ruling, Irish ratification of the EU's major reforming treaties – those of Maastricht, Amsterdam, Nice and Lisbon – has always been deemed to require approval by national referendum: which, as was shown earlier in the chapter, resulted in the entry into force of the Nice and Lisbon Treaties being considerably delayed.

The first German national court involvement occurred when several people – including four Green Party MEPs – appealed to the country's Constitutional Court to declare that the Maastricht Treaty was in breach of the German constitution, the Basic Law. The appeal was made shortly after the Bundestag and the Bundesrat had ratified the Treaty by huge majorities in December 1992, with the consequence that, instead of being one of the first countries to ratify the Treaty, Germany became the very last as the Constitutional Court did not issue its judgment until October 1993. In its judgment the Court declared that the TEU did not infringe Germany's constitution, but made it clear that certain conditions would have to be satisfied in respect of further integration.

The second German court involvement and the Czech court involvement both concerned cases taken before the national Constitutional Courts claiming that the Lisbon Treaty was in breach of national constitutional law. Both cases resulted in delays to national ratifications of the Treaty. In Germany, the Court ruled, in July 2009, that the Treaty would be compatible with German law as long as German law on parliamentary oversight of EU business was strengthened. This was duly done. In the Czech Republic, the Constitutional Court ruled, in November 2009, that there was no conflict between the Treaty and national constitutional law.

Subnational Levels of Government

The parts played and the influence exercised by subnational levels of government in the EU were considered in Chapter 13 (in the section on the Committee of the Regions) and in Chapter 14. Therefore, only a few observations will be made here on key points.

Subnational levels of government have grown in importance within the EU system in recent years, not least as a result of decentralisation and regionalisation in several member states. A consequence of this has been that national authorities, especially governments, have lost some of their power to articulate and advance 'the national position' in EU decision-making forums. The extent to which national authorities' gate-keeping roles have been undermined naturally varies according to a number of factors, most particularly the national constitutional status of subnational levels of government, but even in countries where central powers remain strong – for example Ireland and Denmark – by no means all EU-national official communications are channelled through the central authorities.

Channels of communication between the EU and subnational levels of government include the following:

- Most EU states have subnational levels of government of some kind that have offices or representations in Brussels. For example, all of Germany's länder and Spain's autonomia have offices, as do most of France's regions. The tasks of these offices include lobbying, information gathering, generally establishing contacts and 'keeping in touch' with appropriate officials and decision-makers, and acting as intermediaries between the EU and the regions/localities.
- Many of the subnational levels of government that do not have their own offices in Brussels make use of Brussels-based consultancies and/or have domestically-based EU offices and officers.
- The Committee of the Regions exists for the precise purpose of enabling EU decision-makers to seek the views of regional representatives on regional issues.
- A few governments – including the Belgian, the German and the British – are sometimes represented in the Council of Ministers by regional ministers when agenda items are the responsibility of regional governments.

The EU may be a long way from the Europe of the Regions that some advocate and others claim to detect, but clearly the national dimension of EU affairs has an increasingly powerful subnational element attached to it.

Citizens' Views

Referendums

One way in which citizens can have their say on issues is in referendums. Leaving aside the special case of accession referendums which most, though not all, post-foundation states have held prior to their EC/EU accessions (Cyprus was the only 10+2 state not to hold one), up to the end of 2009 twenty-one referendums had been held in member states on EC/EU related matters. As can be seen from Table 15.2, most of these referendums have been concerned with the ratification of EC/EU treaties.

Whilst referendums do inject an element of direct democracy into public decision-making, it must be doubted whether the referendums listed in Table 15.2 have really done much to deal with the much-publicised and debated problem of the EU's so-called 'democratic deficit'. For a number of reasons:

- Twenty one is not very many give the time period involved and the large number of member states.
- Of the twenty one, twelve – over fifty per cent – have been held in just two states: Denmark (five) and Ireland (seven).
- Many of the referendums have been, or have become, tangled up with national politics and have not been primarily about, or focused on, the EU. For example, the 1972 French referendum was really designed to boost the legitimacy and status of President Pompidou, whilst the 2001 and 2008 Irish referendums focused largely around 'non-EU'

Table 15.2 Referendums in member states on EC/EU issues*

Date	Country	Subject of referendum	Referendum decision
1972	France	Ratification of EU enlargement	Yes
1975	UK	Continued EC membership	Yes
1986	Denmark	Ratification of SEA	Yes
1987	Ireland	Ratification of SEA	Yes
1989	Italy	Transformation of the EC into an 'effective union'	Yes
1992	Denmark	Ratification of Maastricht Treaty	No
1992	Ireland	Ratification of Maastricht Treaty	Yes
1992	France	Ratification of Maastricht Treaty	Yes
1993	Denmark	Ratification of Maastricht Treaty	Yes
1998	Ireland	Ratification of Amsterdam Treaty	Yes
1998	Denmark	Ratification of Amsterdam Treaty	Yes
2000	Denmark	Whether to join the euro	No
2001	Ireland	Ratification of Nice Treaty	No
2002	Ireland	Ratification of Nice Treaty	Yes
2003	Sweden	Whether to join the euro	No
2005	Spain	Ratification of Constitutional Treaty	Yes
2005	France	Ratification of Constitutional Treaty	No
2005	Netherlands	Ratification of Constitutional Treaty	No
2005	Luxembourg	Ratification of Constitutional Treaty	Yes
2008	Ireland	Ratification of Lisbon Treaty	No
2009	Ireland	Ratification of Lisbon Treaty	Yes

* Up to December 2009. Voting figures in the referendums are given in the Chronology.

issues – including dissatisfaction with the government and the protection of 'family values'.

- Few referendums have been on issues that citizens really understand in terms of how the referendum outcome will impact on them. For example, surveys during the 2005 French and Dutch referendum campaigns showed that citizens had little knowledge of the contents of the treaties on which they had voted.
- Most referendums have not been on issues that engage citizens – with the referendums in Sweden and Denmark on euro membership being the clearest exceptions.

The fact is that on major EU issues to which citizens can relate and have an opinion (albeit, often, an ill-informed opinion), few referendums have been held. This is, of course, primarily because the political systems of the member states are based on representative rather than on direct democracy. But, it is also partly because when there have been pressures on member state governments to hold referendums on EU-related issues they have usually not taken the 'risk' for fear of citizens giving the 'wrong' answer. It is significant, for example, that not one referendum on euro membership has been held in the member states that have become euro members, even though – or more precisely because – there was evidence of substantial opposition in several of the states, including Germany. In the two states where euro membership referendums have been held – Denmark and Sweden – the people voted 'no'.

This is not, however, to say that there have not been referendums that have not had a significant impact on the integration process. Four categories of referendums have been especially important.

First, the 2005 referendums in France and the Netherlands produced negative majorities that resulted in the (eventual) abandonment of attempts to ratify the Constitutional Treaty and the Treaty's replacement by the Lisbon Treaty.

Second, some referendums have delayed treaty ratifications: the 1992 Danish referendum on the Maastricht Treaty, the 2001 Irish referendum on the Nice Treaty, and the 2008 Irish referendum on the Lisbon Treaty.

Third, there have been the referendums that have affected public, and especially elite, thinking about the integration process. The 1992 Danish and French referendums on the Maastricht Treaty drew attention to how European integration was essentially an elite-driven process and emphasised that it is important for decision-makers not to get too out of step with public opinion. In recognition of this, the rhetoric of supporters of European integration became more tempered for a while and the importance of the decentralising subsidiarity principle, which was only briefly referred to in the Treaty, was given a greatly enhanced status by decision-makers. The 2001 and 2008 Irish referendums might also be placed in this category in that they drew attention to the 'dangers' in an ever-larger EU of permitting national electorates a decisive influence on EU-wide issues. For, as Rees and Holmes (2002: 49) have observed of the 2001 referendum: 'A country of less than four million people, an electorate of less than three million, a turnout of less than a million and a No vote of slightly over half a million derailed a process designed to allow the EU to enlarge to almost 500 million'.

Fourth, a few referendums have had a very direct and specific policy consequence. Amongst the fall-out of the 1992 Danish referendum was that Denmark was given, as an inducement to approve the Maastricht Treaty, 'opt-outs' from EMU and from the projected common defence policy. The 2000 Danish and 2003 Swedish referendums resulted in those countries not joining the single currency system.

* * *

Of course, there is one way in which referendums could potentially act as a direct and effective channel for citizen's views on EU issues and that is to hold EU-wide referendums on matters of major importance. Such was suggested by many 'pro-integrationists' in the context of the ratification of the Constitutional Treaty. There was, however, never any realistic prospect of an EU-wide referendum being held on the Treaty and nor is there any prospect in the foreseeable future of such a referendum being held on any other matter. The main reason for this is that EU-wide referendums – especially if their outcomes were to be binding – would involve what for most EU governments would be an unacceptable 'transfer' of sovereignty from the national to the EU level.

European Parliament elections

In contrast with the only occasional and localised opportunities for participation offered by referendums, elections to the EP provide citizens with regular and direct opportunities to participate in the political process on an EU-wide basis. (See Chapter 11 for details of EP elections.) As such, the elections are seen by some observers as providing the EU with a democratic base. This view, however, must be counterbalanced by a recognition that EU issues do not directly feature much in the election campaigns and the elections are not in practice contested by European parties standing on European issues. In consequence, the elections can hardly be regarded as occasions when the populace indicate their European policy preferences. The fact that voter turnout is, in most member states, low by national standards, and furthermore has declined across the EU in every set of EP elections since they were first held in 1979 – to such an extent that the overall levels in 1999, 2004 and 2009 were below 50 per cent – raises further questions about the democratic legitimacy given to the EU by the elections.

National elections

Another way in which citizens can exert an influence on EU affairs via the ballot box is through national elections, since most important EU decisions are taken or are co-taken by elected national representatives in the European Council and the Council of Ministers. This influence, however, is indirect in that national elections are two or three stages removed from the EU: voters elect legislatures, from which governments are formed, which send representatives to EU summits and Council meetings. The influence is also somewhat tangential in that voters in national elections usually are not much concerned with 'European issues' or with the competence of candidates to deal with European matters. Beyond some limited attention by far-right and nationalist parties – occasioned by their generally 'anti-Europe' stance – the EU does not normally feature much in national elections.

Public opinion

Public opinion towards the EU and its policies is closely and extensively monitored, both at the EU level through regular Commission-sponsored *Eurobarometer* polls and at national levels through countless polls conducted on behalf of governments, research agencies, and the media. In broad terms it can be said that this ongoing trawling of public opinion reveals three main sets of findings. First, across the EU as a whole just over 50 per cent of citizens are strongly or moderately supportive of European integration, about 30 per cent are ambivalent, around 15 per cent are opposed, and the remainder do not know. Second, there are large variations between countries in their support for the integration process. In recent years Latvia, the UK and Hungary have displayed the lowest levels of support on most indicators, whist Luxembourg, the Netherlands, Spain and Ireland have displayed the highest. Third, there are considerable variations also in terms of the support for EU policy activity between issue areas. Areas with the highest levels of support are those that are either clearly cross-national in nature or that seem to offer the greatest benefits from cross-national policy action. Included amongst these areas are fighting terrorism, protecting the environment, scientific and technological research, and foreign and defence policies. Areas with the lowest levels of support are those that seem to be more naturally national and/or where the implications of EU involvement can seem to be threatening. Prominent here are pensions, taxation, social welfare, education and health.

The extent to which governments respond to public opinion depends very much on their own ideological and policy preferences, their perception of the importance and durability of issues, and the time remaining until the next election. The existence of, for example, less than enthusiastic support for European integration amongst a sizeable proportion of national electorates may both restrain and encourage politicians depending on their viewpoint, but there certainly is no automatic relationship between what the people think about EU matters and what governments do. The UK Conservative government, for example, made no move to withdraw from the Community in the early 1980s even though a majority of the British population thought it should, and it did not weaken its opposition in the 1990s to the Social Charter even though polls suggested that the Charter was supported by about two-thirds of the British people. Similarly, in the late 1990s the German government did not weaken in its resolve to take Germany into the single currency even though polls showed that a majority of Germans were opposed to the Deutschmark being subsumed within the euro.

That said, public opinion does exercise an influence in at least setting the boundaries in which national leaders must operate. For example, anti-Turkish sentiments in France and Germany and very low levels of support for EU enlargement to include Turkey are one reason why French and German leaders have been very wary about the prospect of Turkey eventually acceding to the EU.

Public opinion can also be important in that if an issue is generally accepted as constituting a national interest, or at least commands strong domestic support, then governments of whatever political persuasion are likely to pursue it in the Council. Even if they themselves do not wish to be too rigid, they may well be forced, by electoral considerations and domestic pressures, to strike postures and make a public display of not being pushed around. For example, Irish and French governments invariably favour generous settlements for farmers, Danish and German governments press for strict environmental controls, and CEEC governments argue for increased cohesion operations to enable them to modernise their economies.

Political Parties

Political parties normally wish to exercise power, which in liberal democratic states means they must be able to command popular support. This in turn means they must be able to articulate and aggregate national opinions and interests. At the same time, parties are not normally content simply to act as mirror images of the popular will. Drawing on their traditions, and guided by leaders and activists, they also seek to direct society by mobilising support behind preferred ideological/policy positions. Judgements thus have to be made about the balance to be struck between 'reflecting' society and 'leading' it. Those parties which lean too much towards the latter have little chance of winning elections, although in multi-party systems

they may well still find themselves with strong negotiating hands.

Of course, the precise extent to which parties are, on the one hand, reflecting and channelling opinions on particular issues and, on the other, are shaping and determining them is very difficult to judge since, in most instances, the processes are two-way and interrelated. But whatever the exact balance may be between the processes, both are very much in operation in relation to the EU. The experiences of Denmark, Greece and the UK in the 1980s and early 1990s illustrate this. In each of these countries there was widespread popular scepticism in the early to mid-1980s about Community membership and this found both expression and encouragement at the party political level, with some parties advocating a complete withdrawal from Community membership and others expressing considerable concern about aspects of the implications of membership – especially in relation to sovereignty. As the 'realities' of membership began to seep through, however, both public opinion and party attitudes began to change. So much so that by the early 1990s Greece had become one of the more enthusiastic member states in terms of public opinion and a 'typical' one in terms of the attitudes of its political parties, whilst Denmark and the UK, though still in the slow stream, were not lagging as far behind as formerly they had been.

Apart from their interactive relationship with the attitudinal climate in which EU processes work, political parties also feed directly into EU decision-making. First, by providing much of the ideological base of the policies of governments and most, if not all, of the leading personnel of governments, they do much to determine and shape the attitudes, priorities and stances of the member states in the Council. While it is true that many policy positions are barely altered by changes of government, shifts of emphasis do occur and these can be significant, as was demonstrated in Poland after the November 2007 election when the Law and Justice party headed government led by the somewhat Eurosceptic Prime Minister, Jaroslaw Kaczyński was defeated by the Civic Platform party headed coalition led by the more Euro-friendly, and predictable, Donald Tusk. Second, even when in domestic opposition political parties can influence government behaviour in the Council because governments do not wish to be accused of being weak or not strongly defending national interests. Third, national political parties are the main contestants in the European elections and their successful candidates become the national representatives in the EP.

Interests

Acting either by themselves or through an appropriate Eurogroup, national sectional and promotional interests have a number of possible avenues available to them to try to influence EU policies and decisions. Some avenues are at the domestic level, such as approaches through fellow national MEPs, government officials, and ministers. Others are at the EU level, such as using contacts in the Commission and the EP. These avenues were discussed in some detail in Chapter 14, so will not be repeated here.

In very general terms, the most successful national interests tend to fulfil at least one of two conditions. Either they are able to persuade their government that there is little distinction between the interests' aims and national aims. Or they have sufficient power and information resources to persuade at least some EU decision-makers that they ought to be listened to. A major reason why farmers have been so influential is that both of these conditions have applied to them in some countries. In France, Portugal, Ireland, and elsewhere this has resulted in Ministries of Agriculture perceiving that a major part of their responsibility in the Council is to act virtually as a spokesman for the farmers.

Which States Exercise Most Influence?

As the above sections of the chapter have shown, member states have many opportunities to feed into EU policy processes and play a part in influencing policy outcomes. This is so at virtually all policy stages: agenda setting, policy formulation, decision negotiating, decision-taking, and implementation.

But which states exercise most influence? The seemingly obvious answer to this question is that the larger states do. One reason for the seemingly obvious nature of this answer is that the larger states have a wider range of policy interests, and therefore also a greater desire to be active, across the policy spectrum than do smaller states. Another reason is that the larger states have greater power resources to display and deploy in policy-making processes. Some of these resources emanate from the EU's institutional structure, with larger states having greater voting weight than smaller states in a number of institutions, notably the Council of Ministers and the EP. Other power resources stem from the larger states having greater national political, economic, administrative and other resources to bring to and employ in EU policy deliberations and negotiations. To take just administrative resources, larger states have many more officials available to sit on expert committees advising the Commission, to attend Council working parties, and to prepare for COREPER and ministerial meetings.

The reform of the Stability and Growth Pact between 2003 and 2005, which is described in Chapter 19, provides an example of large state power. In essence what happened was that when a number of small states, including Ireland and Portugal, began to experience difficulties in the early 2000s in meeting the budgetary terms of the Pact they were successfully pressurised by the Commission to initiate reforms to bring them 'back in line'. But when, from 2003, France and Germany began to experience similar problems, the Commission was less successful and France and Germany were able to drive through, against the Commission's wishes, a revision of the SGP rules.

Foreign and defence policies provide another illustration of large state power. These are policy areas where operational capabilities – of various forms, but especially, diplomatic, economic and military – are crucial if policy is to be effective, so it is no surprise that the key member state actors in these areas have been France, Germany, and the UK: the member states with the greatest range of overseas interests, contacts and missions, and the largest military dispositions.

However, although it is certainly true that in general terms the larger states exercise more influence in the EU than do the smaller states, the generalisation requires some important clarifications and qualifications.

First, EU politics have never assumed a large states *versus* small states character, except when institutional issues have been the subject under consideration in recent IGCs. As was intimated in the discussion of national orientations and approaches at the beginning of this chapter, policy cleavages between EU member

Box 15.3

The positions of France, Germany and the UK on key EU issues

Issue	France	Germany	UK
'Vision' of the nature of the EU	A strongly structured regional organisation of states.	A strongly structured regional organisation of states.	Essentially an internal market, but with intergovernmental cooperation in some additional policy spheres.
How should EU decisions be made?	A mix of intergovernmental and supranational processes is accepted.	A mix of intergovernmental and supranational processes is accepted.	On an intergovernmental basis whenever possible.
How 'liberal' (non interventionist) should EU economic and social policy be?	Strong supporter of EU policies bolstering 'the European social model'. Direct state subsidisation of 'national' companies acceptable in some circumstances.	Strong supporter of EU policies bolstering 'the European social model'.	Strong supporter of EU policies being focused on ensuring the market is economically liberal.
What should be the size of the EU's budget?	As a net contributor, wants to see a small budget, but not so small as to endanger CAP support for French agriculture.	As a net contributor, wants to see a small budget.	Supports a minimalist budget.
What should be the EU's spending priorities?	The CAP should remain a central plank of the EU's budget.	The CAP should continue to be an important component of the EU's budget, but could be reduced.	CAP spending should be greatly reduced and more emphasis should be given to policies aimed at improving the efficiency of the market.
How independent should EU foreign and defence policies be of the Atlantic Alliance?	The Atlantic Alliance is important, but the EU should be more independent from the USA within it.	Mid-way between the French and British positions.	Strong supporter of the Atlantic Alliance and of ensuring the EU is closely allied with the US.
Should the EU continue to enlarge?	Only cautiously, and not to Turkey.	Yes, but not to Turkey.	Yes, including to Turkey

states have tended to be cross-cutting rather than cumulative. A consequence of this has been that when there have been differences within the EU over policy matters, the larger member states have rarely constituted a bloc. It is true that over the years France and Germany have worked closely with one another on a number of matters, but even during the heyday of the so-called Franco-German axis in the 1980s and 1990s they sometimes parted company on policy matters. Moreover, they never brought the other two large member states of the 'big four' – Italy and the UK – into their mini-club. The simple fact is that, as with all member states, there are significant policy differences between the large member states. Box 15.3 illustrates this by outlining the general orientations of France, Germany and the UK on a number of key EU matters: these orientations shape the positions taken by the member states in a wide range of policy circumstances.

Second, if attention is switched to the power exercised by the 'big four' on an individual basis, there are major differences between them concerning both the power they have exercised in the EU as a whole and the power they have exercised in particular policy areas. Regarding the power they have exercised as a whole, it is impossible to be precise about this but almost whatever criteria are taken it is clear that Italy has not punched as heavily as the other three. The reasons for this are much debated, but certainly include the frequency of weak and/or unstable Italian governments and the perceived lack of credibility of certain Italian leaders. Regarding the varying power the big four have exercised in particular policy areas, France and more especially Germany have done much to set the pace and direction of EMU from its first stages, France has been to the fore in ensuring the CAP continues to occupy a central policy position, and the UK has been very influential in pressing that the momentum on opening-up the internal market is maintained.

Third, smaller states are not without opportunities to exercise power and influence. Indeed, Javier Arregui and Robert Thomson (2009)) suggest they exercise an influence in EU negotiations that is disproportionate to their size. The reason suggested for this is that, as Box 15.4 shows, a number of factors in the EU's institutional and policy-making systems work to the advantage of small states.

Some of the examples that can be cited of small

Box 15.4

Reasons why smaller states are able to exercise a disproportionate influence in EU policy processes

- They are over-represented in EU policy-making institutions. This is most manifest in their being one Commissioner for each member state, the voting weights in the Council, and the national representations in the EP.
- They are advantaged by the continuity of the availability of the veto in the Council in certain very important policy areas.
- They are advantaged by the prevailing norm in the Council whereby, even when QMV is available, the member states always try to accommodate national interests.
- They have fewer positions than large states on which they wish to take strong stands. This enables them to focus their political and administrative resources on a relatively limited number of issue areas and enables them also to argue more effectively that important national interests really are at stake when strong stands are adopted.

---

states exercising disproportionate influence are not surprising given national policy interests and priorities. So, Luxembourg has been an important policy player in the field of financial services, Cyprus has been so in respect of maritime transport (it has the third largest flagged fleet of all EU states), and Greece and Ireland have in the area of the cohesion funds, Other examples are, however, a little more surprising, For example, Peter Viggo Jakobsen (2009) has shown that Nordic states have exercised a major influence on the 'civilian' aspect of ESDP. Jakobsen concedes that Nordic pressures to advance the civilian ESDP have been assisted by not being resisted by the 'big three' ESDP players – France, Germany, and the UK – but, nonetheless, the fact is that the Nordics have been to the fore in advancing, and participating in, this increasingly important dimension of EU external policy.

That smaller states are capable of exercising power and influence – be it by striking strong positions on particular issues, by being part of 'winning coalitions', or by contributing to the creation of consensual agreements – is crucial to the effectiveness and internal harmony of the EU. For the EU is an organisation that states join because they judge there is more to be gained than is lost from being a member. Were a member state to find its interests constantly being denied and overridden, the rationale for membership would come to be questioned, disillusionment would set in, and the state in question would likely come to be a very awkward and disruptive partner. 'Prizes for everyone' is a key operational principle of the EU.

Concluding Remarks

This chapter has shown the many different sorts of inputs that are made into EU processes by the member states. The existence of these different and frequently conflicting inputs present potential obstacles in the way of the realisation of a smooth, efficient and decisive EU policy-making machinery. But, if the EU is to work it is vital that national views and requirements should be able to be articulated and incorporated into policy processes, for ultimately the EU exists to further the interests of those who live in the member states. If the citizens of the states and, more particularly, the political elites in governments and parliaments were to feel that the EU was no longer serving that purpose, then there would be no reason for continued membership. The member states, in short, need to have confidence in the EU. The EU must therefore be responsive to its constituent parts.

There is an emerging body of evidence to indicate that these constituent parts are becoming increasingly similar in the nature of their inputs into the EU and the way they handle EU business. Though, as has been shown in this and earlier chapters, there still are many significant differences between the member states on both these counts, convergences are nonetheless apparent. This is particularly the case in respect of policy inputs, but there are also signs of some 'institutional fusion'. Such convergences can be expected to increase as the EU and national levels become ever more enmeshed.

Part IV

Policies and Policy Processes of the European Union

Part IV examines what the EU does and how it does it.

Chapter 16 looks at the nature of the EU's policy portfolio. The origins, the range, and the distinctive features of the policies are all considered. Particular themes of Chapter 16 are the breadth and diversity of the EU's policy interests and the less than complete nature of many of its policies.

Chapter 17 focuses on patterns, practices and features of the EU's policy-making and decision-making machinery. Having examined the EU institutions and political actors in Part III, Chapter 17 considers how the various pieces fit together. What sort of policy-making and decision-making systems are they part of and have they helped to create? A central theme of Chapter 17 is that even the most general statements about how the EU operates have to be qualified. For one of the few things that can be said with certainty about EU processes is that they are many, complex, and often vary considerably between policy areas. However, what can also be said is that broad procedural frameworks can be identified.

In Chapter 18, the processes concerned with the making and implementation of EU legislation are examined in some detail. The chapter emphasises, amongst other things, that the institutional balance within legislative processes have changed considerably in recent years as the powers of the European Parliament have grown to such an extent that in most policy areas it is now a full co-legislator with the Council.

Chapter 19 examines the EU's internal policies. They are shown to be multi-faceted in nature, but with the more developed of them usually being directly linked to the operation of the internal market. They are shown also to be, for the most part, relatively cheap for the EU to operate: the biggest spending internal policies, such as health and social welfare, are still largely national responsibilities.

Chapter 20 considers one particular policy area – agriculture – in depth. As such, the chapter offers something of a contrast to the necessarily rather general approach taken in Chapters 16–19. Agriculture is the subject of this chapter not because of any suggestion that it is typical – the variability of EU policy processes precludes any policy area being described as such – but because of its significance in the EU policy context.

The external policies of the EU are increasingly important and these constitute the subject matter of Chapter 21. The examination is undertaken on the basis of the four main component parts of the EU's external policies: trade policy, foreign and defence policies, development policy, and the external dimension of internal policies.

In Chapter 22 the EU budget is examined. From where does the EU get its money and on what does it spend it? The budgetary decision-making processes, which in important respects are distinctly different from the processes that apply in policy areas, are also examined.

Chapter 16

Understanding EU Policies

This chapter introduces the EU's policies. It does so by describing the diverse origins of the policies and by taking an overview of key features of the policy portfolio.

The Origins of EU Policies

The origins of EU policies lie in a number of places. So, for example, at a general level, the changed mood in Western Europe after the Second World War enabled states between which policy cooperation, let alone coordination, would previously have been unthinkable to begin to work closely with one another in policy areas where there appeared to be shared advantages from so doing. Staying at a general level, an increasingly important factor since the Second World War has been the increasingly interdependent nature of the international, and more particularly of the European, systems, which has resulted in national borders becoming ever more ill-matched with political and economic realities and policy needs The combined impact of the changed mood and the pressures of interdependence have been significant in helping to persuade European states to transfer policy responsibilities to a 'higher' level in an attempt to shape, manage, control, take advantage of, and keep pace with the modern world.

At a more specific level, the treaties are generally seen as key determinants of EU policy. However, their influence is not as great as is commonly supposed. Certainly they are important stimuli to policy development and they also provide the legal base upon which much policy activity occurs. For example, such 'core' EU policies as the Common Commercial Policy (CCP), the Common Agricultural Policy (CAP), and the Competition Policy have their roots – though by no means all their principles – in the EEC Treaty (later EC Treaty, now TFEU). Similarly, EU involvement with coal and steel cannot possibly be fully understood without reference to the Treaty of Paris. But treaty provision for policy development does not guarantee that it will occur. The limited progress made towards the establishment of a Common Transport Policy, despite it being provided for in the EEC Treaty, illustrates this. So too does the non-fulfilment of most of the hopes that were held for Euratom. Another, and crucially important in its implications for the nature of the EU, example of limited development of treaty provisions is the only very partial implementation, until the late 1980s, of Part 3 Title 2 of the EEC Treaty, under which member states were supposed to treat their macroeconomic policies 'as a matter of common concern' and were to coordinate, cooperate and consult with one another on key economic and financial questions. In practice, although there was cooperation and consultation in these areas – carried out mainly under the Ecofin Council of Ministers by committees of very senior national officials – the states did not work or act as closely together as the Treaty envisaged. Furthermore, one of the key steps towards economic and financial cooperation – the creation in 1979 of the European Monetary System (EMS) which, amongst other things, was designed to fix maximum and minimum rates of exchange for currencies in the system – was created outside the treaty framework because of concerns in some quarters about the rigidities that a treaty-based approach might entail, and also because not all member states (notably the UK) wished to be full participants. It was only in 1987–8, thirty years after the EEC Treaty was signed, that clear, significant, formal, and Community-based moves towards economic and monetary integration between the member states began to be initiated and implemented.

If treaty provision is no guarantee of policy development, lack of provision is no guarantee of lack of development. Environmental policy illustrates this. Until it was given constitutional status by the Single European Act (SEA), environment was given no specific mention in the treaties. Yet from the early 1970s Community environmental policy programmes were formulated and legislation was approved. Legal authority for this was held to lie in the (almost) catch-all Articles 100 and 235 of the EEC Treaty (now Articles 115 and 352 TFEU). The former allowed the Community to issue directives for the approximation of laws 'as directly affect the establishment or functioning of the common market' and the latter enabled it to take 'appropriate measures' to 'attain, in the course of the operation of the common market, one of the objectives of the Community'. Environmental policy was therefore able to find a treaty base, but it was only a weak one.

However, even the most liberal readings of Articles 100 and 235 could not stretch to some policy areas, but this did not prevent policy development from occurring. Foreign policy cooperation prior to the SEA illustrates this. Aware that there were no treaty provisions for such cooperation, and unenthusiastic about subjecting such a sensitive area to the formalities and restrictions of treaty processes, the EC member states in the early 1970s simply created a new machinery –

which they entitled European Political Cooperation (EPC) – alongside, rather than inside, the formal framework of the treaties. EPC was first given legal (but not EEC Treaty) status by the SEA, and this subsequently provided much of the basis for the Common Foreign and Security Policy (CFSP) pillar of the Maastricht Treaty. This 'constitutional evolution' of foreign policy highlights a key feature of the nature of EU policy development: the treaties are facilitators and enablers of policy development, but they are not always the main causes. Indeed, many of the amendments made over the years to the Founding Treaties have taken the form of acknowledging and giving recognition to changes that have been occurring outside their frameworks.

If the treaties thus provide only a partial explanation for policy development, what other factors have been influential? There has been, and still is, an extensive academic debate on this question. Since much of this debate is examined at length in Chapter 23, suffice it here to focus on three factors that have been especially important: the leadership offered by the Commission; the perceptions of the member states of what is desirable; and the individual and collective capacities of the member states to translate their perceptions into practice.

To begin with Commission leadership, it is generally recognised that the Commissions led by Walter Hallstein (1958–67), Roy Jenkins (1977–81), and Jacques Delors (1985–95) have been the most dynamic and forceful in the Commission's history. This is not to suggest that all their ideas and proposals were translated into practice, but it is to say that they were particularly innovative in helping to bring issues onto the policy agenda and in pointing to what could, and perhaps should, be done. The ability of the Commission, in favourable circumstances, to have a real effect on policy development is no more clearly illustrated than in the way the Delors-led Commissions helped to force the pace on such key issues as the Single European Market (SEM) programme, Economic and Monetary Union (EMU), and the social dimension.

Regarding the perceptions of the states, a fundamental precondition of successful EU policy development has been that the advantages of acting together have been judged by the national governments to outweigh the disadvantages. The advantages have mostly, though not entirely, been seen to be primarily economic in kind. So, there has been a broad consensus amongst the governments that shared policy activity is, on balance, beneficial in respect of the building of a single and integrated internal market, having a common external trading position, and engaging in some collective action and pooling of resources in particular functional and sectoral areas. The principal perceived disadvantages of acting together have been the loss of national decision-making powers and sovereignty that transfers of power and responsibilities to the EU entails and the associated limitations placed on the national room for policy manoeuvre. Policy areas where this disadvantage has been seen as being especially problematical, at least by some member states, have resulted, at best, in only limited convergence in the positions of states in favour of joint policy action. In consequence, in these areas policy development has been slow and limited. Examples of such policy areas include foreign and defence, social welfare, and taxation.

As for the capacity of the member states to operationalise their perceptions of what is desirable, there are many problems. At the individual state level, a government may be favourably disposed towards an EU initiative but be inhibited from supporting it because of opposition from a powerful domestic interest or because it could be electorally damaging. Following this through to the EU level, opposition from just one state, whether it is principled or pragmatic, can make policy development difficult to achieve given the practice of the European Council to take its decisions only by unanimity, the continuing treaty requirement of unanimity in the Council of Ministers in several key policy areas, and the preference in the Council for progress through consensus – especially on major issues – even when majority decisions are legally permissible. This situation whereby a majority of member states is unwilling or unable to oblige states that are in a minority to participate in policy activities against their will has led to 'differentiated integration' becoming increasingly important: that is policy development is increasingly taking place in the EU without all member states being fully involved. Important policy areas where this is occurring include Economic and Monetary Union (EMU), Justice and Home Affairs (JHA), and aspects of foreign and defence policies.

The Range and Diversity of EU Policies

Many of the EU's policies and laws centre on the promotion and defence of an internally free and externally protected market. Hence, there are policies that are designed to encourage the free movement of goods, persons, services, and capital; there is the competition policy, which seeks to facilitate fair and open competition within and across the borders of the member states; and there is the common external tariff and the common commercial policy. In practice, however, not all of these policies are complete or wholly successful. There are, for example, still barriers related to company law and company taxation that can make it difficult for firms in different member states to engage in joint commercial activities. And non-tariff barriers to internal trade still exist, despite strenuous activity on harmonisation and approximation. In consequence, the EU is, in some respects, less than the integrated internal market it is commonly supposed to be.

But in other respects it is more than an internal market in that many of its policy concerns range far beyond matters that are part and parcel of an internal market's requirements. The policy concerns of the EU are not, in other words, just concerned with dismantling internal barriers and providing conditions for fair trade on the one hand, and presenting a common external trading front to the rest of the world on the other. There are two main aspects to this wider policy portfolio.

First, with regard to the EU's economic policies, many of these are not based solely on the non-interventionist/*laissez faire* principles that are often thought of as providing the ethos, even the ideology, of the EU. In some spheres the EU tends very much towards interventionism/managerialism/regulation, and in so doing it does not always restrict itself to 'market efficiency' policies. This is most obviously seen in the way in which the EU's regional, social, and consumer protection policies, plus much of the CAP, have as their precise purpose the counteracting and softening of nationally unacceptable or socially inequitable market consequences. On a broader front, there are the euro-related policies which clearly take the EU – and especially the eurozone – far beyond being 'just' an internal market and give it many of the characteristics of an economic and monetary union.

Second, the EU has developed policies that are not only non-market focused but also non-economic focused. Of these, the most obvious are those where the member states consult and attempt to coordinate their positions on key foreign policy and some defence policy questions. In addition to foreign policy and defence policy, there are many other 'non economic' policy areas – such as public health, broadcasting, and combating crime – which were long thought of as not being the EU's concern, but where important developments have occurred.

The EU's policy portfolio is thus very wide-ranging. The main areas of interest and responsibility within the portfolio can be grouped under five broad headings: establishing the internal market, macroeconomic and financial policies, functional policies, sectoral policies, and external policies. The first four of these are examined in some detail in Chapter 19, whilst external policies are examined in Chapter 21.

The Varying Extent of EU Policy Involvement

The extent of the EU's responsibility for policy-making and policy management varies enormously between policy areas. As Box 16.1 shows, it ranges from very extensive involvement in some areas to very marginal in others.

In those spheres where significant responsibilities are exercised, policy-making arrangements are usually well-established and effective policy instruments are usually available. Where, however, EU involvement is marginal, policy processes may be confined to little more than occasional exchanges of ideas and information between interested parties, whilst policy instruments may merely be of the exhortive and persuasive kind such as are common in many international organisations.

External trade, agriculture and fishing are prominent amongst the policy areas where there is extensive EU involvement. Here, most major policy decisions, such as those on external tariffs, agricultural support mechanisms and payments, and fishing quotas are taken at the EU level, whilst their detailed and supposedly uniform implementation is left to the member states, acting as agents of the EU. In areas where these so-called common policies are not in reality totally common – and both the Common Agricultural Policy (CAP) and the Common Fisheries Policy (CFP) allow room for governments to provide national aids and assistance – decisions of any significance normally require at least clearance from Brussels.

Moving along the spectrum of EU policy involvement, there are many policy areas where the EU's interests and competence, though less comprehensive than in the examples just given, are still very significant and complement and supplement the activities of the states in important ways. Competition policy is one example. This seeks to encourage free and open competition throughout the EU by, for instance, setting out rules under which firms can make and sell their products, laying down conditions under which national authorities may assist firms, and imposing restrictions on certain types of company merger. Employment policy is another example, with much of the EU's focus in this sphere being on job training and re-training, facilitating labour mobility, underpinning safe working conditions, and generally promoting employment.

Turning finally to policy spheres where the EU's involvement is at best limited, examples include education, health, housing, pensions, and social welfare payments. As these examples make clear, many of the policies that fall into this category of low EU involvement are public welfare policies and policies that have major budgetary implications.

This complex mosaic of policy involvement has over the years moved almost unceasingly in an incrementally integrationist direction. The pace of the movement has varied, both over time periods and within policy areas, but it has been constant. So, if one looks back to, say, the mid-1970s, many issues that would have been listed then as being in the category of very limited policy involvement – such as environment and foreign policy – are now by no means marginal. Environment has spawned many policy programmes and much legislation, foreign policy has evolved its own machinery and has seen increasingly coordinated policy development, and both have been awarded treaty recognition. At the same time, some policy spheres which in the mid-1970s the Community would not have been thought of as having any competence in at all have assumed significant places on the EU's policy agenda. Examples include defence policy and the various JHA policies.

Box 16.1

The extent of EU policy involvement

Extensive EU policy involvement	Considerable EU policy involvement	Policy responsibility shared between the EU and the member states	Limited EU policy involvement	Virtually no EU policy involvement
Trade	Market	Regional	Health	Housing
Agriculture	regulation	Industrial	Education	Domestic crime
Fishing	Competition	Foreign	Defence	
Monetary (for		Environmental	Social welfare	
euro members)		Equal opportunities		
		Working conditions		
		Consumer protection		
		Movement across external borders		
		Macroeconomic (especially for euro members)		
		Energy		
		Transport		
		Cross-border crime		
		Civil liberties (especially via the Charter of Fundamental Rights)		

The Varying Nature of EU Policy Involvement

EU policy involvement varies not just in its extent but also in its nature. The most important aspect of this varying nature is whether policies rely heavily on EU law or are more based on forms of intergovernmental cooperation.

It used to be the case that in those policy areas where the EU exercised significant responsibilities, well-established and effective policy instruments resting on EU law were almost invariably in place. It used also to be the case that where EU policy involvement was very limited, policy instruments tended mostly to be of the voluntaristic and persuasive kind. However, over the years these two generalised statements, and especially the first, have become increasingly less accurate as the EU has made use of an increasing number of diverse policy instruments and mechanisms.

More policy instruments and mechanisms have been used because as the EU has expanded its policy portfolio it has moved into areas where member states have seen advantages in working together but have wished to stop short of making laws that would restrict and bind their own policy choices and options. Foreign policy – which began to be developed from the early 1970s, which was given a heightened political importance and a sharper focus by the Maastricht Treaty, and which became increasingly operational 'on the ground' in the 2000s – is a prime example of such a policy area. The benefits of EU states speaking and acting as one on key international issues are recognised, but such are the political sensitivities associated with foreign policy – and even more so with defence policy, which has come to join foreign policy on the EU's policy agenda – that it has not been politically possible to *communitaurise* it. Accordingly, it rests essentially on intergovernmental cooperation, which does not involve the making of laws and in which member states agree to policy positions and policy actions on a wholly voluntary basis. EU foreign policy

Box 16.2

The nature of EU policy involvement

Heavy reliance on legal regulation	Very considerable reliance on legal regulation	A mixture of legal regulation and inter-state cooperation	Some legal regulation but a considerable reliance on inter-state cooperation	Largely based on inter-state cooperation
Trade Agriculture Fishing	Regional Competition Environmental Consumer protection Working conditions Equal opportunities Market regulation	Industrial Transport Movement across external borders Macroeconomic Energy	Social welfare Energy Defence Law and order Lisbon Strategy issues (mainly concerning economic growth and employment)	Health Education Foreign and defence

making processes are described in some detail in Chapter 21.

Much of employment and social policy also illustrates how significant EU policy areas can rely heavily on intergovernmental cooperation. With employment and social policy, however, it is a different form of intergovernmental cooperation than that which applies in the foreign policy sphere. Like foreign policy intergovernmental cooperation, employment and social policy cooperation is based on agreements that are reached by consensus in the Council and, because it too does not involve the making of legislation, it is non-binding. But, intergovernmental cooperation in much of the employment and social policy spheres is different from foreign policy cooperation in that it is largely based on what is known as the Open Method of Coordination (OMC). As compared with 'classic' inter-state cooperation such as exists in the foreign policy sphere, OMC is different in three particular ways: the Commission is extensively involved in the making of much of the policy; the policy itself consists mostly of the identification of broad goals, accompanied by guidelines to member states as to how they should be achieved; and there is considerable devolution of responsibility to the member states as to how each of them operationalises the pursuit of the goals. (OMC is considered at greater length in Chapter 17).

In the same style as Box 16.1, Box 16.2 plots EU

policy areas along a spectrum, in this case according to the extent to which policy areas are based on legal regulation or on inter-state cooperation. Some correspondence between the placement of policy areas in the Boxes can be seen, but so too can some significant differences.

The Regulatory Emphasis

A classic way of distinguishing between policy types is in terms of regulatory, redistributive and distributive policies (Lowi, 1964). Regulatory policies lay down rules governing behaviour. Redistributive policies transfer financial resources from groups of individuals (most commonly social classes), regions or countries to others. And distributive policies also generally involve allocations of financial resources, but not from one 'side' to another (as from the better off to the worse off) but rather between alternative users and usually on the basis of *juste retour* (which in the EU context means member states attempt to draw at least a 'fair share' from the resources available for distributive policies.).

This scheme of policy types is by no means exhaustive or mutually exclusive, but it is much-used and it is helpful in throwing light on the nature of the EU's policy portfolio.

Regulatory policies

EU policies have a strong *regulatory* emphasis. Such indeed is the extent of the emphasis that Giandomenico Majone has suggested that the EU can be thought of as being a regulatory state (Majone, 1992, 1994, 1996; see also Chapter 23 of this book). The regulatory emphasis of EU policies is most obviously seen in respect of the internal market, where an extensive legislative framework exists to govern the operation of the market. This framework covers not just 'pure' market activities, such as the rules governing product specifications and market movements, but also many policies that though partly regulated for their own intrinsic importance are partly regulated too because they have significant market implications. Examples of such policy areas are working conditions, consumer protection, and the environment.

The reason that EU regulatory policy is so wide-ranging and has displayed little sign of slowing down in its advance is that there is both a demand and a supply for it. The demand comes from various quarters, but most especially from large business which wants as integrated a market as possible – which means common rules in all member states – so as to be able to pursue business activities with maximum ease. The supply comes mainly from the Commission, which through its policy and legislative proposals plays a crucial role in setting the regulatory framework. The Commission produces this supply for a number of reasons. One reason is simply that it is much more able to do so than it is with redistributive or distributive policies. This is partly because the technical nature of much regulatory policy tends to make it less contentious than the other two policy types, and it is partly too because most of the costs of implementing regulatory policies fall not on the EU budget but on the budgets of private firms and public authorities in the member states. Another reason why the Commission produces the supply is, in the view of public choice theorists, that expanding EU regulatory powers also expands the Commission's own powers (see, for example, Hix, 2005).

Redistributive policies

The EU does have redistributive policies – most notably in the form of the cohesion funds and the CAP – but nothing like to the same extent as member states have such policies in the form of social welfare, health and educational policies. There are two main reasons why EU redistributive policies are not well developed. First, no pressing reasons have presented themselves for redistributive policies to be transferred to the EU level, so transfers of sovereignty have been seen as being unnecessary. Second, most national governments have wished to keep a tight rein on EU budgetary expenditure, which means the EU has only modest funds to redistribute. Expenditure on the Regional and Social Funds – the two main components of EU cohesion funds – was doubled in 1988 and then again in 1992, but even with the 1992 increase the overall size of the EU budget was capped at 1.27 per cent of total EU GDP. Since the 1992 increase, cohesion spending has hovered at around 40 per cent of total EU budgetary

---

Box 16.3

Reasons why (many) member states have adopted tighter attitudes to EU budgetary expenditure

- Such attitudes conform with the ideological shift that has taken place virtually throughout the Western world since the early 1990s in favour of a more restrictive stance towards all forms of public expenditure.
- The emphasis given in the EU since the early 1990s to the doctrine of subsidiarity weighs against EU budgetary expansion.
- The EMU convergence and Stability and Growth Pact criteria place a strong emphasis on national budgetary discipline, which is a powerful disincentive against being a net EU budget contributor.
- The 2004–7 enlargement, which brought many relatively poor countries into the EU, has not encouraged net budgetary contributor states to expand redistributive policies – from which most of them have little to gain but for which they must pay.
- Germany, for long the major net contributor to the EU budget, has come to suffer from 'donor fatigue' – largely because of the costs incurred by German unification.

expenditure, but overall budgetary spending has been marginally cut as an increasing number of the member states that are net budgetary contributors have adopted tighter attitudes towards EU expenditure. Key factors accounting for these attitudes are set out in Box 16.3.

Distributive policies

Distributive policies are not much developed in the EU. Examples of EU distributive policies include research and technological development, education (where there are some training and exchange programmes), and – if it can be called a policy – the siting of EU agencies. On this last 'policy', many specialised agencies – ranging from the European Agency for the Evaluation of Medicinal Products to Europol – have been created in recent years and their location has almost invariably been the occasion for wrangling and for dispersal amongst the member states.

Much of the explanation for why distributive policies are not well developed at EU level is similar to the explanation for the under-development of redistributive policies: they are seen as being primarily national responsibilities, so only limited budgetary resources are made available for them. In Pollack's view (1994), another key reason is that distributive policies are not so tied-in with the operation of the market as are regulatory or redistributive policies. Whereas regulatory policies are very much a consequence of economic spillover and redistributive policies are at least in part a consequence of member states with specific market difficulties being given compensation or 'side-payments', distributive policies are not so 'advantaged' and are highly dependent on Commission entrepreneurship for advancement.

The Patchy and Somewhat Uncoordinated Nature of EU Policies

The overall EU policy framework can hardly be said to display a clear pattern or coherence. The Lisbon Treaty did insert into the TFEU a new Title on 'Categories and Areas of Union Competence' in which policy areas were grouped into three categories according to the Union's competence within them. However, as can be seen in Box 16.4, the second and third categories – of mixed and supporting competences – are vague, and two extremely important policy areas – macroeconomic and foreign/defence – are not placed in any of the categories.

The closest there is to a clear rationale for the EU's policy competences is via the so-called subsidiarity principle, which holds that only those policies that are best dealt with at EU level rather than at national level become the EU's concern. The problem with this principle, however, both as a description of the present reality and as a prescription for future action, is that it is vague and question-begging. Descriptions of the present and evolving policy framework as being centred on 'managed and tempered capitalism' or 'a controlled open market' are perhaps of more use in capturing the essence of the EU's policy interests, but they too are still far from wholly satisfactory in that they do not embrace the full flavour of the array and varying depths of EU policy interests, nor do they draw attention to the conflicting principles that underlie different parts of the policy network.

The fact is that the considerable national and political differences that exist in the EU make it difficult to develop coordinated and coherent policies based on shared principles and agreed objectives. This is so because any policy development at EU level is usually only possible if searching questions are answered to the satisfaction of a large number of actors. From the viewpoint of the most important actors – the governments of the member states – these questions include: is the national (or at least government) interest being served?; is the cooperation and integration that the policy development involves politically acceptable?; and, if the policy sphere does require closer relations with other states, is the EU the most desirable arena in which it should occur? As the EU's extensive range of policies demonstrates, these questions have often been answered in the affirmative, though normally only after being subject to caveats and reservations which sit uneasily beside, and sometimes clash with, one another. But often, too, the responses have been in the negative, or at least have been so on the part of a sufficient number of decision-makers to severely limit policy cooperation and integration.

Box 16.4

Categories and Areas of Union Competence as Specified in the Treaty on the Functioning of the European Union

- *Exclusive Union competence.* There are five areas in which the EU has exclusive competence: the customs union, the establishment of competition rules, monetary policy for the eurozone, the conservation of marine biological resources under the CFP, and the common commercial policy.
- *Shared competence between the Union and the member states.* There are eleven areas in which competence is shared: the internal market, aspects of social policy, cohesion policy, agriculture and fisheries, environment, consumer protection, transport, energy, the area of freedom, security and justice, research and technological development, and development policy.
- The Union has competence to carry out actions to *support, coordinate or supplement* the actions of the member states in seven areas; human health, industry, culture, tourism, education, civil protection, and administrative cooperation.

In addition, certain general principles are identified for other important policy areas not listed in the above categories. So, for example, the member states are to 'coordinate' their economic and employment policies, and in its external relations the Union 'shall define and pursue common policies and actions and shall work for a high degree of cooperation in all fields of international relations …'.

Source: Adapted from Part One, Title 1, Articles 2–6 of *The Treaty on the Functioning of the European Union*, apart from the reference to external relations which is extracted from Article 21 of the *Treaty on European Union*. The Treaties are accessible on the *Europa* website.

Policy development has consequently been as much about what is possible as what is desirable. In the absence of a centre of power with the authority and internal coherence to take an overall view of EU requirements and impose an ordered pattern, policies have tended to be the outcome of complex and laboured interactions where different, and often contrasting, requirements, preferences, reservations and fears have all played a part. As a result, the EU's overall policy picture is inevitably patchy and rather ragged. A few policy areas – such as agriculture, fishing and the internal market – are well developed, but other areas that might have been expected to be developed, are either developed only in uncoordinated and partial ways or are barely developed at all.

This lack of development has resulted in deficiencies in many EU policies. As Chapter 19 will show, industrial policy, energy policy, and regional policy are but three examples of key policy areas where there are not, if EU effectiveness is to be maximised, sufficiently strong or integrated policy frameworks with clear and consistent goals. The frameworks in these and many other policy areas are too partial and too fragmented. They are also, often, under-funded.

Of course, similar critical comments about under-development and lack of integration can also be levelled against national policy frameworks. But not to the same extent. For, at the individual state level, there is, even when the political system is weak and decentralised, usually more opportunity than there is in the EU for direction from the centre. This is partly because national decision-makers have access to more policy instruments than do EU decision-makers. It is mainly, however, because at state level there is normally some focus of political authority capable of offering leadership and imposing a degree of order: a Head of Government perhaps, a Cabinet or Council of Ministers, a Ministry of Economics or Finance, or a dominant party group. In the EU, there are several foci of political authority and leadership, but none is constituted or organised in such a way as to enable it to establish an overall policy coherence or to enforce a clear and consistent policy direction.

Concluding Remarks

This chapter has emphasised the enormous expansion that has taken place over the years in the EU's policy portfolio. Some of this expansion has involved building on and out from policy areas that were identified in the Founding Treaties, whilst some has taken the form of developing policy areas that did not get a treaty mention until the Single European Act at the very earliest.

Such has been the growth of the policy portfolio that there now are few policy areas with which the EU does not have at least some sort of involvement. But the character of the involvement varies enormously between policy areas. It does so in many ways, not least the balance of policy control between the EU and the national levels and the extent to which policy is based on legal or cooperative policy instruments. The nature of the variations that exist between policy areas will be explored at some length in Chapters 19–22.

Chapter 17
Policy Processes

This chapter examines the nature of the EU's policy processes. It shows that the processes are numerous and highly complex in nature, that a number of factors combine to determine what processes apply in what policy circumstances, that there are four broad frameworks of policy processes, that a number of characteristics regularly feature in most policy processes, and that the processes are by no means as inefficient as they are often portrayed as being.

Broad themes that run through the chapter are the multi-faceted nature of the policy processes and the host of differing sorts of policy actors that interact with one another on the basis of an array of different policy-making rules and procedures. These themes are further examined in the following chapters of this part of the book.

Variations in EU Processes

There cannot be said to be a 'standard' or 'typical' EU policy-making or decision-making process. A multiplicity of actors interact with one another via a myriad of channels.

The actors

There are three main sets of EU policy actors: those associated with the EU institutions, with the governments of the member states, and with Euro-level and national-level non-institutional and non-governmental interests. As has been shown in previous chapters, each of these sets of actors has an array of responsibilities to fulfil and roles to perform. But so variable and fluid are EU policy processes that the nature of the responsibilities and roles can differ considerably according to circumstances. For instance, in one set of circumstances an actor may be anxious to play an active role and may have the power – legal and/or political – to do so. In a second set of circumstances it may not wish to be actively involved, perhaps because it has no particular interests at stake or because prominence may be politically damaging. And in a third set of circumstances it may wish for a leading part but not be able to attain it because of a lack of appropriate power resources.

Take, for example, the Latvian Government. It has a strong direct interest and is actively engaged in EU deliberations in respect of, for instance, issues related to energy supply from Russia and the annual fishing allocations within the framework of the Common Fisheries Policy. It is also much affected by

Box 17.1

EMU policy actors

- *The Ecofin Council of Ministers.* Composed of national Ministers of Finance from all EU member states, the Ecofin Council is responsible for the broad outlines of EU macroeconomic policy. The Ecofin Council also has a number of specific EMU-related responsibilities, including deciding upon whether to take action against eurozone states with excessive government deficits and deciding on a range of issues in connection with external monetary and foreign exchange matters. Under amendments made by the Treaty of Lisbon, only eurozone members can vote when the Ecofin Council takes decisions on matters that just affect the eurozone.
- *The Eurogroup.* The Eurogroup was created in 1998 as an informal and unofficial gathering of Ministers of Finance from eurozone member states. It quickly established itself as an important and permanent forum, and was given legal status – in the form of a protocol – by the Lisbon Treaty.

  The Eurogroup normally convenes monthly, immediately before Ecofin meetings, to discuss matters of shared interest concerning the eurozone. The most striking demonstration to date of its decision-making capacity occurred in the spring of 2005 when it agreed to loosen the terms of the Stability and Growth Pact and then presented its agreement to Ecofin – formally the decision-making body – virtually for ratification. (For a detailed study of the Eurogroup, see Puetter, 2006).

  There have sometimes been suggestions, most notably in recent years from President Sarkozy of France, that the Eurogroup should meet at Heads of Government level. Indeed, following a first ever meeting of eurozone leaders in November 2008 – that was held to discuss a coordinated eurozone response to the international financial crisis – Sarkozy informed the EP that he thought the Eurogroup should be replaced by a 'clearly identified economic government' for the eurozone based on regular meeting of the eurozone Heads of Government. However, his call did not meet with much support from other eurozone national leaders – partly because the notion was seen as being premature and partly because Germany suspected it would be used to develop policies that would draw mainly on German funds.
- *The European Central Bank* (ECB). The ECB operates within the framework of the *European System of Central Banks* (ESCB). The ESCB is composed of the ECB and the EU national central banks (NCBs). NCBs of the member states that are not part of the euro area have a separate status within the ESCB: because they continue to have their own national monetary policies, they do not take part in decision-making on the single monetary policy of the euro area.
- Other EU institutions and actors with significant EMU-related responsibilities are:

  - The *European Council,* which is obliged to discuss, under Article 121 TFEU, 'a conclusion of the broad guidelines of the economic policies of the Member States and of the Union', and in practice can consider anything else that it wishes.
  - The *Commission,* which is responsible for monitoring and producing reports on national economic, and especially budgetary, performances, and for making recommendations to the Council when states are deemed to be in breach of their requirements under the SGP. (In the autumn of 2004 the Council did not accept the Commission's recommendations on action to be taken against France and Germany for breaching the requirements, which led to the Commission taking the Council to the ECJ.)
  - The *Economic and Financial Committee* of the Council, whose remit includes all aspects of EU economic and monetary policies – from the operation of the euro, through macroeconomic policy coordination, to international monetary relations.
  - The *European Parliament,* which has few powers in relation to EMU, but does have a range of consultation and information-receiving rights.

(For a fuller account of the ESCB's institutions, see Chang, 2009: Chapter 4.)

many of the EU's macroeconomic and 'spending' policies, especially in the wake of the global financial crisis which strongly impacted on the Latvian economy, but in this policy sphere its smallness and its precarious economic position has been meant that its role has been more one of policy recipient than policy shaper. By contrast, it is little affected by, and does not involve itself much with, policy negotiations and decision-making related to the EU's Mediterranean strategy.

Box 17.1 further illustrates the range and variety of major actor involvement by showing the unique cast in one of the EU's most important policy areas: EMU. Other policy areas have their own casts.

The channels

The channels vary in four principal respects:

1 *In their complexity and exhaustiveness.* Some types of policy decision are made fairly quickly by a relatively small number of people using procedures that are easy to operate. In contrast, other decisions are subject to complex and exhaustive processes in which many different sorts of actor attempt to determine and shape outcomes.
2 *In the relative importance of EU, member state, and subnational processes and in the links between the three levels.* One of the EU's major structural difficulties is that it is multi-layered, with differing degrees and sorts of power and influence being exercised in different ways at different levels. Moreover, there are often no clear lines of authority or hierarchy between the different levels.
3 *In their levels of seniority.* EU policy processes are conducted at many different levels of seniority, as illustrated by the numerous forums in which representatives of the governments of the member states meet: Heads of Government in the European Council; Ministers in the Council of Ministers; Permanent Representatives and their deputies in COREPER; and officials and experts in committees and working parties.
4 *In their degree of formality and structure.* By their very nature, the fixed and set-piece occasions of EU policy processes – such as meetings of the Council of Ministers, plenary sessions of the EP, and Council of Ministers/EP delegation meetings called to resolve legislative and budgetary differences –

tend to be formal and structured. Partly because of this, they are often not very well equipped to produce the horse trading, concessions, and compromises that are so necessary to build majorities, create agreements and further progress. As a result, they have come to be supported by a vast network of informal and unstructured channels between EU actors, ranging from the after-dinner discussions that are sometimes held at European Council gatherings to the continuous soundings, telephone calls, e-mails, working lunches, and meetings and pre-meetings that are such a part of EU life in Brussels, Strasbourg, Luxembourg and national capitals.

Factors Determining EU Policy Processes

A number of factors can be identified as being especially important in determining the particular mix of actors and channels that are to be found in any particular context.

The treaty base

One of the most important things the treaties do is to lay down different decision-making procedures and to specify the circumstances in which they are to be used. As a result, the treaties are of fundamental importance in shaping the nature of the EU's policy processes and determining the powers exercised by institutions and actors within these processes. Box 17.2 illustrates this point by giving examples of just some of the many and varied policy-making and decision-making procedures provided for in the TEU and the TFEU. (These procedures are all explained at length elsewhere in the book, either later in this chapter or in following chapters).

The proposed status of the matter under consideration

As a general rule, procedures tend to be more fixed when EU law is envisaged than when it is not. They are fixed most obviously by the treaties, but also by Court

---

Box 17.2

Illustrations of different policy- and decision-making procedures laid-down in the treaties

- There are three procedures for non-administrative legislation: the 'ordinary' ('co-decision', pre-Lisbon Treaty), 'consultation', and 'consent' ('assent', pre-Lisbon Treaty) procedures. Key points of difference between these procedures include: 1) the EP can exercise veto powers under the ordinary and consent procedures but cannot do so under the consultation procedure; and 2) there are single readings in the Council and the EP under the consultation and consent procedures, but potentially three readings – or, perhaps more accurately, two readings and a third stage – under the ordinary procedure.
- External trade agreements negotiated under Article 207 TFEU (formerly 133 TEC) have their own special procedure, under which the Commission conducts negotiations under a mandate from the Council and the Council makes final decisions – either by QMV or unanimity depending on the type of decision – subject usually to obtaining the consent of the EP.
- The annual budget also has its own arrangements, under which the Council and the EP are joint budgetary authorities.
- Under the 'flexibility' provisions added to the TEU and the TEC by the Amsterdam Treaty and made easier to apply by the Nice and Lisbon Treaties, it is possible for a group of nine or more member states to establish 'enhanced cooperation' between themselves and to make use of EU institutions, procedures and mechanisms. With the exceptions of those policy areas where the EU has exclusive policy competence and also the CFSP, a decision to so act can be taken by qualified majority in the Council (though with safeguards built in for member states which object to such a decision being taken) and with the consent of the EP. In the CFSP field, there must be unanimity in the Council and the EP only has a right to be informed.
- The CFSP is based on an intergovernmental decision-making framework. Most policy decisions require unanimity in the Council and consultation with the EP, whilst operational and procedural decisions can usually be taken by QMV if the Council so decides and without consulting with the EP. Whether or not the EP is consulted, the Council must keep it regularly informed of policy developments.

---

of Justice interpretations (for example, the obligation specified in the famous 1980 isoglucose case ruling that the Council must wait upon EP opinions before giving Commission proposals under the consultation procedure legislative status) and by conventions (for example, the understanding in the Council that when a member state has genuine difficulties the matter will not normally be rushed and an effort will be made to reach a compromise even when QMV is permissible).

When law is being made, Commission legislation is usually subject to less review and discussion than EP and Council or Council legislation. The reason for this is that Commission legislation is normally of an administrative kind – more technical than political. Indeed, much of it consists of updates, applications or amendments to already existing legislation, often in the spheres of external trade or the CAP. As a result, Commission legislation, prior to being introduced, is

often only fully discussed by appropriate officials in the Commission, and perhaps by national officials in a comitology committee. Some Council legislation, on the other hand, and all EP and Council legislation, is broader in scope and is subject to a full legislative procedure. As such it becomes the subject of representations and pressures from many interests, is assessed by the EP and often also by the EESC and the CoR, and is scrutinised in detail in national capitals and in Council forums in Brussels.

Where policy activity does not involve law making, considerable discretion is sometimes available to decision-makers, especially governments, as to which policy processes will be used and who will be permitted to participate. A common procedure when states wish the EU to do something but do not necessarily wish a new law to be made (which may be because there is no agreement on what the law should be or because, as with foreign policy pronouncements, law is inappropriate), is to issue Council resolutions, declarations, or agreements. These can be as vague or as precise as the Council wishes them to be. Often, resolutions and the like can have a very useful policy impact, even if it is just to keep dialogue going, but because they are not legal instruments they are not normally as subject to examination and challenge by other EU institutions and actors.

The degree of generality or specificity of the policy issue

At the generality end of the scale, EU policy-making may consist of little more than exchanges of ideas between interested parties to see whether there is common ground for policy coordination, the setting of priorities, or possible legislation. Such exchanges and discussions take place at many different levels on an almost continuous basis, but the most important, in the sense that their initiatives are the ones most likely to be followed up, are those that involve very senior officials and politicians – especially if the outcome of deliberations find their way into European Council Conclusions.

Far removed from *grands tours d'horizon* by topmost officials and politicians is the daily grind of preparing and drafting the mass of highly detailed and technical regulations that make up the great bulk of the EU's legislative output. Senior EU figures, especially ministers, are not normally directly involved in the processes that lead to such legislation. There may be a requirement that they give the legislation their formal approval, but it is Commission officials, aided in appropriate cases by national officials, who do the basic work.

The newness, importance, controversiality, or political sensitivity of the issue in question

The more these characteristics apply, and the perception of the extent to which they do may vary – what may be a technical question for one may be politically charged for another – the more complex policy processes are likely to be. If, for example, it seems likely that a proposal for an EP and Council directive on some aspect of animal welfare will cause significant difficulties for farmers, it is probable that the accompanying policy-making process will display all or most of the following features: particularly intensive pre-proposal consultations by the Commission; vigorous attempts by many sectional and promotional interest groups to make an input; very careful examination of the proposal by the EP and the EESC; long and exhaustive negotiations in the Council; considerable activity and manoeuvring on the fringes of formal meetings and between meetings; and, overall, much delay and many alterations *en route* to the (possible) eventual adoption of the proposal.

The balance of policy responsibilities between the EU and national levels

Where there has been a significant transfer of responsibilities to the EU – as, for example, with agricultural, external trade, and competition policies – EU-level processes are naturally very important. In such policy spheres, EU institutions, particularly the Commission, have many tasks to perform: monitoring developments, making adjustments, ensuring existing policies and programmes are replaced when necessary, and so on. On the other hand, where the EU's policy role is at best supplementary to that of the member states – as with education and health policies – most significant policy-making activity continues to be channelled through the customary national procedures, and policy activity at EU level is limited in scope.

Circumstances and the perceptions of circumstances

This is seemingly rather vague, but it refers to the crucially important fact that policy development and policy-making processes in the EU are closely related to prevailing political and economic circumstances, to the perceptions by key actors – especially national governments – of their needs in the circumstances, and to perceptions of the potential of the EU to act as a problem-solving organisation in regard to the circumstances. Do the advantages of acting at EU level, as opposed to national level, and of acting in the EU in a particular way as opposed to another way, outweigh the disadvantages?

The Justice and Home Affairs (JHA) policy area provides an example of how changing circumstances can bring about related changes in policy processes. The policy area began to be initially developed at EU level from the mid-1980s, largely as a result of spillover from the Single European Market project and the opening-up of borders. However, the development was very tentative and was conducted on a strictly intergovernmental basis. Two sets of changing circumstances have, however, resulted in national governments giving JHA issues a much greater priority in recent years and being willing to see intergovernmental policy processes giving way to what in many JHA areas are now supranational processes. One of these changing circumstances has been EU enlargement, which has intensified already existing concerns about border controls and such related issues as illegal inward movements of people (from non-EU states to the EU), cross-border crime, and drug trafficking. The other changing circumstance has been the increased threat to 'the West' from international terrorism, which was first dramatically demonstrated by the September 11 2001 events in the US and has since been brought closer to home by bombings in Europe – notably in Madrid in 2004 and in London in 2005. These changing circumstances have been instrumental in promoting the more 'communitarised' approach to JHA that has been evident since the late 1990s and which saw the Lisbon Treaty 'transfer' what remained of the separate JHA pillar three from the TEU to the TFEU, albeit with the retention of unanimity in the Council for some especially sensitive JHA issues.

The Four Frameworks of EU Policy Processes

As has been stressed above, there are many EU policy processes. Indeed, the Convention that drew up the Constitutional Treaty identified no less than 28 distinct policy-making procedures on the basis of the decision-making rules in the Council, the nature of the EP's involvement, and the consultative status of the EESC and the CoR.

However, notwithstanding this numeracy of policy processes, it is possible to identify broad policy-making patterns. Paul Magnette (2005) suggests that three criteria are especially helpful in enabling such patterns to be discerned. These criteria are: the degree of involvement of institutions that are independent of government; the decision-making rules in the Council; and the legal character of many decisional outcomes.

Using these criteria, four main policy-making frameworks can be identified. Within these frameworks there are variations in the specifics of policy processes, but the fundamental features are shared. The frameworks will now each be examined.

The Community method

When the Community was established in the 1950s a single and relatively simple policy-making system was provided for in the treaties. In the words of what for many years was a much-used maxim, the essence of the system was that 'the Commission proposes, the Parliament advises [on a restricted range of matters], the Council decides [almost invariably by unanimity], and [where laws are made] the Court adjudicates.' This system, which came to be known as the Community method, was designed on the one hand to try and avoid what was seen to be the paralysing effects of the intergovernmental decision-making arrangements of organisations such as the Council of Europe and the OEEC whilst on the other hand ensuring that national governments had the ultimate control of final decision-taking.

Over the years the Community method has evolved in response to changing needs, demands and circumstances. Two changes have been especially important. First, the powers of the EP have been greatly extended in the rounds of treaty reform that have regularly occurred since the mid-1980s. From having initially had only consultative powers, it is now normally a co-decision-maker with the Council where the Community method is used – and it is always used where EU laws are being made. This change has had the effect of transforming the Community method from a system that was primarily based on a Commission–Council tandem to one that is now based on a Commission–Council–EP triangle. Second, the ability of the Council to take decisions by QMV has

The Community method: key features

- The Commission takes the policy lead and has monopolistic power over the drafting and tabling of legislative proposals.
- The Council is always a final decision-maker, either by itself or with the EP. QMV is normally, but not always, available for the taking of Council decisions.
- The EP normally has co-decision-making powers with the Council under the 'ordinary legislative procedure'. Where this power is absent, the EP must be consulted before any final decision can be taken.
- The EU's courts have final jurisdiction over all EU legislation.

been greatly extended – to such an extent that it is available (though, as was shown in Chapter 9, not always used) for most areas of legislative decision-making. Box 17.3 provides an outline of the key features of the Community method in its current form. These features are further considered in Chapter 18, where the EU's legislative procedures are examined.

Because the Community method is the only method that can be used for making EU legislation where a full legislative procedure is required, it is still naturally an extremely important policy-making framework. But, it has declined in relative importance over the years as other frameworks have also come to be used. A key reason for this use of other frameworks is that policy areas and issues have come onto the EU's agenda where law making has been deemed to be unsuitable or has been unacceptable to some member states. In the foreign policy sphere, for example, and much of macroeconomic policy too, member states recognise the need for policy coordination but do not wish to make binding laws and do not want to be subject to the supranational elements which the Community method – to varying degrees – involves. Another reason for the relative decline is enlargement, which by making the EU not only much larger but also much more heterogeneous has meant that more flexible policy processes than the Community method are sometimes more appropriate. And, in the opinion of

Giandomenico Majone, a third reason has been growing suspicions by member states that the supranational institutions, especially the Commission, have over-used the method because the method works so much to their institutional advantage: 'there is clear evidence that the Commission, and arguably also the Court of Justice, on many occasions have used the Community method well beyond the limits envisaged by the drafters of the Treaty of Rome, and that the member states have reacted to this lack of self-restraint by limiting the scope of delegation to the supranational institutions' (Majone, 2006a: 616).

Intensive transgovernmentalism

Intergovernmental cooperation is a form of policy making in which national governments are the key actors, decisions require unanimous approval by participating governments, and many decisional outcomes do not involve the making of laws. In the EU context, intergovernmental cooperation may thus be said to exist when: the European Council and/or the Council of Ministers are the sole decision-makers and the Commission and the EP are, at best, to the margins; QMV is not available and all member states can veto a proposed decision to which they object; and decisions that are taken are political rather than legal decisions and are not enforceable through the EU's courts. Box 17.4 summarises the key features of intensive transgovernmentalism.

This form of decision-making was first used in the early 1970s when the EC began to take steps in the field of foreign policy cooperation. The member states became concerned that whilst the EC was establishing itself as an increasingly important international economic actor, and more especially trade actor, its political voice and influence were largely absent. Accordingly, they began to seek to work more closely with one another on foreign policy issues. But, because of the sensitivities involved in respect of foreign policy – not least the fact that it is a policy area where sovereignty sensitivities run high – the Community method was seen as being unsuitable and unacceptable. The member states wanted to see how far they could cooperate, not integrate. They wanted also to be firmly in charge of developments rather than being dependent in any way on the Commission, the EP, or the ECJ.

Since the taking of the initial steps in the early

Box 17.4

Intensive transgovernmentalism: key features

- The right of policy initiation is not exclusive to the Commission but is held also by the governments of the member states.
- The EP is in a generally weak consultative position, with few formal powers other than the power of consent on some types of international agreements.
- Much policy activity is focused on fostering cooperation between governments rather than on law-making.
- Governments interact with one another on an intensive basis, both at many levels and in many policy areas.
- All key decisions are made by either the European Council or by the Council of Ministers acting by unanimity.

1970s, foreign policy cooperation has developed into a major area of EU policy activity, as is shown in Chapter 21. It is still essentially based on the principles of intergovernmental cooperation on which it was founded, but the policy processes have inevitably become much more intensive in form as the range of foreign policy interests, activities and instruments have grown. Indeed, so intensive have the processes become that it is clear that the term 'intergovernmental cooperation' now no longer fully captures the nature of foreign policy-making processes and that Helen Wallace's term 'intensive transgovernmentalism' is much more accurate (Wallace, 2005: 87–9). This latter term captures the constantly ongoing interactions between representatives of the governments of the member states as they work with one another on a day-to-day basis to make EU foreign policy, and increasingly also the linked area of defence policy, meaningful and effective. These interactions take many different forms, ranging from preliminary and relatively informal discussions on policy matters between middle-ranking officials from member state Foreign Ministries to formal decisions on policy issues made by Foreign Ministers in the Council of Ministers or by Heads of Government in the European Council.

Until recently, the other major policy area where

intensive transgovernmentalism featured prominently in EU policy processes was justice and home affairs. Like foreign policy, JHA was initially developed on a very cautious and tentative basis – in its case from the mid-1980s – and also like foreign policy the sovereignty sensitivities associated with the policy area meant the Community method could not initially be used. However, though in its initial treaty appearance – as pillar three of the TEU which was created as part of the Maastricht Treaty – it was based on firmly intergovernmental principles, pressures quickly built to make JHA more subject to the Community method. This duly occurred, with several JHA policy area – including immigration, visa, and asylum – brought into the EU's first pillar by the Amsterdam Treaty, and then with what remained of the third pillar brought into the TFEU by the Lisbon Treaty. Remnants of intergovernmentalism still remain in the JHA area – with, for example, the Commission not having sole legislative proposing rights in some spheres (the only policy area where this is so) and with unanimity still required in the Council for some types of decision (though, of course, it is not unique in this) – but, for the most part, JHA has been 'communitarised'.

Beyond 'regular' policy areas, there is one other type of policy process that is based primarily on intergovernmental principles: the process that leads to 'history-making' decisions. These are decisions that in some way mark very significant stages or turning points in the integration process. Examples of such decisions include those on the contents of treaties, on the contents of the multi-annual financial frameworks, on enlargements, and on major and new policy initiatives. Decisions of this type have some quasi-supranational features associated with them – they are, for example, often at least partly prepared by the Commission and final adoption of decisions may require the consent of the EP. Furthermore, though history-making decisions do not have the status of being law-making decisions, they are decisions that national governments are required to abide by, and in most cases they are duly transmitted into law by the appropriate procedures. But, notwithstanding such supranational and Community method features, the process that leads to history-making decisions is mainly intergovernmental in character in that national governmental representatives are invariably extensively involved in the preparing of decisions (this is especially the case in respect of treaty making) and, above all, the key decision-makers are very senior members of government, usually the Heads of Government, acting by unanimity.

Open coordination

In the second half of the 1990s the EU began to become involved in a number of policy areas where the governments of the member states felt there was a need to have a policy approach that would fall somewhere between intergovernmental cooperation and the Community method. The former was thought to be too weak for some emerging policy areas whilst the latter was thought to infringe too much on national independence.

The new policy approach that was gradually developed is known variously as open coordination, the open method or, to use its full and official name, the open method of coordination (OMC). Open coordination was initially applied to macroeconomic policy coordination, with a system being developed in the late 1990s, known as the Broad Economic Policy Guidelines (BEPGs), designed to strengthen the coordination of the broad economic policies of all member states, whether they were to be EMU members or not. At much the same time, OMC began also to be applied to aspects of employment policy, where the member states were charged by the Amsterdam Treaty with a responsibility for developing a coordinated strategy and in particular for promoting a skilled, trained and adaptable workforce. The March 2000 Lisbon European Council meeting then gave OMC a major boost by identifying it as a key policy procedure to be used in giving effect to the Lisbon Strategy that was launched at the summit. The Strategy had as its central purpose making the EU economy much more competitive, dynamic, and knowledge-based, and doing so within a framework in which employment and social cohesion are advanced (see Chapter 19 for a fuller account of the nature of the Lisbon Strategy).

What then is the nature of OMC as a policy framework? The broad features are outlined in Box 17.5, but within those features OMC takes a number of forms, with some forms being tighter and more hierarchical than others. Essentially, however, OMC involves the governments of the member states, operating normally, but by no means always, on the bases of ideas and proposals advanced by the Commission,

---

Box 17.5

The open method of coordination: key features

- Broad policy goals and guidelines are set at EU level by the Council of Ministers acting by unanimity. The specificity of the goals and guidelines varies considerably between and within policy areas.
- The policy goals and guidelines are not given legal status, but are essentially voluntary in nature.
- Member states draw up national action plans setting out how they will seek to achieve the goals and be in conformity with the guidelines. In drawing up the plans, member states are granted considerable discretion regarding the policy instruments and mechanisms they are to use.
- Member states submit (to the Commission and the relevant configuration of the Council) annual reports on their progress in achieving the goals and meeting the guidelines.
- The Commission exercises an important role in assisting with and monitoring OMC activities. As part of its activities it produces reports that have, as one of their purposes, encouraging/pressurising member states that fall behind in achieving targets.

---

agreeing (by unanimity) on policy goals – such as reaching target levels for investment in research or launching information technology training programmes for young people – and then seeking to achieve the goals not via legal compulsion but via voluntary action. The nature of the action to be taken is set out in national action plans, which often vary considerably in both ambition and detail. Pressures of various sorts, orchestrated and managed usually by the Commission, are put on the member states to 'fall in line', but national governments are given considerable latitude as to the policy instruments they use and there is no question of legal action being taken against them for failing to meet policy targets. The submission to the Commission and the relevant formation of the Council of annual national reports, peer pressure, bench marking, and the adoption of best practices are amongst the preferred methods of achieving the policy aims and targets.

The main disadvantage of the OMC approach is that it is ultimately voluntary in nature. So, governments are not legally bound by agreements and may not feel very committed to implementing them. Where national implementation is poor, there are no 'punishments' that can be invoked against national authorities, other than them being publicly shown to have 'fallen behind'. Advantages of OMC are that policy remains primarily a national responsibility, national diversities are respected, and governments may agree to commit to orientations and actions they would not accept if stricter and more mandatory policy instruments were being proposed. (Useful introductions to OMC include: Borrás and Jacobsson, 2004; Schäfer, 2004; Heidenreich and Bischoff, 2008.)

Centralised decision-making

There are two very important policy areas where EU supranational institutions have been given extremely strong and relatively independent decision-making powers. The institutions have been given these powers because the policy areas concerned have been deemed to need to be 'de-politicised' in the sense that the decision-makers have been seen to need to be shielded from political pressures. In both cases the powers that have been assigned to the supranational institutions could be seen as constituting a rather special form of the delegation of policy implementation responsibilities, but such is the extent and impact of the implementation that the decisions taken by the supranational institutions regularly have great policy significance.

One of these policy areas is competition, where, as was shown in Chapter 8, the Commission has considerable discretion and powers in relation to a wide range of matters, including abuse of dominant trading positions, proposed company mergers, the existence of cartels, and state aid to public and private companies. The Commission is always lobbied when dealing with competition issues, not least by member state governments when decisions to be taken are seen as having potentially significant consequences for national economies. But though the Commission normally seeks to be sensitive to particular national concerns, final decisions fall to it alone: dissatisfied governments

may appeal Commission decisions to the EU's courts on points of law, but they cannot ask the Council to overturn decisions on political grounds.

The other policy area is eurozone monetary policy where, as was described in Chapter 13, the European Central Bank has very important sole decision-making responsibilities. Like the Commission in respect of competition policy, the Bank is subjected to pressures from member state governments – unsurprisingly given the often different policy needs of eurozone national economies – but it alone takes key interest and exchange rate decisions.

Recurring Characteristics of EU Policy Processes

A number of general features are characteristic of and run through EU policy processes. They include variable institutional roles and powers, compromises and linkages, inter-institutional cooperation, difficulties in effecting radical change, tactical manoeuvring, and different speeds.

Variable institutional roles and powers

The roles and powers of the EU's institutions and of the political actors associated with them vary considerably between policy processes and policy areas. This point was suggested above in the examination of the four policy frameworks, and indeed it may almost be regarded as a theme of this book so often is it made – either implicitly or explicitly – in other chapters. Attention here will, therefore, be confined to the making of a few core observations.

Where legislation is being made, decision-making processes are based on an institutional triangle within which the Commission, the Council and the EP all exercise considerable power and influence and are constantly interacting. But, the precise powers and influence of each of the institutions under the method can vary considerably according to just what is being proposed and what procedure applies. The Commission, for example, has very considerable control over administrative legislation (though with the extent of the control varying according to which comitology procedure applies), but has much less control over the contents of tabled directives that are subject to the ordinary legislative procedure. Indeed, there is a case for saying that once such directives have been tabled, the Commission, though continuing to be a policy participant, is sometimes in a position of doing little more than servicing Council–EP deliberations and negotiations.

Beyond the making of legislation, there is an additional array of varying institutional roles and powers. Where, for example, a 'soft' policy approach is taken, the EP is normally disadvantaged and policy processes resemble more a Commission–Council tandem, as is the case with those parts of the Lisbon Strategy that are based on the OMC. In respect of EMU, the EP is once more on the margins, much of the Council's role is undertaken in practice by the Eurogroup of ministers, and key monetary decisions are taken by the European Central Bank. And in the CFSP and CSDP spheres institutional positions are different again, with the Council dominating. This is because of the intergovernmental nature of these policy areas, which means not only that the unanimity principle prevails in the Council but also that the Commission does not have exclusive proposing rights and the EP is largely restricted to being consulted and being able to tender advice. In addition to the Council, the European Council sometimes also exercises a significant role in respect of CFSP/CSDP (as indeed it does from time to time in other policy areas). Another important CFSP/CSDP institutional actor is the High Representative of the Union for Foreign Affairs and Security Policy who, post the Lisbon Treaty, has a base in both the Council and Commission camps.

Compromises and linkages

The diversity of competing interests across the member states, coupled with the nature of the EU's decision-making systems, means that successful policy development is frequently heavily dependent on key actors, especially governments, being prepared to compromise. If they are not so prepared, effective decision-making can be very difficult.

As part of the process wherein compromises provide the basis for agreements, deals are frequently formulated in which different and sometimes seem-

ingly unrelated policy issues are linked. Linking issues together in 'package deals' can open the door to agreements by ensuring that there are prizes for everybody and not, as might be the case when only a specific issue is taken, for just a few.

The European Council has been instrumental in formulating some of the EU's grander compromises and linked deals. For example, the December 2005 summit, which was focused on the 2007–13 financial framework, pulled together an agreement on a range of matters that had been causing considerable difficulties. They included the overall size of the framework, a proposed review of CAP expenditure, and national net contributions to and receipts from the EU's budget (see Chapter 22).

One of the reasons the European Council has become involved in the construction of overarching deals of the kind just described is that other EU institutions and actors, and EU processes as a whole, are ill-adapted to the linking of different policy areas and the construction of complex package deals. The General Affairs and Ecofin Councils have some potential in this regard, especially the former since its coordinating potential was enhanced by the Lisbon Treaty. However, in practice, these Councils are only occasionally able to 'impose' comprehensive solutions on sectoral Councils. As for the sectoral Councils, they do not normally become involved in discussions beyond their immediate policy concern, and they certainly do not have the means of linking difficulties in their own areas with difficulties being experienced by ministers elsewhere.

Much EU policy-making and decision-making thus tends to be rather compartmentalised, and it is within rather than across policy compartments that the trading, bargaining, linkaging and compromising that are so characteristic of EU processes are mainly to be found. At Council working party level, trading may consist of little more than an official conceding a point on line eight of a proposed legal instrument in exchange for support received on line three. At ministerial level, it may result in what amounts to an exchange of resources as, for example, can happen in the Agriculture Council in respect of decisions on product and income support systems.

A useful case study by Langenberg (2004) of decision-making on the Sixth Framework Programme for Research and Technological Development (covering the years 2000–6) may be cited to illustrate the sort of compromises that frequently have to be made to enable agreements to be reached within policy sectors. Langenberg shows that as decision-making processes have become more complex, not least because of the increasing number of member states and the enhanced part played by the EP in deliberations, then so has it become ever more necessary for political actors, especially the member states, to work collaboratively and flexibly with one another. 'Stubbornly defending an isolated position ... is often costly and ineffective in the end' (p. 67). The Sixth Framework Programme decision-making process, which formally lasted from the Commission's issuing of its proposal in early 2001 to EP and Council agreement in June 2002, was therefore necessarily studded with give-and-take from the outset. Without such an approach by the member states no agreement could have been reached, although of course with the approach no state was completely content with the outcome. Amongst changes that were made to the draft proposal as it proceeded were the removal of some of the Commission's most controversial proposals (including on a number of ethical matters) and the referral of some disputed points to later decision-making when specific programmes could be considered.

Inter-institutional cooperation

As this and other chapters show, policy processes are frequently marked by disagreements and disputes between the EU institutions. These disagreements and disputes mostly concern policy matters, but they can also concern institutional matters – especially if an institution is seen to abuse its powers in some way.

But the extent of inter-institutional disagreements and disputes should not be exaggerated, for EU policy processes are also characterised by close, even intense, inter-institutional cooperation of many different kinds. Indeed, not only are policy processes characterised by such cooperation but they are highly dependent on it. If cooperation was not to be generally forthcoming, policy processes would be much more difficult, protracted and halting than they are. For example, processes would always be highly conflictual if the Commission and Council were seen by MEPs to be over-dismissive of EP amendments to legislative proposals, whilst they would be extremely inefficient if the Commission, the Council, and the EP did not

cooperate with each other on legislative planning and timetabling.

Inter-institutional cooperation has grown over the years as the range of policy activities in which the EU is involved has spread, and more especially as policy processes have become more numerous and more complex. The growth has taken many different forms. So, for example, there has been a mushrooming of informal contacts between officials of the Commission, the Council, and the EP, and it is now commonplace for these officials to liaise closely with their counterparts on policy dossiers. At a rather more formal level, there are tripartite meetings – that is, meetings between representatives of the three institutions – of various kinds. For instance, there is a monthly meeting to monitor the progress of proposals identified in the Commission's annual work programme. There is also a monthly meeting of the Presidents of the three institutions, held during the EP Strasbourg plenary week, to consider relevant issues. At an even more formal level, several inter-institutional agreements have been signed to regularise, clarify and generally facilitate inter-institutional relations. An example of such an inter-institutional agreement is the 2003 European Parliament, Council and Commission *Interinstitutional Agreement on Better Law-Making* which sets out a series of initiatives and procedures to improve the coordination of their legislative activity and thereby improve the quality of EU law making (*Official Journal*, C321/1, 31 December 2003).

The ordinary legislative procedure illustrates in a specific way the growth in interinstitutional cooperation. Amongst its consequences it has: 1) encouraged the institutions to devise/accept a compromise text at an early legislative stage; 2) increased the need for the Council to be sensitive to the EP's views; 3) made trialogue meetings between representatives of the Commission, the Council and the EP a vital feature of much EU law-making; and 4) promoted (the already extensive) informal exchanges between representatives of the institutions to sound out positions, discover what may be possible, and identify areas where progress may be made. In short, the procedure has given a powerful stimulus to a 'cultural' change in the relations between the Commission, the Council and the EP that has been under way since the creation of the cooperation procedure by the SEA. At the heart of this cultural change is the notion that the three institutions must work closely with one another, and when legislation is being made they must operate on the basis of a genuinely triangular relationship.

Figures on the proportions of final legislation that are 'attributable' to the Commission, Council and EP must always be treated with care. They cannot fully measure the dynamics of inter-institutional dynamics and bargaining and the relative 'success' of institutions in championing their policy preferences. There are problems, for example, in evaluating the relative importance of Council and EP amendments, as there are also in assessing precisely what has happened when drafts are re-worked to accommodate some, but not all, of Council and EP amendments. Given, however, that under the ordinary legislative procedure all three institutions must judge a draft to be at least acceptable for it to be approved by the end of second reading, the fact that 85 per cent of legislation is so approved is testimony to the 'give-and-take' that is characteristic of legislative processes. As for the conciliation stage, about one quarter of EP amendments are accepted by the Council (they do not have to be accepted by the Commission in conciliation), about 60 per cent are accepted following compromise, and about 15 per cent are withdrawn (Hayes-Renshaw and Wallace, 2006: 227).

Difficulties in effecting radical change

Partly as a consequence of the prevalence of compromise, much EU policy-making and decision-making displays a deep gradualism and incrementalism. It is just not possible for the Commission, the Council Presidency, a national government, or anyone else, to initiate a clear and comprehensive policy proposal, incorporating bold new plans and significant departures from the *status quo*, and expect it to be accepted without being modified significantly – which usually means being watered down. Ambitious proposals, such as the Services Directive – which is aimed at opening up competition in services industries and which was the subject of long inter-institutional negotiations between 2004 and 2006 – customarily find themselves being smothered with modifications, escape clauses, and long transitional periods before full implementation.

The obstacles to innovation and radical change are powerful, and stem from a range of different national, institutional and ideological positions and perspectives. Moreover, some of the obstacles have increased in force over the years. One reason for this is that the way forward is not as clear as it was in the 1960s, when specific treaty obligations were being honoured and 'negative integration' (that is, the dismantling of barriers and the encouragement of trade liberalisation) was generally accepted as the main policy priority. Another reason is that the EU has become more politically and ideologically heterogeneous. This is partly because of enlargement and partly because the broad Keynesian consensus on social and economic policy that existed in most Western European countries until the mid-1970s no longer exists. Although there has been a measure of consensus on the benefits of moving towards a more liberal model of integration, there have been significant differences between the governments of the member states on the extent to which and the ways in which economic life should be directed and managed. A third reason why some obstacles to change have increased in force is that policy development has inevitably created and attracted interests that have a stake in the *status quo*. This is most obviously the case in agriculture, where Commission proposals for reform invariably produce protests from powerful sectional groups and electorally sensitive governments.

All this is not to suggest that change and reform are not possible. On the contrary, since the mid-1980s there clearly have been major changes and reforms of both an institutional and a policy kind. Additions and amendments to the treaties, the (continuing) internal market programme, the creation of EMU, the enlargement process, the Lisbon Strategy, and the movement of the CAP away from price support towards income support are but amongst the most obvious examples of ongoing changes and reforms. These changes and reforms have been driven by a range of external and internal factors, and have been guided and shaped by complex interactions between EU and national political forces. The existence of obstacles to change does not, therefore, preclude it occurring, but what it does do is to ensure that since just about any policy innovation is likely to meet with at least some resistance from some quarter(s), bold initiatives are always likely to be weakened/checked/delayed.

Tactical manoeuvring

Tactical manoeuvring and jockeying for position are universal characteristics of policy processes. However they are especially apparent in the EU as a result of its multiplicity of actors and channels and the diversity of its interests.

It is not possible to present here a comprehensive catalogue of the tactical options that are available to policy actors. However, a sample of the questions that often have to be considered by just one category of key EU actors – national representatives in the Council – will give a flavour of the intricacies and potential importance of tactical considerations, as can be seen in Box 17.6.

Box 17.6

Tactical options to be considered by national representatives in the Council

- Can a coalition be built to create a positive majority or a negative minority? If so, should it be done via bilateral meetings or in an EU forum?
- Is it necessary, for domestic political purposes, to formally note dissent on a proposal to which the government is opposed? (Although most Council business is conducted behind closed doors, much of what goes on in ministerial meetings enters the public domain, Since the Lisbon Treaty 'the Council shall meet in public when it deliberates and votes on a draft legislative act' (Article 16, TEU). capacity.)
- Is it possible to disguise opposition to a proposal by 'hiding' behind another state?
- Should concessions be made in a working party or in COREPER to ensure progress, or should they be held back until the ministers meet in the hope that this will be seen as conciliatory and helpful, with the consequence that it might reap dividends on another occasion?
- Where is the balance to be struck between being seen to be tough in defence of the national interest and being seen to be European-minded and ready to compromise? (Often, on a particular issue, some states have a vested interest in an agreement being reached, whilst the interests of others are best served by the absence of any agreement and, as a result, the absence of EU obligations.)

Different speeds

EU processes are often criticised for being cumbersome and slow. Unquestionably they can be so, but this is far from always being the case. Procedures exist that allow certain types of decision to be made as and when necessary. So, for example, annual budgetary decisions are made according to a pre-determined timetable, Commission legislation can be issued almost immediately, and Council regulations and decisions can be pushed through via urgent procedures if the circumstances require it.

As for 'standard' EU legislation, decision-making processes have speeded up over the years, despite the movement from the one reading consultation procedure to the potentially three reading co-decision procedure. Whereas the average time between the transmission and adoption of a directive was around 36 months in the mid-1980s, it is now just less than 18 months where conciliation is not necessary (about 85 per cent of co-decisions), just over 29 months where conciliations are necessary (about 15 per cent of co-decisions), and just over 20 months as an overall average (Hayes-Renshaw and Wallace, 2006: 67). There are three main factors determining the speed at which particular proposals are adopted. First, whether or not they command initial general support in the Council and the EP. Second, the legislative procedures that apply and the use that is made of them. Third, whether QMV rules apply in the Council. If QMV is available, ministers are not normally prepared to wait – as they must if unanimity is required – for everyone to agree to all aspects of a proposal. Rather it is customary to give a government that objects strongly to a proposal time to adjust to the majority view – perhaps with encouragement via compromises and derogations – and then proceed, either on the basis of an implicit vote by officials or an explicit vote by ministers.

Voting is used most frequently in established

policy areas such as trade, agriculture and the internal market. As Hayes-Renshaw and Wallace (2006: 298) put it, 'it seems to be the case that routinized explicit voting at ministerial level or implicit voting at official level occurs more readily in those policy fields where there is a settled rhythm to EU decision-making; where the default position is that an existing agreement continues rather than that there is no agreement; where national positions are quite clear; and where habits of doing business together are fairly well established'.

Decision-making is thus likely to be at its slowest when a proposal is in a policy area still under construction, when it is highly contested, when it creates difficulties of principle for members of the Council and/or EP, when it is not subject to the dictates of a timetable, and when QMV cannot be used. In such circumstances the EU's decision-making capacity can be relatively weak and it can be very difficult for progress to be made. There may not even be much of a concerted effort to force progress if it is felt in the Council that one or more minority states genuinely have considerable difficulties with the proposal, for governments tend to be very sensitive to the needs of one another – not least because they are aware that they themselves may be in a minority on a future occasion.

An example of a legislative proposal moving only slowly through the EU's legislative processes is the Commission's proposal of October 2003 for an EP and Council regulation concerning the registration, evaluation, authorisation and restriction of chemicals (REACH), together with the creation of a European Chemicals Agency, which was not adopted until December 2006. Designed to commit firms that manufacture and import chemicals to identify and manage risks, the directive replaced more than 40 existing EU laws and shifted the burden of proof that chemicals on the market are safe from the public to the private sector. The reason why the regulation took over three years to adopt was the existence of sharply differing views within all three institutions: differences that were buttressed by intense lobbying from the chemical industry on the one side and environmental and consumer interests on the other. Very broadly speaking, the Council took a 'business-friendly' approach, the Parliament pressed (not least through the tabling of hundreds of amendments) for a tighter regulatory framework, and the Commission sought, whilst being closer to the Council's position, to find a consensual way forward.

The Efficiency of EU Policy Processes

The EU lacks a fixed, central, authoritative point where general priorities can be set out and choices between competing options can be made. In other words, there is no single framework or mechanism for determining and implementing an overall policy view in which the requirements of agriculture, industry, the environment and so on are weighed and evaluated in relation to one another and in relation to resources. As is shown below, new policy planning instruments have been adopted in recent years, but no EU institution has the power or resources to set a comprehensive EU policy programme and then ensure it is carried through.

Within individual policy sectors there are, as has been shown, many obstacles to coherent and properly-ordered policy development. For example, resistance by states to what they regard as an excessive transfer of powers to the EU has resulted in many policy spheres being less integrated and comprehensive in their approach than is, from a policy efficiency perspective, ideally desirable. Regional policy, industrial policy, and environmental policy are examples of policy areas where policy responsibilities are shared between the EU and the states, where frequently the activities of the two levels (three if subnational authorities are added) are not always properly coordinated, and sometimes where they are not even mutually complementary.

EU policy thus tends not to be wholly the outcome of a rational model of decision-making. That is to say, policy is not normally completely made via a procedure in which problems are identified, objectives are set, all possible alternatives for achieving the objectives are carefully evaluated, and the best alternatives are then adopted and proceeded with. Rather, policy tends to evolve in a somewhat messy way, which means that models of policy and decision-making other than the rational model are often also, or even more, useful for highlighting key features of EU processes. Box 17.7 identifies some of these models.

* * *

Box 17.7

Examples of policy- and decision-making models that can assist in the analysis of EU policy- and decision-making processes[*]

- *Political interest* models can be useful in drawing attention to the interaction of competing interests in the EU, to the variable power exercised by these interests in different policy- and decision-making situations, and to the ways in which decisional outcomes are frequently a consequence of bargaining and compromise between interests.

- *Policy network* models are useful in focusing on the ways in which in some policy spheres EU decision-makers and outside interests come together on an at least semi-regular basis for such purposes as information sharing, reconciling differences, and making decisions. Policy networks can vary considerably in character, with some being tight in structure and making provision for frequent intra-network communications whilst others are relatively loose and provide for only occasional communications.

- *Political elite* models highlight the considerable concentrations of power, at official and political levels, that exist across the EU's policy- and decision-making processes. As at national levels, concentration is especially marked in sensitive policy areas such as monetary policy and foreign policy, where processes are more secret and closed than they are in regional or agriculture policy for example. Political elite models also draw attention to the paucity of mechanisms available to EU citizens to ensure direct accountability on the part of EU decision-makers. The fact is that decision-making in the EU is not so tied to or restricted by elections and electoral outcomes as is decision-making at the national level.

- *Institutional* models emphasise how the rules and understandings via which EU decisions are made do much to shape the nature of the decisions themselves. That is, the institutional structures and processes are not neutral. So, for example, when a wide range of national, regional and sectional interests are entitled to be consulted before policy can be developed and decisions can only be made by unanimity in the Council, progress is frequently slow and the outcome is often little more than the lowest common denominator. When, on the other hand, the process is more streamlined – and permits, for example, QMV in the Council of Ministers or the Commission to disburse funds directly – then policy and decision-making is likely to be more decisive and decisions themselves more adventurous and coherent.

[*] On models and conceptualisations of EU policy processes, see also Chapter 23.

But, having identified weaknesses in the quality of EU policy processes, some re-balancing is now in order lest the impression be given of a system that is wholly and uniquely disordered and undemocratic. There are three main points to be made.

The first point is that, in many respects, EU policy processes are not so different from national processes. This is not, of course, to say that important differences do not exist. The international nature of the EU, for example, makes for more diverse and more powerful opposition to its policy initiatives than customarily exists within states. It is also the case that EU decision-makers are less directly accountable than national decision-makers to those who are subject to their deci-

sions. Another difference is that the EU's policy structures are more complex, and in some respects collectively weaker, than their national counterparts. But recognition of these and other differences should not obscure similarities of type – if not perhaps intensity – between EU and national processes: political interest, policy networks, political elite, institutional and other models of decision-making can, after all, throw light on features of the latter as well as the former. For example, in all member states, especially those with coalition governments (which is the norm in most EU states), political accommodation is an everyday occurrence and policy trimming is common. Furthermore, in countries like Germany and Belgium where there is a considerable geographical decentralisation of power, tensions between levels of government over who does what and who pays for what are by no means unusual. In short, many of the EU's policy-making 'problems' – such as the prevalence of incrementalism and of policy slippages – are by no means absent in national political systems.

The second point is that not all EU policy processes consist of cobbling together deals that can satisfy the current complexion of political forces. This certainly is a crucially important feature, but it does not amount to the complete picture. In recent years greater efforts have been made to initiate rather than just react, to look to the medium-term rather than just the short-term, and to pull at least some of the pieces together into coordinated programmes.

At the level of overarching policy coordination, progress towards more forward-looking and coordinated policy planning has, it must be said, been only modest, but it is developing. For example, as is shown in Chapter 22, the financial frameworks that have framed budgetary policy since 1988 have been based on Commission documents that have sought to deal with at least some central priorities on a multi-annual basis.

The Prodi and Barroso Commissions have further sought to strengthen medium-term planning by issuing at the beginning of their terms of office documents setting out policy priorities. Designed to provide guidelines for their five-year terms, the documents have been followed up by the issuing of annual policy strategies setting out political priorities for the following year. These in turn have fed into the annual legislative work programmes, which are now presented in November rather than, as before, at the beginning of the year in which they are to apply.

Of course, effective EU planning requires that Commission plans and priorities be tied in with those of the other main institutions. This has been something of a problem, with both the Council and the EP being protective of their right to determine their own priorities – as witnessed, for example, by Council Presidencies setting out the goals for their six-months tenure, and by both the Council and the EP specifying their political objectives at the beginning of the annual budgetary process. Nonetheless, collaboration on planning between the institutions is improving, with a variety of consultative and information-exchange mechanisms now in place designed to try and ensure that the three institutions work in the same policy direction.

Medium-term planning mechanisms agreed at the June 2002 Seville European Council meeting have also improved the EU's ability to look beyond the immediate and the pressing, with the European Council adopting three-year multi-annual strategic programmes that are drafted by the six member states that occupy the Presidency over the period and with these programmes informing Council of Ministers operational programmes. Since 2005 these operational programmes have covered three Council Presidencies and have formed a base from which the six-months Presidencies have planned their work programmes. The Lisbon Treaty's creation of eighteen-month 'team' Council Presidencies further strengthens this ability of the Council to plan beyond six-month periods, and the creation of the new post of European Council President should also strengthen planning capacity from the very top.

Coordinated forward thinking and planning has also improved over the years in particular policy sectors, with the existence of medium- to long-term policy objectives and multi-annual programmes. These are drawn up by the Commission, usually in consultation with appropriate consultative committees and committees of experts, and have to be approved by the Council to be given effect. They appear in various forms. For example: Green Papers, such as the 2005 Green Paper *Doing More With Less: Green Paper on Energy Efficiency* (European Commission, 2005d); communications, such as the 2005 communication *i2010 A European Information Society for Growth and Employment,* which set out a strategy for modernising and deploying policy instruments to stimulate the development of the digital economy (European Commission, 2005c); framework and legislation programmes, such as the multi-annual programmes for the environment and for research and technological development (see Chapter 19); and action programmes.

It is worth saying a little about action programmes to illustrate how, within specified fields of activity, a measure of coordinated development over a planned medium-term period is possible. Action programmes vary in nature, from the broad and general to the highly specific. Broad and general programmes typically include measures to improve the monitoring and supervision of existing legislation, ideas for new legislation, running a pilot scheme, and spending programmes. Amongst the fields of activity where such action programmes exist are equal opportunities, public health, and access to educational training programmes. In contrast, specific action programmes are more specialised in their areas of concern and tighter in their provisions. Examples are the social research programmes on such matters as safety in coalmines and industrial hygiene, which are given appropriations for a given period and provide up to about 60 per cent of the cost of approved research projects.

The third and final 're-balancing' point to be made about EU policy processes is that critical judgements of them ought to be placed in the context of the very considerable degree of policy cooperation and integration that has been achieved at the EU level. There is no comparable international development where states have voluntarily transferred so many policy responsibilities to a collective organisation of states, and in so doing have surrendered so much of their national sovereignty. It is hardly surprising, given the enormity of the exercise, that pressures and desires for cooperation and integration should so often be challenged, and held in check, by caution, uncertainty, conflict and competition.

Concluding Remarks

The EU thus has a wide, varied, and in many respects highly complex set of policy processes. Of course, this is to some extent also true of the member states, but not like anything to the same degree. A number of reasons account for the EU's distinctiveness in this respect, of which the varying preferences of the member states regarding which policies they wish to see developed and in what ways are especially important.

The overall policy process picture embraces a number of operating principles that feature to different degrees within particular processes. This is seen most evidently in the varying nature of the intergovernmental/supranational balance.

The chapter has, however, sought to emphasise that notwithstanding the seemingly bewildering overall nature of EU policy processes, some order can be brought to them by recognising that they can be seen as falling within four broad formworks. They are frameworks, moreover, within which a number of recurring features can be detected.

A particularly important dimension of policy processes is, of course, legislative processes. These are examined in the next chapter.

Chapter 18

Making and Applying EU Legislation

This chapter examines the making and applying of EU legislation. Regarding the making of legislation, attention is focused on legislation that is subject to a full legislative procedure, which generally means legislation that is thought to be significant and/or concerned with establishing principles. The reason for this focus is that legislation that does not require a full legislative procedure – which is usually narrow in focus and of an administrative and implementing character – was examined in Chapter 8.

By way of setting the processes that are examined in the chapter in context, Figure 18.1 sets out the key organisational features of EU legislative and application processes and the positions of the main EU institutions within them. Concerning the legislative processes, it is with those to the left of the figure that this chapter is concerned.

Figure 18.1 Principal features of the EU's legislative procedures

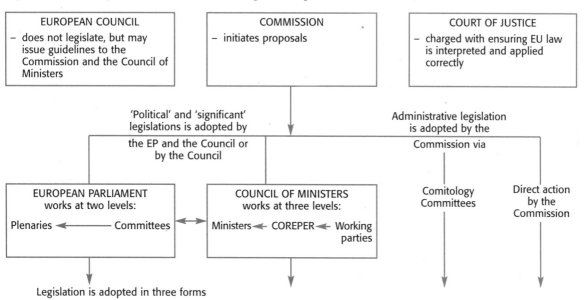

EUROPEAN COUNCIL
– does not legislate, but may issue guidelines to the Commission and the Council of Ministers

COMMISSION
– initiates proposals

COURT OF JUSTICE
– charged with ensuring EU law is interpreted and applied correctly

'Political' and 'significant' legislations is adopted by the EP and the Council or by the Council

Administrative legislation is adopted by the Commission via

EUROPEAN PARLIAMENT works at two levels:
Plenaries ← Committees

COUNCIL OF MINISTERS works at three levels:
Ministers ← COREPER ← Working parties

Comitology Committees

Direct action by the Commission

Legislation is adopted in three forms
1 *Regulations* are binding on member states
2 *Decisions* are binding on those to whom they are addressed
3 *Directives* are binding as to the result to be achieved, but require transposition by the appropriate national authorities

National authorities, subject to a general supervision by the Commission, carry the main responsibility for implementing EU law

The EU's Legislative Procedures

Not counting the special cases of the annual budgetary process (see Chapter 22) and the little-used category of European Parliament acts, since the Lisbon Treaty entered into force in December 2009 the EU has had three legislative procedures: 'consultation', 'ordinary' (called 'co-decision' pre-Lisbon Treaty), and 'consent' ('assent' pre-Lisbon Treaty). Each of these procedures contains internal variations, the most important of which is that QMV is available to the Council for some types of decisions whereas unanimity is required for others.

Prior to the Lisbon Treaty there was a fourth legislative procedure: 'cooperation'. This two reading procedure, which was created by the SEA, was widely used from the entry into force of the SEA until the entry into force of the Amsterdam Treaty, but the Maastricht and Amsterdam Treaties combined to virtually replace it by the co-decision procedure (see Chapter 5). Indeed, the cooperation procedure would have been completely abolished by the Amsterdam Treaty had the member

---

Box 18.1

Special legislative procedures

I   **Ad hoc procedures**
1   Annual budget – joint decision of EP and Council.

II   **European Parliament acts**
2   Statute for Members of the European Parliament. (Adoption by EP after obtaining consent of Council and after consulting Commission.)
3   Provisions governing the exercise of the right of inquiry. (Adoption by EP after obtaining consent of Council and Commission.)
4   Statute of European Ombudsman. (Adoption by EP after obtaining consent of Council and Commission.)

III   **Council acts**

A   *Unanimity and consent of European Parliament*
5   Measures to combat discrimination.
6   Extension of citizenship-related rights. (National ratifications also required.)
7   European Public Prosecutor's Office.
8   Uniform electoral procedure . (On initiative from and after consent of EP. National ratifications also required.)
9   Multiannual financial frameworks.

B   *Unanimity and consultation of European Parliament*
10   Accession to the European Convention on Human Rights. (Council decision on a proposal from the negotiator of the agreement [in principle the Commission], with consent of EP.)
11   Measures concerning social security or social protection.
12   Citizenship: right to vote and stand for election in member state of residence in municipal and European elections.
13   Adoption of measures that constitute a step backwards in Union law as regards the liberalisation of the movement of capital to or from third countries.
14   Measures concerning passports, identity cards and residence permits.

→

states not been reluctant to tamper with the application of the procedure to four aspects of EMU for fear of opening up the whole EMU issue in the Amsterdam IGC. The Lisbon Treaty saw to the procedure's complete abolition. (Should any reader wish to know about the nature of the cooperation procedure, it is described fully in the third edition of this book [1994]).

As its post-Lisbon name implies, the ordinary procedure is the most used of the EU's three legislative procedures. Since its creation by the Maastricht Treaty, its remit has been so extended by the Amsterdam, Nice and Lisbon treaties that it is now used for the great majority of legislation. Indeed, in addition to the telling name change to the procedure made by the Lisbon Treaty, the Treaty further emphasised the procedure's mainstreaming by referring to the other procedures as 'special legislative procedures'. So widely used is the ordinary procedure that rather than list its many applications, Box 18.1 confines itself to listing the legislative acts to which the consultation and consent procedures apply: that is the acts that are not subject to the ordinary procedure.

The nature of the EU's three post-Lisbon legislative procedures will now be described.

Box 18.1 *continued*

15   Judicial cooperation in civil matters concerning measures relating to family law with cross-border implications.*
16   Operational police cooperation.
17   Interventions by the authority of a member state on the territory of another member state.
18   Harmonisation of turnover taxes and indirect taxation.
19   Approximation of provisions with a direct impact on the internal market.
20   Language arrangements for European intellectual property rights.
21   Replacing the Protocol on the excessive deficit procedure.
22   Specific tasks of European Central Bank concerning prudential supervision.
23   Social policy: social security and social protection of workers, protection of workers where their employment contract is terminated, representation and collective defence, conditions of employment for third-country nationals.**
24   Environment: provisions of a fiscal nature, town and country planning, management of water resources, land use and the supply and diversification of energy resources.
25   Energy: fiscal measures.
26   Association of overseas countries and territories with the Union – rules and procedure.
27   Jurisdiction of the Court in the area of intellectual property.
28   Modification of the Protocol on the Statute of the European Investment Bank.
29   Union own resources – ceiling and creation of new resources. (National ratifications also required.)

C   *Qualified majority and consent of EP*
30   Implementing measures of the Union's own resources system.

D   *Qualified majority and consultation of EP*
31   Measures to facilitate diplomatic protection.
32   Research: specific programmes implementing framework programme.
33   Outermost regions.

* The Council may take a unanimous decision, after consulting the EP, to switch to the ordinary legislative procedure (second subparagraph of paragraph 3 of Article 65 [81] TFEU).
** The Council may take a unanimous decision, after consulting the EP, to switch to the ordinary legislative procedure for points (d), (f) and (g) (second subparagraph of paragraph 2 of Article 137 [153] TFEU).

The consultation procedure

Prior to the SEA, the consultation procedure was the only procedure for non-administrative legislation. However, the creation of the cooperation and assent procedures by the SEA and of the co-decision procedure by the Maastricht Treaty, coupled with the 'elevation' of policy areas from the consultation procedure to these other procedures by the SEA and the Maastricht, Amsterdam and Lisbon Treaties, has meant that, as Box 18.1 shows, the number of policy areas to which the consultation procedure applies is now limited. Amongst the areas to which it still does apply are important aspects of social, fiscal, justice and home affairs, and citizenship policies.

The consultation procedure is a single reading procedure in which the Council is the sole final decision-maker. However, it cannot take a final decision until it has received the opinion of the EP. On some proposals it must also await the opinions of the European Economic and Social Committee (EESC) and the Committee of the Regions (CoR).

Initiation

The starting point of any legislative proposal is when somebody suggests that the EU should act on a matter. Most likely this will be the Commission, the Council, or the EP: the Commission because, apart from some JHA areas, it is the only body with the authority formally to table a legislative proposal, and because of its special expertise in, and responsibility for, EU affairs; the Council because of its political weight, its position as the natural conduit for national claims and interests, and its power under Article 241 TFEU to request, by a simple majority vote, the Commission 'to undertake any studies the Council considers desirable for the attainment of the common objectives, and to submit to it any appropriate proposals'; and the EP because of the desire of MEPs to be active and because under Article 225 TFEU 'The European Parliament may, acting by a majority of its component members, request the Commission to submit any appropriate proposal on matters on which it considers that a Union act is required for the purpose of implementing the Treaties'.

Beyond the Commission, the Council, and the EP there are many other possible sources of EU legislation, but little progress can be made unless the Commission decides to take up an issue and draft a proposal. Many factors may result in it deciding to do so, the most frequent being that such legislation is required as part of an ongoing policy commitment or programme. Sometimes, however, it is very difficult, when looking at specific proposals, to determine why the Commission decided to act and to identify precisely who originated the initiative. For example, a Commission proposal that seems to have been a response to a Council request may, on inspection, be traced beyond the Council to a national pressure group influencing a minister, who then gradually and informally introduced the issue into the Council as an option to be considered. Similarly, a Commission proposal may seem to have been a response to points raised in an EP committee or to representations from Europe-wide interests, but in fact the Commission may itself have dropped hints to MEPs or to interests that they should look at the matter (thus reinforcing the Commission's own position *vis-à-vis* the Council).

A further possible source of legislation was created by the Lisbon Treaty: 'the citizen's initiative'. Under Article 11(4) TEU:

> Not less than one million citizens who are nationals of a significant number of Member States may take the initiative of inviting the European Commission, within the framework of its powers, to submit any appropriate proposal on a matter where citizens consider that a legal act of the Union is required for the purpose of implementing the Treaties.

It remains to be seen how this provision will apply in practice but, in the age of the internet, it can be anticipated that the conditions for valid citizens' initiatives will be relatively easily met.

Preparation of a text

In preparing a text, a number of matters must be carefully considered by the Commission in addition to the direct policy considerations at issue.

- The proposal must have the correct legal base – that is, it must be based on the correct treaty article(s). Normally this is a straightforward matter and there is no room for argument, but sometimes disputes arise when a proposal cuts across policy areas and the Commission chooses a legal base that is deemed by a policy actor to be unsatisfactory. For example, a member state that is concerned about the possible implications of a policy proposal is likely to prefer a procedure where unanimity rather than QMV applies in the Council, whilst the EP always prefers the ordinary legislative procedure to be used rather than the consultation procedure because this gives it a potential veto. The question of legal base can therefore be controversial, and has resulted in references to the ECJ.

- Justification of the proposal must be given in terms of the application of the subsidiarity and proportionality principles. This takes the form of answers to a series of questions on subsidiarity and proportionality in the explanatory memorandum that is attached to each proposal.
- Where appropriate, justification must be given in terms of the environmental impact of the proposal. This usually applies, for example, to transport and agriculture proposals.
- The probable financial implications for the EU budget of the proposal must be assessed.

The standard way in which proposals are prepared is as follows. The process begins with a middle-ranking official in the 'lead' DG assuming the main responsibility for the dossier: that is for preparing and looking after the Commission's draft. This way of working emphasises individual responsibility, means that officials are or become highly expert in particular policy areas, and results in the distribution of information about policy proposals being very dependent, in the early stages at least, on the preferred approach of officials responsible for dossiers.

Formal communications within the Commission about a proposal tend initially to be of a vertical rather than of a horizontal kind. That is to say, they tend primarily to be up and down the lead DG – known as the *chef de file* – rather than across and between DGs. This rather hierarchical and compartmentalised approach can make for difficulties, though creative and imaginative officials make appropriate, and if necessary extensive, use of informal communications – through telephone calls, e-mails and meetings – with potentially interested officials elsewhere in the services so as to ensure that there are not too many inter-service problems at a later stage of proceedings.

Whether or not they are kept fully informed of developments from an early drafting stage, other DGs with a possible interest in a proposal must be given the opportunity at some point to make their views known. This may involve the convening of one or more inter-service meetings. Other Commission services with which there must be exchanges and agreements include the Secretariat General (which has amongst its responsibilities the overall coordination of the Commission's work schedule) and the Legal Service (which amongst other things checks the legal base of proposals).

When all directly involved Commission interests have given their approval, the draft is sent to the *cabinet* of the Commissioner responsible for the subject. The *cabinet*, which may or may not have been involved in informal discussions with Commission officials as the proposal was being drafted, may or may not attempt to persuade Commission officials to rework the draft before submitting it to the Commissioner for approval.

When the Commissioner is satisfied, she or he asks the Secretariat General to submit the draft to the College of Commissioners. The draft is then scrutinised, and possibly amended, by the *chefs de cabinet* at their weekly meeting. If the draft is judged to be uncontroversial the Commissioners may adopt it by written procedure; if it is controversial the Commissioners may, after debate, accept it, reject it, amend it, or refer it back to the relevant DG for further consideration.

In preparing a text officials usually find themselves the focus of attention from many directions. Knowing that the Commission's thinking is normally at its most flexible at this preliminary stage, and knowing too that once a proposal is formalised it is more difficult for it to be changed, interested parties use whatever means they can to press their views. Four factors most affect the extent to which the Commission is prepared to listen to outside interests at this pre-proposal stage:

- What contacts and channels have already been regularised in the sector and which ways of proceeding have proved to be effective in the past?
- What political considerations arise and how important is it to incorporate different sectional and national views from the outset?
- How dependent is the Commission on outside knowledge and expertise?
- How do the relevant Commission officials prefer to work?

Assuming, as it is normally reasonable to do, Commission receptivity, there are several ways in which external views may be brought to the attention of those involved in the drafting of a proposal. The Commission itself may request a report, perhaps from a university or a research institute. Interest groups may submit briefing documents. Professional lobbyists, politicians, and officials from the Permanent Representations may press preferences in informal meetings. EP committees and EESC sections may be sounded out. And use may be made of the extensive advisory committee system that is clustered around the Commission (see Chapter 8).

There is thus no standard consultative pattern or procedure. An important consequence of this is that governmental involvement in the preparation of Commission texts varies considerably. Indeed, not only is there variation in involvement, there is also variation in knowledge of the Commission's intentions. Sometimes governments are fully aware of Commission thinking, because national officials have been formally consulted in committees of experts. Sometimes sectional interests represented on consultative committees will let their governments know what is going on. Sometimes governments will be abreast of developments as a result of having tapped sources within the Commission, most probably through officials in their Permanent Representations. But occasionally governments are not much aware of proposals until they are published.

The time that elapses between the decision to initiate a proposal and the publication by the Commission of its text naturally depends on a number of factors. Is there any urgency? How keen is the Commission to press ahead? How widespread are the consultations? Is there consensus amongst key external actors and does the Commission want their prior support? Is there consensus within the Commission itself? Not surprisingly, elapses of well over a year are common.

The opinions of the European Parliament, the European Economic and Social Committee, and the Committee of the Regions

On publication, the Commission's text is submitted to the Council of Ministers for a decision and to the EP and, if appropriate, the EESC and the CoR, for their opinions.

The EP is by far the most influential of the consultative bodies. Though it does not have full legislative powers under the consultation procedure, it has enough weapons in its arsenal to ensure that its views are given serious consideration, particularly by the Commission. Its representational claims are one source of its influence. The quality of its arguments and its suggestions are another. And it has the power of delay, by virtue of the requirement that the EP's opinion must be known before the proposal can be formally adopted by the Council.

As was shown in Chapter 11, most of the detailed work undertaken by the EP on proposed legislation is handled by its standing committees and, to a lesser extent, its political groups. Both the committees and the groups advise MEPs on how to vote in plenary.

The usual way in which plenaries act to bring influence to bear is to vote on amendments to the Commission's proposal, but not to vote on the draft legislative resolution – which constitutes the EP's opinion – until the Commission states, as it is obliged to do, whether or not it will change its text to incorporate the amendments that have been approved by the EP. (Under the consultation, and ordinary procedures, the Commission can amend, or even withdraw, its text at any time, apart from at the third stage of the ordinary procedure.) If the amendments are accepted by the Commission a favourable opinion is issued, and the amended text becomes the text that the Council considers. If all or some of the amendments are not accepted by the Commission, the EP can exert pressure by not issuing an opinion and referring the proposal back to the committee responsible. A reference back can also be made if the whole proposal is judged to be unacceptable. Withholding an opinion does not, it should be emphasised, mean that the EP has a veto power, because it is legally obliged to issue opinions and the ECJ has referred to the duty of loyal cooperation between EU institutions. What the withholding of opinions does do, however, is to give the EP the often useful bargaining and pressurising tool of the power of delay.

For reasons that are outlined in Chapter 11 and which are considered further below, it is difficult to estimate the precise impact the EP has on EU legislation. In general terms, however, it can be said that the record in the context of the consultation procedure is mixed.

Photo 18.1 MEPs voting on a legislative proposal

On the 'positive' side, the Commission is normally sympathetic to the EP's views and accepts about three-quarters of its amendments. The Council is less sympathetic and accepts well under half of the amendments, but that still means that many EP amendments, on many different policy matters, find their way into the final legislative texts.

On the 'negative' side, there are three main points to be made. First, there is not much the EP can do if the Council rejects its opinion. The best it can normally hope for is a conciliation meeting with the Council (not to be confused with a conciliation committee meeting under the ordinary procedure), but such meetings usually achieve little – mainly because the Council has no wish to re-open questions that may put at risk its own, often exhaustively negotiated, agreements. Second, the Council occasionally – though much less than it used to – takes a decision 'in principle' or 'subject to Parliament's opinion', before the opinion has even been delivered. In such circumstances the EP's views, once known, are unlikely to result in the Council having second thoughts. Third, it is possible for the text of proposals to be changed after the EP has issued its opinion. There is some safeguard against the potential implications of this insofar as the Court of Justice has indicated that the Council should refer a legislative proposal back to the EP if the Council substantially amends the proposal after the EP has issued its opinion. Moreover, there is a Council–EP understanding that the former will not make substantial changes without referring back to the EP. In practice, however, the question of what constitutes a substantial amendment is open to interpretation and references back do not always occur.

* * *

The EESC and the CoR are not so well placed as the EP to influence the control of legislative proposals. As was explained in Chapter 13, a major reason for this is that their formal powers are not as great: while they must be consulted on draft legislation in many policy spheres, consultation is only optional in some.

Furthermore, when they are consulted the Council or the Commission may lay down a very tight timetable, can go ahead if no opinion is issued by a specified date, and cannot be frustrated by delays if either the EESC or the CoR wants changes to a text. Other sources of weakness include the part-time capacity of their members, the personal rather than representational nature of much of their memberships, and the perception by many interests and regional bodies that advisory committees and direct forms of lobbying are more effective channels of influence.

Decision-making in the Council

The Council does not wait for the views of the EP, the EESC and the CoR before it begins to examine a proposal. Indeed, governments may begin preparing their positions for the Council, and informal discussions and deliberations may even take place within the Council itself, before the formal referral from the Commission.

The standard procedure in the Council is for the proposal to be referred initially to a working party of national representatives for detailed examination. The representatives have two principal tasks: to ensure that the interests of their country are safeguarded, and to try to reach an agreement on a text. Inevitably these two responsibilities do not always coincide, with the consequence that working party deliberations can be protracted. Progress depends on many factors: the controversiality of the proposal; the extent to which it benefits or damages states differentially; the number of countries, especially large countries, pressing for progress; the enthusiasm and competence of the Presidency; the tactical skills of the national representatives and their capacity to trade disputed points (both of which are dependent on personal ability and the sort of briefs laid down for representatives by their governments); and the flexibility of the Commission in agreeing to change its text.

Once a working party has gone as far as it can with a proposal – which can mean reaching a general agreement, agreeing on most points but with reservations entered by some countries on particular points, or very little agreement at all on the main issues – reference is made upwards to COREPER or, in a few cases a specialised committee – most notably the Special Committee on Agriculture (SCA). At this level, the Permanent Representatives (in COREPER II), their deputies (in COREPER I), or senior officials (as in the SCA) concern themselves not so much with the technical details of a proposal as with its policy and, to some extent, its political, implications. So far as is possible, differences left over from the working party are sorted out. When this cannot be done, bases for possible agreement may be identified, and the proposal is then either referred back to the working party for further detailed consideration or forwarded to the ministers for political resolution.

All proposals must be formally approved by the ministers. Those that have been agreed at a lower level of the Council machinery are placed on the ministers' agenda as 'A' points and are normally quickly ratified. Where, however, outstanding problems and differences have to be considered a number of things can happen. One is that the political authority that ministers carry, and the preparatory work undertaken by officials prior to ministerial meetings, may clear the way for an agreed settlement: perhaps reached quickly over lunch, perhaps hammered out in long and frequently adjourned Council sessions. A second possibility is that a vote is taken when the treaty article(s) upon which the proposal is based so allows. However, as Box 18.1 shows, unanimity is normally required under the consultation procedure. A third possibility is that no agreement is reached and a vote is either not possible under the treaties or is not judged to be appropriate.

If no agreement can be reached in the Council, the legislative process does not necessarily end in failure. The proposal may well be referred back down the Council machinery for further deliberations, referred back to the Commission with a request for changes to the existing text, or referred to a future meeting in the hope that shifts in position will take place and the basis of a solution will be found. If agreement is reached, the decision-making process at EU level ends with the Council's adoption of a text.

The ordinary legislative procedure

The co-decision procedure was created by the Maastricht Treaty. But, it was not named as such in the Treaty but rather was referred to, throughout the Treaty, by reference to the article that set out its provisions – Article 189b. However, since the procedure provided for co-decision making by the EP and

Council, it came to be referred to in everyday use as the co-decision procedure. The Amsterdam Treaty, which amended aspects of the procedure, similarly did not formally name it, with the consequence that under the re-numbered TEC it officially became the Article 251 procedure. The TFEU did finally formally name the procedure, but in recognition of the fact that it was now the dominant procedure, and would be even more so when the Treaty came into effect, called it not the co-decision procedure but rather the ordinary legislative procedure. The procedure is set out in Article 294.

The co-decision procedure grew out of and extended the cooperation procedure, which was created by the SEA. The cooperation procedure was established for two main reasons. First, it was seen as being necessary, especially with the SEM programme in mind, to increase the efficiency, and more especially the speed, of decision-making processes. This was achieved by enabling QMV to be used in the Council when decisions were made under the procedure and by laying down time limitations for the institutions to act during the later stages of the procedure. Second, it was a response to concerns about 'the democratic deficit', and more particularly pressures for more powers to be given to the EP. This was achieved by introducing a two-reading stage for legislation, and increasing the EP's leverage – though not to the point of giving it a veto – over the Council at second reading.

Democratic deficit concerns and pressures from the EP were also very much behind the creation of the co-decision procedure in the Maastricht Treaty. While the cooperation procedure had certainly increased the EP's influence, it did not give the EP the power of veto if the Council was resolved to press ahead with a legislative proposal. The co-decision procedure gave the EP this power of veto.

The application of the procedure was restricted to 15 treaty articles under the Maastricht Treaty, but was extended to 37 by the Amsterdam Treaty. As a result of the Amsterdam extensions, most EU legislation apart from agriculture, justice and home affairs, trade, fiscal harmonisation, and EMU issues now became subject to co-decision. The Treaty also made provision for much of the JHA policy area to be later changed from consultation to co-decision. The Nice Treaty further extended the reach of the procedure, but only marginally: seven additional treaty articles were embraced, but none of these covered a core policy area. However,

two of the core policy areas remaining outside of the remit of the procedure – agriculture and trade – were included in the raft of extensions to the reach of the procedure that was part of the Lisbon Treaty. There are now relatively few policy areas that are not subject to the procedure.

The nature of the ordinary legislative procedure will now be described. It will be seen that it is a one, two, or three stage procedure. Proposals only advance to the third stage if the EP and the Council cannot reach agreement at the first or second stage. It will also be seen that it is a procedure that strongly encourages the EP, the Council, and the Commission to engage in intensive and extensive inter-institutional bargaining. Such bargaining was already developing before the co-decision procedure was established as a result of the creation of the cooperation procedure, and under co-decision it became an absolutely central part of the legislative process. The nature of the ordinary procedure is such that if the three institutions do not liaise and work closely with one another, protracted delays may occur in the early legislative stages and impasses may occur in the later stages. Since, though they may disagree on points of detail, each of the institutions normally wants legislative proposals to become legislative texts, the inevitable requirement is that they spend a lot of time communicating with one another – in forums ranging from a mushrooming number of formal inter-institutional meetings to casual off-the-record conversations between key institutional policy actors. Figure 18.2 provides a diagrammatic representation of the procedure.

First stage

The pre-proposal processes are much as they are under the consultation procedure, though with the Commission taking rather more care as to the EP's likely reactions given its greater powers under the ordinary procedure.

After the Commission has published its proposal, it is examined by the EP and the Council through their normal mechanisms: that is, with most of the detailed work being undertaken by the relevant EP committee(s) and by Council working parties and COREPER.

Prior to the Amsterdam Treaty it was not possible for a text to be adopted at this first legislative stage under co-decision. However, as part of a general attempt to streamline what was widely agreed to be a

Figure 18.2 The ordinary legislative procedure

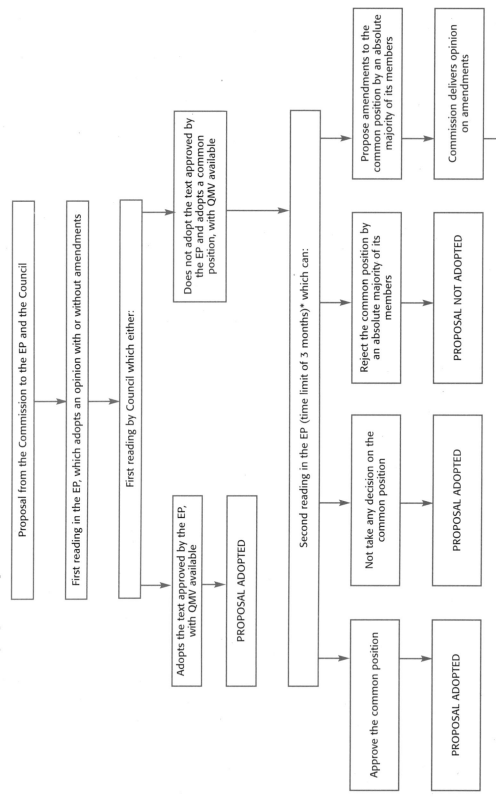

Proposal from the Commission to the EP and the Council

First reading in the EP, which adopts an opinion with or without amendments

First reading by Council which either:

Adopts the text approved by the EP, with QMV available

PROPOSAL ADOPTED

Does not adopt the text approved by the EP and adopts a common position, with QMV available

Second reading in the EP (time limit of 3 months)* which can:

Approve the common position

PROPOSAL ADOPTED

Not take any decision on the common position

PROPOSAL ADOPTED

Reject the common position by an absolute majority of its members

PROPOSAL NOT ADOPTED

Propose amendments to the common position by an absolute majority of its members

Commission delivers opinion on amendments

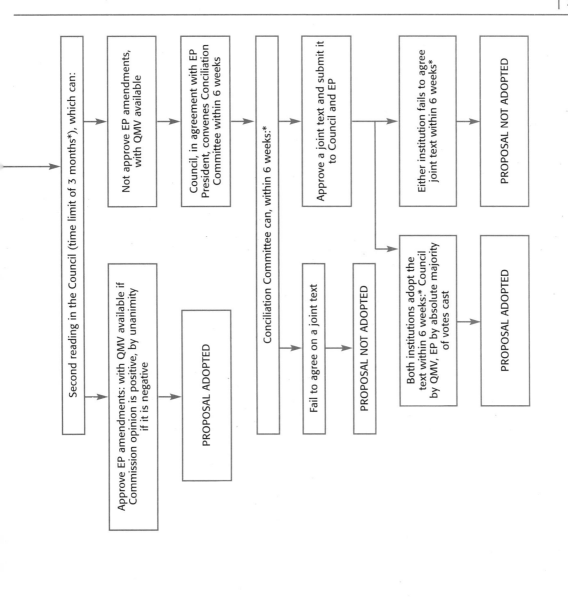

Second reading in the Council (time limit of 3 months*), which can:

Not approve EP amendments, with QMV available

Council, in agreement with EP President, convenes Conciliation Committee within 6 weeks

Conciliation Committee can, within 6 weeks:*

Approve a joint text and submit it to Council and EP

Either institution fails to agree joint text within 6 weeks*

PROPOSAL NOT ADOPTED

Approve EP amendments: with QMV available if Commission opinion is positive, by unanimity if it is negative

PROPOSAL ADOPTED

Fail to agree on a joint text

PROPOSAL NOT ADOPTED

Both institutions adopt the text within 6 weeks:* Council by QMV, EP by absolute majority of votes cast

PROPOSAL ADOPTED

* The periods of three months and six weeks may be extended by a period of one month and two weeks respectively if both institutions agree

somewhat cumbersome procedure, the Treaty made provision for a text to be adopted at first reading providing the Council and the EP agree on its contents and that other 'standard' legislative requirements are met – notably the EESC and the CoR are consulted as appropriate, and amendments with which the Commission does not agree receive unanimous support in the Council. (This latter requirement applies to all stages of all legislative procedures, apart from the final – conciliation – stage of the ordinary procedure.)

Since the Amsterdam Treaty change, around 60 per cent of legislative proposals are agreed at first reading stage (Judge and Earnshaw, 2008: 232). Many of these proposals cover technical matters, consolidated texts, or relations with third countries, though a few are also in 'mainstream' policy areas.

If the Council and the EP do not reach agreement at the first reading, the Council, on receipt of the EP's opinion, adopts a common position – with QMV being available for this purpose.

Second stage

At its second reading, the EP can approve, amend, reject, or take no action on a common position. To assist it in its deliberations, the Council must provide the EP with an explanation of the common position and the Commission must also explain its position, including in respect of whether or not it will accept EP amendments.

If the EP approves or takes no action on a common position the Council can, within three months, adopt it as a legislative act (using the same voting rules as applied at the first reading). If the EP rejects the common position by an absolute majority of its members the proposal falls. (In practice this rarely happens. One example where it did occur in July 2005 when MEPs, dissatisfied with the responses of the Commission and Council to the EP's first reading amendments, voted overwhelmingly to reject the Council's common position on a software patent law.) And if the EP amends the common position by an absolute majority of its members and the Council at its second reading is unable to accept the text approved by the EP, a third legislative stage occurs.

Prior to the entry into force of the Amsterdam Treaty changes, about 60 per cent of legislative procedures were completed by the end of stage two. This figure has subsequently risen to about 90 per cent – with, in addition to the above-noted 60 per cent of completions at first reading, 30 per cent of completions at second reading (Judge and Earnshaw, 2008: 232).

Third stage

This stage opens, within six weeks of the Council failing to approve the text supported by the EP, with the contested proposal being referred to a conciliation committee composed of an equal number of representatives of the Council and the EP. As can be deduced from the figures given above, about 10 per cent of legislative proposals require the convening of a conciliation committee.

In conciliation committees, of which about ten are created in an average year, the Council is normally represented by senior officials from the national Permanent Representations to the EU and the EP is represented by a mixture of semi-permanent conciliation committee members and members of relevant Parliamentary committees. Up to 100 people can be in the room during conciliation meetings, which makes them rather unwieldy and unsuitable for real negotiations.

Accordingly, conciliation meetings are almost invariably preceded by smaller tripartite meetings, known as trialogues, which bring together on a more informal basis key Commission, Council and EP representatives. Normally about 25 people attend trialogues. In around half of the cases that are referred to a conciliation committee, a joint text is agreed in a trialogue meeting, leaving the full conciliation committee to approve the text without discussion. (It might be added here that the success of trialogues at conciliation stage has resulted in them also coming to be much-used 'upstream' at first and second reading stages.)

If the conciliation committee agrees on a joint text – and it normally has six weeks to do so – the proposal is referred back to the Council and the EP for final adoption within a period of six weeks. In this final vote the Council acts by QMV and the EP by a majority of the votes cast. (When the co-decision procedure was created in the Maastricht Treaty, the Council could attempt to impose the common position in the event of non-agreement in the conciliation committee, but this possibility was removed by the Amsterdam Treaty.) Failure by the Council and the EP to agree on a text means the proposal cannot be adopted.

It is unusual for legislative proposals to fail at this third legislative stage. The first failure under the post-Amsterdam co-decision procedure occurred in July 2001, when a proposed directive on corporate takeover bids that had been agreed in conciliation committee failed by just one vote to be given Parliament's approval (the vote was tied at 273 in favour, 273 against, and 22 abstentions). A number of factors contributed to the EP vote, one of them being that the German government, after heavy lobbying from German companies, withdrew its support from the Council's common position and encouraged German MEPs to vote against the agreed text – which virtually all of them did.

When a legislative proposal does fail at the conciliation stage, it is common for the Commission to subsequently re-present it in a form that enables it to be approved by the Council and the EP.

The consent procedure

The consent procedure, which was established as the assent procedure by the SEA, appears at first sight to be simple in form, being a single stage procedure in which proposed measures that are subject to it have to be approved by both the Council and the EP. The procedure does not allow the EP to make amendments.

However, the procedure is in fact rather more complex than initially it appears. This is primarily because although unanimity is normally required in the Council it is not always so, whilst in the EP a majority of those voting suffices for some measures but an absolute majority is required for others. The complexity is extreme in respect of breaches and potential breaches by member states of the fundamental principles on which the EU is founded, as the extracts from Article 7 TEU post-Lisbon on p. 95 show.

The consent procedure is not used for 'normal' legislation but is reserved for special types of decision. In addition to the just-mentioned case of action arising from breaches by member states of the EU's fundamental principles, other types of decision for which it

is used include international agreements of certain kinds, EU enlargements, the multiannual financial frameworks, and the extension of citizenship-related rights.

The precise rules and powers exercised by the EU institutions under the procedure vary according to the type of decision for which consent is being sought. For example, if the decision involves a matter that has involved the preparation of detailed proposals, as with association and cooperation agreements with third countries, the Commission is in a very strong position to influence and shape the outcomes, especially if, as is sometimes the case, unanimity is not required in the Council. If, however, unanimity is required and matters of political principle are of crucial importance, for example with regard to citizenship issues and with the devising of a uniform electoral procedure for EP elections, then the Commission is much less favourably placed and the views of the national governments, and of the Council collectively, are crucial.

As for the EP, it might be thought that because under the rules of the procedure it can only pronounce on final proposals and cannot table amendments, it would be confined to a rather limited confirmatory/withholding role. To some extent it indeed is, but not completely, because by having the power to say 'no' to proposals the EP also has the power to indicate to what it would say 'yes'. It has used this power most notably to take action on the human rights records of third countries that have signed association and cooperation agreements with the EU, and to put pressure on the Commission and the Council to amend and change the terms of some of these agreements.

EU Legislation After Adoption

There are considerable variations in what happens to proposals after they are adopted as EU legislation, what use is made of them, and how they are applied. Many of these variations are considered at some length in other chapters – notably in Chapters 8, 12 and 15 – but it will be useful to pull together the more important variations here in order to give an indication of the overall picture.

The need for additional legislation

Much legislation requires the adoption of additional legislative/regulatory measures:

- Legislation often needs to be supplemented by implementing legislation so as to fit it to particular circumstances, to adapt it to changing conditions, and to keep it up-to-date. Indeed, on a quantitative basis the vast bulk of EU legislation is implementing legislation, usually issued in the form of Commission regulations. The ways in which this legislation is issued are examined in Chapter 8, in the section on comitology.
- Some legislation needs to be followed up not just with implementing legislation but with further 'policy' legislation. This is most obviously the case in respect of 'framework' legislation, which is legislation that lays down general principles and basic rules that states have to follow in a policy area, but which needs usually to be complemented by more narrowly focused legislation that covers in a reasonably detailed manner issues/initiatives/actions that fall within the remit of the framework.
- Legislation that also requires further measures is the 'new approach' legislation that constitutes an important part of the internal market legal framework. Under the approach, the EU does not try to harmonise all the specifications and technical standards of marketed goods, but confines itself to producing relatively short texts that lay down 'essential requirements', in particular requirements relating to health and safety and to consumer and environmental protection. As long as member states abide by the 'essential requirements' they can have their own national standards – subject to them not being protectionist in nature – which are subject to mutual recognition by other states. However, national standards are generally supposed to be replaced by European standards that are agreed by European standards bodies. The main such bodies are the European Committee for Standardisation (CEN) and the European Committee for Electrotechnical Standardisation (CENELEC). Both CEN and CENELEC include non-EU countries amongst their membership, and both use weighted voting procedures for the taking of final decisions on standards. Once European standards are agreed, EU states must adopt them within a fixed time limit, and within the same time limit must remove all conflicting national standards.

The need to transpose legislation

Regulations and most decisions do not require any measures to be taken at national level before they apply, but directives do not normally assume legislative force until they have been transposed into national law by the appropriate national authorities. The member states themselves determine which are the appropriate national authorities in their case and by what process the transposition is to be made. As a result, the mechanisms by which directives are transposed at the national level varies between member states according to differing national legislative procedures and differing perceptions of the importance of particular directives. The general pattern, however, is for transposition to be achieved by attaching the necessary legal text to existing legislation, by introducing new legislation, or by adding new clauses to already planned legislation. States are given anything from a few weeks to a few years to effect the transposition – the final date being specified in the directive – and are obliged to notify the Commission of the national legislation, regulations, or administrative provisions that have been adopted to give formal effect to each directive.

For the most part, transposition is not a major problem for the EU, with Commission 'scorecards' showing average transposition rates for all member states consistently being well over 90 per cent. Some states – including Denmark, Germany, and the UK – do, however, have better average transposition records than others, with the consequence that there are some variations between member states in terms of the speed at which, and extent to which, directives are applied. There are variations too in terms of the frequency with which states are subject to Commission and Court action for non, incomplete, and incorrect transposition of EU law.

The need to apply legislation

Responsibilities for applying EU legislation are shared between EU authorities and national agencies. The main EU authorities are the various DGs that are responsible for particular policies: Agriculture, Fisheries, Regional Policy, Research and so on. Executive agencies (see Chapter 13) also undertake a limited amount of EU-level implementation. The national agencies are mainly the numerous national and subnational authorities whose responsibility it is to collect excise duties, read tachographs, monitor fishing catches, check that agriculture produce for which payments are made is of the quality that is claimed, and so on.

In very broad terms the division of responsibilities between the two levels in terms of day-to-day policy implementation is that the Commission oversees and the national and subnational authorities do most of the 'front line' work. Only in a few policy areas, of which competition is the most important, does the Commission directly implement itself. This means that the Commission needs to move carefully and, because it does not wish to stoke up national resentments, must negotiate and discuss implementing problems with authorities in member states rather than rush to initiate legal proceedings against them.

However, despite – or in some respects because of – the range of agencies that have some responsibility for policy implementation and implementation control, it is evident that all is not well with the application of some EU policies. Three types of difficulty may be taken to illustrate the nature of the implementation challenge. First, the Anti-Fraud Office (OLAF) and the Court of Auditors have identified serious implementation failings in connection with EU spending, especially on the CAP and ERDF. According to some estimates, fraud might account for as much as five per cent of the EU budget. Second, there are a number of high-profile and sensitive policy areas, of which competition and fishing are examples, where national implementation agencies are well aware that vigorous policy implementation could sometimes be damaging to national interests, and are therefore not over-zealous in taking action against suspected irregularities. In respect of such policy areas, the Commission sometimes must, as was shown in Chapter 8, display political sensitivity. And, third, many implementation arise not from deliberate deception but from incorrect understanding and application of the EU's highly complex body of legislation. The control mechanisms and administrative procedures for applying this legislation have been strengthened over the years, not least in respect of flows of information between the Commission and the national agencies. But the fact is that with the Commission being unable to conduct very much direct surveillance of its own because of limited powers and resources, and with much EU legislation being so complicated that it is barely comprehensible even to the expert, it probably will never be possible to ensure that all laws are fully, properly and uniformly implemented.

Taking this last point a little further, some sense of the difficulties the EU has in attempting to apply its policies in a uniform and efficient manner can be gauged by reference to the sheer volume of overlapping laws that exist in some areas of EU activity and the large number of contracts the EU has to deal with in some funded areas. Regarding overlapping laws, there are, for example, over 50 directives in force on labelling, nearly 40 on professional qualifications, over 20 on approval of types of vehicles, and around 15 on packaging. Regarding the large number of contracts, development policy makes the point, with over 40,000 development aid projects running at one time.

Concluding Remarks

Until the mid-1980s, the EC had a unicameral legislative system. That is to say the Council was the sole legislator, with the EP being restricted to a consultative position. Starting, however, with the SEA and continuing through every round of treaty reform since then, the EP's powers have been extended, to such an extent that the EU now has a genuinely bicameral legislative system. Few policy areas now remain in which the approval of both the Council and EP are not necessary to enable legislation to be made.

The main legislative procedure, the now-named ordinary procedure, is formally a somewhat complex three-reading procedure. In practice, however, the EP and the Council agree on the content of most legislative proposals before the third stage is reached. This working flexibility greatly assists with the production of a considerable volume of legislation within reasonable time limits. Of course, particularly controversial legislative proposals can run into considerable difficulties, but that is a consequence not so much of the nature of the EU's legislative procedures as of the political divisions within the EU and of the fact that the EU is not a majoritarian political system.

The implementation of legislation is a problem for the EU. The difficulty is not so much with the transposition of EU laws into national law as with the 'ground-level' application of EU laws. Some of the problems that exist stem from attempts to evade the law, but most are a consequence of unintended administrative irregularities. The reliance of the EU on national agencies for the great bulk of direct application of EU laws is a central underlying reason for many of the difficulties. It just is a fact that, notwithstanding extensive Commission overseeing and promotion of best practice, there remain many differences – of size, competences, working patterns, and cultures – between national administrations.

Chapter 19

Internal Policies

The EU's main internal policy interests and responsibilities can be grouped under four broad headings: establishing the internal market, macroeconomic and financial policies, functional policies, and sectoral policies.

Establishing the Internal Market

The creation of an open European market based on free and fair competition has been at the heart of the policy goals of the EC/EU since the early days of the integration process. Moreover, the rationale for the creation of such a market has remained virtually unchanged over the years, with the central purpose of an open European market consistently having been seen as being to assist economic growth and hence to promote employment and prosperity. The sentiments expressed in Document 19.1, which are taken from a Commission communication of mid-2009 on the internal market, could just as easily have been expressed fifty years previously by the Community's Founders.

But though the creation of an internal market – or common market as it was then called – was provided for in the EEC Treaty, it developed only slowly and for many years only modest progress was made. In the early 1980s, however, a number of factors combined to convince the governments of the member states that a greater thrust was needed: the sluggish economic growth of the second half of the 1970s was continuing; the Community was clearly falling behind its competitors (notably Japan and the United States) in the

---

Document 19.1

The rationale of the internal market

A well functioning single market is essential for creating employment and growth, and for promoting economic stability. The more effective the single market is, the more it will improve the business environment, thereby encouraging firms to invest and create jobs, and the more it will increase consumer confidence and demand.

Source: Commission recommendation of 29 June 2009 on measures to improve the functioning of the single market, (229/524/EC).

new technologies; and there was an increasing appreciation that the continuation of still essentially fragmented national markets was having a damaging effect on the economic performance of the EC's member states.

Against this background, in April 1985 the Commission produced a White Paper *Completing the Internal Market* (European Commission, 1985). The White Paper identified some 300 measures that would have to be taken to enable the internal market to be completed, and suggested that 31 December 1992 should be set as the deadline for the adoption of the measures. The European Council, at its June 1985 Milan meeting, accepted the White Paper, and at its December 1985 Luxembourg meeting agreed that both the internal market objective and the 1992 deadline be included in the Single European Act. Crucially, their inclusion in the SEA involved additions and amendments to the EEC Treaty. Article 13 of the SEA, incorporating a new Article 8A of the EEC Treaty, was especially important:

> The Community shall adopt measures with the aim of progressively establishing the internal market over a period expiring on 31 December 1992 … The internal market shall comprise an area without internal frontiers in which the free movement of goods, persons, services and capital is ensured in accordance with the provisions of this [the EEC] Treaty.

The White Paper sought, in essence, to establish the conditions in which market activities – buying and selling, lending and borrowing, producing and consuming – could be done as easily on a Community-wide basis as they could on a national basis. The hope was that by removing the obstacles and barriers that sectionalised and fragmented the Community market, efficiency, growth, trade, employment, and prosperity could all be promoted. In the context of a general deregulatory approach, three sorts of obstacle and barrier were identified as needing to be removed: physical, technical, and fiscal.

The Commission was not of course starting from scratch with its internal market programme. Some progress towards achieving the free and open market that had been specified in the EEC Treaty had been made. What the White Paper was intended to do was to inject a new focus, impetus and dynamism into a fundamental treaty objective that was proceeding far too slowly and that in some respects had gone rather off the rails. Much of what was proposed in the White Paper was, therefore, not new but had been around for some time – awaiting decisions by the Council of Ministers.

The White Paper and its programme to 'complete' the internal market thus needs to be placed in the context of the Community's long-standing aim to create a common market. That aim was being pursued, but with only limited success, before the White Paper appeared, and it has been vigorously pursued since, not only via the implementation of the White Paper but also via many new measures that did not appear in the White Paper. Today, many years after the formal ending of the '1992 project', the EU's agenda continues to be much taken up with policies, programmes and legislative proposals focused on removing continuing obstacles to free movement in the market place and on ensuring that market efficiency is maximised.

The continuing importance of market-related policy activity in the EU is a consequence of three main factors. First, policy-makers have increasingly come to recognise the importance of the internal market – or Single European Market (SEM) or single market at it is also known. They have done so especially as market liberalisation sentiments have engulfed most of the developed world's economic thinking over the last two decades. Whilst there often is resistance to particular internal market proposals, there is broad consensus amongst both EU-level and national-level policy-makers that an integrated internal market is desirable. Second, many obstacles to full market integration continue to exist. There are several reasons for this, including often a lack of political will – occasioned more often than not by national protectionist motives. And third, policy-makers have taken an increasingly expansive view of what a fully integrated market actually requires – either to make the market function as effectively as possible or to cushion some of the market's costs. So, for example, at the time of the 1985 White Paper the opening up of national infrastructure industries was not seen by most policy-makers as being a priority, or even as being desirable, but views on this began to change greatly in the 1990s.

The EU's internal market rests on four main pillars:

1 The Common Customs Tariff

The purpose of the Common Customs Tariff (CCT), or Common External Tariff (CET) as it also is known, is to further the course of fair and equal trading by surrounding all the member states with common trade barriers so that goods entering the EU via, say, the ports of Liverpool or Rotterdam do so on exactly the same terms as they do via the airports at Tallinn or Prague. No member state can therefore gain a competitive advantage by having access to cheaper raw materials and none can make a profit from exporting imported goods to an EU partner. The CCT takes the EU beyond being just a free trade area – where, at best, external tariffs are only approximated – and makes it a customs union.

The external tariffs were in place by 1968, to coincide with the removal of internal tariffs, and since then governments have had no independent legal authority over the tariff rates on goods entering their country. The terms of trade of the member states are established and negotiated on an EU-wide basis via the Common Commercial Policy (CCP) (see Chapter 20). If a member state wishes to seek exemptions from, or changes to, these terms of trade it must go through the appropriate EU decision-making processes. Naturally there have been frequent disagreements between the states over different aspects of external trade and the CCP – with tariff rates, trade protection measures, and alleged dumping amongst the issues that have created difficulties – but the existence of a clear and binding legal framework has ensured that, for the most part, the common external front – protection system it might be called (though reductions in international tariffs since the 1960s have greatly reduced the protection levels) – has worked.

2 The free movement of goods, persons, services and capital between the member states

Of these four freedoms, the *free movement of goods* was the first to be tackled. It is a freedom that, it might be thought, would be fairly easy to realise: all barriers to trade must be dismantled according to the guiding principles of the TFEU (and its predecessors), which states that customs duties, quantitative restrictions, and measures having equivalent effect are not permitted. Great steps were indeed quickly made in the 1960s with the first two of these and by 1968 customs duties and quantitative restrictions had been removed. Measures having equivalent effect, however, have been more difficult to deal with and have frequently acted, and been used, as obstacles to trade. Attempts to eliminate such measures have generated a considerable amount of EU legislation and much activity in the Union's Courts.

In seeking to establish the conditions for the *free movement of persons,* the Treaty provides for both the employed and the self-employed. The free movement of the former is to be attained by 'the abolition of any discrimination based on nationality between workers of the Member States as regards employment, remuneration and other conditions of work and employment' (Article 45 TFEU). The free movement of the latter is concerned principally with rights of establishment, that is with the right of individuals and undertakings to establish businesses in the territory of other member states. As with the free movement of goods, legislation and Court rulings have done much to clarify and extend the free movement of persons. They have done so in two main ways. First, by providing for mutual recognition of many educational, professional, and trade qualifications. Second, by providing key facilitators, notably in the form of the establishment of various legal entitlements, irrespective of nationality and place of domicile, to education and job training, health care, and social welfare payments.

Some of the legislation and Court judgments that have promoted the free movement of persons, and more particularly rights of establishment, have also helped to give some effect to the Treaty declaration that *there should be free movement of services.* Services, which account for approaching 70 per cent of EU GDP are, however, far from having been wholly liberalised, with many barriers preventing firms from providing services in, or establishing themselves in, other member states. As a central plank in its attempt to tackle this problem, in January 2004 the Commission issued a draft services directive aimed at opening up most of the nonfinancial services market: in total, around 50 per cent of economic activity in the EU would be covered. From the outset, however, the directive was steeped in political controversy, with differences between EU decision-makers turning on two points in particular. First, the Commission's proposal that the directive be based on a country of origin principle – which means that the provider is subject only to the law of the country in which the business is established – met with stiff resistance, not least in the EP. For many, this principle was too liberal and risked standards and levels of social and consumer protection being 'driven to the bottom'. Second, there was intense controversy about which sectors and industries, if any, should be excluded from the directive, and on what grounds. Should, for example, health, educational and cultural criteria be grounds for exclusion, and in what circumstances? Running through both of these areas of disagreement was a mosaic of factors influencing political actors, including ideological preferences concerning regulatory levels in the market and calculations about how national providers would be likely to fare in a more open market. The EP and the Council eventually reached agreement on the directive in November 2006, but only after its contents had been considerably watered down: the country of origin principle was virtually dropped and the number of services excluded from coverage by the directive was extended.

As for financial services (banking, insurance, securities, asset management), progress in opening-up and strengthening markets was made under the 1999–2005 Financial Services Action Plan (FSAP). In December 2005 the Commission issued a White Paper, *Financial Services Policy 2005–2010* (European Commission, 2005f) identifying objectives and proposed actions over the next five years. The focus was mainly on consolidation between service providers, and improving supervisory cooperation and convergence. However, the global financial crisis that erupted in 2008 has inevitably resulted in EU policy-makers giving financial services a much higher and more urgent policy profile than they had hitherto. This has led to a spate of legislative measures and proposals – originating from the Commission working in close cooperation with the European Council and the Ecofin Council of Ministers – designed to tighten the EU regulatory framework in the financial sector and so create greater stability and boost confidence in financial markets. Amongst measures that have been approved by the Council and EP are the Capital Requirements Directive, the Solvency II Directive, and the Credit Rating Agencies Regulation. Amongst proposals that are scheduled to be approved are a package of measures adopted by the Commission in

December 2009 to strengthen financial supervision. The measures will create a new European Systemic Risk Board (ESRB), charged to detect at an early stage risks to the financial system as a whole, and a new European System of Financial Supervisors (ESFS) which will work with three new European Supervisory Agencies for the banking, securities, and insurance and occupational pensions sectors.

Until the late 1980s only limited progress was made in establishing *the free movement of capital*. Treaty provisions partly explain this, since the elimination of restrictions on the movement of capital under Article 67 EEC Treaty (now abolished) was required only 'to the extent necessary to ensure the proper functioning of the common market'. More importantly, however, and notwithstanding the creation of the EMS in the late 1970s, the necessary political will did not exist in the first three decades of the Community's life. For many states, control of capital movements was an important economic and monetary instrument and they preferred it to remain largely in their own hands. However, as part of the internal market programme, much of this former resistance was withdrawn or overcome, and all the major capital markets have – subject to a few derogations and some national protective measures – been more or less open since 1990. (This does not, however, mean that in practice there is complete free movement of capital, since taxation rates have not been made common and banking rules have not yet all been standardised.)

3 The approximation of laws and the principle of mutual recognition

Article 115 TFEU (formerly Article 94 TEC, and before that Article 100 of the EEC Treaty) states that the Council shall 'issue directives for the approximation of such laws, regulations or administrative provisions of the member states as directly affect the establishment or functioning of the internal market.' Until the early 1980s, 'approximation' tended to be interpreted by EC decision makers as meaning 'harmonisation'. However, from the early 1980s a more flexible and less rigid approach developed towards differences in national standards and requirements. This development followed upon the 'breakthrough'

Cassis de Dijon case in 1979, when the ECJ ruled that products conforming with the standards of one member state could not be excluded from the markets of other member states unless they could be shown to be damaging to health, safety, the environment, or other aspects of the public interest. The ruling allowed the Community to be less concerned with the standardisation of technical details and to adopt a 'new approach' under which a simpler and speedier process would apply. The main aspects to this process, which still applies, are: 1) whenever possible, legislation does not seek to harmonise but rather to approximate – which means that attention is restricted to laying down the essential requirements that national standards and specifications must meet (on, for example, product standards and health and safety conditions); 2) as long as the essential requirements are met, member states must mutually recognise the specifications and standards of other member states; and 3) national specifications and standards are gradually being replaced by European specifications and standards drawn up by European standards organisations.

The need for approximation arises because the dismantling of tariff and quota barriers is not in itself sufficient to guarantee free movement. This is most clearly seen with regard to the movement of goods where (especially prior to the 1992 programme) many non-tariff and non-quantitative barriers have inhibited, even prevented, free movement across internal EU borders. These barriers have in the words of the Treaty, the 'equivalent effect' of tariffs and quantitative restrictions, and as such have been obstacles to the creation of a market based on free and open competition. Moreover, they have tended to be barriers of a kind that cannot be removed simply by issuing general prohibitions. Many have taken the form of different national standards, national requirements, and national provisions and practices that have been adopted over the years. Sometimes they have been adopted for perfectly good reasons, but sometimes they have been adopted as a deliberate attempt to protect a domestic market from unwanted competition without actually infringing EU law. Whatever the intent, the effect has been the same: because of the need to adapt products to meet the different national standards of different states, and because of the need for products to be subject to re-testing and re-certification procedures, efficiency has not been maximised and producers in one member state often have been

unable to compete on an equal basis with producers in another. Examples of non-tariff barriers (NTBs) include different national technical specifications for products, different health and safety standards, charges for the inspection of certain categories of imported goods, and taxes that, though nominally general in their scope, have been discriminatory against imported goods in their effect.

Approximation is thus concerned with the removal of NTBs and is vital if free movement across national boundaries is to be achieved. EU directives are the main instruments for achieving approximation, although many Court rulings have also been supportive and helpful. Most approximation law is to be found in relation to the free movement of goods, although there is also an increasing volume covering services. Approximation law consists largely of the setting of common standards on such matters as technical requirements, design specifications, product content, and professional qualifications.

Critics of the EU often present approximation law as seeking unwanted and unnecessary conformity, and sometimes proposals do indeed appear to smack of insensitivity to national customs and preferences. Sight should not be lost, however, of what approximation is all about: creating conditions that allow, encourage and increase the uniform treatment of persons, goods, services and capital throughout the EU.

4 Competition policy

The basic rules on competition are outlined in Articles 101–109 TFEU (formerly 81–89 TEC). As is shown in Box 19.1, they are three main aspects to them.

All of the TFEU prohibitions – on restrictive practices, dominant trading positions, and state aid – have been clarified by subsequent EC/EU law, both in the form of legislation and Court judgments. It has been established, for example, that a 'dominant position' cannot be held to apply on the basis of an overall percentage market share, but only in relation to factors such as the particular product, the structure of its market, and substitutability. Similarly, exemptions to state aid prohibitions, which are only generally referred to in the Treaty, have been confirmed as being legally permissible if they are for purposes such as regional development, retraining, and job creation in potential growth industries.

The main principles of competition policy, as set out in the TFEU

- Under Article 101, there is a prohibition on 'all agreements between undertakings, decisions by associations of undertakings and concerted practices which may affect trade between Member States and which have as their object or effect the prevention, restriction or distortion of competition within the internal market'.
- Under Article 102, 'Any abuse by one or more undertakings of a dominant position within the internal market or in a substantial part of it shall be prohibited as incompatible with the internal market in so far as it may affect trade between Member States'.
- Under Article 107, state aid 'which distorts or threatens to distort competition by favouring certain undertakings or the production of certain goods shall, in so far as it affects trade between Member States, be incompatible with the internal market'.

As was shown in Chapter 8, the Commission's Competition DG is vital to the running of EU competition policy. Over the years its powers have grown and it has become increasingly bold in trying to ensure that the market is as open and competitive as possible. There have been three main aspects to this. First, it has become more active in examining cases of apparent malpractice. For example, using its powers as investigator, prosecutor, judge and jury (though with its decisions subject to appeal to the EU Courts) it has been more willing to take action against member states in connection with state aid. Second, legislation designed to broaden the competition policy base and with it the powers of the Commission have been approved. A particularly important instance of such legislation is the 1989 Merger Regulation, which was revised in 2004, which gives considerable powers to the Commission to disallow or set conditions on mergers that it judges will have an adverse effect on competition. Other examples of legislation, in a very different area of competition policy, are the directives that are designed to open up public procurement – an area of activity that accounts for around 15 per cent of EU

GDP. Third, the Commission has used the momentum provided by the spirit of economic liberalisation that has spread across the Western world since the 1980s to be much more vigorous than it used to be in wielding competition powers to break-up long-established and well protected national monopolies in such policy spheres as energy, postal services and telecommunications markets. This has been a difficult policy challenge that has met with stiff political resistance, but considerable progress has been, and continues to be, made.

But, the Commission's role in advancing competition policy has not been completely unbridled. It has long had to be tempered by the EU's regional and social policies. It has had to be tempered also by political pressures, with care having to be taken, for example, when an anti-competitive ruling on state aid could result in major political problems for the government of a member state. And – perhaps above all – it has had to be tempered by economic realities, as has been no more clearly seen than in positions the Commission has taken in response to the global financial and economic crisis that unfolded in 2008. Working with, and on the basis of instructions given to it by, the European Council and the Ecofin Council of Ministers, the Commission has, since the autumn of 2008, promoted and approved a number of what might be thought of as 'anti-competitive' regulatory measures in the financial sector. These measures have had the objectives of 'of ensuring financial stability and restoring lending to the real economy while safeguarding the internal market, minimising distortions of competition and paving the way to a return to normal market functioning when possible'(European Commission, 2009d: Introduction). Prominent amongst the measures promoted and approved have been public guarantees (amounting to €2.9 trillion between October 2008 and July 2009) and recapitalisations (amounting to €313 billion), and legislation – in such areas as capital requirements, credit rating agencies, and solvency – regulating financial sector institutions and operations.

Problems in 'completing' the internal market

Clearly much has been and still is being achieved in the move towards creating the EU's internal market.

However, there is no foreseeable prospect of the EU market being as open or as integrated as national markets. This is because not all of the barriers to free movement will be removed, and not all of the national policies that serve to fragment the market will be made common. The main obstacles in the way of the establishment of a completely open and integrated market are of seven, inter-related and overlapping, types.

First, there are the somewhat intangible, but nonetheless very important, obstacles arising from different historical experiences, cultures, traditions and languages. These obstacles are unquestionably being broken down, but only slowly. EU laws may, for example, oblige public authorities to receive tenders for contracts from throughout the EU, but laws cannot control the many informal processes that often incline national, regional and local decision-makers to award contracts whenever possible to fellow national companies.

Second, some internal market legislation is rather loose (because this was necessary to overcome opposition in the Council) whilst some of it is only being weakly applied. Spheres of market activity so affected include aspects of financial services, veterinary and phytosanitary controls, and the recognition of some diplomas and professional qualifications.

Third, there is member state resistance to fully opening-up certain market sectors that are judged to be – almost invariably for national protectionist and/or public interest reasons – especially important. Energy, transport and broadcasting are examples of such sectors, as are such 'non economic' sectors as health, education and social welfare.

Fourth, whilst the 'four freedoms' – of goods, services, capital and persons – are fundamental EU principles clearly rooted in the TFEU and developed in an extensive body of EU legislation and case law, responsibility for some policy areas that impact directly on the existence of the freedoms remains largely with the governments of the member states. This is seen most clearly with social and labour policy, both of which are largely nationally controlled. The split in responsibilities between the EU and the national levels inevitably produces variations between member states in some aspects of market functioning, but EU policy-makers cannot always seek to eliminate them – either because they do not have the power to do so or because it would be politically unwise.

An example that serves to illustrate this point is a decision taken by the German Government in December 2007 to announce a minimum wage for the postal sector. The decision was taken as a result of trade union lobbying and pressure from within Germany's coalition government by the Social Democrat Party, which both insisted on the minimum wage decision as a *quid pro quo* for gradually opening-up – as EU legislation requires – the domestic postal market. The EU's Competition Commissioner, Neelie Kroes, criticised the minimum wage decision and claimed it would be at the expense of consumers. But, the Commission took no formal action against Germany for, as a Commission spokesman said, minimum wages lay outside the Commission's competence (*EUobserver*, 13–19 December, 2007: 7).

Fifth, there are ideological differences amongst EU policy-makers concerning where the correct balance is to be stuck between regulation on the one hand and the operation of an open market on the other. In broad terms, 'regulators' tend to come from the political left and 'free-marketeers' from the political right, but there is not a complete match as, for example, the existence of sometimes largely consensual positions on the need to ensure that business is subject to controls on environmental pollution illustrates.

Sixth, economists and politicians dispute exactly what factors constitute market barriers, what their relative importance is, and whether and in what ways EU-level policies are necessary. Prominent amongst the policy areas that are so disputed are: the non-participation of some member states in the single currency system and hence also their non-involvement in the single monetary and exchange rate policies of the eurozone; the only partial development of common regional, social, environmental, transport, and consumer protection policies; and the diversity of corporate direct taxation systems. Taking just the last of these policies to illustrate the point, some EU policy-makers regard a common EU corporate tax base and an approximation of corporate tax rates as being essential if competition is not to result in an undesirable 'drive the bottom', whilst others see corporate tax competition between the member states as being healthy and not requiring regulation.

Seventh, there are problems with policy implementation. The main problem is not so much with the transposition of internal market legislation into national law, for the picture there is relatively good: in mid-2009 the average transposition deficit – that is, the number of directives that were not transposed in time or in full into national law – was less than two per cent (European Commission, 2009a: 3). Rather, the main problem is with the 'front line' application of internal market laws which, as was shown in Chapter 8, is primarily the responsibility of national agencies of various sorts. In its monitoring reports – notably the twice yearly *Internal Market Scoreboard* – the Commission constantly describes policy application as being unsatisfactory and takes many actions against member states – in what are known as infringement proceedings – for incorrect application of EU laws. The worst offenders in recent years have been Italy, Spain, Belgium and Greece.

Macroeconomic and Financial Policies

The background to and creation of Economic and Monetary Union

Notwithstanding declarations by the Heads of Government in 1969 and 1972 that their intention was to establish an economic and monetary union by 1980, only limited practical progress was made until the late 1980s in moving towards Economic and Monetary Union (EMU).

Ministers and senior national officials did regularly convene to consult and to exchange ideas on macroeconomic policy, and at their meetings they periodically considered Commission submissions for the adoption of common guidelines and for short-term and medium-term strategies. A state may have been unwise to fall too much out of step with its partners – as the French government was in 1981–2 when it attempted to stimulate its economy against the general trend – but it was perfectly entitled and able to embark on such a course of action.

Monetary policy was the subject of particularly frequent contacts between the states – at ministerial, official and central bank levels – but, as with other branches of macroeconomic policy, most of what came out of such exchanges was of an exhortive rather than a directionist nature. That said, however, the creation in 1979 of the European Monetary System (EMS) did provide Community monetary policy with

some central structure and some powers, since amongst its features were: a common reserve fund to provide for market intervention; the European Currency Unit (ecu) to act as a reserve asset and a means of settlement; and, in the Exchange Rate Mechanism (ERM) of the EMS, fixed – though adjustable when necessary – bands of exchange for participating currencies.

Until the late 1980s the Community's macroeconomic policies thus had only relatively weak policy instruments attached to them. Attempts to strengthen these instruments and build up a more coherent and effective policy framework met with at least four obstacles. First, there were differences over which – the economic or the monetary – naturally came first and should be accorded priority. Second, the Community's rather sectionalised policy-making mechanisms inhibited an overall and coordinated approach. Third, different aspects of economic and monetary integration had different implications for the states, which resulted in them being viewed with different degrees of enthusiasm. Fourth, for some states the possibility of ceding key macroeconomic powers to the Community raised fundamental sovereignty questions.

But notwithstanding the many obstacles in the way of policy development, real progress towards monetary integration began to be made in the late 1980s. This progress was, as indeed it still is, driven by two main rationales, the relative importance of which has varied amongst policy actors. On the one hand, monetary integration has a political rationale, which is based on a belief that monetary integration inevitably furthers political integration. And, on the other hand, there is an economic rationale, which is based on a belief that monetary integration brings a number of economic benefits and in so doing furthers economic prosperity. Box 19.2 summarises these rationales and also identifies the main perceived disadvantages of monetary integration for states.

With the potential advantages of monetary integration increasingly being appreciated by national leaders and with the EEC Treaty having been amended by the SEA to include a new chapter on 'Co-operation in Economic and Monetary Policy', the Community formally embarked on the road to EMU at much the same time as the SEM programme was beginning to be applied. Differences remained between the states over what precisely EMU should consist of and what should be the timetable for its full implementation,

Box 19.2

The main perceived advantages and disadvantages of European monetary integration.

Advantages

- *Political.* For those who wish to see a more integrated Europe, perhaps a fully federal Europe, monetary integration is an important building block. As with the coal and steel community, the customs union and the internal market, monetary integration offers a potential for creating political integration by economic means.

- *Economic.* There are several potential economic advantages of monetary integration, including: greater price transparency; elimination of currency exchange costs; provision of 'shelter' when international currency rates are volatile; and the removal of exchange rate fluctuations between participating currencies. This last advantage is seen by EMU proponents as being vital in making for greater market stability and in so doing promoting business confidence and hence investment and economic growth.

Disadvantages

- *Political.* Membership of a single currency zone means giving up: the national currency, which in many states has been symbolically important; and sovereignty – in the sense of formal national control – over monetary policy.

- *Economic.* The 'transfer' of monetary policy to a central level means that: national governments have less policy instruments available to them to manage national economies (most particularly, they cannot adjust interest rates or devalue the currency); there is a 'one size fits all' monetary policy, which can result in interest rate and exchange rate policies that are not suitable for some member states; and economic problems in one member state (such as high budgetary deficits fuelling inflation) can more easily spillover into other member states. Some commentators argue that, in the long term, a monetary union cannot work without there also being common fiscal policies and a political union.

but all (apart from the UK) subscribed to the broad outlines of the scheme that was put forward in April 1989 by the Delors Committee in its *Report on Economic and Monetary Union* which laid the foundations for EMU. The Committee proved to be the forerunner of the 1990–1 IGC on EMU in that not only did it clear much of the ground for the establishment of the IGC, but many of its proposals – including the principle of a three-stage transition to EMU – were accepted by the IGC and incorporated in the Maastricht Treaty.

The Maastricht provisions on EMU and their subsequent application were described in Chapters 3 and 5, so will not be repeated here. Suffice it to say that the Treaty established a scheme and a timetable for progression to EMU. The main feature of the scheme was increasing coordination and convergence of the economic and monetary policies of all member states, leading to a single currency in which there would be a common monetary policy to be pursued within the

framework of a European System of Central Banks (ESCB). The main feature of the timetable was a three-stage transitional process leading to the adoption of a single currency by January 1999 at the latest.

The single currency duly came into operation in January 1999, with eleven of the EU's fifteen member states as members – Denmark and the UK used the opt-outs they had been given in the Maastricht Treaty, Greece did not meet the qualifying convergence criteria, whilst Sweden chose not to participate. The eleven became twelve in January 2001 when Greece, having then been deemed to meet the criteria, joined the single currency system. The Danish and Swedish governments also tried to take their countries into the eurozone in the early 2000s, but were unsuccessful when their peoples rejected adopting the single currency in national referendums: in September 2000 in Denmark and September 2003 in Sweden.

Under the terms of their accession treaties, the states that joined the EU in 2004/07 were not eligible

Box 19.3

The EMU convergence criteria (eurozone entry conditions)

- *Price stability.* Inflation should not have exceeded by more than one-and-a-half percentage points that of the three best performing member states for a period of at least one year.
- *Sustainability of the government financial position.* The budget deficit or planned deficit should be no more than 3 per cent of gross domestic product and government debt should be no more than 60 per cent of gross domestic product. (There is some flexibility here if deficits/debts are declining and rates are approaching the two reference values.)
- *Exchange rate stability.* The normal fluctuation margins provided for by the exchange-rate mechanism should have been respected without severe tensions for at least two years. In particular, there must have been no devaluation against the euro.
- *Interest rate stability.* The average nominal long-term interest rate must not have exceeded by more than two percentage points that of the three best performing Member States for a period of one year.

Source: Treaty on the Functioning of the European Union: Article 140, Protocol 12 (on the excessive deficit procedure), and Protocol 13 (on the convergence criteria).

for eurozone membership until they had completed at least two full years of EU membership and had met the eurozone entry conditions – known as the convergence criteria, which are set out in Box 19.3. Since they became EU members, all of the new states have signalled their continued desire and willingness to join the eurozone, but variable economic performances have meant that up to the time of writing – early 2010 – only four have joined: Slovenia (on 1 January 2007); Cyprus and Malta (both on 1 January 2008); and Slovakia (on 1 January 2009). Slovakia's accession raised the eurozone membership to sixteen states, with a combined population of over 325 million people.

The global financial and economic crisis that set in during the late 2000s has had a twofold impact on the prospects for future expansions of the eurozone. On the 'negative' side it has created budgetary deficit and public debt problems for non-eurozone members (as indeed it also has for eurozone members), with the consequence that their ability to meet the eurozone entry conditions has been set back. On the 'positive' side, in some states – including Denmark, the Czech Republic, Poland, and Iceland (an EU applicant state) – it has increased interest in joining the single currency because of the 'protection' that being part of a large currency zone is seen to provide.

The nature of Economic and Monetary Union

There are four principal features of EMU.

First, eurozone members no longer have national currencies. From January 1999 the exchange rates between founding single currency members were irrevocably fixed. In January and February 2002 the national banknotes and coinage of members were replaced by euro banknotes and coins.

Second, as a result of being part of a single currency system, eurozone countries can no longer take individual decisions on what monetary policies – including interest rate or exchange rate policies – they should pursue. The eurozone has common monetary policies, which are determined through the zone's own institutional structures – at the heart of which is the European Central Bank (ECB) (see pp. 238–40). The monetary policies of the Bank have a strong anti-inflationary ethos, tempered (though not sufficiently in the view of some EU governments) by an eye to other needs of the eurozone's economy.

Third, the macroeconomic policies of eurozone countries are aligned, but they are not common as, and are softer in form than, the monetary policies. The framework for this alignment is known as the Stability and Growth Pact (SGP), which is based primarily on the budget and public debt elements of the convergence criteria and which obliges members to practise prudent fiscal policies and, more particularly, to maintain broadly balanced national budgets over the economic cycle. The key SGP rule is that the annual budgetary deficits of eurozone states must not exceed 3 per cent of national GDP. Non-compliance with the terms of the SGP can lead to financial sanctions being imposed on offenders: initially in the form of the lodging of a non-interest bearing deposit and if excessive deficits continue in the form of a fine.

No financial penalties have been applied up to the time of writing, even though several eurozone states have breached SGP rules. In the early 2000s these breaches resulted in sharp differences between the Commission and the ECB on the one hand and some eurozone member states on the other. So, in February 2002 the Commission wanted to issue an early warning to Germany that its budgetary deficit was becoming unsustainable – though there was no breach of the Pact's ceiling of 3 per cent of GDP, Germany's budget deficit was forecast to rise to 2.7 per cent. However, the German Finance Minister succeeded in persuading his British, French, Italian and Portuguese colleagues in the Ecofin Council that the Commission was being too rigid and was not allowing sufficiently for fluctuations in the economic cycle. In a compromise under which Germany undertook to eliminate its budget deficit by 2004, no rebuke was issued and no formal vote was taken by the ministers. Clearly politics had prevailed over tight management of the Pact, with the original main proponent of the Pact able to use its size and power to avoid a political embarrassment.

In 2003, tensions became even sharper, when the Commission proposed taking formal action against both France and Germany for breaching the 3 per cent ceiling. At an acrimonious Ecofin meeting in November, France and Germany managed to persuade Finance Ministers to lift the threat of disciplinary action being taken against them, which resulted in the Commission initiating a case against the Council in the ECJ. In July 2004 the Court ruled largely in favour of the Commission (case C-27/04), but political realities then led not to the disciplinary action being imposed but to the terms of the Pact being changed by Ecofin in March 2005. The key change involved a formal recognition that there were exceptional and temporary circumstances in which the 3 per cent limit could be breached without the risk of a financial penalty being imposed. The circumstances were not listed, as some member states wanted, but rather were left to the discretion of the Commission to judge. The most likely circumstance was generally recognised as being when a national economy is experiencing temporary difficulties, with

low growth and high unemployment, but the underlying structure is sound.

The 2005 'softening' of the SGP rules has come to be much used in the wake of the global financial and economic crisis that set in during the late 2000s. With most EU states adopting aggressive fiscal stimulus measures to deal with rising unemployment and low growth, the crisis inevitably resulted in budgetary deficits and public debts quickly spiralling in many EU states, including eurozone states, and the SGP guideline figures being breached – in some cases by wide margins. The situation was, however, clearly caused by exceptional circumstances and so SGP decision-makers (in the European Council and Ecofin Council) and decision implementers (in the Commission) took the view that whilst the guideline figures should remain in place, states should not be penalised for exceeding them as long as they clearly were making efforts to get back on track and (re)establish firm budgetary positions.

Fourth, there is a 'multilateral surveillance system' involving the economies of all EU states. Under this system, eurozone member states submit to the Commission annual stability programmes and non-eurozone states submit convergence programmes. These stability and convergence programmes are set within broader multi-annual programmes and are supposed to respect the multi-annual Broad Economic Policy Guidelines that are prepared by the Commission and agreed by the Ecofin Council. Amongst information that must be presented in the programmes are medium-term budgetary objectives setting out how the 3 per cent budgetary target figure and the long-term sustainability of public finances will be respected, the underlying economic assumptions of the programmes (especially on growth, inflation and unemployment), and a description of measure to be taken to achieve the objectives of the programme. The Commission, working through the Ecofin Council, assesses the programmes and makes recommendations as appropriate.

Non-eurozone members are thus expected to coordinate their economic policies with the other EU member states. Unlike eurozone members, they cannot be subject to financial penalties for breaching SGP rules, but they are obliged to comply with the multilateral surveillance system and to endeavour to avoid excessive budgetary deficits. For 2004/07 accession states the surveillance system is, of course, part of the preparations they are expected to make for eventual eurozone membership. For the three states that have chosen not to be eurozone members – Denmark, Sweden and the UK – involvement in the surveillance system is an obligation of EU membership: they are subject to the EU's excessive deficit procedure, which means that if they exceed, or seem likely to exceed, the 3 per cent budgetary deficit limit, the Commission can recommend to the Ecofin Council that the state in question be required to adopt appropriate rectifying measures – though neither the Commission nor Ecofin can state, other than in the most general terms, what these measures should be.

The significance of Economic and Monetary Union

Clearly the establishment of the single currency marks a major step forward in the European integration process. On the one hand, it has considerable symbolic significance, with the replacement of the French franc, the German deutschemark, the Italian lira, the Cypriot pound and so on with the euro. It may well be that this will provide much impetus to the development of a common European identity. On the other hand, single currency states have transferred responsibility to Euro-level institutions for two key policy instruments – exchange rate and interest rate levels – and have accepted stiff limitations on what they can do in respect of budgetary policy.

But though the single currency system advances European integration, it still remains to be seen whether it will be judged a success. The rationale is that by creating a more stable European economic and monetary environment and thus providing greater predictability for investments and markets, the single currency will promote growth and prosperity. But to date growth rates have been disappointing, unemployment rates in several eurozone countries have been high, and pre-existing and significant variations in measures of competitiveness between member states have persisted. In consequence, problems have already arisen from the 'one size for all' nature of EMU, with the national economies of eurozone members clearly having required different monetary policy rates at different times.

The fact is that the eurozone system does not contain two key instruments that single currency systems arguably need to deal with problems of internal variations in economic performance, namely mobility of labour and the ability of the centre to effect significant fiscal transfers. The latter, of course, would require more and much stronger macroeconomic policies.

The division of responsibilities for monetary policy and macroeconomic policy has already created difficulties. There have, for example, been open differences over the contents of policies between 'expansionist'

Box 19.4

Requirements for the euro to be able to match the dollar as an international currency

- The euro needs to establish long-term credentials as a stable and successful currency. To date the record has been mixed, with success in that inflation and interest rates have been low but with seeming less success in that growth and competitiveness have not advanced as far or as rapidly as had been hoped.
- There needs to be some flattening of the considerable divergences between the performances of national economies that persist in the eurozone. Highly varied economic performances suggest an over-rigid system, and also one in which some members may become disillusioned.
- A more developed eurozone financial system is required.
- The perceived anti-growth bias of the euro – based on the prioritisation of countering inflation that constitutes a core element of the European Central Bank's remit – needs to be toned down.
- There needs to be clearer and stronger eurozone leadership. As matters stand, there is uncertainty over, for example, who is 'Mr/Ms eurozone': the President of the ECB?; the President of the Eurogroup?; the national Minister of Finance from the member state in the Council Presidency – and therefore the chair of the Ecofin Council?; or the Commissioner for Economic and Financial Affairs?

politicians and 'cautious' bankers in the ECB and 'over rigid' SGP 'guardians' in the Commission. There have been differences too between national governments over policies, with the governments of states with high levels of unemployment showing some reluctance to accept – given that they no longer have interest rate or exchange rate adjustments available to them – tight fiscal policies that are judged to be in the general interest of the eurozone. There have also been differences arising from the desire of some governments to promise tax cuts during election campaigns. Such differences, and the tensions associated with them, show no sign of settling down and could become even sharper if any member states are seen to be seriously endangering the euro system.

As to whether the euro can match the dollar as an international currency, there is a long way to go. There is certainly considerable potential with, for example, a GDP that is comparable in size, a population that is much larger, and an economy that is more reliant on international trade than the US. But, much needs to happen before the international role of the dollar can be seriously challenged. Five things in particular appear to be necessary, as Box 19.4 shows.

Functional Policies

The EU has interests and responsibilities in many functional policies: that is, policies with a clear functional purpose and a more specific nature than the policies considered under the previous headings.

Probably the best known of the EU's functional policies are the justice and home affairs (JHA) policies – which are now becoming known as the area of freedom, security and justice (AFSJ) policies, the cohesion policies, and the research and technological development policies. Less prominent functional policies include education policy, cultural policy, and consumer protection policy. Since it is not possible to examine all of the EU's functional policies here, attention will be directed to six of the more important ones. The examinations that follow will, in addition to explaining the principal features of the six policy spheres in question, also illustrate the range and varying depth of EU involvement in different functional areas.

Area of freedom, security and justice policies

In the mid-1970s the EC member states began to exchange information and cooperate with one another on matters relating to the monitoring and control of terrorism, drugs, and organised crime. A series of mechanisms, which were quite outside the framework of the Community Treaties and which came to be known as the Trevi process, were developed. They brought together, often on a semi-secret basis, officials from Interior and Justice ministries, senior police and intelligence officers, and ministers. Over the years the issues covered by Trevi developed – due in no small part to the need to dismantle internal border controls as part of the SEM programme – and by the late 1980s the original 'threats' of terrorism, drugs and organised crime had been joined by a variety of matters relating to immigration, visas, public order, and customs controls.

This array of policy interests, and the plethora of *ad hoc* arrangements developed to deal with them, were brought together and strengthened by the Maastricht Treaty. They were so mainly under the so-called third pillar of the Treaty – dealing with Provisions on Cooperation in the Fields of Justice and Home Affairs. The contents of the Maastricht third pillar were set out in Chapter 5, so they will be only summarised here. First, the member states were to regard nine policy areas – including asylum policy, immigration policy, and the combating of drug addiction – as 'matters of common interest'. Visa policy was incorporated into the TEC, with the requirement that a common visa policy should be adopted, by qualified majority voting rules in the Council, by 1 January 1996. Second, the Council was empowered to adopt joint positions and joint actions (through, for example, the issuing of resolutions and recommendations), and to draw up conventions. Third, new institutional arrangements to promote cooperation and coordination, and to enable the EU to fulfil its obligations under the Treaty, were to be established.

The Maastricht-created third pillar led to much activity in the JHA field with, for example, the adoption of numerous declarations and conventions and the establishment of a European Police Office: Europol. But progress was only modest in respect of governments becoming committed to adopting tough collective responses to the JHA problems facing them. A major reason for this was that many JHA policies are of a highly sensitive kind, raising deep cultural issues – on, for example, the exchange of sensitive information and individual rights – and touching directly on national sovereignty concerns. Because of this sensitivity, the third pillar was established on an intergovernmental basis, making Council decision-making very difficult. Another reason for the initially slow development of 'hard' JHA policies was – as indeed is still the case – that much of the JHA area is intrinsically complex in nature with, for example, numerous – often non-congruent – national agencies involved and very different national civil laws applying.

Dissatisfaction with the operation of the third pillar resulted in it being much discussed in the 1996–7 IGC and in it being the policy area most strengthened by the Amsterdam Treaty. The ways in which this strengthening was undertaken were set out in some detail in Chapter 5 so, as with the contents of the JHA elements of the Maastricht Treaty, only the major points of the Amsterdam Treaty will be summarised here. First, several JHA policy areas – including immigration, asylum, and refugees and displaced persons – were 'communitarised' by being transferred from the intergovernmental pillar three to the much more supranational pillar one. Within the EC pillar, most decisions were to be taken by unanimous vote in the Council (apart from visa policy), but provision was made for the possible introduction of QMV after five years. Second, policy objectives were clarified. Third, the Schengen Agreement – of which most member states were signatories and which had been developed, on an extra-treaty basis, since the mid-1980s to remove most internal border controls on the movement of people – was incorporated into the EU framework. However, Ireland and the UK, (which had never been full Schengen members) were given opt-outs from the consequences of the incorporation (in Ireland's case this was required because of its common travel area with the UK) and Denmark was given a partial opt-out. Fourth, pillar three, which was to continue to be intergovernmental in character, was re-focused and re-titled 'Provisions on Police and Judicial Cooperation in Criminal Matters'.

As part of the Amsterdam changes, explicit provision was made for the aim of JHA and JHA-related policies to be the creation of 'an area of freedom, security and justice' in which there is free movement of persons behind common external borders. To help give effect to this aim, Amsterdam was followed up by a special European Council meeting on AFSJ matters at Tampere in 1999. At Tampere the national leaders gave further impetus to the policy area by establishing the EU's first multi-annual JHA programme, covering the years 1999–2004. Amongst the goals of the programme were: reaching agreement on the introduction of a common asylum system; the adoption of measures to improve progress in access to justice and in the mutual recognition of judicial decisions; and the creation of two new agencies – a prosecution agency, Eurojust, and a European Police College (European Council, 1999c).

Since Maastricht, and more especially since Amsterdam, the AFSJ policy area has advanced rapidly. The pace has been quickened largely in response to three developments. The first has been the continuing opening of the internal market and the associated greater ease with which internal borders can be crossed. This greater ease of crossing is, of course, intended to bring benefits to citizens, but it also creates problems – concerning, for example, the rights of citizens, residency claims of non citizens, and cross-border crimes – that national political and legal systems cannot adequately manage acting by themselves. As Brendan Donnelly has observed (2008:22): 'The relentless disappearance of national barriers between the Member States of the EU sets the material stage and creates the legal imperatives for most decisions taken under JHA'. The second development has been growing concerns about the porousness of the EU's borders as increasing numbers of people from third counties have sought to enter and settle within the EU. Common, and tighter, policies on immigration, asylum, and visa controls have increasingly been seen as being necessary – all the more so with the already vulnerable southern borders being joined by vulnerable eastern borders with the 2004/07 EU enlargement. Particular attention was given to these matters at the June 2002 Seville summit when political agreement was reached on a package of measures including: closer cooperation between the member states on border controls, including the creation of a network of immigration control officers; closer cooperation with third countries on illegal immigration, with the EU prepared to offer financial and technical assistance where appropriate and prepared also to make it clear that inadequate cooperation could hamper the forging of closer ties; and, so as to make 'asylum shopping' more difficult, the issuing of an instruction to ministers to adopt proposals to make the Dublin Convention – which states that the EU country where asylum seekers first enter the EU is responsible for processing any asylum application – legally binding (European Council, 2002a). The third development quickening the pace of AFSJ policy development has been the revealing, initially through the September 11 2001 terrorist attacks in the USA and subsequently through attacks in Europe – of the extent of the threat posed to the West by international terrorism. The terrorist threat has resulted in the adoption of a number of anti-terrorist measures, including an EU-wide arrest warrant to replace former lengthy extradition procedures.

In November 2004 the European Council approved the Hague programme to succeed the Tampere programme. Covering the years 2005–9, the Hague programme inevitably gave a higher priority to security issues than its predecessor. It was also less innovatory, with most of it being concerned with either completing or extending existing policy developments. Amongst specified policy aims of the programme were the creation of a comprehensive European asylum policy, the provision of crime 'threat assessments' by Europol, and the strengthening of the Schengen information system.

On the institutional front, the Hague programme reiterated earlier commitments that in practice had not been acted upon to change much of AFSJ law-making in the Council from the consultation procedure with unanimity to the co-decision procedure with QMV. In December 2004 the member states eventually made these changes. In consequence, since January 2005, decisions on asylum, illegal immigration, external border controls, and certain civil law cooperation issues have all been subject to co-decision and Council qualified majority voting.

As was shown in Chapter 6, the Lisbon Treaty completed the movement of AFSJ into the EU 'mainstream' by transferring what remained of the third pillar – the Provisions on Police and Judicial Cooperation in Criminal Matters – into the TFEU and bringing most AFSJ policies together in a new Title V of the TFEU entitled 'Area of Freedom, Security and Justice'. Within Title V the 'Community method' is the normal decision-making mode, with QMV available in the Council for all but a handful of policy areas. The Lisbon Treaty thus significantly advanced the shift from intergovernmentalism to supranationalism that

has been underway in AFSJ decision-making since the Amsterdam Treaty.

But, the 'mainstreaming' of AFSJ by the Lisbon Treaty, and especially the widened ability of the EU to make AFSJ laws by QMV, was not acceptable to the UK Government. This was partly because, as an island, the UK has long viewed its position on issues related to movement of peoples as being different from continental European states – hence the UK's opt-out from the Schengen system. It was partly because the nature of the UK's legal system is different from those of most other European states and hence there were concerns that the Treaty changes would affect the UK disproportionately. And it was partly – and arguably mainly – because perceived losses of national sovereignty in important and sensitive policy areas create considerable controversy in UK politics, with the consequence that AFSJ was an area where the Government was resolved in the IGCs that produced the Constitutional and Lisbon treaties to make a stand. Accordingly, the UK pressed strongly in both IGCs for AFSJ 'protections' of various sorts and, in particular, for its existing special status (with the Schengen opt-out) to be not only confirmed but extended. The Lisbon Treaty duly incorporates – in protocols – arrangements for AFSJ policy development that do not necessarily involve all member states. In particular, there are special arrangements for the three states that are not full Schengen members – Denmark, Ireland and the UK. The arrangements are complex, but the key components are:

1 An 'emergency break' applies to some types of AFSJ decisions that allows *any* state to insist that a legislative measure is halted if the measure effects its legal system. The matter is then referred to the European Council and if no compromise can be found the member state concerned can opt-out of the measure. The other member states can proceed with the measure using the enhanced cooperation procedure.

2 Denmark, Ireland and the UK continue to have special positions in relation to AFSJ matters. There are differences in the extent and legal nature of these special positions, with the UK's position being the strongest. In broad terms, however, the three states can decide whether or not they wish to participate in measures designed to strengthen the Schengen system (which includes matters related to borders, immigration and asylum) and also to decide whether or not to opt-in to new measures

concerned with the creation of the area of freedom, security and justice.

3 Under transitional arrangements, the jurisdiction of the EU's Courts in respect of AFSJ is restricted in a number of ways until 2014.

* * *

The factors noted above that have made AFSJ such an important and rapidly expanding policy area in recent years will doubtless continue to ensure that it occupies a key place on the policy agenda. There may now be an extensive body of EU law in place across the AFSJ area – with, for example, no less than 40 or so laws dealing

---

Document 19.2

Key features of the Stockholm Programme

The Stockholm Programme – An open and secure Europe serving and protecting the citizens

The European Council reaffirms its determination to continue the development of an area of freedom, security and justice, serving and protecting EU citizens and those living in this area. Five years after the Hague Programme ... the European Council adopted a new multi-annual programme for the years 2010–2014, the Stockholm Programme.

The Stockholm Programme focuses on the priorities set out below.

Promoting citizenship and fundamental rights: European citizenship must become a tangible reality. The area of freedom, security and justice must above all be a single area in which fundamental rights are protected. The enlargement of the Schengen area must continue ...

A Europe of law and justice: The achievement of a European area of justice must be consolidated so as to move beyond the current fragmentation. Priority should be given to mechanisms that facilitate access to justice, so that people can enforce their rights throughout the Union ...

A Europe that protects: An internal security strategy should be developed in order to further improve security in the Union and thus protect the lives and safety of European citizens and tackle organised crime, terrorism and other threats. The strategy should be aimed at strengthening cooperation in law enforcement, border management, civil protection, disaster management as well as judicial cooperation in criminal matters in order to make Europe more secure ...

Access to Europe in a globalised world: Access to Europe for persons recognized as having a legitimate interest to access EU territory has to be made more effective and efficient. At the same time, the Union and its Member States have to guarantee security for its citizens. Integrated border management and visa policies should be construed to serve these goals.

A Europe of responsibility, solidarity and partnership in migration and asylum matters: The development of a forward-looking and comprehensive European migration policy, based on solidarity and responsibility, remains a key policy objective for the European Union ... The objective to establish a common asylum system in 2012 remains and people in need of protection must be ensured access to legally safe and efficient asylum procedures. Moreover, in order to maintain credible and sustainable immigration and asylum systems in the EU, it is necessary to prevent, control and combat illegal migration as the EU faces an increasing pressure from illegal migration flows and particularly the Member States at its external borders, including at its Southern borders, in line with the conclusions of the European Council in October 2009.

The role of Europe in a globalised world – the external dimension: The importance of the external dimension of the EU's policy in the area of freedom, security and justice underlines the need for increased integration of these policies into the general policies of the European Union.

Source: European Council Conclusions, 10–11 December 2009: 9–11.

just with different aspect of legal and illegal immigration – but there is no shortage of further measures in the pipeline and under consideration. These and other measures will doubtless ensure that the AFSJ momentum is maintained as the EU continues to tackle such ongoing challenges as protecting individual rights, controlling external borders, advancing asylum and migration policy, fighting organised crime and combating drug abuse. For the foreseeable future, the momentum will be framed within the Stockholm Programme, which was adopted by the European Council in December 2009 as the successor to the Hague Programme. Covering the years 2010–14, the key features of the Stockholm Programme are reproduced in Document 19.2.

Cohesion policy

There are a number of policies, grouped under the general name of cohesion policy, that are designed to provide a partial counterbalance to the 'natural' effects of the internal market by promoting a more balanced distribution of resources and economic development across the EU. The central purpose of cohesion policy is thus to reduce economic and social disparities.

Increased importance has been attached to cohesion policy since the mid-1980s. This partly reflects feelings that a vigorous cohesion policy is necessary for reasons of social justice; it partly reflects beliefs that weaker parts of the EU economy can become stronger if they are given focused and directed assistance; and it partly reflects hard political bargaining by the governments of those member states that are the main beneficiaries of cohesion policy – as evidenced by the way in which, prior to the 2004 enlargement, Spain in particular threatened on more than one occasion to cause problems in other policy areas if cohesion policy was not prioritised/protected/structured in a manner that was to Spain's advantage.

The main policy instruments of cohesion policy are the supporting financial instruments, which are generally referred to as the Structural and Cohesion Funds. These are comparable in size to the CAP in the allocation of EU budgetary resources, accounting for over 35 per cent of total budgetary expenditure for the 2000–6 financial period and assigned some €347 billion, or over 40 per cent of total budgetary expenditure, for the 2007–13 period (see Chapter 22 for details). Key prin-

ciples on which the cohesion financial instruments are based are additionality, which means EU resources should add to rather than replace national resources, and co-financing – by which programmes and projects are co-financed by the EU and member states (with member states normally contributing between 15–50 per cent of a project's costs depending on which fund is being used and the economic situation of the recipient state).

Under the 2000–6 financial perspective there were two main financial instruments, or funds, concerned with cohesion policy: the European Regional Development Fund (ERDF), which accounted for 49 per cent of funding and the European Social Fund (ESF) which accounted for 30 per cent. Additional funding was available from four other sources: the European Agricultural Guidance and Guarantee Fund (EAGGF) (mainly for the Guidance Section), the Financial Instrument for Fisheries Guidance (FIFG), the Cohesion Fund, and a number of Community Initiatives managed directly by the Commission. Under the 2007–13 financial perspective, support for agriculture and fisheries was transferred to separate financial instruments and the number of cohesion financial instruments were reduced to three: the ERDF, the ESF, and the Cohesion Fund.

The reduction in the number of financial instruments was part of an attempt to make cohesion policy simpler, more transparent and, above all, more focused. The re-focusing involved the orientation of cohesion policy around three priority themes: innovation and

Photo 19.1 A typical use of cohesion funding: improving roadworks in Malta, between Valetta (the capital) and an industrial/business centre

the knowledge economy; accessibility and services of general economic interest; and environment and risk prevention. These priority themes, which are designed to complement major EU policy initiatives such as the European Employment Strategy and the Lisbon Process, are given practical effect under three operational headings. These headings are set out in Box 19.5.

The scale of the challenge facing cohesion policy is seen in the fact that since the 2004/07 enlargement, no less than one in three EU citizens – about 170 million – live in the poorest convergence regions. The scale of the challenge is seen also in the wide range of incomes across the EU with, in terms of member states, Luxembourg being the richest member state and Romania – with a per capita income about seven times less that of Luxembourg – being the poorest. Of course, cohesion policy is not aimed at completely removing such variations and creating an equalisation of economic activity and economic wealth across the EU, but it is aimed at narrowing the disparities. Increasingly the contribution of cohesion policy to achieving this aim has come to be seen as concentrating on programme and projects that contribute to promote competitiveness and economic growth. As such, there has been what in recent years has come to be called a 'Lisbonisation' of cohesion policy. The nature of 'Lisbonisation' is considered in the next section.

Box 19.5

The operational headings of cohesion policy

- *Convergence:* supporting growth and job creation in the least developed member states and regions. This is the main priority of cohesion policy, with nearly 82 per cent of total cohesion funding being directed at the convergence regions – which are regions whose per capita GDP is less than 75 per cent of the EU average.
- *Regional competitiveness and employment:* anticipating and promoting change. Designed to fund activities outside the least developed member states and regions, this objective aims, through regional and national programmes, to promote competitiveness, full employment, and social inclusion. It accounts for nearly 16 per cent of cohesion funding.
- *European territorial cooperation:* promoting the harmonious and balanced development of the Union territory. Accounting for around 2.5 per cent of cohesion funding, this objective involves supporting joint and integrated approaches to problems being tackled by member states at cross-border, transnational and inter-regional levels. Examples of activities that qualify for funding include joint urban, rural and coastal development schemes, networked and partnership research and development, and integrated water development.

Social, employment, and economic growth policies

The EEC Treaty provided for the development of a Community social policy. It did so in two ways: Articles 117–22 stated that there should be closer cooperation between the member states in the social field, and particularly specified (in Article 119) that member states should apply the principle that men and women should receive equal pay for equal work; Articles 123–8 laid the foundation for the European Social Fund.

Although the ESF was quickly established, little was done for many years to give effect to Articles 117–22, apart from some developments – via legislation and ECJ judgments – in areas linked to employment matters such as working conditions, entitlement to benefits, and equal opportunities. However, in 1989 a major boost was given to Community social policy when the Commission – believing that the SEM programme should have a 'social dimension' – produced *The Community Charter of Fundamental Social Rights for Workers.* The Charter was inevitably somewhat general in character and terminology, but it contained the fundamental principles that should apply to twelve main themes. Amongst these themes were: free movement of workers on the basis of equal treatment in access to employment and social protection; employment on the basis of fair remuneration; improvement of living and working conditions; freedom of association and collective bargaining; and protection of children and adolescents. The Social Charter was adopted by eleven of the EU's then twelve member states – the UK was the exception – at the 1989 Strasbourg summit and formed the basis for the subsequent Social Chapter that the same eleven states had attached to the Maastricht Treaty in the form of a Protocol and Agreement on Social Policy (see Chapter 5).

The Amsterdam Treaty strengthened the treaty base of social policy in two significant ways. First, the UK, now with a Labour government, removed its objections to the Maastricht Agreement on Social Policy, with the consequence that the Agreement was incorporated into the TEC. Second, a new Employment Title was created in the TEC, with a focus on encouraging and exhorting member states to regard the promotion of employment as a matter of high priority and common concern.

To determine how to give effect to the new TEC Employment Title, a special 'jobs summit' was held in Luxembourg in November 1997. At the summit, a procedure for giving employment promotion a higher priority and more focused approach was agreed. The main stages of the procedure were to be, and still are: employment guidelines, which are subject to annual review, are adopted by the Council on the basis of a proposal from the Commission; the guidelines are incorporated into national employment action plans, which are analysed by the Commission; and the Commission draws up an annual employment report for Council approval which, amongst other things, reviews progress, makes suggestions for modifications of the guidelines, and issues country-specific recommendations to the member states. A central theme of the guidelines and of the Commission's reports has been the need to reform labour markets by, for example, the need for active policies to combat youth and long-term unemployment, to increase labour supply and participation, and to have in place a comprehensive lifelong learning strategy.

Employment was also at the heart of a special European Council meeting held in Lisbon in March 2000. At this summit a ten-year strategic goal was set for the Union 'to become the most competitive and dynamic knowledge-based economy in the world, capable of sustaining economic growth with more and better jobs and greater social cohesion' (European Council, 2000a: 2). Amongst specific goals set at Lisbon were raising the employment rate from an average of 61 per cent in 2000 to as close as possible to 70 per cent by 2010 and increasing the number of women in employment from an average of 51 per cent to 60 per cent by the same year. Various devices were identified to enable the summit's goals to be achieved, many of which focused around 'innovation', 'entrepreneurship' and 'the information society'. Progress in achieving the Lisbon strategic goal was to be reviewed and, where appropriate, updated and extended each spring by the European Council.

As the scheduled mid-term review of the Lisbon Strategy – or Lisbon Process or Lisbon Agenda as it came also to be called – approached, it was becoming clear that progress towards achieving the Strategy's aims was disappointing and that the core goals would not be met. Responding to this, the March 2004 European Council meeting established a high-level group of experts under the chairmanship of the former Dutch Minister, Wim Kok, to investigate ways in which the Strategy could be re-vamped. The group presented its report – *Facing the Challenge: The Lisbon Strategy for Growth and Employment* (Kok, 2004) – in November 2004. The central message of the report was that member governments lacked 'the engagement and political determination' to adopt and implement the structural measures that were necessary to enable the Lisbon goals to be met. They further needed to narrow the number of goals and make them more specific and achievable. Difficult matters that needed to be grasped including cutting taxes, liberalising services, and re-structuring social protection schemes, pensions, and labour markets.

Although not all of its recommendations were accepted, the Kok report subsequently provided much of the basis of a Commission communication to the spring 2005 European Council. In its communication, which was entitled *Working Together For Growth and Jobs – A New Start for the Lisbon Strategy* (European Commission, 2005e), the Commission agreed with Kok that the Strategy needed to be given a sharper focus and be made more deliverable. A range of specific measures and actions were identified including further reforms to complete the internal market, more public and private sector spending on research and development, competition rules to be applied more pro-actively, and more direct employment policies to help people into work and to provide incentives for them to stay there.

The March 2005 European Council meeting

welcomed the Commission's communication and agreed to a re-launching of the Lisbon Strategy. As part of the re-launching, the headline goal of making the EU 'the most competitive and dynamic knowledge-based economy in the world' was dropped. Reflecting criticisms from leftist and trade union quarters, the European Council in its Conclusions gave a higher priority to social market aspects of the Strategy than the Commission had done in its communication (European Council, 2005a).

In the second half of the 2000s, however, there was not much evidence of the revised Lisbon Strategy 'working'. Even allowing for the fact that the international recession made Lisbon objectives all the more difficult to achieve, the Strategy was judged by most observers as not having contributed much to such EU-wide problems as high levels of unemployment, low growth rates, under-investment, and insufficient innovation. However, as deliberations got underway in 2009–10 about the Lisbon Strategy's successor and a ten-year plan taking the EU through to 2020, there were few indications that the new plan – labelled *Europe 2020* – would be radically different from its predecessor. There was a lot of – rather familiar – talk about basing growth on knowledge, empowering innovators and investors, aligning labour market skills more closely with employers' needs, creating a more inclusive society and connected economy, and putting a stronger emphasis on 'green growth'. But, there was a general caution about tackling what was arguably at the heart of the Lisbon Strategy's failings: the lack of strong mechanisms to ensure the meeting of set targets. The caution was explained largely by the known sensitivities of some member states to extensions of the Union's powers in such relevant policy areas as employment and education.

* * *

Having described the development and changing nature of social, employment, and economic growth policies, three points particularly merit being highlighted.

First, although the policies remain in important respects separate, they have in practice increasingly become interlinked and intertwined. As has just been shown, this has been most particularly so in the context of Lisbon Strategy discussions and actions.

The tying-in of social policy with employment and economic growth policies builds on the way in which social policy has been viewed in the EC/EU context from the earliest days, and which was encapsulated by the Social Charter. That is, the EU's social policy roles and responsibilities have always been seen as being largely restricted to market-related issues. 'Mainstream' social policy – dealing with the likes of welfare benefits, care for old people, and protection of vulnerable children – is, like health and education policy, thought of as being primarily a national responsibility. This is illustrated by the sort of areas where EU social policy laws are in place: health and safety of temporary workers, safety signs at work, protection of pregnant women at work, the protection of young people at work, parental leave from work, and the organisation of working time. The EU does, it is true, run a few general social policy programmes of various kinds, including public health programmes and programmes to assist the elderly and the disabled, but they are very modest in both nature and funding.

Second, although there are many different preferences and points of view between policy actors on specific aspects of social, employment, and economic growth policies, a broad division exists between those who take a pronounced liberal approach to how the European economy should be framed and those who take a more social market approach. The depth of this division should not be over-stated, for all EU governments are concerned both about market competitiveness and social protections for citizens. So, for example, with all broadly favouring the greater liberalisation of markets, none has been over-willing to adopt new and strong employee protection measures that might threaten labour market flexibility. But, within a very broad consensus that the European market should be both competitive and have a clear social dimension, there have been and still are clear and persisting differences between governments as to where the balance should lie and how extensively EU policies should be involved in laying down the nature of the balance. These differences have led to considerable policy frictions.

Third, policy approaches, especially in the employment and economic growth domains, display significant differences in character from the way in which most EU policies are built. The usual way – which is seen, for example, in the internal market building programme – rests essentially on the top-down approach of the Community method, in which EU laws are made that member states are obliged to implement. By contrast, many employment and economic growth objectives, and some social policy ones too, are being pursued via more voluntaristic and looser approaches. These approaches, which are coming also to be used in a limited way in some other policy areas, are generally based on some form of the open method of coordination (OMC), which was explained in Chapter 17.

Energy policy

Given the existence of the ECSC and Euratom Treaties, the centrality of energy to any modern economy, the disruption and damage that was caused by oil price increases in the 1970s, and the immense savings that the Commission has for years identified as accruing from an integrated energy market, it is perhaps surprising that until the late 1980s very little progress was made towards a common energy policy (as opposed to having some policies for particular energy sectors). The main obstacle to progress was that the member states – with their differing domestic energy resources, differing energy requirements, and large and often state-owned and monopolistic energy industries – preferred essentially national solutions.

Since the late 1980s, however, there has been a greater receptivity to the idea of a common energy policy and in recent years energy policy has come to assume a high profile and priority. This has been stimulated by a number of factors, which are set out in Box 19.6.

As a consequence of the factors identified in Box 19.6, attitudes towards EU energy policy have been changing and there has been a rapid evolution in the extent of EU policy activity and involvement. The policy has a number of aspects:

- *Developing an internal market in energy.* The core aim of this area of policy is promoting internal competitiveness. Progress has been made in a number of areas, including opening-up public procurement in the energy equipment sector, standardisation of energy equipment and products, provision of more effective EU-wide regulatory oversight, and some liberalisation (though not as much as the Commission, and some member states – including the UK, the Netherlands, Denmark and Sweden – would have liked) of the electricity and gas markets.
- *Developing external energy relations and ensuring security of supply.* Initiatives in this sphere largely focus on: establishing binding rules at the international level for the sale and transportation of energy; engaging in an ongoing dialogue and establishing partnerships with major suppliers, most notably Russia and Middle Eastern states; and seeking agreements with new energy suppliers and assisting them with supply arrangements where appropriate – as with EU support for pipelines from Central Asia to the EU that by-pass Russia.
- *Managing demand.* Various schemes and programmes exist to reduce energy consumption.
- *Diversifying sources.* The EU does not exclude any options, including the nuclear energy option, and funds research programmes in renewable sources.
- *Minimising the negative impact on the environment of energy use and production.* The EU has long had a variety of programmes with such purposes as developing alternative sources of non-polluting energy and reinforcing domestic and industrial efficiency. However, several proposals to give the

---

Box 19.6

Reasons for the increased interest in developing EU energy policy

- There has been an increasing acceptance that the energy sector should not be isolated from the internal market but should be subject to the liberalisation policies that affect other sectors.
- There has been a growing recognition of the over-reliance of the EU on external suppliers – the EU depends on non-member countries for almost half of its energy requirements, with this dependence being as high as 70 per cent in the case of oil.
- The 'aggressive' stances adopted by some EU energy suppliers – especially Russia, which has withheld supplies from some EU member states for periods – has contributed to energy supply concerns.
- The heightened attention given to the need to take measures to tackle climate change has led to an increased interest in measures to save energy and promote cleaner energy production.

environmental dimension of energy policy real teeth by establishing fiscal incentives (for energy saving and the reduction of environmental pollution) and disincentives (for polluting) have met with resistance in the Council of Ministers.

Climate change has given this dimension of energy policy an increased importance and urgency in the 2000s. The EU's response has been to increasingly integrate much of energy and climate change policy. As part of this, in 2007 the European Council agreed that the EU would aim to meet the following 'headline' targets by 2020: to cut greenhouse gases (which emanate in very large part from energy consumption) by 20 per cent of 1990 levels, and by 30 per cent if other major emitters agree to assume their fair share of reducing global emissions (no such agreement was reached at the UN international climate change conference in Copenhagen in December 2009, but the EU's conditional 30 per cent offer has been left 'on the table'; to reduce energy consumption by 20 per cent through increased energy efficiency; and to meet 20 per cent of energy needs from renewable sources (such as wind, waves, solar, and biomass). Given the very different positions of the member states regarding energy consumption – with all, for example, having different starting points on the use of renewables, with differing dependencies on heavily-polluting fossil fuels, and with variations in the distribution of energy-intensive based industries (such as steel and bulk chemicals) – the subsequent negotiations on the implementation schemes and arrangements that would enable the headline targets to be met were, unsurprisingly, very difficult. As with most EU negotiations, member states took different positions on particular matters depending on their current situations and their perceived national interests. MEPs, whose approval was also necessary, had their views too. Eventually, however, agreement on the so-called climate and energy package was reached in December 2008.

The challenge of climate change will doubtless remain high on the list of EU energy policy priorities for years to come. But there will also be many other energy issues that will be pressed and given considerable attention. There will, for example, be pressures for the further liberalisation and de-coupling of energy generation and distribution. There will be the establishment of more extensive and stronger infrastructure networks to allow more open access to grids. And security of supply matters are likely to be become ever more urgent: regarding gas, for instance, the EU currently imports 61 per cent of its needs, but the Commission has estimated that this will rise to 84 per cent by 2030.

Research and innovation policy

There was no mention of research policy in the original EEC Treaty, but it nonetheless began to be developed from the late 1970s in response to a growing concern that the EC's member states were not sufficiently promoting innovation or adapting to innovation, especially in high-tech and other advanced sectors. Recognising, and wishing to promote further, the importance of this policy area, the member states added a new title on 'Research and Technological Development' (R&TD) to the EEC Treaty via the SEA. The title has subsequently been strengthened, with the broad objectives of R&TD policy post-Lisbon Treaty being as set out in Document 19.3.

Document 19.3

The aims of research and innovation policy as set out in the TFEU

The Union shall have the objective of strengthening its scientific and technologoical bases by achieving a European research area in which researchers, scientific knowledge and technology circulate freely, and encouraging it to become more competitive, including in its industry, while promoting all the research activities deemed necessary by virtue of other Chapters of the Treaties.

Source: Treaty on the Functioning of the European Union, Article 179 (1).

The EU's R&TD policy – or research and innovation policy as it is increasingly referred to by the Commission – is pursued, on the one hand, by directly managing and financing research activities and, on the other hand, by attempting to create a framework and environment in which research that falls within the EU's priorities is encouraged and facilitated. More specifically, research activity takes four main forms:

1   Research is undertaken directly by the EU itself at its Joint Research Centre (JRC). The JRC consists of seven establishments and has a staff of 1,700. Most of the work of the JRC is concerned with nuclear energy (especially safety issues), materials, energy, biotechnology, computing, environmental issues, and – increasingly – industrial research related to the internal market.
2   The largest part of EU-backed research consists of shared-cost or contract research. This research is not undertaken by Commission employees but by tens of thousands of researchers in universities, research institutes, and public and private companies. The EU's role is to develop and agree the principles, aims, and conditions of the programmes under which the research is conducted, to coordinate activities, and to provide some of the finance (usually around 50 per cent of the total cost of the research).
3   There are concerted action-research projects where the EU does not finance the actual research, but facilitates and finances the coordination of work being done at the national level. The EU's medical research programme takes this form.
4   Some of the research activity takes none of the above three 'conventional' forms, but consists of arrangements in which, for example, only some member states participate, or in which the EU cooperates with non-member states and international organisations. Work undertaken within the framework of the European Research Coordinating Agency (EUREKA) is of this type, with EUREKA'S membership being extended to several non-EU European states, including Russia.

The EU uses multi-annual framework programmes to coordinate and give strategic direction to its research and innovation policies and activities. The First Framework Programme covered 1984–7, the Second 1987–91, the Third (which overlapped with the Second) 1990–4, the Fourth 1994–8, the Fifth 1999–2002, the Sixth 2000–6, and the Seventh 2007–13. The Seventh Programme builds on the Sixth Programme, which was framed within the context of the Lisbon Strategy aim of creating a dynamic and knowledge-based EU economy. As part of this aim, the Sixth Programme began a process of trying to create a European Research Area (ERA). The ERA seeks: to concentrate research support on priority research areas; to strengthen the coordination and coherence of research at European and national levels; to strengthen bridges between research and innovation; to promote the human potential for research and the mobility of researchers; and to advance the particular scientific

---

Box 19.7

The main strands of the Seventh Framework Programme for Research and Technological Development

- *Cooperation.* This is the 'core' of FP7, accounting for around two thirds of the total budget. It promotes transnational collaboration between universities, industry, research centres and public authorities across the EU (and some partner countries) and assists them to 'gain leadership' in science and technology. Research is focused on ten priority areas including: information and communication technologies; nanosciences, nanotechnologies, materials, and new production techniques; energy; environment; and health.
- *Ideas.* This supports 'frontier' research in all areas of science and technology.
- *People.* This assists researchers with skills development, mobility, and career development.
- *Capacities.* This supports research infrastructures, regional research clusters, small and medium-sized enterprises, and science and technology cooperation policy.
- *Nuclear research.* This has long been an important area for EU research policy. It covers a wide range of research activities, including nuclear fusion, nuclear fission, and nuclear waste management.

and technological research needs arising from EU policies.

The total budget for the Seventh Programme (FP7) is €50 billion (at 2006 prices – when the programme was agreed). FP7 has five main 'building bocks', which are set out in Box 19.7.

When the Lisbon Strategy was launched in 2000 with the aim of making the EU economy much more innovative and competitive, research policy was identified as one of the core supporting policy instruments. Accordingly, EU leaders stressed the importance of increasing spending on research and agreed that by 2010 at least three per cent of Europe's GDP should be invested in research. This goal has not been met, with the figure sticking at just below two per cent – which is about one per cent lower than that of both the USA and Japan. Spending in some member states – including France, Finland and Germany – is in the region of the three per cent target, but the overall average is dragged down by many 'laggards' – including the UK, Greece, and most CEECs.

Of course, levels of research spending are but one of a number of factors that shape economic competitiveness and innovation. But, there seems little doubt that the relatively low average level in the EU is at least a significant contributory reason to explaining why, on most indicators of competitiveness and innovation, the EU does not come out well when compared with its principal competitors in the global market.

Environmental policy

As with research policy, there was no mention of environmental policy in the original EEC Treaty. However, it too was incorporated into the Treaty by the SEA. Later treaties have built on the SEA provisions, though not by much.

The broad aims of EU environmental policy are laid down in Articles 11 and 191 of the TFEU, the key parts of which are reproduced in Document 19.4.

Since Community environmental legislation began to appear in the early 1970s, a number of operating principles have been developed, amongst which are sustainability, preventative action, the polluter pays, shared responsibilities of different levels of government,

---

Document 19.4

The aims of EU environmental policy as set out in the TFEU

Article 11
Environmental protection requirements must be integrated into the definition and implementation of the Union policies and activities, in particular with a view to promoting sustainable development.

Article 191
1 Union policy on the environment shall contribute to the pursuit of the following objectives:

- preserving, protecting and improving the quality of the environment,
- protecting human health,
- prudent and rational utilisation of natural resources,
- promoting measures at international level to deal with regional or worldwide environmental problems, and in particular combating climate change.

2 Union policy on the environment shall aim at a high level of protection taking into account the diversity of situations in the various regions of the Union. It shall be based on the precautionary principle and on the principles that preventive action should be taken, that environmental damage should as a priority be rectified at source and that the polluter should pay.

Source: Treaty on the Functioning of the European Union, Articles 11 and 191.

and integration of environmental concerns into other policy areas. As they have been developed, these principles have – as Document 19.4 shows – been given treaty status. They have also been incorporated into EU legislation where possible and as appropriate.

There are now well over 200 environmental policy legal instruments, most of them in the form of directives. They cover matters as diverse as water and air pollution, disposal of chemicals, waste treatment, and protection of species and natural resources. Alongside, and supporting, the legal instruments are several other types of policy instrument, ranging from information campaigns to arrangements for the collection of environmental data. The latter is the particular responsibility of the European Environment Agency, which was established in 1994 and is located in Copenhagen.

Document 19.5, which presents extracts from the official report issued after a typical meeting of EU Environment Ministers, gives a flavour of the very great range of issues that are on the EU's environmental agenda. The report also hints at the sort of differences that exist between member states on many key environmental issues. These differences can arise from such factors as the varying industrial make-ups of the states (and therefore the different concentrations of polluting industries), different views on what constitute environmental threats (for example, there are long-standing differences between member states on the 'threats' posed by genetically modified organisms – GMOs), and different cultural traditions (such as towards the shooting of migratory birds).

Many of the EU's environmental policy instruments, both legislative and non-legislative, have been designed to give effect to the series of Environmental Action Programmes that have been adopted since 1973. The Sixth Programme, entitled *Environment 2010: Our Future, Our Choice,* covers the 2001–10 period. Building on, but also extending, existing practices, the Programme sets out five approaches to be applied across environmental policy. These approaches can be expected to continue to feature prominently in the Seventh Programme:

- Implementation of existing environmental legislation to be improved.
- Integration of environmental concerns into other policy areas to be deepened.
- Working with the market to be intensified, by encouraging business and consumer interests to

contribute to more sustainable production and consumption patterns.
- Individual citizens to be given better quality and more easily accessible information on environmental issues, with a view to making them more environmentally sensitive.
- Development of a more environmentally conscious attitude towards land use.

The first of these approaches – improving the implementation of EU environmental laws – arises as a result of there being particular problems of policy implementation in the environmental sphere. Because of the way in which the EU is structured and because of the Commission's limited resources, implementation of EU laws is, of course, also a problem in other EU policy spheres and sectors. But, for a number of reasons, it is especially so in respect of the environment. One of these reasons is expense. Much environmental legislation requires major capital expenditure – by private industry and/or public agencies – if standards set in EU laws are to be met. It is, for example, very costly for many national authorities – especially in areas of high population density – to fund the measures required to meet the standards specified in the bathing water directive: a directive that is, in consequence, notorious for poor implementation. Another, related, reason why environmental policy implementation is frequently difficult is that member states often have very different starting points on environmental practices. So, for example, the Commission has been pressing for some years for a major strengthening of EU policy on waste management and for the EU to become in the long-term a 'recycling society'. But, member states are in very different positions concerning their current practices regarding the proportions of waste that are recycled, are incinerated, and are sent to landfill sites: the Netherlands, for example, recycles about 65 per cent of its waste, whilst Portugal recycles only about 3 per cent.

Alongside the five approaches prioritised in the Sixth Programme are four priority areas. They can be expected to continue to be prioritised in the future:

- *Tackling climate change.* This was examined earlier in the chapter, in the section on energy policy. Suffice to say here that the EU has taken an advanced position in setting targets for tackling the problem of the emission of greenhouse gases but,

Document 19.5

Items covered at a typical meeting of the Environment Council of Ministers

2953rd Council meeting

Environment

Luxembourg, 25 June 2009

Items debated

Biodiversity and invasive alien species

Industrial emissions

The Council reached political agreement with a view to the subsequent adoption of a common position concerning the recast of the directive on integrated pollution prevention and control.

The IPPC Directive seeks to prevent and control, in a coordinated way, pollution of the air, water and soil resulting from emissions from industrial installations. It regulates emissions of a wide range of pollutants, including sulphur and nitrogen compounds, dust particles, asbestos and heavy metals. The directive is aimed at improving local air, water and soil quality, not at mitigating the global warming effects of some of these substances. Emissions of carbon dioxide are not covered by IPPC.

Soil protection

The Presidency briefed the Council on progress concerning the draft directive establishing a framework for the protection of soil, as set out in its report.

While the European Parliament delivered its opinion in first reading in November 2007, the Council has not yet reached political agreement on this dossier. Several delegations regretted this fact and expressed the need for a Community instrument, whereas others reiterated their opposition to such common measures as well as their concerns in relation to administrative burden and cost-effectiveness.

Soil has not, to date, been subject to a specific common protection policy at Community level. The draft directive aims to fill this gap by establishing a common strategy for the protection of soil, based on the principles of

- integration of soil concerns into other policies and preservation of soil functions,
- prevention of threats to soil through the identification of priority areas and the establishment of action programmes,
- identification of contaminated sites and remediation of such sites.

Climate Change

Ministers held an exchange of views, highlighting their continued commitment to the ultimate objective of achieving an ambitious and comprehensive global agreement in Copenhagen [on tackling climate change]. ...

A number of crucial issues remain unresolved both internally and externally. Therefore the EU will need to employ a parallel approach whereby it

1 Continues to deliver strong messages to negotiating counterparts.
2 Elaborates a vision for the agreement in Copenhagen.
3 Finalises a full mandate well in advance of the Conference in Copenhagen.

→

Document 19.5 *continued*

In doing so the EU must remain united and deliver clear common messages. The value of a coordinated and enhanced diplomatic effort by the EU and its member states with all major negotiating partners, in particular the U.S. and the BRIC countries, was highlighted …

The EU considers it crucial to get agreement in Copenhagen on limiting average global surface temperature rise to below 2°C and for the global emissions pathway consistent with this objective to be incorporated into the agreement including a global reduction in emissions of at least 50% below 1990 levels by 2050 with global emissions peaking by no later than 2020. Mechanisms to ensure developed countries achieve credible pathways to emission reductions of at least 80% by 2050 in relation to 1990 levels, including commitment to comparable robust milestones in the medium term was highlighted. Strenuous actions by developing countries will also need to be enshrined in the agreement if there is to any chance of meeting the 2°C objective.

The EU has adopted an ambitious target for mitigation and the EU should continue to emphasise this commitment and its willingness to move to a reduction of up to 30% subject to adequate commitments from other parties; this offer is a key 'lever' in the negotiations. The EU and its member states will consider in further detail the precise criteria for the interpretation of 'adequacy' in this context and will also agree upon the means by which the 30% reduction would be achieved in practice.

Bio-waste

Other business

Genetically modified organisms

Timber products
The Presidency informed the Council about the progress which had been made on the proposal for a regulation laying down the obligations of operators who place timber and timber products on the market.

Chemicals
The Danish delegation highlighted the importance of a coordinated approach to dealing with combination effects of chemicals (cocktail-effects), including endocrine disrupters. Experts regard the predominant chemical-by-chemical approach in risk assessment as insufficiently protective against the possibility of mixture effects. Denmark urged the Council and the incoming Presidency to start work in order to ensure that due account is taken of the risk of combination effects in EU chemicals legislation.

International environment policy

Environment for Europe

Conferences

EU–China near zero emissions coal plant project

Other items approved

Environment
Adaptation to climate change:
The Council adopted conclusions on 'Climate change: Towards a comprehensive EU adaptation strategy'.

Note: the full agenda is not listed here, and supporting information is given only for some agenda items.
Source: Council of the European Union: 11259/09 (Presse 190).

as the outcome of the 2009 UN Copenhagen conference on climate change showed – no binding targets for restricting emissions could be agreed – has had little success in persuading other major polluters to adopt similar positions.

- *Nature and bio-diversity.* This promotes conservation measures to protect endangered species, natural habitats in decline, landscapes, the marine environment and soils. It also promotes increased sectoral bio-diversity.
- *Environment and health.* This promotes a more holistic approach to environmental improvement, with a particular focus on problems concerning chemicals, water and air quality, and noise.
- *Sustainable use of natural resources and wastes.* This promotes measures that help to ensure the consumption of renewable and non-renewable resources does not exceed the delivery capacity of the environment. In addition, measures advancing the recycling and recovery of wastes are identified and encouraged.

Beyond its 'internal' environmental policy activities, the EU promotes international cooperation on environmental issues and – as, for example, with climate change – actively participates in international environmental forums.

Sectoral Policies

Some EU policies are directed towards specific economic sectors. A few such policies – covering coal and steel, atomic energy, agriculture and transport – were explicitly provided for in the Founding Treaties. Others have their origins in a combination of factors: difficulties in adjusting to changed market conditions; rapid sectoral decline; and effective political lobbying by interested parties.

The most obvious example of a sectoral policy is the Common Agricultural Policy (CAP), which consumes around two-fifths of EU budgetary expenditure and where most major policy-making responsibilities have been transferred from the member states to the EU. The CAP is examined in some detail in Chapter 20. Another, though more modest and less comprehensive example of a sectoral policy is atomic energy where, for example, important research work is

undertaken on the more economical use of atomic energy and on safety standards.

Two of the EU's most important sectoral policies cover fishing and shipbuilding.

Fishing

After years of discussion and the periodic issuing of laws regulating aspects of the industry, a legally enforceable Common Fisheries Policy (CFP) was agreed in 1983. The essential rationale of the CFP, based on reforms that were adopted at the end of 2002, is to ensure that, with resources diminishing, existing fish stocks are exploited responsibly, with due care for the marine ecosystem and with the interests of fishermen and consumers protected as far as possible. The main pillars of the CFP are set out in Box 19.8.

The CFP is widely recognised as being a policy that has major problems. At the heart of the difficulties is, as the Commission recognised in a consultative Green Paper it issued in April 2009 on the future of the CFP, the depleted state of fish stocks (European Commission, 2009b). Nearly 90 per cent of stocks are over-fished, with 30 per cent 'outside safe biological limits'. This over-fishing is a consequence of fishing fleet over-capacity coupled with an inability of Fisheries Ministers to be able to make decisions only on the basis of scientific advice.

Shipbuilding

Rather like fisheries, shipbuilding's central problem has been over-capacity. But whereas with fisheries the over-capacity has been created by insufficient fish stocks, with shipbuilding it has been caused by insufficient competitiveness on world markets. This lack of competitiveness has arisen essentially from two factors: on the one hand, years of state aid by European governments to national shipbuilders so as to keep them in business; on the other hand, very low prices being charged by competitors, especially in Japan and Korea. Today the EU accounts for only around 10 per cent of world production, as compared with Japan's 32 per cent and Korea's 29 per cent.

To deal with shipbuilding's over-capacity and lack of competitiveness, EU shipbuilding policy has

Box 19.8

The main pillars of the Common Fisheries Policy

- *Access.* All waters within the EU's exclusive fishing zone, which extends to 200 nautical miles from its coastlines, are open to all EU fishermen. However, within a 12-mile limit of their own shores member states may reserve fishing for their own fishermen and those with traditional rights.
- *Conservation.* Fish stocks are controlled by the annual setting of total allowance catches (TACs), which are set within multi-annual management framework plans that are designed to protect, and in appropriate cases to enable the recovery of, stocks. TACs are divided into national quotas. The size of TACs and quotas are set in December each year by the Council, on the basis of proposals from the Commission which acts on scientific advice. Domestic political pressures invariably result in the Council setting higher limits for at least some species than are proposed by the Commission.

  TACs and quotas are notoriously difficult to enforce and there is known to be widespread abuse, with the landing of fish that are over quota or undersized. The EU has tried to tackle the problem by strengthening policy implementation mechanisms. Amongst the mechanisms in place are the following: all EU fishing vessels are required to have a fishing licence on board; Commission inspectors (of which there are only a few) have the right of unannounced arrival in ports and on vessels; and use is made of satellite technology to monitor fishing activities. In March 2005 the Council approved the establishment of a Fisheries Control Agency to strengthen enforcement coordination and efficiency. Amongst the responsibilities of the Agency are the development of EU-wide standards for training inspectors and organising the deployment of surveillance resources.
- *Structural measures.* The European Fisheries Fund, with a budget of €3.8 billion for the 2007–13 period, is available for a variety of – mainly structural – purposes. These include processing and market development projects, safety schemes, redeployment measures, and assistance with conversions of fishing boats and equipment so as to remove environmentally destructive fishing practices.
- *External negotiations.* Negotiations with non-EU countries on fishing – which mostly concern access to waters and the conservation of fish stocks – are conducted by EU representatives on behalf of all member states.

been focused around three broad and inter-related objectives:

- *Rationalisation* – by means of a controlled cut-back in capacity.
- *Enhancing productivity and competitiveness* of the industry, especially in those segments of shipbuilding where the EU maintains a world position. These segments are in high technological areas of production such as advanced container vessels, tankers, chemical and gas carriers, and small specialised ships.
- *Providing re-structuring opportunities* for areas affected by rationalisation and *re-training opportunities* for individuals who are made redundant.

A key policy instrument in respect of the first and second of these objectives has been a tightening of rules on state aid. The rules are now comparable to those for other industries, with aid being permissible for some modernisation and restructuring activities but largely prohibited for contract-related operating aid. Another policy instrument, of vital importance in respect of the second objective, has been liaising and negotiating with competitors on ending aid to the shipbuilding industry. In 1994, the EU, Japan, South Korea, Norway and the USA reached an agreement under OECD auspices aimed at eliminating all existing measures or practices constituting obstacles to normal competitive conditions. There have, however, been problems with the full application of this agreement, as there have been with WTO rules on state subsidisation of support. A third policy instrument, used for the third objective, has been ERDF and ESF assistance for regional development and for the re-training of workers.

Concluding Remarks

This chapter has shown the very wide range of the EU domestic policy involvement and has also shown that the extent and the nature of the involvement vary considerably between policy areas. Two factors are particularly important in explaining this varying extent and nature. The first is the relationship of policies to the operation of the market. Broadly speaking it can be said that the more policies directly impact on the market then the more there is EU involvement. So, for example, the EU is heavily involved in setting standards for marketed products and practices, laying down and applying competition rules, and promoting measures that will increase market efficiency, but it is much less involved in areas such as criminal law and road safety. Where the impact of policies on the operation of the market is disputed by the member states and where there are strong differences between member states as to whether competition between them on market-related policies is or is not desirable, then the EU's policy involvement tends to display some mixture of the following: it is only partially developed, as with labour market policy; it is heavily reliant on 'soft' policy instruments, as with much of social and employment policy; and it does not involve all member states, as with the single currency and the Schengen System.

The second factor is cost. The EU does not have, and never has had any prospect of having, a large budget. There is, of course, an element of cause as well as effect here. That is, on the one hand, a cause of the EU not having a large budget is that the traditional areas of high public expenditure – such as social welfare, education and health – are generally seen as being 'naturally' national policies and not candidates for being much developed at EU level. But, on the other hand, there is also an element of effect in that the EU's relatively small budget and the resolve of the budget's main 'paymasters' (northern EU-15 states) to keep the budget small means that it is difficult to develop 'spending policies' except – as with environmental policy – on a basis in which the EU regulates, guides and encourages but the costs of policy implementation are met at national levels.

Chapter 20

Agricultural Policy and Policy Processes

The Common Agricultural Policy in Context

Despite the fact that, even after the 2004/07 enlargement, it accounts for only 1.2 per cent of EU GDP and just over 5 per cent of EU employment, agriculture looms large in the life of the EU. It does so for five main reasons. First, the economic impact of agriculture is greater than indicated by the figures just given, for in addition to farming itself there are many industries that are closely linked to agriculture and are dependent on its success. These industries include agro-chemicals and fertilisers, agricultural equipment, food processing, veterinary medicines, and financial services. Second, the EU has, via the Common Agricultural Policy (CAP), major policy-making and decision-making responsibilities for agriculture. Indeed, agriculture is the most integrated of the EU's sectoral policies. Third, as a major recipient of EU funds – accounting for over two-fifths of total annual budgetary expenditure – agriculture is central to EU budgetary deliberations. Fourth, there is a greater institutional presence and activity in the agricultural field than in any other: the Agriculture Ministers normally meet more frequently than the ministers of all other Councils except for the Foreign and Ecofin Ministers; Agriculture Council meetings are prepared not by COREPER but by a special body, the Special Committee on Agriculture (SCA); the Agriculture Directorate General is the second largest of the Commission's DGs (only Personnel and Administration is larger and that does not deal with a policy sector); and there are far more Council working parties and Commission management and advisory committees in the sphere of agriculture than in any other single policy area. Fifth, agriculture is the most controversial of the EU's policies, with the member states disagreeing on many issues, most notably the extent to which and the ways in which the sector should be protected.

For its supporters, the most important benefits accruing from the CAP are a plentiful and stable food supply and the maintenance of productive activity in the countryside. The CAP is seen also as an important symbol and indicator that real policy integration is possible at EU level. Those who criticise the CAP are thus liable to be attacked both on technical and efficiency grounds – with the claim that national solutions would be much less satisfactory – and more broadly for lacking a European spirit – with the assertion that this most integrated of EU policies should not be undermined. For opponents of the CAP, economic efficiency is the key issue, with criticisms focusing especially on the subsidisation of wealthy farmers and agri-companies, high prices for consumers, the production of farm surpluses, the cost of disposing of the surpluses, and the damage caused to agriculture in the underdeveloped world when the surpluses are disposed of via subsidised 'dumping' on the world market.

Yet even amongst those who are most critical of the CAP, few seriously challenge the view that there should be an EU agriculture policy of some kind. Certainly no member state government believes that the agricultural edifice should be wholly uprooted and policy returned completely to national capitals (though UK governments come close to this position). The view that there is something special about agriculture, something that distinguishes it from other sectoral activities and merits it receiving advantageous treatment, still strikes a chord with EU decision-makers – though it does not command such strong support as in the early days of the EC.

What is Special about Agriculture?

The attention given to agriculture in the EEC Treaty and the subsequent creation of the CAP after long and often tortuous negotiations is often seen as being part of a trade-off between France and Germany. There is some truth to this view. In exchange for the creation of a common market in industrial goods, which the French feared would be greatly to Germany's advantage, France – with its large but uneconomic agricultural sector – would benefit from an agricultural system that, though also in the form of a common market, would be based not on free and open market principles but on foundations that would protect farmers from too much competition.

Important though it was, however, the Franco-German 'deal' is only part of the explanation of why agriculture, from the earliest days of the Community, was given an elevated policy status. For the fact is that when the CAP was being created in the late 1950s and early 1960s, none of the then six member states seriously objected to it in principle – the Netherlands, for example, was a strong supporter – though there were differences between the states on the pace of the CAP's construction and the precise nature of its policy instruments. This consensus on the existence of the CAP was a result of a shared recognition that agriculture required special treatment.

Today, despite the EC and then EU having greatly increased in size, despite the circumstances and conditions of agriculture having dramatically changed, and despite the CAP having caused major difficulties and

disruptions to the whole EU system, agriculture is still generally regarded by the national governments as requiring special treatment. Many of the reasons for this are much the same as they were in the EC's early days. Others are more recent. The reasons can be grouped under two general headings: the distinctive nature of agriculture and political factors.

The distinctive nature of agriculture

Most governments of the industrialised world take the view that agriculture is not like other areas of economic activity. It is special and as such merits special treatment to encourage, assist and protect it. In the EU, five main arguments have been advanced in support of this view, the relative importance of which has varied over time.

The first argument – which, with CAP reforms over the years, is not as important now as formerly it was – stems from the fact that agricultural prices are subject to considerable fluctuation if they are not subject to public intervention and regulation. This is largely because, even with modern farming techniques, agricultural supply is heavily dependent on the weather. Agricultural price instability is seen as being undesirable for two reasons. First, if prices suddenly go up, inflation is immediately fuelled (given that food constitutes around 20 per cent of the budget of the average EU citizen). Second, if prices fall too low, farmers may not be able to make an adequate living and may be forced off the land. Even those who are able to stay in farming may experience severe difficulties as a result of high debt loads on land and capital purchases.

The second argument is that reliance on imports for vital foodstuffs creates a potential vulnerability to outside pressures. In the early years of the EC, when memories were still fresh of wartime shortages and the international trading climate was strained, this argument played an important part in encouraging a drive for greater self-sufficiency. However, in the relatively calm international trading conditions that now exist, and with many of the foodstuffs produced in the EU being in surplus – including cereals, dairy produce and beef – it is an argument that, though still heard, is less weighty than it used to be.

The third argument asserts that because people must have food, insufficient domestic production means the gap between output and demand has to be met by imports, with potentially damaging consequences for the balance of payments. Moreover, since the demand for food is fairly inelastic up to necessity levels (as long as income allows it, food will still be bought even if prices go up) the economic vulnerability of an importing state is high. This balance of payments argument used to be important in helping to underpin the CAP, but it has not been so forceful since the early to mid-1970s when Community prices became significantly higher than world prices and Community production began to move significantly into surplus. Indeed, high domestic prices mean that EU processors cannot maximise their value added exports by buying at the cheapest possible prices and consumers must pay more for food, while surpluses mean that national treasuries have to pay – via the EU budget – for their disposal.

The fourth argument suggests that farmers should be encouraged to stay on the land for social and environmental reasons. Sometimes such calls have an idealistic tone to them, with pleas that a populated countryside is part of the natural fabric or the suggestion that management of the land is a desirable end in itself. Rather more hard-headed perhaps are the arguments that land that is not managed often reverts to scrub which is inimical to bio-diversity, and that it is both undesirable and potentially dangerous to allow farm incomes to deteriorate to the point that poor farmers and agricultural workers are forced to move to the towns in search of employment that often does not exist.

The fifth argument is that agriculture must be treated with particular care because it is intrinsically linked with food health and safety. A series of food scares in Europe since the mid-1990s has brought this consideration firmly onto the political agenda. The BSE/CJD crisis in particular – which first erupted in 1996 and focused on the extent to which BSE in (primarily British) beef was being passed on to humans in the form of CJD – has obliged decision-makers to take a broader view of what should be the content and priorities of agricultural policy.

Political factors

The agriculture sector enjoys political assets that have been translated into influence on EU policy. Four of these assets are especially important.

1 Since the CAP was established, the governments of those states that benefit most from CAP financial transfers have been strong defenders of the system. The line-up of these states has not been wholly consistent over time as circumstances have changed, but in recent years the most prominent opponents of reductions in EU expenditure on agriculture have included France (which accounts for 20 per cent of total EU agricultural production and which is the most notable permanent member of the 'anti-reform' club), Germany (which accounts for 12 per cent), Spain (which also accounts for 12 per cent), and Ireland (which accounts for 2 per cent and where agriculture accounts for just 2 per cent of national GDP, but where agriculture looms large in the national 'psyche'.)

2 At the national decision-making level, Ministries of Agriculture have traditionally tended to be slightly apart from mainstream policy processes, and since 1958 this has been reproduced at the EU level with the position of the Agriculture DG in the Commission. All policy-makers in all areas of policy do, of course, attempt to use their own expertise, knowledge and information to provide themselves with some insulation from the rest of the decision-making system, but agriculture is particularly well placed to do this. Its supposedly distinctive nature, the complexity of much of its subject matter, and the customary close relations between agricultural decision-makers and producers, all combine to make it difficult for 'outside' decision-makers to offer an effective challenge or alternative to what is presented to them. That all said, in a few member states this 'separateness' of Agriculture Ministries is now becoming not quite what it was, with – as in the UK, for example – agriculture becoming part of more broadly based environment/rural affairs departments.

3 Farmers enjoy considerable electoral weight. Even though their relative numerical importance has declined sharply over the years – in 1958 around 25 per cent of total EC employment was in agriculture, by 2002 it was less than 5 per cent, and in the post-2004/07 enlarged EU it is just over 5 per cent – the agricultural vote is still significant. The significance varies from state to state. The size of the domestic population engaged in agriculture is one important factor in determining this significance: proportions

vary considerably, with around 15 per cent of the working population in Poland, 12 per cent in Greece, 11 per cent in Portugal, 2 per cent in Belgium, and 1.5 per cent in the UK. Another consideration is the direction of the agricultural vote. In some member states the agricultural vote is disproportionately directed towards small parties which, benefiting from proportional representation, can be key players in national politics and government. On the whole, farmers, especially richer farmers, incline towards Centre-Right and Right parties, with the consequence that it is they, rather than parties of the Left, that are usually the strongest defenders of agricultural interests in EU forums. But this inclination to the Right does not, in most countries, amount to an exclusive loyalty, so few parties can afford to ignore the farmers: at a minimum, all parties must give the impression of being concerned and solicitous.

4   In most EU countries, farmers have long had very strong domestic organisations to represent and articulate their interests. When it became clear in the 1960s that much agricultural policy and decision-making was being transferred to Brussels, similar organisations were quickly established at Community level. As early as 1963 approaching 100 Community-wide agriculture groups had been formed. Today the number is around 130. The most important of these groups is the Committee of Agricultural Organisations in the European Union/General Confederation of Agricultural Co-operatives in the EU (COPA/COGECA), which is an alliance of umbrella or peak organisations attempting to represent all types of farmers on the basis of affiliation through national farming groups. Beyond COPA/COGECA and a few other overarching organisations, specialist bodies exist to represent virtually every product that is produced and consumed in the EU and also all participants in the agricultural process – farmers most obviously, but also processors, traders, retailers and so on.

The influence of this agricultural lobby has declined over the years, but it is still a significant force in the EU. It is worth setting out the reasons why this is so.

The sheer size of the lobby is formidable

It operates at two levels, the national and the EU.

At the national level there are considerable variations in the pattern and strength of agricultural representation. But in all member states there are groups of some kind that have as part of their purpose the utilisation of whatever devices and channels are available to them to influence both national and EU agricultural policy (within the general principles of the CAP, member states enjoy a considerable policy discretion). Thus, the National Farmers' Union for England and Wales employs a full-time professional staff of 160 at its London headquarters plus around 1,000 staff in over 300 local offices. In addition, the NFU funds – in conjunction with the NFU of Scotland and the Ulster Farmers' Union – a Brussels office, known as the British Office of Agriculture, which has a regular staff of between five and ten who are topped up as and when required.

At the EU level the large number of Euro-agric groups means that lobbying activities across the agricultural sector are almost continuous. COPA/COGECA moves on the broadest front, and with over 50 full-time officials is by far the best resourced and staffed organisation (for further information on COPA/COGECA see Chapter 14, and COPA/COGECA's website at www.copa-cogeca.be). The more specialised groups – such as the mustard makers (CIMCEE) and the butchers (COBCCEE) – are much more modestly provided for and at best may have just one full-time member of staff working in an office made available by a national affiliate. But since the interests of these small groups are usually narrowly drawn this is just about enough to allow basic lobbying and representational requirements to be fulfilled – holding meetings and consultations with decision-makers, feeding information through to the EU institutions and to members, and preparing policy and briefing documents. If necessary, reinforcements are usually available from national and Euro-umbrella associations.

Agricultural interests generally enjoy good contacts with, and access to, decision-makers

Again, this factor operates at both national and EU levels. At the national level, influence with governments is vital, not only because of their control over nationally determined policies but also because they are the route to the Council of Ministers. Most governments are at least prepared to listen to representations from national agricultural interests, and some engage in a virtually automatic consultation on important issues. There are a number of reasons why governments are generally approachable in this way: there may be a pre-existing sympathy for the interests' views; a fuller picture of what is going on in the agricultural world is made possible; policy implementation may be made easier; and political support may be generated by being sympathetic – or at least by giving the impression that the government and the interest are as one. If, despite being seemingly listened to by its government, a national agricultural interest is dissatisfied with what is agreed in the Council of Ministers, the government can always try to blame 'the awkward Italians', 'the impossible Greeks' or 'the immovable Poles'.

At the EU level, the Commission is the prime target for agricultural interests. For the most part it is very willing to listen. Indeed, it has encouraged the establishment of Euro-agric groups and readily makes itself available to them. Close Commission–group relations are viewed by the Commission as being extremely useful: the groups can contribute their knowledge and experience, which may improve policy; the Commission can explain to the groups why it is engaging in certain actions and thus try to sensitise them to Commission concerns and aims; face-to-face meetings can help break down barriers and resistance arising from suspicions that 'the Eurocrats' do not really understand farming practicalities; and if Eurogroups can do something to aggregate the conflicting national interests and demands that inevitably arise in relation to most proposals they can considerably simplify the Commission's task of developing policies that are acceptable and can help to legitimise the Commission as a decision-maker in the eyes of the Council and the EP. All that said, however, it is the case that since the mid-1980s the Commission, though maintaining close links with the agricultural lobby, has been less influenced by it. A major reason for this is that the Commission has been obliged to try to reform the agricultural sector, whilst organisations such as COPA/COGECA have been, in Grant's words, 'seeking to defend the ancient regime' (Grant, 1997: 170).

The agricultural organisations are not counterbalanced by strong and vigorous groups advancing contrary attitudes and claims

'Natural opponents' do exist – consumers and environmentalists most notably – but they are relatively weak in comparison. A major reason for their weakness is that whereas farmers constitute a clear section of the population with a readily identifiable common sectoral interest, consumers and environmentalists do not have such a group consciousness, are more widely dispersed and, in consequence, are just not so easy to mobilise or organise. So although there are many more consumers than there are farmers in the EU, the largest of the Euro-consumer groups – the European Bureau of Consumers' Associations (BEUC) – has a staff of only twenty or so. This is sizeable enough when compared with most Eurogroups, but it pales in comparison with the massed ranks of the agricultural associations. Moreover, the BEUC has to cover the whole spectrum of relevant EU policies: agriculture takes up only part of its time.

Additionally, in terms of access to decision-makers, the farmers' 'rivals' do not as a rule enjoy the 'insider status' granted to much of the agriculture lobby. They rarely have a 'sponsoring' ministry in the way that agricultural interests do. Nor are they necessarily consulted by the Commission on agricultural matters as a matter of routine, nor automatically called in for discussions when something of importance or potential interest arises. The fact is they do not have the political and economic power of farmers, they cannot offer trade-offs in the way of cooperation on policy implementation, they are – in some instances – relative latecomers, and a few – notably the more radical greens – are seen as not conforming to established values and the rules of the game. Some of the more respectable of these 'oppositional' agriculture groups have their foot in the EU door – BEUC, for instance, is a recognised 'social partner' – but none has quite entered the room in the manner of the agricultural lobby.

Agriculture has powerful friends

While farmers and those directly engaged in the agricultural industries have been the most obvious beneficiaries of the CAP, others have gained too, notably the owners of land. Huge profits have been made by investment institutions, financiers, banks, industrial corporations and private landlords from the rising value of land that has been associated with the CAP. Many of these interests have direct access to decision-makers, indeed are themselves amongst the decision-makers in some governments, and have sought to use their influence accordingly.

Unity has been a source of strength

Despite the great range of interests represented, the agriculture lobby was, until the early 1980s, more or less united in its aims: it pressed for comprehensive market regimes for as much produce as possible and it sought the largest price increases it could get. Since that time, however, as significant steps to bring spending on agriculture under control have been taken and as EC/EU enlargements have made the interests of the agricultural sector more divergent, the unity of the lobby has been subject to increasing strains and its effectiveness has accordingly been weakened. Sectors have vied with one another as increasing attention has had to be paid not only to the size of the cake but also to the way in which it is cut. Increasing competition *within* the agricultural sector has been no more clearly demonstrated than by the division in recent years between COPA/COGECA and the European Farmers Coordination (CPE) which represents small farmers. In the context of agricultural reform discussions and negotiations, CPE has been much more in favour than COPA/COGECA of the redistribution of support to small farmers and of broadly based rural development activities.

Farmers sometimes resort to direct action

In some EU countries, farmers sometimes take matters into their own hands if they are dissatisfied with policies and decisions affecting their sector. Disruption of transport networks is a particularly favoured tactic. Whilst decision-makers never care to admit that they have been swayed by direct action, there is no doubt that farmers' militancy has affected at least some of those who are responsible for running EU agriculture.

How the Common Agricultural Policy Works

Title III of the TFEU (Articles 38–44) – the contents of which are still much as they were written for the EEC Treaty, save for the removal of redundant transition measures and some updating (notably on decision-making procedures) – sets out the general rationale and framework of the CAP. The objectives of the CAP, which are reproduced in Document 20.1, are *exactly* as they were in the 1957 Treaty.

Document 20.1

The aims of the CAP as set out in the 1957 EEC Treaty and in the TFEU

The objectives of the common agricultural policy shall be:

(a) to increase agricultural productivity by promoting technical progress and by ensuring the rational development of agricultural production and the optimum utilisation of the factors of production, in particular labour;
(b) thus to ensure a fair standard of living for the agricultural community, in particular by increasing the individual earnings of persons engaged in agriculture;
(c) to stabilise markets;
(d) to assure the availability of supplies;
(e) to ensure that supplies reach consumers at reasonable prices.

Source: Treaty on the Functioning of the European Union, Article 39 (1).

Beyond setting out general aims, the Treaty does not have much to say about the content of agricultural policy. This content rests on four broad operating principles, the first three of which were adopted by the Council of Ministers as early as December 1960. The four principles will now be described.

A single internal market

Agricultural goods are supposed to be able to flow freely across internal EU borders, unhindered by barriers to trade and unhampered by devices such as subsidies or administrative regulations that might distort or limit competition. However, it is not a free trade system based on pure market principles because price and/or income support mechanisms exist for most agricultural products.

The CAP used to be based almost exclusively on a price support system. It was a system that was extremely expensive to finance. This was for three main reasons. First, many products were produced in amounts that were surplus to EU requirements. High guaranteed prices were the main reason for these surpluses, but improved farming techniques and the concentrated use of agri-chemicals also played a part. Second, most products were protected and supported by a market regime, known as a common organisation of the market (COM). Different regimes provided different forms of protection and support – so that in practice there were many agricultural policies rather than just one – but about 70 per cent of products were beneficiaries of support prices of some kind. For some products the support prices were available on an unconditional and open-ended basis, but more commonly, following reforms in the 1980s designed to tackle the problem of surpluses and reduce CAP expenditure, they were subject to restrictions. The nature of the restrictions varied from product to product, but they usually took one, or some combination, of four main forms: quotas, co-responsibility levies, quality controls, and stabilisers – the latter consisting of a mechanism in which production thresholds (maximum guaranteed quantities) were set and if these were exceeded the guaranteed payments were automatically reduced. (For a description of the different forms of COMs, see pp. 393–4 of the fifth edition of this book.) Third, apart from a brief interlude in 1974–5, EU agricultural prices were consistently above

world prices, which meant that it was not possible to export surpluses without suffering a financial loss. Several devices were used to deal with the surpluses: exporting them and providing an export refund to exporters to ensure that no loss was incurred on transactions; storing them until EU prices rose; donating them as food aid; or converting them to animal food-stuffs. All of these devices had to be financed from the EU budget.

The reforms of the 1980s designed to curb agricultural output had some effect, but not enough. Accordingly, internal demands for further reform soon arose, with pressures focused especially on the large proportion of the EU budget – over 60 per cent in the late 1980s – that was allocated to the CAP and the waste of agricultural over-production. At much the same time – the late 1980s and early 1990s – the EC came under increasing pressure from outside – most particularly from the USA – to fundamentally reform the CAP so that the EC market would be made more open and subsidised EC produce would not be 'dumped' on world markets. These twin pressures, internal and external, led, after extensive internal deliberations and external negotiations – the latter in the context of the General Agreement on Tariffs and Trade (GATT) Uruguay Round – to agreement in 1992 on major reforms of the CAP. At the heart of these reforms was a bearing down on prices on the one hand and a shift from price support to income support on the other. Included amongst the income support measures were various compensation schemes designed to enable farmers to take agricultural land out of production, to diversify land use, and to take early retirement.

But just as the reforms of the 1980s alleviated rather than solved the CAP problem, so similarly did the more radical reforms of 1992. By the mid- to late 1990s pressures for further fundamental reform were again building. The pressures came from three directions. First, with the CAP still accounting for around half of the EU budget, several of the net contributor member states started pressing for another attempt to reduce the size of the CAP budget. Second, as enlargement to CEECs loomed, it became clear that the CAP just could not continue in its existing form, or at least not without a very large increase in the EU budget – which would not be politically possible. The large increase would be necessary because most of the CEECs, especially Poland, had (and still largely do have) relatively large and inefficient agricultural sectors and so would be major beneficiaries of an unreformed CAP Third, international pressures, again led by the USA, to open up the EU agricultural market were continuing. The EU was already required, as a result of the Uruguay Round, to partially dismantle its protectionist system, and a further liberalising round was scheduled under the World Trade Organisation (WTO – which replaced the GATT in 1995).

Proposals for responding to these pressures and for further reforming the CAP were set out by the Commission in its July 1997 *Agenda 2000* document (European Commission, 1997a), which was followed up in March 1998 with more detailed proposals. The main features of the proposals followed upon the principles of the 1992 reforms with, on the one hand, further removals of and significant cuts in support prices and, on the other hand, a strengthening of direct compensatory aid to farmers and of incentives for diversification. The Commission also proposed extending rural development policy, by allocating to it around ten per cent of the total CAP budget, by strengthening existing rural development programmes, and by making rural development the 'second pillar' of the CAP (the first pillar being market support measures and direct payments to producers). Following extensive negotiations between the member states, in which there was some dilution of the Commission's proposals, the Agriculture Ministers agreed in March 1999 on a package of reforms based on *Agenda 2000*. A fortnight later, however, some of the key components of the package were further diluted when the Heads of Government met in Berlin to decide upon the whole *Agenda 2000* reform programme. The softening was mainly at the insistence of President Chirac, who – looking to the interests of French farmers and the French exchequer – was not prepared to accept the Agriculture Ministers' agreement as it stood.

As with the 1992 reforms, the 1999 reforms were quickly seen as not having been sufficiently radical. One reason for this was that they did not make provision for any significant overall decrease in CAP expenditure. Indeed, over the period of the 1999–2006 financial perspective there was to be a slight increase. Another reason was that they did not go far enough to meet WTO demands for the reduction of agricultural trade distorting support mechanisms – demands that included the abandonment of export refunds. It was

made clear to the EU, by both developed and developing countries, that the issue would have to be addressed during the new round of WTO trade negotiations that was launched at Doha in November 2001. And a third reason was that they did not address the problem how to manage the increased demands that would be placed on the EU budget by the impending EU membership of CEECs.

This last problem was dealt with in October 2002 by the European Council, on the basis of proposals submitted to it by the Commission. The key element in the resolution of the problem was that the states that would soon join the EU would not receive full CAP support until 2013: that is, until the end of the financial perspective that would cover the years 2007–13. Their 'entitlements' would be only gradually phased-in. This clearly was a major blow for the new member states but then, as was explained in Chapter 4, EU accession negotiations are largely about applicants meeting the EU's terms of admission rather than negotiating what those terms actually are. For the most part, applicants have to 'take it or leave it', and since they are anxious to become EU members they have little choice but to take it.

Ways of dealing with the other post-1999 problems were put forward by the Commission in July 2002 as part of a mid-term review of the 1999 settlement (see p. 365 below). After some modifications to satisfy national interests and preferences, the proposals were accepted by the Council of Ministers in June 2003. The principal measures contained in the agreed reform package continued in the tradition of the 1992 and 1999 reform rounds with: a further bearing down on support prices where they continued to exist; an intensification of support measures for environmental protection and rural development; and a further major movement in the direction of separating – or 'de-coupling' to use the technical term – the provision of financial support for agriculture from production levels. As part of the de-coupling, most financial payments to farmers would henceforth be moved into the Single Payment Scheme (SPS) in which a single payment is made based on (and this varies between member states) past payments, acreage, and land use. In a system known as 'cross-compliance', payments would be conditional on farmers meeting specified standards on a range of farming practice matters, including food safety and animal welfare requirements. To ensure that the much-criticised practice of most of CAP funding being given to large farmers and agri-companies was curtailed, limits would be placed on the maximum size of individual payments. Savings resulting from the imposition of these limits would be directed to rural development – in a system called 'modulation'.

Since the June 2003 settlement, the process of improving the management of the agricultural market has continued. The general framework of the settlement has remained firmly in place, but a variety of specific measures have been taken with a view to streamlining and simplifying CAP operations. As part of this, the remaining 21 CMOs have been replaced with a single CMO (reflecting the continuing movement away from price to income support), simpler rules have been adopted on such matters as market intervention and refunds, and hundreds of legal acts have been either repealed or consolidated.

* * *

A number of factors have thus combined since the late 1980s to produce very strong pressures for fundamental reform of the CAP's market system. The most important of these factors have been: market imbalances arising from the CAP's structure – especially high prices and over-production; the dominating position of the CAP in the EU's budget; rising international dissatisfaction with the distorting effects of the CAP on world agricultural trade; and the increasing importance on policy agendas of newer issues that are of concern to society, notably food safety and environmental protection.

The pressures to which these factors have given rise have been such as to produce major rounds of CAP reform in 1992, 1999, and 2003. These reforms have been so extensive as to bring about a fundamental change in the nature of the CAP's internal market. The three main dimensions of the changes are set out in Box 20.1. In consequence of the changes, income support has generally replaced price support, EU prices are now much closer to world prices, and farmers are now being seen not just as agricultural producers but also as custodians of the land.

However, sight should not be lost of the fact that not all has changed. As Garzon (2006) has observed 'Europe has not fully embraced the new paradigm of market liberalism. Public intervention remains high, in particular in supporting farmer income. The logic of alleviating market instability in the name of the

---

Box 20.1

The principal changes to the CAP system in the 1990s and 2000s

- A movement away from the former policy of high guaranteed price levels. Intervention prices have either been removed or reduced to much lower levels – levels that for most products are, in effect, safety net levels.
- Price level support for farmers has been largely replaced by income support payments that are made by the Single Payment Scheme. Most payments have been de-coupled from payments for production outputs.
- A much higher priority is being given to 'newer' policy concerns, including rural development, environmental protection, and food safety. There is less emphasis on highly intensive and productive farming and more on resource protective farming.

---

social objective of providing farmers with a fair standard of living is still present.' This public intervention, even though it is of a very different kind to formerly, ensures that the CAP will continue to loom large in the EU's budget and ensures too that the EU will continue to be pressed by trading partners to move further in the direction of market liberalisation.

Community preference

The EU market is protected from the international market. Since world prices are normally lower than EU prices, free access onto the EU market would clearly undermine the CAP system. Community preference is, therefore, required. (The term 'Union preference' has not been much used hitherto, though it probably increasingly will be so as the replacement of the word 'Community' by 'Union' in the Lisbon Treaty seeps through into common usage). The mechanics of the preference system and of the tariffs imposed vary according to the market regime for the product concerned.

Protectionist measures do not apply to all agricultural imports into the EU from all states. As is explained in Chapter 21, the EU has negotiated arrangements whereby a large number of countries are given special access to EU markets for at least some of their products, including agricultural products. So, the EU grants 'generalised preferences' to more than 170 developing countries and one effect of this has been the abolition or reduction of tariffs on over 300 agricultural products intended for processing. Under the Cotonou Agreement, virtually all of the agricultural exports of the African, Pacific and Caribbean (ACP) countries are allowed free access to the EU market. (It should, however, be pointed out that these 'concessions' do not stem simply from generosity and goodwill. Much of the produce falling under generalised preferences and the Cotonou Agreement is tropical in nature and not in competition with EU produce.)

Over and above the various special forms of access to the EU market given to developing countries, it should be noted that the general impact and extent of the Community preference system has been greatly reduced since the early 1990s. This has occurred as tariffs have been generally reduced in response to GATT/WTO pressures and as the CAP has moved away from product price guarantees to income support.

Joint financing

The CAP is financed jointly by the member states out of the EU budget. Until 2007 the channel for agricultural expenditure was the European Agricultural Guidance and Guarantee Fund (EAGGF) of the budget. This was divided into two sections. The Guarantee section financed expenditure on direct payments and agricultural market organisations, on certain rural development measures that accompany market support, and on veterinary expenditure and information measures. The Guidance section financed other rural development expenditure. When the CAP was established, the intention was for the Guarantee section to be larger than the Guidance section by a ratio of two or three to one, but in practice this was never even remotely approached and the Guidance section constantly hovered at just under 10 per cent of total EAGGF expenditure. The demands on the Guarantee section, occasioned initially by high EU prices and in later years more by direct payments, explain this imbalance.

In June 2005 the Agriculture Ministers reached political agreement on changes to the CAP funding arrangements from 2007. Their decision was taken partly to modernise financial control and management practices and partly to reflect the changing nature of the CAP – in particular the fact that under the CAP reform programme agricultural policy has come to be more clearly based on two pillars, with pillar one focusing on direct financial support measures and pillar two on rural development. Under the June 2005 agreement, agricultural expenditure was switched into two new funds: the European Agricultural Guarantee Fund (EAGF) and the European Agricultural Fund for Rural Development (EAFRD).

Financial support available for agriculture in the EU is not, it should be stressed, confined to the direct funding provided for agriculture in the EU budget. Some funds are available from other EU sources, including the European Investment Bank (EIB). By far the greatest additional funding source, however, is national exchequers: member states are allowed to assist their farmers in many ways provided they do not – in the judgement of the Commission – distort competition or infringe the principles of the market. In some states national subsidies to agriculture far outstrip those provided by the EU.

Allowance for national variations

As the previous paragraph implies, in addition to the three CAP operating principles that were agreed by the Council of Ministers in 1960, and which still constitute the formal operational principles, a fourth – unofficial – principle may also be said to exist: allowance for national variations.

The CAP is not as common or as integrated as it usually is portrayed as being. To be sure, the CAP lays down a policy framework within which member states must operate. But that framework has never been a complete straitjacket.

One reason for national variations is the differing nature of agricultural economies and structures across the EU: a phenomenon that has increased in scope and intensity as the EU has enlarged. Such are the differences – arising from such factors as topography, weather conditions, and the average size of land holdings – that it has always been necessary to have a policy framework that allows for variations that meets specific needs and circumstances. A second reason for national variations is differing policy choices of governments. Some governments, for example, have been much more inclined than others to make available to their farmers – after receiving Commission approval that CAP rules are not being breached – national financial and other forms of assistance. And a third reason is that, as Greer (2005: 3) puts it, 'There are still important areas that are not covered by EU-level policy making or where the reach of the CAP is weak. These include important supply side matters such as research, education and advice, and some sectors are not subject to common market organisation (potatoes for human consumption, for example)'.

Significantly, the reform rounds since 1992 are resulting in the CAP become ever more diversified and less common. One reason for this is the increased emphasis on 'non-agricultural' aspects of land use. Another reason is that the reforms have built-in a considerable measure of national discretion and allowance. The 2003 reforms in particular made provision for national flexibility with, for example, states having manoeuvrability as to how they calculate direct payments to farmers within the SPS. The main choices here are between a 'historic' approach based on a past reference period, a 'flat rate' approach based on averaged-out payments for land use (though there can be variations within this for arable land and grassland), and a mixed approach.

The calls that are sometimes made for a 're-nationalisation' of agriculture have made little headway, and are unlikely to do so in the foreseeable future. However, it is undeniable that the *Common Agricultural Policy* displays a considerable measure of national variations.

The Impact and Effects of the Common Agricultural Policy

Whether the CAP is to be regarded as a success or not naturally depends on the priorities and interests of those making the judgement. Since, however, the issue has caused so much controversy it is a question that merits some attention here. This will be done initially via assessing the success or otherwise of the five aims that were originally set out for the CAP in the 1957 EEC Treaty and which, in the TFEU, remain unchanged to the present day (see Document 20.1).

- Agricultural efficiency has increased enormously as a result of modernisation and rationalisation. Because of the large number of variables involved, it is difficult to be precise about agricultural efficiency, but one indication of the advances made under the CAP is seen in the fact that at a time when the number of people engaged in agriculture has dropped by well over 60 per cent on average in the EU-12 states (the pre-1995 EU members) since the CAP was created, volume outputs have steadily increased – at an average of approaching 1.5 per cent per annum since the early 1970s. That said, it might be asked whether the overproduction of certain products at great cost, and the encouragement that high levels of support have given to many who would otherwise have left the land to stay on their farms, is wholly consistent with 'ensuring the rational development of agricultural production'.

- Agricultural incomes have grown roughly in parallel with incomes in other sectors. However, this overall average masks enormous variations, both between large farmers (who have done very well for the most part – because they own most of farmland) and small farmers, and between producers of northern temperate products (notably dairy produce, cereals, and beef, which have been the main product beneficiaries of the CAP) and producers of other (mainly Mediterranean) products. The post-1992 direct payment systems have been partly designed to offset these distortions, with support targeted a little more in the direction of small farmers.

- Markets have been stabilised, in the sense that there have been no major food shortages and EU prices have escaped the price fluctuations that have occurred in the world market on some products.

- The EU is now self-sufficient in virtually all of those foodstuffs its climate allows it to raise and grow. In 1958 the then six member states produced about 85 per cent of their food requirements; by the early 1990s the then twelve member states were producing around 120 per cent. This latter figure has now dropped in the wake of the CAP reforms, but surpluses still exist in most product sectors. The movement beyond self-sufficiency to the production of surpluses has been expensive in that it has only been possible to dispose of the surpluses at considerable cost.

- The exclusion of cheaper (often much cheaper) produce from outside the EU means that the aim of 'reasonable prices' to the consumer has had a low priority. The undeniable fact is that within the EU the principal beneficiaries of the CAP have been large agri-companies and farmers, whilst the main losers have been poor consumers.

Beyond an assessment of the CAP through its five Treaty aims, five other significant consequences of the policy are also worth noting.

First, the CAP's strong position in the EU's budget has unquestionably made it more difficult for other policies to be developed. The financial perspectives that have been in operation since 1988, coupled with the series of reforms to the CAP, have brought agriculture under greater financial control, but it still accounts for over two-fifths of the total budget.

Second, the CAP has been the source of many disagreements and tensions both within the EU and between the EU and non-EU states. For example, within the EU, France's generally protectionist attitude towards the CAP has frequently caused it to be at loggerheads with other member states, especially the UK, over aspects of agricultural policy. As for its effect on relations between the EU and non-EU states, the CAP has fuelled many trading disputes between the EU and other agricultural exporters, both within the WTO framework and bilaterally.

Third, the intense farming practices that the CAP has encouraged have had damaging implications for the environment, and arguably also for food safety. It is only in recent years that these damaging implications have begun to be properly addressed. In the case of the environment, this has been achieved by making protection of the countryside a theme of the reform rounds since 1992 – for example, by making some direct aid conditional on farmers adopting production methods that respect the environment and bio-diversity. Food safety issues have been addressed in a number of ways, including by detaching most of the responsibility for it from DG Agriculture and attaching it to DG Health and Consumer Protection and by the creation of the European Food Safety Authority which was established in 2002.

Fourth, protecting the EU market from cheaper world produce, and the release onto the world market of heavily subsidised EU produce, has distorted the international division of labour and the rational utilisation of resources.

Fifth, in international debates and negotiations concerning development policies and the problems of 'the Global South', there has been an increasing emphasis in recent years on the perceived damaging effects of the CAP. This has been partly because NGOs such as Oxfam have given more attention to anti-CAP campaigning.

Policy Processes

Prior to the reform process that began with the 1992 reforms, agriculture was a highly distinctive policy-making sphere. This was mainly because many key decisions were made as part of a regular, and usually highly complicated, process: the annual price review. Many non-price elements were swept up in reviews and became components of what customarily were highly complex and interconnected packages by the time final agreements were made. The core of the packages usually consisted of a range of price increases, adjustments to produce regimes, and statements of intent about future action.

The phased reductions in prices since 1992 coupled with the associated switch from price support to income support have resulted in the annual price review disappearing. As this has happened, policy-making and decision-making processes for agriculture have become more like the processes that exist in other policy sectors. However, the importance, range, and complexity of the CAP, plus the ever-changing nature of the world's agricultural markets, means that there are still significant variations from the 'standard' EU model. The principal variations are as follows.

Commission initiation and formulation: driving for reform

Whereas the policy initiation and formulation responsibilities of the Commission in many sectors are mainly concerned with creating a policy framework, in agriculture they are inevitably directed more towards improving the efficiency of one that already exists.

As part of this drive for greater efficiency, since the

late 1960s the Commission has been proactively in the forefront of attempts to bring about fundamental reform of the CAP. Since the mid-1980s there have four major 'rounds' of CAP reform, each of which has been led by the Commission. The first round resulted in a political agreement on reforms being reached in 1988, the second in 1992, the third in 1999 and the fourth in 2003. The reform rounds have been driven by a number of factors, the most important of which were initially deteriorating market conditions, increasing surpluses, and recurring budgetary problems, and more latterly have been international pressures against the EU's high levels of protectionism and subsidisation. Against the background of these pressures, the Commission has launched and steered the reform processes, with its ideas initially being set out in communications and consultation papers of various sorts (see pp. 473–7 of the sixth edition of this book). The central thrust of its proposals since the early 1990s has been to champion movements towards a more market-based system in which farmers are protected by direct payments.

But though, the Commission has exercised a 'primary role' in putting reforms onto the political agenda and in determining the nature of final agreements (Cunha and Swinbank, 2009: 259), the Commission's proposals have habitually been watered-down by the Council of Ministers – a key reason why agricultural reform has had to be revisited so many times. The latest major round of CAP reform – that which was approved by the Council in June 2003 – was very much in this tradition of picking-up on previous watered-down reforms: in this case the reform package agreed by national leader at the 1999 Berlin summit that constituted part of their broader agreement on the 2000–6 financial perspective. The watering down at Berlin of the Commission's agricultural reform proposals resulted in a planned mid-term review of the 2000–6 arrangements assuming rather more importance than had originally been foreseen. One reason for this was that the 1999 agreement quickly came to be viewed as not having responded sufficiently to international pressures for reductions in agricultural financial support, especially in the form of export refunds. Another reason was that the 1999 reforms had not been sufficiently radical in preparing the EU for enlargement: CAP expenditure in the EU-15 was not planned to fall, whilst applying existing policies to accession states would greatly increase CAP expenditure. Accordingly, in the first half of 2002 the Commission issued two major documents:

In January, in a paper entitled *Enlargement and Agriculture: Successfully Integrating the New Member States into the* CAP (European Commission, 2002a), proposals were made for incorporating acceding countries into the CAP. The key elements of the proposals were: long transitional periods – of up to ten years – before new member states would benefit fully from support measures, with direct aids beginning at just one-quarter of the full level in the year after accession (this being justified with the argument that the immediate introduction of 100 per cent direct payments would freeze existing structures and hamper modernisation in the CEECs); production quotas set at low levels; and confirmation that the immediate costs of accession could be met within the 2000–6 financial framework agreed at the 1999 Berlin summit. These proposals were, with France and Germany taking the political lead in pressing them, accepted by the European Council in October 2002.

In July, a communication to the Council and the EP – *Mid-Term Review of the Common Agricultural Policy* (European Commission, 2002e) – was issued. The Review proposed a range of radical reforms, the most prominent of which were: an end to the array of payments based on levels of output and production; support for farmers to be based on a single direct payment linked to past income, with the maximum amount to be paid to any one farm to be capped at €300,000 and with payments to be reduced over time for larger farmers; payments to farmers to be dependent on them observing environmental, food safety, and animal welfare standards; savings in direct payments to be re-directed towards rural development and environmental protection schemes; and the introduction of a new farm audit scheme. As was widely anticipated, the proposals met with a mixed and predictable reaction. The traditional supporters of CAP reform – most notably Sweden and the UK – broadly welcomed the thrust of the proposals, though regretted they did not go far enough in that they would have little effect on the overall size of the CAP budget. The traditional opponents, by contrast – with France, Ireland and Spain in the lead – expressed concerns bordering on outright opposition, and accused the Agriculture Commissioner, Franz Fischler, of having exceeded his mandate of being restricted to conducting just a mid-term review –

which they understood to mean a technical rather than a policy review. Overall, however, the differences between the member states were less than they had been in respect of the 1992 and 1999 reform rounds. Key reasons for this were that some shifts of policy principle had already been accepted in the earlier rounds and the force of international pressures for further reform was quickly recognised. Accordingly, negotiations on the Commission's proposals lasted just one year – much shorter than with the previous rounds – and the broad thrust of the Commission's proposals were incorporated into the compromise package that was agreed by the Council in June 2003. (For a much fuller account of the Commission's thinking and behaviour, and of the negotiations between the member states on the Commission's proposals in the 1992, 1999 and 2003 reform rounds, see Garzon, 2006.)

* * *

The Commission thus has been and is a crucial agenda setter in the long drawn-out and ongoing process of CAP reform. In this process the lead within the Commission has inevitably been taken by the Agriculture Commissioner and DG Agriculture. However, they no longer have the near-monopoly control over agriculture policy they used to enjoy. As pressures for reform of the CAP have increased and as perceptions of the nature and the implications of agricultural policy have been broadened, so have other parts of the Commission come to have a say and to exercise an influence. Amongst the other parts of the Commission to have inserted themselves, or to have become drawn, into agricultural policy are Health and Consumer Protection, Environment, and Trade. Taking Trade, the Trade Commissioner and DG Trade have become key players as international trade pressures have played an increasing role in driving the agricultural reform process. So, although the Agriculture Commissioner, Marian Fischer Boel, was present at the December 2005 Doha Round negotiations in Hong Kong where agreement was reached, amongst other things, on the phasing-out by 2013 of all first world agricultural export refunds, the EU's 'main player' was the Trade Commissioner, Peter Mandelson.

Council decision-making, and control problems for the Agriculture Council

The formal processes of Council decision-making in the agriculture sphere are relatively straightforward:

- Regarding legislative procedures, until the Lisbon Treaty entered into force, legislation was made mostly on the basis of the consultation procedure, which meant that although the EP could press its policy preferences on the Council its ability to insist on them were much weaker than in policy areas where the co-decision procedure was used. The Lisbon Treaty has changed this situation, by 'elevating' agricultural legislative processes to the newly-named 'ordinary' legislative procedure, which means that laws dealing with agricultural matters can now be passed only if the Council and the EP agree on their content.

- Regarding decision-making in the Council, agriculture was one of the very few areas where the use of QMV was provided for in the 1957 EEC Treaty. Initially because of French resistance and then because of what became a prevailing norm that EC decisions should be consensual, QMV was not in practice used for many years. But, when its use became more acceptable from the early 1980s the Agriculture Council quickly took advantage and became the Council formation to use it most. In terms of the number of usages this continues to be the case – with Agriculture Ministers usually holding at least 50 votes per year. In proportionate terms, however, the Agriculture Council's 'lead' in the usage of QMV is shared with several other Council formations – with around 15 per cent of decisions involving a vote. (On the use of QMV by different Council formations see, for example, Hayes-Renshaw and Wallace, 2006: 279–91; Mattila, 2008: 28–9.)

But though the operation of the Agriculture Council is reasonably 'normal' in terms of formal procedures, it is distinctive in a number of ways. One of these ways is that the Agriculture Council is, of all the formations of the Council, the formation that has traditionally been the most reliant on issue linkages and package deals for the conduct of its business. However, in recent years this use of linkages and packages to increase negotiating flexibility and create room for agreements has not been quite so prevalent. This is because the margins for manoeuvre available to the Agriculture Ministers have been reduced by the use of multi-annual planning within financial perspectives, by the disappearance of the price review, and by the gradual phasing-out of separate product market organisations. But though wide-ranging wheeling and dealing is not now so characteristic of the Council as it used to be, it certainly still exists – most especially when important decisions have to be taken on, for example, Commission reform proposals or positions to be adopted in external agricultural trade negotiations. In such situations, agreements are usually only possible if they are based on a recognition of the different interests and priorities of the member states: some states, for example, are net exporters of agricultural produce whilst others are net importers; some have temperate climates whilst others have Mediterranean; some have mainly large and efficient farms whilst others have many small and inefficient family-based units; and some have vast tracts of 'less favoured' land whilst others have very little.

This diversity of interests and priorities in the Council make it very difficult for it to be a pro-active policy-maker and, in consequence, makes the Council heavily reliant on the Commission for ideas. Of course, this also applies to most Council formations, but not generally to the same extent. As Daubjerg (2009: 399) has observed of CAP reform processes:

> Within the Council of Agricultural Ministers, it is the norm that the Commissioner's proposal forms the basis of the discussions aimed at consensus. After the Commissioner's proposal has been formally presented to the Council, farm ministers seldom put forward alternative proposals ... In the history of CAP reform, the Council, as a whole, has been status quo minded and, thus, not a driving force behind reform; rather it has been an obstacle for farm commissioners to overcome.

A distinctive feature of Council agriculture policy processes that has become less sharp over the years is the relative isolation of the processes from other policy areas. Until the late 1980s, agricultural policy processes were largely confined to a somewhat closed group of specialist policy actors in the Commission and the Council. The specialised nature of these actors was emphasised by the way in which DG Agriculture was widely viewed as being not quite a 'normal' DG and by the privileged position of the Special Committee of Agriculture in undertaking for the Agriculture Ministers the preparatory work that COREPER undertakes for other Council formations. (On the SCA, see p. 146) Agricultural policy-making still remains a little isolated from 'the mainstream', but an increasing enmeshment with other policy areas means it is nothing like as isolated as it was. As Grant (1997: 148) noted over a decade ago, the circle of actors involved in agricultural policy formation in the EU has widened considerably. The most obvious impact of this widening at Council level is that non-Agriculture Councils – especially the Foreign Affairs Council (which is responsible for external trade), Ecofin, and Environment – sometimes express views and make decisions that have direct implications for agriculture. Given the segmented nature of Council structures, this can create problems in terms of developing rounded and properly integrated policy.

Retaining complete control over policy can also be difficult for the Agriculture Council when policy issues assume a high political profile, as they are more prone to do than is usually the case with most other formations of the Council apart from Foreign Affairs and Ecofin. An example that illustrates this is the discussions concerning agriculture in the context of the 2007–13 financial framework. Aware that when the negotiations on the contents of the framework got under way in 2003–4 there would be intense pressures to cut agricultural spending, President Chirac allied with Chancellor Schröder in the autumn of 2002 to pre-empt such pressures. This was done by them jointly putting to, and virtually steamrolling through, the October 2002 European Council meeting the proposition that the proportion of the EU budget assigned to agriculture should be only marginally reduced over the period of the perspective. This October 2002 decision did, as Chirac and Schröder anticipated, effectively preclude the possibility of significant cuts in CAP spending during the lifetime of the financial framework and resulted in the ensuing discussions and negotiations on the expenditure side of the perspective having to focus primarily on the 55 per cent of the budget accounted for by non-agricultural spending.

The role of the European Parliament

As was noted in Chapter 11, the powers of the EP have increased greatly over the years. However, until the Lisbon Treaty came into effect agriculture was one of the areas where the EP's powers remained weak. There were two principal aspects of this weakness. First, although the EP was a co-decision maker with the Council on the EU's annual budget and although agriculture accounted for over 40 per cent of the budget, the EP could do little about agricultural expenditure. This was because whereas the EP had powers to amend what was known as non-compulsory expenditure it could only make recommendations to amend what was known as compulsory expenditure: and compulsory expenditure consisted almost entirely of agriculture. Second, agriculture was one of the very few remaining policy areas where the co-decision legislation procedure did not apply. The consultation procedure which, as was shown in Chapter 17, allows the EP to make recommendations to, and exert pressure on, the Commission and the Council in respect of legislative proposals, but does not permit it to insist that its views be accepted, remained the decision-making process.

This is not to suggest that the EP did not exert influence on agricultural policy before the Lisbon Treaty entered into force. It scrutinised both policy and legislative proposals and it had some successes in helping to shape outcomes. Garzon (2006), for example, suggests that the Agriculture Committee played a crucial role in helping to devise an acceptable formula on de-coupling in the 2003 CAP reform round. It is also the case that the Parliament's influence over agriculture had increased as a result of agriculture policy broadening out to include aspects of related policy areas – such as environment and food safety – where the co-decision procedure applied. Overall, however, agriculture was an area of comparative EP institutional weakness.

The position changed, however, with the Lisbon Treaty because the Treaty 'rectified' the EP's two weaknesses: the distinction between compulsory expenditure and non-compulsory expenditure was abolished, so the EP's budgetary powers over agricultural expenditure were thereby increased; and, as noted above, agricultural law-making became subject to the ordinary legislative procedure, so the EP gained co-equal powers with Council over the making of agricultural legislation.

Management and implementation of the Common Agricultural Policy

Because of the nature of the CAP, the EU is much more involved in the management and implementation of agricultural policy than it is in most other policy spheres. The Commission, and particularly DG Agriculture, are central in this regard. They oversee the operation of the whole system, adjust it as necessary and, as far as possible, try to ensure that the national and regional agencies that undertake the front-line implementation of policy – national Ministries of Agriculture, intervention agencies, customs and excise authorities and so on – fulfil their obligations in a proper manner.

Much of what the Commission does in managing the CAP is of an essentially technical nature. This is no more clearly seen than by looking at the legislation that exists in the agricultural sector. As a result of the Commission's attempts to simplify the CAP system in the 2000s, the volume of this legislation has been greatly reduced, but it is still considerable: in August 2009 there were 3,077 acts in force, which put agriculture far 'ahead' of any other policy area apart from external trade. Box 20.2 provides a summary of the main features of agricultural law. As the Box implies, most of the law is highly specific, covering such matters as product specifications, market intervention instruments and mechanisms, and price-related issues. There is, seemingly, nothing especially 'political' about much of this.

But what may be seemingly technical and 'non-political' may well involve the Commission doing things that amount to rather more than the simple application of tightly drawn rules. Many decisions on, for instance, intervention and support systems are taken within margins of manoeuvre that give the Commission at least some flexibility. This flexibility can result in the Commission's choices having important financial implications for producers, traders, processors, and the EU budget. The Commission also has room for manoeuvre in how it deals with the many national agencies – which include amongst their

---

Box 20.2

EU legislation in the agricultural sector

Number of acts in force in late 2009: 3,077.

Including:

- approximation of laws and health measures: 1,638; animal health and zootechnics matters: 941; plant health matters: 378; animal feeding stuffs matters: 221; seeds and seedlings matters: 154.

   Many of the acts under this heading deal with such matters as the authorisation and non authorisation of products, marketing issues, and preventative and controlling measures in relation to diseases and illnesses.

- concerning products subject to market organisation: 855, including: cereals 67; fresh fruit and vegetables: 65; oils and fats: 67; sugar: 68; wine: 111; rice: 35.

   Taking the 73 in the pigmeat sector as illustration, they include acts on export licences, export refunds, storage, disposal schemes, grading of pig carcases.

   An example of a specific piece of legislation specifying operating rules for a sector – wine in this case – is *Commission Regulation (EC) No. 607/2009 of 14 July 2009 laying down certain detailed rules for the implementation of Council Regulation (EC) No. 479/2008 as regards protected designations of origin and geographical indications, traditional terms, labelling and presentation of certain wine sector products* (*Official Journal*, L193/60, 24 July 2009.) The regulation, which is 80 pages in length, is highly complex and most of it is unintelligible to non experts. However, the following – perfectly intelligible – extract indicates the sort of ground the regulation covers:

   Article 54

   Actual alcoholic strength
   1. The actual alcoholic strength by volume referred to in Article 59(1)(c) to Regulation (EC) No 479/2008 shall be indicated in percentage units or half units.
      The figure shall be followed by '% vol' and may be preceded by 'actual alcoholic strength', 'actual alcohol' or 'alc'.
      Without prejudice to the tolerances set for the reference analysis method used, the strength shown may not differ by more than 0,5 % vol from that given by analysis. However, the alcoholic strength of products with protected designations of origin or geographical indications stored in bottles for more than three years, sparkling wines, quality sparkling wines, aerated sparkling wines, semi-sparkling wines, aerated semi-sparkling wines, liqueur wines and wines of overripe grapes, without prejudice to the tolerances set for the reference analysis method used, may not differ by more than 0,8 % vol from that given by analysis.
      2. The actual alcoholic strength shall appear on the label in characters at least 5 mm high if the nominal volume is over 100 cl, at least 3 mm high if it is equal to or less than 100 cl but more than 20 cl and 2 mm high if it is 20 cl or less.

- agricultural structures 157
- products not subject to market organisation 49

number 85 national or regional paying agencies – that undertake, on the basis of shared management, most of the direct policy implementation. It is, moreover, a room for manoeuvre that has broadened as the CAP has been reformed and, as was noted above, a significant degree of decentralisation has been built into the reform programme. Key features of the decentralisation that have increased management flexibility include: some direct payments are allocated to member states in the form of 'national envelopes' which national authorities manage according to their own criteria and requirements; rural development measures are co-financed with member states; and member states must have in place rural development programmes that require Commission approval before EU funds can be released. Such decentralisation requires the Commission to frame its relations with national agencies more in terms of being a partner than an overseer.

When quick management decisions have to be taken, the Commission is authorised to act. However, as was explained in Chapter 8, the Commission's agricultural management responsibilities are not undertaken by Commission officials alone but via comitology committees made up of civil servants from the member states. There are around twenty such CAP committees, including one for each category of products, and implementing measures that the Commission intends to enact are submitted to the appropriate committees for their opinion. There are usually between 300 and 400 meetings of CAP comitology committees each year. The Commission determines the direction and sets the pace in the committees, but the existence of the committees does mean that the member states have a direct input into, and ultimately a degree of control over, all but the fine details of agricultural policy and the management of that policy.

Concluding Remarks

Despite all the obstacles and hurdles that litter its decision-making processes, the CAP has been the subject of considerable reform in recent years. The core feature of the reform programme has been to replace a system that used to be based primarily on support prices by a system that now is based primarily on direct payments to farmers. Another key aspect of the reform has resulted in the CAP becoming less focused on matters related to food production and more concerned with wider environmental, rural development, and consumer protection issues.

However, the reforms that have been and are being made have not solved all of the CAP's problems. *Outside the EU*, many countries, not least the USA, continue to be dissatisfied with what they regard as a still over-protected EU market and still over-subsidised EU produce on world markets. *Inside the EU*, sharp differences still exist over important aspects of agricultural policy: where should the balance be struck between market efficiency on the one hand and the granting of support to the agriculture sector on the other?; and in so far as support is to be given to agriculture, how ought it to be distributed, and in what form?

Agricultural policy will thus continue to loom large on the EU agenda.

Chapter 21

External Relations

The EU is an important actor on the world stage. It is so partly because of its size and resources and partly because of its ability to act in a united, or at least coordinated, manner in a range of external policy contexts and settings.

There are four main aspects to the EU's external relations: trade; foreign, security and defence; development; and the external dimension of internal policies. Each of these will be examined in this chapter.

External Trade

The EU in the world trading system

The member states of the EU present a united front to the world in respect of international trade and they act as one in contracting the terms of trade agreements. If they did not do so the unified internal market would not be possible.

The main foundations of the united front are the Common Customs Tariff (CCT) – or Common External Tariff (CET) as it is also known – and the Common Commercial Policy (CCP). Together, the CCT and the CCP enable, indeed oblige, the member states to act in common on matters such as the fixing and adjusting of external customs tariffs, the negotiation of customs and trade agreements with non-member countries, and the taking of action to impede imports – this being most likely when unfair trading practices, such as dumping and subsidies, are suspected.

The EU conducts trade negotiations in many forums: with single states; with other regional groupings, such as the European Free Trade Association (EFTA) and the Association of South-East Asian Nations (ASEAN); and in international frameworks, of which the most important is the World Trade Organisation (WTO – which has over 150 members, who collectively account for over 90 per cent of world trade. In these forums the EU is able to bring very considerable economic and trading strengths to bear, as Box 21.1 shows.

The combination of these economic and trading strengths, allied with the fact that in trading forums the EU acts on most matters as a single bloc, means that the EU is an extremely powerful world trading force.

Trade policies

The EU presents itself as being committed to a liberal trade policy and as having as its main priority in external trade negotiations the opening up of

Economic and trading strengths of the EU

- The combined Gross Domestic Product (GDP) of the EU-27 in 2009 was around €13,000 billion, as compared with around €10,500 billion for the USA. In percentage terms this results in the EU accounting for around 24 per cent of world GDP, as compared with around 21 per cent for the USA and 11 per cent for Japan.
- The EU accounts for around one-fifth of world exports and imports (excluding internal EU trade), which is slightly more than the USA and much larger than Japan (which accounts for around 7 per cent).
- The EU market, with almost 500 million people (about one-seventh of the world's population), is much larger than both the US market, which numbers just over 290 million people, and the Japanese market, which numbers around 127 million.
- Many of the countries and groupings with which the EU negotiates on trade matters are heavily reliant on the EU market for their exports – either for reasons of geography (as most obviously with non-EU European countries) or historical linkage (as with former French and UK colonies).

markets. The most important international trade negotiations of recent years – the 1986–93 General Agreement on Tariffs and Trade (GATT) Uruguay Round and the WTO Doha Development Round which was launched in 2001 – are seen as providing evidence in support of this view of the nature of the EU's trading stance. Priorities for the EU during the negotiations have included: the lowering of international customs duties; the removal of non-tariff barriers to trade; and the opening up of hitherto restricted spheres of trading activity, especially those, such as financial services, in which the EU, or at least some of its member states, are strong.

It is a liberal trading policy, however, that is not always pursued with complete consistency or uniformity. The governments of the member states frequently seek to cope with 'special' national economic circumstances and accompanying political pressures by pressing for the EU to adopt protectionist measures. EU trade policy is thus concerned not only with promoting the general liberalisation of trade, but also with ensuring that the consequences of this are not damaging for its member states. This results in trade policy also being much taken up with matters such as the seeking of special exemptions from general trade agreements, the negotiation of 'orderly marketing' agreements with more competitive countries, and the imposition of anti-dumping duties (the latter being taken mainly against Asian countries).

The most obvious sectoral sphere of EU protectionism is agriculture, which has long been sheltered from the full rigours of external competition by domestic support to agricultural producers and traders on the one hand and high tariffs on imports on the other. Under WTO pressures, however, the EU has been changing these policies and since the mid-1990s has been moving away from price support to income support, has been reducing export refunds (which have been a particular target for other agricultural exporting countries because of their distortion of world agricultural markets), and has been lowering agricultural tariffs (see Chapter 20 for details). Other sectors that have attracted EU special protection include the motor vehicle industry, which has been assisted by export restraint agreements with Japan, and textiles, where there have long been restrictions of various sorts on imports from the Far East.

Beyond 'strict' trade issues, the EU often has to deal with, and indeed brings, other issues into trade negotiations. This is part of a general process whereby the international trade agenda has been expanded and politicised over the years. So, politically sensitive trade-related matters such as labour standards and environmental protection increasingly feature in trade talks, as do issues concerning human rights. The EU takes, in relative terms, an 'advanced' position on such matters.

Trade and trade-dominated agreements

The EU has trade agreements, or agreements in which a substantial part of the content is concerned with trade, with just about every country in the world. These agreements take a number of different forms, both in terms of the extent to which they remove barriers to market access and the number and range of non-trade matters that are covered. Some of the agreements are best viewed as being part of the EU's development cooperation policies and, as such, are considered in the section on development cooperation later in the chapter. Trade agreements that are not part of development cooperation policy are of three main types. In 'ascending' order – from minimalist to maximalist – they are:

Trade agreements

These are based on Article 207 TFEU (ex 133 TEC), which obliges the EU to operate a common commercial policy. The opening paragraph of Article 207 is set out in Document 21.1.

Article 207 agreements may be preferential or non-preferential in kind, but they are all subject to the general framework of international trading rules established within the framework of the WTO. These rules prohibit preferential agreements unless waivers are negotiated.

The Lisbon Treaty strengthened the EU's position in respect of negotiating trade agreements by explicitly listing services, intellectual property and foreign direct investment in Article 207 and giving them treaty status as exclusive Union competences. For many years the Commission had sought, with only limited success, to persuade the member states to adopt an expansive approach towards what could be included in Article 133 agreements and not to restrict the Union's exclusive trade policy competence to trade in goods. From the early 1990s in particular the Commission campaigned vigorously for the rapidly expanding trade areas of services and intellectual property to be

located within the framework of Article 133. But, because of the sensitivity of many matters in these areas, the member states preferred to interpret Article 133 narrowly and edged towards a broader approach only slowly. The Lisbon Treaty 'completed' this edging forward, though, so as to provide a measure of continuing national protection, unanimity (rather than the normal Article 207 provision of QMV) was retained in the Council for the taking of decisions in especially sensitive areas – including in respect of cultural and audiovisual services where trade agreements 'risk prejudicing the Union's cultural and linguistic diversity (Article 207: 4(a)).

Trade and economic cooperation agreements

The Treaty base of these agreements depends on their precise nature, but there is usually some combination of Article 207 and at least one other article. So, Article 218 of the TFEU which sets out procedures for the contracting of external agreements, is almost invariably used, whilst Article 209 applies when there is a development cooperation dimension to agreements. The number of trade and cooperation agreements has increased enormously over the years and their scope has steadily expanded. At their core are trade preferences of various kinds and usually also assistance of some sort from the EU to the other signatory(ies). In some cases, as with partnership agreements with states that were part of the former Soviet Union – such as Georgia, Moldova and the Ukraine – free trade is an eventual objective. Since the late 1980s, political conditions – usually concerning human rights and democratic processes – have routinely been part of cooperation agreements.

Document 21.1

Extract from Article 207 TFEU (on the common commercial policy)

1 The common commercial policy shall be based on uniform principles, particularly with regard to changes in tariff rates, the conclusion of tariff and trade agreements relating to trade in goods and services, and the commercial aspects of intellectual property, foreign direct investment, the achievement of uniformity in measures of liberalisation, export policy and measures to protect trade such as those to be taken in the event of dumping or subsidies. The common commercial policy shall be conducted in the context of the principles and objectives of the Union's external action.

Association agreements

These are based on Article 217 TFEU, which states that 'The Union may conclude with one or more third countries or international organisations agreements establishing an association involving reciprocal rights and obligations, common action and special procedure'. Typically, association agreements include highly preferential access to EU markets, the prospect of a free trade area eventually being formed between the signatories, economic and technical cooperation of various sorts, financial aid from the EU, political dialogue, and – in some cases – the prospect of the associated countries eventually becoming members of the EU. There are currently three broad categories of states that either have, or are in the process of negotiating, association agreements with the EU. First, there are countries that are seeking and have realistic prospects of EU membership. Turkey is in this category. So are most of the states of the Western Balkans

– Albania, Bosnia-Herzegovina, Croatia, Macedonia, Montenegro and Serbia. All of these Western Balkan states are part of the EU's Stability Programme for South-East Europe which includes the negotiation of association agreements that contain trade, cultural, and political cooperation aspects that have as their main purpose the promotion of, and assistance with, internal reforms and development. The agreements explicitly hold out the prospect of future EU membership and are very much part of a pre-accession strategy that is designed to assist economic liberalisation, market adjustment, and political democratisation. Second, there are several Mediterranean states – including the Mashreq and Maghreb countries – that constitute part of the EU's Mediterranean policy. The prospect of EU membership is not part of these association agreements. Third, there are the non-EU members of the European Economic Area (EEA) – Iceland, Norway and Liechtenstein. The EEA is the deepest of the EU's

---

Box 21.2

The 'standard procedure' for contracting an external trade (Article 207 TFEU) agreement

- The Commission makes a recommendation to the Foreign Affairs Council that the EU should seek to conclude a trade agreement with a third country or organisation. (There is no separate Trade Council, but at the Foreign Affairs Council trade matters are usually handled by Trade Ministers rather than Foreign Ministers.)
- COREPER discusses the Commission recommendation and places it on the agenda of the Council. The Council takes a decision as to whether negotiations should proceed. In making its decision the Council may, on the basis of proposals drawn up by the Commission and perhaps modified by COREPER, give to the Commission a negotiating directive, set of guidelines or – to use the most commonly used, but not most accurate term – a mandate. The Council normally, though not always, can take decisions by qualified majority vote, but in practice it usually proceeds by consensus.
- Working within the framework of the directive it has been given by the Council, the Commission negotiates on behalf of all twenty-seven EU states. The Trade DG normally takes the lead role on behalf of the Commission but other DGs – including Development, Competition, and Agriculture – are also involved if they have a direct interest. How much room for manoeuvre the Commission has when conducting negotiations varies according to the circumstances. Usually, differences of both principle and special interest between the member states result in negotiating directives being fairly tightly drawn – often reflecting a compromise between those countries tending towards protectionism and those favouring a more free trade approach. While Commission officials acknowledge privately that Council negotiating directives are usually less of a dead weight than is often supposed, the Commission's flexibility in negotiations can be constrained by the necessity of not disturbing compromises that have been agreed only with difficulty in the Council. (Although it should also be said that it is not unknown

→

trading agreements in that it involves not only free trade in goods but also extends the EU's other so-called freedoms (of services, capital, and people) to the three EEA states.

*   *   *

With each of these three types of agreement – trade, cooperation, and association – containing variations in both scope and depth, the EU is thus involved in a wide and complicated range of agreements with trading partners. The agreements can be thought of as constituting a hierarchy of preferences in which the EU and the other signatory(ies) of agreements are, moving from the bottom to the top of the hierarchy, bound together in increasingly open market access arrangements and in an array of complex and varied forms of cooperation.

Policy processes

Trade agreements used to be the responsibility of the Commission and the Council. However, the Lisbon Treaty brought the EP very much onto the decision-making stage. It did so in two ways. First, the adoption of legislative measures defining the framework for implementing the CCP were made subject to the ordinary legislative procedure – under which the EP is a co-decision maker with the Council (see Chapter 18 for a description of the procedure). Second, the EP was given significantly greater powers in respect of the negotiation and contraction of trade agreements, including needing to give its consent before agreements can be ratified.

The normal post-Lisbon procedure for contracting trade agreements is set out in Box 21.2. The powers of and the relations between and within the EU institutions in connection with the making of trade agreements are such that tensions of various

---

Box 21.2 *continued*

for the Commission to use Council reins to the EU's advantage: during negotiations it can be helpful to say in response to an unwanted proposal, 'the Council would never agree to that'. Doubtless, the new powers given to the EP by the Lisbon Treaty will also be used in this way.)

- Throughout the period of the negotiations, the Commission must report regularly to the Council's International Trade Committee, which is known also as the Article 207 Committee (and pre-Lisbon was the Article 133 Committee). This is a committee that normally meets weekly to review, discuss, and make decisions on trade agreements that come within the scope of Article 207. The Committee meets at two levels: full members and deputies. At full members' meetings, which are held at least once each month, national 'teams' are headed by senior officials from the national ministries responsible for trade. The Commission 'team' is headed by the Director General of DG Trade. Full members' meetings focus on general and particularly problematical policy issues. At deputy members' meetings, which are held three times a month, national 'teams' are composed of officials from either relevant national ministries or the permanent representations in Brussels and the Commission is represented by officials from DG Trade. Deputies' meetings deal with detailed policy matters. The International Trade Committee is supported by specialised sub-committees that deal with particular trade matters, including services, textiles, and motor vehicles.
- Since the Lisbon Treaty came into effect, the Commission must also report regularly to the EP (in practice the Parliament's International Trade Committee) on the progress of negotiations.
- During particularly difficult or important negotiations the Commission may return to the Council for clarification of the negotiating directive, or for an amended directive that might break a deadlock. The Council's International Trade Committee can adjust negotiating directives, but anything that is especially sensitive or political is normally referred to COREPER and, if necessary, to the Foreign Affairs Council.
- At the (apparent) conclusion of negotiations the Commission may initial negotiated settlements. But, Council approval and, post-Lisbon, EP consent, is necessary before agreements can be formally authorised and signed.

sorts are by no means uncommon. Four areas cause particular difficulties.

First, the power balance between the Council and the Commission can be very delicate, with the Council trying to ensure that the Commission remains under its control and the Commission wanting and needing enough manoeuvrability to enable it to be an effective negotiator.

Second, the different national interests and preferences of the member states can create difficulties in the Council. Apart from differences that arise on specific issues, there is a broad underlying difference, with some countries – including France, Italy, Spain and Greece – tending to favour a measure of protectionism and other countries – led by Germany and the UK – tending more towards trade liberalisation.

Third, problems can arise within the Commission with disputes between Commissioners and between DGs about where policy responsibilities lie and who has a legitimate interest in particular external trade policies and agreements.

Fourth, until the Lisbon Treaty MEPs were dissatisfied that the Parliament had no automatic right to be consulted, let alone to insist that its views be considered, in connection with trade agreements. Now that the EP's powers have been greatly increased, it can be anticipated that, in customary EP manner, it will strongly assert itself and use its new powers to their maximum.

* * *

As for the making of cooperation and association agreements, there are three ways in which their decision-making processes differ from trade agreement decision-making processes. First, unanimity in the Council is more common, with it being a requirement for all association agreements and also for cooperation agreements that cover areas for which unanimity is required for the adoption of internal rules. Second, because cooperation and association agreements have a broader coverage than trade agreements, more policy actors – in the Commission, Council and EP – are necessarily involved. So, for example, if a CFSP element is included in an agreement the High Representative and the Commission's External Relations DG are amongst those with an involvement, as is the EP's Foreign Affairs Committee. Similarly, if an agreement includes a cultural cooperation element the Commissioner and the DG for Education and Culture, plus the EP's Education and Culture Committee, are

amongst the significant participatory actors. Third, the wider range of policy issues included in cooperation and association agreements means there is more room for cross-policy 'trading' and haggling between EU actors. For example, the EP has long pressed the importance of the political dimensions of association and cooperation agreements and has often sought to pressurise the Commission and Council to give these dimensions greater attention. Where it has been available, the EP's power to block agreements has sometimes been threatened, and occasionally has been imposed, as a protest against insufficient attention being given to lack of democracy and/or abuse of human rights in states with which agreements are proposed. So, in the mid-1990s the EP withheld its assent from the proposed EU–Turkey customs union, which was framed within the EU–Turkey association agreement, because of concerns about the human rights situation in Turkey. The Parliament only 'relented' after Turkey agreed to amend its constitution.

Foreign and Defence Policies

Resources and problems with their usage

Just as it has in respect of trade policies, the EU has considerable resources at its disposal in respect of pursuing foreign and defence policies. The most important of these resources are set out in Box 21.3.

As with trade policy, the resources need to be harnessed and used in an effective manner if the EU's potential as a foreign policy actor is to be realised. The TEU, under which all the treaty provisions regarding foreign and defence policies fall, certainly obliges the member states to try to act in common whenever possible. So, for example, Article 24 of the Post-Lisbon TEU includes:

Within the framework of the principles and objectives of its external action, the Union shall conduct, define and implement a common foreign and security policy, based on the development of mutual political solidarity among Member States, the identification of questions of general interest and the achievement of an ever-increasing degree of convergence of Member States' actions.

Box 21.3

EU Foreign and defence policy resources

- The EU's membership of 27 member states. Some of these states – notably Germany, France, Italy, Poland, Spain and the UK – are, in global terms, of at least middle-ranking size and status.
- Many EU member states, and increasingly the EU itself, have extensive diplomatic experience and skills, and also special links with many parts of the world.
- Two EU states – France and the UK – are nuclear powers.
- Two EU states – again France and the UK – occupy two of the five permanent seats on the United Nations Security Council.
- The collective spending of the member states on defence is second only to that of the US amongst the world's powers. One result of EU defence expenditure is that there are more full-time European troops than there are American.
- The EU's powerful economic and trading positions are becoming all the more important as much of international relations become less focused on 'traditional' political and military issues and more focused on economic issues and economic-related issues such as environmental protection and energy supplies.

The Member States shall support the Union's external and security policy actively and unreservedly in a spirit of loyalty and mutual solidarity and shall comply with the Union's action in this area.

The Member States shall work together to enhance and develop their mutual solidarity. They shall refrain from any action which is contrary to the interests of the Union or likely to impair its effectiveness as a cohesive force in international relations.

The Council and the High Representative shall ensure compliance with these principles.

But, notwithstanding this forceful language, the EU has considerable difficulty in maximising its potential by acting in a united manner. With trade policy the EU is not only able, but is obliged by treaty, to act in a wholly united way, but with foreign and defence policies there are, as Box 21.4 shows, many obstacles in the

Box 21.4

Obstacles preventing the EU from being able to fully utilise its potential foreign and defence policy resources

- The EU is not a state and therefore does not have the (usually) long-established 'givens' that help to focus national foreign policy. Most notably, there is no national territory to protect and no national political, economic, social and cultural interests to promote. The EU's territory does not 'belong' to it in the way national territory 'belongs' to member states, and the EU's political, economic, social and cultural interests are by no means clearly defined.
- Many member states, especially the larger ones with long histories of being influential on the world stage in their own right, are reluctant to lose control of policy areas that are so associated with national influence, sovereignty, and identity.
- Some member states traditionally have had special relationships with particular parts of the world that they are anxious to maintain.
- There are sometimes differences between EU states on foreign policy questions arising from conflicting ideological orientations.
- In the especially sensitive area of defence policy, there are differing national perspectives on whether a distinctive, let alone a comprehensive, European defence orientation and capacity is desirable. This feeds into many specific policy questions, including whether and to what extent the defence resources of individual states should be matched and made mutually compatible. (As long as defence expenditure decisions are taken solely within a national framework, there are naturally major problems at European level of duplications, of the non inter-operability of equipment, and of shortfalls in expensive and sophisticated high-tech hardware.)

way of a joint and effective marshalling of potential power resources.

The fact is that the foreign and defence policy edifice rests essentially on an inter-governmental base in which policies are decided and actions are entered into by voluntary cooperation. Apart from some policy implementation decisions, everything is decided by the governments of the member states acting by unanimity.

Indeed, the continuing ultimate independence of the member states in the foreign and defence policy areas is no more clearly seen than in two declarations on the common foreign and security policy that were attached to the Lisbon Treaty, extracts from which are reproduced in Document 21.2.

Because of the difficulties of fully harnessing and utilising resources, much of the EU's foreign and defence policy potential is thus unrealised. For this reason, the EU is often described as being a 'civilian' or 'soft' international power, which means that whilst it exercises a significant influence on the world stage in

such areas as trade, finance, and the environment, its contribution is relatively modest in the 'traditional' and 'hard' external policy areas of foreign and defence policy. There unquestionably is much in this portrayal of the EU but, as will be shown below, it is a portrayal that is becoming increasingly less accurate. This is because the EU is slowly making better use of the resources it has at its disposal in the foreign and defence policy areas.

The evolution of the EU's foreign and defence policies

Notwithstanding the many difficulties and obstacles that characterise the foreign and defence policy areas, important and significant developments have occurred within them since foreign policy was first launched under the name European Political Cooperation (EPC) in 1970. Although the two policy areas are, of course, closely entwined, they have

---

Document 21.2

Extracts from Declarations 13 and 14 of the Treaty on European Union

13 Declaration concerning the common foreign and security policy

The Conference underlines that the provisions in the Treaty on European Union covering the Common Foreign and Security Policy, including the creation of the office of High Representative of the Union for Foreign Affairs and Security Policy and the establishment of an External Action Service, do not affect the responsibilities of the Member States, as they currently exist, for the formulation and conduct of their foreign policy nor of their national representation in third countries and international organisations.

The Conference also recalls that the provisions governing the Common Security and Defence Policy do not prejudice the specific character of the security and defence policy of the Member States ...

14 Declaration concerning the common foreign and security policy

... the provisions covering the Common Foreign and Security Policy including in relation to the High Representative of the Union for Foreign Affairs and Security Policy and the External Action Service will not affect the existing legal basis, responsibilities, and powers of each Member State in relation to the formulation and conduct of its foreign policy, its national diplomatic service, relations with third countries and participation in international organisations, including a Member State's membership of the Security Council of the United Nations.

The Conference also notes that the provisions covering the Common Foreign and Security Policy do not give new powers to the Commission to initiate decisions nor do they increase the role of the European Parliament.

The Conference also recalls that the provisions governing the Common Security and Defence Policy do not prejudice the specific character of the security and defence policy of the Member States.

tended, until very recently at least, to be developed in somewhat separate ways, so the story of their evolution will be taken separately here too.

Foreign policy

Initially on a tentative basis, and quite outside the framework of the Community Treaties, in the 1970s and 1980s the member states increasingly cooperated with one another on foreign policy matters – to such an extent that by the mid-1980s there were few major international issues upon which the EC did not pronounce. The developing importance of foreign policy cooperation was recognised when EPC was accorded its own section – Title III – in the SEA. Amongst other things, Title III stated that 'The High Contracting Parties [the member states], being members of the European Communities, shall endeavour jointly to formulate and implement a European foreign policy'. However, unlike certain other policy areas that were also recognised in the SEA, Title III was not incorporated into the EEC Treaty. This was mainly because the member states were unwilling to allow the normal Community decision-making processes to apply to foreign policy. As a result, EPC continued to be much looser and more voluntaristic in nature than most other policy areas with which the Community concerned itself. No laws were made within EPC, most decisions were arrived at by consensus, and no state could be prevented from engaging in independent action if it so chose.

But although the SEA signalled the increasing importance of EU foreign policy and facilitated its further development, until the early 1990s the EU's international standing continued to be very much that of an economic giant on the one hand and of a political pygmy on the other. That is to say, it exercised considerable international influence in respect of economic, and especially trade, matters, but its voice did not count for a great deal in respect of political and, more particularly, security and defence matters. Since the early 1990s, however, this situation has been changing as it has come to be increasingly accepted by the member states that the EU ought to be doing rather more than issuing general, and often anodyne, declarations, or, very occasionally, imposing mild economic sanctions against a state to indicate the EU's disapproval of a policy or action. Five factors have been especially important in stimulating this change.

First, the ending of the Cold War and the collapse of communism in the Soviet bloc and the Soviet Union transformed the nature of international power relationships. In particular: the international political context in which Europe found itself changed dramatically, with a shift of focus from the global East–West dimension to regional issues and conflicts; strategically, Europe was no longer squeezed between two superpowers, with little choice but to ally itself to one – the United States – in a more-or-less subservient manner; and the bases of power relationships altered, with nuclear and military capacity becoming less important and economic strength and geographical position becoming more important. In this 'new' world, in which international relations became much more fluid and the nature and future development of the European continent was far from clear, the EU countries naturally increasingly looked to play a leading part in guiding and managing events. In so doing they were given encouragement by the USA which, though sometimes troubled when the EU was seen to be acting *too* independently, was anxious to lighten some of its international and, more especially some of its European, commitments.

Second, German reunification increased the pressure for there to be an EU foreign and security policy EU framework within which Germany was clearly located and to which it was firmly attached. The much-quoted determination of EU leaders, not least German leaders themselves, in the early 1990s to ensure there was a European Germany rather than a German Europe, was seen by many as needing to apply not only to economic policies but also to foreign and security policies given the sensitivities associated with Germany's past and the actual and potential political turbulence to Germany's east and south. That Germany must be 'tied in' more tightly was confirmed for many by the way in which, in late 1991, Germany successfully pressed other EU states to grant diplomatic recognition to Croatia and Slovenia much earlier than most would have preferred, thus obliging the EU states to accept the disintegration of Yugoslavia.

Third, the 1990–1 Gulf War and the events leading up to it demonstrated that EPC would always be restricted in its effectiveness if security and defence policy continued to be kept apart from foreign policy. The Community's response to Iraq's invasion of Kuwait was to coordinate diplomatic action and jointly impose economic sanctions, but on the key issues of the appropriate military response and national contributions to that response, the member states reacted in a piecemeal and uncoordinated fashion.

Fourth, the EU's response to the post-1991 break-up of Yugoslavia and the subsequent hostilities in the Balkans was widely recognised as being inadequately prepared, developed and mobilised. EU states contributed in various ways and through various forums to policy formulation and the setting up of peacekeeping and humanitarian operations, but there was no clear, consistent or coordinated EU response to the situation. What leadership was provided to deal with the turbulence in the Balkans came mainly from the USA.

Fifth, and in response to the factors just identified, starting from the base created by the SEA, treaties have provided for significant advances in foreign and security policy cooperation, albeit on a basis that has maintained their essentially intergovernmental nature. The relevant contents of the treaties were set out in Chapters 5 and 6, so only a brief summary of the most salient points will be given here:

- The Maastricht Treaty provided for a Common Foreign and Security Policy (CFSP) to constitute the EU's second pillar. The key elements of the pillar were: (1) the general objectives of the CFSP, to which member states were expected to conform, were identified; (2) the pillar rested on an intergovernmental decision-making base, with decisions to be taken by unanimity; (3) the CFSP was to include security issues, 'including the eventual framing of a common defence policy, which might in time lead to a common defence'; and (4) the Western European Union (WEU) was to be 'an integral part of the development of the Union'.

- The Amsterdam Treaty strengthened the Maastricht provisions in a number of ways. In particular: QMV became possible for some policy implementation decisions; a 'constructive abstention' device was introduced, allowing a state not to apply a decision that otherwise bound the EU; security policy was advanced a little, with the Petersberg tasks – which were first identified at a 1992 WEU conference and which are focused on crisis management, peace-keeping and humanitarian tasks – incorporated in the TEU and with the Maastricht-inserted reference to 'the eventual

framing of a common defence policy' being upgraded to 'the progressive framing of a common defence policy'; and support mechanisms were strengthened with the creation within the Council of a CFSP High Representative and a Policy Planning and Early Warning Unit.

- The Nice Treaty further strengthened the potential of CFSP, principally by enabling enhanced cooperation – which had been provided for under the Amsterdam Treaty to enable some member states to go forward with an initiative – to be used for the implementation for joint actions and common positions that do not have military or defence implications.

- The Lisbon Treaty sought to give foreign policy a greater coherence, in particular by replacing the two existing main foreign policy posts – of High Representative for the CFSP and Commissioner for External Relations – with a single post of High Representative of the Union for Foreign Affairs and Security Policy (see below).

The various factors that have just been identified have enabled the CFSP to be greatly developed since it was initiated in the early 1970s. The extent of the development should not, however, be exaggerated, for there cannot yet be said to be a coherent and cohesive EU foreign policy based on a united political strategy that stems from shared understandings of what the EU's foreign policy interests and priorities are and should be. It is also the case that for some member states, especially 'the big three' – France, Germany, and the UK – EU foreign policy is not necessarily seen as taking precedence over national foreign policy. Indeed, EU foreign policy is sometimes viewed, and also used, as a sort of 'top-up' to national foreign policy: an additional mechanism for furthering national interests, and sometimes a useful framework for dealing with issues that states prefer not to manage themselves.

However, these reservations notwithstanding, a foreign policy of sorts certainly exists. Its nature will be further examined later in the chapter.

Defence policy

Security and defence policies have been a particularly difficult area in which to develop EU inter-state cooperation, let alone integration. One reason why they have been so is that security and defence are closely associated with the very essence of national sover-eignty. Another reason is the different security and defence capabilities of the member states. A third reason is the varying degrees of willingness by the member states to use armed force when pressed. And a fourth reason is differences between member states regarding their attitudes and degrees of commitment to the various security/defence organisations that exist in the modern world. On this last point, NATO and the transatlantic relationship have been especially problematical, with six EU states not being NATO members (Austria, Cyprus, Finland, Ireland, Malta, and Sweden) and with a range of opinion existing amongst the EU states as to how tightly Europe should be tied in with the USA. Of the large member states, the UK has taken the most pro-US position – as witnessed, for example, in its strong and active support for the military campaign in Afghanistan following the 2001 September 11 terrorist attacks and the spring 2003 invasion of Iraq – whilst France has been the most reticent and the most forceful champion of European independence.

However, notwithstanding these difficulties, the EU did, as was shown above, begin to engage with security and defence policies from the early 1990s, albeit initially somewhat tentatively. The engagement was occasioned largely by Europe's fragmented and hesitant responses to the conflicts in the Gulf and then the break-up of Yugoslavia, where it showed itself to be capable of contributing to post-war stabilisation and reconstruction but only marginally to military intervention during hostilities. Towards the end of the 1990s the continuing turbulence in the Balkans, and especially the crisis in Kosovo, displayed Europe's weaknesses and reliance on the political will and military assets of the USA in a particularly stark manner and fully brought out the need for a greater European independent capability in relation to security operations.

The conflicts in the Balkans were instrumental in producing pressures from the USA for more burden-sharing by Europeans. They also resulted in the Europeans being increasingly obliged to face the unsatisfactory features of their military position: as long as the EU lacked an effective military operational capability, the USA would take the policy lead in dealing with conflicts on the continent of Europe; there might be circumstances in which the EU would wish to adopt a different stance towards conflicts than the USA; and the management of conflicts requires rapid and efficient

decision-making processes – and the EU manifestly did not have these in the security and defence domains.

These considerations led from 1994 to steps being taken to develop a European Security and Defence Identity (ESDI). Based firmly within the NATO framework, the ESDI was concerned essentially with military re-structuring so as to enable the Europeans to exercise a greater, and where necessary more independent, influence within NATO.

The big defence policy 'breakthrough' within the EU framework came in December 1998 when, at a Franco-British summit in St Malo, the two countries that had been almost at opposite ends of the debate about European and American orientations in foreign and defence policy, signalled a convergence in their positions by calling for the creation of a clearer and stronger EU security capability within the NATO framework. The convergence was occasioned by a number of factors, including successful military cooperation on the ground in Bosnia, irritation with American leadership in the Balkans, and frustration – especially on the part of Tony Blair, who in May 1997 became the most pro-European British Prime Minister for over twenty years – that whilst European governments spent two-thirds as much as the USA on defence they could deploy only 10 per cent as many troops (Forster and Wallace, 2000: 481–5). The principal significance of St Malo was that not only did the UK end its opposition to defence policy being considered in the EU context, but it made clear its intention to play a leading role in developing the policy sphere. The references to security and defence in the TEU could thus start to be given some real effect.

Since St Malo, EU security and defence policies have advanced rapidly. Five European Council meetings have been very important in this process:

- At the June 1999 Cologne summit a declaration was issued 'On Strengthening the Common European Policy on Security and Defence'. Included in the declaration was the following:

  In pursuit of our Common Foreign and Security Policy objectives and the progressive framing of a common defence policy, we are convinced that the Council should have the ability to take decisions on the full range of conflict prevention and crisis management tasks defined in the Treaty on European Union, the 'Petersberg tasks'. To this end, the Union must have the capacity for autonomous action, backed up by credible military forces, the means to decide to use them, and a readiness to do so, in order to respond to international crises without prejudice to actions by NATO (European Council, 1999b: Appendix III).

- At the December 1999 Helsinki summit the contents of the Cologne declaration were confirmed and clarified. There was also agreement on a 'Headline Goal' under which, by 2003, a European Rapid Reaction Force (ERRF) of up to 50,000–60,000 persons would be created, capable of being deployed within 60 days, of being sustained for at least a year, and focused on the full range of Petersberg tasks (European Council, 1999d).

  Subsequent to Helsinki, deliberations and negotiations between the governments of the member states led to the 1999 Headline Goal being virtually replaced in May 2004 by a new *Headline Goal 2010*. This resulted in the ERRF concept being enhanced by what were seen to be more flexible policy instruments in the form of rapid reaction 'battle groups', made up normally of around 1,500 personnel from three or four states.

- At the June 2000 Feira summit, a non-military 'headline goal' was added, with member states committing themselves to providing up to 5,000 civilian police officers within 30 days for crisis situations. There was also agreement on the creation of a Rapid Reaction Mechanism (RRM) to enable emergency civilian aid to be available quickly to help stabilise crises (European Council, 2000b).

- At the December 2003 Brussels summit, the national leaders adopted the proposal for a European security strategy – entitled *A Secure Europe in a Better World* – that had been drawn up under the direction of the High Representative for the CFSP (European Council, 2003b). At the heart of the strategy was an emphasis on 'effective multilateralism' through the UN and regional organisations, a focus on conflict prevention and crisis management, maintenance of close relations with NATO, and provision for autonomous EU operations in some circumstances.

- At the December 2008 summit a *Declaration by the European Council on the Enhancement of the European Security and Defence Policy* was agreed

(European Council, 2008). Based on a review by the (pre-Lisbon Treaty) High Representative for the CFSP, Javier Solana, of the 2003 security strategy, it committed 'to make good the shortfall in the resources available in Europe by gradually improving civilian and military capabilities (*ibid*: 16). It re-affirmed the (so far unachieved) 1999 headline goal of Europe being capable of deploying 60,000 personnel within 60 days for a major operation, and added to this other forms of military-civilian operational deployments it would aim to be capable of conducting.

As a further 'contribution' to the policy advancement, the Lisbon Treaty:

1 introduced a – qualified and hedged – mutual defence clause, under which if a member state is the victim of armed attack on its territory the other member states are obliged to provide it with assistance, subject to conditions;
2 accorded security and defence policy its own section in the TEU, whilst emphasising that it is an integral part of the CFSP;
3 symbolically re-named the policy area, which had come to be collectively known since the Helsinki summit as the European Security and Defence Policy (ESDP), the Common Security and Defence Policy (CSDP)

Another important aspect of the policy advancement has been the way in which an increasingly broad view has been taken of what is necessary if the EU is to have effective security and defence policies. The broadening is reflected in the post-Lisbon TEU which, codifying what the EU had increasingly been doing in practice, gives an expansive interpretation of the Petersberg Tasks by stating that the tasks in which the Union may use civilian and military means shall include:

joint disarmament operations, humanitarian and rescue tasks, military advice and assistance tasks, conflict prevention and peace-keeping tasks, tasks of combat forces in crisis management, including peace-making and post-conflict stabilisation. All of these tasks may contribute to the fight against terrorism, including by supporting third countries in combating terrorism in their territories (Article 43:1 TEU).

Box 21.5

Core features of the Common Security and Defence Policy

- The CSDP is limited in its security aims to the Petersberg tasks. 'Traditional' defence is left to NATO or national efforts.
- The CSDP is firmly located within NATO and the transatlantic alliance. The EU will act 'autonomously' only when NATO chooses not to act.
- The main decision-making processes of the CSDP are intergovernmental. (A position that is no more clearly demonstrated than by it being left entirely to national governments to decide to which, if any, EU civilian and military missions they will contribute, by how much and in what ways.)
- There is not to be a European army. Certainly the battle groups are capable of being mobilised by autonomous European action, they do have a European command chain, and they do draw on European military resources. However, they are not to be a standing force, each country retains control over the number and deployment of its troops, and there is no common uniform. Battle groups are best thought of as a mechanism for allowing troops to be called up to undertake military-based fire-fighting operations. (In practice, though fifteen battle groups did exist by the end of 2009, none had been deployed.)
- The CSDP project is open in that the EU wishes to receive contributions from non-EU NATO members and from EU applicant states.

However, extensive though the advancement of security and defence policy advancement has been, it should not be over-stated. As Box 21.5 shows, much of it has been firmly framed within a number of enduring and core features, of which the most important are a clear intergovernmental base, a commitment to the Atlantic Alliance, and a limitation on the sort of operational tasks in which the EU will engage.

A useful way of thinking of just how far EU security and defence policies have developed is to distinguish between three types or levels of policy. *Soft security policy* focuses on the promotion of peace and security and uses non-military tools for this purpose. Examples of EU soft security devices include, at a general level, the EU enlargement process, and at a more specific level the Stability Pact for South Eastern Europe in which a range of trade, aid, and political cooperation instruments feature. The appointment of EU 'special representatives' to address problems in trouble-spots may also be regarded as essentially soft policy instruments. Amongst locations in which such EU representatives have been appointed in recent years are the Balkans, Afghanistan, the Middle East, and Africa. *Hard security policy* involves being prepared to use a capability, including a military capability, for such purposes as conflict resolution, peacekeeping and peace monitoring. These are precisely the

sort of operations that make up the Petersberg Tasks, and the EU has been actively engaged in a number of 'Petersberg operations' – mainly at the 'soft' end – since 2003. By the end of 2009, some twenty-two civilian, military, and civilian–military ESDP missions had been launched, including: an EU police mission in Macedonia in 2005; a border assistance mission in Ukraine/Moldova in 2005; an observation mission in Kosovo in 2006 and a rule of law mission in Kosovo in 2008; and a monitoring mission in Georgia in 2009. To date, the European Force (Eurofor) in Bosnia and Herzegovina, which took over from a NATO-led force in late 2004, has been, with 7,000 personnel, the largest operation to be mounted by the EU. *Defence policy,* as traditionally understood, has at its core using military force, if necessary offensively, for the defence of territory and for 'high security' reasons. The EU is not seeking such a capability.

Policy aims

Having established that the EU has considerable resources at its disposal in the foreign and defence policy spheres, and having established also that the policy areas have – notwithstanding the many obstacles in their way – developed considerably since their

---

Document 21.3

Article 21 of the Treaty on European Union (on the principles guiding its external relations)

1 The Union's action on the international scene shall be guided by the principles which have inspired its own creation, development and enlargement, and which it seeks to advance in the wider world: democracy, the rule of law, the universality and indivisibility of human rights and fundamental freedoms, respect for human dignity, the principles of equality and solidarity, and respect for the principles of the United Nations Charter and international law.

   The Union shall seek to develop relations and build partnerships with third countries, and international, regional or global organisations which share the principles referred to in the first subparagraph. It shall promote multilateral solutions to common problems, in particular in the framework of the United Nations.

2 The Union shall define and pursue common policies and actions, and shall work for a high degree of cooperation in all fields of international relations, in order to:

   a) safeguard its values, fundamental interests, security, independence and integrity;
   b) consolidate and support democracy, the rule of law, human rights and the principles of international law;
   c) preserve peace, prevent conflicts and strengthen international security, in accordance with the purposes and principles of the United Nations Charter, with the principles of the Helsinki Final Act and with the aims of the Charter of Paris, including those relating to external borders;
   d) foster the sustainable economic, social and environmental development of developing countries, with the primary aim of eradicating poverty;
   e) encourage the integration of all countries into the world economy, including through the progressive abolition of restrictions on international trade;
   f) help develop international measures to preserve and improve the quality of the environment and the sustainable management of global natural resources, in order to ensure sustainable development;
   g) assist populations, countries and regions confronting natural or man-made disasters; and
   h) . promote an international system based on stronger multilateral cooperation and good global governance.

3 The Union shall respect the principles and pursue the objectives set out in paragraphs 1 and 2 in the development and implementation of the different areas of the Union's external action covered by this Title and by Part Five of the Treaty on the Functioning of the European Union, and of the external aspects of its other policies.

   The Union shall ensure consistency between the different areas of its external action and between these and its other policies. The Council and the Commission, assisted by the High Representative of the Union for Foreign Affairs and Security Policy shall ensure that consistency and shall cooperate to that effect.

---

origins in EPC, attention is now turned in this and the next section to the aims of the policies and the instruments that are available to try and give them effect.

The first thing that needs to be said about the aims is that those of the CFSP and the CSDP are, of course, one and the same since the CSDP is, in effect, an operational arm of the CFSP. The overall policy aims of the CFSP are based on a number of general guiding principles that are set out in Article 21 of the post-Lisbon TEU, which is reproduced in Document 21.3.

As Document 21.3 makes clear, the EU has a number of foreign policy goals, at the heart of which are such 'worthy' intentions as promoting peace, democracy, liberty, and human rights. The TEU does, of course, identify policy aims only in very general terms and it is left to policy actors – notably the European Council, the Foreign Affairs Council, and the High Representative – to develop more specific aims and objectives and to specify the precise nature of policy instruments and the circumstances in which they should be used.

Although it is not explicitly mentioned in the Treaty, a particular focus of EU foreign policy is cultivating cooperative and stable relations with, and promoting 'western' democratic values and practices in, neighbouring states to the south and east. As such, enlargement policy – which, as Chapter 4 showed, makes much of the political conditions states wishing to accede to the EU must meet – is a key foreign policy focus. So too is the European Neighbourhood Policy (ENP), which was launched in March 2003 with the aim of developing 'a zone of prosperity and a friendly neighbourhood – a "ring of friends" – with whom the EU enjoys, close, peaceful and co-operative relations' (European Commission, 2003). The ENP was not started from scratch but rather built on existing bilateral relations between the EU and mainly former Soviet states to the east and mainly north African states to the south. As such, action plans – covering mainly trade, aid and political and cultural cooperation – have been negotiated with ENP states on an individual basis rather than collectively as part of an overall ENP action programme. The aim of the ENP has been to place the EU's bilateral relations with its neighbours within a more coherent and ordered framework. However, concerns that the ENP focus has been too broad to be effective has resulted in it being 'joined' by two more regionally directed initiatives: the Union for the Mediterranean, which was launched in 2008, and the Eastern Partnership, which was launched in 2009.

Policy instruments

The pre-Lisbon TEU identified common strategies, joint actions and common positions as the key CFSP instruments. The Lisbon Treaty sought to make for greater flexibility by replacing Article 12 TEU, which had set out these instruments, with the more open Article 25 that is reproduced in Document 21.4.

On the basis of Article 25 and also of a number of other treaty articles (both TEU and TFEU), the EU has many potential policy instruments at its disposal for use in specific situations:

- It can adopt actions and positions on the basis of Article 25 (b): (i) and (ii).
- It can use diplomatic channels to exert political pressure: there are few significant foreign policy issues upon which an EU statement or declaration is not issued.
- It can, especially in its relations with states with which it has association or cooperation agreements,

---

Document 21.4

Article 25 of the Treaty on European Union (setting out the means by which the Union shall conduct the CFSP)

The Union shall conduct the common foreign and security policy by:

a) defining the general guidelines;
b) adopting decisions defining:
    (i)   actions to be undertaken by the Union;
    (ii)   positions to be taken by the Union;
    (iii) arrangements for the implementation of the decisions referred to in points (i) and (ii): and by
c) strengthening systematic cooperation between Member States in the conduct of policy.

make use – in both 'offering' and 'withdrawing' ways – of trade benefits, economic and financial assistance, and technical, scientific, cultural and other forms of cooperation. The use of these types of instrument involves the CFSP 'using' the economic strength of the EU.

- It can, as was noted above in the account of the development of EU defence policy, utilise its growing capability in putting together civilian, police and military missions. However, as was also noted above, a military capability is only available for restricted purposes. Furthermore, there are, for the reasons that are set out in Box 21.6, major obstacles in the way of the capability being much further developed. Or, at least, there are major obstacles in the way of it being much further developed on an EU-wide basis, but some states are likely to take advantage of Articles 42 and 46 of the post-Lisbon

Treaty TEU which makes provision for member states 'whose military capabilities fulfil higher criteria and which have made more binding commitments to one another in this area' to establish 'permanent structured cooperation within the Union framework.'

As for the deployment of the EU's policy instruments, figures can give only a very partial impression of the nature and intensity of policy activity since much of foreign and defence policy is, by its very nature, conducted not via formal actions but on an ongoing basis in informal and unrecorded ways. However, with that caveat noted, an indication of the scale of operational activity is seen in the fact that in recent years around twenty new common positions and five or so new joint actions have normally been adopted. In 2008, a total of 54 common positions and joint

---

Box 21.6

Obstacles to the EU developing a fully fledged security and defence policy capability

- A number of member states, especially those with a tradition of neutrality or semi-neutrality, are – for ideological and historical reasons – reluctant to over-develop security and defence policies.
- Security and defence policies raises sovereignty concerns for virtually all member states.
- Security and defence issues still sometimes divide member states in terms of both ends and means. This was demonstrated most dramatically in 2003 when the EU split over the US-led invasion of Iraq: the UK, Denmark, Italy, Spain, and most of the (soon-to-become EU members) CEECs were prominent in supporting the invasion, whilst France, Germany, Belgium and Finland were prominent in opposing it.
- Many member states see no need to take EU security and defence policies too far given the other defence options that are available to them. The most obvious of these options is NATO, to which most EU states belong. There is little desire to downgrade NATO's role or to loosen the EU's bonds with the US. Additional security and defence options include the Organisation for Security and Cooperation in Europe (OSCE), which has been active in the Balkans, and the *ad hoc* coalitions of 'the willing and able' that are constituted from time to time. This variety of security and defence options is seen in the range of ways in which the EU has put military forces 'into the field' in recent years. For example: the Lebanon – mainly a UN operation: Afghanistan – mainly a NATO operation; the Balkans – initially mainly NATO operations, but increasingly EU operations; Iraq – an operation of the willing and able.
- Without significantly higher levels of expenditure on security and defence the EU will continue to be heavily reliant on NATO/the US for such key military resources as satellite technology, heavy airlift, logistical support, and some armaments. Within the EU a variety of means are being used to enhance the capacity of European security and defence – including work by the European Defence Agency (which was established in 2004) to improve the availability, mobility and deployability of forces, the interoperability of equipment, and the procurement of munitions – but the reality is that there is no immediate prospect of the EU being able, let along willing, to embark on a major military campaign without US assistance.

Box 21.7

Examples of common positions and joint actions adopted in 2008

- Extension of the mandate of the European Union special representative in Bosnia and Herzegovina.
- Appointment of the European Union special representative in Kosovo.
- A further contribution of the European Union to the conflict settlement in Georgia/South Ossetia.
- Amendment of Joint Action on the establishment of the European Union policy mission on Afghanistan.
- Restrictive measures against Uzbekistan.
- The launching of the European Union military operation in the Republic of Chad and in the Central African Republic.
- The launch of a European Union military operation to contribute to the deterrence, prevention and repression of acts of piracy and armed robbery off the Somali coast.
- Implementation of Joint Action 2005/190/CFSP on the European Union police mission for the Palestine territories.

Source: European Commission, 2009a: Chapter V, section 4.

---

actions were adopted, over half of which were amendments or extensions to existing positions and actions. Of these 54, fifteen concerned Africa, eleven concerned the Balkans, nine concerned the Middle East, six concerned the South Caucasus, five concerned Asia, two concerned Eastern Europe, two concerned the Indian Ocean, and five concerned other areas (European Commission, 2009a: Chapter V, section 4). Box 21.7, which lists some of these positions and actions, shows how wide-ranging CFSP actions are.

Policy processes

Because of the politically sensitive nature of much of its policy content, the CFSP and its associated policy processes have never been quite part of the 'EU mainstream'. CFSP policy processes have displayed four distinctive features:

- Throughout the rounds of treaty reform that began with the Single European Act, CFSP processes have never been placed within the TEC – now TFEU. In the SEA itself they were 'self standing' and since the Maastricht Treaty they have been located within the TEU. This has meant, amongst other things, that the role of the Commission has never been as strong in relation to the CFSP as it has in relation to most other policy areas and also that the jurisdiction of the EU's Courts has not extended to the CFSP.
- CFSP processes have not been so subject to the 'supranational drift' that has characterised other policy areas, where unanimous decision-making in the Council has generally been replaced by the availability of QMV and where the EP has moved from a position of adviser to co-decision maker. Some QMV is now available in the Council for CFSP matters, but not for significant policy-making decisions, and though the role of the EP has been advanced it is still largely restricted to a consultative role only.
- Whilst virtually all EU policy activity involves extensive consultations between representatives of the member states and relevant EU-level practitioners, CFSP policy processes are particularly centred on an intensive network of consultative arrangements. There are almost constant contacts and rounds of meetings at political and official level, mostly designed to try and ensure there is a maximum information flow and as much cooperative activity as possible. In these ongoing contacts and meetings, policy options and possibilities are discussed, and what is feasible and by what means normally gradually emerges.
- Since the Amsterdam Treaty the CFSP has had, with the High Representative, its own distinctive institutional position. This position was considerably revamped and strengthened by the Lisbon Treaty.

The roles and powers of the CFSP institutional actors, and how they interact with one another in CFSP policy-making processes, will now be described. Figure 21.1 outlines the processes in diagrammatic form.

Figure 21.1 Principal features of CFSP and CSDP decision-making structures

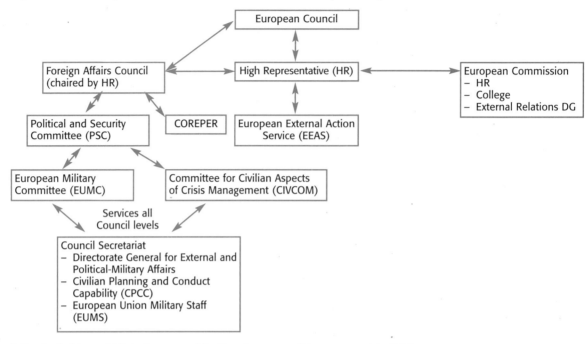

* Situation in February 2010. In time, some of the Council structures will become part of the EEAS.

The European Council

Article 26 of the TEU – most of which is reproduced in Document 10.5 on p. 176 – states that:

> The European Council shall identify the Union's strategic interests, determine the objectives of and define general guidelines for the common foreign and security policy, including for matters with defence implications.

Working through and with the Foreign Affairs Council and the High Representative, the European Council is thus responsible for the overall direction of the CFSP.

In addition to laying down guiding principles, the European Council also commonly pronounces on foreign policy issues of current concern. To cite, by way of example, just one European Council meeting, the June 2009 summit issued statements on Pakistan and Afghanistan, Burma/Myanmar, Korea, and Iran (European Council, 2009a: Annexes 5–8).

The Council of Ministers

The Council is at the very heart of CFSP processes. Most of its work is channelled via a tiered structure of meetings which bring together representatives of the member states. In 'descending' hierarchical order, the nature of the tiered structure is as follows:

- *The Foreign Affairs Council.* Prior to the Lisbon Treaty coming into effect, Foreign Ministers met in the General Affairs and External Relations Council (GAERC). However, as part of the Treaty's attempts to strengthen the CFSP's institutional base, a separate Foreign Affairs Council was created. It normally meets about once a month, but additional meetings are convened when necessary. In addition to formal Council meetings, informal weekend gatherings of Foreign Ministers are periodically held.

  Unlike other formations of the Council which are chaired on a rotating basis by the member state holding the Council Presidency, the Foreign Affairs Council is chaired by the High Representative.

  The Foreign Affairs Council is the main decision-making body of the CFSP. Operating within the

Photo 21.1 A meeting of the Foreign Affairs Council

context of such general policy guidelines as have been issued by the European Council, it makes, or for routine matters formalises, most CFSP decisions. For new and politically important decisions unanimity is the 'default' decision-making requirement, but for operational matters involving the adoption of Union positions, actions and decisions QMV is normally available, though with the proviso that no vote can be taken if a member state objects 'for vital and stated reasons of national policy'. In such circumstances the High Representative searches for a solution acceptable to the member state and if this does not succeed the matter may be referred by the Council, acting by QMV, to the European Council for a decision by unanimity. Another option for a state that is uneasy about a proposed decision is to abstain and to accompany its abstention with a formal declaration. If it does this, it is not obliged to apply the decision, though it must accept that the decision commits the Union and it must 'refrain from any action that might conflict with or impede Union action'.

- *The Committee of Permanent Representatives* (COREPER). As was explained in Chapter 9, COREPER is composed of the Permanent Representatives of the member states to the EU. It meets in two formations – COREPER I (Deputy Permanent Representatives and COREPER II (Permanent Representatives). CFSP matters are dealt with by COREPER II. The Commission is usually represented at COREPER II meetings by the High Representative or her representative.

Meeting weekly, COREPER II acts on CFSP matters primarily as a transmission and filtering agency between the Political and Security Committee on the one hand (whose decisions it can discuss, but not change) and the Foreign Affairs Council on the other.

- *The Political and Security Committee* (PSC, which is often referred to by its French acronym of COPS – for *Comité Politique et Sécurité*) was created in 2000/01 as part of new structural arrangements to handle the ESDP. It replaced the former Political Committee (PoCo) whose membership was headed by the Political Directors of the member states (who are very senior officials based in national Foreign Ministries) and the Political Director of the Commission (who is the Director General for External Relations). The PSC is chaired by a representative of the High Representative and its membership consists of officials at 'senior/ambassadorial level' (European Council, 1999b) from the member states' Permanent Representations to the EU in Brussels. From time to time the PSC meets at the level of Political Directors – though the Directors gather periodically on an informal basis in any event.

Following its creation, the PSC was soon being identified by the European Council as the 'lynchpin' of both the CFSP and ESDP (European Council, 2000b, Annex III to Annex VI). As the lynchpin, it meets normally twice a week to exercise a number of key responsibilities including keeping track of the international situation as it concerns the CFSP, assisting with the definition of CFSP/CSDP policies, providing political direction on the development of military capabilities and on dealing with crisis situations, and monitoring the implementation of agreed policies.

The PSC has been involved in some mild institutional rivalry with COREPER, with both bodies displaying a willingness to assert themselves. Turf battles have, however, always been contained, on the basis of the PSC recognising that its communications with the ministers must be channelled via COREPER and COREPER accepting that it does not interfere too much with the PSC's decisions.

The PSC is supported by a number of specialised groups and committees.

- *The Correspondents' Group.* Composed of those officials who are responsible for the coordination of

CFSP inside Foreign Ministries, and with the Commission in attendance, the Correspondents' Group meets at least once a month. As well as acting as a key liaising mechanism between Foreign Ministries, it regularly deals with business coming up from the working groups with which the PSC does not have the time or the inclination to deal. Correspondents are responsible for much of the day-to-day liaison between the Foreign Ministries of the member states.

- *Working groups.* There are usually around thirty or so working groups in existence, most of which are permanent but a few of which are *ad hoc*. A total of between 250 and 300 working group meetings are held each year. The groups are composed of senior diplomats – often departmental heads – from the member states, plus a Commission representative. Some working groups deal with regions, for example the Middle East, Central and South America, and Africa; some deal with themes, for example the OSCE, disarmament, and human rights; and some deal with operational matters, for example EU representation in third countries, and joint actions.

* * *

Council CFSP meetings are prepared and serviced by the Council's Secretariat, which has a number of organisational units dealing with aspects of CFSP. At the time of writing (February 2010) the principal organisational unit is Directorate General E – External and Political-Military Affairs. Charged with providing administrative and advisory support, about half of the 70 or so officials who work in the DG are permanent Council employees and about half are on secondment from member states. Within DG E are units dealing with such matters as human rights, civilian crisis management, defence, and enlargement. However, the Council's administrative and advisory support roles for CFSP are scheduled to be reduced as a result of the creation by the Lisbon Treaty of a new European External Action Service (EEAS). The EEAS, which is headed by the High Representative, is to recruit its staff from the Council, the Commission and national diplomatic services. It is to be independent of both the Council and Commission.

The High Representative of the Union for Foreign Affairs and Security Policy

The Amsterdam Treaty created a new position of High Representative for the CFSP. The position was created partly for the purpose of raising the profile of EU foreign policy by giving it a human face and partly to strengthen the capacity of the EU to achieve cooperation between the member states on foreign policy matters. So as to ensure that the post would command respect and be high profile, Javier Solana, the Secretary General of NATO, was appointed to be the first (and, as it turned out, the only) occupant of the position.

However, although Solana was quickly seen to be doing a good job, institutional limitations of his post soon became apparent. Three limitations were especially important. First, the Commission continued to have an External Relations Commissioner, which inevitably resulted in uncertainties regarding the leadership positions and the responsibilities of the Commissioner and the High Representative. Second, the GAERC continued to be chaired by the Foreign Minister of the state holding the Council Presidency, which further compounded leadership and responsibility questions. Third, the High Representative had no significant independent powers: he was very much the servant of the national Heads of Government (in the European Council) and the national Foreign Ministers (in the GAERC).

In an at least partial attempt to tackle these problems, the governments of the member states included in the Constitutional Treaty what amounted to a merging of the posts of High Representative and Commissioner for External Relations into a single post, which they titled Union Minister for Foreign Affairs. This new post was retained in the Lisbon Treaty but, for reasons that were explained in Chapter 6, the symbolically charged title – which in popular parlance was quickly shortened to EU Foreign Minister – was dropped and replaced with the more cumbersome title of High Representative of the Union for Foreign Affairs and Security Policy.

The High Representative's institutional position is complex, with the incumbent having a base in both the Commission and the Council. On the one hand the High Representative is a member of the Commission and is the Commissioner for External Relations. On the other hand, the High Representative chairs the Foreign Affairs Council.

This dual position is paralleled in the appointment process. The European Council initiates proceedings by making a nomination, by QMV if necessary, with the agreement of the President-designate of the Commission. As was shown in Chapter 10, at a special summit in November 2009 the European Council nominated the UK Trade Commissioner, Catherine Ashton, to be the first occupant of the post. However, because the High Representative is also a Commissioner, the nomination is only confirmed when the whole College is approved by the EP: which only occurs after all Commissioners-designate, including the High Representative, have given satisfactory accounts of themselves before EP committee 'hearings'.

Regarding the powers of the High Representative, the Lisbon Treaty did not advance these much beyond the powers of the High Representative position that Solana had held. The relevant articles of the TEU are studded with phrases such as: 'The common and security policy shall be put into effect by the High Representative of the Union for Foreign Affairs and Security Policy and by Member States, in accordance with the Treaties' (Article 24); 'The Council and the High Representative of the Union for Foreign Affairs and Security Policy shall ensure the unity, consistency

and effectiveness of action by the Union (Article 26); and 'the High Representative of the Union for Foreign Affairs and Security Policy ... shall contribute through his proposals towards the preparation of the common foreign and security policy and shall ensure implementation of the decisions adopted by the European Council and the Council' (Article 27). The High Representative's roles are thus established in the TEU as being ones of proposer, promoter, facilitator and implementer. The High Representative is not a major independent decision-maker: the making of key policy decisions is left to the European Council and the Council of Ministers.

It remains to be seen whether the High Representative will be able, as many hope, to give the CFSP a significant external boost, not least by giving it 'a human face'. But, the TEU makes for potential problems and uncertainties in this regard with its inclusion in Article 15 – which covers the responsibilities and powers of the European Council President – of the following sentence:

> The President of the European Council shall, at his level and in that capacity, ensure the external representation of the Union on issues concerning its common foreign and security policy, without prejudice to the powers of High Representative of the Union for Foreign Affairs and Security Policy.

The Commission

Since the 1981 London Report the Commission has been 'fully associated' with the work carried out in the foreign policy field. However, the intergovernmental nature and TEU base of foreign policy has meant that the Commission's position has been much weaker in the foreign policy context than it has in respect of external trade policy. This is no more clearly illustrated than by the fact that it was not until the Maastricht Treaty that the Commission gained the right, and then it was a non-exclusive right, to refer foreign policy matters and proposals to the Council.

Concerns within the Commission that the institution should take full advantage of the policy openings provided by the creation of the CFSP pillar by the Maastricht Treaty played an important part in stimulating a number of internal organisational changes – at both College and DG levels – in the 1990s and early

Photo 21.2 The first High Representative of the Union for Foreign Affairs and Security Policy: Catherine Ashton

2000s. In the Prodi and Barroso I Colleges, the approach to the structural question was to divide the external relations portfolios and Directorates General along functional lines and include in the arrangements a Commissioner and a Directorate General with explicit responsibility for foreign policy – though political sensitivities resulted in them being named as being responsible for External Relations rather than Foreign Policy. The creation by the Lisbon Treaty of the joint High Representative–External Relations Commissioner post 'settled' this structural matter.

The Commission's CFSP position is strengthened by the Lisbon Treaty. The External Relations Commissioner now chairs the Foreign Affairs Council and so becomes a key foreign policy player. There is potential for the High Representative to assist the Commission to make much greater, and more coordinated, use of its non foreign policy instruments – notably trade and aid – in foreign policy settings. But, how much influence the Commission as an institution will, in practice, exercise over particular foreign policy matters post-Lisbon is likely to depend, as it always has, on individual circumstances. The Commission is, for example, in a strong position when CFSP actions involve the use of trade policy instruments, such as the use of economic sanctions, for then the Council can only act on the basis of Commission proposals. Similarly, its position can be strong when the Council is reliant on it for specialised information and advice. In this context, one of the ways in which the Commission has sought to enhance its position is by developing policies and policy instruments in the field of conflict prevention and in civilian aspects of conflict management and post-conflict reconstruction. The Commission's position is usually at its weakest when matters in hand are 'purely political' and when the incumbent Presidency is a large member state with a big and effective Foreign Ministry and/or is a member state that prefers foreign policy matters to be conducted mainly on an intergovernmental basis.

The European Parliament

The European Parliament's roles and powers in relation to the CFSP are set in Article 36 of the post-Lisbon Treaty TEU, which is reproduced in Document 21.5.

What the Article 36 provisions amount to in practice is that unless special circumstances apply – as, for example, when a foreign policy issue is linked to an association or cooperation agreement and the consent procedure thus needs to be used – the EP is largely confined to advisory, monitoring and holding-to-account roles on foreign policy.

Of course, these roles are not unimportant, but they are not policy- or decision-making roles. The nearest the EP comes to having a role in CFSP decision-making is during the budgetary procedure when the EP has the opportunity to raise foreign policy issues. It can do this because all CFSP administrative and operational expenditure is charged to the EU budget, except for operations with military and defence implications and cases where the Council acting unanimously decides otherwise.

Document 21.5

Article 36 TEU (setting out the EP's CFSP roles and powers)

The High Representative of the Union for Foreign Affairs and Security Policy Presidency shall regularly consult the European Parliament on the main aspects and the basic choices of the common foreign and security policy and the common security and defence policy and inform it of how those policies evolve. He shall ensure that the views of the European Parliament are duly taken into consideration. Special representatives may be involved in briefing the European Parliament.

The European Parliament may ask questions of the Council or make recommendations to it and to the High Representative. Twice a year it shall hold a debate on progress in implementing the common foreign and security policy.

Embassies, delegations and missions

The development since the Second World War of rapid international travel and instantaneous electronic communications has undermined much of the role and value of diplomatic representations as a means for countries to communicate with one another. Nonetheless, embassies, delegations and missions are still used to promote and defend interests abroad.

Because it is not a state the EU is not able to maintain overseas embassies, but it does have an extensive network of external delegations: nearly 140 in third countries and five delegations to international organisations. (It might be added here – and this exemplifies the importance of the EU to the outside world – that over 170 countries have diplomatic missions officially accredited to the EU.) Prior to the entry into force of the Lisbon Treaty, these external delegations were delegations of the Commission, but the Treaty's granting of legal status to the EU enabled them to become EU delegations. Post-Lisbon, they operate within the framework of the new European External Action Service (EEAS) that is headed by the High Representative.

Overseas representations are, of course, concerned with many issues other than foreign policy – most notably, the promotion of trade and, in the case of national representations, the safeguarding of citizens' interests. The CFSP is, however, a matter that embassies of the member states and EU delegations seek to promote. In this context Article 35 TEU states that:

> The diplomatic and consular missions of the Member States and the Union delegations in third countries and international conferences, and their representations to international organisations, shall cooperate in ensuring that decisions defining Union positions and joint actions pursuant to [the CFSP] are complied with and implemented.

Article 35 underpins the development of processes that have been long underway, whereby embassies of EU member states in third countries and delegations attached to international organisations exchange information and coordinate activities. For example member state ambassadors to the UN meet weekly to coordinate policy, and the member states vote together on around 75 per cent of votes in the General Assembly.

*   *   *

An additional comment needs to be made about CSDP policy processes. Because, as was stressed above, the CSDP is part of the CFSP, the processes are, for the most part, one and the same. However, there are two variations that should be noted. The first is that when CSDP matters are on the agenda of the Foreign Affairs Council, Defence Ministers usually join the Foreign Ministers. Occasionally, Defence Ministers also meet by themselves. The second variation is that, as can be seen in Figure 21.1, there are two bodies that are exclusively concerned with the CSDP. These bodies – which along with the PSC were each created by a Council decision in January 2001 (see *Official Journal*, 44: L27, 30 January 2001) – are:

- *The European Union Military Committee* (EUMC) is composed of the Chiefs of Defence, represented by their military delegates except in circumstances which require the Chiefs themselves to meet. The functions of EUMC include providing military advice and making recommendations to the PSC, acting as the forum for military consultation and cooperation between the member states in the field of conflict prevention and crisis management, and undertaking various evaluative and advisory tasks in crisis management situations. The Committee normally meets weekly.
- *The Military Staff of the European Union* (EUMS) consists of military personnel seconded from the member states. The staff are part of the General Secretariat of the Council, but because of concerns about security they are not based in the same building as the rest of the Secretariat. Working under the direction of the EUMC, the military staff provide military expertise and support for the CSDP, including on early warning, situation assessment and strategic planning.

Development Policy

The EU and its member states are major actors in international development policy. This is no more clearly demonstrated than in the fact that the EU's member states provide around 45 per cent of all international development aid whilst the EU itself provides another 10 per cent. In the related area of international humanitarian aid, the EU's member states provide around 25 per cent of the total and the EU provides around 30 per cent.

Policy content

EU development policy has 'as its primary objective the reduction and, in the long term, the eradication of poverty' (Article 208 TFEU). This objective was at the heart of a major strategy paper – *The European Consensus on Development* – that was adopted in 2005 in a joint statement agreed by the Council, the representatives of the governments of the member states meeting within the Council, the European Parliament and the Commission. The joint statement declared:

> The primary and overarching objective of EU development cooperation is the eradication of poverty in the context of sustainable development, including pursuit of the Millennium Development Goals (MDGs).
>
> The eight MDGs are to: eradicate extreme poverty and hunger; achieve universal primary education; promote gender equality and empower women; reduce the mortality rate of children; improve maternal health; combat HIV/AIDS, malaria and other diseases; ensure environmental sustainability and develop a global partnership for development (European Parliament *et al*, 2005: 4 and 5).

The joint statement also emphasised a number of other values, goals and principles underlying EU development policy, including that development should be based on respect for human rights, fundamental freedoms, democracy, and the rule of law.

The reasons for the EU's active engagement in development policy are a mixture of the historical, the moral, and the economic: historical in that some EU countries, notably France and the UK, have long-established ties with parts of the developing world as a result of their colonial past; moral in that EU governments believe, although with different degrees of enthusiasm, that something should be done about world poverty and hunger; and economic in that developing countries account for around 30 per cent of EU exports, and the EU is highly dependent on the developing world for products such as rubber, copper and uranium.

Some of the forms of assistance made available by the EU apply to the whole of the developing world. Amongst these are:

1 *Generalised preferences.* Under the EU's Generalised System of Preferences (GSP) system, 176 developing and vulnerable countries are given preferential trading access to the EU market in the form of the reduction and/or removal of tariffs (subject to rules of origin requirements and subject also to volume limits for some products). Many agricultural products can also be exported free of duty. As an addition to the GSP scheme, under the 'Everything but Arms' (EBA) system all goods apart from arms and ammunition from the world's 50 Least Developed Countries (LDCs) are given duty free access to the EU market. (It might be noted here that most of the trade preferences under the GSP and EBA schemes are less significant than they used to be as a result of WTO policies and actions to lower trade tariffs and to equalise trade treatment.)
2 *Food aid.* Foodstuffs are sent to countries with serious food shortages.
3 *Emergency aid.* Aid of an appropriate sort is made available to countries stricken by natural disasters and other crises.
4 *Aid to non-governmental organisations.* The EU makes available aid to projects sponsored by non-governmental organisations in a number of developing world countries.

In addition to these general forms of assistance, the EU provides additional assistance and aid to countries with which it has special relationships. Most of these special relationships take the form of economic, trade, industrial, technical and financial cooperation agreements. The most important and most wide-ranging agreement is the Cotonou Partnership Agreement, which was signed in June 2000 and entered into force in April 2003. The Agreement links the EU with 79 African, Caribbean and Pacific (ACP) countries, most of which are countries with which at least one member state has historical links, most commonly as a colonial power. Scheduled to last for twenty years, but with five-year reviews built in (the first review was completed in June 2005 and entered into force in July 2008), the Agreement replaces the Lomé Conventions which framed EU–ACP relations from 1975. The Cotonou Agreement continues with many of Lomé's core features, including: duty-free access to the EU market for virtually all ACP exports; schemes to stabilise export earnings; and the European Development Fund (EDF), which provides financial assistance for development projects in ACP countries.

But Cotonou also involves very significant changes to the Lomé system, which are gradually being phased-in. These changes were, and still are, driven primarily by: a recognition that many ACP states have not improved their economic independence and are not becoming properly integrated into the world economy; an acknowledgement of the increasing diversity of ACP states; and WTO pressures arising from the fact that the non-reciprocal and preferential nature of the trade aspects of Lomé/Cotonou are incompatible with WTO rules. The main changes being introduced by Cotonou are:

- The Lomé system of uniform preferential trade access is being replaced by a phased move towards the creation of reciprocal and regionally based Economic Partnership Agreements (EPAs) involving groups of ACP countries. Cotonou thus allows for more differentiation between ACPs than did Lomé. 'Trade not aid' is the mantra, with greater encouragement being given to more 'South–South' economic activity. The more advanced ACPs are moving quicker with trade liberalisation than are the less developed ACPs. This liberalisaion is seen as being crucial in creating trade development and investment opportunities that match local conditions.
- Increased emphasis is being attached to more self-reliance, with the role of the private sector in stimulating enterprise in the ACP states being given much attention.
- Political cooperation and conditionality is being stepped up, with greater emphasis being given to strengthening democratic processes, good governance, respect for human rights, and civil society in the ACP states.

Development aid is financed in two ways. First, non-EDF aid is funded by the EU budget. Accounting for around four per cent of the budget, about half of this aid is used to provide financial assistance to non-ACP countries and about half is used for food aid purposes. Second, EDF aid is funded by special contributions from the member states. The tenth EDF, covering the years 2008–13, totals nearly €25 billion (at 2010 prices). Taking EDF and non-EDF aid together, the principal beneficiaries are sub-Saharan Africa (which receives almost 60 per cent), southern Asia (about 10 per cent), and Latin America and the Caribbean (also about 10 per cent).

It should be stressed that EU development policy is conducted alongside national policies. Unlike with trade policy, the EU does not have exclusive competence in the area of development policy. In some aspects of development policy the EU takes the leading role whilst in others the member states are the main players and the EU is confined to, at most, supplementing, complementing and coordinating national development policies. So, the trade aspects of development policy are necessarily the EU's responsibility, but the states are much more prominent in respect of financial assistance.

Strains have sometimes arisen between member states and between member states and EU institutions (especially the Commission) regarding development policies. This has been largely because there are differences between the member states regarding their aims, priorities and interests on development policy issues. As Holland (2002: 171) puts it: 'For example, French development policy remains largely neo-colonial, Italy follows a more commercial approach, the UK stresses good governance whereas the Nordic states focus principally on the alleviation of poverty'. Particular problems have arisen when states have used aid for the purpose of promoting national political and economic interests. In an attempt to ensure the policies and activities of the EU and its member states match, much of the focus of development policy in recent years has been on promoting greater cooperation, consistency, coherence and complementarity between EU and member state policy activities.

Policy processes

The EU makes all sorts of decisions in connection with its development policy. Just as in other policy areas, the actors involved and the procedures that apply vary enormously.

With regard to the actors, the most important players are: the Foreign Affairs Council (the separate Development Council was disbanded as part of the 2002 Seville reforms of the Council, so Development Ministers now attend the Foreign Affairs Council when agenda items concern them); the Commissioner for Development; the Development DG; the EP Committee on Development; the diplomatic missions of developing countries in Brussels that are accredited to the EU (which undertake a variety of liaising and information-providing functions); and the EU delegations in developing countries (which, amongst a wide range of functions, have management responsibilities for development aid projects).

With regard to decision-making procedures, these are dependent on the type of decision envisaged. For example, if the Council is simply intending to issue a declaration or a resolution on a matter, it is not obliged to consult the EP and can move at its own pace – which may mean proceeding very cautiously and only after the receipt of proposals from the Commission and/or from a specially convened Council *ad hoc* working party. If a trade-only agreement is envisaged, Article 207 applies – which, as was noted earlier in the chapter, means that the Commission and the Council are the key actors, QMV can be used in the Council, and the EP has the power of consent. If cooperation or association agreements are proposed, QMV is available in the Council for most cooperation agreements, there must be unanimity for association agreements, and the EP again has the power of consent.

As was shown above, the Cotonou Agreement is the most important of the numerous agreements to which the EU is party in connection with its policy on development cooperation. It is therefore worth saying a little about how it functions, for the Agreement has its own institutional structure, which is largely the structure passed down from the Lomé Convention. There are three principal bodies in the structure. The first is the Council of Ministers, which is composed of the members of the EU Council of Ministers, a member of the Commission, and a member of the government of each ACP country. The Council meets at least once a year to take whatever major political and policy decisions are necessary under the Agreement. Decisions are taken by 'common agreement'. If there is a dispute between the 'two sides' binding arbitration applies, with the procedures of the Permanent Court of Arbitration for International Organisations normally being used. The second body is the Committee of Ambassadors, which is composed of a representative of each EU state, a representative of the Commission, and a representative of each ACP state. The

Committee meets at least twice a year and is charged with assisting and advising the Council of Ministers, monitoring the implementation of the Agreement and the progress towards its objectives, and generally supervising and coordinating the work of the many committees and subsidiary bodies that exist under the general umbrella of the Agreement. Finally, there is the joint Assembly, which is made up of equal numbers of MEPs and ACP members of parliament or national representatives. It meets twice a year and acts as a general advisory and deliberating body.

The External Dimension of Internal Policies

Many of the EU's internal policies have significant external dimensions. For example, transport policy involves dealing with neighbouring countries on road transit arrangements and with countries throughout the world on numerous air and maritime transport issues. Energy policy includes dealing with countries that are suppliers of energy to the EU about rights, guarantees, and terms of access. And environmental policy includes dealing with countries near and far on such issues as climate change and many aspects of air, land, and water damage and pollution.

Prior to the Lisbon Treaty, the EU did not have explicit treaty powers to act as the external representative of the member states in such policy areas. However, the Court of Justice established that the EU did have implied external powers in respect of policy areas falling within its internal jurisdiction. Just how extensive these implied powers were, and in what circumstances they applied, was frequently contested, but the key principle of 'parallelism' was firmly established, by which the exercise of internal law-making powers by the EU in a particular policy area was taken to imply that it also had the power to negotiate and conclude international agreements in that area. This principle was acknowledged in a new Article 216 that was incorporated in the TFEU by the Lisbon Treaty:

> The Union may conclude an agreement with one or more third countries or international organisations where the Treaties so provide or where the conclusion of an agreement is necessary in order to achieve, within the framework of the

Union's policies, one of the objectives referred to in the Treaties, or is provided for in a legally binding Union act or is likely to affect common rules or alter their scope.

The procedural arrangements by which the EU contracts external agreements on internal policy issues are set out in Article 218 of the TFEU. Different procedures apply depending on the nature of the agreement concerned. A relatively straightforward agreement with no major institutional or budgetary implications is subject to much the same procedure as applies to trade agreements under Article 207. In contrast, agreements that are constituent elements of more wide-ranging cooperation or association agreements are subject to the 'more difficult' requirement that applies to these latter agreements – that is, unanimity is normally necessary in the Council.

To these already rather complicated arrangements, another complication is that the EU does not necessarily have the exclusive right to negotiate external agreements on internal policies. Rather, there are many mixed competences where policy responsibilities are shared between the EU and the member states. This results in there being two main ways, with variations within each, as to how the EU is represented and conducts itself in international negotiations in such policy areas. On the one hand, where there is exclusive EU competence, as with fisheries, the Commission is the sole EU representative and negotiator. On the other hand, where there is a mixed competence, as with environmental policy, the Commission acts on behalf of the EU and national representatives act on behalf of their member states.

The distribution of competences is highly complex in some policy areas, with overlapping competences that can make it difficult for the EU fully to coordinate its inputs in international forums and negotiations. This can naturally weaken the EU's influence. But, the extent of the weakening should not be overstated. In the environmental policy sphere, for example, the EU is a major global player, as Bretherton and Vogler (2006) show. It is party to, and an influential voice within, more than 30 different multilateral environmental agreements – including agreements on the protection of the ozone layer, the transboundary movement of hazardous wastes and their disposal, desertification, and the protection of the marine environment (there are several marine environment agree-

ments covering different sea areas). Moreover in a few environmental policy areas – including climate change and biological diversity – it is not going too far to describe the EU as virtually a policy leader.

A key reason why the EU is often able to exert a significant external policy influence in internal policy areas is that it is usually well prepared for negotiations with third parties. Even when there have been internal disputes, accommodations – on competences, policy goals, and who is to take the negotiating 'lead' – are usually agreed before external negotiations begin. Furthermore, during the course of external negotiations EU 'coordination' meetings are normally held as and when they are deemed necessary.

The Consistency and Representational Problems

As can be seen in Document 21.3, the concluding paragraph of Article 21 of the TEU emphasises the importance of the Union ensuring consistency in the different areas of its external relations. Clearly, if consistency is not achieved the EU's potential to exercise a significant and effective influence on the world's stages is reduced.

But, ensuring consistency – over time, between individual external relations policies, and between policies at the EU and the national levels – has been a major problem. Amongst numerous examples that could be given of a lack of consistent and coherent policies in recent years are:

- the EU's inability to give a decisive reaction to Kosovo's declaration of independence from Serbia in mid-2008, with some member states giving immediate recognition and others either gradually following or witholding recognition;
- the issuing of only very general CFSP statements following Russia's 'invasion' of Georgia in August 2008, with member states divided on whether Russia should be blamed and pressurised, and if so to what extent and in what ways;
- the lack of a concerted EU position on how to react to Israel's 'invasion' of Gaza in December 2008;
- the lack of consistent 'across the board' policy towards China and Russia, with some EU member states – especially large states – tending to leave

> **Box 21.8**
>
> ## Reasons why external policy consistency can be difficult for the EU
>
> - The great spread of the EU external relations' interests and activities.
> - The diversity of actors and processes that are involved in EU external relations policy processes.
> - The differing powers of the EU in different policy contexts, with particular problems arising when competence is shared between the EU and the member states – as it is for most of the internal policies that have an external dimension.
> - The differing powers of EU actors in differing spheres of external relations.
> - The conflicting orientations and preferences of the member states on many policy issues.
> - The varying levels of EU policy development – from the common commercial policy to the emerging defence policy.

much of the democracy/civil liberties dimension of relations to the EU and downplaying these in bi-lateral relations.

As Box 21.8 shows, there are several overlapping and interrelating reasons why EU policy consistency is often difficult to achieve.

Procedures, mechanisms and arrangements do, of course, exist to try and maximise consistency. Crucial in this respect is the convening, at different levels of seniority, of numerous intra- and inter-institutional meetings that have as their purpose the coordination of external policies and activities. Within the Commission, for example, the coordinating structure is broadly as follows:

- The Commissioners' Relex Group, which brings together the External Relations, Trade, Development, Enlargement, and Economic and Monetary Affairs Commissioners, plus other Commissioners when agenda items require their presence.

- The Directors General Relex Group, which is attended not only by the Directors General of the five DGs covered by the Commissioner's Group but also by the Secretary General, the Head of the Legal Service, and also Directors General from such DGs as Agriculture and Competition when necessary.
- Inter-service groups. These bring together officials from all DGs with an interest in a particular issue. There are a few standing inter-service groups, such as that on the WTO, but most are convened as and when they are deemed to be necessary. So, there are no standing inter-service groups on particular countries, but if a cross-cutting issue concerning a country arises, a paper – probably drafted from the country desk in the External Relations DG – may be circulated, which may then well be followed up by a one-off inter-service meeting in which all interested parties are brought together.

Such coordinating arrangements have become increasingly necessary as many of the EU's external programmes have become increasingly multi-dimensional in character. For instance, the numerous cooperation and association agreements that the EU has concluded with third countries typically include a battery of, as appropriate, trade, development, and democracy-building/human rights measures, plus provisions for a political dialogue between the partners.

The Lisbon Treaty made institutional reforms designed to enable policy inconsistencies to be tackled more effectively at the highest level, notably with the creation of the new High Representative post. But, the closing sentence of Article 21 TEU – see Document 21.3 – does not promise well in this regard, with the responsibility for ensuring consistency still arguably too divided.

The consistency problem is, of course, closely related to the representational problem that is encaptured in the question first allegedly posed by the US Secretary of State, Henry Kissinger, in the early 1970s – who speaks for Europe? When the EU acts on the world stage the nature of its representation can vary considerably according to circumstances. Even after the 'streamlining' of the EU's external representation by the Lisbon Treaty, this situation is likely to at least partly continue. So, for example, in charged political situations the representation is likely to involve some combination of the European Council President, the High Representative, and quite possibly the Head of

Government or Foreign Minister from the Presidency-in-Office. In addition, some member states, especially larger member states, may also seek to act in an individual capacity. Where, by contrast, international monetary matters are under consideration, the representation is likely to involve some combination of the Finance Minister from the Presidency-in-Office, the Economic and Monetary Affairs Commissioner (both of these seeking to represent the EU-27), the President of the European Central Bank, the President of the Eurogroup (both seeking to represent the eurozone), and national Finance Ministers and national Central Bank Governors (especially from the member states outside the eurozone).

Concluding Remarks

This chapter has demonstrated that the EU can be thought of as being a partially constructed international actor in that it has an 'ability to function actively and deliberately in relation to other actors in the international system' (Groenleer and Van Schaik, 2007: 972). The chapter has also suggested that the EU exercises a major influence on the world stage in respect of trade policy, a significant influence in respect of development, environment and certain other policies, and a modest but growing influence in respect of foreign and defence policies. As Ginsberg (1999 and 2001) has argued and demonstrated, the EU not only has external policy outputs but also an external policy impact on non-member state international actors and international issue areas.

A central question that is likely to loom large in the foreseeable future is whether the EU will advance from being a modest player to becoming a major player in the foreign and defence policy fields. Mechanisms to enable it to do so have been strengthened over the years, but they are still essentially intergovernmental in character. As several observers have noted, the CFSP has been 'Brusselised' – with the creation of an extensive institutional system – but it has barely been 'communitarised' in the sense of becoming subject to supranational drive, decision-making, supervision and enforcement.

But the development of a greater institutional capacity will not in itself be enough to enable the CFSP and the related CSDP to deepen. The political will to use and take advantage of the capacity is also required. For reasons that have been outlined in this chapter, such political will is not always forthcoming. To cite just one example of an area where a stronger collective political will is required, it is accepted by virtually all informed observers that defence expenditure in the EU is not used to maximum effect. Amongst the problems are: too many operating systems and forms of hardware that are not interoperable; too many duplications; and in a world where the nature of security threats has changed dramatically in recent years, too many states are spending too much on personnel and not enough on research and sophisticated weaponry. An attempt is being made to improve the situation via the European Defence Agency, but whether it will have much success in persuading EU governments to work more closely together in this highly sensitive policy area remains to be seen.

But however the prospects of the EDA may be judged, it should not be assumed that all political will is lacking and that further integrationist advances cannot be made in the CFSP and CSDP spheres. There may be major obstacles in the way, but many of what used to be seen as almost insurmountable barriers have been removed in recent years. For example: the special relationships that some EU countries have with particular parts of the world have become less problematical as historical ties have been loosened; the difficulties created by the quasi-neutrality of some member states have largely been overcome since the end of the Cold War; and, for a host of reasons, EU member states – including those that have been most concerned about the preservation of national sovereignty – have increasingly come to regard both foreign and defence policy issues as proper and legitimate matters for the EU agenda.

Chapter 22

The Budget

The Budget in Context

Despite the considerable attention it has received over the years and despite the political tensions it has often generated, the EU's budget is relatively small in size. In 2010 it totalled €141.5 billion in commitment appropriations, which though a large sum in absolute terms represented only 1.2 per cent of the total Gross National Income (GNI) of the member states and about 2.5 per cent of their total public expenditure.

The reason why the budget is so small is that most of the policy sectors that make up the bulk of public expenditure – education, health, social welfare, defence and so on – are primarily the responsibility of the member states. Many of the EU's policy activities, such as those concerned with the regulation of the market, involve little in the way of operational costs. When EU policies do involve significant costs, for example when they impose an obligation to invest in large capital expenditure to conform with EU legislation on the quality of air or drinking water, the financial impact usually falls not on the EU budget but on private sector firms and public authorities in the member states.

The relative modesty of the size of EU budget should therefore be borne in mind when assessing the budget's financial and policy impact. The fact is that in overall economic terms the impact of the budget is slight. It cannot and does not serve to bring about a major transfer of financial resources from national exchequers to the EU level or *vice versa*. It does not move great amounts of money around and across the EU on distributive and redistributive bases. And, as Begg (2005: 10) observes:

> compared with established federations in which the federal level has substantial resources and plays an important part in macroeconomic policy, the *economic* significance of the EU budget is minor (italics in original).

That all said, however, the budget certainly merits examination. One reason why it does so is that it generates considerable political heat and attention, especially when the EU's multiannual financial frameworks are being considered and negotiated. A second reason is that whilst the size and economic impact of the budget are small, they are far from being wholly negligible. A third reason is that an understanding of the nature of the debates and discussions surrounding the EU's budget is important to an understanding of the nature of the EU's policy portfolio. And a fourth reason is that budgetary processes are an important component part of what is a theme of this book, and especially of Part IV: the highly variegated nature of EU policy and decision-making processes.

The Multiannual Financial Frameworks

The origins and purposes of the frameworks

In the early 1980s the EC was plagued by budgetary crises, with each annual budget being the focus of sharp and protracted political conflicts between the Commission, the Council and the Parliament, and within the latter two institutions also over the size and nature of both budgetary revenue and expenditure. There were four main reasons why budgetary tensions were never far from the surface. First, the EC was faced with increasing financial obligations, not least in respect of the Common Agricultural Policy (CAP) which at that time accounted for around 70 per cent of total budgetary expenditure and which the UK government thought was over-privileged. Second, budgetary resources – which consisted of customs duties, agricultural levies, and a proportion of Value Added Tax (VAT) up to a one per cent ceiling – could not generate enough income to meet the financial obligations. Third, the UK government under Mrs Thatcher was campaigning vigorously to reduce what it saw to be excessive UK net budgetary contributions. Fourth, the EP, dissatisfied with both limitations on its budgetary powers and with the lack of resources available for non-CAP expenditure, sought to use the annual budgetary negotiations to advance its institutional position and to re-balance budgetary expenditure.

The first three of these reasons for the budgetary crises led to the conclusion of a complicated deal at the 1984 Fontainebleau European Council. Key elements of the deal included new rules on budgetary discipline, a formula for reducing UK budgetary contributions, and an expansion of resources through the setting of a new 1.4 per cent ceiling for VAT from 1986. The Fontainebleau agreement was, however, too little too late, in that no sooner had the 1.4 per cent ceiling been introduced in 1986 than it was exhausted and the Commission was forced to open a new campaign for a further expansion of the revenue base.

That campaign culminated in the 1988 Brussels summit which brought a further, and compared with Fontainebleau much more radical, reform designed to deal with the EC's recurring budgetary difficulties. The Brussels reform was operationalised in an *Interinstitutional Agreement* on *Budgetary Discipline and Improvement of the Budgetary Procedure*, which was signed by the Presidents of the Council of Ministers, the Commission, and – highly significantly in institutional terms – the European Parliament (European Communities, 1987). The importance of the Inter-institutional Agreement was that it contained a formal commitment by all three institutions to the framework of a financial perspective for the years 1988–92. Included in the perspective were: a phased reduction in CAP expenditure, a continuation of special abatement arrangements for the UK, a much tighter framework for ensuring budgetary discipline, and a significant expansion of resources through the creation of a new budgetary resource based on the Gross National Product (GNP) of each state. An increase in resources was thus linked to an expanding spending programme, subject to the limitation that the total amount of resources for any one year could not exceed specified percentages of the total GNP of the Community for the year in question: the perspective started with 1.15 per cent for 1988 and rose to 1.2 per cent for 1992.

The 1988 Inter-institutional Agreement set a precedent for future budgetary decision-making. For since 1988 all of the EU's annual budgets have been set within multiannual financial frameworks (MFFs) – known as financial perspectives until they were accorded treaty status and officially named MFFs by the Lisbon Treaty. What financial perspectives/ frameworks have done is to set for a fixed period – of seven years apart from the five year period of the very first perspective – annual maximum limits (ceilings) on EU expenditure as a whole and for the main categories (called headings) of expenditure. The periods covered by the three perspectives since the 1988–92 perspective have been 1993–9, 2000–6, and 2007–13.

The contents of and the political machinations surrounding the 1993–9 and 2000–6 perspectives are set out in previous editions of this book and will not be repeated here. Suffice it to give just a brief summary of key features of the making of the perspectives and of their contents. Regarding the making of the perspectives, in both cases the Commission set the ball rolling with the issuing of proposals – under the title *From the Single Act to Maastricht and Beyond: the Means to Match Our Ambitions* (European Commission, 1992) for what became the 1993–9 perspective and as part of its *Agenda 2000* package of reforms (European Commission, 1997a) for what became the 2000–6 perspective. The issuing of the Commission's proposals were then followed by long and strongly contested negotiations between the member states, which culminated in deals being struck at European Council meetings at Edinburgh in December 1992 and Berlin in March 1999. In neither case did the EP participate in the negotiations prior to the summits, and it was not able to exercise much influence after the summits when inter-institutional agreements were again contracted. Regarding the contents of the perspectives, the most important features were: a slight increase in spending resources, with an overall ceiling of 1.27 per cent of EU GDP being set for the 1992–9 perspective and this being continued for the 2000–6 perspective; further stabilisation of agricultural expenditure; further increases in funding for structural operations in the 1992–9 perspective and stabilisation of this expenditure heading in the 2000–6 perspective; continuation of the existing four revenue resources, though with some modifications in the 1992–9 perspective to make them weigh less heavily on the poorer states and with, for the same reason, the revenue base being modified in the 2000–6 perspective by reducing the VAT element and increasing the GNP element; and no major changes in the abatement arrangements for the UK.

The making of the 2007–13 framework

The processes leading to the adoption of the EU's fourth financial perspective, covering the years 2007–13, were always likely to be heated. One reason for this was that many national positions that had caused problems in negotiations on previous financial perspectives would inevitably be re-activated, most particularly with net contributors to the budget wanting their contributions cut and net beneficiaries wanting their benefits protected. A second reason was that the states that joined the EU in May 2004 would be party to the negotiations, and since most of these believed they had been treated ungenerously

under the terms of the 2000–6 financial perspective they would be looking for a considerable improvement in their positions. A third reason was that some states, most notably the UK, believed that the 2007–13 financial perspective should tackle a major problem that previous financial perspectives had left largely unresolved – the budgetary imbalance caused by the fact that the CAP accounted for around 45 per cent of budgetary expenditure. And a fourth reason was that 24 of the 25 member states wanted to remove, or at least greatly reduce the size of, the UK abatement, which was seen as being no longer justified given the accession in 2004 of so many poorer states and given too the increased prosperity of the UK since the principle of the abatement had been established in 1984.

The deliberation and negotiation process 'should' have started with the publication of proposals from the Commission. However, before the proposals were issued there were two 'pre-emptive strikes'. The first of these occurred in October 2002, when France and Germany were successful in engineering an agreement in the European Council to the effect that the amount of money spent on the CAP (which is not the same as the proportion of the budget assigned to the CAP) would be virtually frozen during the period of the new financial perspective. This agreement subsequently greatly limited the Commission's room for manoeuvre when devising its proposals for the financial perspective. (See Chapter 20 for further information on the CAP element of the October 2002 agreement.) The second pre-emptive strike occurred in December 2003 when the leaders of the six net contributor states to the budget – Austria, France, Germany, the Netherlands, Sweden, and the UK – sent a joint letter to the President of the Commission, Romano Prodi. In their letter, the leaders urged that a ceiling of one per cent of EU GNI should be set on EU commitments' expenditure in the financial perspective. This one per cent figure was lower than the expenditure ceiling of the 2000–6 financial perspective, but was close to current 'real' expenditure which, because of under-spending, was just under one per cent.

The Commission's proposals were issued in February 2004 in the form of a communication to the Council and the EP under the title *Building Our Common Future: Policy Challenges and Budgetary Measures of the Enlarged Union 2007–2013* (European

Commission, 2004). The main features of the proposals were:

- The total size of the budget to increase by around 35 per cent, with most of this being attributable to the incorporation of new member states.
- The ceiling on total expenditure to be 1.14 per cent for payments and 1.24 per cent for commitments.
- The titles of expenditure headings to be changed to reflect policy developments and priorities. In the 2000–6 perspective there were seven headings: agriculture, structural operations, internal policies, external action, administration, reserves, and pre-accession aid. In the new perspective six headings were proposed: sustainable growth (mainly cohesion and Lisbon Strategy-related policies); preservation and management of natural resources (essentially the CAP); citizenship, freedom, security and justice; the EU as a global partner; administration, and – for three years only – compensations.
- Spending on market-related CAP measures to stay fairly flat in money terms in line with the decision taken at the October 2002 summit, but to gradually decrease as a proportion of the budget – to an average of 29 per cent over the period of the financial perspective and to 26 per cent in 2013.
- Increased spending under the other headings apart from administration to be priorities for the financial perspective. Spending on sustainable growth to increase by 28 per cent over the period, on European citizenship by 122 per cent, and on the EU as a global partner by 38 per cent.
- The UK abatement problem (which was referred to only indirectly) to be tackled within the framework of the creation of a generalised corrective mechanism. The mechanism would be designed to ensure that no state made excessive net contributions to the budget.

Over the following months the Commission's proposals were considered by policy actors in the member states and at EU level. Numerous suggestions/demands for changes were put forward, mostly along predictable lines. The general intention was to try and reach an overall settlement at the June 2005 European Council meeting and to this end the Luxembourg Presidency liaised closely with the member states to

try to find a compromise that would be acceptable. In the event, however, this proved not to be possible, with five member states – Denmark, Germany, the Netherlands, Sweden, and (most strongly) the UK – rejecting the Presidency's final draft. The key features of the draft were: the spending ceiling on commitments to be capped at 1.06 per cent of EU GNI; there to be deliberations in 2010 on ways to cut CAP expenditure, but any agreed reforms not to come into effect during the lifetime of the financial perspective; and the UK rebate to be frozen in 2007 and to be set on a downward path.

The failure to reach an agreement in June 2005 was not a disaster. After all, the financial perspective was not scheduled to come into force for another eighteen months. But the failure did greatly increase the pressures on the succeeding UK Presidency to find an acceptable compromise, not least since a political deal on the perspective would need to be followed by implementing legislation and because also CEECs in particular were pressing for an agreement so they could plan spending programmes. But the UK government was in a difficult position because whilst it was anxious to be seen to have run a successful Presidency and a deal on the financial perspective would be very helpful in that regard, its own national position was the one that was most detached from the positions of other states: it wanted the overall size of the budget to be as near as possible to one per cent of EU GNI, it wanted to retain the UK abatement, and it wanted a review of CAP spending to be both conducted and implemented during the course of the perspective.

As part of its strategy to try and find an agreement, the UK Presidency decided not to issue revised proposals until a matter of days before the end-of-Presidency summit in December 2005. This approach, it reasoned, would reduce oppositional grandstanding and the premature adopting of hard-line oppositional stances. In that an agreement was indeed duly reached at the December 2005 summit it is a strategy that may be said to have worked, assisted by other facilitating factors – most notably the willingness of the leaders to compromise.

Table 22.1 and Figure 22.1 set out an overview of the ceilings on expenditure contained in the agreed 2007–13 financial perspective (adjusted to 2010 figures), using the official expenditure headings. Under what are perhaps more recognisable headings,

Table 22.1 Financial framework 2007–13*

Commitments and Appropriations	2007	2008	2009	2010	2011	2012	2013	Total 2007–2013
1 Sustainable growth	53 979	57 653	59 700	61 782	63 638	66 628	69 621	433 001
1a Competitiveness for growth and employment	8 918	10 386	11 272	12 388	12 987	14 203	15 433	85 587
1b Cohesion for growth and employment	45 061	47 267	48 428	49 394	50 651	52 425	54 188	347 414
2 Preservation and management of natural resources	55 143	59 193	59 639	60 113	60 338	60 810	61 289	416 525
of which: market related expenditure and direct payments	45 759	46 217	46 679	47 146	47 617	48 093	48 574	330 085
3 Citizenship, freedom, security and justice	1 273	1 362	1 523	1 693	1 889	2 105	2 376	12 221
3a Freedom, security and justice	637	747	872	1 025	1 206	1 406	1 661	7 554
3b Citizenship	636	615	651	668	683	699	715	4 667
4 EU as a global player	6 578	7 002	7 440	7 893	8 430	8 997	9 595	55 935
5 Administration	7 039	7 380	7 699	8 008	8 334	8 670	9 095	56 225
6 Compensations	445	207	210	862				
Total appropriations for commitments	124 457	132 797	136 211	139 489	142 629	142 210	151 976	974 769
as a percentage of GNI	1.02%	1.08%	1.15%	1.15%	1.13%	1.12%	1.11%	1.11%
Total appropriations for payments	122 190	129 681	123 858	133 505	133 452	140 200	142 408	925 294
as a percentage of GNI	1.00%	1.05%	1.04%	1.10%	1.06%	1.07%	1.04%	1.05%
Margin available	0.24%	0.19%	0.20%	0.14%	0.18%	0.17%	0.20%	0.19%
Own resources ceiling as a percentage of GNI	1.24%	1.24%	1.24%	1.24%	1.24%	1.24%	1.24%	1.24%

* Adjusted for 2010 prices, in million euro.

Source: European Commission (2009e).

Figure 22.1 Structure and spending ceilings of the 2007–13 financial framework

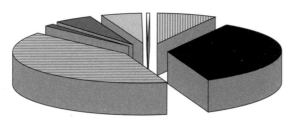

1A   Competitiveness for growth and employment: 8.8%

1B   Cohesion for growth and employment: 35.6%

2   Preservation and management of natural resources: 42.7%

3   A Freedom, security and justice: 0.8%
      B Citizenship: 0.5%

4   The EU as a global partner (excl. EDF): 5.7%

5   Total administrative expenditure: 5.8%

6   Compensations BG/RO: 0.1%

Source: Europa website.

the percentages assigned to the appropriations for commitments are as follows:

– Farm and rural support	42.8
– Cohesion aid	35.4
– Competitiveness	8.3
– Foreign policy	5.8
– Administration	5.8
– Justice and security	1.2
– Other	0.7

The figure appropriated for commitments in the 2005 agreement was 1.045 per cent of EU GNI (since adjusted, as Table 22.1 shows), which was much closer to the 1.0 per cent urged by 'the contributor six' in December 2003 than to the 1.24 per cent originally proposed by the Commission and supported by many beneficiary states. But it was a compromise figure nonetheless. All other aspects of the agreement also involved compromise. One compromise included new arrangements to calculate net contributions, which will have the effect of making for greater parity between the richer states. As part of this, the UK rebate is to be reduced (by about one-fifth), but not eliminated – as the French government in particular wanted. Another compromise involved an agreement

to launch in 2008 a review by the Commission into budgetary expenditure, including on the CAP. The proposal for a review had been resisted by the French, but they gave way when the British agreed not to include a firm commitment that the outcome of the review would necessarily begin to be implemented during the lifetime of the financial perspective.

Features of the making of financial frameworks

A theme of this book is that EU policy- and decision-making processes are highly varied in nature. In this context, four particular characteristics of the making of MFFs merit particular identification.

First, the processes are protracted. If they are measured just from the Commission's issuing of its proposals to adoption by the European Council, each of the last two financial perspectives – those of 2000–6 and 2007–13 – have taken almost two years to resolve. If, however, preparation by the Commission is added on to the beginning of the process and approval by the EP and the adoption of necessary implementing legislation is added on to the end, then the time period is at least doubled.

Second, the processes are highly politicised and contentious – a key reason, of course, why they are protracted. Differences between the states take different forms, reflecting the nature of national economic needs and political preferences, but most boil down to each state wanting to contribute as little as possible to, and extract as much as possible from, the budget. The differences that exist are sharpened by the fact that because decisional outcomes are expressed in numerical figures, it is quite clear who 'the winners' and 'the losers' are when decisions are made – which is not generally so much the case when, for example, internal market or environmental policy decisions are being made.

Third, all final decisions 'on the Council side' are taken at the highest political level on an intergovernmental basis. That is to say, they are taken by the European Council acting by unanimity. This is because of the considerable significance and high-profile nature of the decisions being made: as was shown in Chapter 10, there are now few major EU decisions that are not either made by or at least approved by the national leaders. A related feature of the decision-making process on the Council side is that the overarching nature of matters covered by MFFs coupled with the fact that final decisions are ultimately taken by the European Council means that most of the Council preparatory work is channelled through the General Affairs Council rather than the Ecofin Council.

Fourth, until the Lisbon Treaty the EP had no formal powers in relation to financial perspectives and in practice exercised little influence over them. This was because financial perspectives had no treaty base and were, essentially, political agreements between the governments of the member states. The EP was not a direct participant in the main decision-making processes, though it did have some leverage by virtue of the fact that inter-institutional agreements between the Commission, Council and EP on financial perspectives were deemed to be politically necessary before perspectives could be regarded as having been adopted. So, in January 2006 the EP rejected the December 2005 European Council agreement on the 2007–13 perspective and called for a number of reforms. The reforms requested were, however, somewhat modest in nature, and many of them – such as stronger auditing rules, simpler spending procedures, and a greater role for MEPs in controlling foreign policy expenditure – focused on matters that would not directly affect financial perspective figures. The reason for the EP's seeming 'defeatism' was that it recognised that it would not be realistic to expect the national governments to re-open financial 'basics' that had been resolved only with great difficulty. The Lisbon Treaty strengthens the EP's position by giving it the power of consent over MFFs, which should result in it exercising rather more influence over the contents of MFFs that it has in the past.

The value of and the prospects for the multiannual financial frameworks

As has just been shown, financial frameworks generate much political heat and controversy. In 2005 the two end-of-Presidency European Council meetings, and much of the EU-related political debate before and after them, were dominated by attempts to find an agreement between the member states on the 2007–13

framework. But if the attention given to financial frameworks is perhaps excessive, it should be recognised that they do serve at least three useful purposes. First, by acting as medium-term budgetary planning instruments they allow the EU and the member states to use EU funds in more measured and ordered ways than otherwise would be possible. Second, by specifying ceilings on all categories of EU expenditure they impose budgetary discipline. Third, by greatly restricting what can be done within the annual budgetary process, they help to ensure that although there may be disagreement between the participants in that process there are not full scale political fall-outs every year.

The value of the use of MFFs was formally recognised by the Lisbon Treaty when, for the first time, they were given treaty status. Their binding nature is clearly set out under Article 312 TFEU which specifies:

> The annual budget of the Union shall comply with the multiannual financial framework …
>
> The financial framework shall determine the amounts of the annual ceilings on commitments appropriations by categories of expenditure and of the annual ceiling on payment appropriations.

As for the contents of future MFFS, there seems little prospect of radical changes. Whilst disputes between the member states can certainly be anticipated, they are likely to be over largely familiar issues: the total size of the budget, the proportionate net contributions (including national rebates), and the amounts to be assigned to the CAP, to cohesion polices, and to other policy areas such as research and innovation.

The Annual Budget

The composition of the budget

Revenue

Following a decision by the member states in 1970, the funding of the budget was changed between 1970 and 1975 from a system based on national contributions to one based on 'own resources'. A major reason for introducing this change was that it would provide the Community with greater financial independence. The member states would determine the upper limit of the own resources, but the resources themselves would belong to the Community and not the states.

Since the creation of the GNP-based resource in 1988, the own resources have consisted of the following.

- *Traditional own resources.* These consist of two component elements. First, Common Customs Tariff duties and other duties, which are collected in respect of trade with non-member countries. Second, agricultural levies, premiums and other duties, which are collected in respect of trade with non-member countries within the framework of the CAP. These differ from customs duties in that they are not fixed import taxes, but are fluctuating charges designed to have the effect of raising import prices to EU levels. There are also certain internal agricultural levies and duties, notably connected with the framework of the common organisation of the market in sugar.
- *The application of a uniform percentage rate to the VAT assessment base,* which is determined in a standardised manner for member states (although this still permits states to have some variation in their national VAT rates). In order to reduce the regressive aspect of this element of budgetary resources, rule changes to the uniform rate and the assessment base were included in first three financial perspectives so as to reduce the proportionate share of this budgetary resource.
- *The application of a rate to a base representing the sum of member states' GNI at market prices.* The rate is determined under the budgetary procedure in the light of the total of all other revenue and the total expenditure agreed. Key features of this resource are that it introduces into the EU's revenue system a link with ability to pay, and it can be easily adjusted to bring budgetary revenue into balance with budgetary expenditure. Reductions to the VAT component of budgetary resources, plus declining revenue from customs duties and agricultural levies occasioned by falling world tariffs, have meant this GNI component has become by far the EU's most important income resource.

In addition to these own resources, there is also some miscellaneous income coming from, amongst other

places, income taxes paid by EU staff and contributions made by non-member states to EU programmes in which they participate.

Precisely what proportion of total budgetary revenue comes from each resource is naturally determined primarily by the rules governing the resources. As was indicated above with reference to the VAT resource, these rules change periodically. However, the proportions also vary a little from year to year according to such factors as trade flows, world agricultural prices and output, and national growth rates. Figure 22.2 indicates the considerable shift that has occurred since the mid-1990s in the relative proportions of the VAT and GNI resources. The proportions of the resources for 2009 were: customs duties – 14.0 per cent; agricultural and sugar levies – 2.0 per cent; VAT – 16.9 per cent; GNI resource – 64.5 per cent; miscellaneous – 1.2 per cent.

As regards the member states and budgetary resources, the larger states – Germany, France, Italy, and the UK – are naturally the largest gross contributors to the revenue pool. However, France, Italy and the UK are not so large net contributors: France because it is a major beneficiary of the CAP; Italy because it benefits significantly from the CAP and the Structural Funds; and the UK because of the abatement on its contributions. Germany is by far the

Figure 22.2 EU own resources

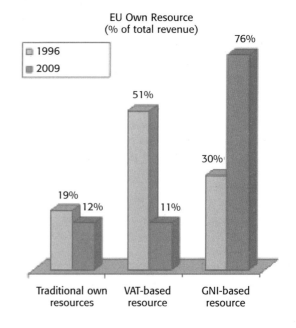

EU Own Resource
(% of total revenue)

□ 1996
■ 2009

largest net contributor, followed by, in relative terms (as a percentage of GNP), the Netherlands, the UK, Sweden, and Austria.

Expenditure

The most striking feature of EU expenditure has long been the very high proportion assigned to the CAP. For much of the 1970s and 1980s the proportion was well over 70 per cent. Even though that proportion has since fallen considerably, agriculture has still accounted in recent years for over 40 per cent of total budgetary expenditure. As was shown in Chapter 20, two main factors account for this very strong position of agriculture in the budget. First, agriculture has seen a greater transfer of financial responsibility from national budgets to the EU budget than any other major policy area. Second, agriculture is heavily subsidised – formerly through price support, now mainly through direct income support.

On a rational and commonsense basis this can hardly be justified. Agriculture appears to be proportionately overfunded, whilst many other policy areas – such as regional policy, research policy and energy policy – appear to be underfunded. Certainly the considerable sum assigned to the CAP means that the EU's financial ability to tackle such pressing problems as research under-investment, technological change, and unemployment is limited. However, budgetary expenditure, like budgetary income, is not determined by 'objective' criteria but by political interplay. And, as was shown in Chapter 20, in that interplay there are many powerful forces that wish to maintain high levels of spending on agriculture: governments anxious to receive farmers' votes do not normally wish to upset this often volatile section of the electorate; net beneficiaries of the CAP (both states and sectional interests) are not inclined voluntarily to surrender their gains; and agriculture is regarded by many decision-makers as 'special'.

However, notwithstanding these obstacles to reform, pressures to 're-balance' budgetary expenditure have been considerable since the mid-to-late 1980s. Attention has focused primarily on the imbalance between CAP and non-CAP spending, on the levels and types of assistance that should be assigned to assisting less prosperous states and regions, and on the financial support to be given to new policy needs and initiatives. Reflecting the outcomes of deliberations and negotiations on these questions, measures

designed to bring about a partial shift in the EU's pattern of expenditure have been important features of financial perspectives. The most important outcome of the measures has been the above-noted proportionate reduction in expenditure on the CAP: from the 70 per cent plus of the 1980s to a projected 33 per cent by the end of the 2007–13 financial perspective.

As for current volumes and proportionate amounts of expenditure, Table 22.1 and Figure 22.1 set out the expenditure figures, in actual and proportionate terms, for the 2000–13 financial framework. It will be noted that although the figures in Table 22.1 are presented in terms of appropriations for commitments, overall figures for payments are also given. Payment appropriations cover actual expenditure during the financial year whilst commitment, or engagement, appropriations cover expenditure during the financial year plus liabilities extending beyond the year. Commitment appropriations are naturally higher than payment appropriations.

Table 22.2 sets out the figures for the 2010 budget, which totalled €141.5 in commitment appropriations. Some brief comments on the budget headings will now be made.

- *Sustainable growth,* accounts for 45 per cent of the budget. Most of this is directed to cohesion via the European Regional Development Fund (ERDF) and the European Social Fund (ESF) (see Chapter 19). The less prosperous member states are the main beneficiaries of the EU's cohesion policies and in 2010, for the first time, the twelve states that joined the EU in 2004/07 received a majority (52 per cent) of this spending.
- *Natural resources* account for 42 per cent of the budget. Nearly three quarters of this 42 per cent is for CAP support, whilst one quarter is for rural development, fisheries and the environment account. Most CAP funding was formerly used for price guarantee purposes but following reforms to the CAP since the early 1990s it is now used mainly for direct income support to farmers (see Chapter 20). Because CAP expenditure in 2004/07 member states is being phased-in, they received only 20 per cent of this spending in 2010.
- *The EU as a global partner.* Accounting for just less than 6 per cent of the EU's budget, this funding allocation is used to support a wide range of external

Table 22.2 2010 EU budget

Commitment Appropriations	billion €	% of total budget	% change from 2009
1 Sustainable growth:	64.0	45.0	+3.0
Competitiveness	*14.7*	*10.4*	*+6.4*
Cohesion	*49.4*	*35.0*	*+2.0*
2 Preservation and management of natural resources:	59.6	42.36	+5.5
Direct payments and market related expenditure	*43.5*	*30.8*	*+16.2*
Rural development, environment, fisheries	*14.8*	*10.5*	*+5.6*
3 Citizenship, freedom, security and justice:	1.7	1.2	+10.4
Freedom, security and justice	*1.0*	*0.7*	*+16.2*
Citizenship	*0.7*	*0.5*	*−2.6*
4 The EU as a global player	8.1	5.7	+0.1
5 Administrative expenditure (for all EU institutions):	7.9	5.6	+2.9
of which Commission	*3.6*	*2.6*	*+2.50*
Total commitments	€141.3	100.0	+3.5
In % of EU-27 GNI	1.18		

activities, from peacekeeping operations to humanitarian aid. Geographically, it is particularly concentrated on the Balkans, the Mediterranean area, and former Soviet states.

- *Citizenship, freedom, security and justice.* Making up just one per cent of the budget, funding under this heading mainly covers matters relating to the protection of external borders and the upholding of law within the borders.
- *Administrative expenditure.* This account for 5 per cent of the budget.

The making of the annual budget

Until the entry into force of the Lisbon Treaty, the procedure for making the EU's annual budget was protracted and rather complicated. Its main features were:

- The Commission issued a Preliminary Draft Budget (PDB) in the spring of the year before the budget was due to come into effect (the EU's financial year runs from 1 January to 31 December).
- The PDB, provided the basis for deliberations in the Council and the EP on the budget. These deliberations involved two readings in both institutions, with

the Council first reading usually being in July, the EP first reading being in October, the Council second reading being in November, and the EP second reading being in December. At each of these readings the Council and the EP would amend the draft budget – with the Council's amendments usually involving net decreases to the overall size of the budget and the EP's amendments involving net increases. Throughout the procedure, there were numerous formal and informal meeting between representatives of the Commission, Council and EP. The final stage of the procedure was, assuming Council–EP agreement on the contents of the budget, a formal vote of approval by the Parliament at its December plenary followed by the EP President formally signing the budget and declaring it to be adopted.

- Although the Council and the EP were co-decision makers in the sense that they both had to give their approval for the budget to be approved, the powers of the two institutions were not quite the same. This was because of a distinction in the budget between compulsory (or obligatory) expenditure, which was expenditure that was a direct result of treaty requirements and which was dominated by CAP spending, and non-compulsory (or non-obligatory), which was spending on everything else. The Council had

The purposes of Lisbon Treaty changes to the annual budgetary procedure

- *To make the procedure simpler*, by changing it from a two-reading procedure to a one-reading procedure with conciliation.
- *To make the procedure shorter*, which the simplification of the procedure facilitates.
- *To give the Council and EP equal powers*, by abolishing the distinction between compulsory and non-compulsory expenditure.

more power than the EP over compulsory expenditure whilst with non-compulsory expenditure the positions were reversed.

A full account of how this procedure, which was given its last 'outing' for the making of the 2010 budget, operated in practice is given in the sixth edition of this book. It will not be repeated here, though it is worth making the general point that, as with all EU decision-making procedures, the formal rules – concerning, for example, the presentation of the PDP and the readings in the Council and the EP – provided but a framework that in practice was fleshed-out and adapted by the budgetary actors in response to pressures, necessities, and convenience.

The Lisbon Treaty made important changes to the budgetary procedure. The changes had the three purposes that are set out in Box 22.1.

Quite how the post-Lisbon Treaty procedure will operate in practice remains to be seen, but its formal features are set out in Figure 22.3 and are now further sketched out.

Preparation of the Draft Budget

As part of its provisions for simplifying and speeding-up the annual budgetary decision-making process, the Lisbon Treaty 'pushed-back' the start of formal proceedings. The Commission does not now have to issue a PDB in the spring but issues a draft budget much later in the year – with 1 September being the last possible date.

The drawing-up of the draft budget by the Commission – which is the most important part of the budget-making process since the budget that is finally adopted does not depart too much from the Commission's initial proposals – will be undertaken post-the Lisbon Treaty much as before, apart from the deadline for the formal presentation of the draft to the EP and the Council being three or so months later.

The prime responsibility within the Commission for drawing up the draft budget falls to the Budget Commissioner and the Budget DG. Inevitably they are subject to pressures from many sides: from other parts of the Commission, which forward their own estimates and bids; from national representatives, both through the Council and on a direct lobbying basis; from the EP, especially leading figures on its Committee on Budgets; and from sectional interests. The Budget Commissioner and officials from the Budget DG hold numerous meetings, both formal and informal, to enable many of these interested parties to have their say. One of these meetings is a formal trialogue meeting, at which delegations from the EP and the Council meet with the Commission to discuss the possible priorities for the budget. Naturally, in these meetings those with the best chance of achieving some satisfaction and influencing the Commission are those that carry political weight and/or are already in tune with the Commission's thinking.

In preparing the draft budget the Budget Commissioner and Budget DG have had to make significant adjustments to traditional ways of working as a result of developments in recent years aimed at improving strategic planning and programming and matching budgetary expenditure more closely with political priorities. The first development involves the College of Commissioners, the Ecofin Council, and the EP each setting out their political priorities for the budget before the draft is finalised. Those responsible in the Commission for preparing the draft are expected to take note of the priorities of the three institutions. The second development, which was first used in 2001 for the 2002 budget and which is framed within the broader development of the use by the Commission of activity-based management for planning, budgeting, managing, and reporting on results, involves the use of activity-based budgeting (ABB). In essence this involves structuring costs and expenditure around policy areas and activities so that a clear

Figure 22.3 The annual budgetary procedure*

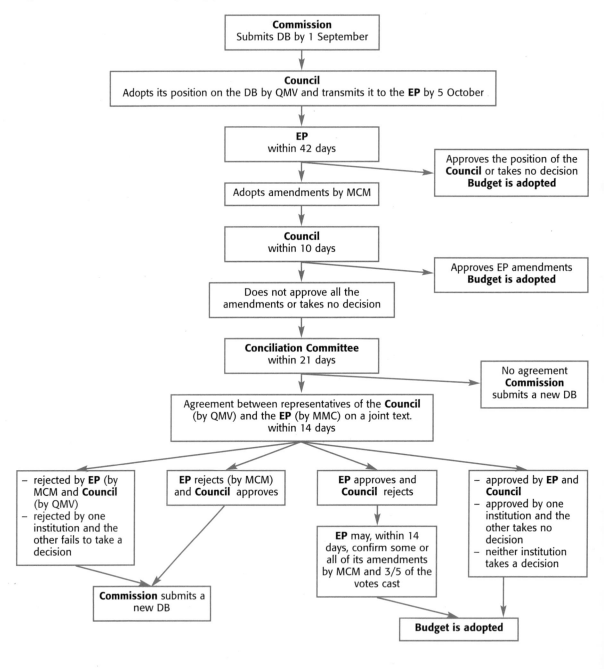

Key: MCM: majority of its component members .
      MMC: majority of its members on the Committee
      DB: draft budget
      QMV: qualified majority vote

* This procedure replaces the pre-Lisbon Treaty procedure. The new procedure was used for the first time in 2010, for the 2011 budget.

comparison can be made between the results achieved for a policy with the resources used for that policy.

Once the Budget DG has its proposals ready, they are presented by the Commissioner to the other Commissioners and all must agree on the package. When they do, the proposals officially become the draft budget.

Since annual budgets must be set within the MFF applying, the ability of the Commission to use them as a vehicle for changing EU priorities is naturally limited. The constraints are not, however, total and the Commission does have some manoeuvrability below expenditure ceilings and it does have options within expenditure headings. Indeed, in recent years the Commission theoretically has had considerable potential manoeuvrability, for budgets have been well below MFF ceilings. But, this potential has not been greatly utilised, and it certainly would have been opposed by the Council had it been so.

The Commission presents the budget in both payment appropriations and commitment appropriations (see above). The spending plans of the budget are grouped under broad headings. Until the 2005 budget these headings were agriculture, structural operations, internal policies, external policies, administration, reserves, and pre-accession aid. As, however, was explained earlier in the chapter, these headings have now been changed and, as Table 22.2 shows, for the 2010 budget the following headings were used: sustainable growth, (sub-divided into competitiveness and cohesion), natural resources (sub-divided into CAP support measures and rural development, environment and fisheries); the EU as a global player; citizenship, freedom, security and justice; and administration. Within each heading, hundreds of budget lines identify the funding proposed for specific policies, programmes and projects.

Council and EP readings

The post-Lisbon Treaty arrangements for the EP and the Council to consider, and ultimately reach agreement on, in making the annual budget are set out in Article 314 TFEU. The key provisions are as follows:

- The Council shall adopt its position on the draft budget by 1 October.
- If within forty-two days of receiving the Council's position the EP either approves the position or has

not taken a decision the budget shall be deemed to have been adopted. (Neither of these eventualities is likely.)
- If within forty-two days the EP adopts amendments by a majority of its component members (the likely eventuality) a Conciliation Committee, composed of an equal number of members of the Council and the EP shall be convened.
- If, within ten days of receiving the EP's amendments the Council approves all of them, the Conciliation Committee will not meet. (This is most unlikely.)
- The Conciliation Committee shall have the task, within twenty-one days of being convened, of reaching an agreement on the budget by a qualified majority of the Council representatives and a majority of the EP representatives. If no agreement is reached within the twenty-one days, the Commission shall submit a revised draft budget.
- The joint text that is agreed in the Conciliation Committee is referred to the EP and Council for their agreement within fourteen days. If one of the institutions rejects the joint text, the Commission must submit a revised draft budget (though in the case of EP approval and Council rejection, EP amendments can be retained only by a vote of the majority of component members and three-fifths of the votes cast.)

Although this procedure marks a very significant departure from the pre-Lisbon Treaty budgetary decision-making arrangements, key pre-Lisbon features will certainly endure. These features are set in Box 22.2.

Non-approval of the budget

If a budget is not agreed between the EP and the Council by December it naturally cannot come into effect at the beginning of the financial year on 1 January. In five of the first nine years after the introduction of direct elections in 1979, this is precisely what happened with the budgets of 1980 and 1984–8.

In such circumstances a fall-back position applies that allows for funding to continue, but only on the basis of what are known as 'provisional twelfths', which means that spending is limited to the monthly average expenditure of the previous year. Therefore policies do

---

Box 22.2

Key features of the making of the annual budget

- MFFs mean the Commission works within quite tight constraints when preparing the draft budget.
- MFFs also mean there are only limited opportunities for increasing or decreasing the draft budget and for cutting or expanding EU policies during the budgetary procedure. In consequence, there is not a huge gap between the positions of the Council and EP. Usually, the Council proposes a budget that is €2–3 billion smaller than the draft budget whilst the EP proposes a budget that is €3–4 billion higher.
- The Commission is actively involved in all decision-making settings on both the Council and EP sides. However, after the presentation of the draft budget it is cast in an essentially servicing capacity: responding to what happens in the Council and the EP and doing what it can to bring the two sides together.
- On the Council side, the detailed work of examining the budget is undertaken by the Budget Committee – a working group of national officials – which reports to COREPER, which in turn reports to the Ecofin Council. Where there is rigidity in the negotiating positions of member states, much of the responsibility for finding a solution falls to the Council Presidency, aided by the Commission.
- On the EP side, the Committee on Budgets is the lead committee. Its work includes bringing coherence to the hundreds of amendments to the draft budget that are customarily put forward from various parts of the EP. Much rests on the liaising, organising, and leadership skills of the chair of the Committee on Budgets and the appointed *rapporteur*.
- There is extensive liaison between the Commission, Council and EP throughout the budget-making process, including the convening of trialogue meetings.
- The annual budgetary procedure is unusual in the EU decision-making context in that it operates according to a stipulated timetable. The existence and exigencies of the timetable introduce an urgency into budgetary decision-making that is not always found in other spheres of EU decision making.

---

not collapse, but some payments have to be suspended, and programmes, especially new ones, may have to be delayed. A speedy agreement on the budget of what by this stage is the current financial year is thus desirable.

There is no formal procedure or set pattern of action in the event of non-adoption. The expectation and assumption is that the process will be resumed at the point at which it broke down. However, the adoption of financial frameworks and inter-institutional agreements have removed, or at least blunted the sharpness of, many of the problems that occasioned the non-adoption of budgets in the 1980s. In particular, MFFs impose limitations on the room available for changing spending amounts, agricultural expenditure has been made subject to stronger budgetary discipline, the relative proportion of the budget assigned to non-agricultural expenditure has been increased, mechanisms have been established to improve the match between income and expenditure, and increases in inter-institutional contacts during budgetary

processes have made the processes less confrontational. All in all, budgetary decision-making just is much less confrontational and dramatic than it used to be, with the consequence that budgets are highly likely to be adopted 'in time'. As Shackleton (2002: 108) has put it, the procedure is now 'more an exercise in joint management than in providing direction for the Union'.

Implementation of the budget

The implementation of, and the monitoring of the implementation of, the budget may also be considered as part of the budgetary process. Only a couple of general points will be made here about these activities, however, since both receive attention elsewhere in the book, notably in Chapters 8, 13 (in the section on the Court of Auditors), and 17.

The first point is that, as with other aspects of EU policy implementation, much of the 'front-line' budgetary implementation is undertaken by national agencies in the member states. The Commission makes transfer payments to the agencies – which are mainly, although by no means exclusively, national and regional governmental bodies – and they manage them on the Commission's behalf. This delegation to agencies does not, however, absolve the Commission from overall responsibility for the execution of the budget, and for this purpose it has a battery of administrative structures and arrangements to deal with such matters as the drawing up of tenders, the issuing of contracts, and the handling – either directly or indirectly – of payments.

An indication of the scale of the activities involved is provided by the fact that the Commission is responsible for some 400,000 or so financial transactions a year, including approaching 300,000 payment orders. These range from large CAP and Structural Fund transfer payments to employees' travel expenses.

The second point is that the implementation of the budget has attracted considerable attention in recent years, not least from the media and the EP. This is partly, perhaps, because attention has been less focused on budgetary decision-making as that process has become much less fraught. It is mainly, however, because the Court of Auditors in a series of reports has exposed mismanagement and fraud in the implementation of EU policies. The Commission is not slow to point out that many of the problems identified by the Court must be laid at the doors of the national agencies that are responsible for around 80 per cent of direct payments, but the fact is that the Court has also exposed inadequacies in the Commission's financial control systems. As was shown in Chapters 11 and 13, it was the exposure of such inadequacies that initiated the events that led to the resignation of the College of Commissioners in March 1999. As was shown in Chapter 8, this resignation and the events leading up to it have resulted in major changes in EU financial management and implementation practices.

Concluding Remarks

The EU budget is necessary for the financing of many EU activities and operations. But it is relatively small in size, and therefore its policy impact is limited. This is no more clearly demonstrated than in the fact that whereas public expenditure by the member states accounts for about 45 per cent of EU GNI, EU expenditure accounts for less than three per cent. Because of the desire of member states, especially net budgetary contributor states, to ensure that EU income and expenditure remain relatively small, budgetary processes have provided only very limited opportunities to forge and drive policy change Financial frameworks have allowed for some use of the budget to guide incremental policy development and have enabled the budget to become the instrument for modest policy reform, but they can hardly be said to have been mechanisms for effecting radical policy shifts.

But notwithstanding its relatively smallness, the EU's budget has been the focus of very considerable political attention and controversy. Since the late 1980s, the multiannual financial frameworks within which the annual budgets are framed have been the main subject of this focus. They have been so because of a mixture of a number of factors, not least the very high political profile that has been given to them. The financial frameworks are essentially the outcome of exhaustive intergovernmental negotiations that culminate in European Council decisions. The Commission does, of course, structure these negotiations with its initial proposals and then helps to facilitate them in association with Council Presidencies. The EP has a role to play too, not least since financial frameworks require its approval. But the national governments are the key decision-makers.

The annual budgets, by contrast, have been negotiated in atmospheres of relative peace. They used to be to be strongly contested, but MFFs and multiannual programming have imposed tight constraints and an ordered framework on what now can and cannot be done within the annual budgetary cycle.

Part V
Stepping Back and Looking Forward

Part V steps back from the detailed study of European integration and the European Union to take an overview of general issues and matters. It also looks forward to how the integration process and the EU might develop.

Chapter 23 is quite different in character from the previous chapters of the book. It examines conceptual and theoretical tools that have been used to capture and analyse the key features of the integration process, the main organisational characteristics of the EU, and particular aspects of the functioning of the EU.

Chapter 24 provides a conclusion for the book. It does so by placing the EU in its global context, by looking at factors that are likely to affect the EU's future development, and by examining the main challenges facing the EU.

Chapter 23

Conceptualising and Theorising

The previous chapters of this book have been concerned with identifying and analysing the principal features of the evolution and nature of European integration and the European Union. This chapter has much the same focus, but takes a different approach. It does so by moving away from logging and analysing 'the facts' to examining the insights that are provided by conceptual and theoretical perspectives.

Conceptualising, which essentially means thinking about phenomena in abstract terms, and theorising, which means positing general explanations of phenomena, have constituted the base of much academic writing on European integration. There are, it should be said, some who question the value of much of this conceptualising and theorising, with doubts and reservations usually focusing on what are seen to be poor, and potentially misleading, 'matches' between over-simplistic models on the one hand and complex realities on the other. This is, however, a minority view and most EU academic commentators take the general social science position that the development and use of concepts and theories enhances the understanding of political, economic, and social phenomena by structuring and directing observation and interpretation. (Fuller arguments for the usefulness – indeed indispensability – of theory in European integration studies can be found in Chryssochoou, 2009: Chapter 1; Rosamond, 2000: Chapter 1; Wiener and Diez, 2009: Chapter 1).

There are three broad types of conceptual and theoretical work on European integration and the EU.

- There are attempts to conceptualise the organisational nature of the EU. Such conceptualisations, which can be thought of as attempts to capture 'the nature of the beast', are explored in the first two sections of this chapter. The first of these sections examines conceptualisations of the EU as a political system and the second examines three key concepts that are habitually employed when assessing the political character of the EU.
- There are attempts to theorise the general nature of the integration process. Such theorising is not as fashionable today as it once was, but it is still seen by many scholars as worthwhile, and it certainly marks the point of departure for a great deal of other conceptual and theoretical work. Grand theory, as general integration theory is commonly known, is studied in the third section of the chapter.
- There are attempts to develop conceptual and theoretical approaches to particular aspects of the functioning of the EU, especially policy and decision-making. Operating at the middle range level, or as it is sometimes called the meso level, rather than at the general level, this has been a major growth area in scholarly work on the EU in recent years. It is the subject of the fourth section of the chapter.

As will be shown, within each of these three broad types of conceptual and theoretical work there is a wide range of different approaches. An underlying theme of the chapter is that the existence of many approaches is inevitable given the multi-dimensional nature of European integration as a process and the EU as an organisation. No single theory is capable of explaining everything. The complexities of the process and the organisation are such that different sets of conceptual and theoretical tools are necessary to examine and interpret them.

Before proceeding, three cautionary notes must be issued. First, there is considerable overlap and intertwining between the many different dimensions of the conceptual and theoretical ideas that are described and analysed in the chapter. Although, for ease of presentation, the dimensions are sectionalised in the account that follows, it should be recognised that in practice there is considerable overlap between the sections. So, for example, most broad theoretical work draws heavily on a wide range of more narrowly focused conceptual work. Second, the range of conceptual and theoretical approaches to the study of European integration and the EU is so great that only some of them can be considered here. Attention is necessarily restricted to examining some of the more important approaches and giving a flavour of their varying characters. Third, the focus here is largely restricted to political science approaches to theorising and conceptualising. Other disciplines do, of course, have their own approaches.

Conceptualising the European Union

What type of political organisation/system is the EU? This is a difficult question to answer. It is so for at least four reasons.

First, the EU itself has never sought to describe or define its political character in any clear manner. The closest it has come to doing so is in the Common Provisions of the TEU, which do say something about the general nature of the EU, but only in rather vague and 'feel good' terms. Since the Amsterdam Treaty, and unchanged by the Nice and Lisbon Treaties, Article 1 TEU states that:

This Treaty marks a new stage in the process of creating an ever closer union among the peoples of Europe, in which decisions are taken as openly as possible and as closely as possible to the citizen.

Article 2 TEU, in its post-Lisbon Treaty form, states:

The Union is founded on the values of respect for human dignity, freedom, democracy, equality, the rule of law and respect for human rights, including the rights of persons belonging to minorities.

Second, as the above extract from Article 1 TEU suggests, the EU is, and always has been, in constant transition. Its character has changed considerably over the years as the integration process has deepened and widened. Its nature has never been settled. For example, its legislative processes have become progressively more supranational since the mid-1980s, as evidenced by the much greater use of QMV in the Council of Ministers and the growing power of the EP.

Third, the EU is a highly complex and multi-faceted system. This means that there are abundant opportunities for different characteristics of the system to be generated by different focuses of analysis. Is, for example, the focus to be on the EU as an actor or as an arena? If the latter, is the focus to be on its territorial or its sectoral character?

Fourth, in important respects the EU is unique. It is so, for example, in the way it embodies both supranational and intergovernmental features in its system of governance, and in the extent to which it embodies shared policy responsibilities between different levels of government and different nation states. A perfectly reasonable answer to the question 'What type of political organisation/system is the EU?' is thus that it is not of any type – or, at least, not of any established type – at all. Rather it is *sui generis* – the only one of its kind.

But recognition of the fact that the EU is in important respects unique, does not mean that attempts should not be made to conceptualise it. The reason for this is that conceptualisation can help to highlight the EU's essential features, and in so doing can draw attention to those features that are distinctive and those that are found elsewhere.

Not all of the conceptualisations that have been offered and developed in the literature can be explored here. Attention is necessarily restricted to some of the more commonly used conceptualisations.

States and intergovernmental organisations

A useful starting point in attempting to conceptualise the EU is to compare it with the most important political unit of the international system, the state, and with the customary way in which states interrelate with one another on a structured basis, the intergovernmental organisation (IGO).

Definitions of the state are many and various. Generally speaking, however, the key characteristics of the state are seen as being those set out in Box 23.1.

The four features of the state set out in Box 23.1 do not all need to be present in a pure, undiluted and uncontested form for a state to exist. They do, however, need to feature prominently and to constitute the essential bedrock of the system. With the EU there is no doubt that all four features are present, but they are so only in partial ways. So, *territoriality* is present in the sense that the EU's territory is the sum total of the member states' territory. But, enlargements mean it is an almost constantly shifting territory. Furthermore, the EU can hardly be said to 'own' the territory in the sense that member states can be said to own their territory. In part to add credence to this territorial dimension of its existence, the EU has created some of the symbols of statehood with a flag,

---

> ## Box 23.1
>
> ## Key characteristics of 'the state'
>
> - *Territoriality* – the state is geographically based and bound.
> - *Sovereignty* – the state stands above all other associations and groups within its geographical area and its jurisdiction extends to the whole population of the area.
> - *Legitimacy* – the authority of the state is widely recognised, both internally and externally.
> - *Monopoly of governance* – the institutions of the state monopolise public decision-making and enforcement.

---

an anthem, and an (almost) common passport. But, the upgrading of the first two of these symbols by giving them official recognition in the Constitutional Treaty was widely seen as being a contributory reason for the difficulties in getting the Treaty ratified, so the Lisbon Treaty removed the references to them – with the consequence that they still have only unofficial status. The EU enjoys some *sovereignty* – as witnessed by the primacy of EU law and the fact that EU jurisdiction applies to the whole EU population – but the reach of that sovereignty is confined to the policy areas where the EU's remit is established. Likewise the EU does command some *legitimacy*, but it is generally weak. Regarding internal legitimacy, there is general agreement amongst observers that there is no EU demos – a shared sense of common identity amongst citizens – whilst opinion surveys show that the internal authority of the EU system is somewhat thinly based. Regarding external legitimacy, this is firmly established and (generally) uncontested only in respect of the Common Commercial Policy. And as for *monopoly of governance*, far from being in a position of dominance the EU monopolises governance in only a very few policy areas, and even then it is highly dependent on the member states for policy enforcement. To these 'weaknesses' might be added the very limited development of EU citizenship, the EU's comparatively limited financial resources, and arguably too its increasingly differentiated character in such core policy areas as monetary and defence policy.

The EU thus falls a long way short of being a state, as statehood is traditionally understood. However, the concept of the state is still of some use in helping to promote an understanding of the nature of the EU. It is so for two reasons. First, as has just been shown, the EU does display some of the traditional characteristics of a state, and the continuing development of the integration process means that some of these characteristics are likely to strengthen. It is, for example, the case that Jacques Delors was not so far off the mark when he predicted in 1988 – to the accompaniment of much scoffing – that by the end of the 1990s 80 per cent of socio-economic legislation applying in the member states would be made at EU level. Second, the realities of traditional statehood are breaking down in the modern world, most particularly under the pressures of international interdependence. So, for example, no modern state can now be regarded as being fully sovereign in a *de facto* sense, and the EU member states cannot even claim that they are fully sovereign in a *de jure* sense. These changes in the realities of statehood mean there must also be changes in how the state is conceptualised. And in such new conceptualisations – involving, for instance, notions of the regulatory state and the postmodern state – the EU displays, as James Caporaso (1996) has argued, many state-like features.

The notion of the EU as a regulatory state is a conceptualisation that has attracted much attention, due in large part to the extensive work of Giandomenico Majone (1992, 1994, 1996) on the subject. The regulatory state model conceptualises the EU in terms both of its functions and its institutional structure. Regarding its functions, the EU is seen as not being greatly involved in distributive or redistributive policies but as being extensively involved in regulating such policy areas as competition, environment, product quality, and health and safety at work. A number of factors are identified by Majone as explaining this regulatory focus, including pressure from business firms for there to be a fully integrated internal market and a reluctance on the part of member state governments to permit the large budget that redistributive policies require. Regarding the EU's institutional structure, Majone argues that a range of regulatory and non-majoritarian institutions exist – most notably in the form of the Commission, the Court of Justice, and regulatory agencies – that collec-

tively constitute virtually an independent fourth branch of government.

Another particular conceptualisation of the state that is helpful is Vivien Schmidt's notion of the EU as a regional state (Schmidt, 2004, 2006, 2009). This conceptualisation, Schmidt readily acknowledges, may be objected to on the grounds that the EU is clearly not a fully developed state, and indeed that 'conventional' states are its component members. But, the combining of the two words 'regional' and 'state' does draw our attention to core EU features. So, 'regional' implies some of the differences between the EU and nation states, such as the shifting nature of the geographical boundaries, the shared powers and sovereignty, the fragmented democracy, and the differentiated participation in some policy areas. 'State' highlights the fact that the EU does have state-like features, including strong central powers in an increasing number of policy areas, a highly developed system of governance, and a legal system in which EU law takes primacy.

* * *

Turning to IGOs, their key characteristics are as set out in Box 23.2.

Paul Magnette (2005) argues for the usefulness of the IGO conceptualisation when trying to understand the nature of the EU. The EU is, he acknowledges, more sophisticated and developed than the likes of

---

Box 23.2

Key characteristics of intergovernmental organisations

- IGOs are based on treaties between states in which representatives of national governments come together to cooperate on a voluntary basis for reasons of mutual benefit. They offer a way for states to work together without formally conceding national sovereignty.
- IGOs usually have very little, if any, organisational autonomy, with decisions customarily made by a consensus between member states. They normally have a permanent secretariat, but it has few independent powers.
- IGOs normally have few instruments to enforce their will on reluctant member states. But, since non-compliance is likely to bring a state's membership into question, there are strong pressures for states to comply. A few IGOs – most notably the World Trade Organisation – adopt a quasi-judicial approach to decision implementation.
- IGOs vary greatly in their focus, purpose, and geographical reach.

There are about 250 IGOs in existence. Amongst the best known are the United Nations, the Organisation for Economic Co-operation and Development, the North Atlantic Treaty Organisation, the International Monetary Fund, and the Council of Europe.

NATO and the Council of Europe but nonetheless 'the best way to understand the EU's structure and functioning is to see it primarily as an intergovernmental organization' (*ibid.*: 3). Central to Magnette's position is that the most useful way of viewing EU institutions is not as external agencies imposing their views on unwilling national authorities but rather as frameworks or networks in which national actors attempt to coordinate their interests and policy preferences. The EU 'is a set of institutions and rules designed to strengthen the European states by encouraging them to cooperate ... The EU is not about depriving the states of their sovereignty. Rather it is about encouraging them to exercise their prerogatives in new and more cooperative ways' (*ibid.*: 3).

Magnette's view, whilst thought-provoking and interesting, is not, it has to be said, widely shared. Most observers see striking differences between the EU and IGOs:

- The EU has a much more developed and complex institutional structure than is found in IGOs. The standard pattern of advanced IGOs – permanent secretariats and attached delegations – is perhaps, in a much grander and more elaborated form, replicated in the EU with the Commission and the Permanent Representations, but to these are added many other features. Among the more obvious of such features are the regular and frequent meetings at the very highest political levels between representatives of the governments of the member states; the constant and many varied forms of contact between national officials; the Court of Justice of the European Union; and the EP – the only directly elected multi-state assembly in the world.
- No IGO has anything like the policy responsibilities of the EU. In terms of breadth, few significant policy areas have completely escaped the EU's attention. In terms of depth, the pattern varies, but in many important areas, including external trade, agriculture, and competition policy, key initiating and decision-making powers have been transferred from the member states to the EU authorities.
- The EU has progressed far beyond the intergovernmental nature of IGOs to incorporate many supranational characteristics into its structure and operation. The nature of the balance within the EU between intergovernmentalism and supranationalism will be examined later in the chapter.

In terms of state and IGO conceptualisation, the EU is thus perhaps best thought of as being less than the former but more than the latter.

Federalism

Interpretations of the nature of federalism vary. This is not surprising when systems as diverse as Germany, India, Switzerland and the United States all describe themselves as federal.

Different interpretations within the EU of the nature of federalism were no more clearly demonstrated than in the run-up to the 1991 Maastricht summit, when the UK government became embroiled in a sharp clash with the governments of the other member states over whether there should be a reference in the TEU to the EU 'evolving in a federal direction'. The clash centred in large part on different understandings of what 'federal' entails and implies, with the UK government giving the word a much more centralist spin than other governments. Indeed, the solution that was eventually agreed upon – to remove the offending phrase and replace it with a statement that the Treaty 'marks a new stage in the process of creating an ever closer union among the peoples of Europe' – seemed to many EU governments far more centralist in tone than did the original formulation.

Academic commentators too have not been in complete accord on the precise nature of federal systems. In broad terms, however, most would regard the key characteristics of such systems as being as set out in Box 23.3

In applying the federal model to the EU it is readily apparent that the EU does display some federal traits:

- Power *is* divided between central decision-making institutions (the Commission, the Council, the EP and so on), and regional decision-making institutions (the governing authorities in the member states).
- The nature of the division *is* specified in constitutional-like documents (the treaties) and there *is* a supreme judicial authority (the EU's Courts) with the authority to adjudicate in the event of disputes over the division.
- Both levels *do* have important powers and responsibilities for public policy – with those of the

Box 23.3

Key characteristics of federal political systems

- Power is divided between central decision-making institutions on the one hand and regional decision-making institutions on the other.
- The nature of this division of power is specified in and is protected by constitutional documents. Disputes over the division are settled by a supreme judicial authority.
- The division of power between the central and regional levels is balanced in the sense that both have responsibilities – although not necessarily wholly exclusive responsibilities – for important spheres of public policy.
- Modern realities dictate that in practice the division of power cannot be over-rigid. Rather, some policy responsibilities inevitably overlap and intertwine. In short, the only viable form of federalism in the modern world is cooperative federalism.
- Whilst the policy content of the division of power can vary, some policy areas are primarily the responsibility of the central level because they are concerned with the identity, coherence, and protection of the system as a whole. Such policy areas normally include foreign affairs, security and defence, management of the (single) currency, and specification and protection of citizens' rights – or at least the more important of these rights.

central level appertaining particularly, but by no means exclusively, to the economic sphere.

At the same time, however, it is also clear that in some respects the EU falls short of the federal model:

- Although power is divided between the central and regional levels, some of the responsibilities that lie at the centre are heavily dependent on the acquiescence of the regional units (the member states) if they are to be exercised. This is most obviously the case where the unanimity rule applies in the Council, as for example, in respect of decisions on

enlargement, foreign and defence policy, and fiscal measures.
- The policy balance is still tilted towards the member states. The degree of tilt is much less than it was before the 're-launch' of the Community in the mid-1980s, but apart from market-related policies the member states are still mostly in control of public decision-making. This is reflected in the fact that policy areas that involve heavy public expenditure – such as education, health, social welfare, and defence – are still essentially national policies. As part of this policy balance, the control of taxation and financial resources is still overwhelmingly with the member states.
- Those policy spheres which in 'conventional' federal systems are normally thought of as being the responsibility of the central authorities, in the EU are primarily national responsibilities. Foreign affairs, security and defence, and citizenship rights are being developed at the EU level, but so far only to a limited degree and on a largely intergovernmental basis. Currency control is the most obvious exception to this, but not all member states are members of the single currency system.
- The central authorities are not able to use 'legitimate violence' in 'EU territory'.

This balance of characteristics combines to suggest a system that does not fully embrace all the traits of the classical federal system, but is not as far removed from the federal model as is usually supposed (for supporting argument along these lines see: Sbragia, 1992; Keleman and Nicolaidis, 2006; Burgess, 2009). At a minimum, the EU may be said to embody the federal principle of combining in a territorial and contractual sharing of power a degree of unity on the one hand with a respect for the interests and partial autonomy of regional units on the other. Moreover, it is clear that over the years the movement of the EU progressively has been in a federal direction. The Maastricht Treaty was, as Koslowski (1999) has observed, especially significant in this respect. It was so most obviously with its provisions for institutional deepening. But it was so also with its establishment of Union citizenship, albeit in a weak form, and its 'codification' of the principle of subsidiarity which may be seen as an embryo federal principle 'governing the scope of EU policy-making and thereby fram[ing] the political relationship between the EU and its member states in federal terms' (*ibid.*: 574).

So the EU may certainly be thought of as at least perhaps being a quasi-federal system. This might lead one to agree with Warleigh (1998, 2000), who suggests that the most appropriate way of labelling the EU at present is as a confederation. The distinction between federation and confederation is fuzzy, but in essence it rests on the amount of power exercised at the central and regional levels, with confederations being systems in which the balance is very much tilted to the regional level. Insofar as the EU is a union of previously sovereign states created by treaty in which supranational institutions exist but whose range of powers fall short of the powers exercised by their counterparts in federal systems, it may be thought of as displaying distinctive confederal traits.

State-centrism and consociationalism

State-centric models of the EU are advanced by those who take an intergovernmental view of the integration process. As such, they portray the EU as having the following features at its core:

- The system rests primarily on states that have come together to cooperate for certain specified purposes.
- The main channels of communication between EU member states are the national governments.
- The national governments control the overall direction and pace of EU decision-making.
- No governments, and therefore no states, are obliged to accept decisions on major issues to which they are opposed.
- Supranational actors such as the Commission and the EU's Courts do not have significant independent powers in their own right, but function essentially as agents and facilitators of the collective will of the national governments.

From this shared core, state-centric models branch out into a number directions, most of which involve some 'softening' of the core's hard edges. Variations occur in respect of such matters as the dynamics of inter-state relations, the nature of the policy role and impact of non-state actors, and the importance that is accorded to national domestic politics.

The last of these variations has produced a conceptualisation of EU policy dynamics as being conducted on the basis of a two-level game, in which state-centrism is combined with a domestic politics approach (see Bulmer, 1983, on this latter approach). In the two-level game conceptualisation, most famously advanced by Putnam (1988), the governments of member states are involved in EU policy-making at two levels: at the domestic level, where political actors seek to influence the positions adopted by governments, and at the intergovernmental level, where governments negotiate with one another in EU forums.

A much-employed variation of the core state-centric model is consociationalism. Originally developed – notably by Arend Lijphart (1969) – to throw light on how some democratic states that are sharply divided internally are able to function in a relatively smooth and stable manner, consociationalism has been championed as a model that can provide valuable insights into central features of the functioning of the EU. Consociational systems, of which the clearest example in Europe is Belgium, are normally portrayed as displaying the features that are set out in Box 23.4.

Just as there are variations of the core state-centric model, so have the main features of the consociational model been developed and directed by analysts in various ways. In the EU context, a leading such analyst is Paul Taylor (1991, 1996), who sees the model as extremely valuable in helping to explain the nature of the balance between fragmentation and cooperation/integration in the EU, the mutual dependence between the member states and the collectivity, and the ability – which does not imply inevitability – of the system as a whole both to advance and maintain stability.

At the heart of Taylor's analysis of the EU is the notion of there being a symbiosis – a mutual dependence – between the participating segments of the consociation (the member states) and the collectivity of the consociation (EU structures and frameworks). This symbiosis is seen as enabling many of the costs of fragmentation to be overcome, whilst at the same time preserving, and in some ways even strengthening, the power and authority of *both* the segments and the collectivity.

A particularly important aspect of this last point is the assertion that EU member states do not lose significant power or authority by virtue of their EU membership. Taylor is quite explicit about this:

> **Box 23.4**
>
> ## Key features of consociational political systems
>
> - There is societal segmentation (which may or may not be geographically demarcated) and there are several politically significant lines of division.
> - The various segments are represented in decision-making forums on a proportional basis, though with minorities often being over-represented.
> - Political elites of the segments dominate decision-making processes. Interactions between these elites are intense and almost constant.
> - Decisions are taken on the basis of compromise and consensus. The majoritarian principle, whereby a majority can proceed even if it is opposed by a minority, is not normally employed, especially when major or sensitive issues are involved. Decisional processes are characterised by bargaining and exchanges, whilst decisional outcomes are marked by compromise and are frequently little more than the lowest common denominator.
> - The interactions between the segments, and particularly between the elites of the segments, can be both positive and negative with regards to promoting solidarity: positive in that links are established and community-wide attitudes can be fostered between the segments; negative in that since the very rationale of consociationalism is the preservation of segmented autonomy within a cooperative system, segments may be tempted to over-emphasise their distinctiveness and moves towards over-centralisation may become occasions for resentment and unease within the segments.

the system works not on the basis of what functionalists, or federalists, would call the Community interest, but much more on the basis of the low level consensus among segmented elites identified within consociationalism. There is a strong sense that the Community exists to serve the member states ... there is no evidence to suggest that common arrangements could not be extended a very long way without necessarily posing any direct challenge to the sovereignty of states (Taylor, 1991: 24–5).

Dimitris Chryssochoou (1994, 1995, 1998, 2009) and Costa and Magnette (2003), who too are exponents of the consociational model, also emphasise this point about the resilience of states within the EU and their retention of fundamental sovereignty. For Chryssochoou (1994: 48), the EU is a confederal consociation in that it is a system in which there is 'the merging of distinct politically organised states in some form of union to further common ends without losing either national identity or resigning individual sovereignty'. The internal mechanisms of the EU – which are seen as being largely under the control of state executive elites – are constituted, Chryssochoou suggests, so as to ensure that vital national interests are

not 'mystically subsumed by the force of common interests in a neofunctionalist fashion' (*ibid.*: 55).

The view that EU membership does not of itself fundamentally undermine the sovereignty of member states is of course widely contested. Some of the contestants suggest that multi-level governance provides a more useful way of conceptualising and modelling the EU.

Multi-level governance

The conceptualisations considered so far are, broadly speaking, located within a comparative perspective. Their concern is whether and to what extent the EU 'matches' established models of governance. However, those who are firmly of the view that the EU is very much *sui generis* – or, as it is sometimes put, $n = 1$ – naturally wish to develop new conceptual ideas and models.

In this context, some EU scholars have drawn on the developing political science interest in what is commonly referred to as 'the new governance' and have given it a particular emphasis and spin. At the general political science level, viewpoints included in the new governance approach are that government now involves a wide variety of actors and processes beyond the state, the relationships between state and non-state actors have become less hierarchical and more interactive, and the essential 'business' of government has become the regulation of public activities rather than the redistribution of resources. As applied to the EU, the new governance perspective

> is that the EU is transforming politics and government at the European and national levels into a system of multi-level, non-hierarchical, deliberative and apolitical governance, via a complex web of public/ private networks and quasi-autonomous executive agencies, which is primarily concerned with the deregulation and reregulation of the market (Hix, 1998: 54).

Taking just one of these strands of the new governance, much has been heard since the early 1990s of the merits of conceptualising the EU as a system of multi-level governance. Advocates of this conceptualisation usually specifically set themselves against the state-centric model, suggesting that the latter is too simple in its emphasis on the pre-eminence of state executives as actors and decision-makers. The great importance of national governments is not denied, but the claim that they dominate and control decision-making processes most certainly is.

Following the scheme initially put forward by Marks, Hooghe and Black (1996) and subsequently developed and used by, amongst others, Bache and Flinders (2004), three main characteristics can be seen as lying at the heart of the multi-level governance model of the EU. These characteristics are set out in Box 23.5.

On the basis of the characteristics identified in Box 23.5, multi-level governance thus conceives of the EU as a polity, or at least as a polity in the making, in which power and influence are exercised at multiple levels of government. National state executives are seen as extremely important actors in the EU arena, but the almost semi-monopolistic position that is ascribed to them by many state-centrists is firmly rejected.

Critics of the multi-level governance conceptualisation naturally focus particularly on whether the supranational and subnational levels really do have the power and influence they are claimed to have.

Box 23.5

The multi-level governance model of the EU

- Decision-making competences lie with, and are exercised by, not only national governments but also institutions and actors at 'higher' and 'lower' levels. At the EU level, supranational actors – of which the most important are the Commission, the EP, and the EU Courts – exercise an *independent* influence on policy processes and policy outcomes. In many member states subnational levels exercise significant powers, with regional and local authorities able to engage in policy activities that are not (wholly) controllable by national governments.
- Collective decision-making by states at the EU level involves a significant loss of national sovereignty, and therefore a significant loss of control by national governments. The intergovernmental view that states retain the ultimate decision-making power is rejected, largely on the grounds that '(l)owest common denominator outcomes are available only on a subset of EU decisions, mainly those concerning the scope of integration' (Marks *et al.*, 1996: 346).
- Political arenas are interconnected rather than nested. So, rather than national political activity being confined to the national arena and national inputs into EU decision-making being channelled via state-level actors, a variety of channels and interconnections between different levels of government – supranational, national, and sub-national – exist and are important. 'The separation between domestic and international politics, which lies at the heart of the state-centric model, is rejected by the multi-level governance model. States are an integral and powerful part of the EU, but they no longer provide the sole interface between supranational and subnational arenas, and they share, rather than monopolize, control over many activities that take place in their respective territories' (*ibid.*: 347).

Supranational levels are seen by state-centric observers as being largely subject to state-level controls (mainly through the various organs of the Council), while subnational levels are considered to have little room or potential to make a significant impact on policy outcomes. Is it not the case, multi-level governance critics argue, that in some member states there is no robust subnational level of government, and is it not also the case that there is little evidence of subnational actors exercising much of a policy role beyond the sphere of cohesion policy from which the advocates of multi-level governance draw most of their empirical evidence?

Three Key Concepts: Sovereignty, Intergovernmentalism and Supranationalism

As indicated in earlier parts of this book and throughout this chapter, much of the debate amongst practitioners and observers about the nature of the EU has centred on the related concepts of sovereignty, intergovernmentalism and supranationalism. These concepts therefore merit special attention.

Defining the terms

Sovereignty is an emotive word, associated as it is with notions of power, authority, independence, and the exercise of will. Because of its emotiveness and its associations, it is a word to which several meanings are attached. The most common meaning, and the one which will be employed here, refers to the legal capacity of national decision-makers to take decisions without being subject to external restraints. This is usually called national, or sometimes state, sovereignty.

Intergovernmentalism refers to arrangements whereby nation states, in situations and conditions they can control, cooperate with one another on matters of common interest. The existence of control, which allows all participating states to decide the extent and nature of this cooperation, means that national sovereignty is not directly undermined.

Supranationalism involves states working with one another in a manner that does not allow them to retain complete control over developments. That is, states may be obliged to do things against their preferences and their will because they do not have the power to stop decisions. Supranationalism thus takes inter-state relations beyond cooperation into integration, and involves some loss of national sovereignty.

The intergovernmental/ supranational balance in the EU

In the 1960s the governments of five of the Community's then six member states were willing to permit, even to encourage, some movement towards supranationalism. President de Gaulle, however, who wished to preserve 'the indivisible sovereignty of the nation state', was not. In order to emphasise this point, and more particularly to prevent certain supranational developments that were due to be introduced, he withdrew France in 1965 from most of the Community's key decision-making forums. The outcome of the crisis that this occasioned was the 1966 Luxembourg Compromise which, though it had no legal force, had as its effect the general imposition of intergovernmentalism on Community decision-making processes: the powers of the Commission and the EP were contained, and decisions in the Council came customarily to be made – even where the treaties allowed for majority voting – by unanimous agreement.

The first enlargement of the Community in 1973 reinforced intergovernmentalism, bringing in as it did two countries – Denmark and the UK – where there was strong domestic opposition to membership and where supranationalism was viewed with suspicion. International economic uncertainties and recession in the 1970s also encouraged intergovernmentalism, since they forced states to look rather more critically at the distributive consequences of Community policies, produced a temptation to look for national solutions to pressing problems, and resulted in greater caution about the transfer of powers to Community institutions.

However, intergovernmental attachments and pressures were never able, and never have been able, completely to stop the development of supranationalism. The treaties, increasing interdependence, and the logic of the EU itself, have all ensured that national sovereignties have been progressively undermined. Indeed, not only has supranationalism become more embedded, but since the mid-1980s it has been given a considerable boost as the states have adopted a much more positive attitude towards its development. They have done so partly because the effects of the delays and the inaction that intergovernmentalism spawns have become more obvious and more damaging, and partly because it has been recognised that as the number of EU member states has grown, over-rigid intergovernmentalism is a greater recipe than ever for stagnation and sclerosis.

The EU thus displays both intergovernmental and supranational characteristics. The principal intergovernmental characteristics are as follows.

- In many of the major areas of public policy – including foreign affairs, defence, fiscal policy, social welfare, education, health, and criminal law – decisions are still mainly taken at the national level. Each state consults and coordinates with its EU partners on aspects of these policies, and is increasingly subject to constraints as a result of EU membership, but ultimately a state can usually decide for itself what is to be done.
- Virtually all major decisions on the general direction and policy priorities of the EU are taken in the European Council: that is, in the forum containing the most senior national representatives. Only rarely does the European Council take decisions by majority vote. As for EU legislation, all important decisions need the approval of ministers in the Council of Ministers, with some key Council decisions, including those of a constitutional or fiscal nature, requiring unanimous approval. Where qualified majority voting is permissible, attempts are always made to reach a consensus – especially if a state declares it has important national interests at stake.
- The Commission and the EP, the two most obvious 'supranational political rivals' to the European Council and the Council of Ministers in that their responsibility is to look to the EU as a whole rather than to specific national interests, are restricted in their decision-making powers and cannot impose policies that the representatives of the member states do not want.

Of the supranational characteristics of the EU, the following are particularly important.

- The Commission does much to frame the EU policy agenda. Moreover, though it may have to defer to the European Council and the Council of Ministers where major decisions are involved, it is an extremely important decision-maker in its own right when it comes to secondary and regulatory decision-making. Indeed, in quantitative terms most EU legislation is issued in the name of the Commission.
- In the Council of Ministers, qualified majority voting is now common. This is partly a result of changing norms and expectations, and partly a result of the treaty reforms that have brought about extensions of the policy spheres in which QMV is permissible.
- The influence of the EP on EU decision-making is considerable. This influence has been greatly enhanced over the years by treaty reforms, especially by the creation of the co-decision procedure by the Maastricht Treaty and its extension by the Amsterdam, Nice, and Lisbon Treaties.
- The force and status of decision-making outcomes is crucial to EU supranationalism, for clearly the EU could hardly be described as supranational if its decisions had no binding force. Indeed, some do not and are merely advisory and exhortive. But many do, and these constitute EU law. It is a law that constitutes an increasingly prominent part of the legal systems of all member states, that takes precedence over national law should the two conflict, and that, in the event of a dispute, finds its final authority not in national courts but in the interpretations of the EU's own courts.

Both intergovernmentalism and supranationalism are thus important features of the functioning and nature of the EU. This is no more clearly demonstrated than in the influence exercised by the Commission: on the one hand it is an important motor in the European integration process, but on the other it is constrained by the preferences of the governments of the member states. As Mark Pollack has put it in analysing the role of the Commission in terms of principal-agent relationships, 'Supranational autonomy and influence … is not a simple binary matter of obedient servants or runaway Eurocracies, but rather varies along a continuum between the two points' (Pollack, 1998: 218).

A pooling and sharing of sovereignty?

The EU is quite unique in the extent to which it involves states engaging in *joint* action to formulate *common* policies and make *binding* decisions. As the words 'joint', 'common' and 'binding' imply, the process of working together is resulting in the EU states becoming ever more intermeshed and interdependent. This is no more clearly seen than in the 'tying' effect of many aspects of their relationships and shared activities: tying in the sense that it would not be possible for them to be reversed without creating major constitutional, legal, political and economic difficulties at both the EU and the national level.

Clearly a central aspect of the intermeshing and the interdependence, and one of the principal distinguishing characteristics of the EU, is the way in which the member states have voluntarily surrendered some of their national sovereignty and independence to collective institutions. However, viewed from a broader perspective, the EU is not only the cause of a decline in national powers but is also a response to decline. This is because much of the rationale of the EU lies in the attempt – an attempt for which there is no international parallel – on the part of the member states to increase their control of, and their strength and influence in, a rapidly changing world. Although all of the states have reservations about, and some have fundamental criticisms of, certain aspects of the EU, each has judged that membership enhances its ability to achieve certain objectives. The precise nature of these objectives varies from state to state, but in virtually all cases the main priorities are the promotion of economic growth and prosperity, the control of economic and financial forces that are not confined to national boundaries, and the strengthening of political influence. Insofar as these objectives are being attained, it can be argued that the diminution in the role of the state and the loss of sovereignty that arises from supranationalism is counterbalanced by the collective strength of the EU as a whole.

Indeed, since international change and developing global interdependence have resulted in all of the member states experiencing a considerable *de facto*, if not *de jure*, loss of national sovereignty quite irrespective of the loss that is attributable to EU membership, it can be argued that the discussion about national sovereignty, in the classical sense of the term at least, is no longer very meaningful. Rather it should be recognised that the only way in which EU states can retain control of their operating environments is by pooling and sharing their power and their sovereignty.

Theorising European Integration: Grand Theory

Many scholars of European integration have explored ways in which the overall nature of the integration process might be theorised. The purpose of such exploration has been to develop a broad understanding of the factors underlying European integration and in so doing to facilitate predictions of how integration is likely to proceed.

This search for what is commonly referred to as 'grand' theory – that is, theory which explains the main features of the integration process as a whole – began soon after the European Community was established in the 1950s, with US scholars leading the way. However, after about fifteen years of considerable activity and published output, interest in grand integration theory declined from the mid-1970s as disillusionment set in with what had been and could be achieved by such theory. Furthermore, the EC itself became less interesting, with its seeming retreat into retrenchment and even sclerosis. There followed a lull of ten years or so in which little was published in the sphere of grand integration theory. This lull ended in the mid-to-late 1980s when interest was re-stimulated by the 're-launch' of the integration process through the SEM and SEA in 1985–6 and with the appearance on the academic scene of new scholars who believed that, though early grand theory may have had its limitations, the *raison d'être* of grand theory – to further understanding of the general character of European integration – was as valid as ever.

A notable feature of the re-awakened interest in grand theory in recent years has been that much of it has centred on debating the respective merits of, and developing more sophisticated versions of, the two theories – the foundational theories one may call them – that dominated the early years of European integration theory: neofunctionalism and intergovernmentalism. Another prominent feature has been the extensive use that has been made of interdependency theory, which is not especially focused on European integration but is widely seen as being helpful in explaining the reasons for, and the course of, the European integration process.

This section of the chapter is thus primarily concerned with neofunctionalism, intergovernmentalism, and interdependency.

Neofunctionalism

The foundations of neofunctionalism were laid in the late 1950s and during the 1960s by a number of US academics, of whom the most prominent were Ernst Haas (1958) and Leon Lindberg (1963).

In its classic formulation, neofunctionalism revolves largely around the concept of spillover, which takes two main forms. The first form – functional spillover – arises from the interconnected nature of modern economies, which makes it difficult to confine integration to particular economic sectors. Rather, integration in one sector produces pressures for integration in adjoining and related sectors. The second form – political spillover – largely follows on from economic integration and has a number of dimensions: national elites increasingly turn their attention to supranational levels of activity and decision-making; these elites become favourably disposed towards the integration process and the upgrading of common interests; supranational institutions and non-governmental actors become more influential in the integration process, while nation states and governmental actors become less influential; and the increasing importance of integration generates pressures and demands for political control and accountability at the supranational level.

With its emphasis on spillover, early neofunctionalism thus suggested, though it certainly did not regard as inevitable, the progressive development of European integration. Drawing heavily on the experience of the ECSC, which had played such an important part in paving the way for the EEC, integration was seen as promoting further integration. The slowing down of the integration process following the 1965–6 crisis in the EC and the world economic recession of the early 1970s was thus something of a jolt for advocates of neofunctionalism. For far from policy integration proceeding apace and political behaviour and decision-making becoming increasingly supranational in character, policy integration did not develop in the manner that had been anticipated whilst political behaviour and decision-making remained essentially nationally-based and conditioned. As a result, neofunctionalism lost much of its gloss and appeal, not least when its foremost figures – Haas and Lindberg – retreated from it and suggested that future integration theory would need to give greater recognition to, among other things, nationalism and the role of political leadership.

Since the late 1980s, however, as the pace of integration has again picked up, there has been a re-assessment and a partial comeback of neofunctionalism, albeit often in a 'disguised' form. As Phillippe Schmitter (2004: 45) has observed 'Real live neofunctionists may be an endangered species, but neofunctionist thinking [is] very much alive, even if it [is] usually … re-branded as a different animal'.

Jeppe Tranholm-Mikkelsen (1991) has argued that much of the 'new dynamism' in Western Europe from the mid-1980s can be explained in neofunctionalist terms, though he also emphasises the importance of factors that were not part of the original neofunctionalist position – such as forceful political actors and changes in the external security environment. His main conclusion is that although neofunctionalism may be dealing only with 'some parts of the elephant … it appears that those parts are amongst the ones that make the animal move' (*ibid.*: 319). Tranholm-Mikkelsen exemplifies those who argue that although original neofunctionalism may have had its limitations and faults – most notably by being overdeterministic and not giving due allowance to the continuing importance in the European integration process of the (often distinctive) interests of member states and their representatives – it still has, especially when updated and modified, considerable theoretical value. Evidence cited to support neofunctionalism's case relates both to functional and to political spillover. In respect of functional spillover, reference is most commonly made to the internal market, where the original 'requirements' for the completion of the market have steadily been expanded to include, amongst other things, the social dimension, the single currency, and a measure of fiscal harmonisation. In respect of political spillover, the great advances in supranational decision-making since the mid-1980s are commonly cited, with 'the motor role' of the

Commission, the common use of QMV in the Council, and the EU Courts' support for much integrationist activity all seen as falling within the neofunctionalist framework. Indeed, with regard to the role of the Court of Justice, Burley and Mattli (1993: 43) have explicitly argued that 'the legal integration of the Community corresponds remarkably closely to the original neofunctionalist model', and that the Court has not only had considerable scope to pursue its own agenda but has frequently done so in a manner that favours integration.

Much of the work of Wayne Sandholtz and Alec Stone Sweet (Sandholtz and Stone Sweet, 1998; Stone Sweet and Sandholtz, 1997) is informed by neofunctionalism, though like Tranholm-Mikkelsen and others they too look on original neofunctionalism as wanting – not least, in their view, in an inability to explain why integration should advance via spillover in some policy sectors and not in others. Building from a broadly neofunctionalist base, Sandholtz and Stone Sweet draw on other approaches and perspectives – notably globalisation and transactionalism – to advance a theory to explain the development of supranational governance in the EU and why the extent of the development varies so much between policy sectors that, they suggest, the EU is best regarded not as a single regime but as a series of different regimes. The starting point of their explanation is that globalisation has led to a growth in cross-border economic transactions (trade, investment, production, distribution) and communications which have produced pressures both for the removal of cross-border barriers and for the creation of EU-wide rules and regulations. These pressures have resulted in the creation and development of EU policies and policy arenas in which supranational institutions have key policy management and policy promotion roles. Integration has thus been sustained in a number of ways, including by a continued expansion of transnational exchanges and by the supranational institutions seeking to widen and strengthen the frameworks with a view to further controlling the transnational exchanges. As Sandholtz and Stone Sweet make clear, the key constituent elements of their theory are thus 'prefigured in neofunctionalism: the development of transnational society, the role of supranational organizations with meaningful autonomous capacity to pursue integrative agendas, and the focus on European rule-making to resolve international policy externali-

ties' (Sandholtz and Stone Sweet, 1998: 6). They build on these elements to develop a theory in which '[t]ransnational exchange provokes supranational organizations to make rules designed to facilitate and to regulate the development of transnational society' (*ibid.*: 25). In seeking to answer the question why integration proceeds faster and further in some policy areas than in others they 'look to variation in the levels of cross-border interactions and in the consequent need for supranational coordination and rules' (*ibid.*: 14).

Neofunctionalism in its various forms has been criticised on a number of grounds, in particular for undervaluing the government-determined frameworks within which supranational actors operate, for not paying enough attention to member state resistance to aspects of the integration process, and for still being implicitly deterministic. But whilst neofunctionalism does clearly have its weaknesses, it continues to have considerable explanatory usefulness. Recognition of this results in many scholars continuing to extol the merits of neofunctionalism and to work within a neofunctionalist framework. Arne Niemann (2006), for example, advances a refined and sophisticated version of neofunctionalism to help explain EU decisions. At the heart of his refinements is the identification of five types of spillover (functional, political, social, cultivated and exogenous) and a clear recognition of the existence of countervailing forces that can result in integrationist advance not being inevitable. And, in an application of neofunctionalism not normally employed – to horizontal integration (that is, to the geographical extension of integration) – Catherine Macmillan (2009) suggests that neofunctionalism provides a useful theoretical framework for enlargement and, more particularly, that neofunctionalist spillover in its various forms has contributed to Turkey's accession process.

(For further introductions to neofunctionalism, see Strøby-Jensen, 2007; Niemann and Schmittter, 2009.)

Intergovernmentalism

Intergovernmentalism has its origins in international relations theory, and more particularly the realist tradition within that theory. Put simply, realism is centred on the view that nation states are the key actors in international affairs and the key political relations between states are channelled primarily via national governments. Unlike neofunctionalism, realism does not accord much importance to the influence of supranational or transnational actors and only limited importance to non-governmental actors within states.

As applied to European integration, intergovernmentalism thus explains the direction and pace of the integration process mainly by reference to decisions and actions taken by the governments of European states. There is a recognition that other actors, both within and beyond states, can exercise some influence on developments, but not a crucial, and certainly not a controlling, influence. This focus on states – and the associated perception of states having their own distinctive national interests which they vigorously defend, especially in the spheres of high politics (foreign policy, security and defence) – has resulted in intergovernmentalists tending to emphasise, as Stanley Hoffmann (1966) put it, 'the logic of diversity' rather than 'the logic of integration'.

For many years Hoffmann was the foremost proponent of this interpretation of European integration, but in the 1990s Andrew Moravcsik (1991, 1993, 1995, 1998) established himself as its leading exponent. (Other exponents of forms of intergovernmentalism include Garrett, 1992, 1993, and Grieco, 1995.) Just as Tranholm-Mikkelsen and others have built on early neofunctionalism to develop a more sophisticated theoretical framework, so has Moravcsik performed a similar service for intergovernmentalism. He calls his framework liberal intergovernmentalism.

There are three main components of liberal intergovernmentalism. First, there is an assumption of rational state behaviour, which means that the actions of states are assumed to be based on utilising what are judged to be the most appropriate means of achieving their goals. Second, there is a liberal theory of national preference formation. This draws on a domestic politics approach to explain how state goals can be shaped by domestic pressures and interactions, which in turn are often conditioned by the constraints and opportunities that derive from economic interdependence. Third, there is an intergovernmentalist interpretation of inter-state relations, which emphasises the key role of governments in determining the relations between states and sees the outcome of negotiations between governments as essentially

being determined by their relative bargaining powers and the advantages that accrue to them by striking agreements. Agreements are deemed to be most likely when there is a convergence of national preferences, especially between the governments of large and powerful states.

Because liberal intergovernmentalism advances such a clear and, in important respects, almost uncompromising framework, and because it is seen by many as just not fitting the facts in an era of multiple international actors and complex interdependence between states, it has inevitably attracted criticism. Four criticisms are particularly worth noting.

First, it is suggested that Moravcsik is too selective with his empirical references when seeking to demonstrate the validity of his framework in the EU context. More particularly, he is considered to focus too much on 'historic' decisions and not enough on more commonplace and routine decisions. To over-focus on historic decisions is seen as distortional, since not only are such decisions untypical by their very nature, they also necessarily emphasise the role of national governments since they are channelled via the European Council.

Second, it is argued that liberal intergovernmentalism concentrates too much on the formal and final stages of decision-making and pays too little attention to informal integration and the constraints that such integration imposes on the formal decision-makers. For example, Wincott (1995) argues that the SEM programme and the SEA, which Moravcsik suggests were the outcome of negotiations between national actors, are in important respects better viewed as the formalisation by national governments of what had been happening in practice for some time.

Third, critics argue that insufficient attention is paid to the 'black box' of the state, and more especially to disaggregating the different parts of government. According to Forster (1998: 364), this means that liberal intergovernmentalism provides an inadequate account of how governments choose their policy options:

> The formation of objectives, the pursuit of strategies and the final positions adopted are every bit as disorderly and unpredictable as domestic policy-making. Politics is not always a rational process: ideology, belief and symbolism can play as important a role as substance (*ibid.*: 364).

Fourth – and this is probably the most commonly voiced criticism of liberal intergovernmentalism, and indeed of any form of intergovernmentalism – it is accused of grossly understating the influence exercised in the European integration process by supranational actors such as the Commission and the EU Courts, and transnational actors such as European firms and interest groups. For example, in a collection of essays edited by Sandholtz and Stone Sweet (1998), several academic commentators provide evidence of EU supranational bodies seeking to enhance their autonomy and influence and having considerable success in so doing. Moravcsik's portrayal of the Commission as exercising the role of little more than a facilitator in respect of significant decision-making has attracted particular criticism, with numerous empirically based studies claiming to show that the Commission does exercise an independent and influential decision-making role, be it as – the metaphors abound – an *animateur,* a policy entrepreneur, or a motor force. Such studies do not, it has to be said, convince Moravcsik that the Commission and other supranational actors are doing much more than responding to an agenda set by the governments of the member states. As he puts it:

> *intergovernmental demand* for policy ideas, not the *supranational supply* of these ideas, is the fundamental exogenous factor driving integration. To a very large extent, the demand for co-operative policies creates its own supply (Moravcsik, 1995: 618, emphasis in original).

Forster (1998: 365) has suggested that liberal intergovernmentalism's weaknesses mean that it is 'perhaps best regarded less as a theory of intergovernmental bargaining, than as a pre-theory or analytical framework'. This may be so, but it should not be forgotten that although weaknesses in liberal intergovernmentalism can readily be identified, the approach has considerable strengths. In particular, it provides a reminder of the role of states and governments in the EU and it does so in a much more nuanced and sophisticated manner than did early intergovernmentalism.

(For further introductions to intergovernmentalism and liberal intergovernmentalism, see: Cini, 2007b; Moravcsik and Schimmelfennig, 2009).

Interdependency

Whilst both neofunctionalism and intergovernmentalism recognise that external factors have at times triggered the pace and nature of European integration, both theories are concerned primarily with the internal dynamics of integration. Interdependency, in contrast, has been used by scholars of European integration to place integration in the wider context of growing international interdependence.

Interdependency theory was initially developed in the 1970s, most famously by Robert Keohane and Joseph Nye (1977). Its central thrust when applied to European integration is that the integration process should not be viewed in too narrow a context. Many of the factors that have influenced its development have applied to it alone, but many have not. This is seen most obviously in the ways in which post-Second World War international modernisation in its various forms – including increased levels of wealth, vast increases in world trade, the technological revolution, and the transformation of communications – has promoted many different forms of political and economic interdependency. These in turn have produced a transformation in the ways in which different parts of the world relate to and come into contact with one another. For example, there has been a steady increase in the number and variety of international actors – both above and below the level of the nation state – and a corresponding weakening of the dominance of states. An increasing range of methods and channels are used by international actors to pursue their goals, with relationships between governments, for instance, no longer being so controlled by Foreign Offices and Ministries of External Affairs. The range of issues on international agendas has grown with, in particular, traditional 'high' policy issues (those concerned with security and the defence of the state) being joined by an array of 'low' policy issues (those concerned with the wealth and welfare of citizens). And paralleling the change in the policy content of international agendas there has been a decline, in the Western industrialised world at least, in the use of physical force as a policy instrument, with conflicts over the likes of trade imbalances and currency exchange rates not being resolved by armed conflict but by bargaining, adjusting and compromising.

Interdependence theory is thus useful in helping to set European integration within the context of the rapid changes that are occurring throughout the international system. This system is becoming, like the EU system itself, increasingly multi-layered and interconnected. Whether the purpose is to regulate international trade, to promote the efficient functioning of the international monetary system, to set international standards on packaging for the transportation of hazardous material, or to control the hunting and killing of whales, states now come together in many different ways, in many different combinations and for many different purposes.

Interdependency theory is distinctive from neofunctionalism and intergovernmentalism in that it emphasises that much of the European integration process is explained by factors that are global in nature, and it emphasises too that many of the systemic features of the EU are found elsewhere in the international system, albeit less intensively. Interdependency is also different from neofunctionalism and intergovernmentalism in that it has been less intensively applied to European integration and partly in consequence is less rigorous and systematic in the explanation it offers. Whilst those who have engaged in the theoretical debate on the nature of the integration process have recognised the importance of global interdependency, they have tended to do so as part of the framing background rather than as central causation. It is not possible to point to any major scholar who has advanced interdependency as *the sole cause* of the European integration process. As Carole Webb wrote in the early 1980s:

> For most students the concept of interdependence has been used to explain the conditions under which governments and other economic actors have to contemplate some form of collaboration; but unlike the approach of integration theory, it does not necessarily help to define the outcome very precisely (Webb, 1983: 33).

This lack of precision in interdependency theory is most obviously seen in the fact that, as O'Neill (2000: 131) puts it, its 'narrative apparently confirms neither an intergovernmental, confederal nor a supra-national prognosis … Governance per se is not the central issue.' Rather, the central issue for interdependency theory is the role of inexorable transnational forces buffeting nation states. As such, interdependency in the European integration context is perhaps best

thought of as an approach and/or a perspective rather than as a theory.

The future of grand theory

Social science theories never satisfy everyone. Whatever phenomena they are seeking to explain and whatever forms they take, they almost invariably attract criticism for being deficient in important respects. Commonly identified deficiencies include focusing on only part of the phenomena under examination, being too general in scope and/or formulation, being excessively time-bound, and being insufficiently empirically grounded.

European integration grand theory has not been exempt from such criticisms. Indeed, it has been especially prone to them given that the European integration process is so complex, so constantly changing, and so capable of being viewed from different angles. But, as with other social science theories, European integration theories do not lose all value because critics can show them to be less than complete and final in the explanations they offer. Rather, grand theories can be of considerable value in furthering understanding of the integration process by offering particular insights into it, by providing partial explanations of it, and by promoting further work and thought on it.

Of course, as long as existing theory is seen to be deficient in certain respects there will be attempts to improve upon it. In this context an increasingly important feature of the theoretical debate on European integration is the attempt by many theorists to move beyond what is now widely viewed as the over-narrow and restrictive nature of the jousting between classical intergovernmentalism and classical neofunctionalism.

One aspect of this new theorising is the development of theoretical explanations that, although emerging from one or other of these two schools of thought, are much more complex, sophisticated and nuanced than the theories in their original formulations. Moravcsik and Sandholtz and Stone Sweet are the best known of those who are theorising in this way, but there are many others.

Another aspect of the new theorising is the attempt to bring together key features of the traditional theories and link them, as appropriate, to relevant parts of other theories. Robert Keohane and

Stanley Hoffmann (1991) were amongst the advance guard in taking such an eclectic and synthesising approach, using it in their analysis of the quickened pace of integration, particularly institutional integration, in the mid-1980s. Essentially they argued that neofunctionalism, interdependency, and intergovernmentalism all had something to contribute to the explanation of why the Community was 'relaunched'. Regarding neofunctionalism:

> [s]pillover took place not as a functional expansion of tasks but rather in the form of the creation, as a result of enlargement, of incentives for institutional change (*ibid*: 22).

Regarding interdependence:

> [t]he 1992 program was ... strongly affected by events in the world economy outside of Europe – especially by concern about international competitiveness (*ibid*: 19).

Regarding intergovernmentalism, they considered that the precise timing of the burst of integration was due

> not only to incentives for the world political economy and spillover but also to intergovernmental bargains made possible by convergence of preferences of major European states (*ibid*: 25).

Janne Matláry (1993) is another who has argued that the limitations of traditional models – especially, in her view, the limitations of intergovernmentalism, which she regards as failing to recognise the crucial interaction between EU institutions and member states and also between formal and informal integration processes – make a synthesising approach essential. There seems, she says, to be

> an emerging view that a comprehensive theory of integration must include not only realist assumptions of state behaviour, but also analysis of domestic politics and the role of the different EC institutions (*ibid*.: 376).

Searching for points of contact and overlap, perhaps even for a synthesis, between ever-more sophisticated intergovernmentalist and neofunctionalist-inspired models are likely to be a feature of future integration theory. Whether, however, synthetic theory will ever be able to escape its basic problem, namely that attempts to develop it are almost inevitably drawn back into one of the dominant perspectives, must be doubted. For as Alexander Warleigh (1998: 9) has observed:

> rapprochement of neo-functionalism and neo-realism would effectively deprive both theories of their respective *raison d'être* and guiding principles, a step which neither set of scholars [advocating the theories] can take without emasculating their theory.

Another likely feature of the future course of integration theory is its placement within the context of wider globalisation theory. As Ben Rosamond (1995) has pointed out, globalisation theory should help to establish how integration is occurring in so many different ways in so many parts of the world: at the 'official' level between international, supranational, national, regional and even local institutions of government, but at the 'unofficial' level too as a result of changes in technology, communications, travel patterns and culture.

Michael O'Neill (1996: 81) has observed that European integration theory

> has been a constantly shifting dialectic between events as they have unfolded on the ground, and the efforts of scholars to track and accurately explain them ... the paradigms and the intellectual tension generated by [the theoretical discourse on integration] have helped to map more accurately the actual developments in European integration, and to clarify our understanding of what the process means.

These observations will doubtless also apply to future theory. Theorising will become more sophisticated and nuanced as new theory builds on previous theory and as the integration process itself continues to unfold. But the essential purpose of grand theory will remain unchanged: to assist understanding and explanation of the integration process.

Theorising the Functioning of the EU: Middle-Range Theory

Whereas grand theory looks at the nature of the integration process as a whole, middle-range theory looks at particular aspects of the process. More especially, it focuses on the politics and policies of the EU: on how the EU functions and on what the EU does.

In recent years, much scholarly attention has shifted in the direction of this less embracing theoretical endeavour. There are two main reasons for this. First, there has been an increasing feeling that grand theory is inherently limited in what it can achieve. It is prone, critics argue, to falling between two stools. On the one hand, if it restricts itself to identifying only major causational factors it inevitably misses, or at least does not adequately recognise, the many different dimensions of the integration process. On the other hand, if it attempts to encompass all the dimensions of integration it becomes too complicated and difficult to operationalise. Better, the argument runs, to be less ambitious and to focus only on parts of the integration process and the EU, especially the more important parts. Second, as the European integration process has intensified, so has the EU attracted the attention of an increasing number and range of scholars. It used to be the case that most of the European integration scholars who were interested in theorising and conceptualising were steeped in and made extensive use of international relations theory. This has become much less so in recent years, with many scholars today taking the view that European integration should be studied not just through a traditional international relations approach but also, and arguably more so, through other subdisciplines of political science. If it is the case, as many of these scholars suggest, that the EU is a polity, albeit one without the usual lines of authority and control, then does it not follow that approaches that are deemed to be suitable for the study of conventional polities – most notably states – might also be suitable for the study of the EU? Those who answer this question in the affirmative have particularly advocated the merits of using comparative politics and public policy studies approaches. As Hix (1994) stated in an influential article advocating the merits of taking a comparative politics approach to EU studies, scholars have used comparative and public policy approaches not to follow the international relations route and examine European integration but rather to examine EU *politics*.

Of course, EU politics are complex, so unsurprisingly a large number and variety of middle-range theoretical approaches have been used to assist explanation of them. This is intellectually healthy for furthering understanding of the nature of the EU since no one approach is likely to be capable of capturing the essential nature of the many different facets of EU politics. To take, for example, the area of activity that has been the main focus for middle-range theorising, policy processes, there is no reason to expect any one theoretical approach to be wholly satisfactory. After all, there are many different types of EU policy process with some, for instance, being essentially intergovernmental in character and others being more supranational. Within each policy process there are several stages – from the initial stages of problem identification followed by policy initiation through to the final stages of policy implementation and then policy evaluation. And each policy area has its own troupe of policy actors.

To illustrate middle-range theorising in the study of EU politics, and more especially on EU policy processes, two of the more important approaches will now be considered: new institutionalism and policy networks. It is to be emphasised that they are both best thought of as being approaches rather than full-blown theories because they are still very much in development, arguably have greater descriptive than explanatory uses and powers, and have only a very limited predictive capability.

New institutionalism

Much has been heard since the late 1980s about the merits of new institutionalism. In essence, new institutionalism has at its core the assertion that institutions matter in shaping the actions of political actors and in determining decisional outcomes. As such, new institutionalism emerged largely as a reaction against the rationalism and behaviouralism which was so influential in social and political science circles in the 1970s and 1980s, especially in the United States.

In what ways is 'new' institutionalism different from 'old' institutionalism? The main difference is that whereas old or traditional institutionalism did not go much beyond analysing the formal powers and structures of decision-making institutions, new institutionalism defines institutions in a very broad sense to incorporate a wide range of formal and informal procedures, practices, relationships, customs, and norms. As such, new institutionalism is much more all-embracing and expansive in its concerns and interests.

Beyond a core shared interest in institutions broadly defined, new institutionalism spreads out in different directions. As Hall and Taylor (1996) have noted, there are at least three analytical approaches within new institutionalism: historical institutionalism, rational choice institutionalism, and sociological institutionalism. The core features of these institutionalisms are set out in Box 23.6.

All three variants of new institutionalism have been employed in respect of European integration and the functioning of the EU. Brief summaries of these employments now follow (for fuller overviews see Dowding, 2000; Pollack, 2003 and 2004; and Schneider and Aspinwall, 2001).

Historical institutionalism has been used most particularly to show how the taking of EU decisions at one point in time constrains the behaviour and policy

---

Box 23.6

The focus of the three new institutionalisms

- *Historical institutionalism* concentrates on the distributions of power that are produced by institutional arrangements, the ways in which these arrangements result in 'path dependencies' and 'unintended consequences', and the relationships between institutions and other factors that shape political activities and outcomes such as economic developments and ideological beliefs.
- *Rational choice institutionalism* is especially interested in the extent to which and the ways in which institutions shape, channel, and constrain the rational actions of political actors.
- *Sociological institutionalism* focuses particularly on how institutional forms and practices can often be culturally explained.

---

options of decision-makers at future points of time. Decision-taking is seen to make for a path dependency which, though possible to be disturbed in certain circumstances, does make for a persistence and endurability of institutional and policy choices. It is seen as making also for an increase in the independence and powers of the supranational institutions which are usually delegated responsibilities for seeing to the application of EU decisions – this increase being one of the unintended consequences of EU decision-making that historical institutionalists make much of. Prominent users and developers of historical institutionalism have included Simon Bulmer (1994, 1998, 2009) and Paul Pierson (1996) who have both advanced the merits of the approach for analysing and, as Bulmer puts it, 'capturing', political and policy activity in the EU's increasingly multilayered system. More specifically, Bulmer has advocated and employed the framework of a 'governance regime' for analysing the EU at the policy-specific or sub-system level.

Rational choice theory has at its core the assertion that political actors behave in ways that enable them to maximise their interests. The interests are exogenously determined (by the 'objective' situations in which actors find themselves) and are mainly focused on economic-related issues. When deciding their courses of action political actors in effect undertake a cost/benefit analysis of what the courses available will produce. As regards the operation of the EU, a much explored theme in the rational choice literature is that governments cede powers to the EU level because they derive a variety of benefits from so doing, prominent amongst which are reducing transaction costs through enhanced policy development, policy effectiveness, and policy compliance. (For overviews of rational choice and EU integration and politics, see: Pollack, 2006; Scully, 2006). *Rational choice institutionalism* is thus naturally much taken up with throwing light on the motivations of member state governments in the integration process, but it also attempts to demonstrate the consequences of different EU decisional rules for actors' behaviour and influence. Amongst the things rational choice institutionalists have shown are the different restrictions placed on policy actors under different decision-making procedures and the varying inter-actor relations and policy impacts that are thereby created (the work of Garrett and Tsebilis is especially notable in this context – see, for example, Garrett and Tsebilis, 1996 and Tsebilis and Garrett, 1997 and 2001). For instance, QMV in the Council has been shown not only to produce the expected increased efficiency in Council decision-making but also to have beneficial effects for the Commission and EP, with policy outcomes being closer to their preferences as a result of dissenting national government positions being more easily by-passed.

As applied to the EU, *sociological institutionalism* is the most under-used of the three branches of new institutionalism. Insofar as it has been used, much of it has been for the purpose of examining the attitudes, motivations and behaviour of people working for and in the EU institutions. There is, for example, now an extensive body of literature on Commission officials, showing amongst other things how they identify much more than do ordinary citizens with Europe and with a supranational perspective of how the EU should function (see: Hooghe, 2001 and 2005; Trondal, 2007). Staying with the Commission, authors such as Bellier (1997) and Cini (2000) have highlighted clashes in the administrative culture of the Commission with, for example, officials in DG Competition displaying a stronger attachment to liberal market principles and less sympathy for selected public intervention in the pursuit of non-market goals than officials in DG Regional Policy and DG Environment. An assumption made by sociological institutionalists is that such cultural values and differences are important because they shape actor choices and behaviour. Whereas rationalist approaches assume actor choices and behaviour are mainly determined by a 'logic of consequences', sociological approaches give greater weight to a 'logic of appropriateness': that is, what is the appropriate thing to do in this situation and this set of circumstances? More broadly, sociological institutionalism has blended with constructivist approaches to the study of European integration and the EU, where attention is directed to examining and establishing how the likes of political space and institutional and individual identities, roles and values are socially constructed. (On social constructivism and European integration, see Checkel, 2006; Wiener 2006; Schimmelfennig 2001 and 2002 provides interesting applications of social constructivism to EU enlargement policy, as is shown below.)

Policy networks

The policy networks approach can be ⟨…⟩ application of new institutionalism in ⟨…⟩ sense. The approach is used to describe and ⟨…⟩ policy processes and policy outcomes.

Simply put, policy networks are arenas in which decision-makers and interests come together to mediate differences and search for solutions. Policy networks vary in character according to three key variables: the relative stability (or instability) of network memberships; the relative insularity (or permeability) of networks; and the relative strength (or weakness) of resource dependencies (Peterson, 1995: 77). From these variables a continuum emerges:

> At one end are tightly integrated policy *communities* in which membership is constant and often hierarchical, external pressures have minimal impact, and actors are highly dependent on each other for resources. At the other are loosely integrated issue *networks,* in which membership is fluid and non hierarchical, the network is easily permeated by external influences, and actors are highly self-reliant (*ibid.*: 77).

The EU is seen by those who champion the policy network approach as particularly lending itself to the emergence of such networks (see, for example, the volume by Kohler-Koch and Eising (1999) which views EU policy processes as being essentially based on a system of network governance). Amongst factors identified as being conducive to policy networks are: the informal nature of much EU policy-making; the multiplicity of interests at EU level that are anxious to have access to policy-makers; the highly technical – almost non-political – nature of much EU policy content; the powerful policy positions held by senior officials, especially in the Commission and especially in the early stages of policy-making; and the heavy reliance of officials on outside interests for information and advice about policy content and policy implementation. As Schneider *et al.* (1994: 480) state on this last point:

> The highly pluralist pattern exhibited by the EC policy networks is a consequence not only of numerous actors' efforts to influence the European

ılation, but
y employed
ıy the

ıe influence of
the policy spec-
ınity type are often
is well established,
exists, and where
the cooperation of
inteɪ... ...licy areas include agriculture and ... ...velopment. In contrast,
issue networks are mo... ...ımon where EU policy is
not well developed, where the policy debate is fluid
and shifting, and where such organised interests as
do exist have few resources to 'exchange' with
decision-makers. Consumer protection policy and
much of environmental and social policy are examples of policy areas where issue networks are
commonly found.

The usefulness of the policy networks approach is
not, it should be said, accepted by all EU analysts.
Amongst the reservations that have been expressed are
that it cannot deal with the making of major directional decisions, it has little predictive capacity, and it
cannot capture the extreme fluidity and fragmented
nature of EU policy processes (see Kassim, 1994, for a
critique of the usefulness of policy networks in
analysing EU policy processes). There is doubtless
much in such criticisms, but they are arguably partly
based on over-stated understandings of what advocates of the model claim on its behalf. As Rhodes *et al.*
(1996: 381) suggest when arguing that the approach is
helpful in the EU context

> Policy networks is a useful tool for analysing the
> links between types of governmental units,
> between levels of government, and between
> governments and interest groups. It aids
> understanding of the policy process but it is only
> one variable in that process.

For other variables to be captured, policy network
analysis often work best, as Peterson (2009) has
pointed out, when deployed alongside other theoretical accounts of EU politics and policy-making.

Using Differing Theoretical Approaches to Explain Decision-Making in a Particular Policy Area: Enlargement

A central theme of this chapter has been that the existence of differing conceptual and theoretical
approaches in EU studies should not be viewed as
being a problem. Rather, the existence and use of
differing approaches furthers understanding by bringing differing perspectives to bear on and by providing
differing insights into the European integration
process and the EU.

The way in which the use of differing theoretical
perspectives can further understanding can be illustrated by taking two of the most important theoreti-
cally-based approaches to EU studies and applying
them to a particular policy area. The perspectives are
rationalism and constructivism, which in recent years
have loomed large in debates on EU theorising. The
policy area is enlargement which has, since the 'easy'
1995 enlargement round, attracted increasing theoretical attention as 'horizontal integration' has become
more difficult to achieve.

Rationalist approaches

As was noted above in the outline of rational choice
institutionalism, rationalist approaches are based on
the assumption that policy actors are motivated by
self-interest to maximise utility. Their interests derive
not from 'within' the actors but rather from the 'given'
circumstances in which they find themselves.
Economic self-interest is usually as being especially
important, not least by proponents of the best known
rationalist approach in EU theorising: liberal intergovernmentalism.

Wholly rationalist actors thus: establish their goals
on the basis of what serves their (largely exogenously
determined and primarily materially based) interests;
identify the possible ways of achieving their goals;
make decisions on the basis of an evaluation of all the
possible options, with a 'logic of consequences' determining final decision-making.

Applying this approach to enlargement policy, to what extent can the 2004/07 enlargement and the opening of accession negotiations with other applicants be explained in terms of net advantages for existing member states? Well, for many EU policy practitioners the challenges and negativities of enlarging the EU to 'difficult' applicants have been, and still are, at least partly offset by positive considerations. Two considerations are especially important:

- *Economic advantages.* A larger internal market creates considerable market and business opportunities for existing EU states. This is all the more so when acceding states have relatively inefficient and under-invested economies, as has been the case since the EFTAn round with all would-be EU states (apart from Iceland). The 2004–07 enlargement added about 105 million people to the EU's population, and therefore also to its internal market, and should Turkey ever become a member there could be another 80 million or so.
- *Political and security advantages.* It is in the EU's interests that neighbouring states – and especially those with which it shares borders – should have solid and stable liberal democratic political systems. More broadly, the promotion of liberal democracy and of respect for human rights has increasingly become a central feature of EU foreign policy, and enlargement policy has virtually become a part of foreign policy. With the CEECs, it came to be accepted by the EU's member states in the early to mid-1990s that early EU membership would assist the CEECs to consolidate their newly based democratic systems – both by bringing them inside 'the democratic fold' and by subsequently opening them up to the possibility of sanctions in the event of any democratic 'slippage' (under Article 7 TEU, which provides for suspension of EU rights if a member state is in serious and persistent breach of the Union's founding principles of liberty, democracy, respect for human rights and fundamental freedoms, and the rule of law).

Beyond promoting the consolidation of liberal democracy, enlargement to CEECs and to South Eastern Europe has also been seen to provide other possible political and security advantages. One of these is that an enlarged EU clearly carries more weight in its external relations and dealings. And in the particular case of Turkey, its accession could provide valuable bridges between Europe and the Middle East and Asia and between the West and the Islamic world.

The extent to which, and the intensity with which, such motivations in favour of enlargement have been felt in member states has varied, both at a general level and in terms of attitudes towards particular applicants. Germany was clearly the EU-15 state with most to gain from admitting the CEECs, primarily because of its geographical position and the market opportunities and security assurances enlargement to the East offered to it. Another EU-15 state with potentially much to gain, though for quite different reasons, was the UK which saw, as it still sees with Turkey, a larger and more heterogeneous EU being less disposed to, and capable of, moving the EU in the supranational direction that some member states support but that UK governments mostly oppose. The EU-15 states with least to gain from CEEC accessions were those less prosperous states on the EU's western side – Spain and Portugal – which would not only be unlikely to gain much from the larger market but would be threatened with reductions in their Structural Fund support as much poorer countries than themselves joined. Such states facing losses were, however, as Schimmelfennig (2010: 48) puts it, 'compensated by discriminatory membership': that is, the EU took advantage of the asymmetrical nature of enlargement processes (in which potentially acceding states are in much the weaker negotiating position) to impose accession conditions that reduced the cost of enlargement for existing member state losers to the point that enlargement became acceptable to them.

So, a rationalist approach is helpful in understanding the EU's approach to enlargement. The approach suggests that existing member states have calculated that while enlargements almost invariably involve some costs for them, these are outweighed by benefits. With Turkey, whose membership is widely seen as bringing far more costs than any previous applicant state, even here a rationalist approach has explanatory value. It rest on a customary cost/benefit analysis, but not on circumstances as they are now but on how they are likely to be in about 2017/18, which is generally seen as the earliest possible time of Turkish membership. By then, it is suggested by rationalists, Turkey probably will have become more economically and politically robust and the EU will be more differentiated in character and therefore more capable of incorporating a state that is in important respects 'different'.

Constructivist explanations

Sociologists, and more particularly constructivists, take as their starting point for explaining recent EU enlargement developments the fact that whilst enlargement has certainly offered opportunities to existing member states it also has presented them with stiff challenges and unwanted consequences. From this, it is concluded that the actions of EU member states cannot be wholly explained in rational or instrumental terms. If they had acted purely on the basis of their own national interests and preferences regarding the future nature of the EU some member states should have voted to reject the applications of at least some of the applicants. That they did not do so means that these member states have not been driven, or at least not completely driven, by 'objective' national political and economic situations and needs. So, a non rationalist explanation must be sought. Constructivists find this explanation in social identities, norms and values.

As applied to the admission of the CEECs, Schimmelfennig (2001, 2002) has emphasised the collective identity and obligations that can exist between liberal democratic states and argues that once the case for a rapid enlargement to CEECs began to be pressed – by the European Commission and some EU-15 states – states that were reluctant became swept up in an unfolding 'rhetorical commitment' to fledgling and neighbouring democratic states that led to a 'rhetorical entrapment':

> By argumentatively entrapping the opponents of a firm commitment to Eastern enlargement, they [the supporters of enlargement] brought about a collective outcome that would not have been expected given the constellation of powers and interests (2001: 77).

Sjursen (2002) argues in similar vein, though for her the key driving factor was kinship-based duty rather than a sense of obligation to fellow liberal democracies. She argues that the 2004 enlargement is to be understood, in part at least, in terms of the existence of a community-based European identity, even though it

is not a fully understood or defined identity. The decision to admit CEECs 'against' many self interests demonstrates, she argues

> that in order to trigger a decision to enlarge, something more than instrumental calculations and something less than a selfless concern for human rights has been at play (p. 509).

Taking Sjursen's argument a little further, it certainly is the case that EU politicians generally have felt that the uniting of most of the continent within the EU framework is a good thing in itself, quite apart from the specific advantages it can bring. In the case of the CEECs, these feelings amounted in the 1990s almost to a moral duty. Having seen the CEECs rid themselves of the communist system that Western Europe so opposed for the forty-plus years of the Cold War, it was seen as an obligation in many EU governmental circles to help CEECs to realise their ambitions to become prosperous and democratic states within 'the European family' of nations. Would it, it was argued, be not only irresponsible and churlish but forgetful and unprincipled not to accommodate such CEEC needs and desires? As Sedelmeier has put it:

> The discourse of a collective EU identify, characterised by a responsibility towards the CEECs, became a central aspect of EU policy (Sedelmeier, 2000: 269).

Constructivist explanations may also be applied to the Turkish application. They can help explain why in the second half of the 1990s and the early 2000s the EU moved from its preferred policy – of being close to Turkey but stopping short of holding out the possibility of membership – to giving Turkey a foreseeable membership perspective. The gradually evolving 'upgrading' of language – which can be traced through European Council Conclusions – produced a situation that made it progressively difficult for doubters and opponents to backtrack. Notions of collective identity and kinship-based duty are by no means as strong in respect of Turkey than they were in respect of the CEECs, which helps explain why the Turkish application is seen as presenting a unique challenge for the EU and why some prominent EU politicians have not hidden their opposition to eventual Turkish membership. But feelings of at least some shared identity with

Turkey – emanating in part from shared membership of European and Western organisations, in part from empathy with Turkey's liberalising and democratising reform programmes, and in part from a sense of responsibility towards an Islamic state that is looking to Europe and the West – do exist in many European governing quarters. (For a fuller examination of this view, see Nugent, 2007.)

Concluding Remarks

A wide variety of conceptually and theoretically informed approaches to the understanding and study of European integration and the EU have been explored in this chapter. All have been shown to be subject to criticism and to expressions of reservation about their usefulness. For example, of the three grand theories that were considered, amongst the central 'charges' laid against neofunctionalism and intergovernmentalism are that both press their side of the case too hard and both disappoint when applied empirically over time, whilst the central weakness of interdependence is seen to be its lack of a regional focus.

But concepts and theories, and the methodological approaches based on them, should be judged not only on their deficiencies but also on what they can contribute to knowledge. In this regard there is, as has been shown, extensive merit in much of the conceptual and theoretical work that has been undertaken on European integration and the EU. There may be no one body of work that has been able to capture and explain all aspects of European integration and the EU reality, but that is only to be expected. After all, as Hix (1998: 46) has observed, there is no general theory of American or German government, so why should there be one of the EU? Rather, we should recognise, as

Sandholtz (1996: 426) puts it, 'that dif theories are appropriate for different p puzzle'.

This notion that different kinds of the be used for different purposes – that different approaches should be seen as potentially complementary rather than competing tools of analysis – is now a working assumption of most EU analysts. It is seen indeed as being essential to ensure that no one type of theory is the victim of over-stretch and that no aspect of integration is analysed via inappropriate conceptual and theoretical tools. To guide thinking on what types of theories might be most useful in what circumstances, a few commentators have suggested frameworks for 'fitting' theories with circumstances. For example, Peterson (1995) and Peterson and Bomberg (1999) suggest a framework based on the level and type of EU decisions being made, with macro theories being most appropriate to analyse super-systemic, or history-making, decisions, new institutional approaches being best for systemic decisions (that is, decisions about policy content), and policy network approaches being best for sub-systemic decisions (that is, decisions about policy details). Alex Warleigh (2000) also provides a three-level framework, but in his case the focus is not just EU decisions but, more broadly, categories of EU activity: confederal theory is advocated to explain the creation and nature of the EU, multi-level governance theory to explain the functioning of the EU, and policy network and new institutional theory to explain EU policy-making and output.

A mixture of conceptual and theoretical tools must thus be utilised when analysing European integration and the EU. This chapter has examined the most frequently used of these tools. They have been shown to further understanding by drawing attention to, and highlighting, key features of processes, structures, contexts, and outcomes.

Chapter 24

Present Realities and Future Prospects

The European Union and the Changing Nature of the International System

The European Union should not be viewed in too narrow a context. Whilst many of the factors that have influenced its development apply to it alone, many do not. This is most clearly seen in the ways in which modernisation and interdependence, which have been crucial to the creation of many of the central features of the EU, have produced similar effects elsewhere in the international system – albeit usually to more modest degrees.

Of the many ways in which modernisation and interdependence have transformed the international system, one of the most important has been in the challenges it has posed to the ability of politicians to control events and forces. Of course, states have never been completely islands in the sense of their leaders being able to act wholly independently and take whatever decisions they liked in the pursuit of national interests and preferences. In Europe this has been so especially for small states such as the Benelux states, but it has applied also to large states such as France and Germany in as much as many of their policies – most obviously their trade policies – have necessitated establishing relations and concluding agreements with other countries.

Since the Second World War, and more especially since the 1970s, international considerations have borne down more strongly than ever before on domestic decision-making in the developed world. This is seen most strikingly in respect of economic and monetary policies, where the increasing importance of non-state actors and of international financial mobility have resulted in the representatives of states having to be extremely watchful when taking what may appear to be purely domestic decisions. So, for example, a government wishing to increase corporate tax rates to help finance social welfare policies has the legal authority to act, but in practice it may well be prevented from doing so for fear that such a decision will result in nationally based multinational corporations transferring investment to other countries that provide more favourable fiscal locations.

The international system has thus become more complex and interconnected. As it has done so, states have come to work much more closely with one another, both in terms of the issues they discuss and negotiate, the mechanisms through which they do business with one another, and the instruments they use to pursue policy goals. Regarding the issues, traditional foreign policy and security issues remain important, but so now are issue areas that used to barely feature on the international agenda, such as the environment and justice and home affairs. Regarding the mechanisms, whereas relations between governments used to be dominated and controlled by national leaders and diplomatic corps, now many branches and layers of government are involved in 'external relations' of some sort. And regarding the policy instruments, policy matters such as trade disputes, sluggish global economic growth, and protection of endangered animal and plant species cannot be tackled by that most traditional policy instrument of larger states, armed force, but rather must rely on international bargaining and compromising.

Another and very important way in which states have reacted to modernisation and interdependence has been via the creation of international organisations. Countless such organisations – each with different memberships, functions, powers, and structures – have been constituted since the Second World War. By way of illustration, the following are just a few of the more important international organisations that have been, and still are, used by European states: global organisations include the United Nations (UN), the International Monetary Fund (IMF), and the World Trade Organisation (WTO); Western-dominated organisations include the Organisation for Economic Co-operation and Development (OECD), the North Atlantic Treaty Organisation (NATO), and the Group of Eight (G8) (though the last of these, which has never been an organisation as such but rather a semi-structured forum for summit and sub-summit level meetings of leading nations, is now seemingly being replaced by the more global Group of Twenty [G20)]); and European organisations include the Council of Europe and the Organisation for Security and Cooperation in Europe (OSCE).

Amongst this array of organisations with which European states have been and continue to be associated, the EU stands out as by far the most important. Within its framework, the transformations in the international system noted above – in issues, mechanisms and policy instruments – have all been developed to an intense degree. This development has made the EU unique amongst international organisations.

The Uniqueness of the European Union

The nature of the EU's uniqueness was explored at length in Chapter 23, but a few key points regarding its uniqueness as compared with other international organisations, including regional organisations, bear further emphasis and development here.

First, the EU is structurally highly complex, with many more institutions, policy actors, and decision-making arrangements and processes than are found in other international organisations. *Regarding the institutions,* there are five 'core' institutions – the Commission, the Council of Ministers, the European Council, the European Parliament, and the Court of Justice of the European Union – and a battery of other institutions, including the European Economic and Social Committee, the Committee of the Regions, and the European Central Bank. The responsibilities and powers of these institutions varies considerably between policy areas, with there being few areas in which there is not a considerable interdependency between at least three of the core institutions. *Regarding the policy actors,* in addition to those associated with the EU's own institutions there are international actors of various sorts plus a host of actors associated with the member states, non-member states, and sectional and promotional interests. *Regarding the decision-making arrangements and processes,* there are nearly thirty distinctive procedures laid down in the treaties, many with their own internal variations.

Second, other international organisations do not have so broad a range of policy responsibilities as the EU. Whereas the EU is involved, to at least some degree, in just about every sphere of public policy, other international and regional organisations tend either to have a very broad focus but with decision-making mechanisms that make it extremely difficult for the potential to be realised – such as the UN and the Council of Europe – or to have a restricted focus – such as the WTO, NATO, and the International Maritime Organisation.

Third, whereas other international and regional organisations are essentially intergovernmental in character, the EU is in many important respects supranational. This supranationalism is seen most particularly in the frequent usage of QMV in the Council of Ministers, in the Commission's wide-ranging executive powers, in the EP's considerable legislative powers, and in the primacy of EU law.

These characteristics do not make the EU a state, but they do make it a highly developed regional organisation and political system.

The Future of the European Union

Factors affecting prospects

Integration in Europe has not evolved in quite the way, or as quickly, as was envisaged by many of the EC's founders. The expectation that policy interests and responsibilities would grow, with achievements in initially selected sectors leading to developments in other sectors, has been partly borne out, but only up to a point, and certainly not consistently. Similarly, the anticipation that the institutions and the political and economic actors of the member states would become progressively entwined with one another has been partially realised, but it has also been partially frustrated – not least because of the continuing reluctance of governments to 'lose control' of particular policy responsibilities and powers. The assumption that the focus of political activities and attentions would switch from national capitals to Europe has happened to an extent, but in many policy areas – particularly those involving heavy government expenditure such as education, health, and social welfare – the national level is still more important than the EU level. And the belief that a European spirit would emerge, based on shared perceptions of a common interest, has proved to be over-optimistic.

There has, in short, been no semi-automatic movement in an integrationist direction. But if integration has not inevitably and of itself led to greater integration, it has certainly stimulated pressure for greater integration. It has done so, for example, by creating 'client groups' – of which, in the EU context, Eurocrats are not the least prominent – that have vested interests in sustaining and extending integration. Integration has also provided an institutional framework into which integrationist pressures, of both an exogenous and an endogenous kind, have been channelled. Among such pressures on the EU today are: the international trade challenge presented by the United States, Japan, and the newly industrialising countries; the transnational character of problem areas such as the environment, energy supply, and terrorism; and the need to respond to the integration that is occurring outside formal EU processes through developments as diverse as industrial mergers, closer cross-border banking and other financial arrangements, and population movements.

How the EU will respond to these and other pressures will depend on a number of factors, the most important of which are perceptions, support and opposition, and leadership.

The importance of *perceptions* is evidenced by the way in which the prospect of progress is considerably enhanced when all of the member states perceive an initiative to be broadly desirable, or at least regard the costs of not proceeding as being too high. Very frequently, of course, there is no such common perception, especially when new types of development are envisaged and/or initiatives have sovereignty or clear distributional implications.

The extent to which key actors are motivated to *support* or *oppose* an initiative depends on many things. Perception of merit is obviously central, but this can be offset by other considerations. For example, a government may fiercely resist a proposal in the Council of Ministers not because it regards it as innately unsound but because acceptance could be electorally damaging or could lead to problems with an important domestic pressure group.

Leadership has long been a weakness of the EU in that there is no strong and central focus of decision-making authority. The Commission, the European Council, and the Council Presidency have long provided the main institutional potential sources of leadership, but their ability to get things done has been subject to limitations. When attempts have been made to provide forceful leadership – by, for example, an informal coalition of states in the European Council and/or the Council of Ministers, by an ambitious Council Presidency, or by a forceful Commission President – there usually has been resistance. But, as well as being a weakness, the dispersed nature of leadership in the EU has also been highly functional in that it has helped to provide for the balance of interests the EU system requires if member states are to have confidence in it.

Perceptions, support and opposition, and leadership are of course not static, but are in constant transition. Since the early to mid-1980s they have undergone significant changes, in ways that have facilitated integrationist developments. The factors accounting for the changes are many and varied, as has been shown at several points in this book. For example, the increasing and inescapable competiveness, interdependence and liberalisation of international economic life have resulted in EU political actors coming to take an increasingly broader view of the required breadth and depth of the internal market programme. Similarly, the collapse of communism in Central and Eastern Europe required a fundamental re-thinking of the EU's enlargement strategy. In such changing situations, some EU political actors have taken advantage of the leadership opportunities that have been provided. So, for instance, the highly dynamic Jacques Delors used his position as Commission President from 1985 to drive forward the opening of the internal market and to lay the foundations of EMU. And the European Commission, working through the European Council, has offered bold leadership on EU enlargement.

But although the integration process continues to move forward, there are still formidable obstacles to further integration. This is no more clearly seen than in the different public positions taken by the governments of the member states on the future shape of the EU. On the one hand, there are those who tend towards a 'maximalist' position – such as the Italians and the Belgians – who are generally enthusiastic about economic, monetary and political union and who do not automatically recoil at the prospect of a federal Europe. On the other hand, there are those who are more cautious – most notably the Danes, the Swedes, the British, and several of the 2004/07 acceding states – who tend to prefer cooperation rather than integration and still make much of the importance of preserving national independence and sovereignty.

Challenges

Of critical importance in determining the future evolution of the EU will be how it handles the many challenges that are facing it. Five challenges feature particularly prominently on the agenda.

Consolidating and extending the eurozone

The launch of the euro clearly marked a major advance in the integration process. Not only do the participating states now share a single currency, but they have ceded national control of monetary policy and have ceded some important controls over macroeconomic policy to central institutions.

Predictions that were made in some quarters that the euro would 'fail' when it faced its first major test –

which turned out to be the global financial crisis and recession that set in during 2008 – proved to be unfounded. However, the financial crisis and recession did highlight problems that can arise when attempting to run a single monetary currency system without having central control of economic policy. Soaring budgetary deficits and public debts in some eurozone states – notably Greece, Portugal and Spain – resulted in early 2010 in the euro coming under intense pressure and eurozone leaders having to issue almost panicky declarations about the solidity of the system.

There are also more general reasons why the euro cannot as yet be judged to have been a success. Growth rates within the eurozone have generally been low, unemployment rates have been high, and the anchor of the euro system – the Stability and Growth Pact – had to be considerably loosened in 2004–5 to accommodate the needs of some states, especially France and Germany, which found it too restrictive. In addition to these 'policy delivery' problems, there have also been institutional difficulties, with the Commission and the Ecofin Council clashing over the SGP and with the ECB clearly disapproving of what it has seen to be the over-lax spending policies of some eurozone states.

The capacity of the euro system to meet the needs of the member states is thus not yet proven. Nor is the ability of the eurozone to accept and absorb the twelve states that joined the EU in 2004/07. All were obliged to become members of the single currency system under the terms of their treaties of accession, but only four – Cyprus, Malta, Slovenia and Slovakia – had joined by early 2010. Moreover, increases in national debts and deficits occasioned by the global recession had resulted in most of the remaining eight being some considerable distance away from meeting the eurozone entry criteria.

Policy development and reform

As was shown in Part IV of the book, EU policies are in constant evolution. In recent years this has been demonstrated with, for example, the shift of the CAP from being a price support system to an income support system, the movement of JHA policies into the EU 'mainstream', and the development of an embryonic external security policy capability.

Many factors fuel debate on and force the pace of policy development and policy reform. Some of the

---

Box 24.1

Factors that are likely to be especially significant in driving foreseeable future EU policy developments

- Europe's continuing lack of relative competitiveness, especially in high-tech and 'knowledge-based' industries.
- Deliberations on the post-2014 financial framework.
- The EU's increasing dependence on the Middle East and Russia for energy supplies.
- Climate change and the need for stronger energy conservation and clean energy policies.
- Demographic trends, and in particular Europe's ageing population.
- Dissatisfaction in some member states with the EU's (continuing) limited political influence in the world.
- The implications for the CFSP and CSDP of: the tensions and security uncertainties on Europe's fringes; pressures from the USA for Europe to make a greater military contribution to international, and especially European, security; the willingness of member states to concentrate their foreign and defence policy activities in an EU framework.
- The growing international muscle of the 'emerging' powers, not least the BRICs (Brazil, Russia, India, China).
- Increasing attempted migratory movements of peoples (especially from the south and the east) to the EU.
- The continuing international terrorist threat and its implications for EU internal and external security policies.

---

factors that are likely to be particular important in the next few years are identified in Box 24.1.

But, of course, different interests and choices between the EU's policy actors will ensure that deliberations on many of the policy challenges facing the EU will be difficult. EU political dynamics are favoured by the fact that many of the policy differences between the member states are cross-cutting rather than cumulative – thus ensuring that the large states do not consistently dominate and also that no state or states are continually in a minority and thus permanently aggrieved. But that does not mean that some of the differences are not significant and capable of threatening policy development. For example, differences between those who take a 'liberal' and a 'social market' view of economic policy may be exaggerated, but they certainly exist and make coordinated and coherent EU-wide macroeconomic and social policy development difficult.

Managing flexibility

In response to the different requirements and propensities of the member states, the EC/EU has long provided for a limited flexibility and diversity in its structures and policies. When 'standard' methods have been judged as inappropriate or over-rigid, inter-state relations have taken other forms. For example, European Political Cooperation was developed from the early 1970s alongside but outside the formal Community structures. This was taken a stage further in the Maastricht Treaty when the three pillar structure was established.

Since the mid-to-late 1990s the increasing use of new modes of governance has further increased flexibility within the EU. The 'new governance', which has impacted widely on Western public policy and administration, has a number of dimensions. One is the 'outsourcing' of public policy functions to agencies that are not fully part of the central administrative system. European agencies such as the European Medicines Agency, the European Environmental Agency, and the European Food Safety Authority are of this sort. The powers and roles of the EU's agencies vary, but most are focused primarily on information gathering and making policy recommendations.

Another dimension of the new governance involves public policy and administration placing less emphasis on traditional, 'top-down', legislation-based forms of operation and more emphasis on flexible, often network-based, and frequently semi-voluntary forms of policy development and practice. In the EU context, use of this approach is seen in the open method of coordination (OMC), which has been used particularly in social and employment policy-related areas. OMC involves a relatively loose form of policy activity, based essentially on the identification of policy targets that member states are pressurised – but are not compelled – to meet by benchmarking and peer review.

A particularly important form of flexibility in the EU is differentiation: that is, policy development and activity in which not all member states are involved. The European Monetary System which was developed from the late-1970s on a partial membership basis, was the first instance of differentiation. It was followed by the development of the Schengen System from the mid-1980s. Differentiation was then given treaty authorisation by the Maastricht Treaty, which identified EMU and the social dimension as policy areas that could be developed without the participation of the full complement of EU states. The Amsterdam Treaty generalised the Maastricht 'dispensation' by providing for 'Provisions on Closer Cooperation', which authorised a majority of member states to develop a policy within the Community framework, subject to conditions. The Nice Treaty then made closer cooperation – which it re-named 'enhanced cooperation' – easier to operationalise by reducing the stipulation that a majority of member states must be involved in an initiative to a stipulation that only eight need be so. With enlargement in May 2004, the proportion of participating member states was thus reduced from over one-half to less than one-third. The Lisbon Treaty increased the number of participating states from eight to nine, but this still left the minimum proportion at just one third – a proportion that will reduce if this number is left intact when future enlargements occur.

In addition to, and more important than, its tinkering with the enhanced cooperation provisions, the Lisbon Treaty considerably widened the treaty base of internal flexibility by including new opt-ins and opt-outs for some states in significant areas of EU activity. So, the UK and Ireland were given the right to choose whether or not they wish to be involved in policies that are designed to strengthen the area of freedom, security and justice. And in a protocol attached to the Treaty, the UK and Poland, later joined by the Czech Republic, were assured that the Charter of Fundamental Rights would create no new rights for their citizens.

Flexibility in various forms has thus become an accepted part of the EU system. It has done so as enlargement and as the expanding policy portfolio have combined to make it increasingly unlikely that all member states will wish to, or will have the capacity to, swim abreast. But, increasing flexibility raises fundamental questions about the nature of the EU. If the EU is to continue to narrow the base of the required *acquis* – that is, the common core that all member states must accept – how far can it go without undermining the Union's very essence? Indeed, is flexibility not raising questions about just what it means to be an EU member state?

Making the Lisbon Treaty work

The Lisbon Treaty mostly disappointed those who would like to see the European integration process further significantly deepened. When set against the high hopes that pro-integrationists initially had for the Constitutional Treaty, the Lisbon Treaty is too routine and modest in character. It is, in essence, another amending treaty in the tradition of all of the EC/EU's revising treaties since the SEA.

But although the Lisbon Treaty is not the document many had hoped to see, it does nonetheless contain, as was shown in Chapter 6, many important changes and provisions. Amongst the more important of these changes and provisions are: the creation of the new posts of European Council President and High Representative of the Union for Foreign Affairs and Security Policy; the creation of the European External Action Service; the incorporation of that part of JHA which had been in the separate third pillar fully into the EU mainstream; the extensions of the availability of QMV in the Council to new policy areas; the strengthening of the powers of the EP – especially in respect of law-making and budget-making; the consolidation of the legal base of the Charter of Fundamental Rights; and, as just noted above, the increased provisions for policy development with not all member states involved.

Doubtless, most of these changes will be absorbed without too much difficulty, as have most of the changes made by previous treaties. But some of the changes will involve considerable adjustments having to be made by EU political actors, and in some cases this may create difficulties. Perhaps the changes presenting the greatest potential difficulties are in respect of the new posts of European Council President and High Representative. The posts were created to address the problem of the EU's so-called leadership deficit, but there is the possibility that they could make the situation even worse by making the field of potential EU leaders even more crowded and complex.

Enlargement

EU enlargement is an ongoing process rather than a series of discrete steps or stages. Since the early 1970s there has never been a time when the EU has not been engaged in some combination of considering membership applications, conducting accession negotiations, and fitting in new member states to EU processes and policies.

There is every reason to assume that this challenge of enlargement will continue into the foreseeable future: the full assimilation of the Central and Eastern European countries that became EU members in 2004/07 will not be completed for some considerable time; in October 2005 the EU opened accession negotiations with Croatia and Turkey; Macedonia, Albania, Montenegro, Serbia and Iceland all have applications on the table at the time of writing; applicants from the remaining Western Balkan states are anticipated; and some former Soviet states, including the Ukraine and Moldova, harbour hopes of eventual membership.

A central problem for the EU in permitting the enlargement process to continue is that it is adding to the EU's diversity. Apart from the special cases of Iceland, Norway and Switzerland, all of the states that could be 'easily' fitted into the EU are now in. As the EU extends further to the east and south east it is inevitably increasingly dealing with countries whose political traditions, economic circumstances, and cultural inheritance are significantly 'different'. Fundamental questions are thus raised about the EU's absorption capacity. They are questions that can only be answered in terms of what sort of EU is envisaged and desired.

Chronology of Main Events in the European Integration Process

1947	March	Belgium, Luxembourg and the Netherlands agree to establish a customs union. Subsequently an economic union is established in October 1947 and a common customs tariff is introduced in January 1948.
	March	France and the United Kingdom sign a military alliance, the Treaty of Dunkirk.
	June	General George Marshall, United States Secretary of State, offers US aid for the economic recovery of Europe.
	September	Sixteen nations join the European Recovery Programme.
1948	March	Brussels Treaty concluded between France, the UK and the Benelux states. The aim is to promote collective defence and improve cooperation in the economic, social and cultural fields.
	April	Founding of the Organisation for European Economic Cooperation (OEEC) by sixteen states.
	May	A Congress is held in The Hague, attended by many leading supporters of European cooperation and integration. It issues a resolution asserting 'that it is the urgent duty of the nations of Europe to create an economic and political union in order to assure security and social progress'.
1949	April	Treaty establishing North Atlantic Treaty Organisation (NATO) signed in Washington by twelve states.
	May	Statute of Council of Europe signed in Strasbourg by ten states.
1950	May	Robert Schuman, the French Foreign Minister, puts forward his proposals to place French and German coal and steel under a common authority. He declares 'it is no longer the moment for vain words, but for a bold act – a constructive act'.
	October	René Pleven, the French Prime Minister, proposes a European Defence Community (EDC).
1951	April	European Coal and Steel Community (ECSC) Treaty signed in Paris by six states: Belgium, France, West Germany, Italy, Luxembourg and the Netherlands.
1952	May	EDC Treaty signed in Paris by the six ECSC states.
	July	ECSC comes into operation.
1954	August	French National Assembly rejects EDC Treaty.
	October	WEU Treaty signed by the six ECSC states plus the UK.
1955	June	Messina Conference of the Foreign Ministers of the six ECSC states to discuss further European integration. Spaak Committee established to study ways in which a fresh advance towards the building of Europe could be achieved.
1956	June	Negotiations formally open between the six with a view to creating an Economic Community and an Atomic Energy Community.

1957	March	The Treaties of Rome signed, establishing the European Economic Community (EEC) and the European Atomic Energy Community (Euratom).
1958	January	EEC and Euratom come into operation.
1959	January	First EEC tariff cuts and increases in quotas.
1960	January	European Free Trade Association (EFTA) Convention signed in Stockholm by Austria, Denmark, Norway, Portugal, Sweden, Switzerland and the UK. EFTA comes into force in May 1960.
	December	Organisation for Economic Cooperation and Development (OECD) Treaty signed in Paris. OECD replaces OEEC and includes Canada and the United States.
1961	July	Signing of Association Agreement between Greece and the EEC. The Agreement comes into effect November 1962.
	July–August	Ireland, Denmark and UK request membership negotiations with the Community.
1962	January	Basic features of Common Agricultural Policy (CAP) agreed.
	July	Norway requests negotiations on Community membership.
1963	January	General de Gaulle announces his veto on UK membership.
	January	Signing of Franco-German Treaty of Friendship and Cooperation.
	July	A wide-ranging association agreement is signed between the Community and 18 under-developed countries in Africa – the Yaoundé Convention, which enters into force in June 1964.
1964	May	The GATT Kennedy Round of international tariff negotiations opens in Geneva. The Community states participate as a single delegation.
1965	April	Signing of Treaty Establishing a Single Council and a Single Commission of the European Communities (The Merger Treaty).
	July	France begins a boycott of Community institutions to register its opposition to various proposed supranational developments.
1966	January	Foreign Ministers agree to the Luxembourg Compromise. Normal Community processes are resumed.
1967	May	Denmark, Ireland and the UK re-apply for Community membership.
	July	1965 Merger Treaty takes effect.
	July	Norway re-applies for Community membership.
	December	The Council of Ministers fails to reach agreement on the re-opening of membership negotiations with the applicant states because of continued French opposition to UK membership.
1968	July	The Customs Union is completed. All internal customs duties and quotas are removed and the common external tariff is established.
1969	July	President Pompidou (who succeeded de Gaulle after his resignation in April) announces he does not oppose UK membership in principle.
	July	Signing of the second Yaoundé Convention. Enters into force in January 1971.
	December	Hague summit agrees on a number of important matters: strengthening the Community institutions, enlargement, establishing an economic and monetary union by 1980, and developing political cooperation (i.e. foreign policy).

1970	April	The financial base of the Community is changed by the Decision of 21 April 1970 on the Replacement of Financial Contributions From Member States by the Communities' Own Resources. The Community's budgetary procedures are regularised and the European Parliament's budgetary powers are increased by the Treaty Amending Certain Budgetary Provisions of the Treaties.
	June	Preferential trade agreement signed between the Community and Spain. Comes into effect in October 1970.
	June	Community opens membership negotiations with Denmark, Ireland, Norway and the UK.
	October	The six accept the Davignon report on political cooperation. This provides the basis for cooperation on foreign policy matters.
1972	January	Negotiations between the Community and the four applicant countries concluded. Signing of treaties of accession.
	May	Irish approve Community accession in a referendum.
	July	Conclusion of Special Relations Agreement between Community and EFTA countries.
	September	Majority vote against Community accession in a referendum in Norway.
	October	Danes approve Community accession in a referendum.
	October	Paris summit. Heads of Government set guidelines for the future, including reaffirmation of the goal of achieving economic and monetary union by 1980.
1973	January	Accession of Denmark, Ireland and the UK to the Community.
	January	Preferential trade agreement between the Community and most EFTA countries comes into effect. Agreements with other EFTA countries come into force later.
1974	December	Paris summit agrees to the principle of direct elections to the EP and to the details of a European Regional Development Fund (ERDF) (the establishment of which had been agreed at the 1972 Paris and 1973 Copenhagen summits). It is also agreed to institutionalise summit meetings by establishing the European Council.
1975	February	Signing of the first Lomé Convention between the Community and 46 underdeveloped countries in Africa, the Caribbean and the Pacific (the ACP states). The Convention replaces and extends the Yaoundé Convention.
	March	First meeting of the European Council in Dublin.
	June	A majority vote in favour of continued Community membership in UK referendum.
	June	Greece applies for Community membership.
	July	Signing of the Treaty Amending Certain Financial Provisions of the Treaties. This strengthens the European Parliament's budgetary powers and also establishes the Court of Auditors.
1976	July	Opening of negotiations on Greek accession to the Community.
1977	March	Portugal applies for Community membership.
	July	Spain applies for Community membership.
1978	October	Community opens accession negotiations with Portugal.
1979	February	Community opens accession negotiations with Spain.
	March	European Monetary System (EMS) (which had been the subject of high-level negotiations for over a year) comes into operation.
	May	Signing of Accession Treaty between Community and Greece.
	June	First direct elections to the EP.

	October	Signing of the second Lomé Convention between the Community and 58 ACP states.
	December	For the first time the EP does not approve the Community budget. As a result the Community has to operate on the basis of 'one-twelfths' from 1 January 1980.
1981	January	Accession of Greece to Community.
	October	Community Foreign Ministers reach agreement on the London Report, which strengthens and extends European Political Cooperation (EPC).
1983	January	Common Fisheries Policy (CFP) agreed.
	June	At the Stuttgart European Council meeting approval is given to a 'Solemn Declaration on European Union'.
1984	January	Free trade area between Community and EFTA established.
	February	The EP approves The Draft Treaty Establishing the European Union.
	June	Second set of direct elections to the EP.
	June	Fontainebleau European Council meeting. Agreement to reduce UK budgetary contributions (which Margaret Thatcher had been demanding since 1979) and agreement to increase Community resources by raising the VAT ceiling from 1 per cent to 1.4 per cent.
	December	Signing of the third Lomé Convention between the Community and 66 ACP countries.
	December	Dublin European Council meeting agrees budgetary discipline measures.
1985	June	Signing of accession treaties between the Community and Spain and Portugal.
	June	The Commission publishes its White Paper Completing the Internal Market.
	June	Milan European Council meeting approves the Commission's White Paper. It also establishes an Intergovernmental Conference to examine various matters, including treaty reform. The decision to establish the Conference is the first time at a summit meeting that a decision is taken by a majority vote.
	December	Luxembourg European Council meeting agrees to the principles of the Single European Act (SEA). Amongst other things the Act incorporates various treaty revisions and confirms the objective of completing the internal market by 1992.
1986	January	Accession of Spain and Portugal to Community.
1987	June	Turkey applies for Community membership.
	July	After several months delay caused by ratification problems in Ireland, the SEA comes into force.
1988	February	A special European Council meeting in Brussels agrees to increase and widen the Community's budgetary base. Measures are also agreed to significantly reduce expenditure on the CAP and to double expenditure on the regional and social funds.
	June	The Community and Comecon (the East European trading bloc) sign an agreement enabling the two organisations to recognise each other. As part of the agreement the Comecon states officially recognise, for the first time, the authority of the Community to negotiate on behalf of its member states.
	June	Hanover European Council meeting entrusts to a committee chaired by Jacques Delors the task of studying how the Community might progress to Economic and Monetary Union (EMU).
1989	April	The 'Delors Committee' presents its report (the Delors Report). It outlines a scheme for a three-stage progression to EMU.
	June	Third set of direct elections to the EP.
	June	Madrid European Council meeting agrees that Stage 1 of the programme to bring about EMU will begin on 1 July 1990.

	July	Austria applies for Community membership.
	September–December	The collapse of communist governments in Eastern Europe. The process 'begins' with the appointment of a non-communist Prime Minister in Poland in September and 'ends' with the overthrow of the Ceausescu regime in Romania in December.
	December	Signing of the fourth Lomé Convention between the Community and 68 ACP countries.
	December	Community and USSR sign a ten-year trade and economic cooperation agreement.
	December	Commission advises Council of Ministers to reject Turkey's application for Community membership.
	December	Strasbourg European Council meeting accepts Social Charter and agrees to establish an Intergovernmental Conference (IGC) on EMU at the end of 1990. Both decisions taken by eleven votes to one, with the UK dissenting in each case.
1990	April	Special Dublin European Council meeting confirms the Community's commitment to political union.
	June	Dublin European Council meeting formally agrees that an IGC on Political Union will be convened.
	July	Cyprus and Malta apply for Community membership.
	October	Unification of Germany. Territory of former East Germany becomes part of the Community.
	October	Special Rome European Council meeting agrees that Stage 2 of EMU will begin on 1 January 1994.
	December	The two IGCs on EMU and on Political Union are opened at the Rome summit.
1991	July	Sweden applies for Community membership.
	August–December	Break-up of the USSR.
	December	The Maastricht Treaty is agreed by the European Council. The Treaty is based on three pillars: the European Communities, a Common Foreign and Security Policy (CFSP), and Cooperation in the Fields of Justice and Home Affairs (JHA). The European Communities pillar includes the strengthening of Community institutions, the extension of the Community's legal policy competence, and a timetable for the establishment of EMU and a single currency.
	December	Association ('Europe') Agreements signed with Czechoslovakia, Hungary, and Poland.
1992	February	The Maastricht Treaty is formally signed by Foreign and Finance Ministers.
	March	Finland applies to join the EU.
	May	After several months' delay caused by a Court of Justice ruling, the EEA agreement between the EC and EFTA is signed.
	May	Switzerland applies to join the EC.
	June	In a referendum the Danish people reject the Maastricht Treaty by 50.7 per cent to 49.3 per cent.
	September	Crisis in the ERM. Sterling and the lira suspend their membership.
	September	In a referendum the French people endorse the Maastricht Treaty by 51 per cent to 49 per cent.
	November	Norway applies to join the EU.
	December	In a referendum the Swiss people vote not to ratify the EEA by 50.3 per cent to 49.7 per cent. Amongst other implications this means that Switzerland's application to join the EU is suspended.

	December	Edinburgh European Council meeting agrees on several key issues, notably: (1) Danish opt-outs from the TEU and any future common defence policy; (2) a financial perspective for 1993–9; and (3) the opening of accession negotiations in early 1993 with Austria, Finland, Sweden and Norway.
1993	February	Accession negotiations open with Austria, Finland, and Sweden.
	April	Accession negotiations open with Norway.
	May	In a second referendum the Danish people vote by 56.8 per cent to 43.2 per cent to ratify the Maastricht Treaty
	June	Copenhagen European Council. It is agreed that CEECs wishing to become members of the EU shall do so once they meet specified economic and political conditions (the Copenhagen criteria).
	August	Following great turbulence in the currency markets, the bands for all currencies in the ERM, apart from the deutschmark and the guilder, are increased to 15 per cent.
	October	German Constitutional Court ruling enables Germany to become the last member state to ratify the TEU.
	November	TEU enters into force.
	December	Settlement of the GATT Uruguay Round.
1994	January	Second stage of EMU comes into effect.
	January	EEA enters into force.
	March	Committee of the Regions meets for the first time.
	March	Austria, Finland, Sweden, and Norway agree accession terms with the EU.
	April	Hungary and Poland apply for membership of the EU.
	June	Fourth set of direct elections to the EP.
	June	In a referendum on accession to the EU, the Austrian people vote in favour by 66.4 per cent to 33.6 per cent.
	June	Corfu European Council. The UK vetoes Belgian Prime Minister, Jean-Luc Dehaene, as the new Commission President.
	July	Jacques Santer, the Luxembourg Prime Minister, nominated as the new Commission President at a special half-day European Council meeting in Brussels.
	October	Referendum in Finland on EU membership. The people vote in favour by 57 per cent to 43 per cent.
	November	Referendum in Sweden on EU membership. The people vote in favour by 52.2 per cent to 46.9 per cent.
	November	Referendum in Norway on EU membership. The people reject accession by 52.2 per cent to 47.8 per cent.
1995	January	Austria, Finland and Sweden become EU members.
	January	EP votes to confirm the Santer Commission: 418 votes in favour, 103 against, and 59 abstentions. The Commission is subsequently formally appointed by the representatives of the member states.
	March	Schengen Accord implemented by seven EU member states: Germany, France, Belgium, Luxembourg, the Netherlands, Spain, and Portugal.
	June	Romania and Slovakia apply to join the EU.
	October	Latvia applies to join the EU.
	November	Estonia applies to join the EU.
	December	Lithuania and Bulgaria apply to join the EU.
1996	January	The Czech Republic and Slovenia apply to join the EU.
	March	The IGC provided for in the Maastricht Treaty is formally opened at a special Heads of Government summit in Turin.

	May	The UK government announces a policy of non-cooperation with EU decision-making following a Council of Ministers decision not to agree to a timetable for the lifting of the export ban on UK beef products.
	June	A formula for ending the UK's non-cooperation policy agreed at the Florence European Council.
1997	June	Amsterdam European Council agrees to the Treaty of Amsterdam. The Treaty fails to provide for the institutional change that enlargement will require, but does contain some strengthening of EU institutions and policies.
	July	Commission issues its *Agenda 2000* programme, which contains recommendations on how enlargement to the CEECs should be handled and how EU policies – especially the CAP and the Structural Funds – should be reformed.
	October	Amsterdam Treaty formally signed by EU Foreign Ministers.
1998	March	Accession negotiations formally opened with Hungary, Poland, the Czech Republic, Slovenia, Estonia and Cyprus.
	May	At a special European Council meeting in Brussels it is agreed that eleven states will participate when the euro is launched in 1999: France, Germany, Italy, Belgium, Luxembourg, the Netherlands, Ireland, Spain, Portugal, Finland and Austria.
	May	Denmark and Ireland hold referenda in which the Treaty of Amsterdam is approved.
1999	January	Stage 3 of EMU and the euro come into operation, with eleven of the EU's fifteen states participating. The non-participants are Denmark, Greece, Sweden and the UK.
	March	The College of Commissioners resigns following the publication of a highly critical report by the Committee of Independent Experts.
	March	At a special European Council meeting in Berlin, the Heads of Government reach agreement on Agenda 2000 measures. The measures include a financial perspective for 2000–6, and CAP and Structural Fund reforms. It is also agreed to nominate Romano Prodi, the former Italian Prime Minister, to succeed Jacques Santer as Commission President.
	May	Treaty of Amsterdam enters into force.
	May	EP endorses Romano Prodi as Commission President-designate by 392 votes to 72, with 41 abstentions.
	June	Fifth set of direct elections to the EP.
	September	Prodi Commission assumes office after the EP endorses it by 414 votes to 142, with 35 abstentions.
	December	Helsinki European Council meeting takes key decisions on EU enlargement. These include that negotiations will be opened in early 2000 with six more applicant states and that Turkey will be viewed as having candidate status. The summit also decides that the EU will establish a Rapid Reaction Force, 50,000–60,000 strong, by 2003.
2000	February	The IGC provided for in a protocol attached to the Amsterdam Treaty is opened.
	February	Accession negotiations are opened with Latvia, Lithuania, Bulgaria, Slovakia, Romania, and Malta.
	June	The Cotonou Agreement, a twenty-year Partnership Agreement replacing the Lomé Convention, is signed by the EU and 77 ACP countries.
	September	In a referendum the Danish people reject membership of the euro by 53.1 per cent to 46.9 per cent.
	December	Nice European Council agrees to the Treaty of Nice. The Treaty consists mainly of a range of institutional reforms designed to prepare the EU for enlargement.

2001	January	Greece becomes a member of the eurozone.
	February	Treaty of Nice is formally signed by EU Foreign Ministers.
	June	In a referendum, the Irish people reject the Treaty of Nice by 54 per cent to 46 per cent on a low 35 per cent turnout.
2002	January	Euro coins and notes come into circulation and the national currencies of the twelve euroland countries are phased out.
	March	The Convention on the Future of Europe opens under the chairmanship of Valery Giscard d'Estaing.
	October	In a referendum the Irish people approve the Treaty of Nice by 63 per cent to 37 per cent on a 48 per cent turnout.
	December	Copenhagen European Council meeting takes key decisions on enlargement. These include: ten states (Cyprus, the Czech Republic, Estonia, Hungary, Latvia, Lithuania, Malta, Poland, Slovakia, and Slovenia) are deemed to have completed accession negotiations and will join the EU on 1 May 2004 subject to ratification procedures having been completed; Bulgaria and Romania will be able to join the EU in 2007 if they make satisfactory progress in complying with the membership criteria; the December 2004 summit will authorise the immediate opening of accession negotiations with Turkey if the Commission makes a recommendation to this effect based on Turkey having continued with its reform process.
2003	February	The Treaty of Nice enters into force. Croatia applies to join the EU.
	March	In the first referendum to be held in the '2004 enlargement' round, the Maltese people vote to join the EU by 53.6 per cent to 46.4 per cent on a 91 per cent turnout.
	April	In a referendum, the Slovenian people vote to join the EU by 89.6 per cent to 10.4 per cent on a 60.3 per cent turnout.
	April	The Treaty of Accession is signed in Athens by representatives of the EU-15 and the 10 applicant states with which negotiations have been completed.
	April	In a referendum, the Hungarian people vote to join the EU by 84.0 per cent to 16.0 per cent on a 45.6 per cent turnout.
	May	In a referendum, the Lithuanian people vote to join the EU by 91.0 per cent to 9.0 per cent on a 63.4 per cent turnout.
	May	In a referendum, the Slovak people vote to join the EU by 92.5 per cent to 6.2 per cent on a 52.1 per cent turnout.
	June	The Convention on the Future of Europe agrees on the contents of the Draft Treaty Establishing a Constitution for Europe.
	June	In a referendum, the Polish people vote to join the EU by 77.5 per cent to 22.5 per cent on a 58.8 per cent turnout.
	June	In a referendum, the Czech people vote to join the EU by 77.3 per cent to 23.7 per cent on a 55.2 per cent turnout.
	July	The Cypriot House of Representatives votes unanimously to approve Cyprus's Treaty of Accession to the EU. (Of the ten states to sign the April 2003 Accession Treaty, Cyprus is the only one not to hold a referendum.)
	September	In a referendum, the Estonian people vote to join the EU by 66.8 per cent to 32.2 per cent on a 64.0 per cent turnout.
	September	In a referendum, the Latvian people vote to join the EU by 67.0 per cent to 32.3 per cent on a 72.5 per cent turnout.
	September	In a referendum, the Swedish people vote against membership of the euro by 56.1 per cent to 41.8 per cent on an 81.2 per cent turnout.
	October	The IGC charged with negotiating a Constitutional Treaty is opened.

	December	The Brussels European Council meeting fails to agree on the contents of the Constitutional Treaty and the IGC is suspended.
2004	March	Macedonia applies to join the EU.
	March	The Brussels European Council meeting decides to re-start the IGC, with a view to the Constitutional Treaty being agreed at the June European Council.
	May	Ten countries become members of the EU: Cyprus, the Czech Republic, Estonia, Hungary, Latvia, Lithuania, Malta, Poland, Slovakia and Slovenia.
	June	Sixth set of direct elections to the EP.
	June	The European Council agrees on the contents of the Constitutional Treaty.
	June	At a special meeting of the European Council it is agreed that Portuguese Prime Minister, José Manuel Barroso, will be nominated to be President of the European Commission.
	July	José Manuel Barroso is approved by the EP by 413 votes to 251.
	October	Barroso withdraws his College-designate from the process of EP approval so as to avoid the possibility of rejection. Following two personnel changes and other portfolio changes the EP gives its approval to the Barroso College by 449 votes to 149, with 82 abstentions.
	October	The leaders of the EU's member states sign the Constitutional Treaty in Rome.
	December	The European Council agrees that accession negotiations should be opened with Croatia in March 2005 and with Turkey in October 2005, provided certain conditions are met.
2005	March	The Spanish people vote in a referendum to ratify the Constitutional Treaty by 76.7 per cent to 23.3 per cent on a 42.3 per cent turnout.
	May	The French people vote in a referendum not to ratify the Constitutional Treaty by 54.9 per cent to 45.1 per cent on a 69.7 per cent turnout.
	June	The Dutch people vote in a referendum not to ratify the Constitutional Treaty by 61.7 per cent to 38.3 per cent on a 63 per cent turnout.
	July	The Luxembourg people vote in a referendum to ratify the Constitutional Treaty by 56.5 per cent to 43.5 per cent on a 90.5 per cent turnout.
	October	The EU opens accession negotiations with Turkey and Croatia.
	December	The European Council agrees on the contents of the 2007–13 financial perspective.
2007	January	Bulgaria and Romania become members of the EU.
	January	Slovenia becomes a member of the eurozone.
	December	The Treaty of Lisbon is formally signed.
2008	January	Cyprus and Malta become members of the eurozone
	June	In a referendum, the Irish people reject the Treaty of Lisbon by 53.6 per cent to 46.4 per cent on a 53.1 per cent turnout.
	December	Montenegro applies for EU membership.
2009	January	Slovakia becomes a member of the eurozone.
	April	Albania applies for EU membership.
	July	Iceland applies for EU membership.
	October	In a referendum, the Irish people endorse the Treaty of Lisbon by 67.1 per cent to 32.9 per cent on a 58 per cent turnout.
	November	The Czech President, Vaclav Klaus, completes the ratification process of the Lisbon Treaty by putting his signature to it.
	December	The Lisbon Treaty enters into force.
	December	Serbia applies for EU membership.
2010	February	The EP gives its approval to the Barroso II College, by 488 votes to 137, with 72 abstentions.

Guide to Further Reading

Official European Union Sources

The EU issues a vast amount of material, most of which is available in paper and electronic forms. Paper copies are usually published by the Office for Official Publications of the European Union (EUR-OP). Electronic copies are usually accessible via the EU's website, Europa, the URL of which is < www.europa.eu >

The treaties should naturally be consulted by all those who wish to understand the nature and functioning of the EU. They have been published in several editions by, amongst others, EUR-OP and Sweet & Maxwell, and are also available on the Europa website.

The *Official Journal of the European Union (OJ)* is issued on most weekdays and provides an authoritative record of decisions and activities of various kinds. It consists of two series. The 'L' (Legislation) series is the vehicle for the publication of EU legislation. The 'C' (Information and Notices) series contains a range of information, including minutes of EP plenary proceedings and resolutions adopted by plenaries, EESC opinions, Court of Auditors reports, Court judgments, Commission communications and notices, and Commission proposals for Council legislation. There is also a supplementary 'S' series which is mainly concerned with public contract and tendering announcements. An index to the 'L' and 'C' series of the *OJ* is available in monthly and annual editions.

The monthly *Bulletin of the European Union* provides a general account of most significant developments. Some of the information contained amounts to a summary of material included in the *OJ* (with appropriate references). Much else is additional: there are, for example, reports – albeit rather brief ones – of Council of Ministers meetings, updates on policy developments, a monitoring of progress in the annual budgetary cycle, and information on initiatives, meetings and agreements in the sphere of external relations.

The General Report on the Activities of the European Union is published annually and provides an excellent summary of both institutional and policy developments. Where necessary it can be supplemented by the annual reports published by most of the institutions.

Information about the annual budget is available in the *Bulletin* and in the *General Report*. The full budget, which runs to about 1,800 pages of text, is published in the *OJ* (L series) about one month after it has been approved by the EP. A useful publication is *The Community Budget: the Facts in Figures*, which usually appears on an annual basis.

The most detailed analysis of and information on EU policies is usually to be found in documents produced by the Commission. Leaving aside one-off publications, these appear in three main forms. First, serialised reports are issued on a regular basis and cover just about every aspect of EU affairs. As an indication of the sort of reports that are produced, four might be mentioned: *European*

Economy covers economic trends and proposals and is issued quarterly, with monthly supplements; *Social Europe* provides information on the many facets of social and employment policy and is issued three times a year; *Eurobarometer* reports on public opinion in the EU, with standard editions appearing in the spring and the autumn and around twenty special editions being issued annually; and the *Agricultural Situation in the Community* is an annual report. Second, an enormous volume of information is issued by the Statistical Office – known as Eurostat – on matters ranging from energy consumption patterns to agricultural prices. Useful general publications from Eurostat include *Europe in Figures* and *Eurostat Yearbook*. Third, there are Commission documents (COMDOCS), which cover many matters including programme reports, policy reviews and, most importantly, proposals for legislation.

Useful material stemming from other EU institutions on a regular basis includes: *Reports, Dossiers,* and *Research Documents* of the EP; the monthly *Bulletin of the EESC*; and *Reports of Cases Before the Court*.

National Government Sources

The governments of the member states produce a considerable volume of documentation on the EU. The precise nature of this material varies, but it mostly consists of a mixture of 'state of play' reports, reports from relevant parliamentary committees, and information pamphlets/booklets/packs. Because many of the latter are intended to stimulate a greater public awareness of the EU, or are designed to encourage business to take advantage of EU policies, hard copies are often available free of charge.

The Foreign Offices of all member states have websites with useful information on the EU.

Periodicals, Newspapers and Journals

A daily bulletin of events is provided in *Europe* – commonly known as *Agence Europe* – which is published by Agence Internationale D'Information Pour La Presse. *European Report*, published by Europe Information Service, provides a similar service.

European Voice, published by the Economist Group, is an excellent weekly newspaper on the EU.

EUobserver provides an extremely useful daily report on issues currently concerning the EU. It is available online at < www.EUobserver.com >

In most member states the 'quality' press provides a reasonable review of EU affairs. In the United Kingdom the most comprehensive coverage is provided by the *Financial Times*.

Academic articles on the EU are to be found in a number of places. Particularly useful academic journals include *Journal of Common Market Studies, Journal of European Public Policy, Journal of European Integration, European Union Politics, Current Politics and Economics of Europe, European Foreign Affairs Review, Common Market Law Review,* and *European Law Review*.

The JCMS Annual Review of the Union is very useful for monitoring each year's developments. It is published by Blackwell and also appears (in the autumn) as a special issue of the *Journal of Common Market Studies*.

Web Sources

An enormous amount of information about European integration and the EU is available on the web. Attention here is directed to a few of the most useful websites, most of which are gateway sites in that they provide links to more specialised sites. All the sites listed have free access.

As was noted above, the Europa website is immensely valuable for accessing official EU information. It provides links to an enormous number of webpages covering EU institutions, policies, documentation and developments. The many different webpages on Europa can be accessed either by logging on to the Europa site and then following links or by accessing webpages directly. So, for example, the URL of EUR-Lex, which gives access to the full text of EU legislation and to the latest editions of the *Official Journal*, is < www.europa.eu.int/eur-lex/ >

Other EU sites well worth visiting include those of the European Commission offices around the world. The site of the Commission's Delegation to the USA, for example, is quite excellent. It is at < www.eurunion.org >

Non-EU websites that cover all aspects of the EU and provide numerous links to other sites include:

- *Europe Sources Online* provides a wide variety of information on the EU and Europe at < www.europeansources.info >
- *The Archive of European Integration,* is a repository of research materials and articles on European integration at < http://aei.pitt.edu >

Online academic papers on European integration, based on several series of research papers, can be accessed at <eiop.or.at/erpa/ >

Two prominent academic associations with helpful websites are:

- The European Union Studies Association at < www.eustudies.org >
- The University Association for Contemporary European Studies at < www.uaces.org >

Finally, Palgrave Macmillan has its own EU web page for this book and other books in the European Union Series. The page provides updating information on important developments and also links to other internet sites on the EU. The URL is < www.palgrave.com/politics/eu/ >

Books

The number of books published on the EU is now voluminous. Only a brief indication of what is available is attempted here, with references being confined to books in English and with preference being given to recent publications.

The titles listed are grouped into very broad sections. The boundaries between the sections are far from watertight.

General books on the government and politics of the EU

McCormick (2008), Bomberg *et al.* (2008), Cini (2007), Ginsberg (2010), Bache and George (2006), Magnette (2005), and Dinan (2005) are all good introductory texts.

Green Cowles and Dinan (2004) and Richardson (2006) are valuable for those who are already familiar with 'the basics'.

Cini and Bourne (2006), Jørgenson *et al.* (2006) and Egan *et al.* (2010) provide advanced overviews (the books are decidedly not introductions) to key issues and debates in EU studies.

The historical evolution

Dinan (2004) provides a highly informed and readable account of the integration process since the Second World War. Stirk (1996) examines the integration process since 1914 and Urwin (1995) does so from 1945. Dinan (2006) includes interesting essays on selected topics.

It is always helpful to consult primary sources and an easy way of doing this is through readers. The following are all useful: Giustino (1996), Harryvan and van der Harst (1997), Salmon and Nicoll (1997), and Stirk and Weigall (1999).

Memoirs of the Founding Fathers merit attention. See especially Monnet (1978) and Marjolin (1989).

Milward (1984, 2000) has written detailed and challenging analyses of the early years of European integration.

On the EU's treaties see Church and Phinnemore (2002) and Christiansen and Reh (2009). On the Maastricht Treaty see Church and Phinnemore (1994), Corbett (1993), and Duff *et al.* (1994). On the Amsterdam Treaty see Dehousse (1999), Duff (1997), and Monar and Wessels (2001). On the Nice Treaty see Bond and Feus (2001), Galloway (2001), and Laursen (2006). On the Constitutional Treaty see Church and Phinnemore (2005). On the Treaty of Lisbon, see Phinnemore (forthcoming).

The institutions and political actors

Peterson and Shackleton (2006) and Warleigh (2002) are the most comprehensive books focused solely on the EU's institutions.

On the Commission see Dimitrakopoulos (2004), Hooghe (2001), Nugent (2000 and 2001). On the Council, see Hayes-Renshaw and Wallace (2006) and Naurin and Wallace (2008). The most comprehensive books on the European Parliament are Corbett, Jacobs and Shackleton (2007), and Judge and Earnshaw (2008). Stevens and Stevens (2001) analyse the administrative apparatus and personnel of the EU institutions. For non-lawyers, amongst the best books on EU law and the EU's Courts are Mathijsen (2007), and Hartley (2010). Greenwood (2007) provides a comprehensive review and analysis of interests in the EU.

Policies and policy processes

Wallace, Pollack and Young (2010) provide an excellent overview of EU policies and policy processes. Chari and Kritzinger (2006) is also helpful.

Useful books on new bases of EU policies and policy processes include Kölliker (2005) on differentiation and Majone (2005), Büchs (2007), and Linsenmann *et al.* (2007) on new modes of governance.

On particular policy areas, the vast literature that is available includes: Pelkmans *et al.* (2008) on the internal market; Chang (2009) and Marsh (2009) on EMU; Garzon (2006) on agriculture; Cini and McGowan (2009) on competition policy; Keukeleire and MacNaughton (2008), Smith (2008), and Bretherton and Vogler (2006) on external policies; Brimmer and Fröhlich (2005) and Nugent (2004) on enlargement.

Amongst the many useful sources in the growing literature on Europeanisation and the impact of the EU on member states are Goetz and Hix (2001), Grabbe (2005), and Ladrech (2010).

The member states and the EU

There is a rapidly developing literature on the member states and the EU, some of which is comparative in nature and some of which consists of single state studies. A good place to start is Bulmer and Lequesne (2005), which combines both comparative and single state approaches and also contains very useful reading lists.

Conceptualising and theorising

Books providing an overview of European integration theory include Chryssochoou (2009), Wiener and Diez (2009), and Rosamond (2000).

Books examining European integration through particular theoretical lenses include Moravcsik (1998) via a liberal intergovernmentalist perspective, Niemann, (2006) through a neofunctionalist perspective, and Beach (2005) via a (qualified) supranationalist perspective.

Much of the debate on integration theory has been conducted through articles in academic journals. Readers that bring together key writings include Nelsen and Stubb (2003) and Eilstrup-Sangiovanni (2006).

Hix (2005) examines the nature of the EU as a political system.

Books using particular conceptualisations and theoretical approaches to analysing policy processes include: Chryssochoou (1998 and 2009) uses consociationalism; Hooghe (1996), Hooghe and Marks (2001), and Jordan and Schout (2006) use multi-level governance; Peterson and Bomberg (1999) and Bache and Flinders (2004) use policy networks; and Schneider and Aspinwall (2001) and Pollack (2003) use new institutionalism.

Bibliography and References

Ackrill, R. (2000) *The Common Agricultural Policy* (Sheffield: Sheffield Academic Press).

Alter, K. J. (1996) 'The European Court's Political Power', *West European Politics,* 19(3): 458–87.

Archer, C. and Nugent, N. (2002) (eds) *Special Edition of Current Politics and Economics of Europe: Small States and the European Union,* 11(1).

Arregui, J. and Thomson, R. (2009) 'State's Bargaining Success in the European Union', *Journal of European Public Policy,* 16(5): 655–76.

Bache, I. and Flinders, M. (2004) (eds) *Multi-level Governance* (Oxford: Oxford University Press).

Bache, I. and George, S. (2006) *Politics in the European Union,* 2nd edn (Oxford: Oxford University Press).

Beach, D. (2005) *The Dynamics of European Integration: Why and When EU Institutions Matter* (Basingstoke: Palgrave Macmillan).

Beatty, A. (2005) 'A Military Pygmy or a Sleeping Giant?', *European Voice,* 17–23 November.

Begg, I. (2005) *Funding the European Union* (London: Federal Trust).

Bellier, I. (1997) 'The Commission as an Actor: An Anthropologist's Views', in H. Wallace and A. R. Young, *op. cit:* 91–115.

Bomberg, E., Peterson, J. and Stubb, A. (2008) *The European Union: How Does it Work?* (Oxford: Oxford University Press).

Bond, M. and Feus, K. (2001) (eds) *The Treaty of Nice Explained* (London: The Federal Trust).

Borrás, S. and Jacobsson, K. (2004) 'The Open Method of Co-ordination and New Governance Patterns in the EU', *Journal of European Public Policy,* 11 (2): 185–208.

Bostock, D. (2002) 'Coreper Revisited', *Journal of Common Market Studies,* 40(2): 215–34.

Bretherton, C. and Vogler, J. (2006) *The European Union as a Global Actor,* 2nd edn (London: Routledge).

Brimmer, E. and Fröhlich, S. (2005) *The Strategic Implications of European Union Enlargement* (Washington: Center for Transatlantic Relations).

Büchs, M. (2007) *New Governance in European Social Policy: The Open Method of Coordination* (Basingstoke: Palgrave Macmillan).

Bulletin of the European Union (monthly) (Luxembourg: EUR-OP).

Bulmer, S. (1983) 'Domestic Politics and European Community Policy-Making', *Journal of Common Market Studies,* XXI: 349–63.

Bulmer, S. (1994) 'The Governance of the European Union: A New Institutionalist Approach', *Journal of Public Policy,* 13(4): 351–80.

Bulmer, S. (1998) 'New Institutionalism and the Governance of the Single European Market', *Journal of European Public Policy,* 5(3): 365–86.

Bulmer, S. (2009) '*Politics in Time* Meets the Politics of Time: Historical Institutionalism and the EU Timescape', *Journal of European Public Policy* 16(2): 307–24.

Bulmer, S. and Lequesne, C. (2005a) 'The European Union and its Member States: An Overview', in S. Bulmer and C. Lequesne (2005b), *op. cit.:* 1–20.

Bulmer, S. and Lequesne, C. (2005b) *The Member States of the European Union* (Oxford: Oxford University Press).

Burgess, M. (2009) 'Federalism' in A. Wiener and T. Diez (2009) (eds) *European Integration Theory,* 2nd edn (Oxford: Oxford University Press): 25–44.

Burley, A. M. and Mattli, W. (1993) 'Europe Before the Court: A Political Theory of Legal Integration', *International Organization,* 47(1): 41–76.

Caporaso, J. (1996) 'The European Union and Forms of State: Westphalian, Regulatory or Post-Modern?', *Journal of Common Market Studies,* 34(1): 29–52.

Castiglione, D., Schönlau, J., Longman, C., Lombardo, E., Pérez-Solórzano, B., and Aziz, M. (2007) *Constitutional Politics in the European Union,* (Basingstoke: Palgrave Macmillan).

Chang, M. (2009) *Monetary Integration in the European Union* (Basingstoke: Palgrave Macmillan).

Chari, R. S. and Kritzinger, S. (2006) *Understanding EU Policy Making* (London: Pluto Press).

Checkel, J. T. (2006) 'Constructivism and EU Politics', in K. E. Jørgenson, M. A. Pollack and B. Rosamond (eds) *Handbook of European Union Politics* (London: Sage): pp. 57–76.

Christiansen, T. and Reh, C. (2009) *Constitutionalizing the European Union* (Basingstoke: Palgrave Macmillan).

Chryssochoou, D. N. (1994) 'Democracy and Symbiosis in the European Union: Towards a Confederal Consortium?', *West European Politics,* 18: 118–36.

Chryssochoou, D. N. (1995) 'European Union and Dynamics of Confederal Consociation: Problems and Prospects for a Democratic Future', *Journal of European Integration,* XVIII(2–3): 279–305.

Chryssochoou, D. N. (1998) *Democracy in the European Union* (London: Tauris Academic Studies).

Chryssochoou, D. N. (2009) *Theorizing European Integration*, 2nd edn (London: Routledge).

Church, C. and Phinnemore, D. (1994) *European Union and European Community: A Handbook and Commentary on the Post-Maastricht Treaties* (London: Harvester Wheatsheaf).

Church, C. and Phinnemore, D. (2002) *The Penguin Guide to the European Treaties: From Rome to Maastricht, Amsterdam, Nice and Beyond* (London: Penguin).

Church, C. and Phinnemore, D. (2005) *Understanding the European Constitution: An Introduction to the EU Constitutional Treaty* (London: Routledge).

Cini, M. (2000) 'Administrative Culture in the European Commission: The Cases of Competition and Environment', in N. Nugent, *op. cit.*: 73–90.

Cini, M. (2007a) *European Union Politics*, 2nd edn. (Oxford: Oxford University Press).

Cini, M. (2007b) 'Intergovernmentalism' in M. Cini (2007) *European Union Politics*, 2nd edn. (Oxford: Oxford University Press): 99–116.

Cini, M. and Bourne, A. K. (2006) (eds) *Palgrave Advances in European Union Studies* (Basingstoke: Palgrave Macmillan).

Cini, M. and McGowan, L. (2009) *Competition Policy in the European Union*, 2nd edn (Basingstoke: Palgrave Macmillan).

Committee of Independent Experts (1999a) *First Report on Allegations Regarding Fraud, Mismanagement and Nepotism in the European Commission* (Brussels: European Parliament), 15 March.

Committee of Independent Experts (1999b) *Second Report on Reform of the Commission: Analysis of Current Practice and Proposals for Tackling Mismanagement, Irregularities and Fraud* (2 vols) (Brussels: European Commission), 10 September.

Corbett, R. (1993) *The Treaty of Maastricht: From Conception to Ratification* (London: Longman).

Corbett, R. (2000) 'Academic Modelling of the Codecision Procedure: A Practitioner's Puzzled Reaction', *European Union Politics*, 1(3): 373–81.

Corbett, R. (2001) 'A Response to a Reply to a Reaction', *European Union Politics*, 2(3): 361–6.

Corbett, R., Jacobs, F. and Shackleton, M. (2005) *The European Parliament*, 6th edn (London: John Harper).

Corbett, R., Jacobs, F. and Shackleton, M. (2007) *The European Parliament*, 7th edn (London: John Harper).

Costa, O. and Magnette, P. (2003) 'The European Union as a Consociation: A Methodological Assessment', *West European Politics*, 23: (3): 1–18.

Council of the European Union (2005) *Note from the Presidency to the European Council: Financial Perspectives 2007–13* (Brussels: Council of the European Union, 19 December, available on Europa website).

Council of Ministers (2008) *Council Decision of 8 December 2008 Amending the Council's Rules of Procedure*, in *Official Journal of the European Union*, L337/92–93.

Court of First Instance (2009) *Statistics Concerning the Judicial Activity of the Court of First Instance*, accessed from the Court of Justice's web pages on the Europa website.

Court of Justice (2009) *Statistics Concerning the Judicial Activity of the Court of Justice*, accessed from the Court of Justice's web pages on the Europa website.

Cram, L., Dinan, D. and Nugent, N. (1999) *Developments in the European Union* (Basingstoke: Macmillan – now Palgrave Macmillan).

Cunha, C. and Swinbank, A. (2009) 'Exploring the Determinants of CAP Reform: A Delphi Survey of Key Decision-Makers', *Journal of Common Market Studies*, 47(2): 235–61.

Dangerfield, M. (2008) 'The Visegrád Group in the Expanded European Union: From Preaccession to Postaccession Cooperation', *East European Politics and Society*, 22 (3): 630–67.

Dangerfield, M. (2009) 'The Visegrad Group and the European Union's 'Eastern' Dimension'. Paper presented to the Conference of the European Union Studies Association, Los Angeles, April.

Daugbjerg, C. (2009) 'Sequencing in Public Policy: The Evolution of the CAP Over a Decade', *Journal of European Public Policy*, 16(3): 395–411.

Dehousse, F. (1999) *Amsterdam: The Making of a Treaty* (London: Kogan Page).

Dimitrakopoulos, D. G. (2004) *The Changing European Commission* (Manchester: Manchester University Press).

Dinan, D. (2004) *Europe Recast: A History of European Union* (Basingstoke: Palgrave Macmillan).

Dinan, D. (2005) *Ever Closer Union. An Introduction to the European Union*, 3rd edn (Basingstoke: Palgrave Macmillan).

Dinan, D. (2006) *Origins and Evolution of the European Union* (Oxford: Oxford University Press).

Donnelly, B. (2008) 'Justice and Home Affairs in the Lisbon Treaty: A Constitutionalising Clarification?', EIAPAS-COPE, 1, 19–23, (Maastricht: European Institute of Public Administration), accessible at <www.eipa.eu>

Dosenrode, S. (2002) (ed.) *Political Aspects of the Economic and Monetary Union* (Abingdon: Ashgate).

Dowding, K. (2000) 'Institutionalist Research on the European Union: A Critical Review', *European Union Politics*, 1(1): 125–44.

Duff, A. (1997) (ed.) *The Treaty of Amsterdam: Text and Commentary* (London: Sweet & Maxwell).

Duff, A., Pinder, J. and Pryce, R. (1994) *Maastricht and Beyond: Building the European Union* (London: Routledge).

Egan, M., Nugent, N., and Paterson, W. (2010) *Research Agendas in EU Studies: Stalking the Elephant* (Basingstoke: Palgrave Macmillan).

Eilstrup-Sangiovanni, M. (2006) *Debates on European Integration: A Reader* (Basingstoke: Palgrave Macmillan).

Ersbøll, N. (1997) 'The Amsterdam Treaty – II', *CFPS Review*, Autumn 1997: 7–12.

European Central Bank (1999) *Organisation of the European System of Central Banks (ESCB)*, <http://www.ecb.int/about/absorg.htm>

European Commission (1985) *Completing the Internal Market: White Paper from the Commission to the European Council*, Com. (85) 310 final.

European Commission (1992) *From the Single Act to Maastricht and Beyond: The Means to Match Our Ambitions*, Com. (92) 2000 final.

European Commission (1997a) *Agenda 2000: For a Stronger and Wider Union*, Com. (97) 2000 final. Also available in *Bulletin of the European Union*, supplement *5/97* (Luxembourg: EUR-OP).

European Commission (1997b) *Communication from the Commission. Towards a New Shipbuilding Policy*, Com. (97) 470 final.

European Commission (2000) *Reforming the Commission – A White Paper* (1 March) (Brussels: European Commission).

European Commission (2001) *Memorandum to the Members of the Commission: Summary of the Treaty of Nice*, Sec (2001) 99, 18 January.

European Commission (2002a) *Enlargement and Agriculture: Successfully Integrating the New Member States into the CAP – Issues Paper*, 1P/02/176, 30 January.

European Commission (2002b) *General Report on the Activities of the European Union: 2001* (Luxembourg: EUR-OP).

European Commission (2002c) *General Budget of the European Union for the Financial Year 2002* (Brussels: EUR-OP).

European Commission (2002d) *Communication from the Commission: The Reform of the Common Fisheries Policy*, Com (2002) 181 final, 28 May.

European Commission (2002e) *Communication from the Commission to the Council and the European Parliament: Mid-Term Review of the Common Agricultural Policy*, Com (2002) 394, 10 July.

European Commission (2003) *Communication from the Commission to the Council and the European Parliament. Wider Europe Neighbourhood: A New Framework For Relations With Our Eastern and Southern Neighbours*, Com (2003) 104 final, 11 March.

European Commission (2004) *Communication from the Commission to the Council and the European Parliament: Building Our Common Future Policy Challenges and Budgetary Means of the Enlarged European Union 2007–2013*, Com (2004) 101 final.

European Commission (2005a) *Report from the Commission on the Working of Committees During 2004*, Com (2005) 554 final, 10 November.

European Commission (2005b) *General Report on the Activities of the European Union 2004* (Luxembourg: EUOP-OP).

European Commission (2005c) *Communication from the Commission to the Council, the European Parliament, the European Economic and Social Committee and the Committee of the Regions: i2010 A European Information Society for Growth and Employment*, Com (2005) 229 final, 1 June.

European Commission (2005d) *Doing More With Less: Green Paper on Energy Efficiency*, Com (2005) 265 final, 22 June.

European Commission (2005e) *Communication to the Spring European Council. Working Together For Growth and Jobs A New Start For the Lisbon Strategy*, Com (2005) 24, 2 February.

European Commission (2005f) *White Paper: Financial Services Policy 2005–2010*, Sec (2005) 1574, 1 December.

European Commission (2005g) *Key Facts and Figures About Europe and Europeans* (Luxembourg: OOPEC).

European Commission (2006) *General Budget of the European Union For the Financial Year 2006* (Luxembourg: OOPEC).

European Commission (2008a) *Communication From the Commission to the European Parliament and the Council: European Agencies – The Way Forward*, Com (2008) 135 final.

European Commission (2008b) *Communication From the Commission to the European Council: A European Recovery Plan*, Com (2008) 800 final, 26 November.

European Commission (2009a) *General Report on the Activities of the European Union: 2008* (Luxembourg: EUR-OP; accessible on *Europa* website).

European Commission (2009b) *Green Paper: Reform of the Common Fisheries Policy*, Com (2009) 163 final, 22 April.

European Commission (2009c) *Report From the Commission on the Working of Committees During 2008*, Com (2009) 335 final. 3 July.

European Commission (2009d) *DG Competition's Review of Guarantee and Recapitalisation Schemes in the Financial Sector in the Current Crisis*, 7 August.

European Commission (2009e) *Communication From the Commission to the European Parliament and the Council: Technical Adjustment of the Financial Framework for 2010 in Line With the Movements in GNI*, Com (2009) 148 final, 1 April.

European Communities (1987) *Interinstitutional Agreement on Budgetary Discipline, Official Journal*, L185/33, 15 July.

European Convention (2003) *Draft Treaty Establishing a Constitution for Europe* (Luxembourg: Office for Official Publications of the European Communities).

European Council (1992) *Conclusions of the Presidency,* Lisbon, 26–27 June (Brussels: General Secretariat of the Council).

European Council (1993) *Conclusions of the Presidency,* Copenhagen, 21–22 June (Brussels: General Secretariat of the Council).

European Council (1994) *Presidency Conclusions,* Corfu, 24–25 June (Brussels: General Secretariat of the Council).

European Council (1997a) *Presidency Conclusions,* Amsterdam, 16–17 June (Brussels: General Secretariat of the Council).

European Council (1997b) *Presidency Conclusions,* Luxembourg, 12–13 December, Europa website.

European Council (1998) *Presidency Conclusions,* Cardiff, 15–16 June, Europa website.

European Council (1999a) *Presidency Conclusions,* Berlin, 24–25 March, Europa website.

European Council (1999b) *Presidency Conclusions,* Cologne, 3–4 June, Europa website.

European Council (1999c) *Presidency Conclusions,* Tampere, 15–16 October, Europa website.

European Council (1999d) *Presidency Conclusions,* Helsinki, 10–11 December, Europa website.

European Council (2000a) *Presidency Conclusions,* Santa Maria Da Feira, 19–20 June, Europa website.

European Council (2000b) *Presidency Conclusions,* Lisbon, 23–24 March, Europa website.

European Council (2000c) *Presidency Conclusions,* Nice, 7–9 December, Europa website.

European Council (2001) *Presidency Conclusions,* Laeken, 14–15 December, Europa website.

European Council (2002a) *Presidency Conclusions,* Seville, 21–22 June, Europa website.

European Council (2002b) *Presidency Conclusions,* Copenhagen, 12–13 December, Europa website.

European Council (2003a) *Presidency Conclusions,* Thessaloniki, 19–20 June, Europa website.

European Council (2003b) *A Secure Europe in a Better World: European Security Strategy,* Brussels, 12 December, Europa website.

European Council (2005a) *Presidency Conclusions,* Brussels, 22–23 March, Europa website.

European Council (2005b) *Declaration by the Heads of State or Government of the Member States of the European Union on the Ratification of the Treaty Establishing a Constitution for Europe,* (European Council, 16–17 June 2005), Brussels, Europa website.

European Council (2005c) *Presidency Conclusions,* Brussels, 15–16 December, Europa website.

European Council (2006) *Presidency Conclusions,* Brussels, 15–16 June, Europa website.

European Council (2007a) *Presidency Conclusions,* Brussels, 21–22 June, Europa website.

European Council (2007b) *Presidency Conclusions,* Brussels, 14 December, Europa website.

European Council (2008) *Presidency Conclusions,* Brussels, 11–12 December, Europa website.

European Council (2009a) *Presidency Conclusions,* Brussels, 18–19 June, Europa website.

European Council (2009b) *European Council Decision of 1 December 2009 Adopting it Rules of Procedure,* in *Official Journal of the European Union,* L315: 51–55, 2 December.

European Investment Bank (2009) *European Investment Bank: Key Statutory Figures,* available on EIB website (which is accessible via the Europa ebsite).

European Parliament (2001) *Draft Treaty of Nice (Initial Analysis)* (Brussels: Directorate General for Committees and Delegations).

European Parliament (2009a) *The European Elections: EU Legislation, National Provisions and Civic Participation,* (Brussels: Directorate-General Internal Policies), PE 410.672.

European Parliament (2009b) *Rules of Procedure:7th Parliamentary Term,* Europa website.

European Parliament (2009c) *Around the European Parliament in Numbers,* Europa website.

European Parliament, Council, Commission (2005), *Joint Statement by the Council and Representatives of the Governments Meeting Within the Council, the European Parliament and the Commission: The European Consensus on Development,* 2006/C 46/01, Europa website.

Featherstone, K. and Radaelli, C. (2003) (eds) *The Politics of Europeanization,* (Oxford: Oxford University Press).

Forster, A. (1998) 'Britain and the Negotiation of the Maastricht Treaty: A Critique of Liberal Intergovernmentalism', *Journal of Common Market Studies,* 36(3): 347–68.

Forster, A. and Wallace, W. (2000) 'Common Foreign and Security Policy', in H. Wallace and W. Wallace, *op. cit.*: 461–91.

Galloway, D. (2001) *The Treaty of Nice and Beyond: Realities and Illusions of Power in the EU* (Sheffield: Sheffield Academic Press).

Garrett, G. (1992) 'International Cooperation and Institutional Choice: The European Community's Internal Market', *International Organization,* 49: 533–60.

Garrett, G. (1993) 'The Politics of Maastricht', *Economics and Politics,* 5(2): 105–24.

Garrett, G. and Tsebelis, G. (1996) 'An Institutionalist Critique of Intergovernmentalism', *International Organization,* 50(2): 269–99.

Garzon, I. (2006) *Reforming the Common Agricultural Policy: History of a Paradigm Change* (Basingstoke: Palgrave Macmillan).

Gehring, T. and Kraphol, S. (2007) 'Supranational Regulatory Agencies Between Independence and

Control: The EMEA and the Authorization of Pharmaceuticals in the European Single Market', *Journal of European Public Policy*, 14(2): 208–26.

German Presidency of the European Union (2007) <http://www.eu2007.de/de/News/download_docs/Maerz/0324-RAA/English.pdf>

Ginsberg, R. H. (1999) 'Conceptualising the European Union as an International Actor: Narrowing the Theoretical Capability-Expectations Gap', *Journal of Common Market Studies*, 37(3): 424–54.

Ginsberg, R. H. (2001) *The European Union in International Politics: Baptism by Fire* (Boulder, CO: Rowman & Littlefield).

Ginsberg, R. H. (2010) *Demystifying the European Union: The Enduring Logic of Regional Integration*, 2nd edn (Lanham: Rowman & Littlefield).

Giustino, D. de (1996) *A Reader in European Integration* (London: Longman).

Goetz, K. and Hix, S. (2001) *Europeanised Political European Integration and National Political Systems* (London: Frank Cass).

Grabbe, H. (2005) *The EU's Transformative Power: Europeanization Through Conditionality in Central and Eastern Europe* (Basingstoke: Palgrave Macmillan).

Grant, W. (1997) *The Common Agricultural Policy* (Basingstoke: Macmillan).

Green Cowles, M. and Dinan, D. (2004) *Developments in the European Union 2*, (Basingstoke: Palgrave Macmillan).

Green Cowles, M., Caporaso, J. and Risse, T. (2001) (eds) *Transforming Europe: Europeanization and Domestic Change* (Ithaca: Cornell University Press).

Greer, A. (2005) *Agricultural Policy in Europe* (Manchester: Manchester University Press).

Greenwood, J. (2007) *Interest Representation in the European Union*, 2nd edn, (Basingstoke: Palgrave Macmillan).

Grieco, J. M. (1995) 'The Maastricht Treaty, Economic and Monetary Union and the Neo-realist Research Programme', *Review of International Studies*, 2: 21–40.

Groenleer, M. L. P and Van Schaik, L. G. (2007) 'United We Stand? The European Union's International Actorness in the Cases of the International Criminal Court and the Kyoto Protocol', *Journal of Common Market Studies*, 45 (5): 969–98.

Haas, E. B. (1958) *The Uniting of Europe: Political, Social and Economic Forces 1950–57* (Stanford, CA: Stanford University Press).

Häge, F. (2008) 'Who Decides in the Council of the European Union?', *Journal of Common Market Studies*, 46 (3): 533–58.

Hagemann, S. (2008) 'Voting Statements and Coalition-Building in the Council From 1999 to 2006', in D. Naurin and H. Wallace (eds) *Unveiling the Council of the European Union: Games Governments Play in Brussels*, (Basingstoke: Palgrave Macmillan): 36–63.

Hagemann, S. and De Clerck-Sachsse, J. (2007) *Old Rules, New Game: Decision-Making in the Council of Ministers After the 2004 Enlargement*, CEPS Special Report, (Brussels: Centre for European Policy Studies).

Hall, P. A. and Taylor, R. C. R. (1996) 'Political Science and the Three New Institutionalisms', *Political Studies*, 44(5): 936–57.

Hallstein, W. (1972) *Europe in the Making* (London: Allen & Unwin).

Harryvan, A. G. and van der Harst, J. (1997) (eds) *Documents on European Union* (Basingstoke: Palgrave Macmillan).

Hartley, T. C. (2010) *The Foundations of European Union Law*, 6th edn (Oxford: Clarendon Press).

Hayes-Renshaw, F. and Wallace, H. (2006) *The Council of Ministers*, 2nd edn (Basingstoke: Palgrave Macmillan).

Heidenreich, M. and Bischoff, G. (2008) 'The Open Method of Co-ordination: A Way to the Europeanization of Social and Employment Policies?', *Journal of Common Market Studies*, 46 (3)): 497–532.

Hix, S. (1994) 'The Study of the European Community: The Challenge to Comparative Politics', *West European Politics*, 17(1): 1–30.

Hix, S. (1998) 'The Study of the European Union II: The New Governance Agenda and its Rival', *Journal of European Public Policy*, 5(1): 38–65.

Hix, S. (2002) 'What Role for the European Parliament in a More Democratic European Union?', *One Europe or Several? – Newsletter*, 7 (Brighton: University of Sussex).

Hix, S. (2005) *The Political System of the European Union*, 2nd edn (Basingstoke: Palgrave Macmillan).

Hix, S (2008) *What's Wrong With the European Union and How to Fix It* (Cambridge: Polity).

Hix, S. (2009) 'The 2009 European Parliament Elections: A Disaster for Social Democrats', *EUSA Review*, 22(4): 3–5.

Hix, S. and Lord, C. (1997) *Political Parties in the European Union* (Basingstoke: Palgrave Macmillan).

Hix, S. and Marsh, M (2007) 'Punishment or Protest? Understanding European Parliament Elections', *The Journal of Politics*, 69(2): 495–510.

Hix, S., Noury, A. and Roland, G. (2007) *Democratic Politics in the European Parliament* (Cambridge: Cambridge University Press).

Hodson, D. and Maher, I. (2001) 'The Open Method as a New Mode of Governance: The Case of Soft Economic Policy Co-ordination', *Journal of Common Market Studies*, 39(4): 719–46.

Hoffmann, S. (1966) 'Obstinate or Obsolete: The Fate of the Nation State and the Case of Western Europe', *Daedelus*, 95: 862–915.

Hoffmann, S. (1982) 'Reflection on the Nation State in Western Europe Today', *Journal of Common Market Studies*, 21(1–2): 21–37.

Holland, M. (2002) *The European Union and the Third World* (Basingstoke: Palgrave Macmillan).

Hooghe, L. (1996) (ed.) *Cohesion Policy and European Integration: Building Multi-Level Governance* (Oxford: Oxford University Press).

Hooghe, L. (2001) *The European Commission and the Integration of Europe: Images of Governance* (Cambridge: Cambridge University Press).

Hooghe, L. (2005) 'Several Roads Lead to International Norms, But Few Via International Socialization: A Case Study of the European Commission', *International Organization*, 59, 861–98.

Hooghe, L. and Marks, G. (2001) (eds) *Multi-Level Governance and European Integration* (Oxford: Rowman & Littlefield).

Howe, P. (1995) 'A Community of Europeans: The Requisite Underpinnings', *Journal of Common Market Studies*, 33(1): 27–46.

Jacqué, J. P. (2004) *Droit Institutionnel de L'Union Europénne*, (Paris: Dalloz).

Jakobsen, P. V. (2009) 'Small States, Big Influence: The Overlooked Nordic Influence on the Civilian ESDP' *Journal of Common Market Studies*, 47(1): 81–102.

Jeffery, C. (2002) 'Social and Regional Interests: The ESC and Committee of the Regions', in J. Peterson and M. Shackleton, *op. cit.*: 326–46.

Jordan, A. and Schout, A. (2006) *The Coordination of the European Union: Exploring the Capacities of Networked Governance*, (Oxford: Oxford University Press).

Jørgenson, K. E., Pollack, M. A. and Rosamond, B. (2006) (eds) *Handbook of European Union Politics* (London: Sage).

Judge, D. and Earnshaw, D. (2008) *The European Parliament*, 2nd edn (Basingstoke: Palgrave Macmillan).

Kaltenthaler, K. (2006) *Policy-Making in the European Central Bank: The Masters of Europe's Money*, (Lanham, MD: Rowman & Littlefield).

Kassim, H. (1994) 'Policy Networks, Networks and European Union Policy Making: A Sceptical View', *West European Politics*, 17(4): 15–27.

Keleman, R. D. and Nicolaidis, K. (2006) 'Bringing Federalism Back In', in K. E. Jørgenson, M. A. Pollack, and B. Rosamond (eds) *Handbook of European Union Politics* (London: Sage): 301–16.

Keohane, R. O. and Hoffman, S. (1991) *The New European Community* (Oxford: Westview Press).

Keohane, R. and Nye, J. (1977) *Power and Interdependence: World Politics in Transition* (Boston, MA: Little, Brown).

Keukeleire, S. and MacNaughton, J. (2008) *The Foreign Policy of the European Union* (Basingstoke: Palgrave Macmillan).

Kohler-Koch, B. and Eising, R. (1999) (eds) *Transformation of Governance in the European Union* (London: Routledge).

Kok, W. (2004) *Facing the Challenge: The Lisbon Strategy for Growth and Employment*, Report From the High Level Working Group Chaired by Wim Kok, November, Europa website.

Kölliker, A. (2005) *Flexibility and European Integration: The Logic of Differentiated Integration* (Plymouth: Rowman & Littlefield).

Koslowski, R. (1999) 'A Constructivist Approach to Understanding the European Union as a Federal Polity', *Journal of European Public Policy*, 6(4): 561–78.

Kreppel, A. (2000) 'Rules and Ideology and Coalition Formation in the European Parliament: Past, Present and Future', *European Union Politics*, 1(3): 340–62.

Kreppel, A. and Tsebelis, G. (1999) 'Coalition Formation in the European Parliament', *Comparative Political Studies*, 38(2): 933–66.

Kuasmanen, A. (1998) 'Decision-Making in the Council of the European Union', in L. Goetschel (ed.), *Small States Inside and Outside the European Union* (London: Kluwer): 65–78.

Kurpas, S. (2007) 'The Treaty of Lisbon – How Much "Constitution" is Left?', *CEPS Policy Brief*, No. 147, Brussels: Centre for European Policy Studies.

Ladrech, R. (2010) *Europeanization and National Politics* (Basingstoke: Palgrave Macmillan).

Laffan, B. (2002) 'Financial Control: The Court of Auditors and OLAF', in J. Peterson and M. Shackleton, *op. cit.*: 231–53.

Langenberg, P. (2004) 'The Role of the Member States in the European Union', in P. W. Meerts and F. Cede (eds), *op. cit.*: 51–70.

Laursen, F. (2006) *The Treaty of Nice: Actor Preferences, Bargaining and Institutional Choice* (Leiden: Martinus Niijhoff)

Lenaerts, K. (1991) 'Some Reflections on the Separation of Powers in the EU', *Common Market Law Review*, 28: 11–35.

Lijphart, A. (1969) 'Consociational Democracy', *World Politics*, 21(2): 207–25.

Lindberg, L. N. (1963) *The Political Dynamics of European Economic Integration* (Oxford: Oxford University Press).

Linsenmann, I., Meyer, C. O. and Wessels, W. T (eds) (2007) *Economic Government of the EU: A Balance Sheet of New Modes of Policy Coordination* (Basingstoke: Palgrave Macmillan).

Lowi, T. J. (1964) 'American Business, Public Policy, Case-Studies and Political Theory', *World Politics*, 16(4): 677–715.

Macmillan, C. (2009) 'The Application of Neofunctionalism to the Enlargement Process: The Case of Turkey', *Journal of Common Market Studies*, 47(4): 789–809.

Magnette, P. (2005) *What is the European Union: Nature and Prospects* (Basingstoke: Palgrave Macmillan).

Majone, G. (1992) 'Regulatory Federalism in the European Community', *Environment and Planning C: Government and Policy*, 10(3): 299–316.

Majone, G. (1994) 'The Rise of the Regulatory State in Europe', *West European Politics*, 17(3): 77–101.

Majone, G. (1996) *Regulating Europe* (London: Routledge).

Majone, G. (2005) *Dilemmas of European Integration: The Ambiguities and Pitfalls of Integration by Stealth*, (Oxford: Oxford University Press).

Majone, G. (2006a) 'The Common Sense of European Integration' *Journal of European Public Policy*, 13(5): 607–26.

Majone, G. (2006b) 'Managing Europeanization: The European Agencies', in J. Peterson and M. Shackleton (eds), *The Institutions of the European Union*, 2nd edn (Oxford: Oxford University Press): 190–209.

Marjolin, R. (1989) *Memoirs 1911–1986* (London: Weidenfeld & Nicolson).

Marks, G., Hooghe, L. and Black, K. (1996) 'European Integration from the 1980s: State Centric v Multi-level Governance', *Journal of Common Market Studies*, 34(3): 341–78.

Marsh, D. (2009) *The Euro: The Politics of the New Global Currency* (London: Yale University Press).

Mathijsen, P. S. R. F. (2007) *A Guide to European Community Law*, 9th edn (London: Sweet & Maxwell).

Matláry, J. H. (1993) 'Beyond Intergovernmentalism: The Quest for a Comprehensive Framework for the Study of Integration', *Cooperation and Conflict*, 28(2): 181–210.

Mattila, M. (2008) 'Voting and Coalitions in the Council After Enlargement', in D. Naurin and H. Wallace (eds) *Unveiling the Council of the European Union: Games Governments Play in Brussels*, (Basingstoke: Palgrave Macmillan): 23–35.

McCormick, J. (2008) *Understanding the European Union: A Concise Introduction*, 4th edn (Basingstoke: Palgrave Macmillan).

McNamara, K. (2002) 'Managing the Euro: The European Central Bank', in J. Peterson and M. Shackleton, *op. cit.*: 164–85.

Meerts, P. W. and Cede, F. (2004) *Negotiating European Union* (Basingstoke: Palgrave Macmillan).

Milward, A. S. (1984) *The Reconstruction of Western Europe 1945–51* (London: Methuen).

Milward, A. S. (2000) *The European Rescue of the Nation-State*, 2nd edn (London: Routledge).

Monar, J. and Wessels, W. (2001) *The European Union After the Amsterdam Treaty* (London: Continuum).

Monnet, J. (1978) *Memoirs* (London: Collins).

Moravcsik, A. (1991) 'Negotiating the Single European Act: National Interests and Conventional Statecraft in the European Community', *International Organization*, 45(1): 19–56.

Moravcsik, A. (1993) 'Preferences and Power in the European Community: A Liberal Intergovernmentalist Approach', *Journal of Common Market Studies*, 31(4): 473–524.

Moravcsik, A. (1995) 'Liberal Intergovernmentalism and Integration: A Rejoinder', *Journal of Common Market Studies*, 33(4): 611–28.

Moravcsik, A. (1998) *The Choice for Europe: Social Purpose and State Power from Messina to Maastricht* (Ithaca, NY: Cornell University Press).

Moravcsik, A. and Schimmelfennig, F. (2009) 'Liberal Intergovernmentalism' in A. Wiener and T. Diez (2009) (eds) *European Integration Theory*, 2nd edn (Oxford: Oxford University Press): 67–87.

Naurin, D. and Wallace, H. (eds) (2008) *Unveiling the Council of the European Union: Games Governments Play in Brussels* (Basingstoke: Palgrave Macmillan).

Nelsen, B. and Stubb, A. C.-G. (2003) *The European Union: Readings on the Theory and Practice of European Integration*, 3rd edn (Basingstoke: Palgrave Macmillan).

Niedermayer, O. (2009) 'The 2009 Elections to the European Parliament: Expectations and Results', paper for the 6th ELAMEP European seminar, Delphi, 25–28 June,

Nieiemann, A. and Schmitter, P. C. (2009) 'Neofunctionalism', in A.Wiener and T. Diez (2009) (eds) *European Integration Theory*, 2nd edn (Oxford: Oxford University Press): 45–66.

Niemann, A. (2006) *Explaining Decisions in the European Union* (Cambridge: Cambridge University Press).

Norman, P. (2003) *The Accidental Constitution: The Story of the European Convention* (Brussels: Eurocomment).

Nugent, N. (2000) (ed.) *At the Heart of the Union: Studies of the European Commission*, 2nd edn (Basingstoke: Macmillan – now Palgrave Macmillan).

Nugent, N. (2001) *The European Commission* (Basingstoke: Palgrave – now Palgrave Macmillan).

Nugent, N. (2004) (ed.) *European Union Enlargement* (Basingstoke: Palgrave Macmillan).

Nugent, N. (2007) 'The EU's Response to Turkey's Membership Application: Not Just a Weighing of Costs and Benefits', *Journal of European Integration*, 29(4): 481–502.

Official Journal of the European Union (various issues) (Luxembourg: EUR-OP, published most working days).

Olsen, J. (2002) 'The Many Faces of Europeanization', *Journal of Common Market Studies*, 40(5): 921–52.

O'Neill, M. (1996) *The Politics of European Integration: A Reader* (London: Routledge).

O'Neill, M. (2000) 'Theorising the European Union: Towards a Post-Foundational Disclosure', *Current Politics and Economics of Europe*, 9(2): 121–45.

Pelkmans, J., Hanf, D. and Chang, M. (2008) *The EU Internal Market in Comparative Perspective: Economic, Political and Legal Analyses* (Brussels: Peter Lang).

Peters, B. G. and Wright, V. (2001) 'The National Co-ordination of European Policy-Making', in J. Richardson, *op. cit.*: 155–78.

Peterson, J. (1995) 'Decision-Making in the EU: Towards a Framework for Analysis', *Journal of European Public Policy*, 2(1): 69–93.

Peterson, J. (2009) 'Policy Networks', in A. Wiener and T. Diez (eds) *European Integration Theory*, 2nd edn (Oxford: Oxford University Press): 105–24.

Peterson, J. and Bomberg, E. (1999) *Decision-Making in the European Union* (Basingstoke: Macmillan – now Palgrave Macmillan).

Peterson, J. and Shackleton, M. (2006) (eds) *The Institutions of the European Union*, 2nd edn (Oxford: Oxford University Press).

Phinnemore, D. (2004) *Treaty Establishing a Constitution for Europe: An Overview* (London: Royal Institute of International Affairs).

Phinnemore, D. (forthcoming) *The Treaty of Lisbon: From Conception to Implementation* (Basingstoke: Palgrave Macmillan).

Pierson, P. (1996) 'The Path to European Integration: A Historical Institutionalist Analysis', *Comparative Political Studies*, 29(2): 123–63.

Pierson, P. (1998) 'The Path to European Integration: A Historical Institutionalist Analysis', in W. Sandholtz and A. Stone Sweet, *op. cit.*: 27–58.

Pollack, M. (1994) 'Creeping Competence: The Expanding Agenda of the European Community', *Journal of Public Policy*, 14(2): 95–145.

Pollack, M. (1998) 'The Engines of Integration? Supranational Autonomy and Influence in the European Union', in W. Sandholtz and A. Stone Sweet, *op. cit.*: 217–49.

Pollack, M. A. (2000) 'The End of Creeping Competence? EU Policy-Making since Maastricht', *Journal of Common Market Studies*, 38(3): 519–38.

Pollack, M. A. (2003) *The Engines of European Integration: Delegation, Agency and Agenda-Setting in the EU* (Oxford; Oxford University Press).

Pollack, M. A. (2004) 'The New Institutionalism and European Integration', in A. Wiener and T. Diez (eds) *op. cit.*: 137–56.

Pollack, M. A. (2005) 'Theorising EU Policy-Making', in H. Wallace *et al.*, *op. cit.*: 13–48.

Pollack. M. A. (2006) 'Rational Choice and EU Politics' in K. E. Jørgenson, M. A. Pollack, and B. Rosamond (eds) *Handbook of European Union Politics*, (London: Sage): 312–55.

Pollard, S. (1981) *The Integration of the European Economy Since 1815* (London: George Allen & Unwin).

Ponzano, P. (2007) 'The New "Reform Treaty"', paper presented to the conference on *The Lisbon Treaty and the Future of the European Union*, University of Glasgow, December 2007.

Preston, C. (1995) 'Obstacles to EU Enlargement: The Classical Community Method and the Prospects for a Wider Europe', *Journal of Common Market Studies*, 33(3): 451–63.

Puetter, U. (2006) *The Eurogroup: How a Secretive Circle of Finance Ministers Shape European Economic Governance* (Manchester: Manchester University Press).

Putnam, R. D. (1988) 'Diplomacy and Domestic Politics: The Logic of Two-Level Games', *International Organization*, 42(3): 427–60.

Rees, N. and Holmes, M. (2002) 'Capacity, Perceptions and Principles: Ireland's Changing Place in Europe', *Current Politics and Economics of Europe*, 11(1): 49–60.

Regelsberger, E., de Schoutheete de Tervarent, P. and Wessels, W. (eds) (1997) *Foreign Policy of the European Union: From EPC to CFSP and Beyond* (Boulder, CO: Lynne Rienner).

Rhodes, R. A. W., Bache, I. and George, S. (1996) 'Policy Networks and Policy-Making in the European Union: A Critical Appraisal', in L. Hooghe, *op.cit.*: 367–87.

Richardson, J. (ed.) (2006) *European Union: Power and Policy-Making*, 3rd edn (London: Routledge).

Risse, T. (2009) 'Social Constructivism and European Integration' A. Wiener and T. Diez, (eds) *European Integration Theory*, 2nd edn (Oxford: Oxford University Press): 144–60.

Robertson, A. H. (1961) *The Council of Europe: Its Structure, Functions and Achievements* (London: Stevens).

Rosamond, B. (1995) 'Understanding European Unity: The Limits of Nation-State-Centric Integration Theory', *The European Legacy*, 1: 291–7.

Rosamond, B. (2000) *Theories of European Integration* (Basingstoke: Macmillan – now Palgrave Macmillan).

Ross, G. (2001) 'France's European Tour of Duty, or Caution – One Presidency May Hide Another', *ECSA Review*, 14(2): 4–6.

Salmon, T. and Nicoll, W. (1997) *Building European Union: A Documentary History and Analysis* (Manchester: Manchester University Press).

Sandholtz, W. (1996) 'Membership Matters: Limits of the Functional Approach to European Institutions', *Journal of Common Market Studies*, 34(3): 403–29.

Sandholtz, W. and Stone Sweet, A. (eds) (1998) *European Integration and Supranational Governance* (Oxford: Oxford University Press).

Sbragia, A. (1992) 'Thinking About the European Future: The Uses of Comparison', in A. Sbragia (ed.) *Euro-Politics: Institutions and Policymaking in the 'New' European Community* (Washington, DC: Brookings Institution): 257–91.

Schäfer, A. (2004) 'Beyond the Community Method: Why the Open Method of Coordination Was Introduced to

EU Policy-Making', European Integration Online Papers (EIoP) 8 13).

Schalk, J., Torenvlied, R., Weesie, J. and Stokman, F. N. (2007) 'The Power of the Presidency in EU Council Decision-Making', *European Union Politics*, 8 (2): 229–50.

Schimmelfennig, F. (2001) 'The Community Trap: Liberal Norms, Rhetorical Action, and the Eastern Enlargement of the European Union', *International Organization*, 55 (1): 47–80.

Schimmelfennig, F. (2002) 'Liberal Community and Enlargement: An Event History Analysis', *Journal of European Public Policy*, 9(4): 598–626.

Schimmelfennig, F. (2010) 'Integration Theory', in Egan, M. *et al. op. cit.*: 37–59.

Schmidt, V. A. (2004) 'The European Union: Democratic Legitimacy in a Regional State?', *Journal of Common Market Studies*, 42:4: 975–99.

Schmidt, V. A. (2006) *Democracy in Europe: The EU and National Politics*, (Oxford: Oxford University Press).

Schmidt, V. A. (2009) 'Re-Envisioning the European Union: Identity, Democracy, Economy', in N. Copsey and T. Haughton (eds), *The JCMS Annual Review of the European Union in 2008* (Oxford: Wiley-Blackwell), 17–42.

Schmitter, P. (2004) 'Neo-Neofunctionalism', in A. Wiener and T. Diez (eds), *op. cit.*: 45–74.

Schneider, G. and Aspinwall, M. (2001) (eds) *The Rules of Integration: Institutional Approaches to the Study of Europe* (Manchester: Manchester University Press).

Schneider, V., Dang-Nguyen, G. and Werle, R. (1994) 'Corporate Actor Networks in European Policy-Making: Harmonizing Telecommunications Policy', *Journal of Common Market Studies*, 32(4): 473–98.

Scully, R. (2006) 'Rational Institutionalism and Liberal Intergovernmentalism', in M. Cini and A. K. Bourne (2006) (eds) *Palgrave Advances in European Union Studies* (Basingstoke: Palgrave Macmillan): 19–34.

Sedelmeier, U. (2000) 'Eastern Enlargement: Risk, Rationality, and Role-Compliance', in M. Green Cowles and M. Smith (eds), *The State of the European Union: Volume 5 – Risks, Reform, Resistance, and Revival* (Oxford: Oxford University Press): 164–85.

Session News: The Week, Brussels: European Parliament Directorate for Press and Audiovisual Services (weekly).

Shackleton, M. (2002) 'The European Parliament', in M. Shackleton and J. Peterson (eds) *The Institutions of the European Union* (Oxford: Oxford University Press): 95–117.

Sjursen, H. (2002) 'Why Expand? The Question of Legitimacy and Justification in the EU's Enlargement Policy', *Journal of Common Market Studies*, 40(3): 491–513.

Smith, K. (2008) *European Union Foreign Policy in a Changing World* (Cambridge: Polity Press).

Spinelli, A. (1986) 'Foreword', in J. Lodge (ed.), *European Union: The European Community in Search of a Future* (London: Macmillan – now Palgrave Macmillan): xiii–xviii.

Stevens, A. and Stevens, H. (2001) *Brussels Bureaucrats? The Administration of the European Union* (Basingstoke: Palgrave – now Palgrave Macmillan).

Stirk, P. M. R. (1996) *A History of European Integration since 1914* (London: Pinter).

Stirk, P. and Weigall, D. (eds) (1999) *The Origins and Development of European Integration: A Reader and Commentary* (London: Pinter).

Stone Sweet, A. and Sandholtz, W. (1997) 'European Integration and Supranational Governance', *Journal of European Public Policy*, 4(3): 297–317.

Strøby-Jensen, C (2007) 'Neo-functionalism' in M. Cini (2007) *European Union Politics*, 2nd edn (Oxford: Oxford University Press): 85–98.

Tallberg, J. (2004) The Power of the Presidency: Brokerage, Efficiency and Distribution in EU Negotiations', *Journal of Common Market Studies*, 42 (5): 999–1022.

Tallberg, J. (2006) *Leadership and Negotiation in the European Union*, (Cambridge: Cambridge University Press).

Tallberg, J. (2008) 'The Power of the Chair: Formal Leadership by the Council Presidency', in D. Naurin and H. Wallace (eds) *Unveiling the Council of the European Union: Games Governments Play in Brussels*, (Basingstoke: Palgrave Macmillan): 187–202.

Taylor, P. (1991) 'The European Community and the State: Assumptions, Theories and Propositions', *Review of International Studies*, 17: 109–25.

Taylor, P. (1996) *The European Union in the 1990s* (Oxford: Oxford University Press).

Teasdale, A. (1995) 'The Luxembourg Compromise', in M. Westlake, *The Council of the European Union* (London: Cartermill): 104–10.

Thomson, R. (2008) 'The Council Presidency in the European Union: Responsibility With Power', *Journal of Common Market Studies*, 46(3): 593–617.

Thorhallsson, B. (2000) *The Role of Small States in the European Union* (Aldershot: Ashgate).

Tranholm-Mikkelsen, J. (1991) Neo-functionalism: Obstinate of Obsolete? A Reappraisal in the Light of the New Dynamism of the EC', *Millennium: Journal of International Studies*, 20: 1–22.

Treaty Establishing a Constitution for Europe (2004), Europa website.

Treaty Establishing the European Community: Consolidated Version (1997), in *Official Journal of the European Communities*, C340, 10 November; also in *European Union Consolidated Treaties* (Luxembourg: EUR-OP).

Treaty of Amsterdam, Amending the Treaty on European Union, the Treaties Establishing the European Communities and Certain Related Acts (1997), in *Official Journal of the European Communities*, C340, 10 November.

Treaty of Lisbon, Amending the Treaty on European Union and the Treaty Establishing the European Community (2007), in *Official Journal of the European* Union, C 306,17 December 2007.

Treaty of Nice, Amending the Treaty on European Union, the Treaties Establishing the European Communities and Certain Related Acts (2001), in *Official Journal of the European Communities*, C80, 10 March 2001.

Treaty on European Union, Together with the Complete Text of the Treaty Establishing the European Community (1992), in *Official Journal of the European Communities*, C244, 31 August.

Treaty on European Union: Consolidated Version (1997), in *Official Journal of the European Communities*, C340, 10 November; also in *European Union Consolidated Treaties* (Luxembourg: EUR-OP).

Treaty on European Union: Consolidated Version (2008), in *Official Journal of the European Union*, C115, 9 May.

Treaty on the Functioning of the European Union: Consolidated Version (2008), in *Official Journal of the European Union*, C115, 9 May.

Trondal, J. (2007) 'Is the European Commission a "Hothouse" for Supranationalism? Exploring Actor-Level Supranationalism', *Journal of Common Market Studies*, 45(5): 1111–13.

Tsebelis, G. and Garrett, G. (1997) 'Agenda Setting, Vetoes and the European Union's Co-Decision Procedure', *Journal of Legislative Studies*, 3(1): 74–92.

Tsebelis, G. and Garrett, G. (2001) 'The Institutionalist Foundations of Intergovernmentalism and Supranationalism in the European Union', *International Organization*, 55(2): 357–90.

Urwin, D. W. (1995) *The Community of Europe: A History of European Integration since 1945*, 2nd edn (London: Longman).

Van Schendelen, M. P. C. M. (1996) 'The Council Decides: Does the Council Decide?', *Journal of Common Market Studies*, 34(4): 531–48.

Wallace, H. (2005) 'An Institutional Anatomy and Five Policy Modes' in H. Wallace *et al.*, *op. cit.*: 49–90.

Wallace, H. and Wallace, W. (2000) *Policy-Making in the European Union*, 4th edn (Oxford: Oxford University Press).

Wallace, H. and Young, A. R. (1997) *Participation and Policy-Making in the European Union* (Oxford: Clarendon Press).

Wallace, H., Pollack, M. and Young, A. R. (2010) *Policy-Making in the European Union*, 6th edn (Oxford: Oxford University Press).

Warleigh, A. (1998) 'Better the Devil You Know? Synthetic and Confederal Understandings of European Integration', *West European Politics*, 21(3): 1–18.

Warleigh, A. (2000) 'History Repeating? Framework Theory and Europe's Multi-Level Confederation', *Journal of European Integration*, 22: 173–200.

Warleigh, A. (2002) *Understanding European Union Institutions* (London: Routledge).

Webb, C. (1983) 'Theoretical Perspectives and Problems', in H. Wallace, W. Wallace and C. Webb (eds), *Policy Making in the European Community* (London: John Wiley): 1–41.

Wessels, W. (2001) 'Nice Results: The Millennium IGC in the EU's Evolution', *Journal of Common Market Studies*, 39(2): 197–219.

Wessels, W., Maurer, A. and Mittag, J. (2001) (eds) *Fifteen into One? The European Union and its Member States* (Manchester: Manchester University Press).

Westlake, M. (1997) 'Keynote Article: Mad Cows and Englishmen. The Institutional Consequences of the BSE Crisis' in N. Nugent (ed.), *The European Union 1996: Annual Review of Activities* (Oxford: Blackwell): 11–36.

Wiener, A. (2006) 'Constructivism and Sociological Institutionalism', in M. Cini and A. K, Bourne (2006) (eds) *Palgrave Advances in European Union Studies* (Basingstoke: Palgrave Macmillan): 35–55.

Wiener, A. and Diez, T. (2009) (eds) *European Integration Theory*, 2nd edn (Oxford: Oxford University Press).

Wincott, D. (1995) 'Institutional Interaction and European Integration: Towards an Everyday Critique of Liberal Intergovernmentalism', *Journal of Common Market Studies*, 33(4): 597–609.

Wincott, D. (1999) 'The Court of Justice and the Legal System', in L. Cram *et al.*, *op. cit.*: 84–104.

Index

Index | 485

Spain, Belgium and Italy v. *Commission* case 224
Special Committee on Agriculture (SCA) *see* Council of Ministers
Spinelli, Altiero 5
Stability and Growth Pact 31, 220–1, 273, 332–5, 448
Stability Programme for South Eastern Europe 374, 383
Standing Committee on Employment 146
state-centrism 425–6
state, the (as a conceptualisation of the EU) 421–3, 446
steel policy *see* European Coal and Steel Community
Stockholm Programme (2009) 338–9
Stresemann, Gustav 5
Structural Funds *see* European Regional Development Fund; European Social Fund, Cohesion Fund
subnational levels of government 231–3, 245, 268
subsidiarity 56, 286
summits
  Hague (1969) 454
  Hampton Court (2005) 168
  Paris (1974) 161–2, 455
  St Malo (1998) 381
  see also European Council
supranationalism 26, 421–34, 446
Sweden 33, 36, 40, 259, 331, 457, 460
Switzerland 40–2, 457, 458

Tajani, Antonio 115
terrorism 337
  see also area of freedom, security and justice
Thatcher, Margaret 172, 258, 402
theory (and European integration) 419–51 *passim*

trade and trade policy 133, 371–6
  see also Common Commercial Policy; internal market
transnational parties 192–3
transport policy 279
transposition (of EU directives) 320
treaties 27–9, 53–101 *passim*, 208–9, 279–80, 291
  Act Concerning the Election of the Representatives of the Assembly (1976) 54
  Single European Act 27–8, 54–5, 92, 267–8, 456
  Treaty Amending Certain Budgetary Provisions (1970) 53–4, 455
  Treaty Amending Certain Financial Provisions (1975) 53–4, 240, 455
  Treaty Establishing a Constitution for Europe (2004) 29, 69–85 *passim*, 421, 460–1
  Treaty Establishing a Single Council and a Single Commission of the European Communities (1965, commonly known as the Merger Treaty) 53, 144, 454
  Treaty Establishing the European Community (1992) 56–8
  Treaty Establishing the European Community (Consolidated Version, 1997)
  Treaty of Amsterdam (1997) 28, 59–62, 92, 336, 380, 459
  Treaty of Brussels (1948) 28, 453
  Treaty of Dunkirk (1947) 453
  Treaty of Lisbon (2007) 28–9, 74–85 *passim*, 92, 337, 380, 391–2, 450–1, 461, 461

Treaty of Maastricht (1992) 28, 31, 55–9, 335, 380, 424, 457
Treaty of Nice (2001) 28–9, 62–7, 92, 380, 459, 460
Treaty of Paris (1951, ECSC) 20, 22, 92, 453
Treaty of Rome (1957, EEC) 23–6, 92, 454
Treaty of Rome (1957, Euratom) 23–6, 92, 454
Treaty of Versailles (1919) 5
Treaty on European Union (TEU) (1992) 56, 92; *see also* Treaty of Maastricht
Treaty on European Union (TEU) (2007) 81–3, 95
Treaty on the Functioning of the European Union (TFEU) (2007) 81–3, 96–7
Trevi process 335
Trichet, Jean-Claude 174, 239
Truman, Harry, and Truman Doctrine 11
Turkey 43, 45–6, 169–70, 261, 272, 441–3, 456, 460, 461

Udre, Ingrida 108–9
UK Independence Party 195
Ukraine 373
Union for Europe of the Nations Group (UEN) 195
Union for the Mediterranean 385
Union of Industrial and Employers Confederation of Europe (UNICE) 124, 247
  see also BusinessEurope
United Kingdom (UK) 90, 258, 264, 271–2, 274
  accession 33–7, 47, 454, 455
  and AFSJ policies 61, 337–8
  and Amsterdam Treaty 60
  and EMU 331
  and enlargement 441
  and EU budget 402, 403, 404, 406, 456
  and inter-war Europe 4
  and Lisbon Treaty 75, 337
  and Maastricht Treaty 57–8, 423